A Historical Phonology of English

Edinburgh Textbooks on the English Language – Advanced

TITLES IN THE SERIES INCLUDE:

Corpus Linguistics and the Description of English
Hans Lindquist

A Historical Phonology of English
Donka Minkova

A Historical Morphology of English
Dieter Kastovsky

Grammaticalization and the History of English
Manfred Krug and Hubert Cuyckens

A Historical Syntax of English
Bettelou Los

English Historical Sociolinguistics
Robert McColl Millar

A Historical Semantics of English
Christian Kay and Kathryn Allan

Visit the Edinburgh Textbooks in the English Language website at www.euppublishing.com/series/ETOTELAdvanced

A Historical Phonology of English

Donka Minkova

EDINBURGH
University Press

Edinburgh University Press Ltd
22 George Square, Edinburgh EH8 9LF

www.euppublishing.com

Typeset in 10.5/12 Janson by
Servis Filmsetting Ltd, Stockport, Cheshire,
printed and bound in the United States of America

A CIP record for this book is available from the British Library

ISBN 978 0 7486 3467 5 (hardback)
ISBN 978 0 7486 3468 2 (paperback)
ISBN 978 0 7486 3469 9 (webready PDF)
ISBN 978 0 7486 7755 9 (epub)

Contents

Acknowledgements x
List of abbreviations and symbols xii
A note on the Companion to A Historical Phonology of English xv

1 Periods in the history of English 1
1.1 Periods in the history of English 2
1.2 Old English (450–1066) 2
1.3 Middle English (1066–1476) 9
1.4 Early Modern English (1476–1776) 15
1.5 English after 1776 17
1.6 The evidence for early pronunciation 20

2 The sounds of English 24
2.1 The consonants of PDE 24
2.1.1 Voicing 26
2.1.2 Place of articulation 27
2.1.3 Manner of articulation 29
2.1.4 Short and long consonants 31
2.2 The vowels of PDE 32
2.2.1 Short and long vowels 35
2.2.2 Complexity: monophthongs and diphthongs 37
2.3 The syllable: some basics 39
2.3.1 Syllable structure 39
2.3.2 Syllabification 40
2.3.3 Syllable weight 43
2.4 Notes on vowel representation 45
2.5 Phonological change: some types and causes 46

3 Discovering the earliest links: Indo-European – Germanic – Old English
FOOT-PODIUM, TOOTH-DENTAL, HILL-CULMINATE, THREE-TRIPLE 54
3.1 Family matters: Indo-European – Germanic – Old English 54

3.2 The Indo-European family of languages 55
3.3 The Germanic branch of Indo-European 59
3.4 Some pre-Old English segmental and prosodic changes 61
3.4.1 Grimm's Law, or the First Germanic Consonant Shift 61
3.4.2 Some IE vowel changes in Germanic 68
3.4.3 Early prosodic changes: stress and syllable weight in Germanic 69
3.4.4 Lengthening of final vowels in stressed monosyllables 70
3.4.5 West Germanic (Consonant) Gemination (WGG) 71

4 Consonantal histories: Old English
KIRK-CHURCH, DAY-DAWN, SAY-SAW-SAGA, SKIRT-SHIRT, SHRIFT-SCRIPT, DISH-DISK-DISCUS, LOAF-LOAVES VS SERF-SERFS, ELF-ELFS-ELVEN, BATH-BATHS-BATHE, BELIEF-BELIEFS-BELIEVE 74
4.1 The consonants of OE 74
4.1.1 Singletons 74
4.1.2 Geminates 76
4.2 Sound-to-spelling correspondences of the consonants in OE 81
4.2.1 The <g>'s of OE 82
4.3 Palatalisation and affrication of velars in OE 84
4.4 Morphophonemic alternations: fricative voicing. CLOSE enough to CLOSE the door? 88

5 Consonantal developments in the second millennium
'AND WOT 'AVE WE 'ERE, GUV'NOR?', WHICH-WITCH, THOUGH-TOUGH, FAR-FA, BRIDGESTOWE-BRISTOL, WRITE-RIGHT, IAMB-IAMBIC, GIGOLO, MATURE-GOCHA, BETTER-BEDDER, MUS GO 99
5.1 H-related histories: AND WOT 'AVE WE 'ERE, GUV'NOR? 99
5.1.1 Phonetic and phonological properties of /h/ in PDE 99
5.1.2 The velar and glottal fricatives of OE 102
5.1.3 Initial glottal fricatives in ME and EModE: ABLE-HABILITATE, WHICH-WITCH, WHINE-WINE 105
5.1.4 Non-initial glottal fricatives in ME: THOUGH-TOUGH 112
5.2 R-related histories 115
5.2.1 Phonetic and phonological properties of the rhotics in PDE 115
5.2.2 Reconstructing the phonetics of <r> in OE 116
5.2.3 Pre-consonantal /r/-loss 121

5.2.4 Post-vocalic /r/-loss 125
5.2.5 The other liquid: BRIDGESTOWE-BRISTOL Historical parallels between /r/ and /l/ 128
5.3 Cluster simplification: KNIGHT-NIGHT, WRITE-RIGHT, IAMB-IAMBIC 132
5.3.1 Initial <kn-, gn-, wr->: KNIGHT-NIGHT, WRITE-RIGHT 132
5.3.2 Final <-mb, -mn, -ng>: IAMB-IAMBIC, DAMN-DAMNATION, SINGER-LINGER 134
5.4 Other inventory changes: the adoption of /ʒ/ 141
5.4.1 More alveolar palatalisations and affrications: s-, t-, d- + -j. GOTCHA, INJUN 143
5.5 The glottal stop [ʔ] and the alveolar tap [ɾ] 145
5.5.1 The glottal stop 145
5.5.2 Voicing of [t] and tapping of [t] and [d]: MATTER-MADDER 147
5.6 Recent trends: [ts-, ʃm-, ʃl-, ʃt-]: MASH POTATO, MANAGE CARE, STAIN GLASS 148

6 The vowels in Old English: spelling, pronunciation. PDE alternations traced back to OE
FOOT-FEET, FULL-FILL, MAN-MEN, CHILD-CHILDREN, HOUND-HUNDRED 151
6.1 The vowel inventories of PDE and OE: a comparison 151
6.2 Orthography and the reconstruction of OE vowels 153
6.3 I-Mutation: FOOT-FEET, FULL-FILL, SELL-SALE 156
6.4 OE homorganic-cluster lengthening: CHILD-CHILDREN, HOUND-HUNDRED 164
6.4.1 Are pre-cluster lengthenings prosodically incongruous? 169
6.5 The late OE vowel inventory in detail 171
6.5.1 The short vowels in late OE 171
6.5.2 The long vowels in late OE: STREET-STRATFORD 173
6.5.3 Diphthongs and diphthongoids 175
6.5.4 Unstressed vowels 179

7 The vowels in Middle English. Dialects. Spelling innovations. Vowel quality and quantity. PDE alternations traced back to ME
DIZZY-BUSY, FURY-BURY, MOON-MONDAY, STEAL-STEALTH, GAME-GAMMON, GRASS-GRAZE 184
7.1 ME dialects 184

7.2 Notes on ME spelling (vowels): <TAXI>-<ATAXY>, <TYRE>-<TIRE>, <COME>-<CUT>, <SEE>-<SEA> 186
7.2.1 Letter-to-vowel correspondences in ME (single letters): SUN-SON, CONE-COME 187
7.2.2 Letter-to-vowel correspondences in ME (digraphs): BEAT-BEET, ROAD-ROOD 190
7.3 Qualitative changes in ME 192
7.3.1 Short vowels: DIZZY-BUSY, FURY-BURY, MERRY-MIRTH 192
7.3.2 Long vowels: GAE-GO, OAKE (Somerset) - AIKE (East Riding of Yorkshire) 200
7.4 The diphthongal system of ME 204
7.5 Quantitative changes: why do they matter? 209
7.5.1 Shortenings: CREEP-CREPT, MOON-MONDAY, MOUTH-PORTSMOUTH, LEEK-GARLIC 212
7.5.1.1 Pre-consonantal shortening: FEED-FED, WIDE-WIDTH, SHEEP-SHEPHERD 212
7.5.1.2 Trisyllabic shortening: HOLY-HOLIDAY, SOUTH-SOUTHERN 216
7.5.1.3 Vowel shortening in unstressed syllables: BUT-ABOUT, LEEK-GARLIC 219
7.5.2 Lengthenings: GAME-GAMMON, GRAZE-GRASS 220
7.5.2.1 ME open-syllable lengthening 221
7.5.3 Orthography and quantitative changes 225
7.6 Reduction and loss of unstressed vowels in ME 227

8 Vowel quality and quantity in Early Modern English and later MOTH-MOTHER, DULL-BULL, LOST-POST, FEAR-BEAR, HERE-THERE, MOOD-STOOD-BLOOD, DEAD-BEAD 234
8.1 Information glut. New sources of phonological reconstruction 234
8.2 Qualitative changes 236
8.2.1 Short vowels: QUASH-QUACK, WASH-WAX, GOD-EGAD, PUTT-PUT 236
8.2.2 The Great/Long/English Vowel Shift 248
8.2.2.1 Chronology and dating 252
8.2.2.2 Mechanism and causation 256
8.2.2.3 Further instability and enrichment: BREW-NEW, DO-DUE, AUNT-HAUNT 267
8.3 The effect of phonotactics on long vowel shifting 271
8.3.1 Shortening in monosyllabic words: LEAD (Pb)-LEAD, V., DEAF-LEAF, MOOD-STOOD-BLOOD 271

8.3.2 Vowels in relation to /r/: PERSON-PARSON, TEAR, v. - TEAR, n., FLOOR-POOR 274
8.4 Continuity or reinvention 281
8.4.1 Canadian or long-vowel 'Raising': ICE [ʌɪs] - EYES [aɪz] ~ [aɛz] ~ [aᵊ] ~ [aː] 281

9 The evolution of the English stress system ALWAYS-CAUSEWAYS, PRÉSENT, n. - PRESÉNT, v., HARÁSS ~ HÁRASS 284
9.1 Preliminaries: definition of some terms 284
9.2 Syllable structure and syllable weight 286
9.3 Historical sources of information for prosodic reconstruction 288
9.3.1 Orthographic evidence for word-stress 289
9.3.2 Verse evidence for stress 290
9.4 OE stress placement 294
9.4.1 OE word-stress 294
9.4.2 OE stress above the word level 298
9.5 ME stress placement: the native component 303
9.6 ME prosodic innovations 306
9.6.1 Grammar, meaning and stress-shifting: PERFÉCT-PÉRFECT, CANÁL-CHÁNNEL 310
9.7 ME compound and phrasal stress 312
9.8 Post-ME prosodic innovations 314

10 Early English verse forms: from Cædmon to Chaucer 323
10.1 Preliminaries: speech prosody vs poetic meter, stress vs ictus 323
10.2 Alliterative verse 326
10.2.1 Classical OE alliterative verse 327
10.2.2 Continuity and reinvention of alliterative versification in ME 339
10.3 Introduction of rhyme, syllable-counting, and binary foot structure 345
10.4 Chaucer and the invention of the iambic pentameter 356

Bibliography 367
Word Index 396
Name Index 412
Subject Index 417

Acknowledgements

This book has grown out of nearly four decades of studying, teaching, and researching the history of English, yet its chronological and thematic breadth presented unforeseen and seemingly endless challenges. It is a pleasant duty to recognise the encouragement and support I have received in dealing with these challenges.

My first acknowledgement goes to the University of Edinburgh's Institute for Advanced Studies in the Humanities for an annual Fellowship, giving an East European beginner a career-changing opportunity to benefit from its library resources and invaluable collegial advice and criticism. Angus McIntosh trusted me with my first Middle English classes and Roger Lass let me loose on his Phonology Two students. During that year I started to think of myself as an English Historical Phonologist. The influence of my first teachers will be obvious throughout the book.

I wish to thank UCLA and more specifically the Council on Research and the Center for Medieval and Renaissance Studies for support throughout the lengthy gestation of this book. The Department of English at UCLA has provided a friendly and accommodating working environment and a steady stream of intelligent and demanding students, without whom such work would be barren. My colleagues in the Department of Linguistics at UCLA have always welcomed me in their seminars and discussions; the analytical rigour and innovation in their work sets the bar high and I feel fortunate to be part of that community.

A generous grant from the Arts and Humanities Research Council of Great Britain on 'The Verse Forms of Middle English Romance' has been providing incentives and opportunities for exciting collaborative projects with Ad Putter and Judith Jefferson of the University of Bristol. Some of the results of our ongoing research are cited in this book.

I am grateful to the ETOTEL team at Edinburgh University Press, Esmé Watson, Sarah Edwards, Vicki Donald, Michelle Houston,

Gillian Leslie, James Dale and my copy-editor Eliza Wright for their sustained support in spite of the many delays. I gratefully acknowledge the assistance of Gillan Adler, UCLA, in the preparation of the indexes.

Special thanks go to Heinz Giegerich, the series editor. His much-tested patience, his encouragement and his unfaltering faith in the value of this project helped me persist stubbornly even when I felt that I had exceeded the limits of metaphorical chewing.

Henry Ansgar (Andy) Kelly, medievalist, Latinist, Satanist, philologist, was characteristically observant and generous with his comments on the overlong first draft. I feel lucky that his state of Emeritude has only enhanced his inexhaustible curiosity, attention to detail and spirited collegiality.

This book should have been co-authored with Robert Stockwell. For many years he and I talked about, argued about and wrote about English historical phonology. After 2006 Parkinson's gradually deprived him of his keen eye and the ability to assert his views. Without the productively critical bouncing back-and-forth of drafts with him, completing the project has been a lonely trip. Dedicating this book to Robert is the least I can do for one of the finest contemporary English historical phonologists and the most important person in my life.

UCLA
Los Angeles, 18 October 2012

Abbreviations and symbols

AAVE	African American Vernacular English
adj.	Adjective
AmE	American English
ANAE	Atlas of North American English
AN	Anglo-Norman
Angl.	Anglian
AS	Anglo-Saxon
AusE	Australian English
BrE	British English
C	Consonant
CE	Canadian English
DOE	*The Dictionary of Old English*
DOEC	*The Dictionary of Old English Corpus*
EModE	Early Modern English
Fr.	French
GA	General American
Ger.	German
Gk	Greek
Gmc	Germanic
Goth.	Gothic
GSR	The Germanic Stress Rule
GVS	Great Vowel Shift
H	Heavy syllable
IE	Indo-European
IPA	International Phonetic Alphabet
L	Light syllable
LAEME	*The Linguistic Atlas of Early Middle English*
LALME	*The Linguistic Atlas of Late Middle English*
Lat.	Latin
LModE	Late Modern English
LOE	Late Old English

LP	Linguistic Profile
LVS	Long Vowel Shift
MDu	Middle Dutch
ME	Middle English
MED	*The Middle English Dictionary*
N	nasal
n.	Noun
NED	*New English Dictionary on Historical Principles*
Norw.	Norwegian
NY	New York
NZE	New Zealand English
OE	Old English
OED	*The Oxford English Dictionary*
OFr	Old French
ON	Old Norse
PDE	Present-Day English
PIE	Proto-Indo-European
PrG	Proto-Germanic
RP	Received Pronunciation
SAE	South African English
Skt	Sanskrit
Sp.	Spanish
SSBE	Standard Southern British English
SSE	Standard Scottish English
V	Vowel
v.	Verb
WG	West Germanic
WGG	West Germanic (Consonant) Gemination
WS	West Saxon
YE	East Riding of Yorkshire
[ ]	phonetic representation
[C]	ambisyllabic consonant
< >	orthographic representation
*	reconstructed form, also unattested form
†	obsolete
.	syllable boundary
:	rhymes/alliterates with
#	word boundary
~	alternates with
≈	approximately the same as
<	previous stage/the input of a change
>	next diachronic stage/the output of a change

For the full names of the Old English texts, their abbreviations, for named authors, and bibliographical information see <http://tapor.library.utoronto.ca/doe/dict/bibl/index.html> (last accessed 27 May 2013).

For the ME authors and titles see <http://quod.lib.umich.edu/h/hyperbib/> (last accessed 27 May 2013).

A note on the Companion to *A Historical Phonology of English*

A Companion to this book is available at http://www.euppublishing.com/page/ETOTELAdvanced/Minkova. The Companion includes additional readings, exercises, comments and further resources. Online resources will be indicated in the text by the icon 💻.

In loving memory of

Robert Stockwell

(12 June 1925–28 October 2012)

1 Periods in the history of English

This book is about the evolution of the phonological structure of English: the history of individual sounds and their representation, the history of syllable structure and word stress. Our very first job is to clarify what we mean by 'English'; one hardly needs a reminder that no two speakers of English sound exactly alike. A phone call from a complete stranger immediately triggers associations based on age, gender, place of birth, education, social status and race. From exposure to the language we know the typical characteristics for each group of speakers; we also know that many or all of these characteristics can be unstable. In spite of the amazing amount of group or individual variation, there are enough shared properties that allow us to construct a mental representation of how an English word, phrase or sentence sounds; thus we can ignore voice quality and accent and communicate in English with people from very different backgrounds and regions. Like all other living languages, English is subject to constant change. What John Donne cherished and bequeathed as 'mine English tongue' (*The Will*, 1633), is a very different-sounding English in the twenty-first century. We start, therefore, by acknowledging that the notion of a single 'English' is a convenient abstraction and a cover term for a multitude of clearly distinct yet mutually intelligible varieties of one language.

The use of the noun *English* with reference to the language spoken by the Anglo-Saxons, as distinct from Latin or Celtic, must have been current from the time of the earliest contacts between the original inhabitants of the British Isles and the 'newcomers', who were speakers of north-west Germanic. Exactly when the first Germanic-speaking settlers arrived in Britain is not known; recent genetic mapping suggests that the Germanic colonisation of the Celts may have begun even before the Romans took administrative control of large sections of the island in the first century AD. What we do know for sure is that large permanent settlements of Angles and Saxons between c. 400–600 justified a separate name for the linguistic identity of the continental transplants. In writing, the earliest record of the noun *English* is found in a ninth-century translation into what we now call 'Old' English of the *Ecclesiastical History of the English Nation*, originally composed in Latin by the historian and scholar Bede (c. 672–735). By the middle of the fourteenth century there appear references to specific regional varieties of English, such as the *English of Kent*, and somewhat later, in the sixteenth century, we find *English* characterised further as *new*, *old*, *northern* and *southern*. In spite of the always-present and growing diversity of English, especially after the language was exported to other continents, it was only early in the twentieth century that *English* began to be treated also as a count noun; the OED records the first such use in H. L. Menken's article 'The Two Englishes', which appeared in the *Baltimore Evening Sun*, 15 September 1910. A hundred years later there are more Englishes than ever before, including blends such as *Chinglish*, *Taglish*, *Frenglish/Franglais*, *Singlish*, *Janglish* and more.

1.1 Periods in the history of English

English as spoken in the twenty-first century is only the latest and the most readily observable stage in a very long history. Like a living organism, our language both carries the marks that identify it as a member of a specific branch of the Indo-European family, Germanic, and has its own peculiarities, setting it apart from its 'genetic' relatives. One of the goals of this book is to describe the phonological features of the modern language in terms of its development, seeking to reveal how the present is indebted to the past. A telescopic view back into the evolution of the language requires us to set up a frame of temporal references and situate the linguistic findings in their historical, literary and social setting. We start with a survey of the main chronological divisions: Old English (OE), Middle English (ME), Early Modern English (EModE) and Present-Day English (PDE). Notice how the divisions become longer as we look back: PDE is the language of roughly the last two centuries, EModE spans about three centuries, ME – four centuries, while the most distant period, OE, stretches over more than six centuries. The further back we go, the less familiar we are with the socio-historical setting of linguistic change, thus the focus in the brief survey below will be primarily on the older periods of English.

1.2 Old English (450–1066)

Traditionally, Old English, also referred to as *Anglo-Saxon*, is assigned a birth date around AD 450. By the beginning of the fifth century prolonged threats from the north, the west and the east contributed to internal strife and disorder within the Roman Empire. In 400 troops were withdrawn from Britain to defend Italy against the invasion of Alaric the Goth and in 407 a large contingent of Roman troops were transferred from Britain to the Continent to bolster the armies fighting against Gaul and Spain. In 410 an appeal for support for the remaining Roman troops in Britain was rejected; that year marks the end point of what we call 'Roman Britain'.

After a hiatus of about forty years, during which time the rest of the Romans must have either left or become assimilated to the local Celtic-speaking population, a new, extensive and permanent occupation of Britain took place. According to an entry for the year 449 in Bede's *Ecclesiastical History of the English Nation*, the first Germanic settlers migrated to Britain within the next seven years. This is the justification for associating the earliest stage of English, OE, with the year 449 in text- and reference books, although, as noted above, there is mounting evidence that members of Germanic tribes had probably lived in Britain since the second century.[1]

The demographic balance after the Germanic invasion was originally in favour of the indigenous Celts who outnumbered the conquerors by a considerable measure. The estimated number of settlers participating in the Germanic diaspora ranges between as little as 10,000 and up to 200,000. In some estimates, most of the three and a half million speakers of Celtic survived the initial conquest.[2] However, the Celts had limited military experience and lacked the organisation to resist the incursions for more than half a century and by c. 550 larger and larger groups of Germanic-speaking peoples moved in, pushing the Celts away – those whom they did not kill or enslave – from the central part of the country west and south towards Cornwall and Wales, and north to the Lothian region. By the end of the sixth century the dominant language spoken on the British Isles was no longer Celtic. Old English had 'begun'. The end of the Celtic territorial and political dominance also determined the direction and the scope of the linguistic influence of Celtic on English: as is often noted, the transfer of lexical items from the language of the conquered into a higher-status language, in this case English, can be expected to be quite limited. This is not necessarily the case with the

[1] See Wakelin (1988: 180); the evidence is addressed more specifically in Oppenheimer (2006).

[2] The distribution of Celtic speakers in the different regions was uneven, with the south more heavily Germanic than the north, where the ratio of Celts to immigrants may have been as much as 50:1; see Tristram (2002: 113–14).

transfer of phonological and prosodic features, though the latter are much harder to isolate. Bilingualism and the physical proximity of Celtic and English speakers in the British Isles has resulted in shared phonological features between the modern languages Irish and Welsh, and Irish English and Welsh English.

In addition to the continuing Celtic–OE bilingualism in the geographical areas of contact, the reintroduction of Christianity called for the study of Latin. Christianity had been practised in Roman Britain, but the Germanic settlers of the fifth and the sixth centuries were pagan, hence the use of 'reintroduction' of Christianity. The conversion began in 597, when a Roman monk, Augustine, and his missionaries were allowed to preach and spread the Christian faith in the southern kingdom of Kent. About thirty years later in the north, a Bishop Aidan came from Ireland to Northumbria, and, through his efforts, the northern kingdoms were converted. What resulted was a dangerous rivalry between the version of Christianity introduced in the south from Rome, and the modes of worship introduced from Ireland in the north. The differences were settled in a convocation known as the Synod of Whitby, which took place in 663–4. The Synod's decision unified the religious practices across England; by 669 the Church acknowledged a single head, a Roman Archbishop named Theodore of Tarsus (602–90). The promotion of the Roman Catholic mode of worship brought the English Church into close contact with the Continent and further enhanced the need and popularity of Latin among English clerics.

The unification of the Church ushered in a period of intense and organised scholarship, known also as 'The Golden Age of Bede'. The study of Latin and the translation of many liturgical and scholastic texts from Latin into OE was a central concern of the officers of the Church, making religion an important channel through which learned Latin borrowings came into the language. Loanwords having to do with trade, warfare and household objects were characteristic of the earlier, Continental contacts between Germanic and Latin, while loanwords from Latin after the middle of the sixth century are mostly associated with religion, books, learning and writing. Characteristically, the words that came into the language through the monks' scholastic culture were introduced through the written language, though the oral aspect of the transmission is also important. Silent reading was not a common practice, and instruction was done mainly through memorisation and repetition. This allowed for a quick adaptation of the more frequently used loanwords to the phonology of the native language. Latin words recorded in OE are of course not restricted to religious terms; there are words from the fields of medicine, biology and the arts, and include plain core vocabulary.

Phonologically, the early loanwords were commonly assimilated to OE: Latin words such as *candēla*, *comēta*, which would have had stress on the penultimate syllable in the source language, shifted their stress onto the first syllable, following the Germanic model of root-initial stress. In OE verse such words alliterate on [k-].

The political and administrative history of multi-kingdom Anglo-Saxon England was unstable.[3] In the first half of the seventh century the kingdom of Northumbria had considerable powers over large areas south of the river Humber. Throughout that century Northumbria and Mercia were in continuous rivalry, with Mercia emerging dominant after 678. The supremacy of Mercia continued into the first quarter of the ninth century, challenged only by Wessex. During the ninth century the rivalry between Mercia and the rising power of Wessex became less important than the need of unity in the face of an outside enemy.

At the same time as the OE language was developing various local and regional varieties whose names are associated with the political and cultural divisions of the Anglo-Saxon kingdoms, large parts of northern Europe were raided and colonised by the Scandinavian seafaring pagan tribes, jointly referred to as the Vikings. Linguistically, the Vikings' language differed from the western branch of Germanic that the Anglo-Saxons spoke; by c. 600 their language was already a distinct northern variety of Germanic, known as Old Scandinavian or *Old Norse* (ON). The Viking Age in Europe is dated c. 750–1050. During that time Old Norse was spoken not just in present-day Scandinavia but also in Iceland, Greenland, the Faroe Islands and in parts of Ireland, Scotland, England, Northern France (Normandy) and Russia. England was not spared: the Scandinavian incursions and the permanent settlements of ON speakers in large parts of eastern England and Yorkshire became an important source of linguistic diversity in OE, though some of the effects of this linguistic contact are not recorded until later.

The invasions started at the end of the eighth century. The *Anglo-Saxon Chronicle*, the most important historical source recording contemporaneous events, describes the first invasion under the year 787 when 'there first came three ships of the Northmen . . . the first Danish ships that came into England'. Throughout the ninth century the incursions and settlements by new ON speakers continued; the Anglo-Saxons

[3] Before the middle of the ninth century, the country was divided into kingdoms whose political importance rose and fell; the seven most important kingdoms of the early period, often referred to as the *heptarchy*, were Northumbria, Mercia, East Anglia, Wessex, Essex, Sussex and Kent. Unlike the kingdoms and states of later history, these kingdoms did not have firmly fixed boundaries and their internal organisation was based on both kinship and perceived merit.

Figure 1.1 England after 886 (public domain image taken from <http://history medren.about.com/library/atlas/natmapengland886.htm>, accessed 16 May 2013)

usually referred to them as Danes, although Norwegian presence is also identifiable in the North-West Midlands.[4] Unable to resist the attacks, in 878 King Alfred of Wessex signed a treaty with the Scandinavian ruler of East Anglia establishing a territory north-east of the river Thames, which came to be called the Danelaw, also spelled *Danelagh* or *Danelaga*, meaning 'Danes' Law'. The treaty suspended the continuous warfare between speakers of OE and ON in that region, allowed the newcomers to set up new households, till the land and trade with the

[4] See Dance (2003: 51, 151); Bibire (2001: 89).

local population, thus putting down permanent roots in England. Most important for the evolution of English, it legitimised the presence of another, northern, strand of Germanic in the country and created conditions for an enduring, and most likely peaceful integration of the two related languages.

Towards the end of the tenth century a new wave of Scandinavian invasions hit the country. Between 1013 and 1016 the English crown passed from Danish to English and back to Danish hands. Between 1017 and 1035 the country was ruled by King Canute, who was also King of Denmark and King of Norway. After the initial takeover turmoil, King Canute's reign appears to have been non-violent and orderly, promoting further linguistic integration. Two of Canute's sons reigned briefly after their father's death. The Scandinavian rule of England continued until 1042, when the English royal line was once again restored. During the decades of Scandinavian reign in England the linguistic contacts between speakers of the two varieties of Germanic were very close, possibly resulting in a kind of mixed, creolised vernacular language.

It is estimated that between the end of the eighth and the beginning of the twelfth century, about one thousand common words were adopted from ON. The new loans were not typically learned words, so they were transmitted orally, and the record of their adoption into English lags behind the actual time when these words must have come into circulation. Words whose presence or form in OE can be traced back to ON are shown in (1).

(1) Words whose presence or form in OE can be traced back to ON:

ceallian 'to call'	*feolaga* 'fellow'
cnif 'knife'	*ragg(g)* 'rough, shaggy'
hæfen 'haven'	*utlaga* 'outlaw'
husbonda 'householder, husband'	*wrang* 'wrong'

Other common words borrowed through contact with Scandinavian are *bank*, *bull*, *cast*, *gape*, *guess*, *hap* 'luck, success', *leg*, *loan*, *score*, *skill*, *sister*, *skin*, *sky*, *wing*. The meanings of many of these words were already fully or partially covered by OE words, thus *sky*, originally in ON meaning 'cloud', developed also the meaning 'firmament' and overlapped with OE *heofon* 'heaven, atmosphere'; ON *vengr* 'wing' replaced one of the meanings of OE *feþer* 'feather', which used to mean 'feather', 'wing' and 'pen'.[5]

[5] The latter meaning was replaced in the fourteenth century by an Old French loan *penne* < Latin *penna* 'feather, quill-feather used for writing'.

Scandinavian and late OE/early ME frequently shared the *Proto-Germanic* (PrG) root of the same word. However, because of the different sound changes within each branch, the forms of the native continuation and the borrowing differ in PDE, so that we get pairs such as ***shirt-skirt***, ***church-kirk***, where the first word reflects late OE changes, while the second word retains the ON pronunciation. The influence of Scandinavian is attested also in the pronunciation of words such as *again* (OE *on-***ġ***ean*), *get* (OE **ġ***ietan*), *give* (OE **ġ***iefan*), in which the bold letters would be pronounced [j], as in PDE *yes*, *yard*, had it not been for the [g-] pronunciation of the Scandinavian speakers (see 4.2.1, 4.3). ON also contributed to some vowel alternations in OE and ME (see 6.2, 6.5.3, 7.4).

The everyday contacts of the Anglo-Saxons with speakers of Celtic and Old Norse and the exposure of clerics to Latin complicated the linguistic realities of Old English. Also, it is logical to assume that the populations of the various historical kingdoms must have spoken distinct dialects, though what we can reconstruct is not strictly area-determined, but based on clusters of texts reflecting the scribal traditions in major monastic centres such as Durham, Lichfield, Winchester and Canterbury (Hogg 2006a: 358). Thus the linguistic situation in Anglo-Saxon England was not unlike the picture we get in any modern language: time, place and sociocultural factors work against the notion of linguistic homogeneity. It is therefore evident that normal dialect divergence and language contact make the single label, *Old English*, inadequate to cover six hundred years of turbulent history. Only a small part of the non-homogeneous OE language can be recovered, however, and in this book we will stay with the traditional umbrella label *Old English* with references to specific varieties whenever needed.

As for resources, the entire surviving body of OE materials, 3,047 texts, is now available in digitised form. Excluded are only some variants of individual texts. Web access was made available by the ongoing *Dictionary of Old English Project*, Centre for Medieval Studies, University of Toronto. The Old English Corpus (OEC) is a research resource which was originally prepared for internal use at the *Dictionary of Old English* (DOE). When completed, this will be the most important and versatile electronic resource for the study of OE. The progress report for 2010 informed us that 'more than one third of the *Dictionary* – eight of the 22 letters of the Old English alphabet – has been published, and more than 60% of the total entries have been written to date'.[6] The

[6] Available at <http://www.doe.utoronto.ca/index.html> (last updated 22 July 2011, last accessed 16 May 2013).

DOE report of May 2011 states: 'The editors are making good progress towards completing the writing of *H* (the next letter to be published). We are also drafting entries for *I*/ *Y*, *L*, *M*, and *N*, and the lemmatization of *S* (the largest letter) is continuing.'

1.3 Middle English (1066–1476)

Deciding when and why it is appropriate to label a reconstructed language as no longer 'old' but 'middle' is not easy. The periodisation of historical English into Old, Middle and Early Modern, originally proposed by the prominent English philologist Henry Sweet in 1874, was based on an important and orthographically testable criterion: the neutralisation of vowel distinctions in final unstressed syllables as attested in prototypical texts. Sweet was also fully aware that strict chronological divisions are unrealistic, and that 'transition' periods during which the linguistic evidence is not clear-cut have to straddle the core periods. In Sweet's schema, *transition* OE stretches from 1100–1200, followed by *early* Middle English from 1200–1300, *late* Middle English from 1300–1400 and, again, *transition* Middle English from 1400–1500. The proposed partitions were later challenged by new evidence for vowel reduction in manuscripts of the second half of the tenth century: 'The transition period from Old to Middle English is not the twelfth century, as the grammarians used to think, nor even the eleventh, as most of them think today, but rather the tenth' (Malone 1930: 117) (see also 6.5.4). At the other chronological end, Kitson (1997) points out the persistence of OE linguistic features in non-literary documents into the early thirteenth century. The problematic nature of such divisions notwithstanding, we still need a label for the linguistic phase that follows OE, so in this book we will follow the *Cambridge History of the English Language* in dating the 'beginning' of ME conveniently, if arbitrarily, from a linguistic perspective, to the year of the Norman Conquest of 1066.

The events surrounding the Conquest are well known: in 1051 William, Duke of Normandy (1028–87) had almost certainly been promised to succeed the childless Edward the Confessor, the last King of the Anglo-Saxon royal line. When Edward died early in 1066, however, a well-liked and powerful English earl, Harold, was elected King. In pursuit of his alleged royal rights, William assembled a force of about 5,000 knights, crossed the English Channel in September, and defeated Harold's army at Hastings in October. The Norman troops then moved on to London and William declared himself King of England on Christmas Day 1066.

The cultural and linguistic consequences of the eleventh-century occupation of Britain by speakers of Norman French were far-reaching. The links to Scandinavia became much less important while contacts with Western Europe were intensified. The political reins of the country passed into the hands of Norman landlords, upper clergy and administrative officers – a foreign minority who spoke little or no English and who maintained strong cultural and linguistic ties to the Continent, especially for the first century and a half after the Conquest. During that same time, and outside the monastic circles, people who had access to writing and the leisure to engage in any literary activity had little or no English. The social layering of feudal England was reflected in linguistic layering too: at the bottom of the scale serfs and peasants would be monolingual English speakers, the most tenacious custodians of the mother tongue. At the top end of the social scale, the sovereign and his barons could barely understand English. Not surprisingly, English was no longer the primary language of record, nor was it the language of upper-class literary entertainment and learning, law or administration; these activities were conducted in Latin and *Anglo-Norman* (AN).

AN is the variety of *Old French* (OFr) spoken in England from the time of the Conquest to approximately the middle of the fifteenth century. The Normans themselves – the word comes from Germanic *Northman* – were an ethnic mixture of Scandinavian and Frankish people whose variety of French was influenced by ON. The ties between the insular and the continental Normans started to weaken after King Philip of France seized the Norman estates of the Anglo-Norman barons in 1204. Being thus cut off, during the thirteenth century and after, more and more members of the upper classes adapted by learning English.

For a linguist digging into the historical records, the ME period matches, and even exceeds, OE in diversity and complexity. This is partly due to the finite nature of the surviving OE material compared with the much richer ME documentation. Another challenge for the study of ME comes from the fact that it was, at least early after the Conquest, the language of unrecorded everyday communication. We are also in the dark about 'colloquial' OE, of course, but at least from the time of King Alfred (871–99) until the Conquest we have evidence of Anglo-Saxon vernacular learning and transmission. Sermons were written and popular Latin texts were translated into Old English to be shared by the laity. The events of 1066 put an end to that practice. Ultimately, the main source of increased complexity is the introduction of multi-tiered and lasting second- and third-language influence on the already diverse base of late OE.

Statistically, the number of monoglot French speakers in England was never very high; it is estimated that it ranged, roughly, between 2 per cent and 10 per cent of the population, and even that group had started shifting to some variety of English by the late twelfth century.[7] The social boundaries within which French was used were narrow. As Ostler puts it:

> The spread of Norman French would have been limited by the very rigidity in the social hierarchy over which the Normans presided. Within the feudal system, the status of every English man and woman was largely determined by birth, with the church providing the only paths for advancement through merit, and that was severely limited through the constraints of celibacy. As a result the French-speaking nobility remained almost a closed society . . . and there was little or no scope for people to better their prospects through aping their masters. In feudal England, people knew their place . . . (Ostler 2005: 461)

This angle on the interaction between English and French speakers excludes, however, the well-attested bilingualism and even trilingualism within the 'closed society' of the aristocracy and the clerics. Spoken transmission of AN, though demographically limited, continued steadily, and indeed the late thirteenth and the early fourteenth century are associated with a temporary expansion of the functions of insular French (Ingham 2012). While Anglo-Norman did not survive as a true vernacular language much beyond the middle of the fourteenth century, the written forms of Anglo-Norman lingered on in legal and parliamentary use until the seventeenth century (Rothwell 2001).

For upwards of two centuries the country's important affairs were conducted in Anglo-Norman or Latin, yet from the middle of the twelfth century onwards, English had to be shared more and more widely even among the nobility. Manuals for instruction in French began to appear in the thirteenth century at the same time as English was gradually regaining ground as a literary language. *The Hundred Years' War* (1337–1453) is a milestone in the development of national consciousness and unity in England, and with that, the re-emergence of English as a new national language. Literary activities in English were resumed, and by the middle of the fourteenth century English was again, and firmly, not just the leading language in the fields and the marketplace, which it had never ceased to be, but also the medium of prose and poetry of interest and lasting value.

The re-establishment of English did not signal the elimination of French as an important second language in medieval England; it held

[7] The demographic details are insightfully summarised in Lass (1987: 56–7).

its position as a learnèd tongue, like Latin. Active political and cultural contacts with the Continent in the fourteenth century meant that French continued to be a language of prestige and culture, only by this time there were two types of French in England: the home-grown Anglo-Norman vernacular, and Old French as it had evolved on the Continent. Both were developments of vernacular forms of Vulgar Latin. The two descendant languages were not identical; their parallel use in England paved the way for the creation of doublet forms of the same etymological form: from AN we get ***Karl***, *cattle*, *warranty*, *warden*, matching ***Charles***, ***chattel***, ***guarantee***, ***guardian*** from OFr (see 4.3).

The most widely recognised effect of the Norman Conquest on English was the rapid absorption of words from all spheres of interaction characteristic of the higher social status of the French-speaking nobility. The new rulers brought with them legal, administrative, military, political and cultural terms which often paralleled existing English words. In some instances the French loans would be indistinguishable from their ultimately Latin prototypes, which makes it difficult to state with precision what the source of the borrowing is. Convenient cover-terms for all of these are 'Latinate' or 'Romance' loanwords. The most common practice of recording the etymological source in dictionaries is to assign 'origin' to a word according to the *immediate* source of borrowing. This means that at times derivatives of the same root will appear under different etymological labels. In the 1150–1450 time-bracket of the *Chronological English Dictionary* (Finkenstaedt et al. 1970) we find: *excuse*, n., v. (OFr), but *excusable* (Lat.); *exemplar* (OFr), but *exemplary* (Lat.); *lineage* (OFr), but *lineation* (Lat.); *violence* (AN), but *violent* (OFr); *visage* (AN), but *vision* (OFr).

What matters to us in the context of this book is that the word-stock was undergoing rapid innovation and growth; words with unfamiliar phonological and prosodic shape were replacing or duplicating words with prototypical Germanic structure. Some examples of such replacements are shown in (2); the dates in parentheses in the second column are the earliest OED records for the new entries, cited in their modern form.

(2) Replacements of Old English words with loanwords from AN/OFr:

OE	**AN/OFr loan**
(ge)mot 'court, council', PDE *moot*	*assembly* (1325)
deman 'to judge', PDE *deem*	*judge*, v. (1290)
deor 'animal', PDE *deer*	*animal* (1398)
treowþ 'truth'	*verity* (1375)
wundor 'wonder'	*miracle* (1230)

As we will see in Chapters 5 and 9, the loanwords from AN/OFr often exhibited features 'alien' to the structure of OE: seemingly underived and uninflected words of more than two syllables (*assembly*, *animal*, *miracle*), word-initial /dʒ-/ (*judge*) or word-initial /v-/ (*verity*). Such features had to be learned by monolingual speakers of English and eventually became integrated into the basic language structure.

Another window into loanword adaptation is provided by their morphological behaviour. More specifically, if a foreign lexical element, either a stem or an affix, combines with native stems and affixes, we can posit a certain degree of 'nativisation' or 'naturalisation' of the borrowed element. Such *hybrid* word-formation is an independent parameter on which one can determine the 'nativeness' of a new loanword. Some examples of hybrid compounds with their first attestations cited in the OED are shown in (3).

(3) Hybrid compounds:

English + AN/French	**AN/French + English**
town-clerk (1386)	*safe-keeping* (1432)
breastplate (1386)	*gravel-stone* (1440)
freemason (1376)	*riverside* (1366)
bedchamber (1362)	*dinner-time* (1371)

Newly derived words could combine borrowed roots with native affixes and native roots with affixes taken from other languages, as shown in (4).

(4) Combinations of roots and affixes:

English + AN/French	**AN/French + English**
husband*ry* (1290)	joy*ful* (1290)
love*able* (1340)	manner*ly* (1375)
talk*ative* (1432)	colour*less* (1380)
wiz*ard* (1440)	*fore*taste (1435)

When we turn to the history of stress-placement in Chapter 9, we will see that one of the channels through which new patterns of accentuation enter English is the adoption of new affixes. While suffixation in OE never changed the stress of the stem, suffixation in PDE can shift the main stress away from the root: *hónour-honourée*, *állergy-allérgic*, *ségment-segmentátion*, *sólid-solídify*).

Another way in which the presence of a French-speaking social elite in England after the Conquest was felt was the shift in modes of versification. As we will see in Chapter 10, OE poetic composition lies firmly within the Germanic alliterative tradition; the verse line was held together by alliteration, which is consistently associated with the first sound of the stressed syllable of a word. In Middle English syllable-counting and end-rhyme, properties characteristic of contemporary Continental versification, became increasingly popular, culminating in the invention of the English iambic pentameter by Chaucer (c. 1343–1400). This culturally based innovation cannot be separated from the prosodic changes in progress towards the end of the ME period and thus offers yet another, albeit indirect, way of calibrating the linguistic effect of the Conquest.

As already noted, the shift of power after 1066 placed English in the position of a demographically dominant vernacular with a relatively low social status. This results in the famous fragmentisation of Middle English. The centralised written 'standard' that had emerged in late OE was abandoned. English obviously continued as a robust vernacular because valuable literary compositions in English did begin to re-emerge around the end of the twelfth century, but the literary language existed and developed without codification. We do not know how local scriptoria taught their scribes to write English, but they must have been allowed the freedom to 'translate' the texts they copied into their own regional pronunciation and grammar. The surviving ME literary documents do not represent a monolithic language with systematic spelling and grammatical rules. Up to at least the middle of the fourteenth century, it is fair to describe English as a conglomeration of dialects, each representing distinct, yet often also mixed, accents, grammar and vocabulary.

Starting roughly in the second half of the fourteenth century, the re-emergence of English as the leading language in all spheres of life led to the formation of more systematic scribal practices, especially in the crafting of official documents in which dialectal differences were levelled out in favour of a unified written standard. The process of standardising English thus has its roots and primary motivation in the events that usher in the re-establishment of English as the language of written communication. The single most important event which accelerated the formation and spread of a written standard and in many ways shaped the future of the English language was the introduction of the printing press in England, in 1476, by William Caxton. Although we know that many linguistic changes associated primarily with Early Modern English started in the fourteenth century, and that some typically ME grammatical features persisted beyond 1500, we can take 1476 as the emblematic 'end' of Middle English; the linguistically arbitrary historical signpost of 1066 that we chose to mark the beginning of the period is thus matched by another datable historical event at its end.

There are rich digital resources for the study of ME. The *Electronic Middle English Dictionary*, in the public domain since 2007, crowns seventy-five years of lexicographical work. It is an indispensable research tool that gives searchable access to more than 15,000 pages of printed material. Two other extremely valuable records of the linguistic landscape of ME are the *Linguistic Atlas of Late Middle English* (LALME), and the *Linguistic Atlas of Early Middle English* (LAEME). Six of the top twenty-five most frequently cited authors and works in the OED are Middle English, including Chaucer in sixth and Caxton in thirteenth place.

1.4 Early Modern English (1476–1776)

The official use of Latin and French decreased rapidly during the fifteenth century. The last French entry from the statutes of Parliament dates to 1489, during the reign of the first Tudor king, Henry VII (1485–1509). Clearly, English was firmly and permanently established as the language of art and literature, the language of trade, administration and the court. In religious and academic discourse, however, Latin and Classical Greek continued to be central to the education of scholars and priests. Intense scholarly engagement with the humanistic heritage of the Classics is one of the most salient characteristics of the two centuries following the introduction of printing.

Academic commitment to Greek and Latin and the development of new areas of scientific inquiry led to an unprecedented rate of adoption of Classical vocabulary in EModE. According to one estimate based on counting entries in the OED, 4,500 new words were recorded in English during each decade between 1500 and 1700.[8] About half of the new words were derivatives of pre-existing native words, but the rest were loanwords: over 20,000 words borrowed from the Classical languages between 1500 and 1700 have survived to this day. The spread of Classical learning and the density of new items make it much more likely that words borrowed from Latin and from Greek via Latin during that period would resist assimilation. For the prosodic history of English a rate of borrowing from Latin ranging from 35–40 per cent of the new lexis (Nevalainen 2006: 53) means that such words would tend to preserve the stress of the original, as in *alumnus*, *antenna*, *cerebellum*, *curriculum*, *lacuna*, *radius*. Affixes were also borrowed from Latin, for example the suffixes *-ence*, *-ancy*, *-ency*, *-y* and the prefixes *ante-*, *post-*, *sub-*, *super-*. In Chapter 9 we will see how the influx of Latin vocabulary in EModE led to the establishment of a new, parallel system of stress placement.

[8] The figures are a recalculation of counts presented in Barber (1997: 220), which cover 2 per cent of the entries in the first edition of the OED.

Among the social and demographic factors influencing the development of the language during the EModE period were rapid population growth and the shift from rural to urban living resulting in the levelling of dialect differences. An early seventeenth-century commentary on English by Alexander Gil, written in Latin, described a variety of English pronunciation, *Communis dialectus*, a 'General' dialect, which is socially and not regionally identified and which exists side by side with the regional Northern, Western, Southern and Eastern varieties. Other contemporary writers were also recommending the pronunciation of the aristocracy and the educated upper class as a model to be imitated. The city of London was the geographic focus of the patterns of pronunciation which became the core of Standard Southern British English (SSBE) in the course of the eighteenth century.

Early Modern English is marked also by the rapid expansion of English across the British Isles and overseas. Although English was spoken in parts of Wales before, and Wales had been annexed to the English crown since 1284, a new measure in 1536 brought the two countries under the same legal and administrative system; the common law of England, rather than Welsh law, was to be used in the Welsh courts, which guaranteed the spread and prestige of English. After the middle of the sixteenth century, economic changes resulted in rapid growth of the use of English in Ireland too, affecting areas beyond Dublin and the original English Pale. The English of medieval Scotland, Scots English, was also under sociopolitical pressure: the Union of the Crowns in 1603, whereby King James VI of Scotland became the first Stuart King of England as James I, and declared himself 'king of Great Britain', brought about wider use of (southern) English in Scotland and accelerated the process of 'Anglicisation' of Scots English. The blending of Welsh, Irish and Scots English with English English has not been completed; it is most advanced in morphology and syntax, while the phonology of the four varieties is still distinct.

The 1607 Jamestown Colony in Virginia and the Pilgrims' landing at Plymouth Rock in 1620 marked the beginning of a new phase in the expansion of English. In the course of the seventeenth century, the New World became the second geographic area where English was the dominant language. 'Colonial' English was far from homogeneous. The demographic strands of the settlers do not correspond exactly to the dialect differences in later American English, but they provide one basis for identifying regional varieties in North America and tracing them back to the speech of the first colonists.

For the first century and a half after the colonisation, the linguistic ties to Britain were very strong, especially along the eastern seaboard.

At the same time, English speakers were exposed to other languages, not just a variety of American Indian languages but also German, Dutch, French and Spanish. In spite of many bi- or multilingual groups and areas, colonial American English is considered more homogeneous than contemporary British English.

1.5 English after 1776

By 1776, when the colonists declared their independence from England, the political, cultural and linguistic conditions for identifying American English as a separate variety were at hand. In 1783 the lexicographer whose name would subsequently become synonymous with specifically American dictionary-making, Noah Webster, published his *American Spelling Book*; he started work on his *American Dictionary of the English Language* in 1807 and completed the first edition in 1828. He was an influential advocate of American spelling and usage and introduced many original American entries in his dictionary, which initially sold more copies in England than it did in the US, contributing much to the perceived legitimisation of American English. The idea of a separate American language was widely accepted in the nineteenth century although British English continued to be admired and imitated well into the twentieth century. The noun *Americanism* was first recorded in 1871 (OED). Predictably, American English itself became more and more diversified. Political contacts between Canada and the US made American English a rival of British English and, of course, French, in Canada, bringing about the formation of a new variety of North American English, Canadian English. In addition to the establishment of identifiable regional varieties of North American English, political and demographic changes in the US have given rise to new ethnic varieties of American English. The best-studied among them are African American Vernacular English and Latino/Chicano English.

The late eighteenth century also marked the expansion of English to other continents. Early immigration to Australia in the 1780s and the settlement of English speakers in New Zealand from about 1840 led to the creation of two other national varieties: Australian and New Zealand English. These varieties have close historical links to southern British English, but they also developed features which distinguish them both from the Cockney dialect of many of the original settlers and from SSBE.

It is impossible to estimate the number of people who spoke Proto-Germanic (see 3.2), but we know how the various branches of Germanic have fared more recently. English has emerged as one of the most widely used native languages: only Mandarin Chinese, Hindi and Spanish have more native speakers than English. Stated very broadly, post-colonial English outside Britain and North America is characterised by the diversity of new features introduced through the contact between colonisers and colonised. The British Raj (1858–1947) fostered the development of Indian English; today South Asia is one of the three largest English-using regions in the world. The establishment of the Cape Colony in 1806 in what is now South Africa and the arrival of American-Liberians in West Africa in 1822 resulted in new English-language communities in Africa. Today, in addition to Liberia, English is the official language of administration in many otherwise multilingual African countries: Botswana, Ghana, Kenya, Lesotho, Malawi, Nigeria, Sierra Leone, Swaziland, The Gambia, Uganda, Zambia and Zimbabwe. Other geographic regions have adopted English too, generating new branches of English such as Caribbean English. English is now both a world language geographically and a global language functionally: it is the language of the airlines, an official language of the United Nations, the dominant language in computing, science and international communication.

This book focuses on the *historical* underpinnings of the Present-Day English phonological system, but as we have seen from the preceding survey, there is no single, or static, entity that can be labelled 'Present-Day English'. Covering the phonological and prosodic details in the huge variety of present-day Englishes is beyond this book's remit; instead, the focus will be on some reference standard accents which will form the starting point for our journey back in time. These prototypical accents are widely recognised and can be easily related to varieties spoken outside the narrow confines of the 'standards'. The two varieties from which we will project backwards are Southern Standard British English (SSBE), also known as Received Pronunciation (RP), and General American (GA), with cross-references to other varieties whenever appropriate.

If the goal of this book is to discover how the past shaped the selected present-day standards, we need some understanding of the genesis of the notion 'Standard English', a topic which has received considerable scholarly attention. First, we have to keep the *written* and the *spoken* standards separate. The orthographic 'standard' is the conformity with a unified written norm that keeps words looking the same on the page or on the screen. Apart from some well-known national differences, such as American English versus British English spelling of *-or*/*-our* or *-er*/*-re* words, the spelling norms are shared by all varieties of English. It is the variation in the *spoken* standards that is our main target of interest, and since we are limiting our scope to phonology, we can talk of 'standard accents'. Here we need to remind ourselves that 'standard' is a socially constructed notion: any accent of English could have become standard under the right cultural and socio-economic circumstances. It is a truism in linguistics that no language is inherently better or worse than any other language; there is no intrinsic value in standards, although standards do carry considerable social and cultural prestige, or baggage, depending on the viewpoint.

Historically, none of the standard varieties we cover can be reconstructed as a linear descendent of one particular historical dialect. The OE standard represented in textbooks is nothing more than a 'high level of agreement in a language community as to what does and what does not constitute "the language" at a given time' – this is what sociolinguists understand by the term 'focussing' (Trudgill 1986: 86). Applied to Old English, the standard is the relatively stable set of forms found in the works of Ælfric (c. 955–c. 1025) and Wulfstan (d. 1023) (Hogg 2006b: 401–3). Yet the ancient origins of Standard English are unknown to us because the particular variety of late West Saxon represented by Ælfric's and Wulfstan's writing is *not* the basis of any one of the emerging late Middle English 'standards'. Those too are most aptly characterised as 'focussed' varieties (Smith 1996: 65–77), preserved only in writing. By the middle of the seventeenth century 'a high degree of uniformity in spelling' was in evidence in contemporary printed materials, though the codification did not extend to private correspondence until much later (Nevalainen and Tieken-Boon van Ostade 2006: 289–91). Pronunciation standards develop much more slowly than the written standard; moreover, a standard accent often coexists with various *-lects* in the repertoire of a single individual. Pronunciation norms emerge under the heavy scrutiny and direction of prominent and respected intellectuals and educational institutions. In England, the educated accent of London and the court became codified during the nineteenth century when the term *Received Pronunciation* (RP) was applied to that accent. This accent, although not native to the large majority of English speakers, is recognised widely and its features are constantly updated to reflect ongoing change. In the US, the corresponding 'standard' is commonly referred to as 'General American'. GA is much less regionally or socially focused and it can be defined negatively: it is identified as the accent that is neither eastern nor southern. It covers a broad geographical area comprising parts of the midlands and the west.

This chapter started with observations on the enormous diversity of Englishes today, making it clear that a single starting point for our telescopic journey back in time is an artificial construct. Yet we have to start from somewhere, and the choice of two accents, GA and SSBE, is motivated by their widespread use, easy identification by speakers of other varieties and by the author's own limitations – these are the two 'standard' varieties that I have been taught and that I have had most exposure to as a non-native speaker of English.

1.6 The evidence for early pronunciation

The inconsistencies of letter-sound correspondences in PDE – pairs like *know-no, scene-seen, reel-real, bass-bass, rough-though* – are frequently remarked on. If PDE spelling is so unreliable, how do we know what sounds correspond to the letters used in the historical documents? Unlike morphology, syntax and word-formation, where the properties of the forms are more tangibly attested in the written texts, the phonological properties of a written form are much less physically 'real'. Nevertheless, rigorous methodologies for phonological reconstruction have been developed and tested repeatedly in the last two centuries. Although scholars will disagree about the precise realisation of specific form, or forms, there is consensus about the validity of many of the histories that have become canonical in describing the evolution of English.

The obvious first step in reconstructing sound systems from written documents is to look at what the scribes recorded and how consistent they were. The main body of surviving Anglo-Saxon manuscripts is based on the Roman alphabet. Along with their conversion to Christianity, starting in 432, the neighbouring Irish had gradually adopted and adapted the Roman script, creating their own version of the letters, known as 'insular' script. That 'insular' script-form was imported into England by missionaries after the adoption of Christianity by the Anglo-Saxons in 597. Monastic culture, not just in Britain, but throughout Western Europe, was dominated by writings in the Roman alphabet. Not surprisingly, the OE orthographic system developed on the basis of Latin writing during the seventh and the eighth century. The Latin connection is helpful in figuring out how the scribes, who were also literate in Latin, matched sound to letter. Not all OE letters are found in Latin: two OE letters, *thorn* <þ> and *wynn* <ƿ>, were borrowed from the runic alphabet; another native addition was the letter *eth* <ð>, also spelled *edh*.[9] The letters <q, k, x, z> were used very rarely in OE; they became part of the regular inventory of consonantal letters after the adoption of

[9] Angled brackets are used to mark letters, as distinct from sounds, which will be enclosed in slashes and square brackets; see Chapter 2.

the Carolingian script in ME. Throughout the history of the language the actual shape of the letters has changed many times, but whether we find <ꝺ, ꝱ, ẟ, 𝕯, 𝔇, D>, or <d>, we can be fairly confident that that letter matches the first and the last sound in *David*.[10] The interpretation of scribal evidence is rarely that straightforward; nevertheless, matching the familiar letter values in the Roman alphabet to the values of the letters used by the scribes is a primary source of information about the older pronunciation.

Consistency or inconsistency of spelling is another fairly good measure of the stability of a particular pronunciation. This presupposes that prior to the introduction of printing and the codification of spelling there was a high degree of letter-to-sound matching – a safe general assumption, though the details, especially the ME details, can falsify such expectations. The variability of spelling and the abandonment of some forms can also be harnessed for phonological reconstruction. Thus the dropping of orthographic <h-> in words like OE <hwil> 'while', OE <hwit> 'white' in some ME texts, where they appear as <wil>, <wit>, as well as the addition of <h-> to words such as OE <wit(t)> 'wit', <wiht> 'wight', ME spellings <w**h**yt(t)>, <w**h**ihte, whith, whyht>, suggests that the scribes could no longer perceive the difference between a 'pure' voiced /w/ and its voiceless counterpart /ʍ/ (<hw>). If they heard the same initial sound in *white* and *wit*, they would be likely to confuse its representation with and without an <h->.

Comparing forms in genetically related languages can be very helpful too. If we find OE <hungor, hunger> 'hunger', and the form in Old Saxon is <hungor, hungar>, Old Frisian <hunger, honger>, Old Norse <hungr>, Old High German <hungar>, German <Hunger>, Middle Dutch <hongher>, Dutch <honger>, Swedish and Danish <hunger>, we can be fairly confident that the OE word also began with /h-/, that the vowel following it was not a long vowel or a low front vowel, that the third sound is /n/ and that the second syllable starts with /g/.

Language universals are another important basis for hypothesising about earlier pronunciation. With appropriate caution, commonly observed cross-linguistic patterns of inclusion or exclusion of particular sounds and sound combinations can be applied to historical reconstruction. Some statistically testable universal properties of language, such as 'languages have fewer vowels than consonants', are too general to be of practical interest. More viable in our plotting of phonological change

[10] The general term for a single alphabet item, irrespective of its shape, is **grapheme**, while the various shapes of a letter are referred to as **allographs**. The terms correspond to the widely used terms **phoneme** and **allophone** (see 2.1).

are the physically testable principles of production and perception, both related ultimately to the way language is learned. This is particularly helpful when we try to reconstruct the direction and the intermediate stages of sound change: we can posit a historical shift of [a] to [æ]; these sounds are phonetically close to each other, but we cannot jump from [a] to [u] without multiple steps in-between. Using the voiced /w/ in *wine* and the voiceless /ʍ/ in *whine* maintains the perceptual difference between two distinct lexical items, but it also requires some extra effort. If we merge the pronunciation of the two words, we create homophones, a perceptual complication arising concurrently with the elimination of the extra effort. The tension between these forces is always present in language; we will see how these general linguistic principles can be applied to the accounts of phonological change in English.

Verse structure is another source of data for phonological reconstruction. Old English verse is based on **alliteration**, or identity of the initial sound or sounds of the first stressed syllable in the word. The matching of OE <**ph**araones> 'of the pharaoh' with <folce> 'to the folk' is evidence that <ph-> in the borrowed word is a spelling for /f/. Similarly, the alliterative pairing of <**F**irgilies> 'Virgil's' and <**f**reond> 'friend' suggests that the poet or scribe replaced the Latin initial consonant in *Virgil* with /f/. Alliterative versification flourished in late ME too; one of the ways we can ascertain that the digraphs <wr-, kn-, gn-> represented real consonant clusters until about 1500 is by their use in fourteenth-century alliterative verse where the first consonants alliterate, for example *writ: wonder, gnaw:* ***God****, knight:* ***kiss***. Rhymes also provide valuable tests for phonological change. A ME rhyme such as *honour: flour* 'flower' suggests that the word *honour* could still be pronounced with stress on the second syllable (see 9.6). Drawing further on the creative use of language we can also go to puns to test the similarity between sounds. Consider the word-play in *Romeo and Juliet* (I, iv):[11]

> Mercutio: 'Nay, gentle Romeo, we must have you dance.'
> Romeo: 'Not I, believe me. You have dancing shoes
> With nimble **soles**; I have a **soul** of lead . . .

Such use is good evidence that Old French *sole* 'sole' and Old English *sawol* 'soul', which had different vowels originally, had already acquired the same value for Shakespeare's audience.

The development of a fixed system of spelling after the introduction of printing in the late fifteenth century did not proceed in step with the

[11] Compare the pun on *reason-raisin* in 'If reasons were as plentiful as blackberries, I would give no man a reason upon compulsion, I' (*Henry IV, Part One*, II, iv).

contemporary phonological changes. The discrepancies between spelling and pronunciation became a major scholarly concern. The people who, from the sixteenth century onwards, were writing manuals for native speakers and for foreigners and who were proposing spelling reforms, are known as **orthoepists**. Although their testimony may be biased and inconclusive at times, since they were influenced by Latin, the orthoepists' works form the backbone of our reconstructions of phonological change in EModE. Their detailed comparisons with Latin, French and Italian and the attempts at phonetic description, albeit imperfect and open to different interpretations, provide a better record of contemporary variation than any of the previous sources mentioned above. The first extensive dictionaries of pronunciation appeared in the second half of the eighteenth century, culminating with John Walker's 1791 *Critical Pronouncing Dictionary*.[12] The scholarly value of Walker's contribution to the history of eighteenth-century pronunciation cannot be overstated; it is a worthy predecessor of the great pronouncing dictionaries of the twentieth century, Daniel Jones's in Britain and Kenyon and Knott's in the US. Beginning with the invention of the phonograph by Thomas Edison in 1877, the technology of speech recording has become more and more sophisticated; the current and future generations of scholars have incomparably superior instruments and methods of recording, quantifying, and analysing phonological change.

Suggested further reading on *Companion* website.

[12] *A critical pronouncing dictionary and expositor of the English language . . .: to which are prefixed, principles of English pronunciation . . . with observations etymological, critical, and grammatical . . . with directions to foreigners, for acquiring a knowledge of the use of this dictionary*, with editions from 1st (1791) to 28th (1826).

2 The sounds of English

2.1 The consonants of PDE

English is not a 'new' language for the reader of this book, but Old and Middle English are different enough to be considered genuinely 'new'. Here is the opening line of *Caedmon's Hymn*, the earliest piece of OE poetry whose composer is known:

Nu sculon herigean	*heofonrices weard*
'now (we) shall praise	heaven-kingdom's guardian'
meotodes meahte	*and his modgeþanc,*
'the creator's might	and his thought'

Even with word glosses in place, the OE text is a challenge to read aloud. If *now* was spelled <nu> in OE, how was it pronounced: like *new*, like *noo*, like *now* or some other way? If *shall* was <sculon>, was it pronounced like *skull-on*, like *shoe-l-on* or some other way? The word <meaht> means 'might', but no word in our modern dictionaries contains the sequence of letters <-eaht>. The pronunciation of earlier stages of English is the topic of much of this book, but in order to establish a common denominator between the past and the present, we need to start with the modern language.

A note on terminology and representation is in order. Throughout the book the terms 'sound' or 'segment' are used to refer more generally to entities of pronunciation, without necessarily assigning them phonemic status, that is, without reference to their ability to distinguish meaning. A **phoneme** is a mental image of all the various realisations of one and the same sound. Thus [v] has always been a sound in English, but in Present-Day English (PDE) it is also a phoneme /v/. Its realisation is not determined by word-structure or by adjacent segments; it can signal meaning contrasts: *fan-van*, *safe-save*, *leafy-Levy*. The **glottal stop** [ʔ], articulated with a constriction of the glottis, occurs between vowels or word-finally in some accents of English, as in *letter*, *bitter*, *sap*, *cat*, *sack*.

Unlike /ʔ/, the glottal stop is *not* a phoneme in English; it is an **allophonic** realisation of the phonemes /t/, /p/, /k/ in our examples. In GA the alveolar stops /d, t/ are realised allophonically as voiced alveolar **taps** [-ɾ-] – *ladder* ["læɾɚ], *capitalise* ['kæpɪɾə'laɪz], *at ease* [ə'ɾiːz] – but the tap is not part of the inventory of contrastive English consonants (see 5.5.2). Similarly, the various types of [r], or the types of [l] used in different regions of the English-speaking world, are allophonic.

This book follows the accepted practice of enclosing phonemes in slashes / /, while square brackets [ ] are used for specific realisations. Previous exposure to the International Phonetic Alphabet (IPA) is assumed.

Some of the familiar observations about phonological inventories and classifications are that:

1. languages have more consonants than vowels;
2. the sounds of any language are either vowels or consonants;
3. consonants are more stable historically than vowels; and
4. the properties of consonants are more easily described and perceived.

All four statements hold for English, although only (1) is truly, and trivially, beyond challenge. As for (2), the difference between consonants, produced with some stricture in the vocal tract and not pronounceable as a syllable, and vowels, produced with little or no stricture and forming a syllable, is mostly clear-cut, yet there are special cases such as the <r> in a syllable such as *nerd* where the consonant [ɹ] can be syllabic; another special case is presented by the sounds known as 'glides' or 'semi-vowels', such as /w/ and /j/.[1] The statement in (3) is also an overgeneralisation; the next three chapters will convince you that consonant (sub-)systems of English offer a rich gamut of variation and change, so overall 'stability' of the consonants can hardly be claimed for the entire inventory. The impression that consonants are easily described is also misguided, although one has to admit that the consonantal features are more accessible to the speaker for self-examination than the corresponding vowel features.

The production of consonants and vowels is commonly described with reference to the vocal tract, starting from the lungs, through the larynx, the pharynx and the upper part of the tract: the oral cavity and the nasal cavity. Most of the action happens in the oral cavity – the chart in Figure 2.1 shows the more detailed anatomy of the upper vocal tract.

[1] 'For many speakers of American English, the approximant ɹ at the beginning of the word "red" bears the same relationship to the vowel ɚ in "bird" as the approximant j in "yes" does to the vowel i in "heed"' (Ladefoged and Maddieson 1996: 323).

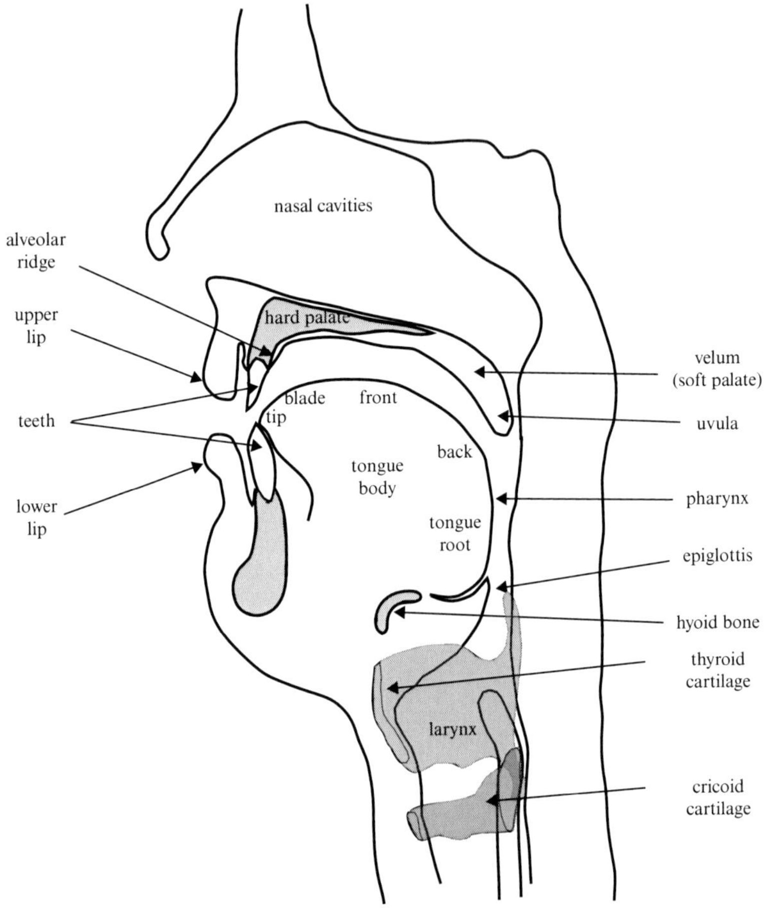

Figure 2.1 Cross-section of the vocal tract (from Ogden (2009) *Introduction to English Phonetics*, Edinburgh University Press, p. 10)

The characterisation of consonants is traditionally done with reference to three physical criteria: *voicing*, *place* and *manner* of articulation.

2.1.1 Voicing

The sounds that one can sing or hum are voiced. Voicing is dependent on the movement of the glottis; it is caused by vibration of the vocal cords and narrowing of the glottis; the glottis itself is the space between the vocal cords. Since the contrast depends on action in the larynx and the state of the glottis, questions of voicing can also be discussed with reference to **laryngeal** or **glottal** specifications. Another related property of note is that voiced consonants require less muscular effort; they are also described as **lenis** consonants, as opposed to **fortis** consonants, which are articulated with stronger effort. The lenis–fortis distinction correlates with voicing, but it is, properly speaking, a distinction based on the manner of articulation (see 2.1.3).

The vibration of the muscular folds triggers voicing. When the vocal cords are spread and not vibrating, as in breathing, the result is a voiceless sound. In English only one subset of the consonants can be voiceless – /p, t, k, f, θ, s, ʃ, tʃ, h/ – so that the voiced sounds outnumber the voiceless sounds. All English **nasals** and **approximants** (/m, n, ŋ, l, r, w, j/, see below) are voiced. The exact phonetic manifestation of consonant voicing in English varies considerably. The 'voiced' /b, d, g/ can be realised phonetically very close to [p, t, k] word-initially, especially after a voiceless consonant as in *this* ***boy***, *this* ***day***, *this* ***guy***. The voiceless /p, t, k/ appear as aspirated allophones word-initially and before a vowel in a stressed syllable, [p^h, t^h, k^h], as in *pin*, *attain*, *cuddle*.

Our knowledge of the degree of glottal opening historically is inferential. It is based on feature compatibility (no co-occurrence of /h/ and aspirated stops, no *hp-, *ht-, and so on), and on the fact that aspirated stops and /h/ occur in the same positions in PDE, as in *pat-hat*, *betoken-behave*. In this book our historical account will follow the tradition and refer to the oppositions /b/-/p/, /z/-/s/, /g/-/k/, and so on as 'voiced' vs 'voiceless', recognising that this shortcut is not always sufficient to account for all the details that one encounters in the records.

2.1.2 Place of articulation

The organs of speech in the vocal tract shown in Figure 2.1 are known as **articulators**. This cover term conflates two separate parameters: the **active** articulators located at the lower area of the vocal tract, for example lower lip and tongue; and the **passive** articulators, that is, the target area towards which the active articulators move and the area in which the articulation occurs, for example upper lip, alveolar ridge and hard or soft palate. Self-monitoring the place of articulation for most consonants is pretty easy if one concentrates on the movement and the place of contact of the lips and the tongue. The places of articulation most relevant for PDE are indicated by arrows on Figure 2.1. Here they are described starting from the front and moving to the back of the oral cavity:

- **BILABIAL**: articulated with the lower lip touching the upper lip. The bilabial consonants in English are the voiceless stop /p/, the voiced stop /b/, and the nasal /m/.
- **LABIOVELAR**: the lips are rounded closer together, the tongue is bunched up, and the sound is produced at the velum. The labiovelars are: the voiced labiovelar approximant /w/, as in *west, sway, glowing*, which appears in all standard varieties of English, and, in some varieties, a phonemically contrastive voiceless labiovelar fricative /ʍ/ as in ***wh**ine, **wh**ale, **wh**istle*, which is a reflex of the OE consonant cluster /hw-/ (see 5.1.3).
- **LABIODENTAL**: articulated with the lower lip touching the upper teeth. The English labiodentals are the voiceless fricative /f/ and the voiced fricative /v/.
- **DENTAL**: articulated most commonly with the tip of the tongue touching the lower edge of the upper teeth, though the articulation can also be **interdental**. The (inter)dental consonants in English are the voiceless fricative /θ/ as in ***th**ick, ba**th*** and its voiced counterpart, the fricative /ð/ as in ***th**is, ba**th**e*.
- **ALVEOLAR**: articulated with the tongue contacting or approaching the bony alveolar ridge behind the upper teeth. English has two alveolar stops, /t/ and /d/, two alveolar fricatives, /s/ and /z/; the nasal /n/, the lateral approximant /l/, and the central approximant /r/ are also alveolar.[2]
- **PALATO-ALVEOLAR**: articulated with the middle of the tongue contacting or approaching the hard palate. The palato-alveolars of English are the voiceless fricative /ʃ/ as in ***sh**ip, da**sh***, the voiced fricative /ʒ/ as in *mea**s**ure*, the voiceless affricate /t͡ʃ/ as in ***ch**air, ma**tch***, and its mate – the voiced affricate /d͡ʒ/ as in ***j**azz, hu**g**e*. These consonants are also called post-alveolar.
- **PALATAL**: articulated with the front part of the tongue body moving towards the hard palate. In English the symbol for the palatal central approximant in ***y**ellow, be**y**ond* is either /j/, following the IPA, used in this book, or /y/, which matches the orthographic representation of the sound (see also 2.2.2 for [j] ~ [i/ɪ]).
- **VELAR**: articulated with the back of the tongue contacting or approaching the soft palate. The English velars are the stops /k/ and

[2] This book follows the practice of previous phonological descriptions of English (Giegerich 1992; McMahon 2002; Kreidler 2004) in using the symbol /r/ for the phoneme whose most common realisation in GA and SSBE is the central approximant [ɹ] (see further 5.2).

/g/, the velar nasal /ŋ/, as in *sing*, and the voiceless fricative /x/ as in *loch*, phonemic only in Scottish English.

- **GLOTTAL**: articulated with the vocal cords moving closer together. The only glottal consonant in English is the voiceless fricative /h/, as in *hill*, *behave*. Its articulation foreshadows the following vowel. A voiceless glottal stop, [ʔ], is used in some varieties of PDE as an allophone of the voiceless stops /p, t, k/. [ʔ] is also inserted optionally before stressed vowel-initial syllables (see further 5.5.1).

Another useful descriptive parameter refers to the active articulators in producing consonants: the lips, the tip of the tongue or the body of the tongue. Involvement of the lips produces labials. When the tongue tip is involved in the articulation, the consonants have the feature **coronal**. The coronal consonants of English are the dentals, the alveolars and the palato-alveolars, while the tongue-body consonants are **dorsal**. All velars are also dorsal.

2.1.3 Manner of articulation

The way in which the airstream travels through the vocal tract determines the **manner of articulation**, that is, the degree and timing of blockage as the air is pushed out of the lungs. During the production of /p, b, t, d, k, g/, there is a brief instance when the air is completely stopped; these consonants are **stops**, also called **plosives**. During the production of the consonants /f, v, θ, ð s, z, ʃ, ʒ/, the airstream encounters a constriction, but the air flows through it generating some noisy friction; these are the **fricatives**, also called **spirants**. English combines stops and fricatives in the production of the consonants /t͡ʃ/ as in *chess* and /d͡ʒ/ as in *joke*, in which the air is stopped for a brief period, and is then released with a certain degree of friction. The consonants that combine the manner of articulation of stops (plosion) and fricatives (friction) are called **affricates**. The only English stops that can be affricated are /t/ and /d/.

A different type of contrast depends on the path through which the air comes out of the vocal tract. Typically, consonants are produced within the oral cavity; they are called **oral** consonants, not marked in Figure 2.2. In the production of /m, n, ŋ/, however, the airflow is blocked from the oral tract and is instead channelled through the nasal cavity, so they are called **nasals**.

The production of the **approximants** /r, l, j, w/ is associated with the lowest degree of constriction. Within that set, the air can exit through the central part of the oral cavity, or it can be diverted: the approximant

/l/ is called **lateral** because during its production the airflow is deflected around the sides of the tongue. Also within this group, /r, l/ are called **liquids**. As noted above, /j, w/ are also identified as **glides** or **semivowels**.

The major manners of articulation relevant to the description of English consonants are:

- **STOPS** /p, b, t, d, k, g/: the air is completely stopped for a brief period heard at the beginning of words (***town***, ***down***), in the middle of words (***upon***, ***cigar***, ***sucker***), or word-finally as in ***rag***, ***rib***, ***sock***.
- **AFFRICATES** /t͡ʃ, d͡ʒ/: the air is stopped, then released with some friction, as in ***chimney***, ***jam***, ***pitcher***, ***Cajun***, ***such***, ***ledge***. The affricates are more 'complex' and are commonly represented with a tie-bar over the two IPA symbols: /t͡ʃ/ and /d͡ʒ/.
- **FRICATIVES** /(ʍ), f, v, θ, ð, s, z, ʃ, ʒ, h/: the air passes uninterrupted, with a degree of friction, as in ***wharf***, ***fan***, ***van***, ***thin***, ***this***, ***sip***, ***zip***, ***sure***, ***Zhivago***, ***hat***. The palatal fricative [ʒ] is a latecomer to English (see 5.4).
- **NASALS** /m, n, ŋ/: the air is released through the nose, rather than the mouth: ***man***, ***numb***, ***hung***.
- **APPROXIMANTS** /w, r, l, j/: the air flows considerably more freely than for the other types of consonants: ***win***, ***ray***, ***low***, ***yes***.

Additionally, the degree of closure of the vocal tract can be important: if the closure is incomplete, the sound is a **continuant**. This feature straddles the dividing line between obstruents and sonorants: stops and affricates are non-continuant, and so are the nasals [m, n, ŋ]. All fricatives and the approximants are continuants, and so are all vowels.

Figure 2.2 presents an inventory of the consonantal phonemes of

			Labial	*Labio-dental*	*Dental*	*Alveolar*	*Palatal*	*Velar*	*Glottal*
Obstruent	STOPS		p b			t d		k g	
	AFFRICATES						t͡ʃ d͡ʒ		
	FRICATIVES		(ʍ)	f v	θ ð	s z	ʃ ʒ	(x)	h
Sonorant	NASALS		m			n		ŋ	
	Approximants	Lateral				l			
		Central	w			r	j		

Figure 2.2 The consonantal phonemes of PDE

PDE. In cells where there are pairs of phonemes the one to the left is voiceless and the one to the right is voiced. Parentheses enclose consonants which are phonemic only in some varieties of English.

The leftmost column in Figure 2.2 shows another important division between consonants based on the configuration of the vocal tract. The upper part of the chart accommodates the class of consonants collectively known as **obstruents**. They are produced with some degree of obstruction of the airstream and they can be voiceless or voiced. One special case in this set is /h-/, which is practically frictionless. In PDE it is a kind of voiceless precursor to the following vowel; it is produced with 'spread glottis', a feature which distinguishes between aspiration and lack of aspiration.

The consonants below the heavy line in Figure 2.2 are **sonorants**. Sonority is a property associated, loosely, with the acoustic loudness of sounds. All English sonorants are voiced. They are high on a **sonority scale** that applies to the entire inventory of English phonemes, not just the consonants. Vowels have the highest level of sonority, followed by glides, followed by nasals and approximants. The least sonorous consonants are the voiceless stops /p, t, k/. In English only consonants at the upper end of the scale of sonority, that is, the sonorants, can function as syllable peaks, as in *kitten*, *bottom*, *muscle* (see 2.3).

The description of the distinctive sounds of any language requires reference to the bundle of **features** that characterise each phoneme. The phonetic properties of the consonants described in 2.1.1–2.1.3 serve as the basis for their phonological representation, so properties such as *nasal*, *labial*, *voiced*, *stop*, *fricative*, *obstruent*, and so on provide the physical substance of the more abstract set of phonological features. It is by reference to the particular features that we can define the classes of phonemes, their interaction and their historical change.[3]

2.1.4 Short and long consonants

Consonants can appear as singletons, or they can be 'long', or **geminate**. In PDE the use of 'long' consonants in pronunciation signals morphological complexity; there are no geminates within the boundaries of a single morpheme. The orthography can be misleading: doubling of consonants in spelling does not automatically signal consonant gemination. Thus the pairs in (1a) do not differ in the length of their consonants,

[3] For a more comprehensive discussion of the set of phonologically relevant features see Giegerich (1992: chs 1, 2, 5); McMahon (2002: ch. 4). Additional features for the description of specific historical changes in English will be introduced in later chapters as needed.

while in (1b) the extra consonantal length is needed to mark off the morphological boundaries.

(1) Short and long consonants in PDE:

(a)		(b)
a**ll**ow	a**l**one	fu**ll-l**ength
fu**rr**y	fu**r**y	barrie**r-r**eef
pa**ss**	pa**c**e	cla**ss s**uit
su**mm**on	le**m**on	bea**m m**e (up)
ba**nn**er	sa**n**er	u**nn**amed

The salience of consonantal length depends on the type of boundary: geminates are realised as shorter at affix-stem boundaries, as in *u**nn**amed, di**ss**atisfied, riva**ll**ess*; they may be longer in compounds, as in *fu**ll-l**ength, cla**ss s**uit*; and predictably, they are quite audibly long within phrases, as in *bi**g g**arden, gri**m m**easure, fiftee**n n**ights, lea**d d**own, sto**p p**outing*. The sequence of identical consonants in these cases is pronounced with only one release and one onset, yet the actual duration of these long consonants may be as long as that of a cluster of two separate consonants. The realisation of geminates in loanwords is a separate issue. Words of classical origin whose components are not recognisable may be pronounced as though they are native words: *su**bb**ie, a**gg**ravate, co**mm**ute, su**ff**er, a**tt**ribute, tra**nsc**end*. When the affix is recognised, however, the consonants can be realised as geminates as in (1b), for example *su**bb**rachial, di**ss**ervice, co**nn**ateness*.

The status of geminate consonants has changed from Old to Modern English; we return to it in 4.1.2.

2.2 The vowels of PDE

The movement of the articulators and the places of articulation for vowels are not so readily open to self-examination. The most important active articulator in vowel production is the tongue body and the actual phonation occurs in the vocal tract. The airstream is allowed free passage through the mouth.

The quality of a vowel sound changes with the movement of the lips and the tongue. Minor shifts in the tongue position, difficult for the speaker to feel, produce quite distinct auditory and acoustic results, described along the dimensions of **height** and **backness**. Height refers to the distance of the tongue from the roof of the mouth: the smaller the distance, the higher (or closer) the vowel. Backness refers to the tongue's distance from the front teeth: the further away the highest point of the tongue is from the teeth, the more pronounced the backness feature is. Some vowels also require reference to the participation of the lips in the articulation: if the lips are rounded, the resulting vowel is also **round**; if not, the vowel is **unround**. Rounding is a feature with limited function in PDE – non-back vowels cannot be rounded, only back vowels can be rounded, that is, a reference to roundness is redundant for the non-back vowels. There are, however, two back vowels that are unrounded: the vowel /ɑ/ in COT in GA, which forms a minimal pair with the rounded vowel /ɔː/ in CAUGHT in those varieties of English that preserve this historical contrast, and the vowel /ʌ/ as in STRUT, which contrasts in roundness with the vowels in THOUGHT, LOT in varieties that have /ɔ(ː)/ in these words.[4]

The IPA vowel chart includes twenty-eight different vowel types, and those can be further modified by diacritics, marking additional properties such as length (macron, breve, colon), nasalisation (tilde), centralisation (umlaut), and so on. Figure 2.3 shows the full version of the IPA vowel chart.

Fitting the IPA chart into a feature-based phonological chart is not a straightforward transfer. Nevertheless, the dimensions of height, backness and rounding allow us to present the contrasts schematically in rows and columns, though with the vowels the positioning is quite different from the categorical placement of the consonants in Figure 2.2

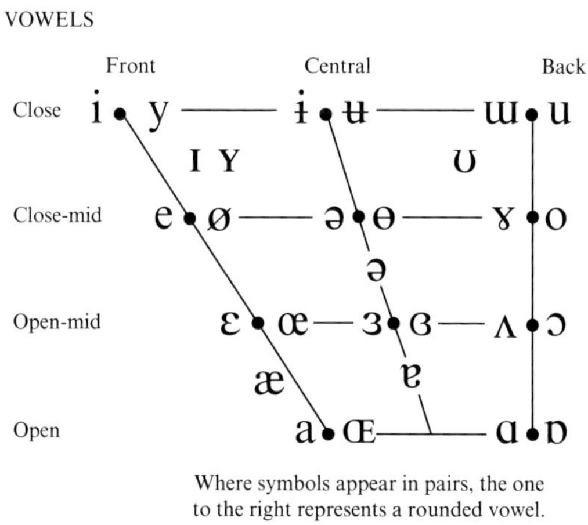

Figure 2.3 IPA Vowel chart, revised to 2005 (from <http://www.langsci.ucl.ac.uk/ipa/vowels.html>, available under a Creative Commons Attribution-Sharealike 3.0 Unported License. Copyright © 2005 International Phonetic Association)

[4] The use of the colon diacritic is addressed in 2.2.1.

	FRONT	CENTRAL	BACK	
			Unrounded	Rounded
Upper high	iː (FLEECE)			uː (GOOSE)
———	———			———
Lower high	ɪ (KIT)			ʊ (FOOT)
Upper mid	eɪ (FACE)	ɚ/ɜː (NURSE)		oʊ (GOAT)
———	———	ə (COMMA)	———	———
Lower mid	ɛ (DRESS)		ʌ (STRUT)	ɔː (THOUGHT)
Upper low	æ (TRAP)			
Low			ɑ (LOT,PALM) (GA)	ɒ (LOT) (SSBE)

Figure 2.4 English vowels

in well-defined cells. Only rounding is treated as strictly binary for the vowels. Realisations with respect to height and backness are scalar and in order to define their unique contrastive properties one has to work with different degrees of the same main features. For height we will use the three levels, **high**, **mid** and **low**, with additional specifications for each of the three levels, **lower** or **upper**. Note that this corresponds to the IPA labels **close**, **mid** and **open**. For backness the main dimensions are **front**, **central** and **back**. Again, positioning of the vowels within the cells is not absolutely fixed; it is a descriptive convenience to highlight contrasts, but the realisations will vary with individual speakers or communities.

Figure 2.4 presents an overview of the vowels of English.

Figure 2.4 provides only a basic frame of reference. Except for the mid central unrounded vowel schwa, [ə], it shows an inventory of the vowels in *stressed* syllables; that inventory is considerably impoverished in the absence of stress, where [ə] may contrast with [ɪ], as in *Rosa's* [-ə-] *roses* [ɪ] or *tilde*, *sal**a**d*, *bal**a**nced*, *cher**u**b*, *welc**o**me*, *hydrang**ea***, *nostalg**ia*** with [ə] vs *spin**a**ch*, *sandw**i**ch*, *ceil**i**ng*, *langu**a**ge* with [ɪ]. In fast speech [ə] can alternate with the syllabic form of the sonorants [r̩, l̩, m̩, n̩]: *mutt**er***, *kett**le***, *bott**om***, *weap**on***. Syllabic sonorants can be functionally equivalent to a vowel only in unstressed syllables. The 'neutral' vowel schwa is the most frequent vowel in the language; its frequency (10.74 per cent) is matched only by the frequency of /ɪ/ at 8.33 per cent.[5]

[5] See Cruttenden (2008: 156), whose counts were based on colloquial SSBE. Reports

The upper mid central symbols /ɚ/ (GA) or /ɜː/ (SSBE), as in NURSE, represent the development of the vowel preceding historical /r/ in such words as BIRD, WORD, HEARD, CURD, SIR. The phonetic realisation of the NURSE vowel in GA is [ɚ], that is, right-hook schwa for the r-colouring, which is present throughout the vowel; in faster speech it could be simply a syllabic [r̩]. In r-less/non-rhotic varieties of English, like SSBE, the realisation of the NURSE vowel is [ɜː] (see 5.2). In eastern New England, parts of the American South and much of African American English, the pronunciation varies and can be [ɜː], [ə] and even [ɜɪ ~ əɪ] (Thomas 2001: 48–9).

In most of the American West and New England, American speakers have identical vowels in LOT, THOUGHT and possibly also in PALM, CLOTH.[6] The low back unrounded vowel /ɑ/ for LOT, PALM is a generalisation for values ranging from the front upper low [æ] to the low back [ɒ]. The fronted variant of [æ] is part of an ongoing chain shift of the vowels /ɔ/, /ɑ/, /æ/, /ɛ/ and /ʌ/ known as the *Northern Cities Shift*, whereby /ɛ/ → /ʌ/ → /ɔː/ → /ɑ/ → /æ/ → /æ̝/.[7] Salient regional or ethnic differences will be highlighted in Chapters 6–8.

2.2.1 *Short and long vowels*

The colon symbol (ː) in Figure 2.4 is an IPA diacritic indicating that the vowel is **long**; all other vowels are **short**. Taken literally, 'length', or 'quantity', refers to the physical duration of vowels. A reference to vowel length as a contrastive feature works well for languages like Classical Latin, where the differences between the vowels are assumed to have been based on duration. However, as happened in Vulgar Latin, and as is the case in PDE, the historical long and short vowels are distinct not only by virtue of duration: they have different articulatory and acoustic properties. In many accounts of PDE sound systems, therefore, the terms 'long' and 'short' have been replaced by **tense** and **lax**, which refer to the manner of articulation of vowels, more specifically, the overall muscular effort involved in the production of a sound. Tenseness involves increased muscular effort, strong spread of acoustic energy and movement away from the centre to the *periphery* of the vowel space,

of measurements in GA produce the same top-frequency vowels. The least frequent vowel shared by both varieties is the diphthong /ɔɪ/ (0.14 per cent).

6 *The Atlas of North American English* (ANAE) (available at <http://www.ling.upenn.edu/phono_atlas/home.html>, last accessed 16 May 2013) shows a map of the merger: invariant responses in production and perception are shown on Map 1 (see also 8.2.1).

7 See Labov (1991, 2008: 37–46); Wolfram and Schilling-Estes (2006: 147–9); Labov et al. (2006: ch. 14).

justifying a reference to another property, **peripherality**, associated with tenseness. PDE high and mid long vowels are peripheral. Length or tenseness are irrelevant for the English low vowels; neither one is used as a phonemically contrastive feature in PDE. Laxness refers to decreased muscular effort and movement; lax vowels are relatively short and they are articulated more towards the central or non-peripheral vowel area; if a vowel is short, it is also lax and non-peripheral.

The short and long vowels in Figure 2.4 are represented by different IPA vowel symbols, since in the basic reference varieties, GA and SSBE, no pair of vowels contrast only in duration; in every instance length distinctions are accompanied by height, backness and peripherality distinctions. Actual duration differences are attested in identical environments. Measurements of RP cited in Cruttenden (2008: 96), for example, show /iː/ + voiced stop, as in *lead*, with a duration of 28.5 centiseconds, while for /ɪ/ + voiced stop, as in *lid*, the duration is 14.7 centiseconds. The durational difference can be reversed, however, depending on the consonant following the vowel: the duration of /iː/ + voiceless stop, as in *meat*, is 12.3 centiseconds against the 14.7 centiseconds of the 'short' *lid* vowel. Therefore, many descriptions of the PDE vowel system rely solely on qualitative differences, using different symbols for the short and long vowels and dispensing with the length mark. 💻

The choice to refer both to the quality and, for the non-low vowels, explicitly to the quantity, of the PDE vowel phonemes in Figure 2.4, is justified mainly historically. If we recognise the relevance of quantity in PDE, with all the caveats above, we can project this quantitative dichotomy backwards as far as we can go. The length dimension thus serves as a consistent common denominator between reconstructions of earlier states of English and PDE (see 6.1, 7.5, 10.2).

Using only qualitative specifications, on the other hand, makes it more difficult to trace the continuity with confidence. First, the phonological function of tenseness is obscured in some PDE varieties.[8] Second, the availability of only five vowel letters in the Roman alphabet is extremely limiting for a language such as English with at least fifteen contrastive vowels at any time in its history, so that the use of identical letters is uninformative with respect to qualitative differences. Very importantly, the agreed-upon reconstructed vowel system of Proto-Germanic is based on quantity: from Proto-Germanic Old English inherited short vowels and long vowels. The short–long dichotomy

[8] The *Scottish Vowel Length Rule* (McMahon 2002: 867) lengthens [i], [o] to [iː], [oː] before [r, v, ð, z, ʒ], before another vowel and before a morpheme boundary, so the vowels in *grief* and *grieve* differ only in duration.

was maintained in the subsequent history of English vowels, which go through a series of changes described traditionally as 'lengthenings' and 'shortenings'. It is for these reasons that the terms *long* and *short* are adopted in this book, bearing in mind that in most cases quantity alone is not sufficient to distinguish the FLEECE and KIT, FACE and DRESS, GOOSE and FOOT vowels of our reference varieties, GA and SSBE.

2.2.2 Complexity: monophthongs and diphthongs

The relatively 'pure', steady-state vowels of English are **monophthongs**: there is usually no perceptible difference in quality between the beginning and the end of the vowel in the syllable *peak* (see 2.3.1). For the long vowels, on the other hand, maintaining a steady state is less typical; the additional duration allows for a transition from one vowel quality to another.

The representations of the upper mid front and back vowels [eɪ] and [oʊ] in Figure 2.4 indicate that the vowels of FACE, GOAT are **diphthongs** – the quality of the vowel changes during the pronunciation of the vowel. The components of a diphthong are not equal: the nucleus is more easily identified with a specific vowel quality, while the glide portion, usually the second vowel position, may or may not reach its end. *Diphthongisation* involves the addition of a glide: with long vowels the gliding is usually towards a higher vowel, as in [eɪ] and [oʊ], while with short vowels the most common gliding is into a schwa-like central vowel, as in KID pronounced as [kɪəd], or New York English OFF pronounced [ɔəf ~ ʊəf]. The degree and the direction of vowel diphthongisation is an important historical index and a salient dialect criterion for PDE.[9]

The dimension of complexity thus refers to the absence or presence of gliding from one position to a second position within a single syllable peak. Only one of the diphthongal components is syllabic; glides are the parts of diphthongs that are non-syllabic. The direction of the gliding and the length of the trajectory vary. In addition to the front and the back glides [ɪ] and [ʊ], diphthongs formed from a vowel + a following /r/ insert a central glide [ə], as in SSBE SQUARE, CURE.

[9] This book follows the common practice – for example, McMahon (2002); Ladefoged (2005: 28–9) – of transcribing the PDE diphthongal glides as [ɪ], [ʊ], [ə] for the front, back (outgliding) and the central (ingliding) elements. This transcription avoids a potential confusion with the palatal and labial approximants [j] and [w]. However, the rationale for choosing [ɪ] over [i], [y], [j] or [ʊ] instead of [u], [w] could be debated, and there is no universally accepted solution. Historically, more 'consonantal' [j] and [w] are precursors of diphthongal glides, and we will use them in transcribing earlier diphthongs in 6.5.3, 7.4, 8.2.2.

All accounts of PDE recognise the existence of three diphthongal vowels, shown in (2).

(2) PDE diphthongs:
/aɪ/ as in PRICE
/aʊ/ as in MOUTH
/ɔɪ/ as in CHOICE

Some analyses of English classify the vowel in CUTE as diphthongal, consisting of a glide, usually represented by [y], followed by [u]/[ʊ]. (Recall that [y] is another way of representing the IPA palatal approximant [j].) The analysis of this sequence is a well-known crux in English phonology. There is no agreement on the tenseness of the vowel when it is not followed by [ə] due to loss of [r] in non-rhotic dialects, as in PURE, nor is there agreement on whether /j/ is (part of) the syllable onset or the syllable peak. Bearing in mind some distributional peculiarities of the palatal approximant – it appears only syllable-initially when preceded by one or more consonants, as in *beauty*, *cute*, *fury*, *skewer*, and the only vowel allowed after it is /uː/ – we analyse /j/ like /w/, that is, as part of the syllable onset, and not as part of a diphthong which occupies the peak/nucleus of the syllable.

For many GA speakers the sequence [-ju] after coronal consonants – *duty*, *dues*, *news*, *sue*, *tune* – is realised as [uː]; the glide-deletion is part of a long historical process that started in the sequence [rj-] and now occurs variably whenever the vowel follows a consonant in the dento-alveolar series [l, n, t, d, s, z], as in *lubricate*, *news*, *Tuesday*, *due*, *suit*, *presume* (see further 8.2.2.3).

Complexity is a scalar property: all long vowels are complex to some degree. The high long vowels in FLEECE, GOOSE are more clearly monophthongal and for them we can use the more abstract representation VV, or [Vː], where V stands for 'any vowel'. The vowels of FACE, GOAT are perceived as changing from beginning to end, but the length of the trajectory between the two end-points varies, and there are varieties in which the vowels are monophthongs, such as SSE in Britain and Louisiana Cajun English, South Carolina, and Georgia in the US. The diphthongal nature of the vowels of PRICE, MOUTH, CHOICE in (2) is generally strong in most varieties of English, except in the American South. The clearly perceived transition from one quality to another in them justifies the more abstract representation VG, where G represents the glide. VV and VG vowels function in very similar ways (see 2.3.3); this similarity is crucial in accounting for the famous long vowel shifting in the history of English (see 8.2.2).

2.3 The syllable: some basics

2.3.1 *Syllable structure*

Phonological segments are not pronounced in isolation – they are organised into syllables. Native speakers have strong intuitions about the division of words into syllables. The way we define a syllable depends on whether we are interested in the production, the perception or the function of the syllable. The most elementary definition refers to production: a syllable is the smallest independently pronounceable unit of speech. In auditory terms, the syllable is a string of sounds of different prominence, where 'prominence' corresponds to the acoustically measurable sonority of the sounds. Functionally, the syllable is a domain which hosts and governs the combinations and distribution of sounds, a domain of prosodic phenomena such as stress and rhythm, and a domain of interaction between phonology and morphology. A brief survey of the basic principles of syllable structure and syllable division will give us the initial reference points for the discussion of historical phonological processes that occur in specific syllabic environments.

The organisation of sounds into syllables depends on the sonority of the adjacent sounds. Vowels are always independently pronounceable, they have higher sonority than consonants and they form the core of a syllable. Structurally, vowels are positioned in the syllable **peak**, also known as syllable **nucleus**. The segment(s) preceding the peak form the **onset** of the syllable, and the segment(s) following the peak form the **coda**. The peak and the coda together form the syllabic **rhyme**. These constituents are illustrated in (3), where C = consonant, V = vowel, G = glide and Ø indicates an empty constituent. The sigma (σ) is a conventional symbol for the whole entity of the syllable.

(3) Syllable structure:

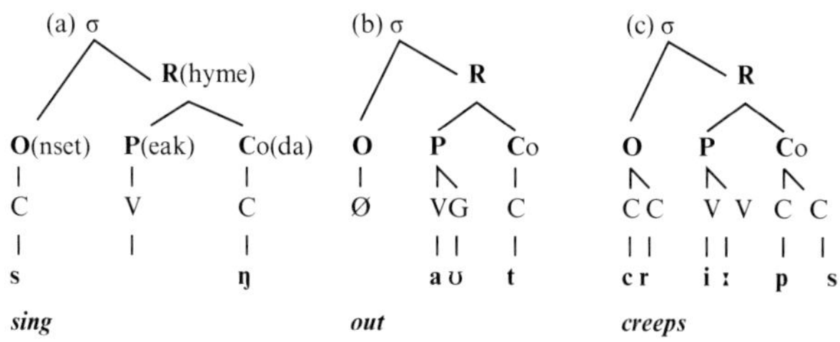

The syllable constituents are not equally important – the only obligatorily filled constituent is the peak. The peak can be filled by any vowel or by a syllabic sonorant [r̩, l̩, m̩, n̩], as in the second syllables of *mutter*, *kettle*, *bottom*, *weapon*. The onset in PDE (but not in OE stressed syllables at least in formal style; see 10.2) can be empty, as in *out* in (3b); it can be filled by a singleton, as in *sing* in (3a); or it can be filled by a cluster, as in *creeps* in (3c). Similar variability is allowed for the coda: it can be empty, as in *my*, *see*, *bow*; it can be filled by a singleton, as in (3a) and (3b); or it can be filled by a cluster, as in ***creeps*** in (3c).

The realisation of one and the same consonantal phoneme typically differs in the onset and the coda, especially in syllables bearing stress. The voiceless stops in the onset of ***tip*** [t^h-], ***pit*** [p^h-] are strongly aspirated, while in the coda position the same consonants are unreleased, that is, there is low vocal-fold activity, no audible burst of air. A well-known case of allophony based on syllable position in SSBE and SAE is the different realisation of the lateral liquid: 'clear' [l] in the onset, as in lick [lɪk], but velarised 'dark' [ɫ] in the coda, as in [kɪɫ] (see further 5.2.5).

Functionally, the onset and the coda are asymmetrical: the onset is more perceptually salient. Onsets can be articulated more forcefully, which contributes to the maintenance of phonological contrasts. The coda, on the other hand, is the location of consonant neutralisation and loss, illustrated by the voicing neutralisation of the /-d/ past tense morpheme in English – ***snapped*** [-pt], ***passed*** [-st], loss of coda <-r> in non-rhotic varieties, or the historical simplification of coda clusters such as <-mb, -ng>. Another asymmetry between the onset and the coda position, observed across the world's languages, has to do with the preference for a single consonant between two vowels to associate with the onset rather than the coda of two adjacent syllables (see 2.3.2).

Yet another difference between onsets and codas has to do with the arrangement of consonants within these constituents. The 'ideal' sonority slope from the onset to the peak is steep, that is, voiceless stops are preferred as onsets, while the reverse holds for the peak–coda slope; codas are preferentially sonorous. When there are consonant clusters, onsets accommodate sequences with **rising sonority** – typically an obstruent followed by a sonorant, for example [pl-, dr-, kr-, gr-], and so on. Coda clusters are a mirror image of the onset clusters in sonority: in monomorphemic words the first coda consonant has to be a sonorant or [s], and the second consonant is typically a voiceless stop, that is, coda clusters show **falling sonority**.

2.3.2 Syllabification

In English a syllable is often a whole word: indeed, English is sometimes referred to as a 'monosyllabic' language, since so many of its core vocabulary words have only a single syllable: *bread*, *child*, *sleep*, *fight*, *green*, *short*. We will see how and why this happened in 7.6. Derived vocabulary and the borrowed word-stock, however, are polysyllabic, and polysyllables, as well as connected speech, present the analytic problem of deciding where to place the syllable boundaries.[10]

Some syllabification principles are universal and some are language-specific. Vowels can be syllable peaks in all languages and must be syllable peaks in English. Another widely shared syllabification rule is that only possible word-initial consonants and consonant clusters can be in the onset of a word-medial syllable. Which consonants are allowed as singletons or as clusters word-initially is a language-specific matter. Thus the fact that English /ŋ/ originates from coda [-ŋg] blocks it from appearing in word-initial position, therefore a word such as *singing* is syllabified *sing.ing* $[\text{sɪŋ}]_\sigma$ $[\text{ɪŋ}]_\sigma$, but this would not be the case in a language like Vietnamese, where the velar nasal is 'legal' word-initially.

Except for /ŋ/, and possibly /ʒ/ (see 5.4), all English consonant phonemes can appear word-initially. Syllabification of intervocalic singletons places them in the onset of the syllable to the right, as in (4).

(4) Syllabification of intervocalic singletons:

VCV	–>	V.CV
ra.**v**en	pho.**n**a.**t**ion	pa.**r**a.**m**e.**d**ic
re.**l**y	me.**ch**a.**n**ic	pa.**l**i.**s**ade

(4) is in accord with a widely attested syllable structure preference for a filled onset: all languages have CV- syllables but not all languages have -VC syllables. This is another instance of the functional asymmetry between onsets and codas. The principle of filling the onset in preference to the coda is known as the *Maximal Onset Principle* or as *Onset Maximalism*.

An alternative way of syllabification in PDE is to assume that at least some singletons preceding an unstressed syllable are *ambisyllabic*. Ambisyllabicity is one way of accounting for the realisation of the dental stops /t/ and /d/ as alveolar approximant taps [ɾ] before an unstressed vowel in AmE, as in *ladder* [ˈˈlæɾɚ], *waiter* [ˈweɪɾɚ] (see further 5.5.2). Our historical account in the following chapters assumes onset-maximal syllabification, which is crucial in the special recitation style of OE verse (see 10.2). One should, however, be aware of the possibility of ambisyllabic analysis of some consonants as early as our earliest OE records.[11]

[10] Following the IPA, we mark syllable boundaries with a period in orthographic forms, or with a subscript sigma in phonetic transcriptions.

[11] For the history of the research on ambisyllabicity in PDE, the phonetic diagnostics and

Onset maximisation may be overridden by morphological considerations. In *dis.able, dis.obey, in.applicable, mis.analyse* the prefixes are likely to retain their final consonant in syllabification.

In addition to placing a singleton to the right of the syllable boundary, onset maximality regulates the syllabic affiliation of the consonants in clusters. As noted, only clusters that can be word-initial can be placed in the onset. Other sequences are split between the onset and the coda. The most common patterns are summarised in (5).

(5) Syllabification of intervocalic clusters:

(a) VC_1C_2V
- $V.C_1C_2V$: *Sea.**gram**, pa.**tron**, ho.ne.**sty**, ver.te.**bra***
- $VC_1.C_2V$: *fi**c.**tion, su**b.m**erge, co**m.pul.**sion, pro.pa.ga**n.d**a*

(b) $VC_1C_2C_3V$
- $VC_1.C_2C_3V$: ***em.bl**em, pa**n.try**,ha**m.st**er, ba**n.qu**et, pi**l.gr**im*
- $VC_1C_2.C_3V$: *gli**mp.s**es, **ant.s**y, mu**nch.k**in, ju**nc.t**ion*
- $V.C_1C_2C_3V$: *in.du.**str**y, re.gi.**str**ar, or.che.**str**a*

In the upper branch of (5a) the division is based on the availability of the cluster word-initially: ***grant, tree, sty, bra.*** The lower branch of (5a) splits the sequences since *[kʃ-, bm-, mp-, ls-] do not appear word-initially.

(5b) follows the same principle. In the top branch [bl-, tr-, st-, kw-] are kept together in the onset when tri-consonantal medial clusters are syllabified. The middle branch of (5b) shows how the division of three consonants in a row avoids [ps-, ts-, tʃk-, kʃ-] in the onset. In the bottom row $C_1C_2C_3$ stick together and are syllabified to the right – *in.du.**stry**, re.gi.**strar**, or.che.**stra*** – again in accord with the existence of [str-] words in English. This carries over to $VC_1C_2C_3C_4V$, where the cluster $C_2C_3C_4$ is cohesive: *mo**n.stro**.si.ty, sea**m.stress**.*

The schema in (5) does not cover all possible cases and theoretical interpretations. For example, the very common word-initial clusters *sp-, st-, sk-* do not behave consistently in syllabification when they follow a stressed syllable, so that speakers are likely to produce *A-**spen***

the rules of ambisyllabicity see the overview in Hayes (2009a). The choice of assuming onset-maximal singleton syllabification in this book is based on the formal style that the our records represent and the lack of well-worked out arguments in the literature in favour of ambisyllabicity in Old and Middle English (see Fulk 1997). Some research into the evidence for syllabification of OE and ME reported in Minkova and Zuraw (forthcoming) reveals similarities between PDE and the earlier stages of English with respect to ambisyllabicity.

or *A**s-p**en*, *hi.**st**o.ry* or *hi**s.t**o.ry*, *ma.**sc**ot* or *ma**s.c**ot*.[12] Further complications arise from the interaction of phonology and morphology: the syllabification of compounds and transparently derived words respects the morphological boundaries rather than the Onset Maximalism, thus *juri**s.pr**udence* not **juri.**spr**udence*, *di**s.pr**ove* not **di.**spr**ove*, *clo**se.n**ess* not **clo.**sen**ess* (in spite of ***sn**ow*, ***sn**ide*, ***sn**ap*), *si**ck.l**y* not **si.**ckl**y* (in spite of ***cl**ose*, ***cl**uster*, ***cl**imb*, but compare *lu.di.**cr**ous*), *to**p.l**ess* not **to.**pl**ess* (in spite of ***pl**us*, ***pl**ay*, ***pl**edge*).

2.3.3 Syllable weight

In 2.3.1 we noted the correlation between allophonic realisation and the position of a segment with respect to syllable structure. Syllable structure is also crucial in determining syllable **weight**: syllables ending in short vowels are **light**, all other syllables are **heavy**. This statement has two entailments:

- All syllables with filled codas are heavy.
- All syllables with long vowels or diphthongs in the peak are heavy.

Long vowels and diphthongs are functionally equivalent because they form the peak of a heavy syllable, as in (3b) ***out*** and (3c) *creeps*, where the peak is represented as branching. If we take the **mora** (**μ**) as the basic unit of weight, the observation that the syllable peak branches amounts to saying that it is **bimoraic**. Non-branching syllable peaks are **monomoraic**, as the peak in *sing* in (3a). Note that there is no necessary correlation between orthography and moraic content. No matter how bimoraic vowels are spelled, with a single vowel letter or with a digraph: <h**i**de, r**o**de, r**ai**d, c**oi**n, n**ou**n>, they are *single* phonemic units, either monophthongal or diphthongal, and belong to the same syllable. Thus *c**oi**-nage*, *g**ui**le-less*, *b**uy**-er* contrast with *g**o**-**i**ng*, *k**i**-**o**sk*, *M**i**-**a**-ta*; in the latter the bold vowel letters correspond to separate syllable peaks.

Short vowels followed by a consonant in the same syllable also form a heavy syllable; such heavy syllables branch at the level of the rhyme, as *sing* in (3a), where the peak is filled by a single mora, and the consonant in the coda counts as a second mora. We can generalise: heavy syllables are represented by branching structures, or: heavy syllables are minimally bimoraic. Put differently, syllables that branch at the level of the rhyme or below are heavy. For the moment, we will stay with the classification of syllables into light and heavy, but we will see in Chapter 9

[12] For a much fuller treatment of syllabification in PDE polysyllabic words see Giegerich (1992: 167–78).

that syllable weight is a gradient property depending on the nature of the segments, especially in the rhyme.

It is important to distinguish between **length**, which is a durational property of segments, and **weight**, which is a prosodic property of the entire syllable. The mora bridges the two notions: both short vowels and light syllables have a single mora, and long vowels and heavy syllables have more than a single mora.

Syllables can also be ***open*** or ***closed***. Any syllable with an empty coda is open: all syllables in *ho.ne.sty*, *pay.ee*, *Le.vi*, *mi.ca* are open, that is, any syllable in which the rhyme does not branch is open. Any syllable with a consonant in the coda is closed. Closed syllables have branching rhymes; they are heavy by definition. Open syllables can be either heavy or light – we return to this in 7.5 when we discuss the history of pairs such as *shade-shadow*, *stave-staff*, *nose-nostril*.

Most of the stressed syllables in the PDE lexicon are heavy; this is in line with a cross-linguistic preference for heavy syllables to attract stress. The tendency to place stress on a heavy syllable in English dates back to Old English, when stress was placed on a heavy syllable in approximately 80 per cent of the words.

The syllable typology sketched out above correlates also with the distribution of long, diphthongal and short vowels. In PDE all vowels can occur in *closed* syllables. However, unlike OE (see 6.1), if a syllable in PDE is *stressed*, *open* and *word-final*, it can accommodate only bimoraic vowels: ***say***, ***decree*** are OK, but forms like ****se*** with [-ɛ], **decrí* with [-ɪ] would be recognised as un-English. In other words, the short, lax, non-peripheral vowels [ɪ, ɛ, æ, ʊ, ʌ] have a more restricted distribution. They are also sometimes referred to as ***checked vowels*** because they must be followed by a consonant when they are stressed, whether in the same syllable or not: *sinful*, *pension*, *monkey* have checked vowels. The peripheral long vowels and diphthongs are known as ***free vowels***. The low back unrounded vowel, namely [ɑ], is neutral with respect to length in GA. It can equally be treated as a member of the long vowel set and though it is not phonetically 'long', it is behaviourally 'long' because it can occur in both free and checked positions: *pa*, *paw*, *God*, *lot*, *saw*, *nought*. In SSBE the vowel [ɒ] in LOT is a checked vowel.[13]

The two types of vowels show some special distributional properties:

[13] The low front vowel /æ/ is also difficult to classify: historically it is the reflex of a phonologically short vowel, but it is phonetically longer than the other checked vowels, especially before voiced consonants. It behaves like a free vowel in at least one very common adverb in GA, *nah* 'not so', which the *Merriam Webster* transcribes with the vowel of *ash*.

monomoraic vowels combine freely with [-ŋ] and [-ʃ]: *ring, flung, mesh, pang, posh, lush*; but bimoraic vowels are generally avoided before these consonants: **feeng, *poung, *coish, *raish* would not be considered 'normal' English words in the standard varieties described here. Another unifying property in the history of the long vowels and diphthongs is the recurrence of changes whereby long vowels develop into diphthongs and vice versa (see 8.2.2); [ɔɪ] is the only English diphthong which has no historical relation to a long monophthong. There is also a distributional difference based on the prominence of the syllable in which the vowels appear: it is only in stressed syllables that we find the full inventory of the vowels, while only monomoraic [ə, ɪ] appear regularly in unstressed syllables in all varieties of English (see 2.2).

2.4 Notes on vowel representation

The English spelling system has not kept apace with the radical and complex historical vowel changes. The resources were inadequate from the start: with only seven vowel letters at their disposal – <i, y, e, æ, u, o, a> – the OE and ME scribes could not represent finer qualitative or quantitative distinctions and one and the same letter could have multiple values (see 6.2, 6.3). Similarly, in PDE there are different values for the same letter: <i> in *hide, hid, machine*, <e> in *pet* and *Pete*, <a> in *grade* and *gradual*, <o> in *sole* and *solitude, come, common*. Such spellings justify the statement that English spelling is 'etymological'. Vowel **digraphs**, two vowel letters representing a single phoneme, such as <ea>, <ou>, <ai> <oo> are useful for marking length, but they can also mask the difference between short, long and diphthongal vowels: <br**ea**d>, <c**ou**sin>, <pl**ai**d>, <f**oo**t> have short vowels, while long vowels are commonly spelled with a single vowel letter: <b**i**te>, <b**o**ne> <s**a**me>, <f**u**me>. This looks like a chaotic situation, but in fact the historical information in the following chapters will reveal that English has a fairly reliable system of orthographic coding of the long vowels. A useful guide when figuring out the phonological history of a PDE vowel from the orthography is that vowel digraphs that represent a single phoneme regularly stand for historically long or diphthongal vowels. Even without looking up their individual histories, we can expect to find that the words spelled <st**oo**d>, <s**ai**d>, <h**ea**d> had long vowels at some earlier period (see further 8.3.1).

Note on diacritics: The **macron** symbol <¯> indicates vowel length in the printed early/etymological form of a word.[14] The macron is not

[14] The use of the macron in the pronunciation guides in many American dictionaries

used in the original texts; it is an *orthographic* convention adopted by modern editors of dictionaries and historical grammars. It is also standardly used in modern editions of OE and some ME texts, a practice which helps the reader figure out the pronunciation. As noted in 2.2.1, the *phonetic* symbol for length is the colon [ː], thus the dictionary entry for Lat. *māter* corresponds to /maːter/; an etymological entry for *we*, OE <wē>, corresponds to /weː/.

2.5 Phonological change: some types and causes

Speech sounds are studied in two interrelated ways. Phonologists explore the sounds' function in speech: how do we learn them, how do we store them, how do we keep them apart, how do we combine them, how do they change? The actual physical aspects of sound: how speech sounds are produced, how they are transmitted as the sound waves travel through the air, and how the acoustic signal is perceived are questions from the domain of phonetics. Since phonetics is an experimental science, **historical phonetics** in reference to the earlier periods is an oxymoron. Only the relatively recent period following the invention of sound recording in the second half of the nineteenth century offers opportunities for observing and analysing phonetic details that lead to change. The absence of historical phonetic records is a discouraging reality, yet no meaningful hypotheses about phonological developments in the past can be formulated without knowledge of the basic phonetic properties of production, acoustics and perception. Consequently, historical phonological analyses have to rely on the phonetic facts established for living languages. The phonetic information that we project back to the older stages of English draws on instrumentally testable patterns of production and perception which provide valuable explanatory angles on phonological reconstruction.

The inventory of contrastive sounds in any language is finite, while the allophonic realisation of phonemes allows quite lavish variation. Variation may or may not produce a restructuring of the inventory, but it is a reasonable assumption that variable pronunciations underlie all categorical innovations. Our access to diachronic variation is limited by the nature of the surviving material, and reconstruction of what happened in the past must be informed by other general principles of linguistic change. One such principle is that change can be triggered both by **internal** factors such as production, perception, acquisition, the

commonly refers to both quantitative and qualitative differences. This is not in accord with IPA usage, nor with the usage in this text.

overall shape of the phonological system and language typology, and by **external** factors such as language contact, sociolinguistic pressures arising from group identity, prestige and education. Separating internal from external factors is analytically expedient. Nevertheless, it has to be acknowledged that in practice the various sources of innovative pronunciations are hard to isolate and identify. The focus of this book is diachronic; the further back we go, the less we know about the external factors of change, and therefore for Middle and especially Old English we will rely primarily on argumentation based on internal factors.

The phonetic properties of adjacent segments and their interactions are important internal triggers of change. When a segmental change is transparently related to the presence of another segment in the word, the change is **environmentally conditioned**. The most frequent environmentally triggered change that we will encounter is **assimilation**. The **target** of assimilation can be one or more of the features associated with place, manner or voicing. The **scope** of assimilation can be complete or partial, and the **direction** of assimilation can be from left to right, also known as **regressive**, and from right to left, also known as **progressive**. In PDE assimilations occur commonly in relaxed speech styles; notice the naturalness of pronouncing *miss Sheila* with [ʃ - ʃ], *this year* as [ʃ - j], to take just one example of regressive assimilation of /s/ to a following palatal. Some historical examples of assimilation are shown in (6).

(6) Assimilation:
OE *hūs* 'house' [-s] + *bonda* 'freeholder' > *husband* [-z]
(Voicing, partial, regressive)
OE *wīf-monn* 'woman' [f - m] > late West Saxon *wimman* [-mm-]
(Manner, voicing, full, regressive)
ME (c. 1225) *questiun* [-stjə-] > question [-ʃtʃə-]
(Place, manner, partial, regressive)
OE *mēt-an* 'to meet' + /**d**/ (past tense) > *mētte* [-tt-]
(Voicing, full, progressive)

The opposite process is **dissimilation**: the avoidance of adjacent or close identical or similar segments. The adjectival suffix *-al* < Lat. *-ālem*, as in *choral*, *mortal*, *natal*, is dissimilated to *-ar* after [-l-], as in *cellular*, *scalar*, *vascular*. An example of dissimilation is the frequent pronunciation of *diphthong* in PDE with [-pθ] (stop-fricative) instead of [-fθ-] (two fricatives). A historical parallel is the change of OE *þēofð*, *þīefð* [-fθ] (<*þēof* 'thief' + **iþa* 'noun') PDE > *theft* [-ft], where the inherited fricative of the suffix becomes a stop; compare also *height*, *sleight*, *drought*, all of them with original [-hθ]. Avoidance of fricative clusters is important in the account of the earliest consonantal changes in Germanic (see 3.4).

Another, relatively minor, pattern of change rearranges the linear order of segments – a process known as **metathesis**. A well-known instance of historical metathesis in English is the verb 'to ask', which in OE had two forms, one starting with <*asc-*> and one starting with <*acs-*>, so that among the more common ME forms we find <*ax, ex, ask, esk*>.[15] Metathesis is found also in OE *cærse* (< **cræsse*), 'watercress'; *Horsa* 'a personal name' < **hross* 'horse' + a; the dialectal (Southwestern) *purty* for *pretty*.

Assimilation, dissimilation and methatesis preserve the number of consonant slots in a word. Other linear phonological processes can add or delete segments. **Epenthesis** is the general term for the insertion of a segment. The epenthesis of a vowel inside a consonant cluster is known as **anaptyxis**. A familiar PDE example of anaptyxis is the insertion of an unstressed vowel between a verbal stem ending in dental stops and the past tense morpheme /-d/: /-t, -d/ + /d/ > [-əd]/[-ɨd], for example *rusted, minded.*

When the segment is added word-initially, the process is called **pro(s)thesis**. Prosthetic initial *e-* characterises French borrowings in English whose roots in Latin had initial *sp-*, *st-*, *sk-*. Thus the Latin root *sta-* 'to stand' appears in two forms in English: as ***estate*** (1225), from Old French, and as *state*, taken directly from Latin. Prosthesis accounts also for the *e-* in loans such as ***espouse*** (1475), ***especial*** (1386), ***escalade*** (1598) vs *spouse* (1200), *special* (1225), *scale* (1330).

The insertion of a consonant within a word is simply a case of epenthesis. Epenthetic consonants may fill a structural position and improve the overall shape of the syllable, for example *bra.mel, spi.nel, þu.nor*, with empty first-syllable codas and sonorants in the onset of the unstressed syllable alternate in OE and ME with ***bram.ble***, ***spin.dle***, ***thun.der***, where the insertion of the voiced stops causes resyllabification whereby the syllables *bram-*, *spin-*, *thun-* have filled codas, and the stops, the least sonorous of all consonants, form the onset of the unstressed syllable.

Segments can be added word-finally, though the examples of this type of change in English are not very numerous. In ME we find forms such as <ino**h**t> for *enough*, <bogh**t**> for *bough*, <borch**t**> for *borough*, and after final nasals *margen**t*** ~ *margin* (sixteenth century and after), *vermin* ~ *varmin**t*** (dialect and US). Among the ones that have become codified are: *poun**d***, v. < OE *punian*; *soun**d***, n. < AN *soun*, OFr *son*; *boun**d***

15 The form *ax* was the regular literary form until c. 1600. It is still used in Midlands and Southern dialects, though supplanted in standard English by *ask*, originally the Northern form (OED). In the US the metathesised form *axe* is characteristic of the South and African American English.

'a clamp of wood' < early ME **houn*. The final consonant in such unetymological additions is called **excrescent**. Analogy with the superlative affix *-est* is the OED explanation of final [-t] added to the OE adverbial ending *-es* in *against*, *amidst*, *amongst*, *betwixt*, *whilst*.

The deletion of segments at the beginning of words is called **aphe(re) sis**. A widely recognised historical example of apheresis is the loss of the initial consonant in the clusters <kn-, wr-, gn->, as in *knight*, *wrong*, *gnaw* in English, which stand for singletons today, but were real clusters in earlier English (see 5.3.1). Some early aphetic forms are ME *ches*, *chess* 'chess' < AN and OFr *eschès* (c. 1180); *fray* < AN and OF *affray*, *effray* (1300); *tend* < ***a**ttend* (1370), *ply* < ***a**pply* (1393), *gypsy* < ***E**gyptian*, n. (1514).

Word-medially, the consonants of English have been fairly stable except in isolated instances of cluster simplification. Some early simplifications are reflected in the spelling: OE *blosma* < *blos**t**ma* 'blossom', OE *elboga* < *el**n**boga* 'elbow', OE *Sæterdæg* < *Sæter**n**dæg* 'Saturday', OE *en**d**leofan* 'eleven'. The orthography does not reflect consonantal losses that were not completed at the time when spelling began to be codified, towards the second half of the fifteenth century: *fasten*, *thistle*, *castle*, *fight*, *sought*, *talk*, *walk*.

The loss of a vowel word-medially is known as **syncope** ['sɪŋkəpɪ]. Syncope affects unstressed vowels: consider the rapid speech pronunciation of *silvery*, *family* as disyllables, and of course *every* is no longer trisyllabic, *pace* OED's recorded pronunciation ['ɛvərɪ]. Syncope can therefore be a diagnostic for the position of the stress at the time of the vowel loss, as in the case of ME *corúne* 'crown' < OFr *corone*, *corune*, Lat. *corōna*), for which we find the spelling <cruness> 'crowns' (c. 1200). When two vowels are adjacent, the vowel which bears a lower degree of stress may be syncopated, as in *marr**ia**ge*, *carr**ia**ge*. The most common case of syncope in English occurs in inflectional morphemes, as in the formation of the <-est> and <-es> of the second and third person singular present tense, and the noun plural <-es>.

The dropping of word-final segment(s) is known as **apocope** [ə'pɒkəpiː]. The term can apply to consonants, vowels and whole syllables. Some cases of consonantal apocope are the loss of [-n] after unstressed vowels – OE *ā**n*** > *a* (indef. article), OE *mī**n*** > *my* (adj. pronoun), the loss of the voiceless affricate [-t͡ʃ] in the pronoun *I* < OE *iċ*, and cluster simplification as in [-ŋg] > [-ŋ-] (*sing*, *thing*) (see further 5.3.2). Syllabic apocope is illustrated by adverbial *-ly* < OE *liċe*, [-ən]-loss in real or pseudo-suffixal *-en*, *-on*, *-an*, resulting in pairs such as *ev**en**(ing)-eve*, *maid**en**-maid*, *gamm**on**-game*.

The effect of such segmental changes on the overall phonological structure varies. Original allophones can become separate phonemes –

this would be a case of **phonemic split**. For example, [v], the voiced allophone of the OE fricative /f/, appearing originally only word-medially between voiced segments, became contrastive everywhere in ME, as in *vast-fast*, *coffin-coven*, *leaf-leave* (see 4.4). The loss of [-g] in the [-ŋg] cluster, where [ŋ] is an allophone of /n/, as in *sing*, *thing*, resulted in the addition of a new phoneme /ŋ/ to the consonantal inventory (see 5.3.2). For Shakespeare's contemporaries the vowels of *lush* and *bush* would have been allophones of /ʊ/, as they still are in some varieties of English, yet today the /ʌ/ of *lush* and the /ʊ/ of *bush* are phonemes, as is clear from the contrast of *putt-put* (see 8.2.1). Conversely, separate phonemes can lose their distinctiveness and merge into one distinctive unit – this would be a **phonemic merger**. In many North American varieties the vowels of COT and CAUGHT, which are distinct phonemes historically, have merged into a single vowel. AmE is in the process of losing the voiceless labial fricative /ʍ/, as in *wharf*, *whine* – it is currently merging with /w/ (see 5.1.3).

Inventories can be augmented by borrowing. Famous historical additions to the English phonemic inventory are the voiced palatal fricative /ʒ/ as in *beige*, *leisure* (see 5.4), and the diphthong /ɔɪ/ as in *choice*, *toy* (see 7.4).

Another aspect of the diachronic behaviour of segments refers to the notion of segmental **strength**, that is, historical phonological processes can result in **weakening/lenition** or **strengthening/fortition**. The strength of a segment can be described in reference to its sonority. Recall from 2.1.3 that segments differ in sonority. Lower sonority, which corresponds to a higher degree of stricture in the vocal tract, means that the sound is 'more consonantal' or 'stronger'. If there is less obstruction and less effort in the production of the segment, the sonority rises. Consonants are *lenited* when they involve less stricture and when they are voiced. Lenited consonants are more vowel-like. The 'strongest' consonants are stops, and the weakest are the sonorants, and especially the oral sonorants [r, l, w, y]. In the vowel system, the most open vowels are also most sonorous, while the high vowels are least sonorous – in that sense, they are more 'consonantal'.

The historical probability of weakening may be measured in terms of intrinsic articulatory and acoustic properties such as degree of constriction for the consonants. Fricatives, for example, are weaker than stops. Another parameter is constriction duration for the vowels: high vowels take longer to articulate, they are stronger than the mid vowels. Complexity is another correlate of weakness: schwa [ə] is the weakest vowel because it lacks the featural complexity of peripheral vowels, thus the change of any vowel in English to schwa is also weakening or **vowel**

reduction. In diachronic terms, weakening can be defined as propensity towards deletion, the resulting zero being the ultimate 'weak' segment.

Weakening and strengthening may be associated with the properties of an individual segment, with the context in which the segment appears, or, with both inherent properties and context. Segments are organised into hierarchical prosodic units – we already looked at one such unit, the syllable, in 2.3. The syllables themselves are organised into higher-level domains: prosodic feet, prosodic words, clitic groups (see 9.4.2). Typically, domain-initial positions resist weakening processes, while domain-final positions are more vulnerable to weakening. A very important interaction between prosodic structure and weakness relates to the presence or absence of stress. The syllable is a stress-bearing unit and there is a well-established correlation between weakening and lack of stress; one such weakening, the reduction and loss of final unstressed vowels in English, has had pervasive consequences for the entire phonological, prosodic, morphological and even syntactic history of English (see 7.6).

Another factor that can influence the implementation of sound change is **frequency**. The role of frequency in language change is a rapidly developing area of research. When the phonetic motivations are relatively transparent, the prediction is that the most frequent words will change first, but as Phillips (2006) reports for English, if there is further involvement of other components of the grammar, sound change can affect the least frequent words first. The availability of electronic historic corpora has made such hypotheses testable on a broad set of changes, but one should still bear in mind that the reliability of quantitative data diminishes rapidly the further back we go in time.

Changes affecting the contrastive and relational status of sounds: replacements, additions, deletions of segments, phonemic merger and split, and the positioning of a segment on a strength scale, are closely linked to the physical correlates of sounds: their articulatory, acoustic and auditory properties. The phonetic grounding of sound change is universal, though the individual paths of optimisation in the production and perception of sounds are language-specific. One of the main mechanisms driving phonological change, therefore, is the diachronic selection of optimal realisations, where the demands on production and perception are in constant conflict.

A description of language in terms of its sounds and prosodic units is an analytical convenience, but it is also highly idealised and artificial. In practice, phonemes and syllables matter only in so far as they are part of the communication process. Phonological segments are the building blocks of **morphemes**, the smallest meaningful units in language, and morphemes build words. Although morphological structure and change is a separate area of inquiry, the interaction between phonology and morphology is a major factor in the initiation and propagation of phonological processes. Phonological alternations occurring in conjunction with morphological processes are known as **morphophonemic** alternations, whereby one and the same morpheme assumes different phonetic shapes, or **allomorphs**. Taking a very simple example: /-d/, /-t/ and /-əd/ are allomorphs of a single past tense morpheme in English. Allomorphy always involves a phonological difference. If the difference is systematic, we seek to establish an underlying form and the rules or constraints that produce the derived form. Ideally, these refer to general principles of production and perception. Using the same example, we do not store in our memory all verbs that take /-d/, /-t/ or /-əd/; instead, we store a single affix /-d/ and change it in those verbs in which the voiced /d/ is incompatible with the final voiceless consonant of the verb stem, as in *stacked, paced, limped*, with [-t]. For stems ending in dental stops, *waited, bonded, raided*, the affix is realised as [-əd] to avoid a sequence [-dd] which English disallows word-finally (see further 4.4 for this and other cases of allomorphic variation).

The sources of phonological change discussed so far – phonetic characteristics, structural relations within the sound system, and prosodic and morphological alternations – are all 'internal' to an idealised theoretical construct, the 'linguistic system'. Obviously, linguistic systems do not exist in isolation; language is a social act and the initiation and propagation of new linguistic forms is accomplished by speakers. The relationship between language and society is studied by **sociolinguistics**. Modern sociolinguistic methodologies involve collecting and analysing live data from speakers. Crucially, these data are testable and replicable. Historical sociolinguistic research, on the other hand, has to rely on written sources. The further back in time we go, the scantier the sources. For Old English there is an unfillable gap between the language of the texts and the range of possible forms and variations used by the speakers. The availability of early sources is predicated on accidents of social and military history. The records of linguistic variation are limited also by the purposes for which texts were written and copied: highly stylised verse compositions, chronicles, religious, archival, administrative texts survived, while we have no casual correspondence, or the equivalents of short stories or drama for OE and much of ME. Literacy is another problem because while 'illiterate' spellings are a boon for the historical phonologist, the bulk of the written records for OE are filtered through standardisation associated with the *Schriftsprache* in late West

Saxon, where considerable levelling of the written forms may obscure spoken variants in contemporary OE.

With these caveats in mind we can still take account of the historical and social context of the changes under discussion. Loanword phonology is essential in plotting the phonological histories of English sounds – from pre-fifth-century exposure to Continental Latin, to the continuing Celtic, Latin, Old Norse, Anglo-Norman, Old French bi- and trilingualism in Britain. Although commonly measured by the number of borrowed words, the effect of medieval multilingualism stretches beyond the adoption of lexical items; the introduction of new words means new phones in new places, and ultimately a reanalysis of the entire phonological and prosodic system. This is evident from the recent history of the palatal fricative /ʒ/ (see 5.4), the acceptability of previously unattested [ts-, ʃm-, ʃl-] (see 5.6) and the prosodic differences between OE and PDE (see 9.6, 9.8). Dialect mixture in ME is another area where system-internal factors interact with social factors, and in Early Modern English and after, the social forces of standardisation can be as instrumental for the selection of variants as is their intrinsic phonological structure.

Suggested further reading on *Companion* website.

3 Discovering the earliest links: Indo-European – Germanic – Old English

FOOT-PODIUM, TOOTH-DENTAL, HILL-CULMINATE, THREE-TRIPLE

The core meaning in the **cognate** word-pairs in our title is obviously shared; most speakers will also recognise *foot, tooth, hill, three* as **native** words, that is, they have been in the language since OE. As is evident from the dates of the first attestations of their semantic mates in the OED, *podium* (1743), *dental* (1594), *culminate* (1647), *triple*, v. (1375) are newer words; they were borrowed from Latin. What is not immediately evident to a non-specialist is that these pairs exhibit a pattern of regular consonantal correspondences: /p/ and /d/ in ***pod****(ium)* correspond to /f/ and /t/ in ***foot***; /t/ in ***dent****(al)* and ***tri****(ple)* corresponds to /θ/ (<th>) in ***tooth*** and ***three***; and /k/ in ***cul****(minate)* corresponds to /h/ in ***hill***. There are also vowel correspondences in cognates that are striking, too: ***mother-maternal*** (1481), ***wind-vent****(ilate)* (c. 1440), originally 'to blow away'. The roots of these correspondences go deeper than the recorded history of the language; they are pre-Old English.

This chapter will describe some of the most salient phonological changes accounting for the difference between PDE words attested in Germanic and OE, and their cognates borrowed in English from Greek and Latin and their descendants. Before we address the specific changes, we need to position OE in a more extended historical timeline.

3.1 Family matters: Indo-European – Germanic – Old English

Recall from 1.2 that the beginning of (Old) English is dated roughly to the middle of the fifth century AD. The Germanic dialect of the Anglo-Saxon settlers that became identifiably 'English' fifteen hundred years ago was related to other Germanic dialects, and Germanic itself was related to other branches jointly forming a set of languages known as **Indo-European** (IE); IE is the metaphorical 'family' to which English belongs. As will become clear in 3.4.1, family *matters* when we seek to explain the puzzle presented by pairs of cognates such as *three-triple*, *tooth-indent* and *foot-podium*.

Cognate, literally 'born together', means that we need to identify the common origin of words such as *(in)dent-tooth*. It is convenient to refer to them as representing languages that belong to the same family. The representation of genetically related language groups as a 'family tree' is just a helpful metaphor and not an exact parallel of biological models of identity and transmission. Languages are clustered together depending on their shared features. We focus here on the similarities in phonological and prosodic structure of cognate words in PDE, but there are many other features that are very important in establishing common origin; they include vocabulary and word-formation, grammatical structure, territorial proximity and a long list of ethnic and cultural markers: shared religion, rituals and customs, mythology, fables, chanted verse, architecture, food, clothing, jewellery, weaving. Archaeological artefacts such as tools and weapons, wagons and coins can also point to ancient contacts among the speakers of now separate languages. The identification of common linguistic ancestry has been pursued also in terms of human genetics by tracing the Y chromosome in male populations as the material basis of shared origin. Such research efforts add to the testable criteria for relatedness and for the classification of the world's languages into families. Among the better-studied families are Native American, Hamito-Semitic, Niger-Congo, Austronesian, Finno-Ugric, Dravidian, Sino-Tibetan, Korean, Japanese, Vietnamese and, closest to us, **Indo-European**, of which Germanic is one of the surviving branches.

3.2 The Indo-European family of languages

The study of Indo-European has a long history. The ancient Greeks and Romans were aware of the similarities between their languages. Throughout the Middle Ages and the Renaissance, the European vernaculars had been compared with the Classical languages, but not in any systematic way, and the usual goal of the comparisons was to point out the disadvantages of the vernaculars. The first scholarly reference to 'familial' resemblances among European and south Asian languages (Persian and Sanskrit), was made by a British judge stationed in India, **Sir William Jones** (1746–94). A Welshman by birth, he was intensely interested in language and is reported to have mastered over twenty-five languages before he died, including French, Italian, Spanish, Portuguese, Latin, Greek, Persian, Hindi, Sanskrit, Hebrew, Arabic and Chinese. Addressing the Bengal Asiatic Society in 1786, he announced that the affinity between Sanskrit, Greek and Latin could not 'possibly have been produced by accident'; the languages had to 'to have sprung from some common source, which, perhaps, no longer exists'. Throughout the nineteenth and into the twentieth century, scholars discovered new similarities among these and other languages, and more branches were added to the Indo-European family tree. Today the descendants of the 'common source', **Proto-Indo-European** (PIE), have been identified and agreed upon, though the representations of the family vary from branches that resemble a genealogical diagram to spokes on a wheel, to images of trees with bigger and smaller branches.

Some form of Indo-European, the presumed original, or **proto-language**, was spoken in the Black Sea–Caspian Sea area until, roughly, 4500–3500 BC. The latter part of the fifth millennium BC is therefore considered 'the latest possible date for the community of Proto-Indo-European proper' (Watkins 1992: 2,088). Thereafter, geographical separation of the speakers following tribal migrations resulted in divergence of the proto-language into many mutually unintelligible languages. This is also the approximate date archaeologists have established for the spread of the wheel through Europe, thus the dating of the IE diaspora coincides with the initiation of transport in wheeled carts. The **Anatolian**, **Indo-Iranian** and **Greek** languages are the earliest attested individual branches of Indo-European. It is believed that the split between them and other branches occurred between c. 3500 BC and 3000 BC. By c. 2500 BC most of the other branches were beginning to take shape. The diversification of Indo-European is such that today as many as 439 separate language codes are assigned to Indo-European (Lewis et al. 2013).

There are no written records of the reconstructed parent language, Proto-Indo-European. Except for the tablets in **Hittite**, an extinct Anatolian language, which date back to the fourteenth to the twelfth century BC, the earliest texts preserved from any language in the IE family are in **Sanskrit**, the religious language of the Hindus, in India. The oldest literary work in Sanskrit is the *Rigveda*, or *Veda of the Stanzas / Wisdom of the Verses*, a collection of religious hymns composed c. 1400–1000 BC, and preserved only in documents of a later date. Greek, whose speakers had moved away to the south-west, is recorded from c. 850 BC in the largely historical account of the Trojan Wars fought between the city-state of Sparta and the City of Troy in Asia Minor. The *Iliad* and the *Odyssey*, ascribed to Homer (c. 850–750 BC) include myths and legends that must have been part of the Greek tradition of oral transmission long before they were written down in the form with which we are familiar.

Figure 3.1 shows the division of Proto-Indo-European into some of its main branches; the dates are necessarily approximate. The vertical connecting lines are *not* intended to suggest that the upper branches develop

Retreat of glaciers in northern Europe

(c. 8000 BC)

*Proto-Indo-European (c. 4500–3500 BC)

|

*Indo-Iranian -----------**Greek**

|

Celtic---------------Later European – I ------------ **Italic/Romance**

|

Balto-Slavic --------------- Later European – II ------------ Northwest European

(***Proto-Germanic** c. 750–250 BC)

Figure 3.1 Some branches of the IE family of languages

into the lower ones; the branches evolve independently from each other, though the cessation of human linguistic contact cannot have been abrupt or complete, and therefore some linguistic continuity must be assumed.

The chart is simplified.[1] An asterisk (*) is used to mark languages of which we have no physical record, but which are reconstructed on the basis of the forms found in the daughter languages. Bold are the branches whose daughter languages have played some role in the development of Germanic or English.

Starting from the geographically most distant IE relative, we can say that the influence of Greek on the phonological shape of English is minimal. Most etymologically Greek words came into English via Latin, or via Latin and Old French. Some orthography, but not the pronunciation, carries through, so only the spellings <ch-, ph-, pn-> in ***chorus***, ***physics***, ***pneumonia*** signal their Greek origin. Further, words spelled with <chth, phth, hy-, ps-, rrh, chr-, pt-, ct-, rh-, x-, sth-, mn-, bd->, are almost exclusively of Greek origin, but the non-native clusters have been simplified to fit the system of English consonants. In some rare cases when a direct Greek loanword survives with its original pronunciation – for example, ***chthonic*** or the combining form ***ichthi(o)-*** with /kθ-/, ***phthisis*** with /(f)θ-/, ***sthenic*** with /sθ-/ – recognisably foreign consonant clusters can be added to the periphery of the inventory of allowable consonant groupings in English (see 5.6). Some words have variable realisations: ***asthma*** can be ['æ**z**mə], ['æ**s**mə], ['æ**sθ**mə], earlier ['æ**st**mə], and ***isthmus*** is ['ɪ**sθ**məs] ['ɪ**st**məs], ['ɪ**s**məs] (OED). The initial cluster in

[1] For a complete chart of the Indo-European language family see the inside of the back cover of the *American Heritage Dictionary of the English Language*, any edition.

the combining form ***pneo-*** 'related to breathing' is simplified today, but *The New English Dictionary* (1907), as the OED was then known, gives the pronunciation as /pn-/. The Greek stem ***phthi*** 'coughing' as in *phthisic*, was borrowed first via Latin as /t-/, but pronunciations with /θ-/ or /fθ-/ are recorded in PDE (OED). In clusters such as <ps-, pt-, mn-> the foreign sequence is nativised by dropping the first consonant: ***psy****chology*, ***pt****erodactyl*, ***mn****emonic*. Greek initial <x-> is pronounced /z/, as in ***x****ylophone*. Consecutive vowels often form the peaks of adjacent syllables, for example *th**ea**tre*, *id**ea***, *id**io**m*.

The Celtic branch of Indo-European, and especially the Brythonic languages Cornish and Welsh, were territorially closest to OE. As noted in 1.2, the presence of Celtic speakers in the British Isles prior to the fifth-century Germanic incursions and settlements does not appear to have influenced the Germanic word-stock significantly, at least as attested in the surviving records. The transfer of phonological and prosodic features from Celtic into Old English is still a matter of debate (see also 6.5.3, 9.6).

The Italic branch, with its illustrious principal language Latin, has a very long recorded history; there are Latin inscriptions dating back to the sixth century BC, and literature in Latin flourished after the third century BC. As the primary language of religion and learning in England for at least a thousand years after the adoption of Christianity in the sixth century AD, Latin has been an important contact language throughout the history of English. The influence of Latin on OE phonology, if any, is hard to identify. Latin loans whose phonological shape did not fit the OE system were apparently assimilated. Thus, the native system disallowed word-initial [v-] (see 4.4), so that we find spellings such as <fers> for Lat. *uersus* 'verse', *Firgilius* for *Virgilius* (see Campbell 1959: 212). Prosodically, OE Latin loans such as *candēla*, OE *candel* 'candle', *comēta*, OE *cometa* 'comet' were also adapted to the native model of root-initial stress. The situation changed in late ME and the Renaissance (see 9.6, 9.8) so that PDE has a layered stress-system.

Within Italic, Anglo-Norman and Old French provide an important source of phonological innovation in Middle English. Both the consonantal and the vowel inventories were augmented: /v/ and /z/ became independent phonemes, the diphthong /ɔɪ/ as in CHOICE was added to the vowel system (see 7.4). English–French bilingualism is one of the main early conduits of a new system of stress-placement, allowing main stress on the final syllable of nouns and adjectives: *degree*, *abysm*, *entire*. Another Italic language, Spanish, has become increasingly important for the development of PDE. In the last century, Spanish–English bilingualism in the American Southwest has resulted in the formation

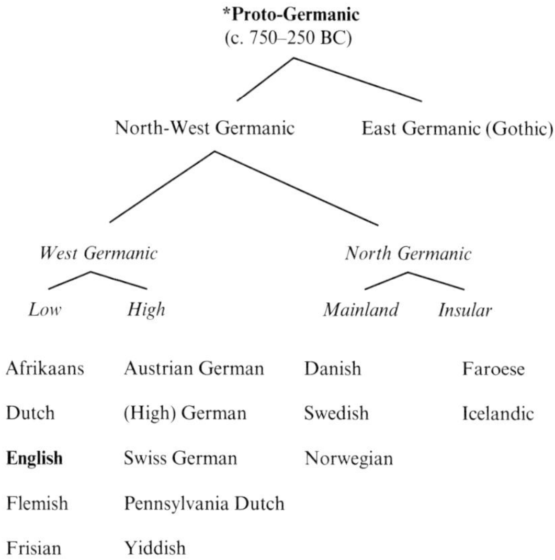

Figure 3.2 Proto-Germanic and its descendants

of new varieties of Latino Englishes, which in their turn influence GA. One such influence is the acceptability of initial and stem-internal [h], as in *jojoba*, *rioja*, *fajita*.

3.3 The Germanic branch of Indo-European

Using the family metaphor again, English is a descendant of the North-West European branch of Indo-European. Figure 3.2 shows the modern Germanic languages that share that genealogical line.

Proto-Germanic (PrG) remained a relatively homogeneous group of languages spoken in the north-western parts of Europe. After c. 250 BC, speakers of Proto-Germanic settled large areas of Central, Western and Eastern Europe, from southern Scandinavia, the North Sea and the Baltic coasts, present-day Holland, east to the Vistula River in what is now Poland and in the lands along the rivers Rhine, Weser and Elbe to the south.

The most important **East Germanic** branch of PrG is **Gothic**, which became extinct during the sixteenth century. Gothic is important for the study of the history of the Germanic language family because, except for a few scattered runic inscriptions, Gothic records antedate those of the other Germanic languages by three to four centuries. The earliest Gothic writings date back to the fourth century AD, when a Christian bishop named **Wulfila** (c. 311–c. 382) is credited with putting together a new, Gothic, alphabet, based on Greek and Latin letters for the purpose of translating the Bible into a Germanic language. The best-preserved Gothic manuscript copy of Wulfila's translation, the Silver Bible, or *Codex Argenteus*, with 188 leaves surviving, dates from the sixth century. This translation of the Bible is by far the oldest lengthy text we have in any Germanic language. Although it gives us little information about syntax, since it is a rather close glossing of the Greek, and most of the time follows Greek word order, it is very informative about early Germanic morphology and is indeed the main source of our reconstruction of the earliest details of the Germanic inflectional systems. Gothic provides the phonological anchoring for the reconstruction of the prehistory of all Germanic languages, both because of the earliness of the written record, and because of apparent similarities of sound-to-spelling in Gothic to the better-documented contemporary Greek system.

The living daughter-languages of Proto-Germanic are grouped further into **North Germanic** and **West Germanic**. West Germanic is further subdivided into 'High' and 'Low', where 'low' refers to the lowlands of northern Germany. The Low West Germanic group does not include any of the standard languages referred to as 'German' today. Historically, the languages in this group, especially **Frisian**, **Dutch** and **Flemish**, are most closely related to Old English. The 'youngest' offshoot of Low West Germanic is **Afrikaans**, also known as 'Cape Dutch'. It is based on the language of the Dutch and other European settlers of South Africa after the middle of the seventeenth century.

The original High West Germanic dialects of the mountainous central and southern parts of Germany have evolved into **High German** (Ger. *Hochdeutsch*), used as a standard language throughout Germany. The national varieties of German spoken in Austria and Switzerland also belong to this group. German and Swiss refugees in the US in the nineteenth century developed another variety of High German, known as **Pennsylvania Dutch** < *Deitsch* 'German', an important Germanic 'heritage' language in North America. Another High West Germanic language is **Yiddish**, which arose as a fusion of Germanic and Slavic in the last millennium. Yiddish loan phonology has led to the recognition and integration of new consonant clusters in English: [ʃm-, ʃl-, ʃt-] (see 5.6).

In the North Germanic branch, **Icelandic**, **Faroese** and **Norwegian** are descended from Old Norse. There were only minor differences between Old Norse and the precursor of modern **Danish** and **Swedish**. As noted in 1.2, Old Norse is of particular interest because it was spoken by the Scandinavian invaders and settlers of England between the eighth and the eleventh centuries. ON influence is evident both in the consonantal system (see 1.2, 4.2.1, 4.3) and in the vocalic system (see 6.2, 6.5.3, 7.4) of OE and ME. The most recent addition to the North Germanic branch is **Nynorsk**, or **New Norwegian**, a language created in the mid-nineteenth century, which combines many rural dialects and which functions as the second official Norwegian language, the first being **Bokmål**, a language heavily influenced by Danish.

We have now looked at the genealogical history of the language up to the point when it became English nearly sixteen hundred years ago. The next section introduces some phonological processes that characterise the Germanic branch of Indo-European as distinct from the other contact languages.

3.4 Some pre-Old English segmental and prosodic changes

The separation of Proto-Germanic from Indo-European is posited on the basis of archaeological findings, shared lexicon, grammatical structures and verse tradition. Most relevant in our context, however, is the phonological identity of the Germanic group – the features shared by the Germanic languages, but not found in the other IE branches. The topics included here – the First Germanic Consonant Shift, some vowel changes from PIE to Germanic, early prosodic changes, final vowel lengthening in monosyllables in Germanic and consonant gemination in West Germanic – are chosen because these processes can be usefully invoked in the recognition and account of cognates, allomorphic relations and prosodic properties in the modern language.

3.4.1 Grimm's Law, or the First Germanic Consonant Shift[2]

The most salient phonological difference between Germanic and its ancestors was discovered in the nineteenth century. It refers to a set of changes affecting three sets of IE obstruents, known as ***Grimm's Law***, though the term 'law' was not used by its discoverer. The changes covered by Grimm's Law are also more neutrally and more descriptively referred to as the **First Germanic Consonant Shift**, where 'first' distinguishes it from a second set of changes, the 'Old High German' or the 'Second Consonant Shift', which affects only Continental West Germanic, more specifically Old High German.

The correspondences included in the First Germanic Consonant Shift are the key to the puzzle referred to at the beginning of this

[2] Material presented in this section is treated also in Minkova and Stockwell (2009: 142–5).

chapter: recall the 'teaser' pairs ***pod(ium)-foot***, ***tri(ple)-three***, ***cul(minate)-hill***. A simplified overview of the main consonantal correspondences which identify the Germanic languages as a separate Indo-European branch is shown in (1).[3]

(1) The First Germanic Consonant Shift:

***Proto-Indo-European**		**Proto-Germanic**	
***p t k**	→	f θ h	(voiceless stops→voiceless fricatives)
***b d g**	→	**p t k**	(voiced stops→voiceless stops)
*b^h d^h g^h	→	**b d g**	(voiced aspirated stops→voiced stops)

The time-span during which the First Germanic Consonant Shift occurred is reconstructed as extending roughly between 750–250 BC, and possibly as late as the turn of the first millennium AD. In the course of at least five centuries the Germanic branch was moving further away from the proto-language. At the same time, various dialects must have evolved, they must have acquired new distinct properties, but all Germanic dialects were still probably mutually intelligible. Since all modern Germanic languages show its effects, it is logical to assume that the Shift was under way prior to the split of Proto-Germanic into separate Germanic sub-branches.

As shown in (1), the Shift involves three sets of stops in the parent language, reconstructed PIE. Within all three sets the original distinctions in place of articulation are well preserved: before and after the shift labials remain labials, dentals remain dentals and velars remain velars. In addition, the change of voiceless stops to fricatives involves also a change from a bilabial /p/ to a labiodental /f/, a dental /t/ to an inter-dental /θ/, and a velar /k/ to a glottal /h/.

Looking at the top row in (1), the original voiceless stops */p, t, k/ changed their manner of articulation and emerged as the voiceless fricatives /f, θ, h/, most likely going through an intermediate stage of aspirated voiceless stops: /p^h, t^h, k^h/. In the second row, the voiced stops */b, d, g/ became voiceless: /p, t, k/. Unlike Germanic, in Latin and the old Romance languages, as well as in Greek, the consonant sets in the first

[3] The asterisk (*) is used for forms established by comparative reconstruction. In the PIE reconstructed consonant system the velar stops */k, g, g^h/ can also appear in a labialised version: */k^w, g^w, g^{wh}/; in Germanic the secondary labial articulation is interpreted as the lip-rounded vowel /u/, while the primary velars develop into /h, k, g/.

Consonant class	*PIE	Latin	Greek	English	Examples
VOICELESS STOPS	*p	p	p	f	*pedal, podiatry, **f**oot*
	*t	t	t	θ	*triple, triad, **th**ree*
	*k	k	k	h	*cordial,[5] cardiac, **h**eart*
VOICED STOPS	*b	b	b	p	*Very rare*
	*d	d	d	t	*endure, dryad, **t**ree*
	*g	g	g	k	*cognition, prognosis, **k**now*
VOICED ASPIRATED STOPS	$*b^h$	f	p^h	b	*refer, eu**ph**oria, **b**ear*
	$*d^h$	f	t^h	d	***f**orum, **th**yroid, **d**oor*
	$*g^h$	h	k^h	g	***h**orticulture, **ch**orus, **g**ird*

Figure 3.3 PIE cognates in Latin, Greek and English

two rows, /p, t, k, b, d, g/, kept their quality, or a quality very similar to the original PIE input.

The third set involving the PIE aspirated voiced stops */b^h, d^h, g^h/ represents a more complex development. 💻 In Germanic the aspirated stops are reconstructed as going through an intermediate stage of voiced fricatives /β, ð, ɣ/; they result ultimately in voiced stops /b, d, g/ in West Germanic/Old English. PIE */b^h, d^h, g^h/ first get devoiced to /p^h, t^h, k^h/ in word-initial position, which is the result of the shift we find attested in Greek. In the Italic branch, as attested in Latin, the aspirated voiceless stops /p^h, t^h, k^h/ become voiceless fricatives /f, f, h/. Of special note for the shift in Latin is the merger of the labial and the dental, where the place difference is neutralised in favour of the labial.[4]

Figure 3.3 illustrates the First Consonant Shift with native English words and cognates borrowed from Latin and Greek.

[4] The confusability of the fricatives /f/ and /θ/ and their merger is perceptually motivated. A parallel merger of /θ/ and /f/ is attested in some English dialects. Though 'generally associated with Cockney and London pronunciation . . . it is in fact characteristic not only of the Home Counties as a whole but of areas further afield. It can, for example, be heard in Leeds' (Wakelin 1972: 98). Wells (1982, II: 329) illustrates the variability of [f] ~ [θ] in Cockney with a pun: 'Advertisements for beer award the brand in question "thirst prize".' 💻

[5] The spelling for /k/ in Latin is <c>: as in *cor* 'heart', *centum* 'hundred', *celer* 'swift', *culmen* 'summit', and so on.

The correspondences shown in Figure 3.3 represent the results of a **chain-shift**, an important type of change in historical phonology. A chain-shift differs from an ordinary 'shift' of a single sound, for example /ʍ/ 'shifting' to /w/ in *whale*, *white*, where 'shifting' is simply a synonym for 'merging with'; no other consonants are involved. A chain-shift, on the other hand, entails the maintenance of some of the original contrasts within a related set of sounds, known as **natural classes**. The three sets in the PIE column – voiceless stops, voiced stops and voiced aspirated stops – are natural classes because they share manner of articulation and voicing; the contrast among the members of each set is based on different places of articulation. Similarly, the output sets of consonants in the English column are natural classes; they share manner of articulation and voicing and their members maintain the place of articulation contrasts of the input sets.

The order in which the sets shifted is not certain, but as in other cases of chain-shifting, for example the English Vowel Shift (see 8.2.2), one can posit more than a single starting point; the end results can be reached via more than one possible route. If the voiceless stops changed their articulation first, creating a full set of fricatives – PIE is reconstructed as being rather impoverished in that area, having only [s]- and [h]-like sounds – then the /p, t, k/ slots in the system would have been vacated. This would trigger the devoicing of /b, d, g/; it is well known that consonantal systems typically disallow voiced obstruents if the corresponding voiceless obstruents are missing. Vacating the voiced /b, d, g/ slots in its turn makes possible the shifting, or loss of breathy-voice, of the original voiced aspirated stops. This scenario can be described as a **drag chain-shift**.

The avoidance of perceptually undesirable mergers of previously distinctive entities allows an alternative direction for the shift. In that reconstruction, the voiced aspirated stops */b^h, d^h, g^h/ are the initial focus of change since they are universally 'marked', that is, they are rare across the systems of the world's languages.[6] If the voiced aspirated stops */b^h, d^h, g^h/, shifted to /β, ð, ɣ/ and then to /b, d, g/ first, the addition of new items with /b, d, g/ would motivate the devoicing of the pre-existing PIE /b, d, g/ to maintain earlier contrasts. One way in which merger can be avoided is by shifting the original /b, d, g/ to /p, t, k/. Further, one way of avoiding homophony would be for the 'new'

[6] Informally, markedness correlates with the strong tendency across languages for some elements to be avoided or to become 'unmarked'. Markedness is part of the human linguistic competence. In the consonantal system, markedness is associated with voicing, coronality, aspiration and nasalisation.

/p, t, k/ set to be differentiated by reanalysis of aspiration as distinctive followed by a change of the manner of articulation, where one enabling factor would be the fact that /f/ and /θ/ were unfilled slots in the PIE system of fricatives. This alternative sequence of events would constitute a **push chain-shift**. The documentation for either scenario is lacking, however, and even in cases where we know much more about the intermediate stages, as with the English Vowel Shift, push chains and drag chains remain controversial.

In the nineteenth century the Shift was taken as a paradigm case of the regularity of sound change, yet it does not apply in all environments. The most common and phonetically well-defined exception to the shift is when */p, t, k/ follow another voiceless obstruent in reconstructed IE. Thus, /g^h/ in PIE ***g^hosti-*** 'guest, stranger' is shifted as expected, while /t/ remains a stop after /s/. (2a) shows more examples of the regular operation of the shift from IE to OE, while (2b) illustrates the 'blocking' of the shift by the preceding sibilant fricative /s-/.

(2) IE voiceless stops in Germanic:

(a) **Regular shifting**		(b) **No shifting**	
****pleu-***,	OE ***flowan*** 'to flow'	**spe-*,	OE *spēdan* 'to prosper, speed'
**tā-*,	OE ***ðāwian*** 'to thaw'	**sta-*,	OE *standan* 'to stand'
****kerd-***,	OE ***heorte*** 'heart'	****skei-***,	ON ***skífa***, PDE ***skive*** 'to cut'

The rationale behind the preservation of /p, t, k/ in (2b) is easy to understand: the implementation of the shift would result in two adjacent voiceless fricatives, /sf/, /sθ/, /hθ/; such clusters require additional articulatory effort and their acoustic closeness would make it hard to perceive the difference between them. Since /p, t, k/ remain unchanged in Greek and Latin, loans which contain /sp, st, sk/ are the same in English and the borrowed item; compare IE ****hesti*** '(s)he is', Lat. ***est***, Goth. ***ist***; IE **sta-* 'stand', English ***stool***, ***stead***, and the loans ***stance***, ***static***, ***status***, ***statistics***; IE ***$skab^h$*** 'to scratch', OE (ON) ***sceabb*** 'scab', and the loans ***scabies*** (c. 1400) 'scabies, itch', ***scabrous*** (1657); IE ***spe**- 'to prosper', OE ***sped*** 'success, (God)speed', later loans ***prosper*** (c. 1350), ***despair*** (1325).

After the operation of the First Consonant Shift, a prosodically motivated set of changes resulted in correspondences that look like apparent exceptions to the shift. The key to the changes in question is the position of the stress in the original word. It is generally held that in PIE the accent could fall on any syllable in the word (see 3.4.3). In Proto-Germanic the voiceless fricatives /f, θ, h/ resulting from the First Consonant Shift were voiced to /β, ð, ɣ/ intervocalically when the IE stress did not fall on the immediately preceding syllable; /β, ð/ merged with the corresponding voiced stops (/b, d/) in OE. This regularity in the phonology of early Germanic was explicated by **Karl Verner** in 1876 and is known in the literature as **Verner's Law.**

(3) Prosodically triggered post-Grimm's Law fricative voicing in PrG (*Verner's Law*):

(a)	Skt *bhrátar*,	OE *brōðor* 'brother'	Lat. *frater*
(b)	Skt *pitár-*,	OE *fæder* 'father'[7]	Lat. *pater*

In (3a) the Shift operates following the model in (1): /-t-/ becomes /-θ-/, which has a voiced allophone /ð/ between vowels (see 4.4). In (3b) the intervocalic /-t-/ follows an unstressed syllable, where the reconstructed chain of events is /t/ > /θ/ (Grimm's Law) > /ð/ > /d/ (Verner's Law).

The changes covered by Verner's Law are shared by all dialects of Old Germanic except Gothic. Chronologically, the voicing must have preceded the shift of stress to the first root syllable in Germanic (see 3.4.3). The effects of fricative voicing after an unstressed syllable are recognisable in OE in the strong verb paradigm of class 2 weak verbs, where the past plural and past participle show the voicing; compare OE *flēon* 'to flee' < **flēohan* 'flee' with intervocalic loss of /-h-/ in the initially stressed infinitive, vs *flogen* (past part.) 'flown'; OE *sēoðan* 'to seethe' – past participle *sodden*.

Under the same prosodic circumstances, original /z/, an allophone of /s/ between vowels, became /r/, possibly passing through a palatal fricative stage [ř], like Czech /ř/, as in *Dvořák*. The transition from /s/ to /r/ is known as **rhotacism**, familiar outside Germanic from paradigmatic alternations in Latin, for example *os* 'mouth', gen. sg. *oris* 'of the mouth', *opus* 'work', pl. *opera*. In Germanic some pairs of cognates also show the effect of rhotacism. Disregarding vowel changes, the PrG root **rīs-* corresponds both to OE *rīsan* 'to rise' and to OE *rǣran* 'to rear'; the OE form *lār* 'lore' corresponds to PrG **laiz-* 'to teach'; the /z/ ~ /r/ alternation in the past tense forms of the verb *to be* – sg. *was* - pl. *were* – and the present tense and the adjectival participle of the verb *lose-(for) lorn* from earlier *(for)loren*, are pairs which illustrate historical rhotacism.

An interesting parallel stress-dependent voicing is the so-called 'Verner's Law in English', a sixteenth-century tendency to voice fricatives after unstressed syllables, manifested in the voicing of /s/ to /z/ in loanwords, mostly, but not exclusively after prefixes – *resign, transact, example, Alexander* – and even against the spelling in *possess, dessert, dissolve.*

[7] For the change of [-d-] to [-ð-] in *father* see 5.2.3, 5.5.2.

Within Germanic, the regular results of the First Consonant Shift are still in evidence in English, Dutch, other Low German languages and the Scandinavian languages. The shift took place within a restricted span of time prior or up to the beginning of the Christian era. This entails that already in OE speakers and writers familiar with Latin would encounter pairs of cognates where the borrowed item and the Anglo-Saxon word exhibit the relevant correspondences, as the following pairs show; they did not, of course, know about Indo-European or Grimm's Law.

(4) Cognates showing *Grimm's Law* in OE:[8]
tripartita istoria, þæt is, ***þ**ryfeald* 'threefold' (gereccednyss.)
***p**ater noster qui es in celis*. þæt is ure ***f**æder* 'father' (þe eart on heofenum.)
*in **c**or**d**e suo*; þæt is on Englisc . . . on his agenre ***h**eor**t**an* 'heart'

For a PDE speaker, the way in which the obstruents in words of shared Indo-European origin appear today is a good chronological indicator: if a word existed in Germanic prior to the development of its separate dialects, it shows the effects of the First Consonant Shift, but if the word was borrowed after the split, it preserves the consonants of the donor language, most commonly Latin or Greek. What we know about the Shift makes it evident that in a pair such as ***kn**ow*-*i**gn**orant*, the latter was borrowed after OE, and so were *a**gn**ostic*, *pro**gn**osis*, *dia**gn**osis*, *i**gn**ore*, while the related ***c**a**n***, ***c**o**n***, ***c**u**nn**ing*, ***k**e**n***, ***k**e**nn**ing*, are Germanic.

We have now traced the two possible paths of entry of cognates into PDE: one is the direct continuation of the PIE form into Germanic, Old, Middle and Modern English. Then, independently, and after Grimm's Law had stopped operating, the language could borrow a word from Greek, Latin and other IE languages. Such later borrowings are obviously not subject to any Germanic changes, though they may undergo their own shifts specific to their branch, as we saw in Figure 3.3 with the voiced aspirated stops in Greek and Latin. This dual route that the same root has taken historically in entering English is responsible for the correspondences in so many interesting pairs of the type *FOOT-PODIUM*, *TOOTH-DENTAL*, *HILL-CULMINATE*, *THREE-TRIPLE*. The list in (5) includes more examples of PIE cognates coexisting in PDE; in the second column, the root consonants illustrate the results of the First Germanic Consonant Shift. The dates in parentheses are the first attestations of the words in English cited in the OED.

[8] The examples are from the homiletic writings of Ælfric (c. 955–1020).

(5) Grimm's Law and the chronology of cognates in English: [9, 10]

PIE	Germanic/ English	Later loan
*pod-/ped-	foot, fetter	**p**o**d**ium (1743), **p**e**d**al (1611)
*trei-	three	**t**riple, v. (1375), **t**riplex (1601)
*kl-/kel-/kol-	hill	**c**ulminate (1647), **c**olumn (1440)
*dent-/dont-	**t**oo**th**	**d**en**t**al (1594), (perio)**d**on**t**al (1899)
*gal-	call, clatter	**g**lasnost (1972)[9]
*b^{h}er-	bear, **b**airn	fertile (1460), eu**ph**oria (1684)
*d^{h}wer-	door	forum (1460), **th**yroid (1693)[10]
*g^{h}os-ti-	guest	**h**ost (1290), **h**ospitality (1375)

Consonantal changes in cognates represent only one aspect in which the Germanic languages differ from the Indo-European parent language. The next section turns to some vowel correspondences between IE and early Germanic.

3.4.2 Some IE vowel changes in Germanic

In the vowel system, the line of transmission from PIE to Germanic to OE and later is interrupted or diverted much more often than with the consonants. Therefore, it is only rarely that we can recognise continuity in the vowels from PIE to PDE without the additional knowledge of the processes covered in Chapters 6–8. For now, we will just summarise some relevant changes from IE to Germanic, skipping over some complex IE interactions between the class of laryngeal sounds and the vowels.

(6) Some vowel mergers from PIE to Germanic:

PIE	Germanic	Examples
a	PrG a	PIE **al-* 'grow', Lat. *aliment*, Gmc **alda* 'old'
o		PIE **g^{h}os-ti-* 'guest', Lat. *hostis*, Goth. *gasts*
ā	PrG ō	PIE **māter-*, Lat. *māter*, OE *mōdor* 'mother'
ō		Lat. *plōrare* 'weep', OE *flōd* 'flood'

[9] From Slavic *glas* 'voice'; *glasnost* is 'giving something public voicing and transparency'.

[10] Lat. *foras, foris* 'out of doors'; Gk *thura* 'door', *thureos* 'shield'; hence the seventeenth-century formation *thyroid* 'door/shield-shaped'.

i		PIE *tit-/kit- 'tickle', Lat. *titillate*, ME *kittle*
	PrG i	
e		Lat. *ventus*, OE *wind* 'wind', Lat. *sedeo*,Gmc**sitjan* 'sit'[11]

This selective list of changes may be quite mystifying at this early stage. It is intended primarily as a bridge between the unfamiliar PIE forms and the cognate forms that one will see cited in an etymological dictionary.

A final set of segmental changes that may help one recognise some etymological connections refers to the set of syllabic sonorants in PIE.

(7) The syllabic sonorants of Indo-European:[12]

PIE	Germanic	Examples
r̥	→ <ur>	PIE *mr̥-ti-*, Lat. *mortal*, Gmc *mur-þra* 'murder'
l̥	→ <ul>	PIE *wl̥k^{w}o-*, Lat. *lupus*, OE *wulf* 'wolf'
m̥	→ <um>	PIE *g^{w}m̥-*, Lat. *venire*, OE *cuman* 'to come'
n̥	→ <un>	PIE **n̥ter*, Lat. *inter*, OE *under* 'under'

3.4.3 Early prosodic changes: stress and syllable weight in Germanic

Another important phonological difference between Indo-European and Germanic is observed in the stress system of the Germanic group. PIE is reconstructed as having a free accentual system, where accent was marked by high pitch. In principle, PIE accent could be placed on any syllable of the word. An IE noun like **pətér-* 'father' had accent on the second syllable, while the noun **bhrā́ter-* 'brother' was accented on the first syllable.

The prosodic properties of PIE are still debated. What is agreed upon with regard to Germanic is that all early dialects of that branch developed a stress-based system of marking prominence. Moreover,

[11] The raising of IE /e/ to /i/ occurs before a covered, and occasionally, before a single nasal, and before /j, i/ in the following syllable, which was commonly lost in OE.

[12] The syllabic sonorants of PIE are represented here with an under-ring following the common practice by Indo-Europeanists, for example Watkins (1985). Elsewhere in this book we follow the IPA practice marking syllabicity by a subscript vertical stroke under the corresponding letters: r̩, l̩, m̩, n̩. Sonorants functioning as syllabic peaks can be treated as equivalent to the more familiar schwa /-ə-/ followed by a sonorant – /-ər, -əl, -əm, -ən/ – as in PDE *mutter*, *kettle*, *bottom*, *weapon*.

Germanic stress became fixed on the first syllable of the root. The establishment of the innovative system has to be dated later than the operation of Verner's Law, because the latter requires IE-type accentuation. One likely approximate date for the fixing of Germanic stress on the first syllable is about 500 BC (Salmons 1992: 162–4).

Initial prominence in native roots continues to be a defining prosodic feature of English to this day. This prosodic characteristic present throughout the history of English is known as the **Germanic Stress Rule** (GSR). The GSR refers to the default root-initial stress in non-monosyllabic words inherited from Old English, the pattern of *áfter, hállow, blóssom, becóme.* The preference for marking the left edge of nouns in English persists and it can affect loanwords whose first syllable was originally a prefix; such are the synchronically monomorphemic nouns: *cóntrast, cónflict, éscort, óbject, présent, próduce, súrvey.*

Primary prominence on the first syllable of the root entails that syllables following the root in non-derived words were unstressed. Already by c. 100 BC fully unstressed syllables were undergoing *reduction*, that is, the vowels and consonants in these syllables were losing their distinctive properties. In English the process of vowel and consonant reduction in unstressed syllables developed more fully than in other Germanic languages. Reduction in unstressed syllables eventually resulted in merger and loss of unstressed vowels from the final syllables of polysyllabic words, so that all short unstressed final vowels were dropped (see 6.5.4, 7.6). To this day English maintains a full inventory of vowels only in syllables bearing primary and secondary stress, while the set of vowels allowed in fully unstressed syllables is limited (see 2.2).

3.4.4 Lengthening of final vowels in stressed monosyllables

In 2.3.3 we noted the absence of word-final stressed short, lax, non-peripheral vowels [ɪ ɛ æ ʊ ʌ] in PDE; words such as **se* with [-ɛ], **decrí* with [-ɪ], **bru* with [-ʊ] are ill-formed. This constraint on the shape of the final stressed syllable in English can be traced back to OE and even earlier. In all North-West Germanic languages the final vowels of lexical monosyllables became uniformly long, that is, they were lengthened if the original vowel was short. In some instances the long vowel appears to be a compensation for the loss of PrG final /-z/: PrG */hwaz/ > OE *hwā* 'who', PrG /wiz/, OE *wē* 'we'. Lengthening without loss of a syllable coda is attested in OE *nū* 'now', Goth. *nu*, OE *swā* 'so', Goth. *swa*; in this second set the process is evidently driven by the preference for co-occurrence of stress and syllable weight noted in 2.3.3. Lengthening under stress is the inverse of the reduction of final vowels in unstressed syllables: having a long vowel in a stressed monosyllabic word *increases* the word's perceptual salience.

The length of the vowel in some of the pronominal monosyllables in OE – *he* 'he', *me* 'me', *þu* 'thou' – fluctuates depending on the position of the pronoun in the phrase or clause: the long vowel goes with stressed position, but when the pronoun was unstressed, the vowel was short. The subsequent history of the vowels in these particular pronouns is based on their pronunciation in stressed position; the vowels are long and they go through the English Vowel Shift. The opposite process, shortening, can occur if a monosyllabic pronoun ends in a consonant, as in OE *ūs* 'us' (see 7.5.1.3). What is important for us here is, again, that the pre-OE constraint on the distribution of word-final stressed vowels is still active in PDE and renders monosyllables other than function words, like *bi* *[bɪ], *lo* *[lɔ], *se* *[sɛ], *ru* *[rʊ] unacceptable. Similarly, underived words of the shape **ponrí* with [-ɪ], **sebrú* with [-ʊ], could not occur in OE and are still blocked from the PDE lexicon. The lengthening of short final vowels in stressed monosyllables is thus the earliest stage in a long process of regularisation of the weight of stressed syllables in the language history. By eliminating lexical monosyllables ending in a short vowel, it is arguably also the process that makes English subject to the constraint on *word-minimality*, whereby a minimal lexical word should be prosodically heavy – either -VV or -VC.

3.4.5 West Germanic (Consonant) Gemination (WGG)

Recall from 2.1.4 that PDE disallows the use of geminate consonants within the boundaries of a single morpheme, and therefore long consonants in PDE serve as a juncture signal in compounds and transparent derivatives; compare *pen-knife* [-nn-], with *Pennines* [-n-], *midday* [-dd-] with *middle* [-d], *misspell* [-ss-] with *missive* [-s]. In this respect PDE differs from OE, where geminate consonants appeared freely in word-medial position (see 4.1.2).

The geminate consonants of OE can be traced back to various sources. Some consonantal geminates arose already in PrG from assimilation.

(8) Proto-Germanic assimilations resulting in geminates:

IE	PrG	OE	Gloss
**wl̥ə-nā-*	**wullō*	*wull*	'wool'
**ster-la*	**sterron-*	*steorra*	'star'
**kl̥-ni*	**hul-ni*	*hyll*	'hill'

By far the most important source of consonant gemination in Old English is a process known as **West Germanic (Consonant) Gemination**

(WGG), which was under way, but not necessarily completed by the early fifth century. The gemination is in evidence in the earliest OE written records, around the first quarter of the eighth century; compare Goth. *sibja* 'amity' with OE *megsibbi* 'affection among relatives' in the *Épinal Glossary* (c. 700?).

The process can be described as doubling of single consonants other than /r/ in the environment V̆ – /j, w, r, l/: a short vowel followed by a single consonant (= light syllable), followed by an approximant or a liquid. The process is most regular before /-j/. Since there was no gemination in Gothic and in Old Norse it was restricted to the velar stops /k, g/, we can use actual recorded forms as evidence for the pre-gemination status of the consonants. The examples in (9) show how gemination works in the large group of OE verbs formed with the *-jan* suffix.

(9) West Germanic Consonant Gemination:

PrG	**OE**	**Gloss**
ON *sitja*	*sittan*	'to sit'
Goth. *saljan*	*sellan*	'to give, to sell'
Goth. *hlahjan*	*hlæhhan* (Angl.)	'to laugh'
Goth. *bidjan*	*biddan*	'to bid'

The examples in (9) may appear straightforward, but they also oversimplify a very complex set of phonological events. While /j/ triggered gemination in all consonants except /r/, gemination occurred in other environments, but in a more limited way. The other triggers of WGG, /w, r, l/, operate only on voiceless stops, for example OE *æppel* 'apple' < PrG **apl*, OE *bit(t)or* 'bitter', ON *bitr*. Further complications arise from the gemination of the velar stops, where the end results are not /-kk-/ and /-gg-/, but /tʃ/ written <-cc->, as in PrG **wak-jan*, OE *weccan* 'to wake, watch'; WG **strakkjan*, OE *streccan* 'to stretch'; and /dʒ/ written <cg> as in Goth. *bugjan*, OE *bycgan* 'to buy'. On the interpretation of /tʃ/ and /dʒ/ as singletons or geminates see 4.1.2.

As the examples in (9) show, one source of opacity in the distribution of geminates is that the attested results in OE show no trace of the trigger /-j-/. Clearly, the loss of this approximant in word-medial position also belongs to the pre-OE period, most likely after, possibly even during, but *not before* the consonant gemination was well under way. The absorption of /j/ cannot have happened much before the seventh century. The loss of the approximant is directly related to syllable structure. In 2.3 we discussed the principle of syllabification which disallows word-medial syllable onset clusters that are not also attested word-initially. Projecting this principle to the stages of West Germanic Gemination suggests that the lack of word-initial /Cj-/ in Germanic can be the structural reason for the loss of /j/ following WGG, thus *bid.jan* > **bid.djan* > **bid.dan*. The intermediate stage **bid.djan* could have developed into **bid.di.an* by vocalisation of the /j/, but instead, /j/ was deleted and the form retained its original disyllabic structure.

The preference for the disyllabic solution is related to a process known as **High Vowel Deletion** (HVD). HVD is sensitive to the prosodic shape of the word: /i/ deletion occurs only after a heavy syllable. The foot structure of the stem of the reconstructed **bid.di.an* would be H(eavy)L(ight), triggering deletion of the high vowel /i/. Compare this with *e-ri-an* 'to plough' where the first foot is LL and it exhibits no HVD. Since /r/ resisted gemination, it would be syllable-initial; /rj-/ is an impossible syllable onset, however, which results in the vocalisation of /j/ to /i/. Thus in PrG, /V̆r-/ stems + /j/ > /V̆-ri-/. The option realised in OE is /i/ or /e/ after /r/: PrG **arjan* > OE *erian* 'to plough', PrG *harjaz* > OE *here* 'army'. As we will see in 6.3.1, Proto-Germanic medial /j/ is one of the triggers of *I-Mutation*, another major co-articulatory change which affected the vowels of the preceding syllables.

Another related question has to do with the orthographic representation of the geminates that OE inherited: what makes us confident that the double consonant spellings in OE words such as *æppel* 'apple', *sellan* 'to give, sell', *biddan* 'to bid' reflect genuine 'long' consonants, compared with PDE *apple, sell, bidding*, where the doubling is only orthographic? A simplistic, but still credible response would be that the literate people recording Old Saxon, Old English, Old Frisian, Old Low Franconian and Old High German could not have had shared training, and therefore the scribal practices of doubling consonants we find in all of these Old Germanic dialects must reflect actual geminate pronunciations. Within English, the argument for positing geminates in OE and subsequent loss of gemination are quite subtle. As we will see in 7.5.2.1, the short vowels before medial geminates, for example OE *æppel* 'apple', behave differently from the short vowels before singletons, for example OE *apa/ape* 'ape'. Another important indicator of the reality of geminates in medial position in OE relates to the patterns of heavy and light syllables found in OE verse (see 10.2.1). Finally, the 'solid' arguments for the existence of geminates in OE refer to consonantal length in word-medial position. There were no word-initial geminates in Germanic. Whether word-final geminates were actually realised in OE, or whether spellings such as *pytt* 'pit', *hyll* 'hill' were, or became, conventional, remains an open question.

Suggested further reading on *Companion* website.

4 Consonantal histories: Old English

KIRK-CHURCH, DAY-DAWN, SAY-SAW-SAGA, SKIRT-SHIRT, SHRIFT-SCRIPT, DISH-DISK-DISCUS, LOAF-LOAVES VS SERF-SERFS, ELF-ELFS-ELVEN, BATH-BATHS-BATHE, BELIEF-BELIEFS-BELIEVE

Some consonantal correspondences in Indo-European non-Germanic and Germanic cognates: ***plenary-full***, *cordial-**hearty***, and so on, were covered in 3.4.1. This chapter turns to a different set of consonantal correspondences in cognates, as in ***kirk-church***, the inherited alternations in *day-dawn*, *say-saw-saga*, and the fricative voicing in the paradigm of a single stem, as in *loaf-loaves*, *bath-bathe*, *grass-graze*. Understanding the origin of these correspondences takes us back to Old English, so we start with an overview of the OE consonantal system (4.1). Some background information on OE consonant spelling is provided in 4.2. Section 4.3 explores specific sound changes: palatalisation and affrication in (late) OE involving the velars [k, g], relevant for the differences in cognates such as ***kirk-church***, *shrift-script*, *dish-disk-discus*, *skirt-shirt*. The voicing alternations in three OE fricatives – [f ~ v], [s ~ z], [θ ~ ð] – and their continuity and marginal survival in PDE in pairs such as *loaf-loaves*, *bath-bathe*, *grass-graze*, are covered in 4.4.

4.1 The consonants of OE

4.1.1 Singletons

Figure 4.1 shows the set of consonant phonemes reconstructed for OE; the classification matches the PDE chart in Figure 2.2.

Whenever there are two consonants in a single cell, as is the case with all stops, the affricates and the velar fricatives, the one to the right is voiced. Shaded cells indicate that the respective consonants are reconstructed as functionally different from their PDE counterparts, including the unfilled shaded cells corresponding to the PDE voiceless labial fricative /ʍ/ and the velar nasal /ŋ/. The parentheses around the affricates [tʃ] and [dʒ] and the glottal fricative [h] also signal differences from PDE (see 4.3 for the affricates and 5.1 for [h]).

			Labial	Labio-dental	Dental	Alveolar	Palatal	Velar	Glottal
Obstruent	STOPS		p b			t d		k g	
	AFFRICATES						(tʃ dʒ)		
	FRICATIVES			f	θ	s	ʃ	x ɣ	(h)
Sonorant	NASALS		m			n			
	Approximants	Lateral				l			
		Central	w			r	j		

Figure 4.1 The consonantal phonemes of Late Old English (singletons)

The inventory in Figure 4.1 makes it obvious that the bulk of the differences between OE and PDE affects the obstruent set and within that set, the subset of fricatives. In terms of place of articulation, it is the consonants in the palatal and the velar area that have been most prone to change. The only difference in the inventory of the sonorant set is the empty cell for the velar nasal /ŋ/ in OE. Phonetically, the nasal /n/ is predictably velarised before a following velar in the same syllable; it is a straightforward case of regressive assimilation. Although [ŋ] must have existed as an allophonic realisation of /n/ before tautosyllabic velar stops in OE in words such as ***cyning*** 'king' [-ŋg], ***lang*** 'long' [-ŋg], ***þank*** 'thought' [-ŋk], it was the loss of final /-g/ in Early Modern English (see 5.3.2) that resulted in the phonemicisation of /ŋ/, evidenced by PDE contrasts such as *fang-fan, thing-thin.*

Within the obstruent set, the stops have been fairly stable. The voiced velar /g/ is shaded; its addition as a contrastive element was an innovation within the OE system. In Germanic and early OE the corresponding consonant was a voiced velar fricative /ɣ/. By the middle of the tenth century, as evidenced by the alliterative practice, initial /ɣ/ merged with pre-existing /j/ before front vowels, but before back vowels and the sonorants /r, l, n/ it was subject to fortition, that is, it became the voiced velar stop /g/. A singleton voiced velar fricative [ɣ] was preserved until late OE only between back vowels (see further 4.2.1).

The palatal fricative /ʃ/ developed in late OE from the etymological sequence /s + k/, usually spelled <sc> in OE, as in *sceadu* 'shade', *scearp* 'sharp', *flesc* 'flesh' (see 4.2). The coarticulation of vowels with velars in OE and the origin and status of the affricates /tʃ/ and /dʒ/ are discussed in 4.3.

The shaded empty cell for the voiceless labiovelar fricative /ʍ/ in Figure 4.1 highlights the absence of contrastive /ʍ/ in OE, while some PDE varieties have different onsets in ***whale-wail, whet-wet*** (see 2.1.2, 5.1.3). Historically, /ʍ/ goes back to an OE bi-segmental cluster /hw/, spelled <hw>, for example <*hwæl*> 'whale', <*hwīt*> 'white'.[1] The evidence that the onset in such words was identified as a velar/glottal, and not a labial, comes from verse, where <hw> alliterates regularly on [h-].

(1) OE <hw> alliteration:
Ac se **hw**ita **h**elm / **h**afelan werede — *Beowulf* 1448
'but the white helm / head guarded'
hea hornscipe, / ofer **hw**æles eðel — *Andreas* 274
'high horned (beaked) ship, / over the whale's dominion'
Hwalas ðec **h**erigað, / and **h**eofonfugolas — *Daniel* 386
'whales hear you, / and heavenly birds'[2]

The [h-] in this position must, however, have been weak, close to marking just aspiration, which allows an allophonic interpretation of <hw-> as [ʍ]. Already by late OE, we find the first spellings of <hw> with just <w> (<ƿ>) and alliterations of <hw> with <w>-initial words.

(2) Late Old English alliteration of <hw->:
þa **hw**ile þe hi wæpna / **w**ealdan moston[3] — *Maldon* 83
'as long as they their weapons / could wield'
and he þar **w**unode / ða **hw**ile þe he lyfode — *Death of Alfred*[4] 21
'and he lived there / for as long as he was alive'

The variation between /ʍ/ ~ /w/ has been in the language for the whole of the second millennium, and the situation continues to be unresolved (for more on this see 5.1.3; for the history of the fricatives /f, θ, s/ see 4.4).

4.1.2 Geminates

Figure 4.1 includes only the single consonants of OE. Most of these consonants could also appear as geminates arising both from WGG

[1] The letter <w-> is a modern convention; the Anglo-Saxon scribes used a runic letter known as *wynn*. Its manuscript form in Old and early Middle English is Ƿ, ƿ.

[2] Here and throughout, for the full names of the Old English texts, their abbreviations, for named authors, and bibliographical information see <http://tapor.library.utoronto.ca/doe/dict/bibl/index.html> (last accessed 27 May 2013). For the ME authors and titles see <http://quod.lib.umich.edu/h/hyperbib/> (last accessed 27 May 2013).

[3] Also *Maldon* 272.

[4] *The Death of Alfred* is dated 1036.

(see 3.4.5) and from various assimilations. The only consonants that did not appear as geminates in OE were the approximants /w/ and /j/. In addition, in words in which the velars /k/ and /ɣ/ were subject to WGG, the result was not *[kk] and *[ɣɣ] but [tʃ], spelled <cc>, and [dʒ], spelled <cg>, for example WG **jukkjan* > OE *gyccan* 'itch', PrG **brugjō-* > OE *brycg* 'bridge'.

Phonetically, the palatal affricates [t͡ʃ, d͡ʒ] are combinations of stops and fricatives, not unlike PDE /t͡ʃ/, /d͡ʒ/ (see 2.1.3). In view of the origin of these affricates, however, it is of relevance to establish when the original bi-segmental clusters started to function phonemically as singletons, as they clearly do today.[5] There is no direct evidence on which such a reconstruction can be firmly based, but some indirect evidence is supplied by later changes in open syllables (see 7.5.2.1): the stressed syllables of words with medial geminates developing into affricates resisted lengthening, for example OE (ge)*mæcca* 'spouse, match'; compare with OE *wacian* 'to wake'. Also, in OE verse words with medial affricates appear to resist resolution, which requires that the stressed syllable should be light (see 10.2.1). Such phonological behaviour can be interpreted in two ways: the affricates were either still perceived as 'composite' and rendered the syllable to the left heavy, or they were treated as ambisyllabic singletons, again rendering the stressed syllable heavy. The latter interpretation is of considerable interest since it provides historical evidence for the possibility of variable contribution of consonants to syllable weight – a question that has not been explored for the history of English.

As noted in 2.1.4, 3.4.5, today long consonants occur only when two identical consonants are positioned back to back across a morphological boundary, as in *pace-setter*, *set terms*, *grim monster*, *unneeded*, *dissatisfied*, *rivalless*. Since the morphological compositionality of such words or phrases is transparent, the two consonants are independently identifiable, while 'real' geminates are fully cohesive, meaning that they cannot be separated by an epenthetic vowel or otherwise interrupted. In the morphologically created long consonants, only one of the consonants can go through a phonological process, while real geminates behave in a unitary way, in spite of the fact that the closure duration for geminate stops in languages that have consonantal length contrast is up to three times longer than for the singleton stops.[6]

The reconstruction of consonantal length in OE relies on comparative evidence, orthography, minimal pairs and the behaviour of geminates in various phonological processes.

[5] See Cruttenden (2008: 180–4).

[6] See Ladefoged and Maddieson (1996: 92).

Recall from 3.4.5 that some Proto-Germanic assimilations resulted in long consonants, for example IE **ster-la* > PrG **sterron-* > OE *steorra* 'star'. West Germanic (Consonant) Gemination (WGG) is another source of inherited geminates, thus Goth. *saljan*, OE *sellan* 'to give, to sell'. These well-studied processes are shared by other dialects of Germanic, making the reconstruction of geminates in OE more plausible. As for orthography, we can appeal again to the logic of widely shared assumptions: OE spelling was closer to being phonemic than the etymologically based spelling of PDE. This increases the likelihood that the pronunciation of OE *æppel* 'apple' was with /-pp-/, *sellan* 'give' with /-ll-/, *cyssan* 'kiss' with /-ss-/, and so on, while in PDE *apple*, *sell*, *kiss*, and so on, have the same consonants as *ape*, *seal*, *rice*. In isolation, spelling might not be a strong indication of consonantal length even in OE, yet consistency of double-consonant spellings in a much freer orthography also works in favour of positing consonantal length: of well over a thousand <bb> spellings for *abbod* 'abbot', there is only one attestation of <abud> in the DOE.

Turning to the test of minimal pairs, we find a small number of items where the presence of a stem-internal geminate after a short vowel is contrastive.

(3) Singletons and geminates in OE (minimal pairs):

bitela 'beetle'	*bitter* 'bitter'
bite 'bit, morsel, cut'	*bitte* 'bucket'
hopian 'to hope'	*hoppian* 'to hop'
manu 'mane'	*manna* 'man'
sæp(e) 'sap'	*sæppe* 'spruce, fir'
tela 'well, thoroughly'	*tellan* '(re)count'

Since WGG occurred only after short vowels, the most common co-occurrence was of a short vowel followed by a geminate (-$\breve{V}$ C_1C_1-), though geminates due to assimilation, usually across a morpheme boundary, could arise also after long vowels, for example *cȳþan* 'to make known' > past sg. *cȳþ-de* ~ *cȳdde*; *lǣdan* 'to lead > 3rd sg. *lǣd-þ* > *lǣdt* > *lǣt(t)* ~ *lǣd*; *mētan* 'to meet' > 3rd sg. *mēt-þ* > *met(t)*. Such morphologically conditioned assimilations are the source of the most notable set of 'new' geminates in OE, one that has had a lasting effect on the structure of some weak verbs in English. The long consonant in the past tense of weak dental-final verbs with a long vowel in the stem – *lǣdan* 'to lead' > past sg. *lǣdde* 'led'; *mētan* 'to meet' > *mētte* 'met'; also *blēdde* 'bled', *brēdde* 'bred'; *fēdde* 'fed', *spēdde* 'sped' – triggers shortening of the stem vowel, creating a new pattern of 'irregular' past-tense formation for originally 'regular' verbs (see 7.5.1).

A distributional restriction on OE geminates noted above was the absence of */ww/ or */jj/, a typologically predictable situation, because of the closeness of these approximants to vowels. WGG of the voiced velar fricative /ɣ/ resulted in OE [dʒ]. A medial /-gg-/ did occur, albeit rarely, as in OE *frogga* 'frog', though its source is unclear.[7] The rarity of /-gg-/ correlates well with the aerodynamics of voicing, combined with the additional factor of difficulties associated with the back articulation of [g]. This results in a scale of difficulty, where [gg] is harder than [dd] and [dd] is harder than [bb].[8]

The voiced fricatives [v, ð, z] were allophones of /f, θ, s/ between voiced sounds in OE, from which it follows that voiced fricative geminates are also precluded. Phonetically, geminate fricatives are more 'effortful' than geminate stops.[9] Hogg (1992a: 32) remarks on the rarity of /-ff-/, describing it as a 'marginal member of the normal phonological inventory of OE'. The phonological significance of this fact is not obvious; since other fricative geminates are common, it could simply be an accidental gap in the lexicon.

There were no word-initial geminates in Germanic, or Indo-European. This is not surprising: word-initial geminates in particular are typologically rare, though initial long stops are attested in some non-Indo-European languages.[10]

Another sequential distributional restriction on the occurrence of geminates in OE was that they could occur only post-vocalically within the confines of a single word, where 'single word' is defined to include inflectional suffixes, that is the environment (-)VC_1C_1-. Thus we find *nǣddre* 'adder', *winneð* 'strives', *libban* 'to live', *þridda* 'third'. Again, the restriction is typologically supported: geminates are most common intervocalically and least common when adjacent to a consonant. This restriction does not apply in compounds, where gemination occurs freely at the juncture of two roots, as in *beorhhliþ* 'city-slope', *gærsstapa* 'grasshopper', *handdæda* 'perpetrator', *feorhhus* 'body', *woruld-dream* 'earthly joy'. Similarly, geminates are sequentially unrestricted at the prefix–root junction, as in *ymbboren* 'surrounded', *þurhhefig* 'very heavy'. As in PDE, the long [-bb-] and [-hh-] in these words serve as a morphological boundary signal.

7 The OED tells us that in OE 'the ending *-gga* occurs in several other names of animals: cf. *stagga, docga, wicga*. It is possible that *frogga* may owe its form to the analogy of other animal names with this termination.' Other items in this set of words of uncertain etymology are *pig* and *hog*.

8 See Hayes and Steriade (2004: 7–12).

9 Kirchner (2004).

10 Ladefoged and Maddieson (1996: 91–5).

The strongest argument for positing phonemic word-internal geminates in OE comes from the different treatment of singletons and geminates in the verse, and their different effect on the preceding vowel: singletons provide the proper context for lengthening, while geminates cause vowel shortening or block lengthening (see 7.5.1.1, 7.5.2.1).

In spite of the minimal pairs in (3) and the occasional appearance of long consonants after a long vowel, it is evident that already in OE the contrastive function of the geminates was limited both by the nature of the consonant and by position. By the tenth century, geminates became unstable in unstressed medial syllables, for example *gyldenne* 'golden' with earlier [-nn-] > *gyldene* with [-n]. The functionality of geminates in the present tense verbal inflectional system, the difference between, for example, *hlyhhe* 'I laugh' and *hlihe* 'laugh!', was no longer maintained, as the orthographic records show. Consonantal length is unstable at domain-edges; there were no word-initial geminates, and by the eleventh century the spelling of word-final geminates indicates that they were also simplified, so words like OE *bed(d)* 'bed', *sib(b)* 'relationship', were pronounced as in PDE. Nevertheless, the full simplification of stem-internal geminates is an ME development.

Degemination in ME was a function of multiple factors. The set of words in which medial geminates were phonologically contrastive with the corresponding singleton was quite limited already in OE. There were no geminates following long vowels in ME, because original geminates triggered shortening of the preceding long vowel, as in OE *mētte* > ME met(t)(e) 'met', *blēdde* 'bled', *brēdde* 'bred', and so on. Another factor, not yet explored in the literature, is the possibility of language contact in this process. Of the languages that speakers of ME could have been exposed to, AN and Latin had no long consonants, and in British Celtic voiceless geminate stops had merged with the singletons.

Most importantly, the progressive loss of final unstressed vowels in all types of words, and the syncope and loss of inflectional syllables, jeopardised the status of the original geminates. To illustrate: when *steorra* 'star' lost its <-a>/[-ə], the original geminate would be in final position, and therefore it would not be differentiated from a singleton (no geminates at domain-edges). Similarly, when an inflection, for example <-eð>/[-əθ] in *winneð* 'strives', is syncopated to [-θ], or <-est>/[-əst] in *dippest* 'dipst' becomes [-st], the resulting *[-nnθ] or *[-ppst] would be phonotactically ill formed. Since the loss of final unstressed vowels in ME was apparently more advanced in Northern ME than in the south, the full demise of word-internal geminates is equally regionally bound. In the north, Orm's (late twelfth-century) orthographic innovation to use double consonants to indicate that the preceding vowel was short is the first reliable test of

Letter	Value	Examples
<ð>/<þ>	[θ]	***ð****rēo* 'three', ***þ****īn* 'thine', *bæ****þ*** 'bath' (at word-edges and before C)
	[ð]	*hwæ****þ****er* 'whether', *ba****þ****ian* 'bathe', *hræ****ð****e* 'rather' (between voiced sounds)
<c>	[k]	*bō****c*** 'book', ***c****ræft* 'craft', ***c****weðan* 'say' (adjacent to back vowels and C)
	[kʲ/c]/[tʃ]	*ċild* 'child', *ċīese* 'cheese', *rīċe* 'kingdom' (adjacent to front vowels)[11]
<g>	[j]	***ġ****iet* 'yet', *mæ****ġ****den* 'maiden, *dæ****ġ*** 'day', *re****ġ****n* 'rain' (next to <i>/front vowels)
	[g]	***g****rund* 'ground', ***g****ast* 'ghost', ***g****nætt* 'gnat' (initially before back V and sonorant)
	[ɣ]	*dra****g****an* 'draw', *la****g****u* 'law' (between back vowels)
<-g> ~ <-h>	[x] ~ [h]:	*mear****g*** ~ *mear****h*** 'marrow', *dā****g*** ~ *dā****h*** 'dough' (finally after back V and sonorant)

Digraphs

<cg>	[dʒ]	*bry****cġ*** 'bridge', *se****cġ*** 'sedge'
<sc>	[ʃ]	***sċ****ip*, 'ship', ***sċ****ulan* 'must', ***sċ****ieppan* 'create'

Figure 4.2 Some letter–sound correspondences for OE consonants

the loss of phonemic gemination in his dialect. The south lags behind, but degemination there must have been very advanced or even fully accomplished by the end of the fourteenth century.

4.2 Sound-to-spelling correspondences of the consonants in OE

Projecting the present into the past inevitably requires information on the written shape of the words in the older language. Linking spelling to pronunciation provides the philological foundation for figuring out the intended pronunciation of OE. With some extra effort and time, one can develop the skill to read edited OE texts aloud and appreciate the 'sound' of the older language. To complement the classification of the OE consonants in Figure 4.1, Figure 4.2 lists some common correspondences between consonant letters and letter combinations used in OE

[11] The overdot on the letters <**ċ**> and <**ġ**> is not in the manuscripts. It is a common editorial practice indicating palatalisation in OE scholarly and pedagogical materials. This text will use the overdot only when the palatality of the consonant is of some consequence.

and the sounds that they represent. Figure 4.2 does not include letters that had the same value in OE as they do today: <b, p, d, t, f, m, n, r, l, h-, w>. In the interest of simplicity, we eschew references to the actual handwritten shapes of the letters – the reference here is to the letters commonly used in modern editions of the surviving texts.

The first set of letters, **<ð>** ('edh') and **<þ>** ('thorn') were used by the Anglo-Saxon scribes indiscriminately for both the *voiced* and the *voiceless* dental fricative allophones, [ð] and [θ]. Both letters were gradually replaced by the digraph <th> in ME, though thorn continued in general use up to the fifteenth century, and it can be found in private papers and in some printed books up until the seventeenth century.[12]

The letter <c> was the only commonly used letter for the voiceless velar stop /k/ in Old English. The letter <k>, though used occasionally in OE, was not fully adopted until after the Conquest when it was popularised by Anglo-Norman scribes. The only possible pronunciations of <c> in classical OE were either [k], the realisation of <c> when adjacent to back vowels or consonants, as in *carian* 'to care', *cuman* 'to come', *cnēo* 'knee', *clerc* 'clerk', *meoluc* 'milk', or the palatalised variant [k^j] (= IPA [c]) when adjacent to etymologically front vowels (see 4.3), where it can be the precursor of the late OE/early ME [tʃ], as in *ċēosan* 'to choose', *dīċ* 'ditch', *līċ* 'body'. The value [s] for the letter <c>, as in PDE *city, cell, race, mice, decision*, is another innovation in ME due to Anglo-Norman scribal practices. The spelling <cc> represents the West Germanic gemination of /k/ where the end result was not /-kk-/ but [tʃ], as in PrG **wak-jan*, OE *weċċan* '†wecche, watch', WG **strakkjan*, OE *streċċan* 'to stretch' (see 3.4.5, 4.3).

4.2.1 *The <g>'s of OE*

The letter <Ʒ,ʒ>, known as **yogh** and used in some editions of OE texts, descends from <ᵹ>, the insular form of <g>. For OE, the distinction between <ʒ> and <g> is, however, unnecessary, and <g> will be used instead of yogh in citing OE forms in this book. Yogh began to alternate with the Continental <g> in early ME. In the ME manuscripts yogh was commonly replaced by <z> or <y>, but some forms of yogh survived throughout ME. In fifteenth-century vocabularies the words beginning with yogh are at the end of the alphabet. Caxton uses the

[12] See Scragg (1974: 2). After 1400 <þ> 'fell more and more out of use, and in some scripts was represented only by the y-form in the compendia y^e, y^t or y^{at}, y^{ei}, y^m, y^u = *the, that, they, them, thou*, and the like, many of which continued to be extensively employed in manuscript in the 17th and 18th centuries' (OED).

symbol sparingly, chiefly before final <-t>. The use of <z> for the palatal realisation [j] continued in Scotland as in the spelling of names like *Menzies* [mɪŋɪz] and *Dalziel* [diː ˈɛl].

The letter <g> stands for three etymologically distinct categories in OE. First, it is used for the palatal approximant /j/ from PrG, as in ***ġ**ēar* 'year', ***ġ**eoc* 'yoke', ***ġ**eōmor* 'sad', ***ġ**eong* 'young', ***ġ**iest* 'yeast'. All of the numerous inherited /j/-initial pronouns and function words in OE – ***ġ**e* 'and, either, or', ***ġ**ē* 'you', ***ġ**ea* 'yea', ***ġ**eon* 'yon', ***ġ**ief* 'if', ***ġ**iese* 'yes', ***ġ**it* 'you two' – belong in that etymological group. Second, it was used for the palatalised allophone [j] of the PrG voiced velar /ɣ/ < IE /g^{h}/, as in *****ġ**eonian* 'yawn', ***ġ**iefan* 'to give', ***ġ**iernan* 'to yearn'. Third, word-finally after back vowels and sonorants /ɣ/ was subject to devoicing, most likely to the voiceless velar fricative [x].

As shown in Figure 4.2, pre-OE /ɣ/ developed variable realisations depending on the adjacent segments; the forms are contextually determined. As with fricative voicing (see 4.4), such contextual constraints are responsible for the different shape of morphemes within the same paradigm. As a basic guide to reading aloud, here is how the realisation of <g> in OE was conditioned by the phonological environment:

- Adjacency to <i> and other front vowels results in palatal assimilation, as in ***ġ**iernan* 'yearn', *hāli**ġ**dæ**ġ*** 'holiday', ***ġ**earn* 'yarn', *mæ**ġ**den* 'maiden', *mani**ġ*** 'many'. The 'new' /j/ merged with the pre-existing /j/. The reconstruction of the palatalisation to /j/ is based on the subsequent history of the sound and on variant spellings <i> ~ <ig>: *dæ**i**, me**i**den, wæ**i**.*
- Adjacency to a sonorant and a following back vowel (/a/, /o/, /u/) results in /g/, thus *Engle*, ***g**rowan* 'grow', ***g**adrian* 'gather', ***G**ota* 'Goth'. As noted in 4.1, the addition of the voiced velar stop phoneme /g/ was an OE innovation after the middle of the tenth century. The rare OE <gg> stands for geminate /gg/ (see 4.1.2): *fro**gg**a* 'frog', *sta**gg**a* 'stag'.
- The only unfamiliar value for the letter <g> in OE was the voiced velar fricative [ɣ]. It occurs initially before c. 950, as in ***g**āt* 'goat', ***g**ōd* 'good', ***g**rāfa* 'grove', and medially between back vowels /a/, /o/ or /u/: *dra**g**an* 'to draw', *ō**g**a* 'terror, awe', *la**g**u* 'law'. In initial position the fricative became a stop /g/ after c. 950. The normal development of medial [ɣ] in late OE and ME is further lenition to the approximant [w], ME, for example OE [laɣu] > ME [law(ə)] 'law', which formed a diphthong with the preceding vowel (see 7.4). The preservation of medial [-g-] in later borrowings from Old Norse could result in etymological doublets (see (4) below).

- In word-final position after back vowels or the sonorants /r-, l-/, Germanic /ɣ/ was devoiced and realised as [x], thus WS spellings <burg ~ burh ~ burgh> '-burgh, city', <beorg ~ beorh> 'hill, barrow', <plog ~ ploh> 'plough'. This devoicing was part of a more general avoidance of voiced fricatives in the coda of stressed monosyllabic words in OE, which in itself is a subset of a strong trend for final consonant devoicing, including stops, characteristic of West Germanic.

4.3 Palatalisation and affrication of velars in OE

2.4.1 makes it evident that the OE inherited velars were particularly sensitive to phonological context. Drawing a parallel with PDE, the conditions for palatalisation were similar to the conditions for the process known as 'velar softening', characteristic of paradigmatic alternations between [k] ~ [s] and [g] ~ [dʒ] in the Romance vocabulary of PDE, as in *critic-criticise*, *medic-medicine*, *fragment-fragile*. The specific palatalisation results were different in OE, however.

The contextual variability of PrG /ɣ/ in OE is shown in (4); the third column lists later borrowings of the same Germanic etymons, mostly in Old Norse loans.

(4) OE <g> in OE, ME, and ON:

Old English	**Middle English**	**Loanword**
dæġ 'day'	*dai, dei*	
dagian 'dawn'[13]	*dauen, dawen*	
dragan 'to draw'	*draw(en)*	*drag* (1440) < ON draga
dræġe 'drag-net'	*dray*	
haga 'enclosure, hedge'	*haw* (now dial.)	*hag(g)* (1470) < ON hagi
heġe 'enclosure, fence'	*hay* (now dial.)	*(The) Hague* (< Dutch)
sagu 'saying, saw'	*saw(e)*	*saga* (1709) < ON saga
sæġe 'say', v. imp.	*say*	

The different realisations of PrG /ɣ/ in OE allow some three-way correspondences in modern English, as in *draw-dray-drag*, *saw-say-saga*. The first item shows the development of OE [ɣ] between back vowels (*draw*, *saw*), and the second item has palatal [j] in the context of front vowels which may arise independently in the same stem (*dray*, *say*).

[13] The form *dawn* may be from the past tense *dagode* 'dawned' with [ɣ]; compare OE infinitive *herġian* 'to harry' - p.t. *hergode*, the latter base producing 'harrow'. The failure of <-i> in the verbal derivational affix *-ian* to trigger palatalisation is addressed in 6.3.

The palatalisation of the original Germanic velar stop [k] to the voiceless palatal stop [c] (= [k^j]) when adjacent to the high front vowel [i] or to [j], was already under way in OE. Phonetically, it is a case of assimilation, whereby a non-coronal segment becomes coronal. The step following palatalisation was affrication to [tʃ]. The exact dating of the affrication of [c] to [tʃ] is not reliably reflected in the orthography and is hard to establish. The process of palatal assimilation must have started with the allophonic realisation of [k] as [c] in typically weak positions: in unstressed syllables and in coda position. The allophone [c] was a complex segment simultaneously preserving the fronted dorsal place of articulation of [k] (involving the back of the tongue), and having also the feature coronal (involving the blade of the tongue). In the onset of stressed syllables, affrication appears to have been delayed. At least until the late tenth century, and even later, the alliterative practice allows matching of [k-] to the palatalised allophone [c-], for example *ðe clene Cudberte* / *on cildhade* ('The clean Cuthbert / in childhood', *Durham* 16).[14] This treatment of <c-> by poets and their scribes prompts the assumption that [tʃ] was not phonemic until after c. 1000.

The history of the adjacent front vowel is also important: palatalisation and affrication are carried through in the environment of adjacent original front vowels, as in OE ***ċild*** 'child' < PrG **kilþo-*; OE ***ċin*** 'chin' < PrG *kinnjo-*; OE ***dīċ*** 'ditch' < PrG **dīk-*; OE ***benċ*** 'bench' < PrG **banki-z*. If initial [k-] was positioned before 'secondary' front vowels derived from PrG back vowels through I-Umlaut (see 6.3), the fronting of the consonant remained allophonic, as in OE *cyning* 'king' < PrG **kuningaz*; *cymeþ* 'arrives' < PrG **kum-iþi*. The development of [k] to [c] to [tʃ] was also blocked by a following obstruent, thus *spricþ* 'speaks', *ricsode* 'ruled', *uictor* 'victor'. Affrication does not occur in the Old Norse cognates. This produces paradigmatic alternations which have come down to PDE: OE *sp(r)æċ* 'speech' vs *sp(r)ecan* 'to speak', where the words are clearly etymologically related but their consonants have different histories with respect to palatalisation. Two such pairs are shown in (5).

(5) Pronunciation of OE <c>:

(a) PrG *kara-

[k] — [c]/[tʃ]

OE *caru* — OE *ċeariġ*

'care' — 'chary, careful'

(b) WG *kirika < Gk kūriakon

[c]/[tʃ] — [k]

OE *ċiriċe* — ON *kirkja*

'church' — 'kirk'

[14] *Durham* is dated c. 1100. A full account of the velar palatalisations in OE is found in Minkova (2003: ch. 3).

In (5a) the vowel following PrG /k/ remains a back vowel in the OE noun *caru* 'care', while in *ċeariġ* 'chary' the vowel undergoes early fronting to **cæriġ*, hence the resulting palatalisation of the initial velar. (5b) illustrates the OE palatalised reflex of WG /k/ in *ċiriċe* 'church', while the ON form of the word preserves the original velar. The PDE vocabulary shows many such pairs. The presence or absence of palatalisation of an etymological [k] to [tʃ] is responsible for the different initial consonants in *cold-chill*, *kettle-chettel* (dial.). Alternative pronunciations in a derivational set or in OE and ON are also behind the [k] ~ [tʃ] alternation in the histories of *bench-bank*, *birch-birk*, *chest-kist* (Scots and Northern), *milk-milch*, *muckle* (dial.)-*much*, *drink-drench*, *stink-stench*, *seek-beseech*, *wake-watch*, *wreak-wretch*, place-names in *-wick* vs *-wich* (Berry*wick* vs Green*wich*), *-caster* vs *-chester*, and surnames whose second element ends in OE *-rīċ* < *rīċ(e)* 'power, rule': *Goodrick-Goodrich*, *Aldrick-Aldrich*, *Rickman-Richman*.[15]

In the orthography, the affricate [tʃ] was typically represented as <c>, or <cc> in the words with historical geminates, for example OE *gyċċan* 'itch' < WG **jukkjan*. Some <ch> spellings appear for the palatalised consonant already in late OE, for example <ælche> 'each'. The most common ME spellings for [tʃ] were <c, ch, cch>.

Yet another source of early [k-] ~ [tʃ-] alternations are found in some lexical items independently borrowed from Anglo-Norman and Old French, where AN preserved /k/ and OFr had /tʃ/: AN *catch*, *Karl*, *cattle* vs OFr *chase*, *Charles*, *chattel*.[16]

As shown in Figure 4.2, the digraph <cg> stands for [dʒ], as in OE *bryċg* 'bridge' < PrG **brugjō-*, OE *eċg* 'edge' < PrG **agjā-*. The origin of the affricate is gemination, palatalisation and affrication of WG /ɣ/ (see 3.4.5). Not just the early but also the later OE verse treats [dʒ] as bi-segmental, as in *on þa briċge stōp* 'on the bridge stepped' (*Maldon* 78b), where the first syllable of *briċge* 'bridge' must be heavy, otherwise the verse is defective.

The digraph <sc> represents the West Germanic cluster [sk] in Old English. Once again, dating the palatalisation is difficult. Some items with etymological [sk] show metathesis, thus <ascian> ~ <acsian> 'to ask' < PrG **aiskōjan*; <fiscas> ~ <fiscas> 'fishes', Goth. *fisks*. In the verse <sc> is treated as compositional, blocking resolution after short vowels, thus *asca þryþe* 'glory of ashes' (*Wanderer* 99b); *ofer fisces bæð* 'over the fish's

15 *Ælfric*, the prominent Anglo-Saxon writer (c. 955–c. 1010), is now most commonly pronounced with [-k], but the reversal to [k] from an earlier [tʃ] must have happened in Middle or even Early Modern English, possibly under the influence of the Latin form of the name, *Ælfricus*.

16 Differences in the consonantal systems of AN and OFr are also reflected in the shape of PDE *warranty*, *warden* from AN vs *guarantee*, *guardian* from OFr.

bath' (*Andreas* 293b). Post-vocalic [ʃ] continues to be treated as compositional in ME, where it appears only after short vowels in native words, a restriction that does not apply to any singletons in the system.

The palatalisation must have spread gradually, but by the end of OE <sc> is assumed to stand for (conservative and Northern) [sc], alternating with a fully palatalised [ʃ] in all environments. Since this was a specifically OE development, the absence of palatalisation of [-k-] in the cluster [sk-] in Scandinavian is the reason for etymological doublets exemplified in (6).

(6) [*sk-] in Old English and Old Norse:

PrG	LOE/EModE	ON	PDE
**scaf-/scab-*	*sċeafian*	*skabb-*	shave, scab
**skaljō-*	*sċell, sċiel*	*skāl* 'bowl'	shell, scale, skoal
**skipa*	*sċip*	*skipari* 'shipman'	ship, skipper (1390)
**skot*	*sċ(e)ot*	*skot*	shot, scot (-free)
**skraw-*	*sċrēade*	(MDu) *schrode*	shred, scrod (1841)
**skrub*	*sċrybb*	(Norw.) *skrubba*	shrub, scrub
**skuf-*	*sċufan*	*skuff*	shove, shuffle, scuffle
**skurt-*	*sċyrte*	*skyrta*	shirt, skirt
* –	*sċīr*	**skir-*	shire, Skirlaugh (YE)

A similar pairing of [ʃ] and [sk] is found in etymological cognates, one of which existed in OE, and the other of which was a post-OE borrowing from outside Germanic, thus ***fish-piscatorial***, ***mesh-mask***. Later loans from Greek, and Latin loans where the <sc> is followed by a back vowel or a consonant, preserve [sk], while palatalisation to [ʃ] occurs if the cognate form was inherited from OE.

(7) [*sk-] in Old English and later loans:[17]

OE	Later loan	Source
sċēadan 'to separate, shed'	*schism* (1382)	Gk *skhizein* 'to split'
	schizo- 'to split' (1870)	
sċrift 'prescribed penalty, penance'	*script* (1375) *scripture* (1300)	Lat. *scrīpt-* 'to write'

[17] The history of [sk] in words borrowed via French varies since the cluster was simplified in Old French as in *disciple, discipline, visceral, rescind,* and so on. Both in French and in English, direct reference to the original etymological [sk] can restore the cluster or produce doublets; compare *sceptre* with [s-] and *sceptic, skeptic* with [sk-].

fisċ 'fish'	*piscary* (1475) 'fishing right' *piscator* (1674) 'fisherman'	Lat. *piscā-ria*
disċ 'flat round plate'	*discus* (1656) *disc/disk* (1715)	Lat. *disc-us* < Gk

The digraphs <cg> and <sc> were abandoned after the end of OE. In ME, the post-vocalic affricate [-dʒ] was represented most commonly by <gg>, <g> and <dg(e)> from French after the fifteenth century. Word-initial [dʒ-], a ME innovation based on the adoption of French vocabulary, was represented by <g>, or <j-> ~ <i->. The letter <j> was a variant of <i> and was treated as such until the seventeenth century, when the shape of <i> was preferred for the vowel and <j> for the consonant, not unlike the similar differentiation of the value of <u> for the vowel and <v> for the consonant, from earlier <v> in initial position, <u> in medial and final position.

Palatal [ʃ] had multiple representations in ME: <sc, ss, sh, sch> are found in the earlier texts. Later ME spellings for [ʃ] include also <ch, ssh, ssch, schch, schs, sshs>.

4.4 Morphophonemic alternations: fricative voicing. CLOSE enough to CLOSE the door?

The consonantal alternations producing pairs such as *draw-drag*, ***church-kirk***, ***shirt-skirt***, ***shrift-script***, are based on differences in cognate forms in OE and non-OE/borrowed words. A reference to divergent phonological histories in different languages is not the only way in which morphemic alternations arise. As is clear from the examples in (4) and (5a), the difference between, say, OE *caru* 'care' with [k]- and OE ***ċ****earig* 'chary' with [c] > [tʃ] is not a matter of different pedigree; in that pair the palatalisation and affrication in *chary* occurs within the same language and it is conditioned by the different vowels in the second syllable of the words. In ***ċ****earig* the adjectival ending *-ig* causes the fronting of the vowel following the original [k-] (see 6.3); the secondary front vowel then triggers palatalisation and affrication of [k-] > [c] > [tʃ]. Put differently, the front vowel /i/ in the derivational morpheme *-ig* creates a phonological context responsible for the different pronunciations of the same original morpheme. OE *car-* in 'care' [k-] and OE *ċear-* in 'char-y' [c/tʃ] are *allomorphs* of the same morpheme; the alternation itself, as noted in 2.5, is known as *allomorphy*.

It is a common assumption in linguistic theory that we store the basic forms of morphemes in the **lexicon**; they are our lexical entries. When we speak, we use the lexical entries to produce words by assembling roots, derivational and inflectional morphemes. Building words from the base forms of these morphemes is the morphological component of our grammar. Once the morphology of a word is in place, the phonological rules and constraints of the language are activated and we come up with a surface phonetic realisation of the segments in the word. The final phonological shape of the word therefore reflects changes reflecting the different morphological composition of words derived from the same lexical entry.

A familiar example of allomorphy at work in PDE is provided by the morpheme /-d/, spelled <-ed>, forming the past tense of regular, or weak verbs; the final shape of that morpheme depends on the properties of the final segment of the verbal stem.

(8) PDE past tense allomorphy:

Stem ends in	Past tense	Realisation	
Voiceless		[t]	*i**c**ed, la**ck**ed, lau**gh**ed*
Voiced	/-d/	[d]	*fra**m**ed, tr**i**ed, na**gg**ed*
[-t, -d]		[-əd]/[-ɨd]	*a**dd**ed, rus**t**ed, lau**d**ed*

A more restricted instance of paradigmatically induced phonological change in PDE is the voicing of the final fricative [-f] of some singular nouns: *shelf, loaf, wife*, to [-v] in their plural forms *shelves, loaves, wives*. A similar voicing may accompany the derivation of verbs, as in *belief-believe, grief-grieve, proof-prove*. Voiceless-voiced fricative pairs are found also in *house*, n.-*house*, v.; *grass-graze*; *glass-glaze*, *peace-appease*; *cloth-clothe*; *bath-bathe*. These are marginally productive morphophonemic alternations, which may appear unmotivated to a modern speaker. The alternation of the labial fricative [f] ~ [v] is somewhat familiar; the alternation [θ-] ~ [ð-] less so; and [-s] ~ [-z] appears to be fossilised in pairs such as *close*, *adj.-close*, *v*. In cases like this reference to the history of the forms is quite illuminating: the current alternations are relics of a robust Old English morphophonemic pattern of voicing of fricatives in well-defined environments.

As noted in 4.1.1, one of the striking differences between PDE and OE is the absence of *contrastive* voiced fricatives in the older language. There were no minimal pairs in OE in which only the presence of a voiced or a voiceless fricative was sufficient to signal a new meaning, similar to *fine-vine*; *sit-zit*; *mouth*, n.-*mouth*, v. in PDE. This does not mean that the Anglo-Saxons could not produce or hear the voicing contrast in the pairs [f-v], [s-z], [θ-ð]; it means only that the voiced allophones were not functional independently of the environment in which they appeared. In linguistic terms, there were three fricative phonemes, /f, θ, s/, in OE. The realisations [f-v], [θ-ð] and [s-z] were *allophonic* – they appeared in mutually exclusive environments. Voiceless and voiceless fricatives were in **complementary distribution** (see 2.1).

A legitimate question regarding allophones in complementary distribution is why the voiceless allophones in OE are assumed to be more 'basic' than their voiced counterparts. There are two reasons for selecting /f, θ, s/ as the unmarked state of the fricatives in OE. First, the voiceless variants appear in most environments: word-initially, word-finally and when adjacent to other obstruents (stops, affricates and fricatives), while the voiced allophones have a much more restricted distribution. Second, taking /f, θ, s/ as the unmarked case is in line with the observation that voiced fricatives are more effortful from an articulatory point of view; they are also cross-linguistically less frequent.[18] Other than that, the choice is not analytically significant; the crucial point is that in Old English the voiced allophones appeared only when they were flanked by voiced segments; otherwise the fricatives were realised as voiceless.

The distribution of voiced and voiceless fricatives in OE is illustrated in (9), using angled brackets for spelling and square brackets for pronunciation.

(9) The realisation <f, s, ð, þ> in OE:

	<f>		<s>		<ð>/<þ>	
	[f]	[v]	[s]	[z]	[θ]	[ð]
OE:	*wulf*	*wulfas*	*græs*	*grasian*	*bað*	*baþian*
	'wolf	wolves'	'grass	to graze'	'bath	to bathe'

Orthographically, the representations for the labial and the sibilant were <f> and <s>. The angular allograph of <u>, the letter <v>, was introduced only in ME. The letter <z> was used only rarely in OE to represent /ts/. Somewhat surprisingly from a modern point of view, in spite of the availability of two letters for the dental fricative, <ð> 'edh' and <þ> 'thorn' (see Figure 4.2), the OE scribes used them indiscriminately, so there is no systematic orthographic correspondence between

[18] See Flemming (2004); Simon (2008) and references therein.

the letters and their phonetic values; <ð> does not have to represent [ð].

The phonetic nature of the process is straightforwardly accounted for by coarticulation: when the fricative is flanked by two voiced sounds (vowels or sonorants), the configuration of the vocal cords remains stable throughout and the input fricative consonant is partially assimilated to its neighbours. Voiced allophones occur in the onset of an unstressed syllable either stem-internally – OE *ofer* 'over', *broðor* 'brother', *nosu* 'nose', or across a stem and an inflectional boundary – OE *wif-a* 'of wives', *að-as* 'oaths', *hus-es* 'of the house'.

The voicing patterns show clearly the asymmetrical nature of affixes: in OE only inflectional affixes can supply the appropriate voicing environment. No voicing occurs if the fricative is the onset of the stressed root syllable, so in OE *befǽstan* 'to fasten', *biþéncan* 'bethink, recall', *gesǽlig* 'happy, silly', the fricatives are not voiced because *be-*, *bi-*, *ge-* are prefixes. Derivational suffixes, both when they are fully unstressed and when they carry non-primary stress, behave like roots in this respect; thus the fricatives in the onset of OE *-sum* '-some', *-ful* '-ful', *-fæst* '-fast' *-feald* '-fold' are not affected in OE *wilsume* 'desirable', *synful* 'sinful', *twifeald* 'twofold'.[19] There is no voicing in compound words at the boundary of the two roots: OE *tóðæ̀ċe* [-θ-] 'toothache', OE *hláf-æ̀ta* 'loaf-eater', OE *gærs-ierþ* 'grass-earth, land'. The lack of voicing in such forms is a confirmation that OE treated the elements of compounds as prosodically independent entities, a property also testable in the verse (see 9.4, 10.2.1).

The phonemic split (see 2.5) of [f-v], [θ-ð] and [s-z] occurred in Middle English. It resulted in six fricative phonemes in PDE, where voicing or lack of it differentiates between *ferry-very*, *fast-vast*, *life-live*, *seal-zeal*, *sink-zinc*, *race-raise*, *thistle-this*. The development of the fricatives in ME is of considerable interest because it highlights the importance and interaction of multiple factors: (a) the influence of loanword phonology, (b) the effect of system-internal phonological changes obscuring the evidence for previously existing complementary distribution, (c) the role of prosody in the categorisation of the contrast, and (d) the spread of independently occurring initial fricative voicing from limited dialect areas (Kentish, possibly late OE West Saxon) to the emerging supra-regional variety. It is instructive to look at these factors in some more detail.

(a) *Loanword phonology.* The impact of loanword phonology is not

[19] Voicing *can* occur in nouns derived from the verb base, where the fricative was voiced, as in PDE *teeth-ing*, *teeth-er*, *hous-ing*, *hous-er*, *shelv-ing*, *shelv-er*, *glaz-ing*, *glazier*.

equally important for the three pairs of fricatives. Latin and OF/AN loans appear to have been the main driving force behind the phonemicisation of the [f]-[v] contrast to /f/ and /v/. The influence of such loans is most clearly observed in word-initial position. Old English had already borrowed some [v-] words, but these isolated items were assimilated early to the native template of initial voicelessness, thus OE *fann* 'fan' < Lat. *vannu*, OE *fiddle* < Lat. *vidula*, OE *fers* 'verse' < Lat. *versus*. In ME, the influx of [v-] words was much more vigorous and pervasive. It was the adoption of over 800 items with word-initial [v-] after the eleventh century that disabled the earlier constraint on voiced labial fricatives in that position. Already in LAEME, prior to c. 1325, we find many contrasting minimal pairs.

(10) Early ME [v-]-[f-] minimal pairs:

Old French	**Middle English**
vēle 'veal'	*fēle* 'many' (OE *fēla*)
verrien 'validate'	*ferien* 'to transport' (OE *ferian*)
veyn 'vain'	*fain* 'glad' (OE *fægen*)
vile 'vile'	*file* 'file' (OE *fil*)

The nativisation of /v/- initial words is further confirmed by the ability of the loans to combine with native affixes, thus *varīe* 'different' < OFr *vairié*, produces *vārī-en* (v.), *variant-lī* (adv.), *vārī-inge* (ger.), *various-nesse* (n.), *variāble-nesse* (n.).

Word-medially, it is again the labial fricatives for which the borrowed vocabulary contributed most significantly to the demise of the OE pattern of voicing. If the ME loanword had a *voiceless* labial fricative between voiced sounds, this would obscure the inherited coarticulation pattern.

(11) Word-medial inter-voiced [-f-] in ME loanwords:

Middle English	**Compare with**
cofin (1330) < Lat. *cophinus* < Gk 'coffin'	OE *cofa* 'cove'
ofice (c. 1250) < Lat. *officium* < OFr *ofice*	OE *ofer* 'over'
sacrifice (1250) < Fr *sacrifice*	OE *drifan* 'to drive'
sulphur (12th c.) < AN *sulf(e)re*	OE *culfer* 'culver, dove'
wāfer (1212) < AN wafer 'wafer'	OE *wǣfre* 'wavering'

In word-final position the conditions for voicing in OE and OFr were the same; if the labial fricative appeared in the coda, it was realised as [-f], as in ME *bref* 'brief', *chef* 'chief', *motif* 'motive', *serf* 'serf'.

Compared with the labial fricatives, the share of loanword phonology on the history of the sibilants [s]-[z] is less critical. There are only about thirty <z>-initial words in ME, many of them infrequent items, for example *zephyr, zeal, zone, zeugma*. Latin did not have initial [z-], so most of the borrowings in this set are from Greek. Since OFr intervocalic [-s-] was voiced to [-z-], and final [-z] was devoiced to [-s], there was no difference in the native and loanword phonology with respect to the sibilants.

The development of the dentals [θ]-[ð] into independent phonemes in ME was not influenced by loanword phonology.

(b) *System-internal phonological changes* also obscure the evidence for the earlier complementary distribution of voiced and voiceless fricatives in Middle English. The changes most closely associated with the phonemicisation of the voicing contrast for the fricatives were **degemination** and the loss of final unstressed vowels.

Recall from 4.2.1 that OE geminate fricatives could only be voiceless, [-ff-, -ss-, -θθ-]. Degemination started in OE in word-final position and in unstressed medial syllables, but geminates persisted in the sequence VC_1C_1V, for example ME *blissen* 'to bless', *syþþen* 'since', *graffe* 'graft, twig' < OFr. By the early thirteenth century, however, the vowels in final unstressed syllables were subject to loss, especially in hiatus and in inflectional endings, destroying the inter-voiced environment for the original geminates which became word-final, where gemination was not sustainable (see 7.6). Thus <blisse> would have variants in [-ɪssə] ~ [-ɪsə] ~ [-ɪs].

The gradual degemination of the sequence -VC_1C_1ə to -VC_1 did not occur in isolation. As schwa loss gets under way and spreads to more environments, single fricatives in historically intervocalic position (VCV), where the vowel to the right was [-ə], would have the voiced variant appear word-finally, creating minimal pairs such as <blis(se)> with [-**s**] vs <wise> with [-**z**]; <graffe> 'graft' with [-**f**]- vs <grave> 'grave' with [-**v**]. More abstractly, the voicing contrast between $V\mathbf{C}_1\mathbf{C}_1$ə (voiceless) and $V\mathbf{C}_1$ə (voiced), where C_1 = [f, s, θ], used to be signalled by the geminate versus singleton realisation of the consonant, while after the loss of [-ə] voicing became a property of the word's lexical form, not dependent on the phonetic context.[20]

In principle, the system-internal phonological factors should be considered equally important for all three pairs of consonants in final position, though as noted in 4.1.2, word-medial /-ff-/ was rare in OE and therefore [-ff] to [-f] degemination would not be a major driving force behind the establishment of a word-final /f/-/v/ contrast. Geminate [-θθ-] was also rare in OE. However, since [-ð] did not appear in loanwords, all of the word-final [-ð] instances in PDE are directly attributable to historical schwa loss: *bathe, breathe, seethe, swathe, smooth,*

[20] For the stress-related voicing in *dessert, dissolve, possess* see 3.4.1.

loathe, *clothe*, *mouth*, *soothe*, *teethe*, *wreathe*, and so on. Indeed, the only [-ð] items without the possibility of analogy from a verbal form are the preposition *with* and the adjective *lithe*, both of which are variable.[21]

The /s/-/z/ contrast in final position was also reinforced by the loss of final [-ə], for example *lease* 'glean' (now dialectal), with [-z] < OE *lesan*, v. vs *lease*, v. 'grant' (1292) < AN *lesser*, *phase*, n. 'Passover' [-z] (OE) vs *face*, n. [-s] (1300); *nose* [-z] < OE *nosu* vs *gross* [-s] < Fr. *grosse*. New verbs with the suffix *-ize* (< Lat. *-izāre*, Fr. *-iser*) borrowed especially freely after the sixteenth century consolidated the contrast in word-final position. Interestingly, the sibilants continue to show some variability in word-medial position; compare PDE *usage*, *unison*, *gosling*, *greasy* both with [s] and with [z].[22]

(c) *Prosody*. The third factor in establishing a voicing contrast is prosodic: fricatives were voiced in prosodically weak positions in ME. The role of prosody is most prominent with the dentals. Initial voicing of the dental fricatives – outside the dialect voicing discussed in (d) below – is limited to function and pronominal words: ***the***, ***this***, ***these***, ***those***, ***that***, ***there***, ***thus***, ***thine***, ***then***, ***thy***, ***thou***, ***thence***. All major-class <th-> words in English are [θ-]-initial: ***thumb***, ***thin***, ***thrust***, ***three***, ***thatch***, ***thunder*** (OE), ***theme*** (Lat. < Gk), ***thyroid*** (Gk), ***thermos*** (trade name based on Gk), and so on. We know that the voicing in these words was an innovation and cannot be projected back to OE because of the alliterative practice of the OE versifiers. The featural identity of voicing for the consonants in OE alliterative verse was stringently observed. There are no instances of alliteration of [p-]:[b-], [t-]:[d-] or [k-]:[g-]. Alliteration of the type shown in (12) is therefore a fairly reliable indication that the poets were alliterating on [θ-].

(12) OE alliteration of initial dental fricatives:
ðys dogor **þ**u / ge**þ**yld hafa — *Beowulf* 1395
'This day thou / patience have'
þær ic, **þ**eoden min, / **þ**ine leode — *Beowulf* 2095[23]
'There I, chieftain mine, / thy people'

The voicing of [θ-] to [ð-] in the function and pronominal words must have been gradual, with the definite article leading the way, since it would be the least stressable item in the set. The scribal practice is not

[21] The OED gives only [-ð] for the now infrequent adjective *lithe*, but *Merriam Webster Online Dictionary* gives both. The letter-name *edh*, first recorded in 1846, is clearly an echo of the sound it represents.

[22] Also *exclusive* vs *excluzive*; the full form of *Mrs* with medial [-s] or [z] (see Ching 1996); note also *electrizity* for *electricity* for some young speakers of AmE.

[23] Similarly *Beowulf* 2131.

revealing, but we know that voicing is an option in the late fourteenth century because it is attested by rhymes in Chaucer's southern variety of ME;[24] the dating of the change in the north is not clear.

The voicing of [-s] to [-z] in the inflection <-es> and in prosodically weak *is*, *has*, *was*, *his* must also have been under way during the fourteenth century. The evidence for that is the use of <ʒ> to represent the French letter <z> by the scribe of the *Pearl* manuscript; it is usually transcribed as <z> in print: <cloudez> 'clouds', <hillez> 'hills' <rennez> 'runs', <watz> 'was'. Note, however, that if the inflectional vowel in <-es> was lost earlier, <-s> would be word-final and voiceless in a monosyllabic word, as in *hence* < *hennes*, *twice* < *twies*, similarly *truce*, *thrice*, *pence*.

Prosodically induced voicing of [-f] and [-θ] is also attested in function words, as in *of* [əv], *with* [wɪð], where the increase of sonority is associated with the lower degree of effort and absence of stretching in the lower laryngeal area in unstressed syllable codas. More specifically, phonetic studies show that stretching the cartilages at the bottom of the vocal cords is linked to voicelessness, while lack of stress correlates with no stretching, as in *of* pronounced with [-v], or *was*, *is* with [-z].

(d) *Dialectal developments* account for the occurrence of initial fricative voicing in Kentish, possibly late West Saxon in OE, and the south and south-west Midlands in ME, where we find spellings <valle> for *fall*, <vox> for *fox*, <zwyn> for *swine*, <zwo> for *so*. In these areas it was initial [f-] and [s-] that had to be imported from the emerging supra-regional variety. Only a few dialectal forms were eventually adopted by the standard: *vane*, *vat*, *vixen*. The area of initial fricative voicing has been shrinking; it is no longer a feature of the dialects of Kent and Sussex, although it is still attested in Somerset, also Devon, Dorset, parts of Cornwall, Gloucestershire, Wiltshire and Hampshire (Trudgill 1999a: 30–1). The only trace of this feature in the emigrant communities of North America is recorded in Newfoundland and Labrador English: *vish*, *vin*, *varket*, *vir* for *fish*, *fin*, *forked*, *fir* (see Kirwin 2001: 446–7). The long-term effect of the historical initial fricative voicing in the southern dialects is thus mainly local; it changed the distribution of voiced and voiceless fricatives by limiting the latter to word-final and obstruent-adjacent positions, but it did not contribute independently to the establishment of phonemically contrastive fricatives in the standard language.[25]

[24] The statement is based on infrequent rhymes such as *soothe*: *to the* 'the truth: to thee' (*The Canon Yeoman's Prologue* 662–3), *swithe*: *by thee* 'swiftly: hasten thee' (*The Canon Yeoman's Tale* 1294–5).

[25] Another historical dialectal change, well attested in south-eastern dialects from the middle of the fifteenth century, and considered characteristic of Cockney until the end of the nineteenth century, is the interchange of /v-/ and /w-/ (see further Wyld

The extent to which fricative voicing survives as a morphologically triggered change today: *shelf, loaf, wife* - *shelves, loaves, wives*, is hard to determine. Arguably, for the labial alternation [f] ~ [v], morphological conditioning is a recognisable pattern, both in noun-verb and especially in singular-plural alternations, as in the examples in (13); as usual, the dates in parentheses are first dates cited in the OED.

(13) Continuity of [f]:[v] alternations:

Noun	**Verb**	**Singular**	**Plural**
belief (1175)	believe (OE)	hoof	hoofs/hooves (OE)
grief (1225)	grieve (1225)	dwarf	dwarfs/dwarves (OE)
proof (1225)	prove (1175)	elf	elven, fem. and pl. (OE)
relief (1330)	relieve (1375)	turf	turfs/turves (OE)[26]
serf (1483)	serve (1303)	scarf (1555)	scarfs/scarves

In the noun-verb set in (13) the voicing context was present and preserved longer in the verbs: verbs had more vowel-initial inflections, and the OF/AN loans were modelled after recognisable correspondences that replicated the *reif*, n. - *reave* v., *grass*, n. - *graze*, v. pattern inherited from Old English. The second set in (13) is the more common pattern of voicing in the plural. Here belong also historical doublets such as sg. *cloth*, pl. *clothes* (OE), *cloths* (after c. 1660); *kerchief* (< AN *courchief* c. 1300), pl. *kerchiefs* ~ *kerchieves*; *roof* (OE *hrōf*), pl. *roofs* ~ *rooves*. The OED lists the forms *dwarves* and *elven* as being brought back and popularised by Tolkien; the mere fact that this can happen testifies to the continuing 'reality' of the voicing alternation in the modern language.

The synchronic picture is further complicated by a slightly different pattern: the pairing of members of the same derivational or inflectional set, where the fricative in the first form is historically flanked by vowels, the one on the right now 'silent', while in the other form it is followed by an obstruent.

(14) Continuity of [-v]: [f + obstruent] alternations:

(be)reave	(be)reft	leave	left
cleave	cleft	shrive	shrift
five	fifth	sieve	sift
give	gift	thrive	thrift
heave	heft	weave	weft, woof

1949: 210; Wakelin 1972: 95–6). This interchange is most famously recorded in Sam Weller's/Sam Veller's speech in *The Pickwick Papers*; the 'vulgarism', as it is described in Wyld, died out in the first part of the twentieth century.

26 The verb *turve* 'to cover with turf' is recorded for the fifteenth to seventeenth century (OED).

Further evidence for the historical continuity of complementary distribution of [f] ~ [v] is provided by double borrowings from French such as *naif*, n. adj. (1531, 1598); *naive*, fem. (1614); *digestive*, adj. (1532); *digestif*, n. (1908). Such examples of apparent complementarity in PDE reinforce the familiar sg.-pl. model of *wife-wives*, *leaf-leaves*.

For the sibilants, the old pattern of *glass-glaze*, *grass-graze*, *brass-brazen* originally 'made of brass', is mirrored in the variability in word-medial position in the ME noun-verb pattern *peace* n. (1160)-*appease* (1330); *grease*, n. (c. 1340 < OFr *graisse*)-(variable) *grease*, v. (1440); or *goose* (OE *gōs*)-(variable) *gosling* (1425).

Paradigmatic voicing of [θ] is found not just in inherited *mouth*, n. - *mouth*, v., but, as noted above, regularly in verb forms derived from native [-θ]-final words, as in *bathe*, *breathe*, *seethe*, *wreathing*, and so on.

While such alternations testify to the partial survival of the OE model of complementary distribution, there is also good evidence that the development of a context-free contrast between voiced and voiceless fricatives in ME, especially in word-initial position, undermined significantly the recognition of historical voicing correspondences based on the phonetic environment in verbs or the plural of nouns. The plural inflection of Romance loans, originally just [-s] (unlike the native [-əs]), and the derived verb forms of the nouns, the latter all of relatively recent vintage, as in the last column of (15), generally block morphologically driven voicing correspondences.

(15) Paradigmatic preservation of [f]:

Noun sg.	**Noun pl.**	**Verb**
brief, n. (1225)	briefs	brief, v. (1837)
beef, n. (1300)	beefs/beeves	beef, v. (1870)
carafe, n. (1786)	carafes	
coif, n. (1325)	coifs	coif, v. (1530)
golf, n. (1457)	–	golf, v. (1800)
oaf, n. (1638)	oafs/oaves	oaf, v. (1876)
surf, n. (1685)	surfs	surf, v. (1831)
serif, n. (1785)	serifs	serifed, adj. (1889)

The mixed evidence above suggests that the correspondences discussed in this section changed from fully productive to only marginally productive in PDE. It is difficult to determine a cut-off point for the shift because of the strong intuition that native speakers of PDE continue to show for the plural voicing of [f] to [v]. A productivity experiment (*wug test*), reported in Hayes (2009b: 198) confirms this: the subjects gave the plural of the nonce word [hif] as [hifs] 58 per cent vs 42 per cent of

[hivz].[27] Nevertheless, new words that have entered the language in the last two centuries tend to preserve the same form of the fricative [-f] in plural nouns, for example *pouff* (1817), *chef* (1842), *spoof* n. and v. (1889), *digestif* n. (1908), *gaffe* (1909), *smurf* (1958), *boyf* (1990).

In conclusion, the history of the three fricatives [f, s, θ] illustrates the complexity of the interaction between phonology, morphology, loanword phonology and prosody. To those interested in etymology, knowing that OE disallowed voiced fricatives word-initially offers a window into the origin of all [v-, z-] words in PDE: such words are loanwords or recent formations; for example, *vagrant, vahana, valet, vase, vodka, zephyr, zloty, zone, zombie.*

The next chapter turns to consonantal changes associated primarily with the history of the language in the last millennium.

27 See also Becker et al. (2012), who found some level of voicing in, for example, *myth, vermouth, plaintiff, pontiff,* also *giraffes* ~ *gira[v]es, photographs* ~ *photogra[v]es, psychopaths* ~ *psychopa[ð]s.*

5 Consonantal developments in the second millennium

AND WOT 'AVE WE 'ERE, GUV'NOR?', WHICH-WITCH, THOUGH-TOUGH, FAR-FA, BRIDGESTOWE-BRISTOL, WRITE-RIGHT, IAMB-IAMBIC, GIGOLO, MATURE-GOCHA, BETTER-BEDDER, MUS GO

This chapter starts with a discussion of the fate of the glottal fricative /h/, a notoriously unstable segment in many varieties of PDE. Then we move on to the history and present state of the English rhotics, another major regional and social marker in PDE. The next topic is the simplification of consonantal clusters. The rest of the chapter covers other inventory changes: the addition of /ʒ/ and /ŋ/ to the phonemic system, innovative patterns of palatalisation and affrication, alveolar stop tapping and contact-induced influences on the consonantal phonotactics of PDE.

5.1 H-related histories: And wot 'ave we 'ere, guv'nor?[1]

5.1.1 Phonetic and phonological properties of /h/ in PDE

The consonant [h] in PDE presents an interesting case of instability which can cause insecurity and social anxiety in some speakers. Unlike other letter-sound correspondences in the consonantal system, typically transparent as <f>-[f], <m>-[m], <h> can be 'silent'. We drop the [h-] in ***heir*** but not in ***heritage***, in ***honour*** but not in ***honey***, and ***herb***, ***hostler***, ***humour*** can be pronounced either way. The words *ma**h**araja*, *pro**h**ibition*, *ve**h**icle*, *ve**h**ement* have two fully acceptable pronunciations: with or without the medial [-h-]. As recorded in John Walker's famous *Pronouncing Dictionary* (1791), the first such dictionary of English, the words ***host***, ***humble***, ***hospital*** were pronounced without the initial [h-] two centuries ago. Though somewhat old-fashioned, it is still acceptable to treat the initial sounds in ***historic***, ***humorous*** as vowels and write ***an** historic event*, ***An** Humorous* (*Day's Mirth*).

How one sounds one's *(h)aitches* can be one of the more subtle signals of a foreign accent. French speakers show a predictable

[1] Cartoon by by Ariel Molvig from *The New Yorker*, 8 February 2010.

"And wot 'ave we 'ere, guv'nor?"

Figure 5.1 'And wot 'ave we 'ere, guv'nor?' (© Ariel Molvig (2010) *The New Yorker*)

tendency to replace English [h] with strong aspiration, while speakers of Chinese, Greek, and many Semitic and Slavic languages, whose native phonology includes the velar fricative /x/, tend to add more friction to [h], producing [x]. The [x] is, of course, a notable feature of SSE, as in *loch, dreich* 'dreary'; it is found in place names in Scotland, South Africa (influenced by Afrikaans), and in the unassimilated pronunciation of loanwords, as in *Bach* with [-x] rather than the common [-k], *chutzpah* with [x-], rather than the usual [h-]. Then there are areas in the English-speaking world where *all* <h->'s are commonly dropped. In England *h-dropping* occurs in all dialects outside Northumberland and the Eastern Counties. Australian English, New Zealand English and occasionally even South African English also show *h-dropping*, especially in varieties considered 'non-standard', so that the retention of [h] has become a socially significant linguistic shibboleth.

The fugitive nature of /h/ has given rise to different analyses. As the changing realisation of <h> is an excellent example of how history rationalises a seemingly unmotivated discrepancy between sound and spelling, we will take some time to explain how this situation came about.

The ***phonetic*** roots of variable *h-dropping* and its different interpretations lie in the segment's nature. Ladefoged describes it as follows:

> In English [h] acts like a consonant, but from an articulatory point of view it is simply the voiceless counterpart of the following vowel. It does not have a specific place of articulation, and its manner of articulation is the same as that of a vowel, only the state of the glottis is different. (Ladefoged 1982: 33–4)[2]

The lack of place and manner features motivates the exclusion of [h] from the inventory of PDE consonants (Ladefoged 1982: 33). Further, the articulatory basis for the instability of /h-/ in English lies in the shape of the vocal tract, which for /h/ is the same as that of the following vowel. Acoustically, spectral information on English [h] shows that it has the least energy of all the fricatives, which provides further confirmation that [h] is effectively a voiceless cognate of the following vowel (Tabain 1998). Alternatively, and when [h] *is* included in the system, which is the more common practice, it can be given a slot with either the obstruents or the sonorants, which highlights the difficulties inherent in fitting this sound within the current taxonomic grids.

Turning to function: within the English consonantal system, /h/ aligns in many ways with the other consonants, so it 'acts' like a consonant, as in the selection of the indefinite article allomorph *a hedge - a ledge - an edge*. A possible argument for treating /h/ as [+ consonantal] comes from its retention in borrowings in the onset of unstressed syllables: *alóha*, *màharája*, *fáham*; in this context note twentieth-century AmE colloquial *doohickey* ['duːhɪkɪ] (1914), *yeehaw* ['jiːhɑ] (1929), formed natively.

In terms of distributional restrictions, /h/ is not isolated in the system; compare the restrictions on the sonorants /m, n, l, r/, which cannot be followed by another consonant in the syllable onset: *hat*, *mat*, *rat* are fine, but **hlat*, **msat*, **rdat* are not. Another symmetry argument which prompts classifying /h/ as a consonant on a par with the other English obstruents is voicing: all English sonorants are voiced, while /h/ is voiceless. It has to be acknowledged, nevertheless, that within the obstruent system as a whole, PDE /h/ is still asymmetrical: it is the only obstruent that does not have a voiced counterpart in any variety

[2] See also Ladefoged and Maddieson (1996: 325–6), who describe [h-] as a voiceless or breathy voiced counterpart of the vowel[s] that follow it.

of PDE, in contrast to the glottal state pairing of all other obstruents /p/:/b/, /t/:/d/, /f/:/v/, and so on.[3] Since the origin and the earlier history of /h/ in English warrant its analysis as a consonantal entity, throughout this book /h/ will be treated as [+ consonantal] [-sonorant], that is, as a voiceless fricative.

5.1.2 The velar and glottal fricatives of OE

Except for synchronically still marginal items (*maharaja*, *pahit*, *vehicle*), the distribution of /h-/ in PDE is almost exclusively found in (a) the onset of stressed syllables (***h**appy*, ***h**eather*, *be**h**ave*, *in**h**ibit*) and (b) word-initially, both in stressed and in unstressed syllables (***Ha**.vána*, ***h**a.bítual*, ***h**a.llúcinate*, ***h**e.llénic*, ***h**e.lló*, ***Hun**.gárian*). This restricted distribution is the result of a series of historical changes whereby /h/ in all other positions was gradually lost. Let us look again in Figure 5.2 at the inventory of consonants in late OE, here repeated from Figure 4.1.

Old English had two velar fricatives: voiceless /x/ and voiced /ɣ/. The glottal fricative [h] is in parentheses because it was possibly an allophonic realisation of /x/ in the onset of stressed syllables. Another allophone, not shown in Figure 5.2, but see (1) below, is the voiceless palatal fricative [ç]. The two velar fricatives, /x/ and /ɣ/, were fully contrastive only in early OE, as in *hramma* [xr-] 'cramp' vs *grama* [ɣr-] 'rage'; *hāt* [xaːt] 'hot' vs *gāt* [ɣaːt] 'goat'; *hōd* [xoːd] 'hood' vs *gōd* [ɣoːd]

			Labial	*Labio-dental*	*Dental*	*Alveolar*	*Palatal*	*Velar*	*Glottal*
Obstruent	STOPS		p b			t d		k g	
	AFFRICATES						(tʃ dʒ)		
	FRICATIVES			f	θ	s	ʃ	x ɣ	(h)
Sonorant	NASALS		m			n			
	Approximants	Lateral				l			
		Central	w			r	j		

Figure 5.2 The OE consonantal inventory

[3] The only other obstruent without a voiced counterpart is the voiceless labiovelar fricative /ʍ/ in *whine*, *whale*, *whistle*, in some varieties of PDE, a continuation of the OE consonant cluster /hw-/ (see 5.1.3).

'good'. After the middle of the tenth century, the voiced velar /ɣ/ in initial position, and when adjacent to consonants, was no longer a fricative – it was subject to *fortition* or 'strengthening' to /g/ (see 4.2.1). In medial position between back vowels [ɣ] remained a fricative, as in *dragan* 'to draw', *ōga* 'terror. In late OE and ME this [ɣ] underwent *lenition*, or 'weakening' to [w]; the approximant [w] formed a diphthong with the preceding vowel, so OE *dragan* 'to draw' > ME *drawen*, OE/ON *ōga* 'awe' > ME *awe.* In final position [ɣ] merged with the voiceless velar fricative /x/, as in *burg* '-burgh', *beorg* 'hill, barrow' (see 4.2.1). (1) summarises the status of the OE velar and glottal fricatives.

(1) The velar and glottal fricatives in OE

Pre-c. 950	**Allophones**	**After c. 950**	**Allophones**	**Examples**
/x/	[h]	/x/ or /h/	[h]	*heard* 'hard'
	[ç]		[ç]	*niht* 'night'
	[x]		[x]	*sohte* 'sought'
/ɣ/	[j]	/j/		*giellan* 'to yell'[4]
	[ɣ]	/g/		*grund* 'ground'
	[ɰ][5]	[ɰ] or /w/		*lagu* 'law'
	[x]	/x/ or /h/		*dāg* ~ ***dāh*** 'dough'[6]

The somewhat simplified summary of a more complex situation in the velar and glottal area in OE in (1) will serve as the starting point for the description of the ME and EModE changes which shape the outcomes in the PDE system. As usual, the decision to assign specific allophonic realisations of the contrastive entities is based on spelling, subsequent history and typological considerations. The logic of positing an optional

[4] The stem *yell*, also *yelp*, *-gale* (as in *nightingale*), corresponds to IE *g^hel 'to call', so the OE /j/ here is a case of merger of the allophone [j] < /ɣ/ < IE */g^h/ with a pre-existing Germanic /j/, as in *gēar* 'year', *geong* 'young' corresponding to IE **yēr-* 'season, year', *yeu-* 'vital force'.

[5] The IPA symbol [ɰ] stands for a voiced velar approximant. It is posited here as the intermediate stage between /ɣ/ and /w/ when /ɣ/ was flanked by back vowels, as in *dragan* 'to draw', *lagu* 'law.

[6] The lenition to [-x] ~ [-h] is indicated by the spelling of etymological /ɣ/ word-finally after back vowels and sonorants, as in *mearg* ~ ***mearh*** 'marrow', *dāg* ~ ***dāh*** 'dough'.

/x/ for early OE is based on two arguments: the fact that it corresponds to IE /k/ (see 3.4.1) and the fact that [x] is the most frequent realisation of the velar fricative cross-linguistically. The reconstruction of the three allophones [h, x, ç], as in Modern German, is defensible on the basis of observable phonetic effects of coarticulation: initially, <h-> is likely to have been the same as PDE [h-], and post-vocalic <h> is likely to have been velar [x] after back vowels and palatal [ç] after front vowels.

Using only /x/ for early Old English but allowing the indeterminacy of either /x/ or /h/ by the end of the tenth century is justified by some early evidence of initial <h-> dropping, which suggests that in the syllable onset the consonant was undergoing lenition to a glottal [h-]. The assumption that [h-] was pronounced with reduced friction is supported by early evidence of loss in unstressed syllable onsets between voiced segments, which presupposes a shift from [x] to [h], as in PrG *_sehw-_ > *_seohan_ > *_seo-an_ > OE _sēon_ 'to see'. Word-initially too, there is scribal omission in pronominal and other unstressed forms: OE <æfð> for <hæfð> 'hath'; <is> for <his> 'his'; <hefre> for <æfre> 'ever'. Such spellings suggest that the situation was similar to the PDE omission of /h-/ in _'im_ for _him_, _'er_ for _her_, _'ve_ for _have_, all of which are normal casual-speech variants for all varieties and registers of English today, where _pass him_ and _passim_, _Calder_ and _called her_ are homophones. In stressed-syllable onsets orthographic h-dropping is rare in OE, though admittedly a limited number of manuscripts do show occasional forms such as <ondweorc> for <hondweorc> 'handiwork', <yngrade> for <hyngrade> 'hungered', <happel> for <appel> 'apple'.

At first sight such evidence prompts the question whether the letter <h> in late OE stood for an entity which is as difficult to classify as that of PDE /h/. The answer for OE appears to be easier, and that is not a corollary of the limited nature of the evidence. The status of earlier /x/, later /h/, as an _obstruent_ phoneme in OE is supported independently by orthographical and by phonological arguments. In spite of the possible interference from Latin, the OE scribes did preserve initial <h-> with considerable regularity. Forms such as <ondweorc> for <hondweorc> 'handiwork', <yngrade> for <hyngrade> 'hungered' are infrequent: there are two attestations of <yngr-/ungr-> for the stem 'hunger' against 364 attestations of <hyng(e)r-/hung(e)r->; the ratio is characteristic for other such orthographic doublets in the corpus of OE texts.

Phonologically, the consonant spelled <h> was fully integrated into the system. It could appear in onsets as a singleton, as in _hū_ 'how', _hēah_ 'high', or as the first member of onset consonant clusters such as /hr-, hl-, hn-, hw-/, as in *hring* 'ring', *hlot* 'lot', *hnappian* 'to nap', *hwīt* 'white'. It was found word-medially followed by another voiceless obstruent, as in *mihtig* 'mighty', *wrohte* 'wrought', and it could appear in codas by itself or in the clusters /-rh, -lh/, as in *þeah* 'though', *þurh* 'through', *holh* 'hole'. Like all other consonants except the approximants /w/ and /j/ (see 4.1.2), the voiceless velar fricative could be geminated, as in *hlæhhan* 'laugh', *cohhetan* 'cough'. It paralleled the stops /p, t, k/ in that in early OE it was in phonological contrast with the voiced velar fricative /ɣ/, as in *hāt* [xaːt] 'hot' vs *gāt* [ɣaːt] 'goat'. Not least, the alliterative practice confirms further the strong obstruent nature of the segment: in the poetry <h-> behaves like any other consonant, namely it alliterates with itself, irrespective of the nature of the following consonant or vowel. Thus <hr-, hl-, hn-, hw-> words alliterate freely among themselves and with <h->; the practice is the same in the earlier and the later OE verse (Minkova 2003: 339–45).

5.1.3 Initial glottal fricatives in ME and EModE: ABLE-HABILITATE, WHICH-WITCH, WHINE-WINE

Whether the OE inventory of fricatives is analysed as including either the velar /x/ or the glottal /h/, it is evident that after the middle of the eleventh century, the segment written with <h> must have been /h-/ in initial position. Orthographic records and the alliterative practice of the fourteenth century show that starting in early ME to PDE, the history of /h-/ is one of loss and instability. The phonetic grounds for this were discussed in 5.1.1: when followed by a vowel, the vocal tract configuration for /h/ is the same as that of the vowel itself. Phonologically, after the split of the voiced velar fricative /ɣ/ into /g/, /j/ and /w/ (see 5.1.2), and the development of voicing contrasts for /f/:/v/, /s/:/z/ and /θ/:/ð/ (see 4.4), /h/ remained the only fricative with no voiced counterpart in the system.

Another dimension of the change involves the exposure of English speakers to phonological systems lacking the corresponding segment. The presence of /h-/ in onset position in Latin, the main source of borrowing in OE, was inconsistent. Latin had already started abandoning the fricative in the third century, and the loss was complete by the end of the seventh century, but <h-> was often preserved in the orthography. In words whose transmission was not exclusively literary, Latin *h* is lost in OE: *iācin(c)tus* (< *hyacinthus*), *istoriam*. It was also lost in popular proper names, for example *Ercol* (*Hercules*), *Elene*. In purely literary words it is retained in the spelling and pronounced like English *h-*: *hōlocaustum*, *Hōlofernus* (see Pyles 1943: 909).

Though socially stigmatised, /h/-dropping was spreading in the Gallo-Roman regions.[7] This meant that for post-Conquest Anglo-Norman speakers /h/ would be a foreign element and would pose acquisition problems. Second-language learners and speakers of Anglo-Norman would also be aware that the segment was not common in the French vocabulary. We say 'not common' because the language contact situation is further complicated by the fact that OFr had reintroduced [h-] in initial position in some words borrowed from Germanic, such as *haste*, *hardy*, *heron*; these items were possibly [h-]-ful in AN too. The ME options, based on etymological source and prosodic prominence, are shown in (2).

(2) The pronunciation of <h-> in Middle English:

Etymology	Anglo-Saxon stressed words	Anglo-Saxon unstressed words	French words of Germanic origin	Romance words
Examples	*hold, heaven, high, hundred*	*(h)ave, (h)im, (h)e, (h)er*	*haste, hardy, heron, herald*	*horrible, humour, hermit, humble*
Pronunciation	[h-]	Ø	[h-]	Ø

In the first three columns, the situation as a whole does not differ from what we encounter today in SSBE and GA. The parentheses around (h) for the unstressed words indicate that in addition to etymological source, prosodic prominence is an important factor in the retention of [h-]. If <h-> is in the onset of a stressed syllable, it is much more likely to preserve its consonantal properties, in line with the universal syllable-structure preference for a filled onset and a sonority increase from the onset to the peak (see 2.3.1, 2.3.2). In unstressed syllables, however, lenition of [h] to Ø is much more likely; unstressed syllables are the typical 'weakening' domain; compare '*Yes, we **have***' with '*We (h)ave shown*'.

The distributional details are much more complex than the overview in (2) suggests. 'Middle English' is a convenient chronological label which covers a range of quite distinct regional, and obviously,

[7] St Augustine (AD 354–430) wrote that 'it was deemed a greater offence to drop the *h* of *hominem* than to disregard the law of Christian charity' (*Confessions*, I, Section 181, cited in Pope 1961: 91).

social, varieties. Information about socio-linguistic variability in ME is sketchy, but it is well established that the Northern dialects resisted /h-/ loss, while the rate of /h-/-lessness in the Midlands and the south was much higher.

The last column in (2) refers to h-dropping in Romance loanwords. Throughout ME, [h-]-dropping in such words was a feature of the spoken language, though it could be resisted by the scribes and the educators. Variability between [h-] and Ø was widespread: words like *able* (1325), *ability* (1380), *ostler* (1325), *arbour* (1300) 'a bower of trees and shrubs' (Lat. *herba* 'grass') came into English without [h-], directly from Anglo-Norman/Old French. Many of their cognates, however, show the orthographic influence of the Latin etymon and preserve *h-* both orthographically and in pronunciation: *able*, *ability* (1380) vs *habil*, adj. (1425), *habiliments* 'appropriate garments' (1491), *habilitation* (1612); *ostler*, but *hostel* (1250); *arbour*, but *herbage* (1390), *herbal* (1516). In this group the effect of stress is also noticeable: *(h)istóric* is much more likely to be h-less than stressed [h]-initial ***hístory***; ***hármony***, but the <h> in *philharmónic* is realised variably, with silent <h> dominant in AmE. Thus both in native and in borrowed h-initial words the instability of /h-/ is well attested.

Orthographic standardisation, especially through printing after the end of the 1470s, was an important factor shaping the later fate of ME /h-/. Until the beginning of the sixteenth century there was no evidence of association between *h*-dropping and social and educational status, but the attitudes began to shift in the seventeenth century, and by the eighteenth century [h-]-lessness was stigmatised in both native and borrowed words (Mugglestone 2003: 98ff.). In spelling, most of the borrowed words kept initial <h->; the expanding community of literate speakers must have considered spelling authoritative enough for the reinstatement of an initial [h-] in words with an etymological and orthographic <h->. New Greek loanwords in <h->, unassimilated when passing through Renaissance Latin, flooded the language; learned words in *hept(a)-*, *hemato-*, *hemi-*, *hex(a)-*, *hagio-*, *hypo-*, *hydro-*, *hyper-*, *hetero-*, *hysto-* and words like *helix*, *harmony*, *halo* kept the initial aspirate in pronunciation, increasing the pool of lexical items for which *h*-dropping would be associated with lack of education. The combined and mutually reinforcing pressure from orthography and negative social attitudes towards *h*-dropping worked against the codification of *h*-less forms. By the end of the eighteenth century, only a set of frequently used Romance loans in which the <h-> spelling was preserved were considered legitimate without initial [h-]. Here is Walker's instruction on how to pronounce the letter <h>:

> At the beginning of words, it is *always* sounded, except in *heir*, *heiress*, *honest*, *honestly*, *honour*, *honourable*, *herb*, *herbage*, *hospital*, *hostler*, *hour*, *humble*, *humour*, *humorous*, *humoursome*. Ben Johnson leaves out the *h* in *host*, and classes it in this respect with *honest*. (Walker 1791–1826: 53)

Today *heir*, *honest* and *hour* (and *herb* in AmE) and some of their cognates are the only surviving instances of a once widespread phonetic attrition. Along with [h]-less *heir* we find ***heritage***, ***inherit*** with [h-]; along with *honest* we get ***honorarium*** with [h-] ~ Ø; and along with *hour* we find ***horary***, ***horæ*** 'a book of hours', ***horology*** with [h-]. All OE <h>-initial words that are still used in PDE, except, possibly, the pronoun *it*, OE <hit>, preserve /h-/ in careful speech in the 'standard' varieties to this day Irrespective of etymology, initial <h> in all words has become an important shibboleth, and a 'symbol of the social divide'.[8] In Victorian England, *h*-dropping and its counterpart, unetymological insertion of [h-] in onsetless syllables (as in *Harab* for *Arab*, *Hirene* for *Irene*), was stigmatised as 'vulgar'. The great nineteenth-century phonetician Henry Sweet characterises the 'proper' pronunciation of [h-] as 'an almost infallible test of education and refinement'. In his authoritative treatise on *The Letter H*, Leach states:

> it is no exaggeration to say that, socially, H is of English letters the most important, and that a systematic trifling with half the vowels and consonants of the alphabet would not be visited with such severe social reprobation as is the omission or misplacement of an H. (Leach 1880: 9)

Our focus so far has been the pre-vocalic loss of [h-], because its variable survival is most easily recognised by speakers of PDE. However, loss in pre-vocalic position did not occur in isolation from the developments of /h/ in other contexts. Indeed, the earliest stage of h-loss is attested in onset clusters of /h-/ + sonorant, for example *hlot* 'lot', *hring* 'ring', *hnappian* 'to nap', *hwīt* 'white' (see 5.1.2). The loss of [h-] in word-initial consonant clusters was already under way in the eleventh century and it progressed rapidly in the next century. LAEME and the MED show no <hr-, hl-, hn-> spellings after c. 1250.

(3) Early ME loss of /h-/ + sonorant:

OE <hlot>	ME <lot>	'lot'
OE <hring>	ME <ring>	'ring'
OE <hnappian>	ME <napp(en)>	'to nap'

The bi-segmental realisation of the clusters in (3) is testable in OE

[8] The phrase is the title of chapter 4 in Mugglestone (2003).

alliterative verse.[9] Since there is no comparable method of testing the transitional period between c. 1000–1150, and since the orthographic traces of such clusters after 1150 are found in documents copied from OE, it is safe to assume that h-loss in these clusters had been completed by the beginning of the thirteenth century.

The simplification of /hw-/ to /ʍ/ to /w-/ started around the same time as in the other clusters. The history of this cluster, however, is more complex and more interesting from the point of view of the modern speaker. As noted in 4.1.1, OE <hw-> represented a fricative-initial bi-segmental onset, as attested by the alliterative choices. The most common practice found in the main body of OE verse was for the poets to match <hw-> to <h->, also to <hr-, hl-, hn->. Assuming that /x-/ was lenited to [h-] in late OE, it is not very surprising that there is some evidence in late OE verse that the sequence [hw-] started losing its initial fricative, and coalescing with etymological /w-/, allowing alliterations such as ***hwile*** 'while', ***wæpna*** 'weapons': ***wealdan*** 'wield' (see 4.1.1, (2)). Such practice can only be ascertained for compositions from the southern parts of the country.

The tendency for simplification became more pronounced in early ME. Loss of [h-] was especially common in weakly stressed interrogative words: *what, which, where.* The map in Figure 5.3 shows the distribution of <h->-less forms of *which* in LAEME.

In the Midlands and in the South, cluster simplification affected also major class words whose initial sound, historically, had been a [hw-]: *wheat, white, whale, wharf,* and so on. The continuing rivalry between [(h)w-] and [w-] is confirmed by some sixteenth- and seventeenth-century respellings of original <w-> words: OE *wōs*, n., *wēsan* 'ooze' appears as <wheeze>; *whiff* < early ME *weffe*; *whisk* < ON *visk*.[10] In one limited subset of original <hw-> words – *who* < OE *hwā*, *whose* < OE *hwæs*, *whom* <OE *hwām* and *whoop* ~ *hoop* (onomatopoeic) – the fricative is preserved and the [w] is lost before the following high back rounded vowel.

The merger of the two previously distinct entities, /hw-/ and /w-/, persists in PDE varieties in which there is no contrast in the onsets of, for example, ***whale-wail, which-witch, whine-wine.*** However, in ME the merger in fully stressed words was never complete, and it did not occur in the Northern varieties of Middle English, where it was represented in spelling by <qu(h), qw(h)>. This particular spelling is one of the ways in

[9] The evidence is discussed in Minkova (2003: 342–9).

[10] The OED comments that in *whip* < the base *wip-* and in *whisk* 'The spelling with *wh* was adopted as being symbolic'. The [hw] ~ [ʍ-] in these words is a spelling pronunciation.

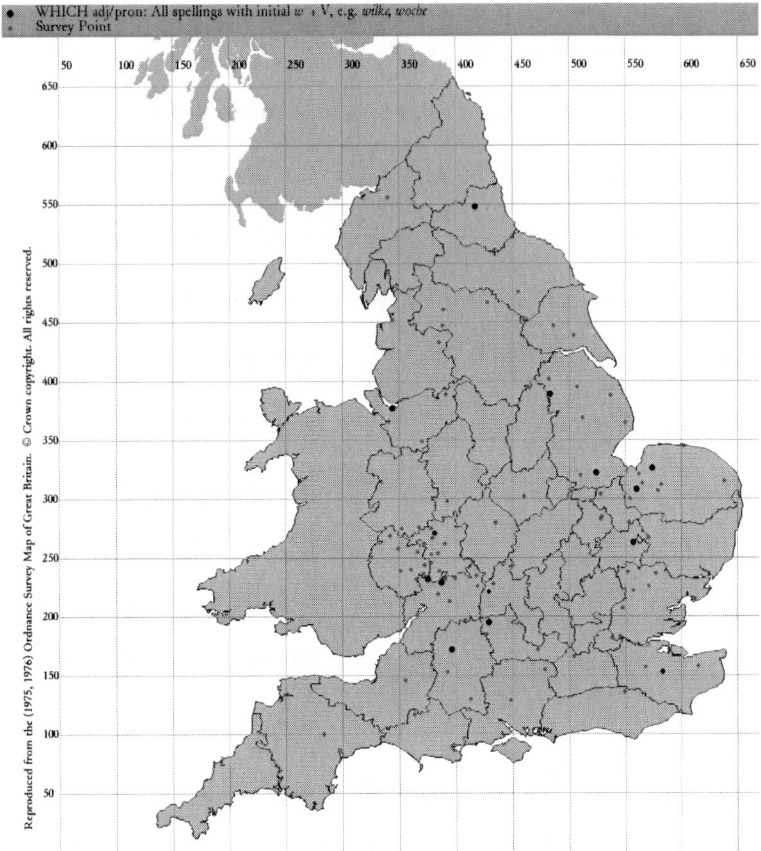

Figure 5.3 WHICH spellings with initial <w> and <ƿ> in EME (from *A Linguistic Atlas of Early Middle English* © 2007–, The University Court of the University of Edinburgh, Old College, Edinburgh. Reproduced with kind permission of Margaret Laing)

which we can ascertain the stable nature of <hw-> in the north, where its realisation was probably [xw-]. Another confirmation of the different status of the cluster in the north and in the south comes from the practice in fourteenth-century alliterative compositions: ***behold***: ***quareon*** 'whereon', ***quilke*** 'which': ***hert*** 'heart' are unmistakably Northern alliterations. Indeed, the matching of etymological <wh-> onsets with <w-> onsets, as in ***await***: ***white***, ***word***: ***where*** is an indication of non-Northern origin of a composition.[11]

[11] The areas of preservation of [xw] in Middle English are Scotland, Northumberland,

A note on spelling: recall that by the seventh century /h/ was lost in Latin, whereby <h> was 'freed' for use as a diacritic in combination with other consonant letters. The digraphs <ch> and <th>, both familiar to the OE scribes, are derived from Latin orthography.[12] The <ph> digraph from Greek was also used in OE loanwords and names (*pharaoh*, *philosoph(e)*, *Phillipp*, *Joseph*, *Stephanus*). In ME the practice of spellings using the letter <h> in second position was extended to include <gh, rh, sh>. These spellings were not uniquely or necessarily associated with the fricative [h], so at a time when [xw-] > [hw-] > [w], the scribes reversed the order of the letters in the old spelling <hw-> to <wh->, thereby aligning the digraph with all other <consonant + h> digraphs. The <wh> spelling helps reinforce the impression for the literate speaker that there could, or *should* be an [h-] in the pronunciation of <wh-> words.

The sociolinguistic reaction to the *which-witch* merger in early Modern English was parallel to the attitude to initial *h*-dropping. Throughout the eighteenth and nineteenth centuries the [wh-] ~ [w-] alternation was 'a socially sensitive variable';[13] as late as 1880, the popular treatise on pronunciation mentioned above, *The Letter H*, identifies one of the book's goals as 'to seek redress for the digraph WH' (Leach 1880: 5). It was only during the last century that the historically based identity of *which-witch* became standard for most varieties of British English, except for Scotland, Northumberland, partly Welsh and Irish English, but even in those historical strongholds of *which-witch* contrast, recent studies indicate a tendency for weakening of the contrast in large urban areas such as Edinburgh and Glasgow. For New Zealand English, Bauer (1994a: 395–6) reports that the contrast is receding, adding that 'This feature is kept alive by overt teaching: /hw/ is perceived as being a prestige pronunciation.'

The merger of the originally distinct sounds is also increasingly popular in North America. In Canadian English the *which-witch* homophony is fully established (Brinton and Fee 2001: 430). The merger has also been spreading in the US. According to reports on early/colonial American pronunciation, [hw-] was widespread, especially in the South. This feature of early AE is attributed to the influence of settlers coming from areas other than southern England, especially during the eighteenth century (Montgomery 2001: 143). By the middle

Cumberland, Durham, Westmorland, large sections of Lancashire and Yorkshire (see Minkova 2004).

12 Scragg (1974: 46–7).

13 See further Mugglestone (2003: 186–9, 196).

of the twentieth century, it was mostly the American South that preserved the contrast, but by the end of the century the preservation was no longer cleanly localised.

In summary, the phonological history of the bi-segmental /hw/ cluster from OE to the present is part of the overall history of /h-/ in the syllable onset. The alternation [h-] ~ Ø, first in weak prosodic positions, and then in any onset position, undermined the stability of [hw-]. The next stage in southern ME was dominance of [w-], while in the north the original [hw-] continued to be realised as a complex segment. /w/ and /ʍ/ are both complex labiovelar segments and the place identity between them increases the chance of merger in spite of the different glottal states: constricted vs spread glottis. Phonologically, /ʍ/ is isolated in the sense that its voiced counterpart, /w/, is the only approximant that has a *contrastive* voiceless realisation; this could be another reason for the historical instability of /ʍ/. The tension between the phonetic and structural factors promoting loss of /ʍ/, and the sociolinguistic and possibly semiotic factors promoting its retention and restoration, continues. The timeline of the changes of OE /hw-/ is presented in (4); the current variables are enclosed in square brackets and bold indicates dominant realisations.

(4) Variability of /hw-/ ~ /w/ in the history of English:

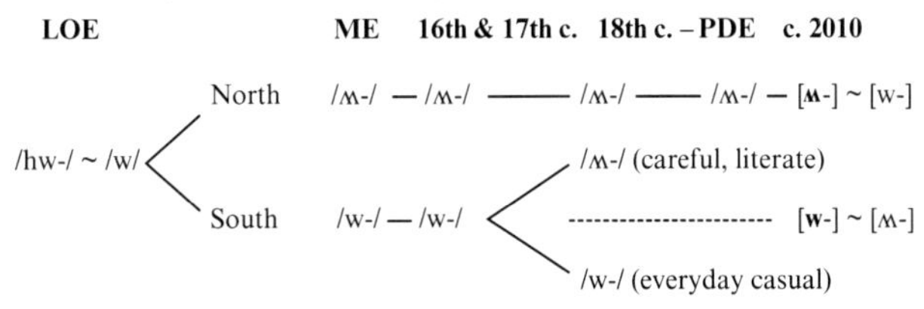

5.1.4 *Non-initial glottal fricatives in ME:* THOUGH-TOUGH

In intervocalic position [-h-] had been lost in early OE, as in PrG **sehw-* > **seohan* > **seo-an* > OE *sēon* 'to see'; PrG **teuh-an* > OE *tēo(ha)n* 'to tug'. The glottal fricatives were preserved in word-internal geminates: *hlæ**hh**an*> 'laugh', *co**hh**etan* 'cough', *genea**hh**e* 'enough', but such geminates were rare. When geminate consonants were simplified in ME (see 4.1.2), the resulting single fricative developed in the same way as <-h> in any coda position.

The parallelism of what happened to [h] in word-medial and in final position is based on two factors. First, when word-medial [h] was followed by another consonant, it would automatically be in the coda, as in *soh.te* 'sought'. Second, the attrition of final unstressed vowels in ME (see 7.6) led to the placement of intervocalic [-h] in the syllable coda. In words like ME *laughen* 'to laugh', the fricative [-h-] was originally either ambisyllabic or in the unstressed syllable onset, but in the paradigm of the stem *laugh-*, past tense *lough-*, the inflection was increasingly missing, so that [-h] was also increasingly frequently just the coda of the monosyllable. The number of items with coda /-h/ was augmented by words in which the Germanic voiced velar fricative /-ɣ/ was devoiced and realised as [-x] in word-final position after back vowels or the sonorants /r, l/: <burg/burh> '-burgh'; <beorg/beorh> 'hill, barrow'; <plog/ploh> 'plough' (see 4.2.1).

In coda position, both the single fricative and the fricative in <-ht> clusters were subject to changes based on coarticulation with the preceding vowel. The realisation of <-h> after back vowels was probably a velar [-x], while after front vowels it would have been a palatal [ç], not unlike the Modern German *ach-Laut* [x] and *ich-Laut* [ç]. This coarticulation is likely to give rise to transitional glides: a back glide [w] before [-x], and a front glide [j] before [-ç]. These glides are interpreted as part of the syllable peak, forming diphthongs with the original vowel (see 6.5.3, 7.4).

The developments of non-initial [-x] and [-ç] are behind one of the most striking discrepancies between spelling and pronunciation in the consonantal system of PDE, illustrated by the realisation of <-gh> in the pair THOUGH-TOUGH. As noted already, <-gh> is a ME re-spelling of <-h>; this only tells us that the presence of a fricative was stable long enough to be encoded in the orthography. There is more to say, however, about the difference in the PDE reflexes of the ME <gh>, as in *high*, *bough*, *sought*, with a complete loss of the fricative, vs *enough*, *laughter*, with the labial fricative [f].

Full lenition of /-h/ in the syllable coda is a typologically predictable change, though it is obviously not a necessary one. The realisation must have been variable [-h] ~ Ø, starting as early as the thirteenth and fourteenth centuries, as evidenced by incidental orthographic loss of coda <-h>: <hei(e)> 'high', <brit> 'bright', <bow(e)> 'bough', <brout(e)> for 'brought', with full-scale evidence found during the fifteenth century.

The variability of [-x(t)] ~ [-f(t)], as in *enough*, *rough*, *draught*, is also attested orthographically in the fourteenth century, both in items in which PDE has [-f], as in <ruff> 'rough'; <inowf> 'enough', and in items in which the [-f] variant was abandoned in favour of the vocalised pronunciation: <þof> ~ <thouh> 'though', <þurf> ~ <trugh> 'through'; <dofter> ~ <douter> 'daughter'. The timeline of these changes is shown in (5).

(5) Development of [ç, x] in Middle English:

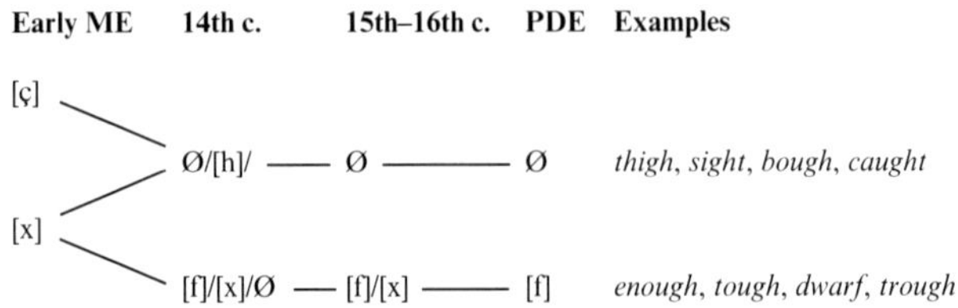

The vocalisation of the lenited [-h] occurs after both front and back vowels, while the change of [-x] to [-f] can only occur after back vowels. For medial [x] following a back vowel, there was widespread variation between Ø and [-f]. The phonetic motivation for the shift to [f] involves an acoustically based reanalysis which 'strengthens' the consonant. Specifically, the trigger of the [-x] > [-f] change is plausibly attributed to perceptual confusion; the two consonants shared acoustic feature [+ grave], which correlates with the fact that the development is attested exclusively after back vowels.

Both the lenition of [x] > [h] > Ø, and the shift of [x] > [f], shown in (5) are phonetically grounded. The triggers refer to different aspects of sound production: ease of articulation in the case of vocalisation, and similarity of the acoustic signal in the case of [f]. The latter 'mishearing' was initially socially stigmatised. It has been characterised as originating in 'dialectal and vulgar speech'; in words like *laugh, cough, rough* [x] was 'the normal pronunciation of good speech' until the seventeenth century (Dobson 1968: §371). Dialectal forms such as <*barf*> < OE *beorh* 'hill, mound', <*dofter/dafter*> < OE *dohtor* 'daughter' were abandoned, but the fully lenited pronunciation and the [-f] pronunciation survive in the pair *dough-duff* 'a dumpling', the latter a continuation of an earlier Northern form, OE *dah*.

The various options in the realisation of the voiceless velar fricative in the history of English are summarised in (6).

(6) Realisations of OE <h> in PDE:

Position of /h/	PDE outcome	OE	ME	PDE gloss
Onset: -V	[h-]	*hus*	*hous*	*house*

Coda: V-	Ø	*sihð*	*sight(e)*	*sight*
		þeah	*þough*	*though*
	[-f]	*ruh*	*rugh*	*rough*
Onset: -C	Ø	*hlot*	*lot*	*lot*
	[w-]/[ʍ]	*hwit*	*whit*	*white*
Coda C-	Ø	*þurh*	*þrough*	*through*
	[-f]	*dweorh*	*dwargh*	*dwarf*

The overall picture is clear: in native words /h-/ remains stable only if it forms the single onset of a stressed syllable, which is tantamount to saying that in the native vocabulary this consonant is historically restricted to stem-initial position.[14] The distribution of /h-/ is broadening, however. In the last century, Spanish–English bilingualism in the American Southwest has resulted in the formation of new varieties of Latino Englishes, which in their turn influence AmE. One such influence results in the acceptability of stem-internal /h-/, as in *jojoba*, *mojo*, *fajita*. Also, as noted in 5.1.1, /h-/ is retained in borrowings in the onset of unstressed syllables: *rioha* (1611), *alóha* (1825), *mája* (1832), *fáham* 'an orchid native to Mauritius' (1850), and it is formed natively as in *Soho* (1818), colloquial AmE *doohickey* ['duːhɪkɪ], *yeehaw* ['jiːhɑ], most recently the blend *WeHo* ['wiːhoʊ] 'West Hollywood' (2006).

5.2 R-related histories

Doe, a deer, a female deer
Ray, a drop of golden sun
Me, a name I call myself
Far, a long, long way to run . . .

5.2.1 Phonetic and phonological properties of the rhotics in PDE

The term 'rhotics' comes from the name of the Greek letter *rho* <ρ>, Roman <r>. Using /r/ as a generalised phonemic representation for orthographic <r>, we start the historical account of the English rhotics by recognising that the realisation of /r/ in PDE is not uniform; the various dialects of English exhibit at least six of the eight different

[14] The suffix *-hood* goes back to a noun – OE *hād*, ME *had(e)*, *hōd* 'person, condition, quality, rank'; it carried secondary stress, as is clear from the shift of the vowel [oː] to [uː] to [ʊ].

forms of rhotics found in the world's languages.[15] Perhaps the most widespread articulation of <r> is the alveolar approximant [ɹ], used in RP and in AmE, but we also find the alveolar coronal trill [r] (in some accents of Scots), alveolar tap [ɾ] (intervocalically in 'Refined RP', also the most common rhotic in Scots), the retroflex [ɻ] (South-West British English, North American, similar to [ɹ]), the uvular continuant [ʀ], or the uvular fricative [ʁ] (North-East England, Lowland Scots), and even the realisation of /r/ as a labiodental continuant [ʋ] or [ɰ], the velar approximant similar to an unrounded [w] in London/Estuary English.[16] Moreover, in varieties of English that undergo historical /r/-loss, the *non-rhotic* varieties, the effect of the loss goes well beyond the consonantal system and leads to a restructuring of the vowel system (see 8.3.2). This justifies elevating /r/ to the 'single most salient factor differentiating today's varieties of English' (McMahon 2009: 113).

5.2.2 Reconstructing the phonetics of <r> in OE

Although the most broadly used articulation of /r/ in PDE is as an approximant [ɹ] or retroflex [ɻ], this may not have been the case historically, at least for all dialects. For a start, in the North-West Germanic dialects, /r/ came from two distinct sources: original IE */r/, and the /r/ that resulted from the voicing of IE */s/ by Verner's Law (see 3.4.1). For the latter some runic inscriptions have a special symbol, distinct from the letters for /r/ and /s/, usually interpreted as /z/ (Wakelin 1988: 41). There is no evidence, however, suggesting that the etymological distinction between the two types of /r/ was maintained in OE. Two conflicting interpretations of the phonetic nature of OE /r/ are found in the literature: OE <r> reconstructed as velar/velarised/uvular, or, more loosely, some back variety of /r/, or as an apical/anterior/coronal/alveolar approximant or tap. Such contradictory reconstructions of the phonetic properties of OE /r/ are due to the intrinsic variability of the rhotics: their stability, realisation and coarticulatory effects in the modern Germanic languages and dialects vary significantly.

An important argument in favour of reconstructing a velarised allophone of /r/ in OE comes from the process known as *OE Breaking*, orthographically recognisable by the insertion of a back-vowel letter, usually <o, a>, after the short front vowels /i, e, æ/ if <-r> was in the

[15] Ladefoged and Maddieson (1996: 235–6). Magnuson (2007) provides a comprehensive phonetic account of the rhotics and their connection with the laryngeal and oral vocal tract.

[16] Cruttenden (2008: 221–2); Davenport and Hannahs (2010: 32).

syllable coda and adjacent to another consonant to the right. Thus, in West Saxon, we find the forms in (7).

(7) OE Breaking before <-rC>:

Source	**West Saxon**	**Gloss**
*arma-	earm[17]	'arm'
*hertan	heorte	'heart'
*lirnojan	liornian[18]	'learn'

Whether the vowel spellings in the second column represent phonemic contrasts in this or any variety of OE is not of interest here – we return to the question of Breaking in 6.5.3. What matters for now is that such digraph spellings are fairly consistent and allow the assumption of a uvular/velar version of the rhotic. This is not the only possible interpretation, however. Typologically, apical rhotics, for example [r], and the uvular rhotics, for example [ʀ], are acoustically close and they can have the same effect on the preceding vowels leading to the development of a glide (Howell 1987: 325). In articulatory terms, arguably a clear way of characterising the PDE rhotics, it has been shown that rhotics are produced with *both* dorsal and coronal constrictions in English, which also allows for the realisation of a transitional glide, especially since the front/coronal gesture is delayed with respect to the dorsal gesture.[19]

Another observation relating to the historical nature of /r/ has to do with the geographical area where PDE has the uvular continuant [ʀ], or the uvular fricative [ʁ], namely North-East England and Lowland Scots. This dialectal area is presumably a continuation of Northumbrian OE, that is, part of Anglian, where Breaking before <rC> is unstable, especially after <a>: Anglian *warp* 'threw', *barn* 'bairn' for WS *wearp*, *bearn*.[20] Of interest in the context of reconstructing a single velar rhotic for OE is also the fact that clusters that should have exerted the strongest velar effect, namely <r> + velar consonant in Anglian, in fact repair the clusters not by weakening of the rhotic, but by inserting an epenthetic vowel between /r/ and the velar, thus <bu**ru**g> ~ <byrig> for <burg> 'city'.

Such observations support the assumption that OE had different rhotic allophones in different dialects and in different structural positions. The higher scribal stability indicating Breaking in the 'focused'

[17] The orthographic <a> of the source would have been fronted to [ɑ] > [æ] prior to Breaking.

[18] The <io> spelling is early West Saxon.

[19] See Delattre and Freeman (1968). For full details on the gestural overlap of liquids in English and elsewhere see Proctor (2010).

[20] These objections are recorded in Lass and Anderson (1975: 89–90, fn. 1); see also Howell (1987).

classical and late West Saxon records would be consistent with the reconstruction of a central approximant, a type of [ɹ], in the syllable coda. The reconstriction of a coronal trill [r] is also appealing because it is the most common type of rhotic across the world's languages (Maddieson and Ladefoged 1996: 217). Comparison with the other Germanic languages is also suggestive: in Afrikaans, Faroese, Frisian, Icelandic, Norwegian and Swedish the dominant realisation of <r> is also a coronal trill. This would be in line with the documented behaviour of both RP English (Heselwood 2009) and American English. The realisation of /r-/ in stressed-syllable onset in OE probably involved more friction. Dialect differences in that position are beyond reconstruction; all we can say is that there is a high likelihood of a strong apical component and greater constriction, matching the historical stability of the rhotic in onsets.

The effect of /r/ on the preceding short vowel shown in (7) is usually interpreted as 'diphthongisation' due to the nature of the OE rhotic. OE Breaking is constrained by the properties of the preceding vowel – it occurs only after short front vowels. This constraint is compatible with interpretation of the transitional glide either as creating a positional diphthongised allophone of the short vowel, or as marking the post-vocalic rhotic as a velar allophone. The higher probability of a transitional element after front vowels is associated with a relatively high tongue position for the rhotic and the rounded quality of the glide (Stockwell 2002a; Denton 2003: 29). The absence of orthographically recorded /r/-adjustments after long vowels is unsurprising, since the extra phonation time for the long vowel will mask the special nature of the coda.

In the majority of instances of Breaking, either the stem, or high-frequency derived or inflectional forms, are non-monosyllabic, as in *heorte* 'heart', *liornian* 'learn'. Since the sequence (C)VRCV, where R stands for a rhotic, will be syllabified VR.CV, the environment for OE Breaking can be defined as short vowel + tautosyllabic /r/. There are also the instances of stem-final geminate /r/, for example *feorr* 'far', where the -/r/ is most likely a singleton coda. This modifies the common assumption that Breaking requires a 'covered' /r/, but further considerations regarding OE and phonetic considerations from current studies of rhotic effects warrant this slight amendment of the canon.

The position that coda /-r/ is a sufficient condition for OE Breaking does not negate the importance of the following consonant in the long-term history of English /r/. There are clear cases of Breaking where the /r/ is followed by a consonant in the same syllable: *wearp* 'threw', sg., *heord* 'custody'. The cluster -RC# alternated paradigmatically with -R.C- as in the past sg., 1st and 3rd pers. of Class 3 strong verbs: *ċeorfan* 'cut', *steorfan* 'die', *weorpan* 'throw', *weorðan* 'become'. The significance of such paradigmatic alternations has not been explored. The progressive weakening of the final vowels would also bolster the -RC# group, another source of the inclusion of the consonant in the traditional description of Breaking. As we will see below, however, the real significance of -RC# can only be established in post-OE records.

Two other processes in OE relate directly to the properties of /r/: metathesis and epenthesis. Some examples of metathesis are shown in (8).

(8) Metathesis involving /r/ + short vowel in OE:

brinnan ~ *birnan* 'to burn'	*timbrede* ~ *timberde* 'built'
cerse ~ *cresse* 'cress'	*(to)þræsċ* ~ *þærsċ* 'threshed'
(Sige)-*ferð* ~ (Reð)-*frið*[21]	*ðirdda* ~ *ðridda* 'third'
ræn ~ *ærn* 'ran', sg.	*worhte* ~ *wrohte* 'worked, wrought'

Hogg (1992b: 110–11) describes this process as 'perhaps more structurally organized' than metathesis not involving /r/. The alternation of (C) VRC ~ (C)RVC is indicative of the strong sonority of /r/, not surprisingly so, as /r/ is the consonant of highest sonority in PDE, except for the glides /j/ and /w/. If the short vowel in the sequence -VRC- was realised as a rhotacised vowel [ɚ], as in PDE *bird*, the perceptual similarity of the transition of [ɚ] to the following consonant and [ɹ] + short vowel + C would make metathesis likely. Note that the process continues into PDE: *bright*, *burn*, *burst*, *cress*, *crud*, *dirt*, and so on are survivals of metathesised forms, and throughout ME and in many PDE dialects one often finds /r/-based metathesis.

(9) Metathesis results in ME and metathesis in PDE:

ME spellings	**PDE regional variants**
frist ~ *first* (OE *fyrst*)	*burches* ~ *breeches*
gridel ~ *girdle* (OE *gyrdel*)	*cross* ~ *corse*
grost ~ *gorse* (OE *gorst*)	*garston*[22] ~ *grass*
-*thorp* ~ -*throp* (OE *ðrop*)	*grin* ~ *girn*
thrist(e) ~ *thirst* (OE *þyrst*)	*purty* ~ *pretty*

The cases of metathesis in (8) and (9) are phonetically 'natural' in the sense that the lower F3 of the rhotic overlaps with an adjacent short

[21] The shared Germanic root in the names is *frið* 'peace', as in *Frederick*, *Friedman*, *Friedrich*, and so on.

[22] Dialectal, 'a grassy enclosure, a paddock' (OED).

vowel, thus obscuring the sequencing of the rhotic and the vowel.[23] Therefore, the persistence of metathesis from OE to PDE points to salience of the rhotic, making the proposed coda-weakening of /r/ in OE (Howell 1991; Lutz 1994) an unlikely scenario. Metathesis is a structure-preserving process; focusing on the 'inherent weakness' of the rhotic as its determining property in OE is not enlightening in terms of its effect and it contradicts the OE orthographic records, which are remarkably uniform in preserving scribal <r> in *all* positions. Another suggestion relating to /r/ metathesis, that it improves the syllable structure by reducing the weight of the coda by shifting the cluster to the onset (Windross 1994), fails to account for the bidirectionality of metathesis we find in English – the coda would be 'lightened' in the case of OE *fyrst* > *frist*, but that motivation does not apply to, for example, OE *cros* > ME *cors* ~ *cros*, or the survival of items such as *gorse*, *first*, *girdle*, *thirst*.

Epenthesis or anaptyxis (see 2.5) is another process associated with the perceptual similarity between -CRV- and -CVR-. In this case, a short, schwa-like vowel is inserted into a -CR- cluster, in effect increasing the number of syllables in the original word; for example, inflected forms of the WG root **wɑtr-* 'water' when followed by a vowel alternate between <wætr-> (x406) ~ <wæter-> (x892). Other examples of anaptyxis involving /r/ in different environments in OE are shown in (10).

(10) OE anaptyxis involving /r/:
 (a) Onset CR- > -CVR
 ǣfre ~ *æfere* 'ever'
 bremel ~ *beremel(e)* 'bramble'
 broþor ~ *beroþor* 'brother'
 wrohte ~ *worohte* 'wrought'

 (b) Coda RC(C) > RVC(C)
 beorht ~ *beoroht* 'bright'
 beorc ~ *berec* 'birch'
 burg ~ *buruh* '-burg'
 fyrn ~ *firen* 'transgression'

 (c) Coda -CR > -CVR
 apuldr ~ *apuldur* 'apple-tree'
 bebr ~ *beber* 'beaver'
 frofr ~ *frofor* 'consolation'

[23] Blevins and Garrett (1998); Denton (2003).

Ignoring details regarding the etymology, chronology and dialectal distribution of the epenthetic forms in OE, we can say that the variation illustrated in (10) was 'persistent and continuing' (Hogg 1992a: 239). The motivation for the process is perceptual: the transition from high-sonority /r/ to the low-sonority adjacent obstruent. The sonority is falling in the case of initial clusters and in stressed syllable codas (10a, b), and rising in unstressed syllable codas (10c). The unifying principle in all instances is that the /r/ in the cluster mimics the transition from an obstruent to a vowel, rendering the epenthesised CVR and RVC strings perceptually confusable with CR or RC strings.[24]

The processes discussed in this section are associated with /r/, but the other liquid, /l/, and the sonorants /n, m/ can produce similar effects – we return to these below. Staying within the topic of the past and the present of the rhotics in English for now, we turn to the most salient process for speakers of PDE: the historical loss of coda /r/.

5.2.3 Pre-consonantal /r/-loss

Although there are no systematic indications of <r>-loss in the OE corpus, some early forms foreshadowing later changes should be recognised. As shown in (11), /r/ due to rhotacism (see 3.4.1) could be dropped in OE; the loss could result in lengthening of the preceding vowel.

(11) OE loss of /r/ < PrG /z/:
Gothic *mizdō* > OE *meord* ~ *mēd* 'meed, reward'
PrG **twizna* > OE *twīn* 'twine', compare German *Zwirn*
PrG **hwaz* > OE *hwa* ~ *hwā* 'who', compare German *wer*
Gothic *weis* > OE *we* ~ *wē* 'we', compare German *wir*

Sporadic loss of <r> occurs in some onset clusters: *sp(r)ecan* 'to speak', *sp(r)æċ* 'speech', *p(r)ǣtiġ* 'clever, pretty'; and in unstressed syllables: *cwearte(r)n* 'prison', *bere(r)n* 'barn' < *beretærn* 'barley-house'. Such examples are isolated, however; more significant numbers of forms in which one can detect a definite pattern of loss appear only in post-Conquest records. Some of the earliest instances of /r/-loss are shown in (12).

(12) Early instances of /r/-loss before dentals:[25]
OE *cerse* - ME *cesena* 'of cress. pl.' (c. 1050)
OE *gorst* - ME *gost* 'gorse' (11th c.)

[24] Bermúdez-Otero and Hogg (2003) provide a comprehensive account of the data on anaptyxis in OE in relation to the theoretical issues of sound change.

[25] Cited in Hill (1940).

ON *karskr* - ME *kaske* (c. 1300) 'active, vigorous'
OI *fors* - *fosse* (1440) 'waterfall'
ME *harsk* - *haske* (1440) 'rough'
ME *mornings* - *monyngys* (c. 1452) 'mornings'
ME *horse* - *hosse* (1473) 'horse'

Place names (1086 entries are from *The Domesday Book*):
OE *Deorling-tun* > *Dallingtune* 'Darlington' (1086)
OE *mersc* > *Messe* (1086)
ON *Þorst-* > *Tostenland* (1086)
ME *Wurðsteda* > *Wosted* (1330)

Pre-consonantal loss of /r/ had occurred in some OFr dialects and in AN, attested in thirteenth-century rhymes such as *sage*: *large*, *cors*: *enclos* (Pope 1961: §1,172). Variant forms such as AN *morsel* ~ ME *mossel* (1290), *ordinance* ~ ME *odinance* (1389), *parcel* ~ *passel* (c. 1468), *tarsel* ~ *tassel* (1459) reinforce the native tendency towards /r/ + dental simplification illustrated in (12). To this one can add inverse spellings such as OE *wæter*, ME *water* spelled *warter* (MED, 1156–7, 1463). A strong indication of the potential for perceptual confusion of the sequence /-rC/ comes also from some ME rhymes (Jordan 1974: §166; Ikegami 1984: 341).

(13) ME rhymes showing /r/-loss:
bass 'perch' (< OE *bærs*): *wers*: *mess* (1330)[26]
fors: *clos* 'prison' (1400–25)[27]
worst: *adust* 'treated with heat' (1450)[28]
ars 'arse': *was*: *passe*; *neke-verse*: *casse* 'box': *fers* 'fierce'[29]

The common denominator in the early instances of /r/-loss is the adjacency of a dental consonant to the right of the rhotic (Hill 1940). The path of loss Hill proposes is (a) assimilation, and (b) simplification of the long consonant. Assimilation is indeed the most plausible account of the process. Its likelihood is supported by the exclusion of heterorganic consonants from the environment for early /r/-loss. Hill defined the set triggering /r/-loss 'loosely' as [t], [d], [n], [l], [θ], [ð], [s], [ʃ], [dʒ] and [tʃ]: this is the full set of the coronal consonants of ME. This suggests that the rhotic was also coronal, which does not tell us much about its

[26] *Guy of Warwick* (Language of London/Middlesex border. LALME Middlesex Linguistic Profile (LP) 6510).
[27] *Castle of Perseverance* 1400–25, Norfolk, LALME: LP 58.
[28] Cited in Wyld (1953: 298).
[29] From the morality play *Mankind*, fifteenth century, Norfolk.

manner of articulation – all we can say is that there is a strong probability of /r/ being an alveolar trill. We should also note that while bundling together all coronals as triggering early /r/-loss is a convenient generalisation, the data point to /-rs/- cluster-being simplification as 'ahead of the curve'. In the words of a sixteenth-century commentator, /r/-loss before /s-/ is a 'widespread vulgarism' found in East Anglian texts.[30]

Labelling the process 'assimilation' does not address the question of whether it was triggered by articulatory factors, perceptual factors, the more abstract notion of syllable structure optimisation, or maybe all three. The loosely shared place of articulation involving the blade of the tongue for the rhotic and the dentals could be an assimilatory factor. Both [ɹ] and [s] involve some lip-rounding, also conducive to coalescence, yet articulatory similarity is hardly sufficient to account for the entire development. The noise spectrum of sibilants compared with other coronals after /r/ would contribute to stronger perceptual cues for [s]. Perceptual place assimilation involving apicals is 'invariably progressive' (Steriade 2001); following that approach, an assimilation account must involve an intermediate stage of retroflex [ʂ, ɖ, ɳ], and so on, so [baɾs] > [baʂ], where the [-ʂ] is unstable and merges with the pre-existing [s]. The articulation of retroflex consonants is more complex than plain coronal/alveolar articulation (Hamann 2005), therefore one phonetically likely change is loss of retroflexion: [baʂ] > [bas]. In terms of sonority, clusters of /r/ + obstruent are well-formed codas, so that parameter offers no compelling phonological reason for simplification. In terms of syllable structure, one can treat the end-result of the assimilation as preference for simple codas over complex codas, and /r/-loss rather than /s/-loss as preference for a sharper sonority drop in the syllable coda – the transition from the peak to /s/ is preferable to the transition from a vowel to /r/, in line with the postulates of 'The Coda Law' (Vennemann 1988: 21). Since none of the potential triggers excludes reinforcement from the others, a full account of the process must evaluate each of these factors.

Surprisingly, the instances of pre-consonantal loss shown in (12) are not traditionally considered precursors to a general /r/-loss in coda clusters (Hill 1940; Wyld 1953: 298–300; Dobson 1968: §427; Lass 1992a: 66–7; Lass 1999: 114–15). One reason for that is that loss before non-coronals – labials and velars – is incipiently attested only in the late seventeenth century. Another reason for separating the two types of /r/-loss is that early loss may leave a preceding short vowel unaffected,

[30] Dobson (1957: 112); the commentator is William Bullokar (c. 1531–1609).

while later loss appears to trigger lengthening, thus *ass* < *arse*, *cuss* < *curse* with short vowels vs *arm*, *turf* with long vowels in the non-rhotic varieties.

The occasional survival of an unlengthened vowel is only a tenuous argument against continuity, however: early instances of /-rC/ simplification often show PDE forms with a lengthened vowel, as in *gorse*, *horse*, *morning*, *Darlington*. Of relevance also are the small number of pre-/-rC/ lengthenings in early ME, in which the vowel digraph spellings indicate lengthening before **-rC** clusters, as in *board* (OE *bord*), *hoard* (OE *hord*), *earl* (OE *e(o)rl*), *hearken* (OE *he(o)rcnian*), *heart* (OE *he(o)rte*), *mourn* (OE *murnen*).[31] Further, some arguably 'late' cases of /-rC/ simplification fail to result in a long vowel in the peak: *gal* < *girl*, [klʌdʒɪ] for *clergy*, [wʌdʒɪn] for *virgin*, and so on (Hill 1940). Predictably, in unstressed syllables simplification of /-rC/ clusters does not trigger lengthening, as in *-wards* [-wədz], or in *scissors*, *colours*, *letters*, *lectern*, *yogurt* in non-rhotic varieties. It is likely, therefore, that the earlier and the later cases of /-rC/ simplification represent a single historical process stretching over more than six centuries and affecting different dialects and different lexical items unevenly. Vowel lengthening is one possible outcome rather than an essential stage in the process of /r/-loss. Delayed codification in the non-rhotic varieties, the occurrence of hyper-rhoticity, as in *warsh* for *wash*, *larst* for *last*, incipient derhoticisation in essentially rhotic varieties of English, and reversal to rhoticity in previously categorically non-rhotic accents, are clearly points on one historical continuum.

While we can subsume early /r/-loss in coda clusters under the general umbrella of assimilation, many questions remain: the nature of the rhotic in various dialects, the exact distribution of /-rC/ forms, the position of the cluster – within the same syllable, stressed or unstressed, or straddling two adjacent syllables – the relevance of lexical frequency, are some of the areas that await further research.

Another coarticulatory change involving /r/, and occasionally /l/, resulted in variation between the voiced intervocalic dental stop /-d-/ and the fricative /-ð-/ in the onset of /-ər, -r̩/ and /-əl, -l̩/ syllables. In front of syllabic /r̩/ the variation was first recorded in the fifteenth century, when core-vocabulary items in etymological <-**d**er> began to be spelled <-**th**er>, the form in which they have survived to this day. The list of original [-d(ə)r̩] words includes *father*, *mother*, *gather*, *weather*,

[31] These items are usually 'filed' under 'homorganic-cluster lengthening' (see 6.4), but they can equally well be pre-/r/ schwa-insertion, resulting in a lowered and lengthened /r/-coloured vowel which resists the Long Vowel Shift (see 8.3.2).

hither, thither, together, whither. They were subject to extensive variation in the sixteenth to eighteenth century. Britton (2007a: 261) cites the forms <al**th**erman> 'alderman', <el**th**er> 'elder', and <chyl**th**eryn> 'children' in Machyn's written language (1550–63). In some items the fricative is preserved only regionally today: *adder, bladder, ladder, fodder* are attested with [ð] in Yorkshire, Leicestershire, Scottish and Irish English (Jespersen 1909: 208–11). The variability between the stop and the fricative can be motivated on both articulatory and perceptual grounds. Fricative articulation and loss of occlusion of [-d-] before an apical trill is assimilatory. It would be facilitated by the acoustic similarity of [dr̩] ~ [ðr̩].

The reverse development, namely /-rðər, -rðr̩/ > /rdr̩/ as in *burden, murder, afford* (OE *byrðen, morðor, geforðian*), is also attested. The other liquid, /l/, can have a similar effect. One item in this group goes back to OE, *næðl* ~ *nedl* 'needle'; here belong also *spider* < OE *spiðre*, first <d> spelling c. 1440, and *fiddle* < OE **fiðele*, first <d> spelling c. 1450. The change in these instances is dissimilatory, also facilitated by the confusability of [d] and [ð] in the context of syllabic liquids. In *murder, spider, fiddle,* the second syllable acquires a phonologically preferred onset, since /d/ is more strongly consonantal than /ð/.

The discussion of the history of rhotics in English so far has revolved around strategies of avoiding suboptimal transitions from and to an /r/ and an adjacent consonant. Now we turn to general post-vocalic loss, the process which justifies the consensus that rhoticity is the most salient dialect criterion in PDE.

5.2.4 Post-vocalic /r/-loss

Early spellings, as in (14), indicating that coda /r/ in unstressed syllables was unstable, have been taken as evidence that historically coda /r/-loss was most advanced in prosodically weak syllables.

(14) Loss of /-r/ in unstressed codas:
<mero> (1434), <merowe> (1475) 'mirror'
<fathe> 'father', <mothe> 'mother' (*The Cely Letters*, 1472–88)

An account which associates consonantal weakening with a weak prosodic position is appealing on typological grounds, yet the evidence adduced in support of this hypothesis in the case of post-vocalic /r/-loss in English is sparse. The examples in (14) are isolated; word-final <-r> appears to be quite stable in the fifteenth and sixteenth century. The hypothesis of early /r/-loss in unstressed syllables is largely based on seventeenth-century orthographic insertion of <r>.

(15) Early <r>-insertion:
<winder(e)s/wynders> 'windows' (1601, 1613)
<feller> 'fellow' (*Vernay Letters*, 1639)
<pillars> 'pillows' (1673)

As Britton (2007b) argues, such spellings are just as likely, or even *more* likely, to represent the analogical insertion/sandhi of an unetymological rhotic in high-frequency common-core words in unstressed <-ow> [-ə] words: *arrow, borrow, fellow, narrow*, and so on. The analogy is based on the perceptual similarity of [-ə] and [-ɹ]. Britton points out that equating the occurrence of early sandhi to early loss is problematic on two scores: first, hyper-rhoticity in PDE is most prominent in those dialect areas in England where rhoticity is still strong, and second, there are no accents where rhoticity is in decline and where /r/-loss is better attested in unstressed final syllables than in stressed syllable codas. To this we can add the findings in Hay and Sudbury (2005) regarding loss of rhoticity in NZE, where the decline of linking /r/ lags significantly behind the development of non-rhoticity – an asymmetry which suggests that spellings such as the ones cited in (15) are not necessarily prima facie evidence for early /r/-loss.

After the seventeenth century the evidence for coda /r/-loss becomes somewhat clearer. The dating varies depending primarily on the data source. Dobson found that 'only sources which reflect vulgar pronunciation give evidence of the change before 1700, and even they give little' (1968: §332). In stressed syllables 'the change could not have occurred in good speech before . . . c. 1800' (§427). There is clearly a very important socio-linguistic component to the change, where literacy is a major factor. This is to be expected; good parallels with many more social variables from PDE are offered by studies of ongoing decrease or increase of rhoticity. The dating of the vocalisation in SSBE is most helpfully surveyed in Windross (1994), whose analysis of the orthoepists' commentaries 1791–1836 shows that there cannot have been codification of /r/-loss in standard speech in the eighteenth century. Variable /r/-vocalisation in SSBE continued as late as the 1870s, and its spread continued in NZE during the twentieth century, with female speakers lagging behind in developing /r/-sandhi (Hay and Sudbury 2005).[32]

The accents in which the fully consonantal realisation of /r/ became restricted to the syllabic onset are 'non-rhotic'. Along with SSBE, non-

[32] For ongoing changes in rhoticity see Hay and Sudbury (2005) for NZE; Lawson et al. (2008) for Scottish English; Nagy and Irwin (2010) for AE. For variable /r/-vocalisation in SSBE as late as the 1870s see Lass (1999a: 115); Trudgill (1999); Mugglestone (2003: 86–94).

rhotic English is spoken today in parts of the US eastern seaboard and the Gulf Coast, South Africa, Australia and New Zealand. The main rhotic varieties are spoken in Scotland, Ireland, South-West England, extreme West Lancashire, most of the USA and Canada. This is the overall picture; as noted earlier, many regional and social varieties show that the state of rhoticity is not fixed and allows progressive /r/-vocalisation or reversal of /r/-loss.

In terms of articulation, the vocalisation of /r/ can be accounted for as a gradual separation of the gestural components of constricted /r/, as proposed in Heselwood (2009). If the palatal gesture is temporally delayed until after the pharyngeal gesture, it could lead to its loss in non-prevocalic contexts. The suggested path of realisation of coda /r/ is from bi-gestural to uni-gestural; the change from a rhotic to a non-rhotic state is from a bi-gestural [ɹ], to bi-gestural [əɹ], to uni-gestural [ə]. The perceptual similarity between the sonorant /r/ to schwa based on the F3 has already been discussed. Thus articulatory and acoustic factors go in tandem in advancing the vocalisation.

The phonological representation of <r> in, for example, *doctor*, *summer*, *poor*, *sheer*, is a matter of debate because of complications surrounding the realisation of /r/ in pre-vocalic contexts, where it is not vocalised. Arguably, following Heselwood (2009), even in the most advanced non-rhotic varieties of PDE, /r/ can be analysed as present in all positions as an underlying segment, and word-final schwas are the surface realisations of a vocalised rhotic.

The vocalisation of coda /r/ in non-rhotic varieties is blocked if a word-final <r> is followed by a vowel-initial word in the same prosodic domain. This 'preserved' /-r-/ is widely known as a 'linking' /r/, illustrated by the pronunciation of the <r> in the first column of (16).

(16) Linking /r/ in non-rhotic English:

summe**r i**n Spain	vs	. . . that summe**r**.
poo**r A**ndy	vs	poo**r M**andy
shee**r a**we	vs	shee**r b**oredom

Another process related to the history of coda /r/ is the insertion of an unetymological /r/ in words ending in non-high vowels when the next word or even the next morpheme is vowel-initial. This type of /r/ is known as 'intrusive' /r/, a feature of non-rhotic varieties which is still regarded as 'incorrect' and avoided by the 'speech-conscious' (Wells 1982, II: 284).

(17) Intrusive /r/ in non-rhotic English:

F**a[r] a** long, long way vs fa, sol, la

Emma**[r]** is	vs	Emma saw
aphasia**[r]** and	vs	aphasia problems
withdraw**[r]**ing	vs	withdrawnness

Intrusive /r/ is typical of non-rhotic varieties, but not exclusively so. Its appearance has triggered many different analyses, all of them in some way relying on the perceptual similarity of syllables ending in non-high vowels [ə, ɔː, ɑː, ɜː] and syllables ending in alternating /r/ ~ /ə/. In an analogical account the avoidance of intrusive /r/ after high vowels is predictable because there is no similarity between /r/ and the high vowels /i/ and /u/.[33] The analogical mechanism behind the historical spread of /r/-sandhi in non-rhotic varieties is worked out in Sóskuthy (2010), whose extensive eighteenth-century corpus demonstrates the strikingly higher density of <r>-final words compared with neutral- or central vowel-final words (*Emma*, *idea*). Phonetic similarity and frequency of the source of alternation are shown to result in the extension of the alternation to words which never had etymological <r>.

Whether /r/-loss in word-codas is the same type of change that affected the rhotics in pre-consonantal position is a hard question. The general phonetic properties of the rhotics – their gestural complexity, their high sonority, and their acoustic similarity to central vowels – are clearly involved in both the loss of /r/ in /-rC/ clusters and in the loss of coda-/r/. On the other hand, the actual mechanism of the loss is different: assimilatory in the case of pre-consonantal loss, and analogical in the case of post-vocalic word-final coda loss. The processes seem to have originated at different times, with assimilation before coronals occurring first, though they do overlap eventually – late pre-consonantal loss and early post-vocalic loss are both active in the eighteenth century, and the variability of their realisation continues to this day.

5.2.5 *The other liquid: Bridgestowe-Bristol. Historical parallels between /r/ and /l/*

In some varieties of PDE, namely SSBE and South African English, the realisation of the lateral liquid /l/ is a paradigm case of allophonic distribution: it is velarised to [ɫ] in the coda, as in *pill* [pɪɫ], while the 'neutral' [l] is restricted to the onset, as in *lip* [lɪp] (see 2.3.1). In addition to velarisation, some varieties of English show 'vocalised' /l/ in word-

[33] Specifically for /i/: high front vowels have high first formants, rhotics have lowered F2, usually lower F3, which would predict that the transition in /i-r/ would be optimised by the insertion of a schwa, so /i - ə - r/ >> /ir/. On the cross-linguistic avoidance of adjacent high front vocoids and rhotics see further Hall and Hamann (2010).

final position and pre-consonantally: for example, *feel* is realised as [fiːw], *cool* as [kuːw], *knealt* as [nɛwt], and *people* as [piːpu]. The process of vocalisation is ongoing; in Britain it is most pronounced in the south-eastern dialects, but it is observed also in AmE, AusE, NZE and Falkland Island English, and in 'near' RP speakers and speakers of SSE and non-regional AmE. Moreover, /l/ is also active as an 'intrusive' segment, as in *paw is* [pɔːlɪz], homophonous *Saul*: *saw*, spellings such as <falcet, falcit> for *faucet*, <papal> for *papaw* 'grandfather', <seasowl> for *see-saw* in AmE (Gick 2002). Wells (1982, II: 344–5) reports that for some Bristol speakers *idea*: *ideal*, *area*: *aerial*, *mango*: *mangle*, and *tango*: *tangle* are homophones. The etymology of the name *Bristol* itself is based on OE *brycg* 'bridge' + *stow* 'place'. Sóskuthy (2010) reports on the much higher density of word-final /-ɔ:l/ tokens in PDE (110,874) than word-final /-ɔ:/ tokens (12,219), and uses this as an argument supporting the idea of analogical extension of the intrusive consonant: /r/ is intruded after schwa because of the density of /-ər/# tokens, while the likelihood of /l/ insertion is highest after /-ɔ:/ and lags behind after other vowels.

The parallels between the two liquids are obvious; indeed, the similarity of the effects of /r/ and /l/ can be traced back to the earliest stages of Germanic, where the IE syllabic sonorants developed in a parallel way (see 3.4.2).

(18) Syllabic sonorants in PIE and Germanic:

PIE	Germanic	Examples
/r̥/	→ <ur>	PIE *mr-ti-*, Gmc **mur-þra*, OE *morðer* 'murder'
/l̥/	→ <ul>	PIE *pl-no-*, Gmc **fulla*, OE *full* 'full'

Like <-r>, the lateral /l/ in OE is associated with OE Breaking (see 5.2.2, 6.5.3).

(19) OE Breaking before <lC>:

Source	West Saxon	Gloss
Go. all-s	eall	'all'
*halƀoz	healf	'half'
*selho-z	seolh	'seal'

Breaking before /-l/ in OE is even more restricted than before /-r/: it does not occur after /i-/, it is sporadic after /e-/, and its occurrence after /a-/ > /æ-/ is limited to West Saxon and Kentish. Anaptyxis (see 5.2.2) involving /l/ is attested in, for example, *wylif* 'she wolf' < *wylf*, *yleca* 'ilk, same'. Similarly, in heterosyllabic /-Cl-/ clusters the transition from the first consonant to the lateral liquid is facilitated by an intervening consonant: PrG **ainlif-*, OE WS ***endleofan***, OE Northumbrian *ællefne* 'eleven', *bræmlas* > *bræ**mb**las* 'brambles', OE

þȳml- > ME *thimble*; compare the epenthesis in, for example, Goth. *timrjan* > OE *timbrian* 'to build', or, going outside Germanic, OFr *cha(u)**mbre*** < Lat. *camera.* There are also cases of metathesis involving /l/, as in *seld* ~ *setl* 'seat', *aðl* ~ *ald* 'disease', *spatl* ~ *spald* 'spittle' (Minkoff 1972: 92–3; Hogg 1992a: 256

Like /r/-loss, the first instances of /l/-loss date back to the early post-Conquest records.

(20) Early instances of /-lC/-loss:

OE	**ME**	**Gloss**
hwylċ	hwich	'which'
ælċ	ech	'each'
wenċel	wenche	'wench'
myċel	muche	'much'

These are examples from non-Northern thirteenth-century texts: *The Lambeth Homilies*, *Poema Morale*, *St Katherine.* The loss must be traced through velarisation of /l/ to [ɫ] in the coda, where its perceptibility would have been minimised when adjacent to the highly salient [-tʃ]. The high frequency of these words could also have been a contributing factor to the loss.

Coda-loss of /l/ + other coronals is recorded early in high-frequency words of low prosodic prominence: *as(e)* < *ealswa* 'as'; compare with stressed *als*, *also.* By the fifteenth century spellings such as *shud*, *sud* 'should' and *wud* 'would' indicate /l/-loss in the modals.

Another indicator of the instability of /l/ comes from unetymological insertion of <l> in the environment back vowel + /lC/.

(21) Early unetymological <l-> insertion (data from MED):[34]
<palker> for <packer> surname < 'packer' (1282)
<walke> for <wake> 'wake' (c. 1384)
<salme> for <same> 'same' (a. 1399)
<salke> for <sake> 'sake' (c. 1400)

The next step, fully covered in documents from and after the fifteenth century, involves loss of coda-/l/ flanked by a back vowel in the peak and a velar or a labial in the second coda slot (Wyld 1953: 297; Dobson 1968: §425).

(22) Extended /lC/-loss:

Spelling	**Gloss**

[34] The MED uses a. ('ante') before a date to indicate the latest presumed date of composition, as distinct from c. ('circa'), which refers to the approximate date of the manuscript.

hafpenny	'halfpenny', note [heɪ-] pronunciation[35]
fok(k)(e)	'folk'
scowk	'skulk'

'Loss' in these instances implies vocalisation of the dark [ɫ], eliminating the constriction component and preserving the backness of its secondary component. This development is attested earlier in Northern sources. Its spread southwards, where it was apparently originally stigmatised, was still under way at the end of the sixteenth century.[36]

The same mechanism of loss of constriction leads to complete loss of single-coda /l/; it is attested after back vowels in the seventeenth century in Northern, Scots and Northern Irish English. Indeed, <a'> 'all' is 'the current spelling in modern literary Scots' (OED), with precursors in seventeenth-century <pow, pou, pu> for 'pull', <faa, fawe, fa> for 'fall'.

An important, though often ignored contributing factor in the history of /l/-loss in English is the fact that Old French and Anglo-Norman had undergone an independent vocalisation of /l/. Vocalisation of [ɫC] clusters, similar to [rC] clusters, started in OFr in the ninth century, and although the change in AN seems to have been somewhat delayed (Pope 1961: §§390, 1,179), the absence of /lC/ in bilingual speakers would undermine the stability of the cluster in ME. Thus we find *Pamer* (personal name, 1207) < AN *palmer*, *paumer* 'palmer, pilgrim', OE *palm* 'palm' < Lat. *palma* ~ OFr *paume*, ME *sauder*, *sawder* < OFr *soud(i)er*, *saudier* 'soldier', *sauf* 'safe' < Lat. *salvus*. The retention of the /l/ in some modern forms, as in *fault*, *vault* is an Early ModE reversal to the original Latin form, and in some cases we find interesting alternations such as *Wat*, *Watson* < *Walter*.

Again, as has often been pointed out (Jespersen 1909; Dobson 1968; Lutz 1991, 1994; Lass 1992a; Sóskuthy 2010), the historical developments of the liquids have much in common, based on their shared properties. Both liquids have high sonority and they are bi-gestural, where the secondary dorsal component involves minimal obstruction and is therefore perceived as more vocalic than consonantal, so that some similarities in the processes triggered by /r/ and /l/ are phonetically and phonologically predictable. On the other hand, there are some

[35] The loss of /l/ causes lengthening of the preceding vowel prior to its diphthongisation to [eɪ].

[36] In *Love's Labour's Lost* (V, i) the pedantic Holofernes says that he abhors 'such fanatical phantasimes, . . . such rackers of orthography, as to speak *dout*, fine, when he should say *doubt*; *det*, when he should pronounce debt, – d, e, b, t, not d, e, t: he clepeth a *calf*, *cauf*; *half*, *hauf*.

notable differences: complete pre-consonantal loss of more obstruent-like /l/ is less advanced historically, and it has not become the definitive dialect marker that /r/-loss is considered to be; intrusive /r/ is more advanced than intrusive /l/; and the environments in which intrusion is most salient are different: schwa for /r/-sandhi (*Emma[r] is*) and /ɔː/ for /l/-sandhi (*paw[l] is*).

5.3 Cluster simplification: KNIGHT-NIGHT, WRITE-RIGHT, IAMB-IAMBIC

Compared with OE, PDE is a language with relatively restricted sets of consonantal clusters. Some early simplifications were discussed in 4.3: LOE/EModE /sk/ > /ʃ/, thus OE *sċip* > ME *ship*, OE *disċ*, ME *dish*. In 5.1.3 we covered the loss of initial /h-/ when followed by sonorants: OE *hlot* > ME lot, OE *hring* > ME ring, OE *hnappian* > ME *nappen*. Recall also that OE was a language where geminate consonants were phonemically contrastive: OE *hoppian* 'to hop' vs *hopian* 'to hope' (see 2.1.4, 3.4.5, 4.1.2), but stem-internal geminates were lost in ME. The next two sections will cover more instances of cluster simplification in English.

5.3.1 Initial <kn-, gn-, wr->: KNIGHT-NIGHT, WRITE-RIGHT

The tendency to simplify consonant clusters at word-edges, which started with /h/-initial clusters and word-final geminates, spread to other clusters in ME and after. Unlike the pre-fourteenth-century /hr-, hl-, hn-/ simplifications, later simplifications are not reflected in the spelling.

During the fourteenth century, initial <kn-> and <gn-> were probably still realised mostly as /kn-/, /gn-/. The evidence for that is found in alliterative verse where [kn-] is matched to [k-], thus in *Piers Plowman* (fourteenth century) Langland alliterates *clothed*: *copes*: ***k**nowen*; ***k**nytten*: *coler*: *commune*.[37] Orthographic anaptyxis is another diagnostic of continuing separability of <kn-> in ME.

(23) Early anaptyxis in /kn-/ onsets (from LAEME):
<k**i**nicht, cinth> 'knight'
<kinf> 'knife'
<k**e**neleden> 'kneeled'

Such spellings, though not very frequent, show that one way of resolving the non-cohesiveness of the cluster was to separate the consonants, in the same way that the German surname of American popular culture

[37] For more details see Minkova (2003: 330–9).

hero *Evel Knievel* became [kə ˈniːvəl]. Another strategy, the first signs of which appear in the fourteenth century, is occasional simplification by dropping initial <k->, or adding it unetymologically before [n], suggesting uncertainty about the velar in the scribe's speech.

(24) (a) Etymological /kn-/ spelled <n->:

<neyg>	'knew'	c. 1300 (?c. 1225)
<(horse)nave>	'stable-boy/-knave'	(1314)
<nobbes>	'knobs'	(a. 1398)

(b) Etymological /n-/ spelled <kn->:

<knoynge>	'noying, annoyance'	(a. 1425)
<know>	'now'	(a. 1475)

The spread of the simplified forms continued in the fifteenth and sixteenth century, and by the latter half of the seventeenth century, the innovation was already recognised by the grammarians. Intermediate stages in the simplification include [-tn], [hn], and possibly [ŋ̥n] (see Lass 1999: 123).

The non-cohesiveness and, ultimately, the simplification of the /kn-/, /gn-/ onsets is both phonetically and lexically grounded. In terms of sonority, /kn-/, /gn-/ are well formed, but there are other factors that undermine the stability of these clusters. A major factor is the articulatory effort of producing a sequence of two non-continuants. There are no other onset clusters in ME, or in PDE, that require both of the adjacent onset consonants to be produced with full closure. Distributionally, /kn-/ is isolated: after the loss of /hn-/, there were no other velar + nasal onsets in the system. Perceptually, /kn-/ and /gn-/ were often confused, and the long transition of the velar into the nasal allows alternative interpretations of the signal, as in (23) and (24). Not least, the overall number of items with initial /kn-/ was not high, if one excludes the verb *to know*, and the number of /gn-/ lexemes was vanishingly small.

Two other initial clusters, /wl-/ and /wr-/, were also subject to anaptyxis and simplification. Words with initial /wl-/ were very rare in the OE and ME lexicon, and the only survival is *lisp* < OE **wlispian*. Early examples of splitting the cluster <wr-> can be found in OE example *wrohte* ~ *worohte* 'wrought', as in (10a) above, early ME *werangus* 'wrong' (Jordan 1974: 148).

(25) Early anaptyxis in /wr-/ onsets:[38]

wreche ~ *werche* 'wretch' (13th c.)

[38] For further examples and discussion see Minkova (2003: 365–8).

wartȝe ~ *wredȝe* 'wrath' (13th c.)
wernches ~ *wrenches* 'wrenches' (13th c.)

The other option of realising the original cluster was by simplification. Some fourteenth-century evidence from southern texts suggesting instability is shown in (26).

(26) (a) Etymological /wr-/ written <r->:
wrynkul ~ *runkel* 'wrinkle' (c. 1400)

(b) Etymological /wr-/ alliterating with /r-/:
riche: ryden: wrathe *Piers Plowman* (14th c.)

(c) Etymological /r-/ written <wr->:
wright ~ *right* 'right' (14th c.)

The process of simplification was more advanced in the southern varieties and it probably proceeded step-wise. One possible path of change involves an initial merger of the rounded labiovelar approximant [w-] with the following coronal trill [-r-] into a doubly articulated, labialised coronal *[r^{w}-]. The complex articulation is then simplified to [ʋ], the voiced labiodental approximant heard today in some RP speakers, in popular London speech, and even further afield, making *red* and *wed*, *wreck* and *reck* homophones (see Jespersen 1909: 354–5; Cruttenden 2008: 221). The [ʋ]-realisation must have persisted into the nineteenth century, evidenced by substitutions of <r> by <w> as in *Wichard*, *Twinity*, *thwee*. The final step would be loss of the labial component of [ʋ-] and a merger with the pre-existing variety of /r-/.

The simplification of /hn-, hr-, hl-, kn-, gn-, wr-/ in English results in a consonantal system with clear phonotactic limits: except for the sequence obstruent + liquid, initial clusters in English cannot involve two non-continuants. Also, as noted in 2.3.1, except for clusters involving initial /s-/, onset clusters are well formed only if the sonority of the cluster is rising, banning onsets such as */kt-/, */gd-/, */kf-/, */gv-/, and so on. Deliberate preservation of original Greek /(f)θ-/, /sθ-/, /tm-/, occasionally /pn-/, as in ***phthisis***, ***sthenic***, ***pneu-***, ***tmesis*** (see 3.2), is rare and does not affect the native phonotactics.

5.3.2 *Final <-mb, -mn, -ng>: IAMB-IAMBIC, DAMN-DAMNATION, SINGER-LINGER*

Well-formed coda clusters involve a drop in sonority. All final clusters in English, unless they involve coda /-s/ (*apse*, *axe*, *ellipse*, *blitz*, *kibbutz*, *larynx*), show a falling sonority profile. Another property of English coda clusters is that two voiced obstruents are disallowed at stem-ends, *adze* being the single notable exception; this phonotactic constraint does not apply across inflectional boundaries, thus *sheds*, *legs* with /-dz, -gz/, *robbed*, *obliged* with /-bd, -dʒd/. Comparing the PDE with the OE system, the most conspicuous difference is the simplification of final <-mb, -mn, -ng>, reflected in standard speech. Like the initial clusters <kn-, gn-, wr->, the history of these final clusters is revealed by the spelling, see below. In both onset- and coda-cluster simplification, the deletion affects the edge-most lower-sonority consonant and preserves the sonorant adjacent to the syllable peak.

The simplification of [-mb] is phonetically motivated by the fact that it is a **homorganic cluster**: the pre-pausal labial stop would be realised as an unreleased allophone [b˺], with a weaker acoustic signal. The identical place of articulation would favour assimilation, so perceptually the whole cluster is very close to the bare nasal [m]. The regularity of <mb> in OE and early ME orthography suggests that the [-mb] was more or less intact, primarily due to the fact that stem-final <-mb> rarely occurred word-finally, which resulted in the cluster straddling two syllables in the paradigm of the few eligible words: *clim-ban* 'to climb', *lom-bes* 'lamb, gen. sg. or pl.', *dum-be* 'dumb, pl.' Even so, some scribal uncertainty can be detected early: the DOE records instances of <dum(e), duman> 'dumb'; <ge-camde> 'combed' < OE *cemban*, and inverse spelling such as <þumbes> 'thumbs' < OE *þuma* appear in the twelfth century.[39] The paucity of rhymes and the limited number of lexical items with stem-final <-mb> make the dating difficult, but it is clear that by the beginning of the seventeenth century /-m/ was the accepted coda for *lamb*, *dumb*, *climb*, *womb* (Jespersen 1909: 216).

The simplification of stem-final [-mb] in native words was matched by the behaviour of the cluster in borrowed words. The base forms of *tomb* (1225), *succumb* (1490),[40] *bomb* (1588), *rhomb* (1575), *hecatomb* (1598), *aplomb* (1828), *iamb* (1842) have lost the final [-b]. In the set of native words the simplified shape of the base is completely stable and persists in the derivatives, for example *lambie*, *lambiness*, *lambly*, *lambskin*, *lamb's-wool*; *climber*, *climbing*, *climbable*. In the loanwords the picture is more complex: ***bomb*** and ***bombable*** have [-m], ***tomb***, also ***entombing*** are always

[39] The spelling <thumb> is predominant in the fourteenth century. For OE *cruma* 'crumb', the first <-mb> spellings in LAEME and the MED are fifteenth century. OE *lim* 'limb' is not recorded with <-mb> spelling in LAEME or the MED; the modern spelling spreads in the eighteenth century.

[40] John Walker (1791–1826) still recommends that *succumb* should keep [-mb].

with [-m], but the adjectives ***tombic*** (1874), ***tombal*** (1900) retain the [-b-]; ***rhomb*** and ***iamb*** have [-m] ~ [mb], but ***rhomboid***, ***rhombic***, ***iambist***, ***iambic*** preserve [-b]. This is a case where multiple factors interact: resyllabification of the stop into the next syllable, as in *rhom.boid*, *iam.bic*, will favour preservation of [-b-], while lexical frequency will favour preservation of the shape of the base in the derivatives, as in *bombable* and *entombing*.

The cluster <-mn> in word-final position appears only in non-native words: *autumn*, *column*, *condemn*, *damn*, *solemn*. In some instances of early borrowings, the <-mn> was avoided from the start, thus Lat. *hymnus*, Late Lat. *ymnus*, OE epenthetic ***ymen***; in *damn* the input was Old French *dampn-er* ~ *damn-er*, the ME adopted forms are predominantly with <-mpn->, but <dam(e)> is already in evidence c. 1440; note also the spelling <dambd> for 'damned' (1611). The phonetic nature of this simplification is based on avoidance of similarity: the cluster [-mn] is perceptually opaque because of the overlapping features of the two adjacent nasals. As in the case of /-mb/-simplification, morphological composition may affect the realisation: *damner*, *damning* have no [-n-], but *damnation* (1300), *damnable* (1303) preserve it; *hymner* 'a singer of hymns' is both ['hɪmə(r)] ~ ['hɪmnə(r)], but *hymnal* has [-n-]. We preserve [-m.n-] in *alumnus*, *alumna*, but not in the shortened form *alum* (1683). The realisation of [-n] requires a vowel-initial suffix, but it is not sufficient: (rare) *autumny*, no [-n-], unlike *autumnal*, *solemnity*, where [-n-] is resyllabified in the syllable onset.

Another case of historical cluster simplification affects the coda cluster [-ŋg]. The phonemic inventory of the OE consonants in 4.1 lacks the velar nasal /-ŋ/ (called *eng* [ɛŋ], or *agma* ['ægmə], or *angma* ['æŋmə]). The velarised *allophone* of the nasal is of course reconstructed in words in which <n> was followed by a letter indicating a velar stop, thus OE *singan* [siŋgən] 'to sing', *tunge* [tʊŋgə] 'tongue', *ðanc* [θɑŋk] 'thought'.

The historical loss of the voiced velar stop in [-ŋg] in word-final position justifies the inclusion of the velar nasal /ŋ/ in the inventory of contrastive sounds in 'standard' Present-Day Englishes. The distinctive function of /ŋ/ is testable today in minimal pairs such as *rang-ran*, *thing-thin*, *sung-sun*. The simplification of the cluster started in the north of England, first in unstressed syllables, as attested by the rhyme *fechtyn*: *syn* (Barbour's *Bruce* 1375), gradually spreading south in the fifteenth century (Jordan 1974: 162). The suffix *-ing* is at the forefront of the change. The instability of [-ŋg] and the perceptual confusion between /-n/ and /-ŋ/ in that suffix is shown in some early inverse spellings and rhymes.

(27) (a) <ng> spelling for <n> (data from the MED):

<birthing>	'burden'	a. 1400 (a. 1325)
<Hethyng (strete)>	'heathen'	(1380)
<kelsyng>	'keelson/kelson'	(1402)
<coming>	'cumin'	a. 1450 (?c. 1421)
<chappinge>	'chopin, half-pint'	(1455)

(b) <-ng> rhyming with <-n>[41]

<Mapyne: endinge>	(2347:2349)
<serpentyne: endyng>	(3171:3173)
<tyþinge: appolyne>	(84:86)

The mechanism of the merger is similar to the development of /-mb/, except that in this case the assimilation of the obstruent results in a complex segment combining properties from both the nasal sonorant and the obstruent, involving velar closure. The further option, namely a complete loss of the velar coarticulation and retention of just /n/, has been taken only partially. It is well attested with the unstressed suffix *-ing* during the sixteenth century, when even Queen Elizabeth writes <besichen> for 'beseeching', although teachers were urged not to let pupils pronounce [ɪn] for <-ing>. Well into the eighteenth century, Wordsworth, Byron, Keats and Tennyson rhyme <-in>: <-ing> (Lass 1999: 120). In SSBE [-ɪŋ] began to be preferred in educated speech by the end of the nineteenth century, and it is now the recognised SE pronunciation.[42]

Some forms which we have inherited in the simplified variant are *midden* < ME *midding* 'a refuse heap, dunghill' and *tarpaulin* < *tar* + *pall* + *ing*.[43] A related development in late ME is the epenthesis of /-n/ or [-ŋ] in the coda of unstressed syllables before the voiced velar stop /-g/ or the affricate /-dʒ/ in (mostly) loanwords: *farth**in**gale*, *harb**in**ger*, *mess**en**ger*, *pass**en**ger*, similarly native *night**in**gale*. Dobson (1968: §438) calls the nasal 'a species of consonantal glide', easing the passage between the preceding unstressed vowel and the following consonant, but this is not the sole trigger of the epenthesis which is possibly also analogical to frequent native variability of [-ɪŋ] ~ [-ɪŋg].

The [-ɪn] pronunciation of <-ing>, as in *sittin'*, *walkin'*, continues as a variant in all of the central areas of England, plus peripheral areas of

41 From *The Sowdone of Babylon* (Yorkshire, end of fourteenth century).

42 The stigmatisation of [-ɪn] both in British and American English is undoubtedly due to orthographic prescriptivism. On the preservation of [-ŋg] in the suffix *-ing* in places like Birmingham, Manchester and Liverpool see Wells (1982, II: 365).

43 The OED warns that this etymology must 'remain conjectural'.

the north, the south-western peninsula, the eastern counties and Essex (Trudgill 1999: 48). In the southern US [-ŋ] is replaced by [-n] in many socially prestigious varieties, while [-ŋ] is the norm in many working-class varieties. More typically, however, the [-n] pronunciation for [-ŋ] in *-ing* is associated with lower-working-class speech habits; it is also a typical marker of deliberately affected casual speech style.[44]

In stressed codas, the replacement of [-ŋg] by [-ŋ] is supposed to have occurred later than in *-ing*, but in *The Sowdone of Babylon* we find *everychone: among, distruccion: wronge*, compare with (27b). The existence of both [-ŋg] and [-ŋ] in stressed syllables was recognised by contemporary commentators in the middle of the seventeenth century. As in PDE, consistent [-g]-dropping was observed only word-finally (Luick 1964: §767; Lass 1999: 119).

The distribution of contrastive /ŋ/ prompts some interesting phonological questions. Like PDE /h-/, which can appear only in onsets, /-ŋ/ is a 'defectively distributed' phoneme: it can be distinctive only in coda position. The restriction reflects its historical origin since it is only through the loss of the voiced velar stop in the coda that /ŋ/ became contrastive: *kin-king, ban-bang, run-rung*. Before /k/, as in *plank, sink, hunk*, [-ŋ] remains a positional allophone followed by the voiceless stop. Thus, we get a three-way opposition in *pin* [pɪn]-*ping* [pɪŋ]-*pink*-[pɪŋk], *sin, sing, sink*, and so on.

Another peculiarity of contrastive /ŋ/ is that it has to be domain-final, that is, the [-g-] is preserved stem-internally, rendering [-ŋ-] allophonic, as in *Bangor, bingo, tango, single, hungry, Hungary*, all with [-ŋg-]. Note that the preservation of [-g-] does not depend only on syllabification, because in forms derived with *-ing* or the agentive suffix *-er*, the [-g-] of the stem is not realised, and the derived form copies the shape of the base form: *singing, singer* with just [-ŋ-]. In addition to the most frequent *-ing* and *-er*, the majority of the native suffixes such as *-y, -dom, -hood, -ness, -ish, -less, -ling*, also *-let* (OFr), preserve the shape of the base: *slangy, kingdom, thinghood, youngness, strongish, fangless, kingling, ringlet* have [-ŋ-]. The addition of a comparative suffix, *-er* or *-est*, as in *longer, strongest, youngly*, however, results in heterosyllabic [ŋ].[g]. The addition of Latinate suffixes generally preserves the [g], as in *fungation, diphthongal*, but not always, as in *ringette, nothingism*. Then there is vacillation with

[44] A study of the substitution of [-ŋ] by [-n] in words ending in <-ing> by Detroit speakers shows that [-n] forms are used by 19.4 per cent of the upper middle class, 39.1 percent of the lower midddle class, 50.5 per cent of the upper working class and by up to 78.9 per cent of the lower-working-class speakers (Wolfram and Schilling-Estes 2006: 174–5).

some derivatives: *prolong* and *prolonging* are always just [-ŋ], *prolongation* varies between [-ŋ-] and [-ŋg-], and *prolongate* is always [-ŋg-]. There are some idiosyncrasies: *dinghy, hangar* allow both pronunciations, and so do *English* and *England.* The behaviour of [-ŋ] in clitic groups and phrases is also variable; the variability of [-ŋ] is of continuous theoretical interest. In our diachronic context, the deletion of the [g] and the possibility of phonemic /ŋ/ in narrowly defined contexts in late ME and EModE is most notable as an addition to the inventory of contrastive sounds in English.

Although there are no [ng-] or [ŋ-] words in the native Germanic vocabulary, or in loans from Latin and its descendants, the OED lists more than twenty <ng-> words, all of them first recorded in the last two centuries: *ngaio* 'evergreen shrub', *ngaka* 'doctor', *ngapi* 'Burmese pressed fish', *Ngbandi, ngiru-ngiru,* and so on. The accommodation of the initial cluster in such words can result in three different pronunciations.

(28) Accommodating initial <ng-> in PDE:

<ng>
- [n-] *ngaio* 'NZ shrub', *ngawha* 'hot spring' (Maori)
- [ŋə-] *ngapi* 'Burmese pressed fish' (unassimilated)
- [əŋ-] *ngwee* 'Zambian monetary unit', *ngege* 'fish', *Ng* (name)

In borrowings from Maori, SSBE and AmE favour simplification to [n-]. Occasionally, the dictionary records unassimilated pronunciations, as in *ngapi* [ŋə'piː], *ngaio* [ŋaio], *ngawha* [ŋafa]. By far the most common strategy, shown in the bottom row, is the insertion of a schwa to the left of the cluster, making a new unstressed syllable, placing the cluster conveniently in the syllable coda and therefore within the pattern of native [-ŋ]. A similar strategy of schwa insertion can be observed also with the initial cluster <mb->: *mbongo* 'a political stooogе' (from Zulu and Xhosa), *mbari* 'an extended family unit' (from Swahili) pronounced [əm-].[45]

The processes discussed above present only a partial picture; the focus has been on the main innovations separating ME from PDE. There are a number of 'smaller' changes that affect a limited number of items. In ME the final [-tʃ] of OE *ānlic* 'only' and OE *ic* 'I', *-lic(e)* -'ly' were gradually dropped. The bilabial approximant [w] was lost in the onset cluster [sw-] followed by a back vowel: OE *swā*, 'so', OE *swylc*, ME *suche* 'such', similarly OE *sweord* 'sword', *twā* 'two', where the spelling does not reflect the change. Along with the simplification in nasal +

[45] The initial <x> in *Xavier* ['zeɪvɪə(r)] is sometimes taken to represent [ks-] as in *X-ray*, triggering prosthetic [ɛ-/ə]: [ɛg'zeɪvɪə(r)] (see 3.4.1 for [ks] > [gz]).

non-continuant coda clusters (*-mb*, *-mn*, *-ng*), *-nd* tends to lose the dental, as in ME *scande/scanne* 'scan', v. < Latin *scand-*, *woodbine* < OE *wudubinda*, which gives rise to hypercorrect *sound* < OFr *soun*, *pound*, v. < OE *punian*, similarly *compound*, *expound*, *tyrant*, *peasant*, *ancient*.

Figure 5.4 presents a survey of the major consonantal changes covered so far. It shows typical spellings for the consonants and consonant clusters in ME, followed by ME examples, the reconstructed value of the consonant(s) and the PDE realisation.

ME Representative Spellings	*Examples*	*14th-c. Value*	*PDE Value*
g, h, gh, hg, ȝ, ȝh, ch, gȝ, ȝg	*sigh(en)* 'sigh'	[-ç]/[-h]	Ø
	bough 'bough'	[-x]/[-h]	
	ynogh 'enough'	[-x]/[-h]	[f]
h-, Ø	*helpen* 'help'	[h-/Ø]	[h-]
	humour 'bodily fluid' *(h)ure* 'hour'	Ø	[h-]/Ø
wh-, w-, qh-, qw-, qwh-, ȝw	*whete* 'wheat' *whil(e)* 'while'	[hw-]/[w-]	[ʍ]/[w]
gn-	*gnawynge* 'gnawing'	[gn-]	[n-]
kn-	*knyght* 'knight'	[kn-]	
wr-	*wroght* 'wrought'	[wr-]	[r-]
-mb	*dumb* 'dumb'	[-mb]	[-m]
-mn	*autumn(e)* 'autumn'	[m(p)(n)]	[-m]
-ng	*song* 'song', *yonge* 'young'	[ŋg]	[-ŋ]
-lC-	*half* 'half', *almesse* 'alms'	[ɫ]	Ø/[l]
-rC-, -r#	*farm*, *ferther* 'further'	[r]/	[-r-]/Ø

Figure 5.4 Fourteenth-century consonants and their PDE reflexes

The consonantal system has moved from more complex to simpler phonotactics at syllable edges. This contributed to the progressive disjunction of written and spoken English in the last six centuries, most often commented on in connection with the vowels. The changes are driven by articulatory and perceptual factors, in spite of the persistence and standardisation of the conventions of etymologically based orthography. The only notable exception to this pattern is the reversal of the

ME /h-/-less realisations in Romance loanwords of the type *humour*, *humble*, where the model of regionally stable /h/-fulness, and the orthographic preservation of <h> in (re)-borrowings from Latin, result in a very restricted lexical set of /h/-less stems: *heir*, *honour*, *hour*, GA *herb*. The reinstatement of /h-/ was facilitated by the large number of /h-/-initial Renaissance Greek loans (see 5.3.1) and the intrinsic phonetic weakness of /h-/, which makes the alternation Ø ~ /h-/ perceptually innocuous. In all other instances, the realisations selected in PDE are phonetically and phonologically motivated.

5.4 Other inventory changes: the adoption of /ʒ/

As noted in 2.1.3, the palatal fricative [ʒ] was a late addition to the consonantal inventory of English. It is also the rarest of all English consonants (Cruttenden 2008: 232), and indeed of all English phonemes (Ladefoged 2005: 91). Its distribution is limited to loanwords, except across word-boundaries (see (31) below).

In ME borrowings from OFr, words which have Modern French /ʒ/ appear regularly as /dʒ-/: *jargon*, *juice*, *jealousy*, *abridge*, *rage*, *cage*, *courage*, *plunge*, *village* are all early loanwords. The simplification of the OFr affricate /dʒ/ to /ʒ/ was in progress in the thirteenth century in Continental OFr, but the parallel change appears to have been delayed in Anglo-Norman (Pope 1961: 93–4, 450). Thus in the fourteenth and the fifteenth century the sound [ʒ] would have been familiar to a minority of well-travelled speakers of French, but [ʒ] in loanwords would still be assimilated to the pre-existing /dʒ/. The potential for [dʒ]- pronunciations is reinforced by the very robust historical presence of [dʒ] in core vocabulary words like *bridge*, *edge*, *ridge*, which go back to OE. Indeed, as we will see below, the tendency to assimilate /ʒ/ to /dʒ/ in post-ME loanwords has continued to this day; compare PDE *garage*, *prestige*, *melange* with both /ʒ/ and /dʒ/ as recognised 'standard' pronunciations.

Exposure to French loans with /ʒ/ was only one of the sources of [ʒ] in English. The allophone [ʒ] could arise in borrowed words in which the voiced alveolar fricative [z] was followed by a palatal glide [j], triggering assimilatory palatalisation of [z] to [ʒ] with concurrent loss of the palatal glide, as in *division*, *treasure*, *usual*. The time-depth of this assimilation is hard to judge, because neither spelling nor rhymes are informative, but orthoepistic evidence from the middle of the seventeenth century onwards indicates that the palatalisation was common, though not stable. 💻 Some examples illustrating the continuing variability of the results of palatalisation are shown in (29). As usual, parentheses indicate the first recorded entry date in the OED.

(29) Palatal assimilation: [z] + [j] > [ʒ]

[ʒ] **only**	[z] ~ [ʒ]	[z] **only**
measure (1225)	*osier* (1175)	*symposium* (1586)
confusion (1290)	*glazier* (1385)	*gymnasium* (1598)
vision (1290)	*nausea* (1425)	*paradisian* (1615)
occasion (1382)	*Elysian* (1579)	*trapezial* (1681)
closure (1386)	*transient* (1607)	*magnesium* (1781)
usual (1387)	*amnesia* (1786)	*nasion* (1879)

In terms of the consonantal system as a whole, the addition of [ʒ] can be seen as a process which would have been facilitated by the functionality of the voicing contrast in the obstruent set: the stops /p/-/b/, /t/-/d/, /k/-/g/ and the affricates /t͡ʃ/-/d͡ʒ/ were paired in voicing from OE onwards. In ME voicing became contrastive for the fricatives too (see 4.4), thus /f/-/v/, /θ/-/ð/, /s/-/z/. After the palatalisation of /sk/ to /ʃ/ in late OE, early ME, the voiceless palatal fricative was the only voiceless obstruent unmatched by a voiced counterpart, except for /h/, which, as shown in 5.1, is quite different from the other obstruents. It is hard to argue that the balance of the system with respect to obstruent voicing contrasts is the driving force behind the rise of /ʒ/, but it undoubtedly increases the likelihood that the speakers would perceive, produce and learn the /ʃ/-/ʒ/ contrast. As we will see in 5.4.1, the palatal assimilations in the first column of (29) are not isolated either – they are part of a more general process of coronal dental palatalisations in English.

The integration of /ʒ/ in the consonantal system has been progressing gradually in the last centuries as new borrowings continue to introduce the speakers to items with [ʒ-] in initial and final position: ***zho*** 'a Tibetan bovine' (1841), ***Gitane***, ***Giselle***, ***Zdanovism/-ist*** (1957), ***zhoosh*** (1977); ***ménage*** (1325),[46] ***cortège*** (1679), ***espionage*** (1793), ***beige*** (1858), ***camouflage*** (1917). The word-initial occurrence of [ʒ-] is more restricted and it tends to be more prone to variation between the palatal fricative and the affricate: ***genre***, ***gendarme***, ***gigolo***, ***georgette*** show [ʒ] ~ [d͡ʒ-]. If peripheral vocabulary additions, for example ***gigue*** (1685), ***(au) jus*** (1865), ***(beau) geste*** (1920),[47] become frequently used items, they may slow the rate of nativisation, strengthening the position of /ʒ/ in the system. It is likely that the globalisation of English will bring in more /ʒ/-initial words, as suggested by a long list of <zh>-initial words on the (unmonitored)

[46] *N.E.D.* (1906) gives only /meɪˈnɑːʒ/, though OED allows /ʒ/ ~ /dʒ/. Retention of word-final /ʒ/ is matched by the retention of the stress on the final syllable, reinforcing a word's 'foreignness'; compare *ménage* with *manage*, v. (1561).

[47] Compare *jig*, 'often assumed to be identical with Old French *gigue*' (OED), *juice* (c. 1290), *jest* (1300).

online *Urban Dictionary*.[48] The extent to which /ʒ/ signals 'foreignness' therefore varies greatly among the speakers of PDE.

5.4.1 *More alveolar palatalisations and affrications: s-, t-, d- + -j.* GOTCHA, INJUN

The development of [z] + [j] to [ʒ] shown in (29) is part of a more general pattern of palatal assimilation in EModE affecting all alveolar obstruents in that environment.

(30) EModE palatalisations and affrications of alveolar obstruents + /j/:

[s j-]	>	[ʃ]:	*mission, sugar, passion*
[-z j-]	>	[ʒ]:	*occasion, derision, measure*
[t j-]	>	[t͡ʃ]:	*mature, mutual, rapture, sculpture*
[d j-]	>	[d͡ʒ]:	*soldier, verdure, procedure*

Of the four parallel developments in (30), the palatalisation of the fricatives appears to have occurred first. For [s] + [j] it is attested in correspondence already in the fifteenth century: *sesschyonys* (*Paston Letters*, 1422–1509), *consederraschons, oblygashons* (*The Cely Letters*, 1472–88). The change would be more advanced in unstressed syllables. We can assume that the stressed syllable onset sequence [sj-] in ME had not coalesced into /ʃ/: a word like ME *sure* would have /sj-/ and it would be homophonous with PDE *sewer*. In stressed position the preservation of [s] is suggested by fourteenth-century alliterative pairings such as *suren* 'to assure': *sithen* 'since': *serven* 'to serve' (*PP* 5.540) and *asoyled* 'absolved': *surely*: *sette* (*SGGK* 1883).

Tautosyllabicity of the alveolar and the glide was the first step towards palatalisation; the completion of the process involves loss of the glide /j/. The sequence alveolar obstruent + [ju-] in primary stressed onsets, as in *suit, pursue, zeugma, Zeus, tune, Tuesday, due, dune*, can be simplified either by the absorption of the palatal into the consonant, as in *sure, sugar* with [ʃu-], and *tune, Tuesday* with [tʃu-], or by preservation of the features of the alveolar and loss of palatality, as in *suit, Sue, suet* with [suː], *due, dune* with [du-]. In the sequence [sju-], as Walker (1791–1826: 60) noted, the only two items in English with stressed stem-initial [sj-] to [ʃ-] change are *sure* and *sugar* and their derivatives.

In unstressed position the sequence [-sj-] occurred most commonly in the French suffix *sio(u)n/cio(u)n*, where /s-/ was a singleton onset and the suffix was disyllabic; the orthographic <i> was [ɪ] and not a glide,

[48] <http://www.urbandictionary.com/> (last accessed 23 May 2013).

so in Chaucer *condicion, devocion, nacion, proporcion* still had [-sɪ.ən], not [-sjən]. In Chaucer and throughout the fifteenth century the suffix was disyllabic, rhyming on *-on*, for example *destruccion: person, proporcion: upon, scorpioun: confusioun.* Disyllabic <–ion> [ɪ.ən] continues into the Renaissance, though only as an archaic feature in verse.

The affrication of the alveolar stops was first reflected in informal sixteenth-century spellings *sawgears* 'soldiers', seventeenth-century *teges* 'tedious' (cited in Lass 1999: 121). It was still a matter of debate in the eighteenth century. Walker (1791–1826: 61) makes a distinction between the behaviour of the dentals in stressed and unstressed syllables: he writes that *nature, creature, feature, fortune* 'have the *t* pronounced like *ch, or tsh*', but he objects vigorously to word-initial [t͡ʃ] in *tutor, tumour, tumult,* which his contemporary, the actor and elocution guru Thomas Sheridan (1719–88) respelled in his *Dictionary* (c. 1774) as <tshootur>, <tshoomour>, <tshoomult> – what was respectable from the stage had not reached acceptance in the more purist academic circles. Walker disapproves of [tʃ] before native suffixes: he expects [t] in *(thou) pitiest, mightier, twentieth,* and so on. He recommends the affricate in *righteous, plenteous, piteous,* where the last two items have reverted to /t/, yet he opts for [t͡ʃ] in *bestial, celestial, frontier,* where the PDE norm is [t] + [ɪ]. The variability of [tj] ~ [t͡ʃ] continues, and the recommended pronunciations can be puzzling, so the OED lists *latitude, longitude* only with [-tjuːd], while *multitude* is given as both [-tjuːd] and [tʃ(j)uːd]. For non-word-initial [-dj] Walker (1791–1826: 50–1) says that *soldier, grandure, verdure* are 'universally and justly pronounced as if written *j*' (= [d͡ʒ] in his system); for stressed-syllable initial [dj-], as in *duke, reduce,* his verdict is that the pronunciation with [-dʒ] 'cannot be too much reprobated'.

The degree of acceptance of the innovative palatals and affricates still varies, and their realisation often differs in casual and in careful speech. For over-cautious speakers the palatal assimilations can be reversed for some lexical items, probably an influence from the spelling, so one can hear *appreciate, negotiate* with [-s-], *Parisian, Tunesia* with [z-], *literature, overture, mature* with [–t-], *ordure, endure* with [-d-]. In some instances doublet forms are reflected in the spelling and one of the forms, not necessarily the one showing palatal assimilation, has become a distinctive stylistic marker, as in *creature ~ critter* (1815), *Indian ~ Injun* (1812), *idiot ~ eejit* (1919).[49]

Regressive palatal assimilations can occur in PDE across word boundaries.

[49] In informal speech the dentals in initial <tr-> and <dr-> can undergo palatalisation, for example [t͡ʃrai] for *try*, [d͡ʒrai] for *dry*.

(31) Palatalisations and affrications across word boundaries:
[-s] + [j-]: [ʃ]: *this year, unless you*
[-z] + [j-]: [ʒ]: *as you say, as yet*
[-t] + [j-]: [t͡ʃ]: *got you* (*gotcha*), *not yet*
[-d] + [j-]: [d͡ʒ]: *had you, said yes*[50]

Above the word-level, the assimilation of the alveolar obstruents to a following palatal is even more gradient than within the word. The presence of [j-] at the beginning of the next word is not a sufficient condition for the assimilation. If the two words do not form a unified prosodic domain, a clitic group with a single stress, but preserve their independent stress, palatalisation and affrication do not occur. Thus, there is usually no change in slow speech to the final [-s] in *paints yellow*, the [-z] in *reads Yeats*, the [-t] in *liked yoga* and the [-d] in *rigged yacht*, though coarticulatory effects do occur, especially in fast, relaxed speech.

5.5 The glottal stop [ʔ] and the alveolar tap [ɾ]

The history of [ð] ~ [d] variation in conjuction with /r/, as in PDE *father* < OE *fæder*, PDE *burden* < OE **byrðen* was covered in 5.2.3. This section turns briefly to two other processes: glottal stop insertion and substitution, and the intervocalic tapping of /t/ and /d/ to [ɾ]

5.5.1 The glottal stop

The glottal stop [ʔ], articulated with the vocal cords pressed together, sometimes likened to the sound of coughing, is not part of the inventory of contrastive consonants in English (see 2.1, 2.1.2). It is, however, a sound of long Germanic lineage. It is commonly reconstructed as present in the onset of orthographically vowel-initial stressed syllables in OE. The OE alliterative practice of matching non-identical stressed vowels: *ǣnne ofer ȳðe / umborwesende* 'alone over waves / child-being' (*Beowulf* 46), suggests strongly that the insertion of a glottal stop before the stressed syllables ['ʔæːnnəː 'ʔyːðəː 'ʔʊmbor ˌwɛzɛndə] was what satisfied the

[50] Hence '*round yon virgin*' in the Christmas carol lyrics is (mis)heard as '*round John Virgin*', or *wouldn't you* becoming *wooden shoe* (*wooden chew?*) in the once popular children song *Mairzy Doats* (*Mares Eat Oats*). Such reanalyses are popularly known as *mondegreens*. The word *mondegreen* itself has its origin in such a 'mishearing'. It is based on 'the name *Lady Mondegreen*, a misinterpretation of the phrase [they have slain the Earl of Murray and], *laid him on the green* in the ballad "The Bonny Earl of Murray"' (OED).

identity requirement in onsets, so strictly observed elsewhere in the OE and the Germanic alliterative corpus. The phonological justification for the insertion of a consonantal onset is syllable-structure optimisation – throughout its history, the vocabulary of English shows a strong preference for onset-ful stressed syllables.

The insertion of a glottal stop in stressed vocalic onsets became much more variable in ME, allowing maximal onset resyllabification across word-boundaries in clitic groups. A late fifteenth-century gloss of Lat. *spica* 'spike, an ear of corn' reads *Hec spica:* ***a ner***, compare also the history of *tother* < *þet oþer*, *nuncle* < *an uncle*, *newt* < *an ewt*. Such resyllabification could occur only if the onsets of *ear*, *other*, *uncle*, *ewt* were empty. Absence of glottal stop insertion is also associated with the development of allomorphy: the loss of [-n] in the OE numeral *ān* 'one', weakened to *an* before vowels and *a* before consonants. Loss of [-n] in the OE forms *mīn* 'mine' and *þīn* 'thine' is involved in the alternation of *my-mine* and *thy-thine*. The selection of the adjectival pronominal forms in EModE was based on the nature of the following sound, as in *my sister* vs *mine uncle*.

The more recent history of pre-vocalic glottal-stop insertion is related to style of delivery. In SSBE and GA the glottal stop is realised in stressed vocalic onsets after a syntactic break, as in the exclamation spelled *uh-uh*, meaning 'no'. It is a feature of emphatic pronunciation of stressed vowel-initial syllables, as in *is this art* [ʔɑɹt]?, *the word's ample* ['ʔæmpl̩], not *sample*. In RP the insertion is more widespread, occurring between an unstressed and a stressed vowel in hiatus as in ***co-opt***, ***reac**tivate*, *pre-**aortic***. Since there is no Roman letter for [ʔ], no glottal stop in Latin or French, and the sound is not contrastive, the testimony of the orthoepists is scant, but it was apparently noted in the seventeenth century. Glottal 'reinforcement' is implicit in descriptions of singing techniques referring to 'hard attack' in vowel-initial words (Cruttenden 2008: 181).

Another process involving the glottal stop is *glottalisation*, the substitution of a coda voiceless stop by a glottal stop: ***that*** [ðæʔ], ***lap*** [læʔ], ***sack*** [sæʔ], similarly intervocalic [t] in *bitter* ['bɪʔə], *matter* ['maʔə], whereby the oral closure is weakened to a very short glottal closure. The glottal stop realisations are more common in British varieties of English. In RP the strongest tendency for replacement affects /t/ before homorganic consonants: *great table*, *sat down*, *not now*. The environments for the replacements of [t] are broader for some speakers, and there is evidence that [ʔ] for [t] is no longer stigmatised in London Regional RP.

The chronological depth of glottal substitution is hard to assess since there are no contemporary commentaries before the second half of the nineteenth century. The replacement is considered primarily British, and of recent vintage, since it is absent from AusE and not present in older speakers of NZE, though it is showing up in the pronunciation of younger NZE speakers.[51] Recent reports on AmE also point to a trend towards word-final glottalisation of /t/, more pronounced before consonant-initial words (*submi**t** **f**ive*, *faul**t** **b**ecause*), but occurring also before vowels (*lo**t** **o**f*, *tha**t** **a**ny*, *shu**t** **u**p*, *tha**t** **a***). This innovative tendency is most strongly associated with the western US, with younger and/or female speakers (Eddington and Taylor 2009; Eddington and Channer 2010). The full diachronic dimension of this change has yet to be researched, but as Wales (2006: 176–7) points out, it probably originated much earlier in the north and could have been latent in many speech communities.

5.5.2 *Voicing of [t] and tapping of [t] and [d]:* MATTER-MADDER[52]

Another pattern of replacement, characteristic of AE, found also in some Northern Irish varieties of English, is the realisation of the dental stops /t/ and /d/ as the alveolar approximant tap [ɾ] between (a) a stressed and an unstressed vowel word-medially, as in *ladder* [ˈˈlæɾɚ], *waiter* [ˈweɪɾɚ], *bidder* [ˈbɪɾɚ], *setting* [ˈsɛɾɪŋ], (b) between two unstressed vowels as in *abnormality* [ˌæbˌnɔrˈmæləɾi], *capitalise* [ˈkæpɪɾəˌlaɪz], or (c) between vowels across a word boundary, as in *at ease* [əˈɾiːz], *get úp!* [gɛɾ ˈʌp]. Phonetically, tapping involves voicing and a single rapid contact of the tongue with the alveolar ridge. Since the replacement affects both /t/ and /d/, the allophonic [ɾ] can neutralise the surface forms of lexically distinct entities, resulting in homophonous pairs such as *matter-madder*, both [ˈˈmæɾɚ], *kitty-kiddy*, both [ˈkɪɾi] or [ˈkɪɾɪ].

The change to [t] to [ɾ] may be reconstructed as proceeding stepwise from intervocalic /t/ > [d] > [ɾ]. Possible very early indications of voicing are found in OE *botm*, ME variant spellings *boþom*, *boddom*, *bodme*, *boden*, PDE Northern English and Scots *bodome*, *bodom*, *bodum*, *boddem* (OED); LOE *witter* 'wise' spelled *wiþer* (MED, c. 1275); *water* spelled *warter*, *wader* (MED, 1156–7, 1463); *federyn* 'fetter' (1440).[53] Jespersen (1909: 340–1) cites *pottage* > *porridge* from the early sixteenth century,

[51] See Cruttenden (2008: 180–1) for AusE; Trudgill (1999b: 236) for NZE; Wales (2006: 175–7) for Northern English and the glottalising influence of urban Scottish English.

[52] Although in some languages *flaps* and *taps* are functionally distinct, there is no such distinction between them in English. The process described in this section can be referred to as either *tapping* or *flapping*.

[53] The MED labels <wader> an 'error'.

also *neverberrer* 'never better' in Dickens, *nor a bir of it* 'not a bit of it' in Meredith, *wasermarrer* 'what's the matter' in Jerome, representing speech under the influence of alcohol or sleep. Variability between [d] ~ [ɾ] is the most likely account for the current form of *paddock* < OE *pearroc* 'park, enclosed place'; the [d] and [ɾ] forms have coexisted since the middle of the sixteenth century. Although tapping is commonly considered an innovation in AmE, such data justify the assumption that tapping in AmE is a feature which was indeed inherited from the mother country, as suggested by Haugen (1938) and Montgomery (2001: 139). Tapping is also attested in Australian and New Zealand English. Its robustness is due partly to the current lack of social stigma associated with it, which must have facilitated its codification.

5.6 Recent trends: [ts-, ʃm-, ʃl-, ʃt-], MASH POTATO, MANAGE CARE, STAIN GLASS

Our diachronic survey of the English consonantal system will conclude with observations on some recent trends of enrichment and simplification.

Like <ng->, <mb->, the homorganic onset <ts-> is not found in any native vocabulary items, nor in loanwords from French or Latin. Initial /t/ in PDE can only be followed by /-r, -j, -w/ in the native vocabulary, so /ts/ is phonotactically non-native but *not* universally unattested. The earliest <ts->-initial borrowing in English is from Slavic: *tsar* (1555); the voiceless alveolar affricate onset [t͡s-] in this word and its many derived forms is most commonly assimilated to a singly articulated [z-], though the affricate [t͡s-] pronunciation is also recorded. Only three more [t͡s-] words were added in the sixteenth to seventeenth century, nine in the eighteenth century, and twenty-three between 1901 and 1975, with sources from languages from all over the world: Burmese, Chinese, German, Greek and Japanese. All of the most recent borrowings preserve the [t͡s-]; apparently the phonotactic constraint which generated the [z-] in *tsar* is no longer part of the system: no one would say ['zɛtsə] or [zuː 'nɑmi]. In other words, [t͡s-], although of more recent lineage, is likely to join [ʒ] (see 5.4) as an addition to the consonantal inventory. The still marginal acceptability of a [t͡s-] onset can be related to its relative complexity and lower frequency of occurrence, though *tsunami* is hardly a rare item in English after 2011.

The situation with initial <s(c)hm->, <-s(c)hl> <sht->, as in *schmooze, schmeer, shlep, shlock, shtick, shtetl* is somewhat different, in that these clusters identify the origin of the words not just as non-Anglo-Saxon or Romance, but as specifically Yiddish. After World War II,

Yiddish is spoken by more people in English-speaking countries – US, Canada, Australia and Great Britain together – than in Continental Europe or Israel. Large Yiddish communities in New York, Los Angeles, Melbourne and Montreal have contributed to the recognition and integration of new vocabulary and new consonant clusters: [ʃm-, ʃl-, ʃt-], which have become productive **phonaesthemes** in PDE.[54] With at least a quarter of a million Yiddish speakers in North America, and a strong presence of Yiddish culture in film, TV and literature, familiarity with these clusters is to be expected and there is no attempt to assimilate them to some native sequence. What is more, the onset <schm-> [ʃm-], treated as a 'combining form' since 1929 by the OED, is clearly productive in playful reduplication, generating mildly disparaging or comic attention-getters: *madam-shmadam*, *able-shmable*, *holy-shmoly*, the *Libros Schmibros* lending library in Los Angeles. Additions to the phonetic and phonological inventory are predictable in a language with a constantly expanding vocabulary. Onset [ts-, ʃm-, ʃl-, ʃt-] are well on their way to being integrated into the PDE consonantal system.

The final process, reminiscent of the series of cluster simplifications described in 5.3.2, is known as dental or, more broadly, *coronal stop deletion*. In PDE it is noticeable and much discussed for AmE, but there are parallel processes in BrE (Tagliamonte and Temple 2005). The essence of the ongoing change is that coda clusters of consonant + dental stop are often simplified, resulting in homophony: *packed-pack*, *paste-pace*, *lost-loss*, generating spellings such as *left lane **close*** for *clos**ed***, *W**es** Coast* for *W**est** Coast*, *mana**ge** care* for *mana**ged** care*. Dental stop deletion is now legitimised in forms such as *ice cream* (first OED record 1744), *mash potato* (1797) and even *stain-glass* (2012).

The simplification is phonetically 'natural' in the sense that the dental stop in the coda is unreleased – the allophonic realisation is [-t̚] or [d̚]. The absence of a release stage renders further lenition and eventual deletion perceptually likely, as the difference between an unreleased stop and zero is minimal. Historical records of this deletion are scarce, but occasional spellings such as *bes* 'best' (*Havelok*, c. 1325) and rhymes such as *wirschip* 'worship': *Egipt* 'Egypt' (*The Northern Homily Cycle*, c. 1315); *frek* 'quick': *effec* 'effect' (Castelford, *Chronicle of England*, fourteenth century) are informative. Fifteenth-century loss of coda <t>, especially in Scotland, is found in *excep(t)*, *stric(t)ly*, *nex(t)*, and *feck* (1488), *feckful* (1568), *feckless* (1586) < *effect*. The addition of a non-etymological <-t> in the coda is also indicative of insecurity about the

[54] A phonestheme is 'a phoneme or group of phonemes having recognizable semantic associations, as a result of appearing in a number of words of similar meaning' (OED).

realisation of consonant + dental codas: OE *behǣs* > ME *bihese* ~ *biheste* 'behest'. Among the unetymological additions of <-t> that have become standard are *behest*, *against*, *amidst*, *amongst*, all attested in ME, and later *whilst*, *hoist*, *tuft*, *graft*, *tyrant*, *peasant*, *pheasant*, *pennant*, *pageant*, *ancient*.

In PDE the rate of dental stop deletion varies according to the nature of the preceding consonant, the morphological affiliation of the dental – whether it is part of the stem or inflectional – and the presence or absence of a following consonant. The deletion is most pronounced for stem-final dentals after liquids or coronals and before another consonant.[55] In the US, the rates of reduction vary along social and ethnic lines: in the position of strongest vulnerability, that is, non-inflectional [-d] or [-t], followed by a consonant (*behin**d** **th**e*, *bes**t** **m**ovie*), it is estimated at 66 per cent in 'standard' AmE. It is extremely common among speakers of AAVE (88–97 per cent), New York City Puerto-Rican (93 per cent), Native American Puebloan English (98 per cent), Vietnamese English (98 per cent), Chicano working class (91 per cent) and Appalachian working-class speakers (74 per cent).[56]

Suggested further reading on *Companion* website.

[55] Further commentary on the hierarchy of the environments for stop deletion is addressed in Labov et al. (1968), Côté (2004), Schreier (2005), Tagliamonte and Temple (2005).

[56] Data from Walt Wolfram & Natalie Schilling-Estes (2006: 253).

6 The vowels in Old English: spelling, pronunciation. PDE alternations traced back to OE

FOOT-FEET, FULL-FILL, MAN-MEN, CHILD-CHILDREN, HOUND-HUNDRED

6.1 The vowel inventories of PDE and OE: a comparison

As this is the first of three chapters that survey vowel histories, we start with a brief review of the PDE vowel inventory. Figure 6.1, combines Figure 2.4 and the diphthongs of 2.2.2 (2).

Recall from 2.2.1 that in GA and SSBE vowel length by itself is not phonemically distinctive: long and short vowels differ in height, backness and peripherality, and these parameters are sufficient to define the phonemic contrasts in the inventory. It is nevertheless the case that functionally, and above the level of the atomic segment, the PDE vowels fall into two major types: short/lax and long/tense. The parameter of length or tenseness is essential for the prosodic behaviour of vowels: (C)V syllables are *light*, while (C)VV syllables are *heavy*.

	FRONT	CENTRAL	BACK		DIPHTHONGS
			Unrounded	Rounded	
Upper high	**iː** (FLEECE)			**uː** (GOOSE)	**aɪ** (PRICE)
Lower high	**ɪ** (KIT)			**ʊ** (FOOT)	**aʊ** (MOUTH)
Upper mid	**eɪ** (FACE)	**ɚ/ɜː** (FUR)		**oʊ** (GOAT)	**ɔɪ** (CHOICE)
		ə (COMM<u>A</u>)			
Lower mid	**ɛ** (DRESS)		**ʌ** (STRUT)	**ɔː** (THOUGHT)	
Upper low	**æ** (TRAP)				
Low			**ɑ** (LOT, PALM) (GA)	**ɒ** (LOT) (SSBE)	

Figure 6.1 An overview of PDE vowels and diphthongs

The 'short' vowels in Figure 6.1 are transcribed in an IPA form, while the 'long' vowels are marked with the length diacritic (ː). This is a typographical convenience, which allows one to identify more readily the lineage of short and long vowels and their eligibility for specific historical processes. PDE contrastive diphthongs are functionally the same as the long vowels.

Turning back to OE, we follow the long tradition of separating the short from the long vowels and diphthongs. Wherever relevant, the descriptive parameters in Figure 6.1 – height, backness and rounding – are also preserved. As in the idealised system shown for PDE, the OE vowel system is idealised in that it is based on classical and late West Saxon, the variety from which the most written materials survive. It is also the variety of OE that is most commonly used for etymological references. Since the focus of this book is to trace the major patterns of correspondences between OE and PDE and to place the 'outliers' in a historical context, details regarding the OE dialects are avoided. A note of warning is due, however: the West Saxon OE, on which the Anglo-Saxon grammars written in the last two centuries draw, does not have a direct and localisable linear descendant. With this disclaimer in mind, Figure 6.2 presents an overview of the (late) OE vowels:

		Short vowels				Long vowels			Diphthongs
		Front		*Central*	*Back*	*Front*		*Back*	
		Unround	*Round*			*Unround*	*Round*		
High	*Upper*					iː	yː	uː	iə
	Lower	ɪ	ʏ	ə	ʊ				ej
Mid	*Upper*					eː		oː	eə
	Lower	ɛ			ɔ				æj
Low		æ		ɑ		æː		ɒː	æə

Figure 6.2 An overview of late Old English vowels

All vowels except for the central [ə] appear as nuclei of stressed syllables. The IPA symbols used for OE are familiar from Fig. 6.1, except for [ʏ] and [yː], which are not found in SSBE and GA. The 'small capital ʏ' stands for a lower high rounded vowel, a counterpart of unrounded 'small capital ɪ'. The pronunciation of [ʏ] in OE is as the <ü> in German *küssen* 'to kiss', *Münster* 'minster', or as <u> in French *début* 'debut'. The pronunciation of the long front rounded vowel [yː] is as in German *kühl* 'cool' or French *juge* 'judge'.

The choices for categorizing the low back vowels are based on subsequent history: short [ɑ], whose contrastiveness with respect to [æ] in OE is a matter of uncertainty, must be assumed to have been at least quite central in late OE, since in early ME it merged with [æ], except before nasals (7.3.1). Positing a long back rounded [ɒː] is similarly a projection of later history: except in the northern dialects, OE [ɒː] was raised to [ɔː] in ME (7.3.2).

The final column in Fig. 6.2 shows the diphthongal nuclei in late OE. The entries [iə], [eə], and [æə] are important for the phonology of Germanic and OE, but they cannot be traced forward to PDE, which is why they are highlighted. All three were monophthongized in ME and they merged with pre-existing vowels. To avoid any confusion, it should be borne in mind that PDE/RP [ɪə] as in *HEAR*, or [ɛə] as in *HAIR*, are innovations based on the historical rhotic in such words; there is no direct association between them and the OE [iə] and [eə].

The discussion of vowel histories will follow the approach used in the outline of consonantal histories: we compare the two admittedly highly variable end-points, PDE and OE, and we isolate and focus on processes which have contributed to the shape of the modern system. While some of the vocalic processes, such as I-Mutation (6.3.1) are period-specific, their phonetic underpinning and their structural triggers and effects are not. It is therefore important to read the rest of this chapter both as a selective description of the synchronic components of the phonology of OE, and as the diachronic fabric giving rise to to the phonology of ME, EModE, and PDE.

6.2 Orthography and the reconstruction of OE vowels

PDE spelling is largely *etymological.* Among the languages using the Roman alphabet, English is notorious for violating the sound-letter correspondences of Classical Latin. In many instances the five vowel-letters and their combinations are more likely to reflect historical sources and morphological affiliations than actual sounds. In contrast, it is generally held that OE spelling was more or less *phonemic*, and that inconsistent or innovative spellings indicate deviations from a pronunciation 'norm'. Using hedge-phrases such as 'more or less' is justified because reconstructing the pronunciation of vowels in OE is even more problematic than the reconstruction of consonantal values. Though not fully systematically, the contrastive consonants in OE were associated with specific letters (see 4.1). In addition to orthographic consistency, the identity of consonants can be tested in the verse, where stressed alliterating syllables have matching onsets. The situation is more complex with the vowels, where we do not have the evidence of rhymes to supplement the orthographic evidence. Ælfric, writing about letters in 995, identifies five vowel-letters:

> Five of those [letters] are vowels, that is, *clypiendlīce* 'callings out': **a e i o u**. These five letters are by themselves their own names, and without them no word may be written. Therefore they are called the **five vowels**. To these is added the Greek **y** for the sake of Greek words and **y** is very usual in English writing. All the other letters are called **consonants** . . . (Throop 2008: 19)

Ælfric's testimony that the 'five letters are by themselves their own names' supports the assumption that the values of the vowel-letters in OE match roughly the range of the phonetic values of the corresponding letters in Latin, or, from our perspective, the values of the same letters in languages like Italian, German and Polish. The capital Greek upsilon <Y> had the high front rounded value [y] in the Attic-Ionic dialect, and later in classical Greek.[1] The 'ligature' of Roman <a> and <e>, ash <æ>, was a rendition of a runic symbol, named helpfully after the first sound in the OE word *æsc* 'ash(-tree)', IPA [æ].

Even adding <y> and <æ>, seven vowel-letters are inadequate for the representation of the twenty vowels in Figure 6.2. Like all other early Germanic languages, OE had short and long vowels, yet the scribes did not mark vowel length: the letter sequence <f**o**r> can stand for [fɔr] 'for' or [f**o**ːr] 'travelled'; <m**e**tan> represents both [mɛtən] 'to measure' and [m**e**ːtən] 'to meet'. Note that in this book, as well as in many edited texts and textbooks, macrons are inserted to help lexical recognition, for example <g**o**d> [gɔd] 'God' vs <g**ō**d> [goːd] 'good'.

The doubling of vowels to mark vowel length is used in some early OE manuscripts, but it is not a regular feature of the main body of OE texts; it became a common practice only after the end of the thirteenth century.

Some diacritics, a superscript curl, a circumflex, and an extra-long macron marking short vowels, do appear in the eleventh century (Hogg 1992a: 17), but the credit for the first consistent attempt to represent vowel length in English belongs famously to the monk Orm, whose 10,000-line autograph translation and commentary of the Scriptures, c. 1180 uses double consonant letters to mark short vowels in closed syllables, thus <goddspelless> 'Gospels', <heffness lihht> 'heaven's light'. Orm's innovative system was an isolated example; there were no followers.

[1] Gnanadesikan (2009: 214–16).

In addition to using the same letter to mark different vowels, the OE scribes sometimes used different vowel-letters in the same word; for example, in early WS 'giver' occurs with equal frequency as both <gifa> (x44) and <gyfa> (x45). The vowel-letters are used in both stressed and unstressed position. The letter <e>, for example, stands for [ɛ] and [eː], and it is also the commonly used letter representing any unstressed vowel in late OE. <e> is also used as a diacritic marking the palatal quality of the preceding consonant, producing the impression that the vowel was diphthongised, for example *ġieldan* 'yield', *sċieran* 'shear'. Figure 6.3 shows the most frequent correspondences between the vowel-letters and the simple vocalic nuclei posited for late OE.

Letter	SHORT		LONG	
	Value	Example	Value	Example
<i>	ɪ	*binn* 'bin'	i	*rīdan* 'to ride'
<y>	ʏ	*fyllan* 'to fill'	y	*fȳr* 'fire'
<e>	ɛ ə	*settan* 'to set' *dǣlere* 'dealer'	e	*swēte* 'sweet'
<æ>	æ	*þæt* 'that'	æ	*mǣl* 'meal'
<a>	ɑ	*bannan* 'to ban'	ɒ	*bāt* 'boat'
<o>	ɔ	*(ge)boren* 'born'	o	*dōn* 'to do'
<u>	ʊ	*drunken* 'drunk'	u	*hūs* 'house'

Figure 6.3 Letter-sound correspondences in OE

Unlike PDE, where single vowel-letters can be silent, it is generally held that all single vowel-letters in OE represent syllable peaks: *swēte* 'sweet' is a disyllabic word, and *dǣlere* 'dealer' has three syllables. The horizontal line separating the <i> and <y> rows is dashed both because they were often graphic variants, as in <gifa> ~ <gyfa>, and because of the later merger of short [ʏ] and [ɪ] and long [yː] and [iː] in large areas of ME (see 7.3.1).

The dashed line separating [æ] and [ɑ] is justified by their ambiguous phonemic status. At least originally, they were in complementary distribution: they were both reflexes of West Germanic /a/, which was raised to /æ/ in OE unless it was followed by a nasal, /w/, or a back vowel in the following syllable. Moreover, the subsequent history of the two vowels also points to a merger (see 6.3.1). However, an argument in favour of phonemic /ɑ/ comes from cases of <a> + nasal, as in OE *mann* ~ *monn* 'person', *fann* ~ *fon(n)* 'fan, winnow', *gram* ~ *grom* 'hostile' (Hogg 1992b: 86, contra Colman 1983). The <a>~<o> variable spellings suggest a shift to the back vowel area, possibly pre-nasal [ɑ̃~ɒ̃]. OE Merican and Northumbrian texts regularly represent PrG /a/ + nasal as <o> + nasal, for example *monn* 'man', *gongan* 'go', *lomb* 'lamb'. In late West Saxon the <a> spellings are the more common, though in ME the Northern and West Midlands spelling favours <o>.

The spelling-pronunciation correspondences for the OE digraph spellings are very complex. We will get to some details of interpretation in 6.5.3; for now we list the most common digraph spellings and their reconstructed values in two rather vaguely defined 'early' and 'late' stages. As in Figure 6.3, the editorial macron indicates etymological length.

	Value		Example
Digraph	*Early*	*Late*	
<ēa>	æʊ	æə	*strēam* 'stream'
<ea>	æ^{ə}	æ	*heall* 'hall'
<ēo>	eʊ	eə	*sēon* 'to see'
<eo>	ɛ^{ə}	ɛ	*ġeolu* 'yellow'
<īe>	iʊ	iə, iː	*(ġe)līefan* 'to believe'
<ie>	ɪ^{ə}	ɪ	*ġiefan* 'to give'

Figure 6.4 OE digraph spellings and reconstructed realisations

Since our focus is on late West Saxon, omitted from Figure 6.4 is the spelling <io>, found primarily in Northumbrian and Kentish. Only three of the six realisations of digraph spellings in the third column – [æə], [eə] and [iə] – are uncontroversially considered contrastive. The phonetic values assigned to these contrastive diphthongs are different in the early and late stages of OE, and the exact phonetic interpretation of the diphthongal end points have been and can be debated. Although the matching orthographic sequences with supplied macrons and without the macrons – <ēa>-<ea>, <ēo>-<eo> and <īe>-<ie> – seem to invite a parallel interpretation of long and short diphthongs, we will see in 6.5.3 that positing such a parallel is neither necessary nor compelling.

The next two sections will address two important OE processes that contributed to the shaping of the system in Figure 6.2: the early process known as I-Umlaut, and a selective vowel lengthening known as *Homorganic Cluster Lengthening*.

6.3 I-Mutation: FOOT-FEET, FULL-FILL, SELL-SALE

I-Mutation, also known by its German moniker *I-Umlaut*, is the most important coarticulatory process affecting the vowels of early Old English. It had a far-reaching effect on the structure of the late Old English vowel system and produced paradigmatic alternations in the lexicon which survive to this day. Deservedly, I-Mutation takes pride of place in all phonological histories of English; excellent discussions can be found in Campbell (1959: 71–85); Hogg (1992a: 121–38); Lass (1994: 59–71) among others. We will not cover all of the specifics here; the goal of the section is to present a simplified account of the mechanism and scope of the process, with particular emphasis on patterns whose survival accounts for otherwise 'irregular' or 'unexpected' inflectional and derivational alternations of the type *FOOT-FEET*, not **FOOTS*, *FULL-FILL*, not **TO FULL*, *MAN-MEN*, not **MANS*.

The *triggers* and the *mechanism* of I-Mutation are well defined: a high front vowel /i/, or a palatal approximant /j/ in a post-tonic syllable cause anticipatory, or regressive, assimilation of the vowel in the preceding syllable: PrG **ubilaz*, Goth. *ubils* > OE *yfel* 'evil'; PrG **dōmjan* > OE WS *dēman* 'to judge', compare OE *dōm* 'judgement, doom'; WG **taljan* > OE *tellan* 'to tell', compare OE *talu* 'tale'. The resulting vowels are more similar to the conditioning factor in terms of tongue-height/palatality, hence the term 'assimilation', but since there is no good argument for contiguous spreading of palatality, the process is more appropriately classified as a type of *vowel harmony* (Hogg 1992a: 121). In most cases the harmonisation triggers /i, j/ are not preserved in the written records; their historical presence is reconstructed from comparative evidence. Because of the loss of the triggering environment, some new mutated vowels acquire independent phonemic status (Lass 1992b). 💻

The shifts of the monophthongs involved in I-Mutation are shown in Figure 6.5.

The parenthesised length mark in Figure 6.5 indicates that the changes affect both the short and the long monophthongs. It is assumed, along with the standard representations of the pre-Old English vowel systems (Campbell 1959; Reszkiewicz 1973; Hogg 1992a; Lass 1994), that the difference between the short and the long vowels at that early period was based crucially on duration, so that the contrasts were /i/ - /iː/, /e/ - /eː/, and so forth. If any height or backness differences

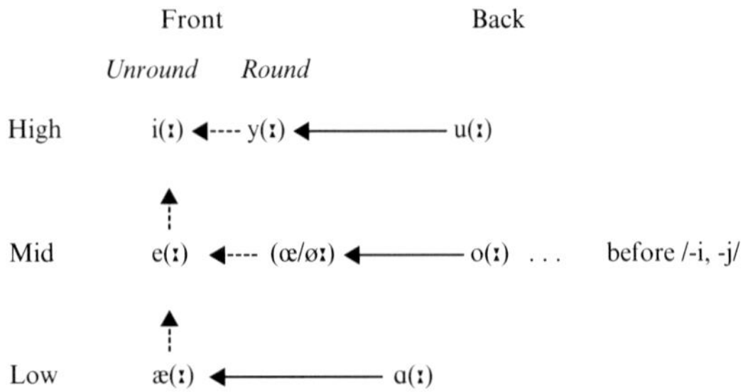

Figure 6.5 OE I-Mutation of monophthongs

existed in these pairs in pre-OE, they cannot be tested in the records. Therefore, no qualitative differences between the short and the long vowels are shown in Figure 6.5.

The parenthesised symbols in the mid round set (œ/øː) are new and call for a comment. The 'slashed o' [ø], commonly used for the I-Umlaut of both short and long /o/, is the IPA symbol for the upper/close mid front rounded vowel. The [œ] 'o-e ligature' is the IPA symbol for a lower/open mid front rounded vowel, as in French *œuf* or German *göttlich*. This symbol is similar to the ligature <œ> found in some non-West Saxon texts (Kentish and Anglian). Since the assumption is that there was no height difference between the short and the long input to I-Mutation of the mid back vowel [o], the choice of either [ø] or the ligature [œ] is arbitrary.

The use of dashed arrows linking the high and mid rounded [y(ː)] and [ø(ː)] to the front [i(ː)] and [e(ː)] is justified by diachronic instability within OE. The rounded vowels [y(ː)] and [ø(ː)] combined the frontness of the trigger and the rounding of the input vowels. Such front rounded nuclei were innovations resulting from I-Mutation, and they were 'intermediate' in a long-term perspective. Their existence is not in question, but crucially, they end up merging with the corresponding high and mid front unround vowels. The merger between [ø(ː)] and [e] occurred earlier, and by the time of late West Saxon only the unrounded mid front vowels are attested. The unrounding and high-vowel merger of [y(ː)] and [i(ː)] was well under way in late West Saxon, but as we will see in 6.5.1, the [y(ː)] can be realised differently in different dialects.

The dashed vertical arrow in Figure 6.5 – between the low front vowel /æ(ː)/ and the mid front /e(ː)/ – flags internal differences in this set. West Saxon /æː/, ultimately going back to PrG /ai/, remained unchanged, so that it was only short /æ/ that participated in I-Mutation, but not in all environments. The dashed vertical arrow connecting /e(ː)/ and /i(ː)/ is there to indicate another complexity: long /eː/ in

Pre-I-Mutation		Post-I-Mutation		Examples (editors' spellings)
Spelling	*Value*	*Spelling*	*Value*	
<ēa>	[æʊ][2]	<ie, i, y, e>	[iː, eː][3]	OE _ġe-lēafa_ 'belief' < PrG *_galauƀon-_ _ġelīefan_ 'to believe' < Goth. _galaubjan_
<ea>	[æᵊ]	<ie, i, y, e>	[ɪ, ɛ]	_wearm_ 'warm' < PrG *_warmo-_ _wierman_ 'to warm' < Goth. _warmjan_
<ēo>	[eʊ][4]	<ie, i, y>	[iː]	_fēond_ 'fiend' < Goth. _fijands_ _fȳnd_ 'fiends' < PrG *_fiund-iz_
<eo>	[eᵊ]	<ie, i, y>	[ɪ]	_feorr_ 'far' < WG *_ferro-_ _fyrran_ 'to drive away' < PrG _ferrian_

Figure 6.6 OE I-Mutation of diphthongs

WS was primarily the result of I-Mutation of PrG /oː/, so there are no further shifts. Paradigmatic alternations between short /e/ and /i/ – as in OE _beraþ_ < PrG *_ber-a-nþi_ 'they bear' vs OE _bireþ_ < pre-PrG *_ber-i-þi_ 'he bears' – could be due either to the earlier raising of /e/ before high vowels, or to mutation of the original /e/ vowel in pre-OE.

The triggers associated with I-Mutation, /-i, -j/, have a fronting and palatalising effect on the diphthongs of OE too. Once again, we omit some details and focus on the forms that feed into the phonology of ME. Figure 6.6 shows the shifts posited for the diphthongs subject to I-Mutation. In summary: all back vowels, short and long, are subject to the harmonising process, and so are the diphthongs. The front vowels undergo I-Mutation much more selectively: the long vowels /æː/ and /eː/ are

[2] This diphthong comes from Germanic /au/, for example PrG. *_strauma-_ > OE _stream._

[3] The spellings with <e> are found in Kentish and Anglian texts. The reconstructed [eː] in these varieties is the basis of the ME forms with <-e-, -ee-, -i-e->, from which we get PDE _belief._

[4] In PrG, original IE */eu/ + /i, j/ was raised to /iu/. We simplify further by glossing over the fact that <eo> digraphs and <io> digraphs (as well as the corresponding vowels) coalesced when subject to I-Mutation. For details see Hogg (1992a: 121–2).

never affected, the results for [e] are uncertain and the shift of [æ] to [ɛ] is not fully carried out.

As for the timeline of I-Mutation, it must have been under way prior to the earliest OE texts. It was not fully completed until the late eighth to the early ninth century. Some early Latin borrowings show I-Mutation: *glesing* 'gloss' < Lat. *glossa* 'marginal note'; OE *cælic* 'chalice' < Lat. *calyx*, WG **kalik*; OE *ynce* 'inch' < Lat. *uncia*. Late Latin borrowings are unaffected: OE *aprilis* 'April' < Lat. *aprilis*; *OE paradis(e)* < Lat. *paradisus*; OE *organe* 'marjoram' < Lat. (herba) *origanum*.

Under the rubric of 'scope' we should also include another topic of interest: *where* does I-Mutation show up in the grammar, that is, what are the morphophonemic implications of the change? As noted above, the triggers of the change are most often missing even in the earliest texts, though /-i-/ may survive in some suffixes, notably *-il*, *-ir*, *-in*, *-ing*, for example *yfel* 'evil', compare Goth. *ubils*; *cyning* 'king', compare Goth. *kuni* 'tribe'. Many of the orthographic <-i->'s found in the classical OE texts can be misleading because they do not represent /i/'s that were in existence at the time of I-Mutation, and therefore the preceding vowel remains unchanged. Such is the case with the derived class 1 weak verbs in <-ian>, where the original form of the suffix was **ōj-an*, as in OE *lufu* 'love' - *lufian*, without I-Mutation. Another relevant factor can be the prosodic domain: typically, the harmony operates within the domain of the prosodic word, which implies that compounds will behave differently. This is indeed the case: the presence of /-i-/ in the second half of a transparent compound is insufficient to cause mutation. Some examples of unmutated OE forms are shown in the second column of (1).

(1) Late OE unmutated forms before /i/

Input	**Late OE**
blōd 'blood'	*blōdig* 'bloody'
lufu 'love'	*lufian* 'to love'
–	*arabisc* 'Arab, adj.'
āc 'oak' + *rind* 'rind'	*āc-rind* 'oak-bark'
blōd 'blood' + *drynce* 'drink'	*blōd-drynce* 'bloodshed'
tūn 'town' + *scipe* '-ship'	*tūnscipe* 'township'

The projection of an originally allophonic process into the morphology is accompanied by the loss of the trigger and the phonologisation of the original allophones. Once this happens, mutated forms become associated with specific functions. A paradigm that shows the effects of I-Mutation and that has prominent survivors in PDE is the 'root' or 'athematic' declension. In that set the PrG inflections were added directly to the root with no intervening 'theme'-vowel. Consequently, if the inflection contained /i/, as it did in the dative singular (*/-i/) and nominative plural (*/-iz/), an eligible root vowel would be mutated, as illustrated in (2).

(2) I-Mutation in PrG athematic noun stems:

	Nom. sg.	**Dat. sg.**	**Nom. pl.**
PrG	*fōt-s	*fōt-i	*fōt-iz
OE	fōt 'foot'	fēt	fēt 'feet'
PrG	*mannz	*mann-i	*mann-iz
OE	man(n) 'man'	men(n)	men(n) 'men'
PrG	*mūs-s	*mūs-i	*mūs-iz
OE	mūs 'mouse'	mȳs[5]	mȳs 'mice'

About two dozen nouns, mostly feminine but also some high-frequency masculine nouns, belong to the OE root declension. Although the type-frequency of root-stems is low, and the triggering /i/ not in evidence in OE, this fossilised group included common core-vocabulary items of high token-frequency, which may have allowed them to resist the pressure of analogy for the formation of an alternative plural in *-(e)s*. Other survivals in this group are OE *tōþ* 'tooth', OE *gōs* 'goose', OE *lūs* 'louse' and the now obscure compound *woman-women* < OE *wīf-man(n)*, where the second element replicates the plural of *man(n)*.

In pre-OE, PrG inflectional /i/ could also affect masculine *-nd* stems (*frēond* 'friend', *fēond* 'fiend') and *-r* stems (*mōdor* 'mother', *dōhtor* 'daughter', *brōdor* 'brother'), which show I-Mutation in the dative singular and occasionally also in the nominative plural: *frȳnd*, *mēder*, *dēhter*, *brēþre(n)*.[6]

Another set of I-Umlaut fossils in PDE is exemplified by FULL-FILL. These are noun or adjective vs verb pairs, where the base preserves the vowel in its original form in the noun or adjective, but in the verb the same vowel shows I-Mutation triggered by a historical derivational suffix **-j-an* for the infinitive and a connecting vowel **-i-* in the preterite.

[5] The form *mȳs* was also gen. sg. fem., where I-Mutation was triggered by PrG *-iz*.

[6] *Breþ(e)ren*, *brethren* was the standard plural until c. 1600. *Brothers*, after an isolated appearance in the thirteenth-century Lagamon's *Brut*, does not reappear until the end of the sixteenth century. Shakespeare uses *brothers* ~ *brethren* indiscriminately. Starting in the seventeenth century, *brothers* became the plural of the literal sense and *brethren* was retained in reference to spiritual or ecclesiastical relationship (OED). For more details on the transition of mutated plurals to *-es* plurals in the nouns of relationship see Krygier (1996).

(3) OE I-Mutation in weak class 1 verbs in *-*j-an*:

	Base		**Class 1 weak verb**
(a)	f**u**ll 'full'	*f**u**lljan >	f**y**llan 'to fill'
	l**u**st 'desire'	*l**u**stjan >	l**y**stan 'to desire'[7]
	f**ū**l 'foul'	* f**ū**ljan >	f**ȳ**llan 'to defile'
	c**ū**þ 'known'	*k**u**nþjan >	c**ȳ**ðan 'announce, kithe'[8]
(b)	g**o**ld 'gold'[9]	*g**u**lþjan >	g**y**ldan 'to gild'
(c)	bl**ō**d 'blood'	*bl**ō**djan >	bl**ē**dan 'to let blood, bleed'
	d**ō**m 'doom, judgment'	*d**ō**mjan >	d**ē**man 'to deem, judge'
	f**ō**d 'food'	*f**ō**djan >	f**ē**dan 'to feed'
	(ġe)m**ō**t 'meeting'[10]	* m**ō**tjan >	m**e**tan 'to meet'
(d)	s**a**la 'gift, sale'	*s**a**ljan >	s**e**llan 'to give, sell'
	t**a**lu 'tale'	*t**a**ljan >	t**e**llan 'to tell'
	h**ā**l 'whole, healthy'	*h**ai**ljan >	h**ǣ**lan 'to heal'
	h**ā**t 'hot'[11]	*h**ai**tjan >	h**ǣ**tan 'to heat'

The pattern in (3) was robust in pre-OE, but after the loss of the front-vowel triggers, in many instances the base forms were analogically restored in the previously mutated verbs. Had it not been for analogy, presumably to the more frequent form, for OE *hunger*, n. - *hyngran*, v. (< **hungrjan*) we would have *hunger*, n. - **hinger*, v.; for *sprūt*, n. 'sprout' - *sprȳtan*, v. we would have *sprout*, n. - **sprite*, v.; for OE *rūm* 'room, space' - *rȳman* 'make room' the PDE verb would be *rime*. There were many instances in OE in which I-Mutation is recognisable *within* the noun and verb paradigms, where unmutated and mutated forms can coexist depending on the presence of /i, j/ in the PrG inflections, for example 2nd and 3rd pers. sg. present tense indicative and the past subjunctive of strong verbs: *cuman* 'to come' – *cymest*, *cymþ*, *cyme(n)*.

Of interest from the point of PDE is the history of present and preterite forms in English as in *sell-sold*, *tell-told*. As seen in (3d), the infini-

[7] Compare PDE *listless* 'without desire or spirit'.

[8] The long vowel in the base is due to the loss of the nasal /n/ before the fricative in pre-OE; compare Goth. *munþs* - OE *mūþ* 'mouth', Goth. *uns* - OE *ūs* 'us'.

[9] The /o/ in this word is a reflex of PrG /u/ which was harmonically lowered to /o/ in West Germanic before a non-high vowel, thus PrG **gulþam*, Goth. *gulþ*, OE *gold*.

[10] Compare the adjective 'moot' – originally a legal term for a case to be discussed at a meeting, generalised to 'debatable; uncertain, doubtful; unable to be firmly resolved' (OED).

[11] The expected PDE reflex of the OE long vowel in this word is the vowel of GOAT, but already in ME it was shortened before a dental (see 8.3.2).

tives, and also the present tense forms of these verbs show I-Mutation, but the preterite of a subset of class 1 weak verbs was formed by adding the dental suffix /-d/ directly to the root, leaving the base vowel unchanged. Such verbs are considered 'irregular' by PDE criteria, yet as shown in (4), they reflect a pre-OE pattern of I-Mutation in the present tense paradigm and no I-Mutation in the past.

(4) OE I-Mutation in weak class 1 verbs present and preterite forms:

Base	**Present (I-Mutation)**	**Preterite (no I-Mutation)**
*bug-	*bugjan > b**y**ċġan 'buy'	*boh-ta[12] > b**o**hte 'bought'
*wur-	*wurkjan > w**y**rċan 'work'	*worh-ta > w**o**rhte 'wrought'
*sōk	*sokjan > s**ē**ċan 'seek'	*sōh-ta > s**ō**hte 'sought'
*sal-	*saljan > s**e**llan 'sell'	*sal-da > s**ea**lde 'sold'
*tal-	*taljan > t**e**llan 'tell'	*tal-da > t**ea**lde 'told'

Other such pairs in OE were (Kentish) *brengan-brohte* 'bring-brought', *þenċan-þōhte* 'think-thought',[13] *tǣċan-tāhte* 'teach-taught', and the now 'regularised' *dwellan-dwolde* 'dwell', *streċċan-streahte* 'stretch'.

Another set of morphophonemic alternations due to I-Mutation was found in the comparative and superlative forms of some adjectives before the suffixes *-ir-*, *-ist-* < PrG *-*iz-*, *-*ist*. Once again, the high vowel trigger is not in evidence in OE, where the comparative marker is *-ra*, and the superlative *-ost* or *-est*. Some mutated adjectival forms in OE are: *eald* 'old' - *(i)eldra/yldra* 'elder', *(i)eldest* 'eldest'; *hēah* 'high' - *hīerra* 'higher' - *hīehst* 'highest'; *lang* - *lengra* - *lengsta*, 'long-longer-longest'. The comparative forms *ELDER* ~ *OLDER* were interchangeable in ME; the semantic differentiation started only in late ME; the superlatives can be interchangeable to this day. The <o> forms (*older*, *oldest*) are clearly copies of the unmutated base form on the analogy of the dominant model of *-er*, *-est* comparatives.

The PDE derivational pairs *STRONG-STRENGTH*, *FOUL-FILTH*, *LONG-LENGTH* are another echo of OE I-Mutation. The nouns were formed with the PrG suffix *-iþō*, used for feminine abstract nouns from adjectival bases. Although only a few sets have survived, the pattern was quite frequent in OE, including pairs such as *mōd* 'courage, pride' - *ofermettu* < *ofer-mōdiþ(o)* 'pride, insolence'; *þēof* 'thief' - *þīefþ* 'theft'.

As noted already, derivational suffixes containing /-i-/ could also cause I-Mutation. The vowels in the PDE pair FOX-VIXEN differ because *fox* descends from WG **fuhs*, Skt *puccha*, while *vixen* is the derivative of **fuhs* + PrG *-inī*, a suffix forming feminine nouns from masculine

[12] For Germanic /*o*/ and /*u*/ before /*a*/ in **boh-ta*, **worh-ta* see n. 9 on *gold* above.

[13] The PDE form of *think* with <i> is from the cognate verb *þynċan* 'seem'.

bases, OE *fyxen* 'she-fox'; compare OE god 'god' - *gyden* 'goddess', *munuc* 'monk' - *mynecen* '(obsolete) minchen, nun'. Other suffixes where I-Mutation can be encountered are *-il*, *-ing*, *-ig*, *-isc*, where analogical levelling of forms within the paradigm often results in unmutated forms, for example *ānlic*/*ǣnlic* 'only'. The strongest I-Mutation triggers are the historical inflections and stem-formative elements in pre-OE, which are subsequently lost, while 'live' suffixes such as the diminutive *-incel* are more 'word-like' and are typologically more likely to behave like the second elements of compounds. Whether the typological prediction is borne out by the OE data remains an open question.

We have described I-Mutation as an anticipatory segmental assimilation of height and frontness within the domain of the prosodic word. The process adds complexity to the vowel system by generating previously unattested contrastive front rounded vowels. Height harmonisation parallels exists in the earlier history of Germanic. Why did I-Umlaut cease to be productive in OE and why has it not recurred later in the history of English? One obvious factor is that the preservation of the properties of the base, 'faithfulness' to the base, tends to inhibit the operation of phonetically driven changes, but there can be other factors. Seeking an explanation for something that has *not* happened is of course an ontological problem, yet knowing that such coarticulatory processes are widespread in the languages of the world, we can take their presence *or* absence as diagnostics for other properties of the system.

In the case of OE I-Mutation, the valuable secondary information we can extract refers to the properties of the triggers. Ideally, in harmonic processes, the trigger either has to be prominent, or it has to have contrastively specified features (Hyman 2002). For I-Mutation these features were frontness and height. The prominence and the contrastive features of the trigger interact dynamically with the domain of application: inflectional suffixes or thematic elements, as in (2) and (3), have a higher probability of influencing the base, but as the domain extends to include derivational suffixes, the results become erratic. The picture is further complicated by type- and token-frequencies. Still, a hypothesis that can be entertained is that the loss of I-Mutation correlates with the beginning of reduced prominence of the post-tonic syllables where the triggers reside. A related fact here may be the fact that /i/ is the least sonorous of the vowels. Reduced prosodic prominence is associated with fewer contrasts; put differently, the phasing out of I-Mutation can be seen as a diagnostic for the prosodic developments within OE leading to weakening of the contrastive properties of the unstressed vowels. While the suffixal <i>'s were generally not weakened, stem-internal post-tonic <i>'s – as in the verbs *lufian* 'to love', *lōcian* 'to look', *hopian* 'to hope' – were not viable triggers, in spite of the fact that they are in the right domain. As we will see in 6.5.4, this fits in with a more general picture of unstressed vowel reduction in late OE.

6.4 OE homorganic-cluster lengthening: CHILD-CHILDREN, HOUND-HUNDRED

The lengthening of final vowels in monosyllables in North-West Germanic (see 3.4.4) was seen as an early manifestation of the universal tendency for stressed syllables to be heavy. Already in pre-OE monosyllabic content words ending in a short vowel were disallowed. This early lengthening was one of many historical adjustments of the weight of stressed syllables, and has been analysed as the first link in a chain of quantity changes in English cumulatively resulting in optimally weighted stressed syllables.

A prominent OE quantitative change whose initial stages are traced to the latter half of the eighth century (Luick 1964: §§267–8), or even earlier (Liberman 1992a), is *Homorganic Cluster Lengthening*. All historical phonologies of English recognise the lengthening. We keep the traditional label for the sake of continuity, although it will become clear that the label covers parallel, but not necessarily identical processes, whose differences are as significant as their similarities.

Descriptively, the lengthening affected short vowels before clusters of liquid or nasal plus a homorganic voiced obstruent. 'Homorganic' means that the two consonants forming the cluster have identical or very close places of articulation. The clusters associated with this lengthening are *-ld*, *-nd*, *-mb*, and possibly /r/ + coronal clusters: *-rd*, *-rn*, *-rs*, *-rl*, *-rð*. While some ME spellings do indicate sporadic lengthening before -rC – *board*, *hoard*, *yearn*, *earl*, *earth* had short vowels in OE – the observed vowel length before these clusters may be due either to pre-cluster lengthening or to /r/-vocalisation before a coronal (see 5.2.3). Because of the convergence of effects, we postpone the discussion of lengthenings before /r/ + coronal clusters to 8.3.2. Some sporadic lengthening effects are reconstructed in early ME before [-ŋg], but it is ignored here because there are no traces of the lengthened forms in PDE.

The necessary segmental condition for pre-cluster lengthening was the presence of a sonorant in the stressed syllable coda. Additionally, lengthening required that the sonorant was followed by an obstruent either as the second consonant of the coda in monosyllabic forms, for example *blind* 'blind', or it could be the onset of a following weak syllable, for example *bin.dan* 'to bind'. Obviously, within the paradigm of a single item the syllabic structure can vary between monosyllabic and non-monosyllabic, thus *blind*, sg. - *blin.de*, pl., or *bin.daþ*, imperative pl. - *bind*, imperative sg. After the loss of inflections, the paradigms show uniform vowel length, so it is unclear how or whether syllable-structure variability interacts with the lengthening. Until we have a fine-grained statistical picture of the density of monosyllabic and non-monosyllabic forms and the type of coda in the stressed syllable at the time of lengthening, we can assume that tautosyllabicity of the cluster provided the optimal condition for the lengthening. The assumption is dictated by the absence of lengthening in forms in which a short vowel is followed by a single sonorant, for example OE *fell* > PDE *fell* 'skin', but OE *feld* > PDE *field*.

The effects of Homorganic Cluster Lengthening are most clearly traceable in early ME. Some typical examples of the process are shown in (5).

(5) OE Homorganic Cluster Lengthening:

OE[14]	**ME**
ċild [c**i**ld] 'child'	child [tʃ**i**ːld]
mild [m**i**ld] 'mild'	mild [m**i**ːld]
feld [f**e**ld] 'field'	feld [f**e**ːld]
hund [h**u**nd] 'hound'	hound [h**u**ːnd]
(be)hindan [-h**i**ndən] 'behind'	bihinde [h**i**ːnd(ə)]
climban [kl**i**mbən] 'climb'	climb(e) [kl**i**ːm(b)(ə)]

The lengthening was blocked if the homorganic cluster was followed by a liquid word-internally, hence no lengthening in OE ***ċildru*** 'chi**ldr**en', OE ***hundred*** 'hundred', OE ***sund*** 'sound, swimming water', but OE ***sundrian*** 'to sunder'. This is in line with the balancing of syllable weight by shortening long vowels before -CCC- clusters, associated with late OE, - early ME, that is, either simultaneously or somewhat later than Homorganic Cluster Lengthening (see 7.5.1).

Another factor influencing the results of the lengthening is morphological structure. In suffixed words and compounds the addition of a third consonant is not sufficient to change the shape of the base and the lengthened forms persist, as in OE ***blindnes*** 'blindness', ***ċildliċ*** 'childlike', ***grundleas*** 'groundless', ***goldsmið*** 'goldsmith'. The details regarding

[14] The [i], [e], [u] allophonic transcription for the OE short vowels /ɪ/, /ɛ/, /ʊ/ is prompted by the earliness of the process, the possibility that the sonorant-obstruent cluster in the coda triggered a short tense allophone, and the post-lengthening results [iː], [eː], [uː].

vowel height will be noted below, but here it should be added that the template of long vowels before *-ld*, *-nd*, *-mb* continues beyond ME. Thus -VCCC- words of later date, such as ***Cambridge*** (1580?), ***cambric*** (1530),[15] ***laundry*** (1533), ***foundry*** (1601), ***doldrum(s)*** (1811) preserve the long vowel irrespective of their compositionality.

Focusing just on the non-rhotic clusters *-ld*, *-nd*, *-mb*, we now turn to the specifics of the implementation and causation, and the contingent issue of unity of the lengthening.[16] The least problematic data are presented by the small set of items in which the stressed vowel was eligible for lengthening before <-mb>, a total of nine words: *climb*, *comb*, *coomb*, *dumb*, *December*, *lamb*, *timber*, *tumble*, *womb*. Only four of these show lengthening in PDE: OE *climban* 'climb', OE *camb/comb* 'comb', OE *cumb* 'comb/coomb',[17] OE *wamb/womb* 'womb'. This is too small a set to warrant any generalisations. The best we can say is that there could be sporadic, item-specific lengthening, possibly compensatory for the loss of [-b], developing simultaneously with the simplification of word-final *-mb* (see 5.3.2). Recall that the evidence for [-mb]-simplification goes back to late OE, as in *dum(e)* and *duman* 'dumb', *ge-camde* 'combed', and inverse spelling such as *þumbes* 'thumbs' < OE *þuma* (1154), *ember* < ON *eim(y)rja*. There is no compelling argument for classifying *-mb* as a lengthening cluster.

The case of *-ld* as a lengthening cluster is much stronger. The lengthening applied systematically to the low and back vowels: all surviving OE <-ald-> and <-old-> items – words such as *bold*, *cold*, *fold*, *hold*, *mold*, *old*, *sold* – had short vowels in OE, but the vowels were long by c. 1200.[18] In addition, there are items in which front vowels were lengthened: *child*, *mild*, *field* (OE *feld*), *shield* (OE *sceld*), but these are narrowly outnumbered by forms in which the short nucleus of OE is preserved in PDE: *seldom*, *elder*, *build*, *gild*, *guild*.[19] The systematic nature of pre-[-ld] lengthening of <a> and <o> suggests a phonetic basis: if the post-vocalic realisation of the liquid was a dark [ɫ], the transition from the vowel to the liquid plus dental stop coda could be mediated by the insertion of a linking

15 The stressed vowel in this word, based on Flemish *Cambray* < Latin *Camaracum*, can be both [-æ-] and [-eɪ-] (OED).

16 This section updates arguments presented in Minkova and Stockwell (1992).

17 The phonological history of the homophones *comb/coomb* [kuːm] 'vessel' and 'valley' is identical; there is also a possible etymological link between the two nouns (OED).

18 The evidence for that is the special spelling system devised by Orm, who used double consonant letters after short vowels (see further Anderson and Britton 1997; Fulk 1999).

19 The spelling of *should*, *would*, *could* suggests a long vowel; auxiliaries/modals are prosodically weak, which accounts for the short vowel in PDE. The [-l] in them continued to be pronounced until the late seventeenth century (Minkoff 1972: 336).

l-coloured non-syllabic glide, reanalysed as an extension of the vowel. The new bimoraic nucleus would then be identified with the phonetically closest pre-existing long vowel. The details of this hypothetical development are tentatively reconstructed in (6), bearing in mind, as always, that such narrow phonetic details remain untestable.

(6) Reconstructing pre-<-ld> lengthening in OE:

OE (Angl.) *ald* 'old':	[ɑɫd] > [ɑᵊɫd] > [ɒːɫd] > (ME) [ɔː ɫd]
OE *gold* 'gold':	[oɫd] > [oᵊɫd] > [oːɫd] > (ME) [oːɫd]
OE *mild* 'mild'	[miɫd] > [miᵊɫd] > [miːɫd] > ME [miːɫd]
OE *feld* 'field'	[feɫd] > [feᵊɫd] > [feːɫd] > ME [feːɫd]

The only possible instance of lengthened <u-> before [-ld]in a PDE word is *shoulder*, OE *sculdor*. As for the domain of lengthening, it has to be restricted to -Vld forms in which the vowel and the cluster are in the same syllable. This is crucial because there is no lengthening in monosyllables ending in a single liquid; as noted above, OE *fell* > PDE *fell* 'skin', but OE *feld* > PDE *field*. The morphological domain of the lengthening is also restricted: the entire cluster has to belong to the stem. Thus inflectional *-d(e)* for the past tense of weak verbs attached to V + [-l] stems has no lengthening effect: *fill*, *swill*, *spill*, all attested in OE, preserve the short vowel in the past tense. Indeed, in some instances the addition of the /-d/ past tense morpheme causes pre-consonantal shortening, as in the past tense forms of *deal*, *feel*, *kneel* (see 7.5.1.1).

The third cluster associated with Homorganic Cluster Lengthening is [-nd]. The long-term effect of this cluster is limited. It applies systematically only to the high vowels [i] and [u].[20]

(7) OE <-ind> and <-und> lengthening:

Early OE	**ME**
blind [blind]	blind [bliːnd] 'blind'
grindan [grindən]	grind(en) [griːndən] 'grind'
(be)hindan [-hindən]	bihinde [-hiːnd(ə)] 'behind'
grund [grund]	ground [gruːnd] 'ground'
hund [hund]	hound [huːnd] 'hound'
pund [pund]	pound [puːnd] 'pound'

[20] The association of <-nd> spelling and a preceding [uː] was extended to some [-n] codas: AN *soun* 'sound' (compare Chaucer's rhyme in *The Miller's Tale*: *And softe he cougheth with a semy* ***soun*** *– / What do ye, hony-comb, sweete ali****soun***); similarly OE *pūnian*, ME *poun(en)* 'to pound'; ON *būinn*, ME *boun* 'bound for, ready'; OE *þunor*, *þunre*, ME *thonder* 'thunder'; ME *kin* + *reden* (suffix) > 'kindred'.

The pair *wind*, n. - *wind*, v. is a special case, probably best explained on the grounds of homophony avoidance. Rhyme evidence suggests that the forms were actually homophonous into the late seventeenth century. The restriction of the lengthening effect to the high vowels leaves a whole set of common OE lexemes such as *band*, *hand*, *land*, *sand*, *bend*, *blend*, *end*, *rend*, *send*, *spend*, *tender*, *wend* with short vowels in PDE.

As with [-ld] lengthening, the mechanism of lengthening before [-nd] is still under scrutiny. An important factor in the process must have been the sonority of the first consonant in the cluster following the short vowel and the possible gestural overlap between the nasal and the voiced coronal stop. It is logical to assume with Phillips (1981a) and Jones (1989) that the lengthening was the result of phonologisation of coarticulatory lengthening. One could speculate that the presence of a nasal + voiced stop would trigger allophonic lengthening before all vowels, but because of the intrinsic shorter duration of the high vowels, it was only the 'longer' [i] and [u] that were reanalysed as 'long', while the lengthening remained allophonic with the mid and the low vowels. Another possible direction of inquiry could be to look further into the nature of the nasal: as shown in Lavoie (2009: 35), the intensity of /n/ in the neighbourhood of a reference /i/ vowel is actually greater than that of the vowel, and the intensity could be perceived as length. Since the coarticulatory effects of nasals are language-specific (Cohn 1993), however, these hypotheses are not testable. The oddity of pre-*nd* lengthening in OE remains to be accounted for.

Summing up: the shared environment for OE Homorganic Cluster Lengthening is a tautosyllabic sonorant followed by a voiced homorganic stop. It is a more restricted version of a broader process of glide insertion and lengthening before sonorants, singly or followed by obstruents, that recurs in some varieties of later English, with or without sonorant loss, as in *art*, *cord*, *first*, *curse*, *false*, *bolt*, *boulder*, *aunt*, *chance* (see Chapter 8).[21] Taken by itself, however, OE Homorganic Cluster Lengthening is hardly a unified process. The scope, the targets and the mechanisms of implementation of the OE changes are highly specific, and it is only in the most general sense that we can classify them as being different manifestations of the same process, where the presence of a sonorant increases the probability of a glide transition,

[21] Broadening further the chronological range of lengthening before nasal + obstruent will include the pre-OE lengthening contingent upon loss of nasals before spirants, thus PrG **gans-* > OE *gōs* 'goose', PrG **fimfi* > OE *fīf* 'five', PrG **munþaz* > OE *mūð* 'mouth'.

misperceived as a portion of the vowel, leading to reanalysis of the vowel as long.

6.4.1 Are pre-cluster lengthenings prosodically incongruous?

Another aspect of the OE pre-cluster lengthenings has to do with the overall prosodic shape of stressed syllables in the history of English. Translated into units of prosodic weight, where a short vowel has one mora (μ), and a long vowel or a diphthong has two moras (μμ), the *minimal* major-class word in OE was bimoraic (see 3.4.4). OE -VC syllables are bimoraic too; the coda consonant in OE can be shown to add to the way the syllable weight is computed in verse (see 9.3.2). This does not tell us what the *upper* weight limit of a stressed syllable in OE was, and indeed OE stressed syllables could be light, heavy and superheavy.

Counting the first consonant in the coda as a mora, superheavy syllables are syllables with long or diphthongal nuclei and a filled coda: OE *ēast* 'east', *āc* 'oak', *þīeft* 'theft', *ūt* 'out', *fȳlþ* 'filth', *prēost* 'priest' can be analysed as tri-moraic and superheavy. The superheavy grade can be recognised in various quantitative processes in ME (see 7.5.1), leading to the long-term vision of regularisation of syllable weight by elimination of superheavy syllables (Luick 1898; Lass 1992a: 70–83). For early OE, however, the upper limit of weight of the stressed syllable was not regulated: there is no evidence that -VC, -VCC, -VV, -VVC and even -VVCC syllables were functionally different, though they clearly represent a continuum of 'heavyness', with VVCC being longest/heaviest. We know that all five types jointly were strongly favoured in the stressed syllables of OE: for disyllabic words Getty (2002: 213–14) reports 17.8 per cent of light stressed syllables; the other 82.2 per cent are heavy syllables, though the counts do not differentiate the heavies further. The universal bias towards co-occurrence of weight and stress was thus in evidence already in OE, yet that does not tell us how much weight is 'good' weight. Criteria such as the weight of a minimal word, or the overall ratio of lights to heavies in stressed syllables are uninformative with respect to the difference between -VC, -VCC, -VV, -VVC and -VVCC.

All OE pre-cluster lengthenings generate forms that are 'superheavy', or at least heavier than the input -VR([C])- or -VRC syllables, where R = sonorant. The lengthened syllables are -VVR([C]) ([**biːn**[**d**]an]) or -VVRC ([**biːnd**]). Since other VVC([C]) and -VVCC syllables undergo shortening to VC([C]) and -VCC (see 7.5.1), one unexplored line of inquiry would be to see whether the homorganic lengthening clusters -RC- contribute an intermediate degree of weight between that of a singleton coda and an obstruent-initial coda cluster. Put differently, the question is whether the make-up and cohesion of *-ld*, *-nd*, *-mb* renders them 'lighter' than other -CC clusters, bringing the weight of the lengthened syllables closer to the very common -VVC stressed syllable shape. The commonness of the -VVC shape can then be taken as motivating shortenings in -VVCC(C) syllables or lengthenings in -VC syllables, unifying all of the major quantitative changes in late OE and ME. 💻

The hypothesis of unidirectional prosodic weight adjustments first formulated by Luick (1898) treats all shortenings and lengthenings in terms of an 'optimal' bimoraic syllable. In that context, the -VVCC outputs of OE Homorganic Cluster Lengthening are anomalous and require special explanations. Lass (1992a: 75) labelled pre-cluster lengthening a quantitative 'misfit', and is content to leave it out of the 'conspiratorial' picture of goal-oriented quantitative changes. Within a theory of phonologically gradient weight, most recently explored by Gordon (2006) and Ryan (2011a), the weight difference between -V, -VC, -VVC and -VCC becomes a matter of phonetically testable degree, not an abstract numerical correspondence between a segment and a mora. The cut-off between heavy and light syllables can be different for different phonological processes, and it is also language-specific. Within the theory of gradient phonological weight we should also reconsider the proposal (Phillips 1983) that there was a discontinuity in the application of the 'optimal syllable' principle between early OE, when it was ignored, and late OE and ME, when it was respected. As we will see in Chapter 8, the ideal of a bimoric syllable continued to be ignored in early Modern English. The question in the title of this section, 'Are pre-cluster shortenings prosodically incongruous?', should therefore be answered in the negative.

6.5 The late OE vowel inventory in detail

In preparation for the discussion of later developments, the final sections of this chapter provide more details on the OE vowel system at the end of the eleventh century.

6.5.1 The short vowels in late OE

Figure 6.7 reproduces the short-vowel portion of the overview of the OE vowel system in Figure 6.2.

		Short vowels			
		Front		*Central*	*Back*
		Unround	*Round*		
High	*Upper*				
	Lower	ɪ	ʏ	ə	ʊ
Mid	*Upper*				
	Lower	ɛ			ɔ
Low		æ		ɑ	

Figure 6.7 The short vowels of late Old English

Except for [ə], to which we return in 6.5.4, the vowels in Figure 6.7 appeared in stressed position. Some typical forms illustrating them are shown in (8).

(8) Examples of OE words with short stressed vowels:

Front unround	**Front round**	**Back**
s**i**ftan [sɪftən] 'to sift'	f**y**llan [fʏllən] 'to fill'	l**u**fu [lʊvə] 'love'
s**e**ttan [sɛttən] 'to set'		g**o**d [gɔd] 'God'
bl**æ**c [blæk] 'black'		c**a**tt(e) [kɑtt(ə)] 'cat'

From a PDE perspective, the front unround and the back short vowels are straightforward: their realisations are identical or close to familiar PDE vowels. Of note is that for the high and mid short-vowel inputs to I-Mutation and pre-cluster lengthening in Figure 6.5, and in (5)–(7), we used the same symbols as the long vowels: [-ild] > ME [-iːld] as in *ċild* 'child'; [-eld] > [-eːld] as in *feld* 'field'; [-und] > [-uːnd] as in *grund* 'ground', that is, they are treated as qualitatively identical, differing only in duration. The rationale for that is that the vowels lengthened in early OE merged with pre-existing long vowels at the same height.

The use of the high and mid non-peripheral vowel symbols [ɪ, ʊ, ɛ, ɔ] in Figure 6.7 assumes a qualitative difference from the corresponding long vowels, implying lowering and centralisation of the short vowels between early and late OE. Positing a qualitative shift of the high and mid vowels is defensible on the grounds of later quantitative processes, whereby lengthened [ɪ, ʊ, ɛ, ɔ] merged with long vowels at a lower height: so that [ɪ] > [eː] as in OE *wicu*, ME *wēk(e)* 'week'; [ʊ] > [oː] as in OE *duru* > ME *dōr(e)* 'door', and so on (see 7.5.2). In addition, ON /ɛ/ is identified with OE and ME [ɛ] and is consistently found as <e> in ME spelling.[22] The exact date of the lowering cannot be established, and some unresolved questions remain, yet it is reasonable to accept, with Hogg (1992a: 199–202), that late OE West Saxon had non-peripheral, or 'lax' high and mid short vowels.

The high front rounded [ʏ], as in *fyllan*, which was most commonly the result of I-Mutation of /u/ (see 6.3), is the only OE short vowel which does not survive contrastively in SSBE and AmE.[23] Initially a fronted allophone of the high back vowel spelled <u>, it had become phonologised in all dialects of OE by the mid ninth century (Lass 1992b: 103). The loss of the I-Mutation trigger in the paradigms shown in (2)–(4) makes the new sound an exponent of morphological alternations. Phonetically [ʏ] must have been perceived as being much closer to the unrounded [ɪ] of late West Saxon than to the original back vowel: the spelling records show <i> and <y> used interchangeably (<dyne ~ dine> 'din' (PrG **dunjan*), <*dysiġ* ~ *disiġ*> 'foolish, dizzy'), while there are no records of 'confusion' between <u> and <y>. By the end of OE, [ʏ] was treated differently in the different dialect areas: it merged with [ɪ] in the East Midlands and the Northern dialects, it was lowered to [e]/[ɛ] in Kentish, and the rounded realisation became characteristic of the West Midlands (see 7.3.1).

6.5.2 *The long vowels in late OE:* STREET-STRATFORD

Except for the front rounded [yː], the values of the long vowels in OE are also familiar sounds. Unlike the short stressed vowels in Figure 6.7, however, which have been more resistant to qualitative changes, not a single OE long vowel survives in PDE with all of its original features. Figure 6.8 shows the long-vowel portion of the OE vowel survey of Figure 6.2.

Rounding is shown only for the front vowels. The origin of the high front rounded [yː] parallels that of [ʏ] – it is most frequently the result of I-Mutation. As we will see in 7.3.1, the subsequent history of the two vowels is also parallel. All back vowels are round. Keeping the editorial macrons over the long vowel-letters, (9) shows examples of words with long stressed vowels in late OE.

[22] Dance (2003: 117, 122).

[23] This is a simplification. For other sources of the high front rounded vowel see Hogg (1992a: 167–70). SSE has a front rounded vowel for the vowels of GOOSE and FOOT.

		Long vowels		
		Front		*Back*
		Unround	*Round*	
High	*Upper*	iː	yː	uː
	Lower			
Mid	*Upper*	eː		oː
	Lower			
Low		æː		ɒː

Figure 6.8 The long vowels of late Old English

(9) Examples of OE words with long stressed vowels:

Front unround	**Front round**	**Back**
mīn [miːn] 'mine'	mȳs [myːs] 'mice'	nū [nuː] 'now'
dēma [deːmə] 'judge'		dōm [doːm] 'doom'
mǣl [mæːl] 'meal'		hāliġ [hɒːli] 'holy'

Some information on the sources and the allophones of the low vowels will help us link the spelling and the etymology of otherwise puzzling ME and PDE forms. In pre-OE, West Germanic /aː/ – using <a> as a generic symbol for a low non-front vowel – was raised and fronted to [æː], for example **slāp-* > OE *slǣp* 'sleep'. The raising was paralleled by short /a/ > /æ/ (see 6.2); in both instances the low front vowel is a new addition to the pre-OE vowel inventory. The most notable aspect of the fronting was that in Anglian the fronted /æː/ was raised further to /eː/, so we get WS <ǣ> - Angl. <ē>, a difference not just in spelling but in vowel height: WS *slǣp* - Angl. *slēp* 'sleep', WS *dǣd* - Angl. *dēd* 'deed', WS *sǣd* - Angl. *sēd* 'seed'. The split survived in ME. This is relevant to the history of the pair *STREET-STRATFORD*: Lat. *strāta*, an early loanword, is recorded as *strǣt* in West Saxon, *strēt* in Anglian. When shortened (see 7.5.1), [æː] became [æ] ~ [a], while [eː] became [ɛː] (see 7.3.2); the OE compound *Strǣtford* became *Stratford*, but compare *Stretham* (Cambridgeshire). The spelling <ee> for PDE *street* goes back to the Anglian form with [eː].

The OE dialect split in the treatment of pre-OE /aː/ has a long-term effect on its orthographic representation in PDE. There was no necessary continuity between WS and ME, and the incipient late ME standard inherited mostly the Anglian forms with the upper mid front [eː]. After the two long mid front vowels of ME, [ɛː] and [eː], began to be differentiated in spelling, <ea> for [ɛː] and <ee> for [eː], the system ended up representing identical etymological entities with either <ee> or <ea>, depending on whether the spelling was based on the continuation of the WS or the Anglian form.

The fronting of /a/ was prevented by a following nasal: WG /-aːn/ in OE appears to have retained its backness, that is, we can posit an intermediate stage [ɒ̃ː], which subsequently merged with pre-existing /oː/, thus Gmc **mān-* > OE *mōna* 'moon', Gmc **sān-* > OE *sōna* 'soon'.[24] Coarticulation with a following labial approximant [-w] also blocks the fronting, so that WG *-āw-* can be reconstructed as a low rounded [ɒː], thus Gmc **blā-* > OE *blāwan* 'blow'. These developments are summarised in (10).

(10) Germanic /a:/ in OE and ME:

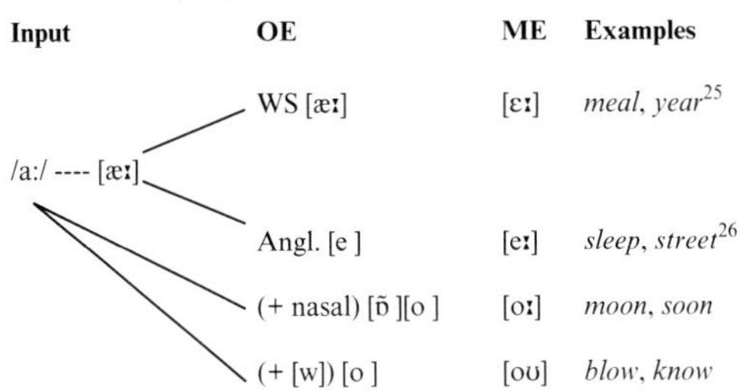

The Long Vowel Shift (see 8.2.2) obscured the differences between the West Saxon and the Anglian forms for the standard varieties, but the dialectal split shown in (10) is of considerable etymological and orthographic interest nevertheless. It is also a major test for the identification of dialect features of ME texts.

As (10) indicates, Germanic /aː/ did not survive in late OE, which raises the question of the source of the low back vowel [ɒː] in our inventory in Figure 6.8. That vowel results from monophthongisation of the West Germanic diphthong /ai/, held to have occurred after the fronting of /aː/ to /æː/. Examples of this process are Gmc **stain-*, **haim-*, **aigan-* > OE *stān* 'stone', *hām* 'home', *āgan* 'own' (see the first row in (11) below). The presence of the high front /-i/ in the WG diphthong suggests that initially the monophthongal long vowel would have been more central than [ɒː], but since the next step in the history of that

[24] Regressive nasalisation can cause either raising or lowering depending on the height and backness of the vowel. Low back vowels are typically subject to raising (see Beddor et al. 1986).

[25] Compare German *Mal/Mahl*, *Jahr*.

[26] Compare German *schlafen*, Lat. *strata*.

vowel in the southern dialects of ME shows definitely a back rounded vowel, reconstructed as [ɔː], we can posit [ɒː] in late OE.

6.5.3 Diphthongs and diphthongoids

The correlation between orthographic representation and reconstructed values for the OE diphthongal nuclei is one of the most controversial topics in the study of English historical phonology.[27] This is unsurprising in view of the instability of complex nuclei in general, the difficulty of perceiving and representing the transitions of the stressed part of the nucleus to the syllable coda, and not least, the confounding variability of digraph spellings found in the OE dialects. The effect of I-Mutation on diphthongs complicates the system further (see Figure 6.6). Agreement exists, however, that OE inherited a set of diphthongs from pre-settlement Germanic. Focusing just on late West Saxon, (11) shows the West Germanic diphthongs and their OE counterparts.

(11) West Germanic diphthongs in OE:

WG	**Late WS**	**Examples**
/ai/	[ɒː]	*hām* 'home'
/au/	[æə]	*strēam* 'stream'
/eu/	[eə]	*þēof* 'thief'
/iu/	[iə]	*ġe-līefan* 'believe'

Since WG /ai/ was monophthongised (see 6.5.2), late WS [æə], [eə], [iə] are the core inherited diphthongs. They are not 'long diphthongs' (though that is their traditional name), just simply diphthongs. The reconstruction shown in (11) assumes evolution of an original high back glide to, most probably, a schwa-like glide. The plausibility of the values [æə], [eə], [iə] is based on their later pronunciation: they merged with the corresponding long vowels [æː, eː, iː]. Indeed, the diphthongal nature of the reflexes of WG /au/, /eu/ in early OE is clear, but variation between [æə] ~ [æː] and [eə]~[eː] must have come into existence during OE, because <æ> ~ <e> spellings for [æə] as in <stræm>, <strem> 'stream', and <e> for [eə] as in <tre> for more common *trēo* 'tree' are documented in late OE.

By virtue of their compositionality, diphthongs can be *falling*, when the first element is more prominent, as in PDE [aɪ], [aʊ], or they can

[27] The controversy goes back to at least the first half of the twentieth century, and it continues today. Good surveys of the earlier literature are found in Wełna (1978: 21–7); Wełna (1987: 44–56); Hogg (1992a: 16–24); Lass (1994); White (2004).

be *rising*, when the 'stressed' part is in second position, as in [jɑː]. The compositionality of the unit allows a shift of the prominence within the two elements of a diphthong, a switch known by its German name *Akzentumsprung*. In some OE words the second element of <ēo>became more prominent at the expense of the first element; the switch was triggered by the properties of adjacent consonants. More specifically, palatal onsets palatalised and absorbed the first element, which presumably passed through an intermediate stage of being a palatal glide, while the second element remained a bimoraic monophthong: OE *sċēotan* > ME *shōte(n)* 'to shoot'. A following /-w/ could also result in shift of the prominence onto the second element, thus OE *fēower* > ME *four(e)* 'four', OE *trēowþ* > ME *trowþe* 'troth'.

At least two other falling diphthongs belong to the diphthongal set of late OE (see Figure 6.1). The diphthongs in question are [æj] as in *dæġ* 'day', whose uninflected form is also spelled <dæig, deig, daig, deih, dæi, dei, dai> (DOE), and [ej] as in Angl. *grēġ* 'grey', also spelled <greig, grei> (DOE). The glide [-j] in these diphthongs was originally a palatalised allophone of the voiced velar consonant representing PrG /ɣ/ (see 4.2.1). The difference between the inherited diphthongs and the ones arising by glide vocalisation in OE is that the [æj], [ej] preserve their diphthongal character much longer, most likely due to the more perceptually distinctive end point [j].

The formation of [æj], [ej] presupposes that the vowel and the glide are in the same syllable; it is therefore logical to expect that diphthongisation would be delayed in forms realised predominantly as disyllables. This is one of the reasons why these diphthongs are generally treated under the rubric of 'New ME diphthongs' (Lass 1992a: 49–53) – the loss of the final unstressed vowel in many forms in ME increases the incidence of tautosyllabic vowel + palatal glide. Another reason why these diphthongs are chronologically (dis)placed in ME is that contextual diphthongisation due to the emergence and vocalisation of post-vocalic glides is broader in the transitional period and in ME, involving not just the original palatal [j], but also the voiced velar fricative [ɣ] (see 4.2.1), the labial approximant [w] and the different realisations of the voiceless fricative /h/ (see 5.1.4). Another reason to postpone the discussion of a significantly enriched diphthongal system is loan phonology: Old Norse had a set of [-j, -w] diphthongs, but the ON phonological influence is not clearly traceable before early ME (Dance 2003). In addition to the ON influence, ME borrowed /oi/ and /ui/ from Anglo-Norman. We will revisit these new and not so new diphthongs in 7.4.

One final comment on the OE contextual diphthongs: vocalisation of the glide obscures the etymological length of the original vowel; whether the input was a short vowel, as in *dæġ* 'day', Gmc **dag-*, or a long vowel, as in *grēġ* 'grey', Gmc **grǣ-*, the result is a falling diphthong of the same type as the inherited [æə], [eə], [iə]. The neutralisation of the original vowel length in favour of simply 'a diphthong' is an argument against positing a fully developed system of diphthongs contrasting in length in OE: had there been a pattern of well-integrated monomoric diphthongs (see below) vs bimoric diphthongs (all of the inherited diphthongs), it is hard to explain why the length distinction of the input would not be maintained in [-j, -w] diphthongs.

This last point takes us to one of the greatest uncertainties in reconstructing the OE vowel system: the interpretation of the digraphs <ea>, <eo>, <ie> representing historical short vowels as in <earm> 'arm', <geolo> 'yellow', <seolh> 'seal', <hliehhan> 'laugh'.[28] The digraphs, which are appealingly similar to the digraphs for the inherited diphthongs in (11), show up before coda /-h/, coda liquids, heterosyllabic back vowels and in identifiable palatal contexts. The spellings <ea>, <eo>, <ie> are commonly taken as representing innovative monomoric *phonemic* short diphthongs /e͝a/, /e͝o/, /i͝e/ specific to OE. However, the reconstruction of underlyingly contrastive short diphthongs faces a series of objections.

First, typological comparison calls in question an analysis of coexisting mono- and bimoric diphthongs which are otherwise identical. In addition to the general paucity of languages with contrastive long and short diphthongs, phonemic short diphthongs would make OE unique within its own language family. No other Germanic language, past or present, has contrastive long and short diphthongs that do not differ in some other feature. Another objection, based on the OE system of contrasts, was mentioned above: if diphthongal length was contrastive elsewhere in the system, there is no reason why the etymological length in [ej] as in OE *hēġ* 'hay', also spelled <heig>, and (presumably) [e͝j] as in OE *weġ* 'way' < Gmc **weg-*, should not have been preserved as /eːj/ in *hay* and /e͝j/in *way*, in conformity with the hypothesised length contrast /ea/ and/e͝a/, /eo/ and /e͝o/.

The third, and probably the most damaging argument against the phonemic status of /e͝a/, /e͝o/, /i͝e/, comes from subsequent history: in late OE and ME these 'short' diphthongs merged with short monophthongal counterparts: <ea> merges with <æ>, and <eo> merges with <e͝o, e, o, ue>, the latter representing [œ/ø] ~ [e] (see 6.5.1). Ignoring /i͝e/ because of scribal instability (see Figure 6.6), (12) shows some

[28] This section follows the arguments in Minkova (2013).

characteristic examples of the orthographic mergers in late OE–early ME.

(12) Merger of <ea>, <eo> with short vowels:

OE	**Early ME (based on LAEME)**
mearc; *æppel*	*mark(e)*, 'mark'; *appel* 'apple'
healf; *bæþ*	*half(e)*, *halue* 'half'; *bað*, *bath* 'bath'
deorc; *berie*	*derk(e)*, 'dark'; *berie* 'berry'
ġeolu; *elles*	*yelewe*, *geleu*, *geluwe* 'yellow'; *elles* 'else'

Finally, the evidence from actual minimal pairs is quite limited and open to alternative accounts. Frequently cited minimal pairs are unconvincing: the orthographic distinction between *bearn* 'child' vs *bær* 'bore,' p.t. sg., is not necessarily interpretable as [-e͡ar-]: [-ær] because the form *bær* could be influenced by the past plural form *bǣron* [bæːr-], and by the related form *-bǣre* as in *leohtbǣre* 'light-bearing, luminous', *lustbǣre* 'joy-bearing'. We also find the spellings <barn>, <bærn> for 'child'. Another pair, *ærn* 'house' vs *earn* 'eagle' (Smith 2009: 56–7), is dubious because the spellings <earn> for 'house' and <ærn> for 'eagle' are firmly in evidence; they could have been homophones.

The strongest defence of the phonemic status of /e͡a/, /e͡o/ is consistency of spelling, but this does not apply to all dialects. The digraph spellings are fairly uniform in the 'focused' variety of late West Saxon OE, where some orthographic homogeneity can be attributed to the strong normative tendencies characteristic of the Winchester school and the stability of the Ælfrician texts. Scribal codification notwithstanding, it appears that since the diphthongal spellings occur in well-defined phonetic environments, it makes good sense to treat them as representing allophones of the respective non-diphthongal vowels with which they later merge.

The 'digraph controversy', one of the most 'complex and acrimonious debates in the history of OE scholarship' (Lass 1994: 45), was conducted in terms of a theory of phonology that separates phonemes from allophones categorically. Current phonological theory recognises that segmental inventories are comprised of units that can range from fully contrastive to fully allophonic, with intermediate stages (Goldsmith 1995: 12). In principle, the OE situation parallels the gradience illustrated by the tensing of [æ] to [eːᵊ] in AE. The process is gradual in some northern dialect areas, categorical in the Mid-Atlantic cities, and lexically idiosyncratic before /d/ in Philadelphia.[29] Seen in the context of scalar contrastiveness, the OE short digraphs never stood for

[29] The three words that have the tense vowel in Philadelphia are *bad*, *mad* and *glad*. See

stable and fully phonemic entities. The realisations /ĕa/, /ĕo/ or, more likely phonetically [εᵊ], [eᵊ], are best analysed as 'not-yet-integrated semi-contrasts', a status half-way between a phoneme and an allophone (Goldsmith 1995: 12).[30] From the point of view of the subsequent history of the sounds spelled with the digraphs <ea>, <eo>, <ie>, then, calling them 'diphthongs' is justified only for the vowels marked here (but not in the manuscripts) with the macron diacritic.

6.5.4 Unstressed vowels

So far our survey has focused on vowels in stressed position; it is only in prosodically prominent syllables that one expects to find the full set of vowels shown in the inventory in 6.2. Under stress, phonetically associated with the degree of loudness, length and pitch in the pronunciation of a syllable, the vowels are most likely to be realised with their full set of features. Phonologically, stress plays a decisive role in the maintenance and survival of contrasts. Stress is perceived in relation to adjacent syllables: we identify [-d͡ʒeɪ-] in *a.dja.cent* and [sɪ-] in *sy.lla.ble* as *more* prominent than the neighbouring syllables. In non-monosyllabic words one syllable carries the primary stress; other syllables may have *reduced* stress, or they can be completely unstressed. The lower the degree of stress in a syllable, the more likely it is that the nuclear vowel will lose some of its characteristics, resulting in *vowel reduction*.

Recall from 3.4.3 that the system of free pitch accent characterising Proto-Indo-European was replaced in Germanic by stress on the first syllable of the word root. The entailment of prominence fixed on the first root syllable is that the vowels in inflectional syllables, post-tonic root syllables and commonly in affixes (see 9.4.2), were pronounced less forcefully. This leads to a series of vowel reductions in unstressed position in all Germanic languages. The details in the branches of Germanic differ, but taking Gothic as a model, all final vowels lost a mora: monomoric vowels except **u* were lost, long vowels were shortened and overlong vowels became long/bimoric (Ringe 2006: 75).

Further, reduced force in the pronunciation of vowels in unstressed syllables in Germanic led to the elimination of length distinctions.

Thomas (2001: 19–23) for further details on the split, which he describes as 'not truly phonemic in the traditional sense'.

30 The schwa glide is a short cut. The reconstruction of a rounded glide allophonically induced by the following consonant, with the degree of rounding variable depending on the height of the vowel is convincingly presented in Stockwell (2002a).

Some of the original short vowels were lost, and all long vowels were shortened. The reconstruction of the set of unstressed vowels in early OE (Campbell 1959: §§369, 371; Reszkiewicz 1973: 89–99; Hogg 1992b: 119–22) shows only four vowels in the so-called 'little' vocalic system.

(13) The unstressed vowels of early OE (pre-c. 700):

Front	Example	Back	Example
/i/	*cyning* 'king'	/u/	*duru* 'door'
/æ/	*endæþ* 'ends'	/ɑ/	*nefa* 'nephew'

A general lowering of /i/ to /e/ (or possibly /ɪ/ to /ɛ/) in all unstressed syllables – except in the derivational suffixes *-iġ*, *-isc*, *-ing*, which were heavy syllables and were possibly carrying a degree of stress – created an unstable three-way contrast in the front set: /i/ - /e/ - /æ/. As Crosswhite (2004) has shown, vowel reduction is not a unitary phenomenon and it can be driven by different factors. The scale of reduction may be related to accentual prominence, syllable weight and to vowel sonority. One way in which lack of prosodic prominence affects vowels is loss of sonority; in the case of the early OE unstressed /e/ and /æ/ this resulted in merger of these two front vowels into a single mid vowel represented by <e>. The next stage in the elimination of front vowel contrasts is their convergence into the low-sonority /ə/.

As for the back vowels, /u/, when followed by a consonant, tended to be lowered to /o/ unless the following consonant was a labial, as in the dat. pl. inflection *-um*: *stānum* 'stones', *heofenum* 'heavens'. The merger of the back vowels, like the earlier lowering of fully unstressed /i/ to /e/, may be attributed to the phonetic phenomenon of 'undershoot', 'a situation in which a given speech sound is articulated in a manner that does not fully instantiate the canonical realization of that sound' (Crosswhite 2004: 216). The articulation time for the high vowels is short, which can prove insufficient for the full realisation of the sound. From the point of view of perception, too, the lowering of /i/ and /u/ in unstressed position can be related to the nature of the vowels: high vowels are shorter than low vowels; the quality of the shorter vowels would be harder to perceive.

Still, in early OE the unstressed vowels maintained *some* distinctive qualities, and one can assume that vowel-letters in unstressed syllables represent syllabic peaks. Starting in the ninth century, and definitely by the end of the OE period, however, there is ample evidence that the contrasts in unstressed final syllables were obscured. Thus late OE–early ME orthographic records indicate that most unstressed vowels were subject to blurring and confounding of phonetic contrasts. Phonologically, this means that the vowels were losing distinctive height and backness feature specifications, merging into a single schwa /ə/, using /ə/ as an umbrella identification consistent with a wide range of articulations in a wide range of contexts. The diagnostic of vowel reduction is the replacement of earlier vowel-letters by <-e>. Such replacements occurred both in the unstressed syllables of monomorphemic words and in inflections. Some examples are <*nosu*> ~ <*nose*> 'nose', <*nama*> ~ <*name*> 'name', <*fana*> ~ <*fane*> ~ <*fanu*> 'vane', <*heofon*> ~ <*heofen*> 'heaven', <*biscop*> ~ <*biscep*> 'bishop', <*lufian*> ~ <*lufien*> 'to love', which were probably pronounced with a type of /ə/-compatible vowel in the second syllable. Such variant spellings are found in pre-Conquest documents, in spite of the conservative nature of late OE orthography and the expected time lag between sound change and its written representation. Indeed, scribal evidence for vowel reduction is found in literary manuscripts as early as the second half of the tenth century, prompting a reconsideration of the dating of the OE to ME transition period: 'The transition period from Old to Middle English is not the twelfth century, as the grammarians used to think, nor even the eleventh, as most of them think today, but rather the tenth' (Malone 1930: 117).

Not all contexts were equally conducive to reduction. Inflectional suffixes are more prone to reduction and even syncopation. Initially syncope was prosodically conditioned by the presence of a stressed heavy syllable, but by the end of OE syncopation of inflectional unstressed vowels was more general. This is particularly noticeable in the 2nd and 3rd pers. sg. present indicative of both strong and weak verbs, where dropping the <-e-> in the inflections *-(e)s(t)* and *-(e)þ* was the dominant pattern in West Saxon texts. There is also frequent confusion in the paradigm of originally monosyllabic stems ending in a sonorant, as in *wǣpn* ~ *wǣpen* 'weapon', in originally disyllabic stems such as *engel* ~ *englum* 'angel', and even syncope of internal vowels in derivatives as in *dyslic* ~ *dysiglic* 'dizzy', *eft-selenes* ~ *eft-selnes* 'reward'.

Heavy derivational -VC(C) syllables appear to preserve the quality of the unstressed vowel distinct into early ME: the suffixes in, for example, *(ge)bēorscipe* 'beership', *brosnung* 'corruption', *dǣdliċ* 'deed-ly, active', *manig* 'many' do not show orthographic variation of the vowels. A difference should be made between the pre-tonic and post-tonic vowels. An unstressed initial syllable in OE was prefixal by default, but only the light prefixes: *be-*, *ge-*, *a-*, uniformly unstressed in the lexicon, can be treated as fully reduced, for example <*be-*> ~ <*bi-*>, <*ge-*> ~

<*gi-*>. Other prefixes, such as *un-*, *mis-*, *wiþ-*, which had reduced stress only in verbs and adverbs, preserve their spelling unchanged.[31]

The next instalment in the history of final vowels in English is 7.4, where we look at the details and the profound phonological and orthographic consequences of the reduction and ultimate loss of unstressed vowels. As this section has shown, however, the amalgamation of vowel characteristics in many unstressed contexts was a necessary first step in the later process of schwa loss. In addition to the scribal testimony that fully unstressed vowels were similar, there is also a strong probability that in faster and more relaxed speech final schwas were ignored. Some lexical items have doublet uninflected forms with or without a final vowel: *adela* ~ *adele* ~ *adel* 'filth', *(a)dun* ~ *(a)dune* ~ *(a)duna* 'downward', *bæc* ~ *bece* 'stream', *cat* ~ *catte* 'cat', *cǣġ* ~ *cǣġe* 'key', *drync* ~ *drynca* 'drink', *eall-rihte* ~ *eall-riht* 'exactly', *earc* ~ *arc* ~ *earce* ~ *arce* ~ *earca* ~ *arca* 'ark', *ēare* ~ *ēar* 'ear', *fǣhþ* ~ *fǣhþu* 'hostility'. Though tentative, there is some evidence from verse suggesting that inflectional final vowels could be elided before another vowel, as in *Beowulf* 1997b *Gode ic ðanc secge* 'to God I thanks say', a verse which would be a vanishingly rare type if the sequence *gode is* ... is scanned as trisyllabic. It is also the case that the final vowel of the first elements of compounds, generally held to be stable until ME, is in fact missing in many OE compounds; thus we find *cēap-mann* ~ *cȳpe-mann* 'merchant', *dūne-stīgan* ~ *dūn-stīgan* 'descend', *dyrn-licgan* ~ *dyrne-licgan* 'commit adultery' (DOE). There can be no doubt that the roots of the pervasive ME schwa loss are in evidence in OE. Therefore, if we associate the 'middle' period in the history of English by levelling of the vowels in final unstressed syllables, which existed already in the second half of the tenth century, and their incipient loss, 'the beginning of the Middle English period ... must be put at A. D. 1000 or thereabouts' (Malone 1930: 110).

[31] The patterns of prefixal stress in OE are discussed in Minkova (2008a).

7 The vowels in Middle English. Dialects. Spelling innovations. Vowel quality and quantity. PDE alternations traced back to ME

DIZZY-BUSY, FURY-BURY, MOON-MONDAY, STEAL-STEALTH, GAME-GAMMON, GRASS-GRAZE

7.1 ME dialects

Linguistic change is continuous and uneven, and putting an exact date to an innovative pronunciation or a variant grammatical form is impossible. The beginning of the 'middle' period in the history of the English language is a stretchy notion (see 1.3, 6.5.4). Bearing in mind that the entire eleventh century is 'transitional', we still talk of pre- and post-Conquest English, taking a major historical event, the Norman Conquest of 1066, as the symbolic start of the 'middle' period.

The reference variety that we used in describing the phonology of late OE was based on clusters of texts reflecting the scribal traditions in major monastic centres at the end of the first millennium. While there was no 'standard' OE, there was at least a template of accepted and codified forms, a 'focused' variety, commonly referred to as Ælfrician English, which could serve as a model for other scribes and authors. Geographically, that variety of OE is associated primarily with Winchester. Turning to ME, we find that the input to what will eventually be recognised as Southern Standard British English (SSBE) is rooted in forms characteristic of documents produced in the Midlands and East Anglia towards the end of ME (Samuels 1963). The discontinuity is even more striking if we add that the documents identified as Mercian in OE, one potential ancestor of ME Midlands and East Anglian varieties, come from Worcestershire and Warwickshire, and are thus essentially West Midlands in origin. This leaves us in the dark about the provenance of Standard English – all we can say is that it is *not* based on any particular variety of OE.[1]

This perplexing labyrinth of dialectal tracks is unsurprising in view of the historical and linguistic context. The Norman Conquest led to

[1] This is a summary of the fully argued agnostic conclusions in Hogg (2006b) and Laing and Lass (2006).

new administrative and cultural practices: the use of the vernacular for legal records was replaced by Latin and to some extent French, though some copying of texts in the late OE-focused model continued for about a century. There is virtually no surviving original writing in English for several generations after the Conquest. The second continuation of *The Peterborough Chronicle* (1154/5) is considered the first document in 'truly Middle English language – that is, language that reflects how the spoken language of this region had developed in the preceding century' (Laing and Lass 2006: 419). When the metaphorical curtain on English is lifted in the second half of the twelfth and the early thirteenth century, the records are very patchy: the majority of the extant texts are from the West Midlands, the East Midlands, and the Southeast. For early ME, the period covered by LAEME (c. 1150–c. 1325), there are large geographical areas for which the information is either lacking or very sparse: almost nothing from the North or the North Midlands, from the Central Midlands or from the extreme South-West. It is this patchiness and discontinuity that makes the designation 'Middle English' even more of an agglomeration than 'Old' or 'Early Modern' English: Middle English is a convenient composite of a range of unevenly documented dialects, often remarkably unlike each other. The textual coverage after the middle of the fourteenth century is fuller, but even LALME (c. 1350–c. 1450) is thin on more northern sources. A special problem is presented by multilingual/mixed-language texts, where there is code-switching between English, Latin and French (Schendl 2002). There is also the complication of multiple copies of lost originals, where the language of the manuscript may show a mixture of authorial forms, forms native to the copyist and forms reflecting the standard(s) that the scribe was following.

Interesting as the detective work in this historical area is, it is not our remit in this book, so we will take a very general view of the periodisation and varieties of Middle English. We will follow the traditional chronological designations of 'early' and 'late' ME, and as for dialect areas, we will refer to the divisions in the map in Figure 7.1: Lowland Scots, Northern, West Midland, East Midland, South-Western and South-Eastern.

Put crudely, then, the linguistic situation in post-Conquest England can be characterised with reference to a shift from records primarily in English, to records in Latin and Anglo-Norman, the suppression and subsequent re-emergence of English as a language used in the production of literary and administrative documents, and the fragmentisation of English into dialects, followed by incipient formation of a national written standard in the fifteenth century.

Figure 7.1 Schematic map of the dialects of Middle English, Figure 4.4 in Horobin and Smith (2002: 51), *An Introduction to Middle English*, Edinburgh University Press

7.2 Notes on ME spelling (vowels): *<TAXI>-<ATAXY>*, *<TYRE>-<TIRE>*, *<COME>-<CUT>*, *<SEE>-<SEA>*

The reconstruction of sound histories from the surviving ME written records poses a myriad of challenges: scarcity of twelfth- and thirteenth-century records in English, lack of a relatively unified orthographic practice, the scribes' exposure to Latin and French writing, their own uneven command of the three languages, and the fact that in most cases they were copying not just original English compositions but translations and copies made by others. Until at least the middle of the fourteenth century the basic training for the scribes would have been for them to write Latin or French and not in the vernacular.

The expanding use of English in the fourteenth century makes it possible to identify clusters of texts which are less obviously idiosyncratic, and which can serve as the basis for establishing the lineage of the incipient fifteenth-century written standard. Two of these clusters – Type I, Wycliffite texts, mostly stemming from the Central Midland counties, and dating from the mid fourteenth century on, and Type IV, the 'Chancery Standard' used in government documents after c. 1430 – are 'focused' varieties. It is important to bear in mind that there is as yet, and for more than three centuries to come, no 'fixed' standard, but at least by the middle of the fifteenth century ME was a language represented more reliably by scribes trained to follow a more rigid orthographic tradition, in principle not unlike the Ælfrician tradition of late OE.

7.2.1 Letter-to-vowel correspondences in ME (single letters): SUN-SON, CONE-COME

Acknowledging that there is no single stable spelling system that can be taken as a continuation of the late OE system, and that 'middle' English comprises four hundred years of phonological variation and change, one can still draw hypothetical connecting lines between the letter-sound correspondences of ME. Some of the recurrent correspondences between vowel letters and the sounds they represent most commonly in ME are summarised in Figure 7.2.

The values shown in 7.2 are neither static nor exhaustive – the chart only highlights differences between the OE representation of vowels and ME, in order to provide a link to the values of vowel-letters in EModE.

The letters <i> and <y> (and also the digraph <ie>) were used interchangeably already in OE (see 6.5.1), and indeed the choice of <i> or <y> in PDE can still be unstable, as in *tyre* ~ *tire*, especially in names: *Robin* ~ *Robyn*, *Judi* ~ *Judy*, *Cindi* ~ *Cindy*, *Kelli* ~ *Kelly*, *Joni* ~ *Jony*. In spite of the convention to use <y> word-finally – *ataxy*, *namby-pamby* – <i> shows up in clippings and prefixes as in *taxi*, *maxi*, *combi*, *ambi-*. The potential for <i> ~ <y> variability is exploited commercially as in the attention-getting *Citi(bank)*, *Cristal* (champagne), *Infiniti (car)*, *Sereniti (records)*. The phonetic values [ʏ] and [yː], preserved mainly regionally in ME (see 7.3), could also be represented by <y>, <u>, <ui>, <yu>.

The letter <y> shape-shifted with <þ> in ME – this is familiar from

Letter	SHORT		LONG	
	Value	Example	Value	Example
<i> <y>	ɪ	*bin* 'bin' *synn(e)* 'sin'	iː	*rid(en)* 'to ride' *fyr(e)* 'fire'
<e>	ɛ	*sett(en)* 'to set'	eː ɛː	*swet(e)* 'sweet' *del(e)*'deal'
<æ> <a>	æ/a ɑ	*bæð/bað* 'bath' *fall(en)* 'fall'	æː/ɛː ɑː/ɔː	*ræd(en)* 'read' *bat*, *bot(e)*'boat'
<o>	ɔ ʊ	*(i)bor(e)n* 'born' *son(e)* 'son'	oː ɔː	*mon(e)* 'moon' *bot(e)* 'boat'
<u> (<v>)	ʊ	*drunken* 'drunk' *vnder* 'under'	uː	*hus(e)* 'house' *vt(e)* 'out'
	y	*furst* 'time'	yː	*duk(e)* 'duke'

Figure 7.2 Letter-to-stressed-vowel correspondences in ME (single letters)

archaising modern spellings of <the> as <y^{e}> or, more frequently, <ye> as in *Ye Olde King's Head.* On the shape-shifting of <y> ~ <þ> see Laing and Lass (2009), who describe the paleographic basis of the confusion and define the importance of the different scribal practices with respect to <y> ~ <þ> in establishing the regional provenance of texts. The runic *þ* fell into disuse in the fourteenth century though the use of <y> instead of <th> continued in hand-writing into the nineteenth century.

The letter <e> was the most common letter for unstressed vowels, and it was also used for at least three contrasting stressed mid vowels in ME: the front upper mid [eː], the front lower mid short [ɛ] and long [ɛː]. In the fifteenth century and after, historical [eː] and [ɛː] began to be differentiated in spelling, using <ee> for [eː] as in *flee*, *see*, *sweet*, and <ea> for [ɛː] as in *flea*, *sea*, *seat.* The reliability of the <ea>-<ee> spelling as an indicator of etymological [eː] and [ɛː] respectively is much lower if the vowel is followed by /-r/ (see 8.3.2).

The ligature *ash*, <æ>, is preserved only in the earliest documents; by the end of the thirteenth century the scribes were no longer using it. It was replaced by either <a> or <e>. The letter <o> represented three contrasting stressed mid vowels in ME: the back upper mid [oː], the back lower mid short [ɔ] and the corresponding long [ɔː]. As with [eː] and [ɛː], the upper mid [oː] and the lower mid [ɔː] began to be spelled differently in late ME, with [oː] represented by <oo> and [ɔː] represented by <oa>.

The letter <u> continued to be used for [ʊ] and also [uː], though see 7.2.1 for <ou> and <ow> replacing <u> for [uː]. An ME innovation is the addition of <v> to the inventory of letters. It was used both for the consonant /v/ and for the vowels [ʊ] and [uː], usually in word-initial position, as in *vnder* 'under', *vt* 'out'.

Of particular interest because of its effect on the spelling of PDE is the scribes' practice of replacing etymological <u> with <o> when adjacent to <i, u, m, n> within the same word: OE <*sunu*> > ME <*son(e)*> 'son', OE <*cuman*> ME <*com(en)*> 'come', OE <*druncen*>, ME <*dronk(en)*> ~ <*drunk(en)*>, similarly *some, cover, hover, honey, monk, tongue, wonder, worse,* shortened *month, dove, glove.* The substitution was intended to avoid a confusing sequence of downstrokes in the writing of letters with vertical strokes: combinations such as <-um-, -un-> are harder to read than <-om-, -on->. This is a purely visual stratagem: the spelling change does not indicate a shift in the pronunciation of the vowel, so *son, come* have the same PDE vowel as *luck, cut* (see 8.2.1).

Recall from 6.2 that vowel length in OE is not represented in the orthography. This situation began to change in ME. The most famous innovation in this respect was the system introduced by the monk Orm in his extensive verse translation and exegesis of scriptural texts. He devised a system whereby short vowels were marked by doubling of the consonants: *follc* 'folk', *þiss* 'this', *þennkenn* 'think'. Long vowels can be marked by acute accents, as in *fór* 'fared', *tíme* 'time'. The system was not perfect, but as the earliest attempt at a 'spelling reform' in the history of the language, it was remarkably forward looking.

Orm's highly informative spelling conventions were not adopted by other scribes. Vowel length continued to be ignored by thirteenth-century scribes, though some alternative ways of marking long vowels gradually came into being in the fourteenth century. One way of indicating length was by doubling the vowel letter: <*aa*> 'aye',[2] <*see*> 'sea', <*stoone*> 'stone(s)', <*ook*> 'oak', are some early examples found in LAEME. Another innovative way of marking long vowels, related to the lengthening of stressed vowels in disyllabic words in the environment <-Ce> (see 7.5.2), was to code length by preserving or adding the final <-e>, as observed in uninflected forms of ME *wife* (OE *wīf*), *stone* (OE *stān*), *hale*/*hole* (OE *hāl*) 'whole'. This is, of course, the 'silent <-e>' familiar to any schoolchild – <-e> is now established as the diacritic

[2] This adverb, OE *ā* 'always, ever', is recorded as <*aa*> already in OE (DOE). Occasional doubling of <i> for [iː] in OE is found in *wiif* 'wife', *tiid* 'time', *liif* 'life'.

that distinguishes the vowels in *pal – pale*, *pet – Pete*, *pin – pine*, *rob – robe*, *cut – cute*, *lyric – lyre* (see further 7.5.3).

7.2.2 Letter-to-vowel correspondences in ME (digraphs): BEAT-BEET, ROAD-ROOD

Yet another way of distinguishing vowel length was by using digraph spellings. Some digraph spellings were inherited from OE: <ea>, <eo>, <ie>. They continued in use in OE documents copied until the thirteenth century. Subsequently, the same graphs were adopted for the representation of new values: <ie> for [eː], <eo> for [eː] or, perhaps, for a front rounded [œ]/[øː] in the West Midlands and the South-West.

It must be kept in mind that the PDE use of the digraphs <ea>, <oa> does not go directly back to OE. Towards the end of ME, when [ɛː] and [eː], and [ɔː] and [oː] were still contrastive (see 7.3), the letter <a> was employed as a diacritic to mark the low/open mid vowels. As noted above, <ea> was associated with [ɛː] (*beat*, *sea*, *meat*). A parallel innovation was to use <oa> for [ɔː] (*boat*, *coal*, *road*). Doubling of <e, o> marked the high mid vowels [eː] (*beet*, *see*, *meet*) and [oː] (*boot*, *cool*, *rood*).

One further regional peculiarity in the marking of long vowels is that the letter <i>, in addition to marking the second element of diphthongs, as in *dai* 'day', *pleinten* 'complain', *boi(e)* 'boy', was also used as a length diacritic. In that function too, <i> alternates with <y>. In ME this scribal practice is characteristic of northern dialects, including Lowland Scots, for example <ai> for [aː] as in *baith*, *bayth* 'both', *laith*, *layth* 'loath', *stain*, *stayn* 'stone'; <ei> for [eː] as in *keip* 'keep', *heid* 'head', *weill* 'well'; <ui> for [yː] as in *bluid* 'blood', *buik* 'book', *guid* 'good', *puir* 'poor'.

The repertoire of the post-Conquest scribes was expanding; it was also remarkably fluid, allowing multiple variant spellings of the same lexical item. To illustrate: the OE word <*prēost*> 'priest' is recorded in the MED as '*preste*, *presth*, *priest*, *prist*, (late) *preast*, (chiefly N) *preist*, (SWM) *pruest* (chiefly early or S or W) *preost*, *prust*, *prost*, (early SWM) *proest*, (early SW) *præst* . . . and (in names only) *pres*, *presse*, *preos*, *pris-*, *presti-*, *purs-*.'

Figure 7.3 presents an overview of some of the most frequent vowel doublings and digraphs in ME and their main sound correspondences.[3]

[3] Digraphs with <y> and <w> as a second element are not included in the chart. The letter <w>, which was introduced by Anglo-Norman scribes to replace the OE wynn (<ƿ>), was also interchangeable with <u> and <uu>: *hous(e)* ~ *hows(e)* 'house', *fouel* ~ *fowel* ~ *fouul* 'fowl'. Recall from 2.2.2 that the rationale for transcribing diphthongal

Letter	Some typical values	Examples
<aa>	[ɑː], [aː]	*baas* 'base', n. and adj.
<ai>	[aj], [ej], [aː]	*dai* 'day', *þai* 'they', *stain* 'stone'
<au>	[ɑw]	*clau* 'claw', *drau* 'draw'
<ea>	[ɛː], [eː]	*sea* 'sea', *beand* 'being'
<ee>	[eː] or [ɛː]	*been* 'be', *eet* 'eat'
<ei>	[ej], [aj], [eː]	*dei* 'day', *þei* 'they', *theif* 'thief'
<eo>	[eː]	*feond* 'fiend'
<eu>	[ɛw], [ew]	*reume* 'realm', *deu* 'dew'
<ie>	[eː], [iᵊ]	*trie* 'tree', *fiet* 'feet', *fier* 'fire'
<iu>	[iw]	*niuwe* 'new', *bliu* 'blue'
<oa>	[ɔː]	*woa* 'woe', *toa* 'toe'
<oi>	[oj]	*boi(e)* 'boy', *boil(en)* 'boil'
<oo>	[oː], [ɔː]	*good* 'good', *stoon* 'stone'
<ou>	[uː], [ow]	*hous* 'house', *stou(e)* 'stow'
<ui>	[uj] (AN)	*puint* 'point', *puisun* 'poison'

Figure 7.3 Doubling of vowels and some digraph spellings in ME

Of relevance to the spelling of PDE is that for the value [uː] the <ou> spelling was 'borrowed' from Anglo-Norman, where <ou> was the normal digraph for [uː]. In the course of the adaptation the <ow> spelling was preferred word-finally and when the [uː] is adjacent to a 'vertical strokes' letter such as <l, n>; otherwise the spelling is kept as <ou>; compare OE <*nū*>, <*tūn*> with ME *now, town*; OE <*(a)būtan*>, <*mūþ*> with ME *about(e), mouth*. As noted above, <u> continued in use for [ʊ], occasionally also [uː], but the introduction of <ou, ow> 'freed' <u> for the representation of the sound written <y> in OE (see 7.3).

glides as [ɪ] for the front glide and [ʊ] for the back glide can be debated. We have kept these for PDE, but we switch to [j] and [w] in the context of the 'new' ME diphthongs because of the clear association between the consonantal sources and the new glides.

7.3 Qualitative changes in ME

7.3.1 Short vowels: DIZZY-BUSY, FURY-BURY, MERRY-MIRTH

This section addresses the major qualitative shifts of the short vowels from Old to Middle English, summarised in Figure 7.4.

Late Old English		Late Middle English		Examples[4]
(ɪ ʏ)	ʊ	ɪ	ʊ	OE [sʏnn] ME [sɪn] 'sin'
ɛ	ɔ	ɛ	ɔ	
(æ	ɑ)	æ/a		OE [θæt] ME [θ**a**t] 'that'

Figure 7.4 Short vowel changes from late OE to late ME

Three of the stressed short vowels, [ɛ], [ʊ] and [ɔ], remained relatively stable in most environments: OE *lettan* – ME *let(en)* 'hinder, let', OE *botm* – ME *bot(te)m* 'bottom', OE *full* – ME *ful* 'full'. The hedge 'in most environments' is because coda [-ŋg], or single or covered nasal codas, had the effect of raising the nuclear mid vowels, so LOE <-eng> and <-ong> were raised to <-ing> and <-ung>. Thus we find early fourteenth-century rhymes such as OE *genge*, ON *gengi* 'troop', ME *gyng*, rhyming with *coming*, *kyng*; EModE *weng(e)* < ON *vǣngr* 'wing' rhyming with gerunds in *-ing*.[5] Only the front vowel raising is attested reliably in the orthography because of the ambiguity of <o> and <u> spellings before <n>, so OE *(on)ġemang* ~ *ġemong* 'among' appears in ME spelling with <-ong>, rarely <-ung>, but the [-ʊŋg] value can be inferred from its later pronunciation: *among* rhymes with *lung*, OE *lungen*, not with *strong* < OE *strang* ~ *strong*.

The most notable example of the raising of the front mid vowel is the adjective and noun *English*, for which there are no <ing-> spellings in OE, but in LAEME's thirteenth-century database we find twenty-two tokens of *Inglis(s)*. Other items in this set are ON *vǣngr* > ME *wenge* ~ *winge* 'wing', ON *flengja* > ME *flengen* ~ *flingen* 'fling', AN **vencir*, OFr *guenci(e)r* > ME *wincen* 'wince', OFr *enque* > ME *enke* ~ *ink* 'ink'. The raising of <-en(C)> > <in(C)> started in early ME, continued into EModE (late ME *lenger* > EModE *linger*), and is mirrored by the PIN-PEN merger throughout the American South, in southern California, central Ohio, Kansas and elsewhere in the US.

[4] The examples cover only vowels which underwent some qualitative changes from OE to ME.

[5] For more examples of rhymes showing raising before nasals see Ikegami (1984: 330–1).

The major changes, enclosed in the dashed ovals in Figure 7.4, are mergers of pre-existing vowels. In the high front portion of the vowel space the unrounding of [ʏ] and its merger with pre-existing [ɪ] for a large portion of the input items is paralleled by the unrounding of [yː] to [iː], so we can follow the practice of previous studies in treating them together in this section.

Recall from 6.5.1 that the OE spelling records show <i> and <y> used interchangeably. Even before the end of OE, [ʏ] and [yː], the output of I-Mutation (see 6.3), were treated differently in the different dialect areas: they were lowered to [e]/[ɛ] and [eː] in Kentish and they were in the process of merging with [ɪ] and [iː] in the East Midlands and the Northern dialects. For forms such as OE *cyss(te)* 'kissed', the recorded spellings for the vowel in OE are <y> ~ <i> ~ <e>: *cys-te* ~ *cis-te* ~ *kes-te*, and for OE *hȳdan* 'to hide' we find *hyden, hiden, heden*. To these the early ME records add a new spelling <u> for the short vowel and <u>, <ui> for the long vowel, as in *cus-te, hude(n)* ~ *huide(n)*.

The interchangeability of <i> and <y> makes it hard to judge whether <-y-> spellings in early ME represent a rounded vowel or not, but the use of <-u-> in words which had the front rounded vowel in OE has traditionally been considered an indication that the vowel preserved its rounding, so that <*custe*> 'kissed' is reconstructed as representing [kʏstə], and *hude(n), huide(n)* 'to hide' as [hyːdə(n)], parallel to the pronunciation of French loans, such as *bugle* 'bugle', *duc(e)/duk(e)* 'duke'. The spellings of OE <y> with <u>, suggesting preservation of front rounded vowels, are characteristic of texts originating in the West Midlands. It is commonly held that the rounded quality of the vowels descending from the OE front rounded vowels persisted into the fourteenth century; the [ʏ] and [yː] realisations were supposedly reinforced by the existence of the same vowels in French loans. The most common description in the textbooks is that OE <y> had three regional manifestations in ME, roughly as shown in Figure 7.5.

		Examples	
		OE *fyrst* 'first'	OE *cȳnde* 'kind', n.
OE [ʏ], [yː]	[ɪ], [iː] (N, East Midl.)	<first>	<kind(e)>
	[ʏ], [yː] (West Midl.)	<furst>	<cund(e)>
	[ɛ], [eː] (South-East)	<f/verst>	<kend(e)>

Figure 7.5 Commonly posited realisations of OE [ʏ], [yː] in ME

This tripartite division is entrenched in the canonical studies of ME, but it is also debatable on several scores. As shown in Lass and Laing (2005), a fresh examination of the presumed sound-spelling correspondences in West Midland ME belies the claim that a front rounded realisation [ʏ], [yː] was systematically associated with particular spellings. Instead of positing continuing [ʏ], [yː] in the Western dialects, which previous researchers link to scribal practices based on French, Lass and Laing suggest that in those areas the OE front rounded vowels were retracted, merging with pre-existing [ʊ] and [uː]. The realisation of front rounded vowels in French loans did exist, but the textual evidence fails to confirm the 'neat geographical tri-partition for /y(ː)/'. There are further aspects of the reconstruction that need clarification. For the short vowel it is indeed the case that the retraction of [ʏ] to pre-existing [ʊ] in specific environments goes back to the twelfth century (Jordan 1974: 70–2); many of the forms surviving in PDE reflect this merger.

(1) West Midlands form of OE [ʏ] in PDE:

OE	ME	PDE
clyċċan	*clicchen/clucchen*	clutch
ċyriċe	*chirch(e)/church(e)*	church
dyncge	*dung(e)/ding(e)*	dung[6]
myċel	*mich(e), mech(e), much(e)*	much

For the set in (1), which includes also PDE *blush*, *bush*, *crutch*, *churn*, *cudgel*, *furze*, *hurdle*, *shut*, *shuttle*, *such*, *sundry*, *thrush*, *thud*, *trust*, the merger with [ʊ] was sufficiently early and widespread to affect the embryonic early fifteenth-century standard. Even some French loans such as OFr *buf(f)et*, *iug(g)e* 'judge', *iust* 'just', *punish(en)* 'punish', *ruser*, *ruiser* 'rush' join the backing to [ʊ],[7] so there is no compelling argument from orthography or later forms in support of OE [ʏ] continuing as phonemically contrastive in the West Midlands areas of ME.

On the other hand, positing a parallel backing of the long [yː] of OE to [uː] based on <u>-spellings in the Western area is much more problematic: there are no surviving lexical items reflecting the presumed change – one would expect the nucleus OE *brȳd* 'bride', *dȳfan* 'dip, dive', *hȳdan* 'hide', and so on to emerge as [uː] > [-aw] in *some* lexical items in *some* PDE varieties, but it is not the case. This is surprising in view

[6] For this and the following item spellings with <o> for <u> (see 7.2) are ignored.

[7] Similar to the native high front rounded vowel, the [y] in French loans could be unrounded to [ɪ], for example OFr *escumer* > ME *skimmen* 'skim'. One interesting etymological pair is *brisk-brusque*. The OED notes suggest that '*brisk* is identical with French *brusque* (which appears as *bruisk* in Scots *c*1560, and as *bruske* as early as 1600); . . . the words appear to have influenced each other in early use.'

of the remarkably high rate of adoption of the West Midlands reflexes of the corresponding short vowel in PDE as shown in (1). It is therefore probable that the <u> spellings of the etymological long front rounded vowel and in the French loans in the West Midland dialects represented a range of realisations: conservative [yː], possibly [juː], and also [uː] and [iː] – the latter based in the eventual absorption of OE [yː] by [iː] in all areas except the South-Eastern areas, where the reflex was [eː], as in OE *bȳtel* > ME (South-East) <be(e)tel> 'beetle'. It is relevant that the French front rounded vowel [yː]/[juː] as in *endure*, *fume*, *use* did not merge with the vowel of OE *brȳd*, *dȳfan*, *hȳdan*. So we know that in the West Midlands OE [yː] was kept separate from French [yː], we know that it was commonly spelled <u> (also <ui>), we know that it joined the [iː] of the neighbouring regions, but we are not close to a convincing reconstruction of a single quality of that vowel. The identification of the reflexes of OE <y> in ME in Figure 7.5 is thus open to more research, which should take into consideration the uneven distribution of surviving texts in the various geographical points, the effect of the different consonantal contexts on the merger with the front or the back vowel, the token and type frequencies of loanwords with the relevant sound, and the numerous lexical idiosyncrasies of spelling and survival.

The great majority of lexical items that had a front rounded stressed vowel in OE do end up as [ɪ] or [iː] in late ME, as in OE *synn* > ME *sin* (see 7.4). This is in line with the observations that the emerging southern standard was based primarily on Midlands and East Anglian forms (see 7.1). There are, however, a substantial number of items that do not fit the OE *synn* > ME *sin* pattern in spelling, pronunciation or both. For these items the OE <y> vowel can emerge with unexpected West Midlands <u> or South-Eastern <e> in spelling, and a possibly unmatched [ɪ], [ɛ], [ʊ] in the pronunciation. This apparently unmotivated mixture of ME developments of OE [ʏ] is illustrated by the pairs in the title of this section: *dizzy-busy*, *fury-bury*, *merry-mirth*. *Dizzy* and *busy* are a perfect rhyme, and the identity of the vowel goes back to OE: *dysiġ* – *bysiġ*, but in *busy* the spelling is West Midlands. *Fury* < French *furie* and *bury* < OE *byrian* are only an eye-rhyme – the [-ɛ-] in *bury* is South-Eastern. In *merry-mirth* the adjective has the South-Eastern spelling and pronunciation, but the noun is East Midlands. Post-ME standardisation has obscured much of the variability of the ME reflexes of OE <y>, but place names, which commonly resist regularisation, are a strong reminder of the options in ME. The third and the fourth columns in (2) show the orthographic and phonological sources of these and of some other related items in PDE.[8]

[8] All place-name etymologies are from Ekwall (1960).

(2) Mixed regional forms of OE <y>:

OE form	Gloss	ME spelling source	ME pronunciation source
(be)*byrian*	'bury'	burie	[-ɛ-]
bysig	'busy'	busie	[ɪ]
myriġ	'merry'	meri(e)	[ɛ]
myrġð	'mirth'	mirth(e)	[-ɪ-] or [-ʊ-] (8.3.2)
ċyriċe	'church'	church(e)	[-ʊ-] or [-ɪ-] (8.3.2)[9]
byriġ	'-bury'	bir-	[-ɪ-] or [-ʊ-] (*Birstall*, W. Yorks)
		ber-	[ɛ] (*Berry* Pomeroy, Devon)
		bur-	[ɛ] (*Bury* St Edmunds, Suffolk)
hrycg	'ridge'	rug(ge)	[-ʊ-] (*Rugeley*, Staffordshire)
hyll	'hill'	hull(e)	[-ʊ-] (Bishop's *Hull*, Somerset)
hǣþ-*hyll*	'heath-hill'	Het*hell*a	[ɛ]/[ə] (Het*hel*, Norfolk)
mylen	'mill'	melle	[ɛ] (*Mellis*, Suffolk)

There is clearly no seamless uniform development of the OE front rounded vowels in ME, but the common denominator in all of the outcomes is loss of rounding. The observed instability raises interesting theoretical questions. Including both the short and the long vowel, why should the high peripheral [ɪ] and [ʊ] be preferred over [ʏ], and [iː] preferred over [yː]?

The causes of unrounding of [ʏ] to [ɪ]/[yː] to [iː], or retraction of [ʏ] to [ʊ] can be addressed from different phonetic and related phonological angles. In terms of phonological feature typology, one approach could be to treat [ʏ] and [yː] as intrinsically more complex because they involve the additional phonological feature of rounding, which is considered more 'marked' for non-back vowels (for example, Chomsky and Halle 1968: 409ff.). Across the languages of the world front rounded vowels are less common than the 'primary' vowels such as [ɪ]/[iː] and [ʊ]. Typically, backness and rounding are mutually enhancing, and the disassociation of backness and roundness in [ʏ] and [yː] adds to the motivation for their avoidance.

Phonetically, lip-rounding for the high back vowels maximises articulatory ease; the flip side of this is that maintaining lip-rounding for the high front vowels requires more effort. Perceptually, the oppositions based on height, manifested in the acoustic frequency of F1, are more basic and salient than the backness oppositions whose acoustic manifestations involve the frequency of F2; F2-based contrasts are inherently

[9] Compare the place name *Cheriton* (Devon) with the South-Eastern spelling and pronunciation.

weaker (see Kaun 1995: 5.3.1 and the references there). In discussing F2 contrasts and vowel dispersion, Flemming (2004: 4.1) also finds that F2 contrasts involving non-peripheral vowels such as front rounded vowels are 'sub-maximal' and 'dispreferred'. In his dispersion framework there are markedness relations over contrasts as well as over sounds – and the contrast between [ɪ] and [ʏ] is more marked than the contrast between [ɪ] and [ʊ], that is, [ɪ] and [ʏ] are less distinctive than [ɪ] and [ʊ]. Thus the instability of ME [ʏ] and [yː] can also be seen in terms of the vowel inventory as a whole. An additional contrast in the set of high vowels makes for a crowded vowel space while the loss of rounding optimises the perceptual distance between the vowels.

Two other points related to the history of the front rounded vowels need further clarification. What is it that determines whether the input [ʏ] will be unrounded to [ɪ], as in OE *synn* > ME *sin*, or whether [ʏ] will emerge as [ʊ] as in OE *blyscan* > PDE *blush*? It has been suggested (Jordan 1974: 70–2) that there is an association between the ME [ʊ] realisation and adjacency to /t͡ʃ, d͡ʒ, ʃ/, possibly before a rhotic. The correlation is not stable, however, because we find divergent results from the same input, so OE *bryċġ* > PDE *bridge* vs OE *cyċġel* > PDE *cudgel*. It is possible that the affricates and the sibilant had a secondary articulation involving lip-rounding which would enhance the probability of a [-ʊ-] outcome. There is as yet no detailed study of the entire corpus of OE [ʏ] in ME which takes account of the exact phonetic environment and the frequency of the relevant items. It is not clear whether the selection of the back vowel over the front vowel can be related to the later simplification of [yː]/[juː] to [uː] (*yod-dropping*) as in *sue*, *chew*, *Jew*, *rue* (see 8.2.2.3).

Another area which will profit from further study is the different behaviour of short and long vowels. Why do all of the OE long [yː]'s end up as [iː] (OE *hȳdan* > ME *hīde(n)*), while the phonetically quite similar [yː] in early loanwords merged most frequently with /iu/, as in *duke* (1129), *use* (1225), *huge* (1275), *jewel* (1290)?[10] Is it a historical accident that West Midlands variant forms in presumably early and conservative [yː], later [uː], were ignored in the selection of forms that survived locally or in the standard language? Finally, how do we address the fact that while the front rounded [yː] was ultimately unrounded in the Southern varieties of ME, late thirteenth- and early fourteenth-century Northern [oː] was first fronted to [œ] and then raised to [yː], which is the reconstructed ME reflex of OE [oː] in words such as *foot*, *soon*, spelled <fut>, <sun(e)>, recognisable (after shortening, see 7.4.)

[10] One notable exception is PDE *trifle* from ME *trufle* < Old French *trufle*.

in the modern Scottish realisation of the vowel in the FOOT lexical set as [ʏ] (Wells 1982, II: 401–2). Clearly, the newly generated Northern front rounded vowels are incompatible with accounts which rely on the intrinsic markedness of such vowels without reference to the whole system, the density of lexical items with front rounded vowels and the influence of the phonetic environment. Furthermore, front rounded vowels, both [ʏ] and especially [œ], are very much in evidence in PDE: rounding of the GOOSE vowel may be a change in progress in RP, and the rounding of the NURSE vowel is attested in South African English, Australian English, New Zealand English, and in the UK in Tyneside, Liverpool, London, the West Midlands and South Wales (see Mayr 2010: 94 and the references there). The inconsistencies of survival, assimilation and (re)introduction of front rounded vowels in the history of the language and its current varieties is open to further study.

Moving on to the changes of the low vowels: the circle around [æ] and [ɑ] in Figure 7.4 indicates another possible merger in ME.[11] In 6.1 we noted that the contrast between OE [ɑ] and [æ] is a matter of uncertainty, though following Hogg (1992a: 14, 98) we assumed that they were contrastive, at least in West Saxon. The presence of a coda nasal presents a special case: <a> ([ɑ]) is characteristic of West Saxon, while Anglian has <o> ([ɔ]) in words such as OE *bana* ~ *bona* 'killer', *camp* ~ *comp(e)* 'battlefield'. This distinction continues into ME, but the area of <-on-, -om-> spellings is confined to the West Midlands, with <-an-, -am-> spellings much more broadly distributed; it is from the East Midlands, the South and the North that PDE has emerged with the <a> forms in *man*, *hand*, *lamb*, *camp*, and so on (see Jordan 1974: 50–4).

The letter *ash* <æ> was used only in the earliest ME documents (see 7.2). In Anglian OE as well as in Kentish OE [æ] shows raising and fronting to [e]/[ɛ].[12] Elsewhere the [æ] must have started lowering to [a] in late OE; moreover, the phonological basis of the historical difference between [æ] and [ɑ] was often obscured in the paradigms of the same word, and variant <æ> ~ <a> spellings are commonly attested, for example OE *bæð* ~ *bað* 'bath', *fæder* ~ *fader* 'father', *fæst* ~ *fast* adj. 'fast'. During the thirteenth century the letter <æ> was completely replaced by <a>, or <e> in the areas where the Anglian and Kentish forms were preserved or adopted. Based on the orthographic substitution of <æ> by <a>, the usual textbook accounts posit a general lowering and retraction of OE [æ] to [a]. This would cover the additional merger of [ɑ],

[11] The complexities of the merger of the OE dipthongoid [æᵊ] with [æ]/[ɑ] as in OE *feax*~*fæx* 'hair', *heall*~*hall* 'hall' (see 6.5.3) are ignored here.

[12] Compare OE *bæc* 'back, ridge' in *Backbarrow* (Lancashire) with *Beckhampton* (Wiltshire).

spelled <a> in OE, and [a] spelled <æ> in OE. The assumption that the result of the merger is phonetically [a] is not necessary, however; the merger could be anywhere in the [a] ~ [æ] range and it can be seen as allophonic variation based on the phonetic closeness of the two low vowels. Spellings such as *beth* 'bath', *sed* 'sad', *weter* 'water' are easy to find in the ME records. OE [-ɑ-] and [-æ-], if subject to open-syllable lengthening (see 7.5.2), emerged as a long vowel reconstructed as [aː] in late ME: OE *cnafa* > ME [knaːvə] 'knave', OE *hatian*, ME [haːt(ən)] 'hate', OE *hæsel* > ME [haːzəl] 'hazel'. Reconstructing low front [aː] is supported from later history: it is raised and diphthongised and eventually merges with pre-existing [ej]. The intermediate steps for lengthened OE low vowel [a] ~ [æ] to EModE [æj]/[ej] are a matter of conjecture and one should be sceptical about the accuracy of the <a> spellings as representing a uniformly low vowel if there was no <æ> in the scribes' repertoire, and <e> stood for a contrastive sound. The point to take away is that there is nothing in the phonetic or phonological history of the 'generic' short /a/ phoneme in ME to exclude continuing allophonic [æ] in ME in words such as OE *æppel* 'apple', OE *glæd* 'glad', OE *hæt* 'hat'. This is a case where neither spelling, nor rhymes, nor system-internal evidence can make the reconstruction testable. Still, positing continuity of allophonic [æ] in ME is appealing in view of the long-term instability of the 'main' allophone of the low short vowel in the history of the language, as shown in (3).

(3) Long-term perspective on the instability of short /a/:

PrG/WG	**OE**	**ME**	**EModE**	**PDE**
*/a/	/**æ**/	[a] ~ [æ]	[**æ**] ~ [a]	/**æ**/
*apl-	/**æ**p-/	[ap-] ~ [æp-]	[**æ**p-] ~ [ap-]	/**æ**p-/ 'apple'
*baco-	/b**æ**k/	[bak] ~ [bæk]	[b**æ**k] ~ [bak]	/b**æ**k/ 'back'
*þat	/θ**æ**t/	[θat] ~ [θæt]	[ð**æ**t] ~ [ðat]	/ð**æ**t/ 'that'

Seen from this macro-perspective, the fully open pronunciation [a] has been in competition with the neighbouring higher or backer vowels throughout the history of the language. The realisations of PDE /æ/ and its most recent fluctuations are quite telling: Gimson (1970: 106) identifies the allophones of /æ/ for British English as [ɛ ~ æ ~ æ^{ə} ~ a ~ ä ~ ɑ̈]; one generation later Cruttenden (2008: 112–14) adds an even higher diphthongoid [e^{ə}] for 'refined' RP, and marks *both* [æ] and [a] as standard RP. In New World English the vowel of BACK and THAT also shows a variety of realisations: while generic /æ/ is widespread, one finds also a slightly raised [æ$^{\wedge}$], strongly raised [eə ~ eɛ ~ iə] and slightly lowered [æ^{v} ~ æ] (Thomas 2001: 19–21). In view of OE <æ> ~ <a> ~ <e> dialectal and paradigmatic alternations – for example, *bæc* ~ *bec(es)* ~ *bacu(m)* 'back, n.' – and continuing variability attested by forms such as ME *appel* ~ *eappel* ~ *eppel* 'apple', there is no reason to assume that there was an across-the-board lowering of OE [æ] to [a] in ME. The 'middle' period is not different from EModE; crucially, a stable phonemic contrast between [æ] and [a] cannot be reconstructed for any dialect at any time. The low front vowel is extremely susceptible to contextual, regional and social variability, so for 'generic' ME /a/ it is reasonable to reconstruct realisations ranging from a higher [æ] to a retracted realisation [ɑ], the latter most likely to occur before liquid codas, as in *stark(e)* 'stark', *warnen* 'warn', *barbour* 'barber', *salven* 'to annoint'. The relevance of this to a PDE speaker is that the coexistence of [a] and [æ] as non-contrastive realisations of the same phoneme can be projected all the way back to OE.

A final short-vowel merger, part of the processes discussed in 8.3.2, has to do with the effect of a tautosyllabic rhotic on late ME <-er>, which begins to appear as <ar> in the fourteenth century, starting in the North (Jordan 1974: 98–9, 234): OE/early ME *(ge)beorc* 'bark of a dog', *herġan* 'harry', *sterr(e)* 'star', *teru* 'tar' > late ME *bark(ing)*, *barye(n)*, *star(re)*, *tar(re)*. By the end of ME the lowering had begun to appear also in the Southern dialects. It has been suggested that the path of change was via [æ] (Dobson 1968: §64, n.2), but positing an intermediate front value is not necessary, especially in view of the well-attested centralising effect of /r/ on the preceding vowel. The spread of the lowering was enhanced by the parallel change in OFr and Anglo-Norman: AN *merveille* ~ *marvaille* 'marvel', *(h)erber* ~ *arber* 'arbour', *persil* ~ *parsel* 'parsley'. The orthographic representation of the change can be erratic; the word *parsley* in the various manuscripts of Chaucer's *Cook's Tale* appears as <*parsel*, *percely*, *persle*, *persele*, *percelly*, *parselee*, *persly*>. The [-ar] pronunciation in native words was more stable and advanced, and was fully established in EModE (Dobson 1968: §64, §§67–9). However, in many loanwords the Latin spelling with <-er-> was preserved and a spelling-based pronunciation with [-ɛr] eventually replaced earlier [-ar] in loanwords such as OFr and AN <*mercant* ~ *marchand* ~ *marchant* ~ *merchand*, *merchant* ~ *mercheant*> 'merchant', but notice the surname *Marchand*, or OFr and AN *parfit* ~ *perfit* < classical Latin *perfectus*, 'perfect'; compare PDE *parfait*, a recent (1884) borrowing from French.

7.3.2 Long vowels: GAE-GO, OAKE (Somerset) - AIKE (East Riding of Yorkshire)

The OE set that served as an input to the ME long-vowel set (see 6.5.2 and Figure 6.8) included two high vowels [iː] and [uː], two upper mid vowels [eː] and [oː], two low vowels [æː] and [ɒː], and the high front rounded [yː], discussed along with its short counterpart in 7.3.1. Figure 7.6 shows the correspondences between the OE and the ME long-vowel sets.[13]

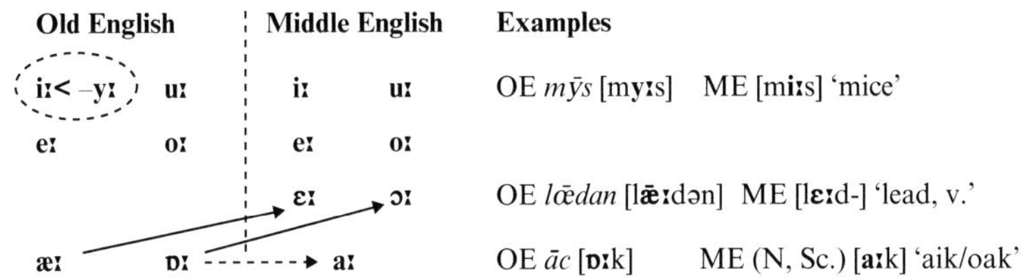

Figure 7.6 Long vowel changes from late OE to ME

A comparison of the inventories in 7.4 and 7.6 shows a reduction of the number of short-vowel contrasts through mergers, while the membership of the long-vowel system remains numerically the same as in OE in spite of the unrounding of [yː] to [iː]. Except for the high front vowel merger whereby the nuclei of OE *mīn* [miːn] 'mine' and OE *mӯs* [myːs] 'mice' were no longer contrastive, the high and upper mid long vowels remain relatively stable: OE *mīn* [miːn] > ME [miːn] 'mine', OE *nū* [nuː] > ME [nuː] 'now', OE *dēman* [deːmən] > ME [deːm(ən)] 'deem', OE *dōm* [doːm] > ME [doːm] 'doom'. Monophthongisation of OE [eə] as in *þēof* 'thief', *ċēosan* 'choose' (see 6.5.3) also resulted in either [eː] or [oː]. The diphthongised and raised fourteenth-century allophones of these four vowels – [iː] ~ [ij]/[ɪi], [uː] ~ [uw]/[ʊu], [eː] ~ [e˔(ə)], [oː] ~ [o˔(ə)] – are at the core of the changes associated with the initial stages of the chain shift, known commonly as the *Great Vowel Shift*, described in Chapter 8.

The low front [æː], which had different sources and different realisations in OE (see 6.5.2), appears to have been raised a notch to [ɛː] in most dialects. The raising, evidently allophonic in its initial stages, can be seen as a precursor of the more general tendency of the long monophthongs of ME to shift upwards, ultimately resulting in an across-the-board upward shift of all non-high long monophthongs (see 8.2.2). In late OE the diphthong [æə] as in *strēam* 'stream' had started to monophthongise, and so we find both <æ> and <ea> spellings for [æː] in early ME texts. Yet another source of ME [ɛː] is the lengthening

[13] The examples in the third column are only of vowels that changed from OE to ME. The ME forms are given only in the reconstructed pronunciations that provide the input to the EModE long-vowel changes.

of OE [ɛ] in open syllables, as in OE *stelan* [stɛlən] 'steal' > ME *stel(e)* [stɛːl(ə)] (see 7.5.2).

After the end of the thirteenth century, the spelling with <e>, later <ee>, is used to represent both the inherited [eː] and the new [ɛː] vowel, so that in Chaucer's manuscripts one can find both [eː] < OE [eː] or [eə], and [ɛː] < OE [æː] or [æə], spelled <ee>: OE *drēam*, ME *dreem* 'dream', OE *mētan*, ME *meete* 'meet'. The identical spellings can be deceptive: Chaucer, whose rhyming practice is an important test for late fourteenth-century London/Southern pronunciation, tends to keep ME [ɛː] and [eː] apart, rhyming OE [æː] and [æə] with themselves, for example *meene* 'mean': *clene* 'clean', and OE [eː] and [eə] also with themselves as in *queene* 'queen': *ysene* 'seen'. For someone reading Chaucer it is important to keep in mind that in spite of the uninformative, identical spellings, and the coalescence to [iː] in later English, the open and close front-mid vowels have different histories.

The two types of mid vowels were kept separate long enough for them to be represented differently in fifteenth-century spellings: as noted in 7.2, the lower mid front vowel [ɛː] was associated with <ea> as in *mean, clean, meal, meat*, while the upper mid vowel [eː] was represented by <ie> as in the French loanwords *brief, piece*, and in native *thief, fiend*, and by <ee> as in *queen, seen, heel, seek*. In practice this makes the second letter in the digraph <ea> a diacritic for openness of the vowel (see 7.3.2); as we will note again below, the diacritic use of <-a> to mark openness is mirrored by the pair <oa> for [ɔː] - <oo> for [oː] for the back vowels.

Metaphorically speaking, the raising of late OE [æː] to [ɛː] adds a new rung to the ladder of vowel heights in the set of long front vowels. Looking at Figure 7.6 again, we see that the new lower mid vowel in the front set is matched by a lower mid back vowel [ɔː]. This innovation results from the raising of the OE low back [ɒː] to [ɔː] in the non-Northern dialects, as in OE *āc* [ɒːk] > ME [ɔːk] 'oak'. The shift of [ɒː] to [ɔː] started in the latter half of the eleventh century in the West Midlands, the Berkshire/Oxfordshire area, the South Midlands and the South-East (Liebl 2006; Stenbrenden 2010: 531). It was a slow, lexically specific process, not fully developed before the end of the thirteenth century. Raising of OE [ɒː] was one of the sources of [ɔː]; the other source was lengthening of OE [ɔ] in open syllables, as in OE *nosu* [nɔzu] 'nose' > ME *nose* [nɔːz(ə)] (see 7.5.2). The new long vowel in the back series is represented initially by <-o-> or <-oCe->, and, after the middle of the sixteenth century, as <oa> (Scragg 1974: 77) as in *oak* (OE *āc*), *boat* (OE *bāt*), *coal* (OE *col(u/a)*), *toad* (OE *tāda*).

In the North the OE low back [ɒː] vowel was fronted to [ɑː] >

[aː], represented in the spelling as <a>, <aCe> and <ai>, where the <-Ce> and <-i> are the Northern/Scots markers of vowel length (see also 7.5.3). The dotted arrow in Figure 7.6 indicates the fronting; it is a regional development recognisable in Scots forms and Northern place names in PDE, as in *both* ~ *baith*, *do* ~ *dae*, *go* ~ *gae*, *home* ~ *hame*, *more* ~ *mair*, *toes* ~ *taes*, *whole* ~ *hail*. The raising and fronting of the long low monophthong [aː] possibly to [ɛː] in the North, pre-dates the raising of the low vowel in the South, and it is arguably the first step in a front-vowel chain shift, identified as the 'Northern Shift' (Smith 1996: 99–101), a set of changes comparable to, but not identical with the (Southern) Vowel Shift. The preservation of the low vowel, its fronting and raising and later diphthongisation to [ej] was most likely influenced by the existence of parallel ON forms with [ej] < *[aj]. Examples of the different outcomes of the split of OE [ɒː] are shown in (4).

(4) Regional developments of OE [ɒː] in ME:

OE	**ON**	**PDE Southern**	**PDE Northern**
āc	eik	**oa**k	**ai**k
		Oake (Somerset) -	**Ai**ke (East Yorkshire)
brād	breiðr	br**oa**d	br**ai**d
		Br**oa**dway (Somerset)	Br**ai**thwaite (Cumbria)
stān	stein	st**o**ne	st**a**ne
		St**o**nehenge (Wiltshire)	St**ai**nborough (Yorkshire)
		Folkest**o**ne (Kent)	(Dwarfie) St**a**ne (Orkney)

The addition of an extra level of height contrasts for the front and back long mid vowels is a systemic innovation in ME. As noted at the beginning of this section, one should also consider the strong probability of variable purely monophthongal and slightly diphthongal realisation of inherited long vowels, which is tantamount to initial long vowel shifting. The earliest orthographic evidence for diphthongisation of [iː], namely <ei/ey> spellings for the vowel in *abide*, *betide*, appearing also in rhyme position, goes back to the first half of the thirteenth century, especially in the West Midlands. More such spellings are found in the next century, and there is no doubt that by the early fifteenth century the change was well under way. The evidence for the diphthongisation of [uː] is confounded by the introduction from French of <ou> and <ow> spelling for [uː] (see 7.2), but since the raising of [oː] is attested from the thirteenth century, and there was no merger with [uː], the initial steps in the direction of diphthongisation to [uw] can be dated to approximately the same time. For this vowel too, the shift of OE [uː]

to PDE [əw]/[aʊ] is firmly rooted in Middle English. We will return to these issues in 8.2.2.

The premise of a fourteenth-century start of diphthongisation of the high vowels means that Figure 7.6 is quite conservative. It is a representation of the long-vowel system found in all introductions to Chaucerian English; however, it conceals the option of initial diphthongisation, which would bring the vowels closer to their PDE values. A less archaising reconstruction of the system for reading Chaucer aloud would allow the vowel of OE *mīn* [miːn] > ME [miːn] 'mine' as [ij]/[ɪj]/[əj], and the vowel of OE *nū* [nuː] > ME [nuː] 'now' as [uw]/[ʊw]/[əw].

7.4 The diphthongal system of ME

Recall from 6.5.3, also 7.3.2, that the core inherited diphthongs of late WS [æə] and [eə] merged with the corresponding long vowels [æː]/[ɛː] and [eː] in early ME. Ignoring the instances of diphthong-internal prominence shifts resulting in rising diphthongs (OE *ċēosan* > ME *chesen* ~ *chose(n)* 'choose'), the mergers of diphthongal and simple long vowels are shown in Figure 7.7.

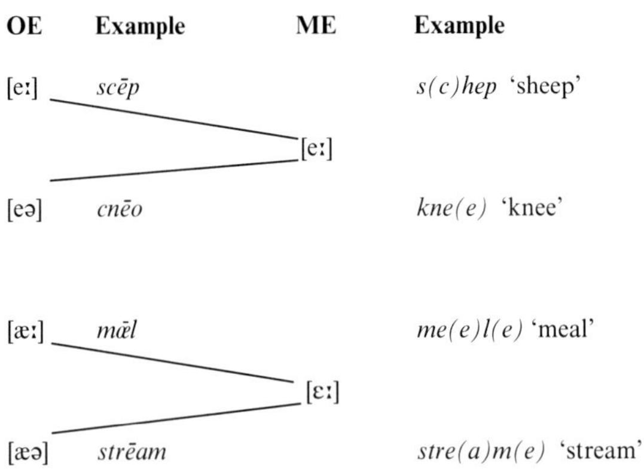

Figure 7.7 Monophthongisation of the OE diphthongs in ME

The removal of the diphthongs [æə] and [eə] from the system does not mean that ME had no diphthongs. This would be a strange situation, given the rich diphthongal presence in the vowel systems of OE and all varieties of PDE. A set of simple long vowels without any diphthongal realisations would also be peculiar in view of the functional unity of diphthongs and steady-state long vowels throughout the history of the language. Diphthongal vowels can be reconstructed for OE both from inheritance and in cases where the nucleus was followed by the palatal glide [-j] based on an earlier palatal fricative. Thus Gmc **daǣ-*, OE *dæġ* 'day', with recorded OE spellings <dæig, deig, daig, deih, dæi, dei, dai>, is interpreted as representing [æj], and spellings such as <greig, grei> for OE (Angl.) *grēġ* 'grey' are interpreted as [ej] (see 6.5.3).

The pattern of glide vocalisation and diphthong formation illustrated by *day* and *grey* is not an isolated change – it is just the change most clearly discernible in the orthographic records. The palatal glide [-j] was drawn into any front-vowel nucleus when it was in the same syllable or in the same stem: early OE **briġdel* > late OE *brīdel* 'bridle', *drȳġness* ~ *drīġness* > late OE *drinesse* 'dryness', *flȳġan* ~ *flȳan*, p.t. *fliġde* '(cause to) fly', all with [-ij].

The trajectory within a diphthong involving a high front vowel + [j] is minimal; it is perceptually difficult to keep [ij] apart from the simple long [iː]. While the merger of [-ij] with [iː] already in OE is beyond doubt, there is no principled way of deciding whether the dominant post-merger realisation was [iː] or a slightly diphthongal [ij] – the latter could easily be the input to the vowel shift that occurred later. The fact that OE scribes commonly use both <i> and <ig> as representing 'pure' [iː] in word-final position as in <bi ~ big ~ bii> for OE *be/bi* 'by, prep.', <hwy ~ hwig> for *hwȳ* 'why', <sie ~ sy ~ sig> for *sȳ* 'be, pres. subj.' confirms the merger and allows a reconstruction of [ij] as the primary allophone of the long high front vowel in early ME.

A process parallel to the diphthongisation of front vowels + [j] involves also the OE voiced velar fricative [ɣ] (see 4.2.1), the labial approximant [w] and the different realisations of the voiceless glottal fricative /h/ (see 5.1.4). The voiced velar fricative [ɣ] in OE was always preceded by a back vowel. The further lenition of [ɣ] to [w] and subsequent merger under [w] was under way in late OE/early ME, evidenced by variant spellings such as *gnagan* ~ *gnawen* 'gnaw', *lage* ~ *lawe* 'law', *boga* ~ *bowe* 'bow'. When the approximant [-w] appeared in the coda, increasingly likely at a time of general weakening of the final unstressed vowels, it was vocalised and the glide became the second element of a diphthong: OE *bo.ga* ~ *bo.we* (with possibly ambisyllabic intervocalic consonant) > ME *bow(e)* > *bow* [bow] 'bow', OE *būgan*, ME *bouen* ~ *buwe(n)* [buwən] 'bow down'. The result for the vocalisation of [ɣ] after back vowels is indistinguishable from the vocalisation of original [w], as in OE *stōw* > ME *stou* [stow] 'spot'. Vocalisation of etymological [-w] occurs also after [æə], [eə] and [iː]: OE *dēaw* ~ *deau* > ME *deu* [dɛw] 'dew', OE *brēowan* > ME *breu* ~ *brew* [brew] 'brew', OE *nīwe* > ME *niw(e)* ~ *new(e)* [niw] 'new'.

It is evident that although these diphthongs are commonly referred to as ‘new’, they were rooted in the phonology of late OE. They are ‘new’ only in terms of the nature of their second elements: the diphthongs [æə] and [eə] inherited from WG have a rather short and flat trajectory, ending in the non-distinctive [-ə], while the [-j] and [-w] endpoints of the ‘new’ diphthongs give them a longer trajectory and make them perceptually more salient. As we will see in 8.3.2, a return to, or perhaps a replication of, diphthongal nuclei with [-ə] as their second element, the so-called *centring diphthongs*, occurs again in the environment of a coda /-r/, lenited to [-ə] as in RP *beer*, *dear*, *there*, *moor*, *cure*.

Another source of diphthongisation in ME is the presence of the voiceless glottal fricative [-h] in the coda, originally realised in agreement with the nature of the nucleus: [-ç] after front vowels, as in EME *niht* ‘night’, or [-x] after back vowels, as in *sohte* ‘sought’; the details were discussed in 5.1.2, 5.1.4. The most common spelling for the fricative in non-initial position was <gh>. Already at the beginning of the fourteenth century forms such as <mit> for OE *miht* ‘might’, <brit> ‘bright’, <nit> ‘night’ testify to variable [-ç] ~ Ø in these words. The coarticulation of front vowel + [ç] results in the epenthesis of a transitional palatal glide [-j-], so that phonetically <miht> ~ <mit> ‘might’ can be reconstructed as [mijçt] ~ [mijt]. Inputs with the mid vowels [-ɛç], [-eːç] result in [-ɛjç] ~ [-ɛj] (later [ej]), and [-ejç] ~ [ej] (later raised, merging with [ij]): OE *ehta* > ME *ehte* ~ *eihte* ‘eight’, OE *nēh* > ME *neh*, *neih*, *nih* ‘nigh’.

A parallel process of glide epenthesis occurs between a back vowel + [-x]; in this case the inserted glide is [w]/[ʊ]: OE *drūgoþ* > ME *druȝt* ~ *drout(e)* [drʊxt] ~ [druwt] ‘drought’, OE *tahte* > ME *tahte* ~ *tauhte* ‘taught’, OE *bohte* > ME *bohte* ~ *bouhte* [bɔʊht(ə)] ‘bought’. The initial evidence for the back glide epenthesis before the velar fricative is also dated to the fourteenth century with the full-blown developments in evidence during the fifteenth century.

Figure 7.8 presents an overview of the diphthongal vowels emerging from glide vocalisation in late ME.

Input	**OE/EME**	**LME**	**Examples**
(a) V (front) + [-j]	[-ij-]	[-ij-]	OE **brīġdel*, ME *bridel* ‘bridle’
	[-eːj]	[-ej]	OE (Angl.) *grēġ*, ME *grei* ‘grey’
	[-ɛj]	[-ɛj] ~ [-æj]	OE *weġ*, ME *wei* ~ *wai* ‘way’
	[-æj]	[-aj] ~ [-æj] ~ [-ɛj]	OE *dæġ*, ME *dai* ‘day’

Figure 7.8 The diphthongal vowels in late ME

Input	OE/EME	LME	Examples
(b) V + [w]	[-iːw]	[-iw] ~ [-ju]	OE *nīw(e)*, ME *niwe* ~ *newe* 'new'
	[-eəw]	[-ew]	OE *brēowan*, ME *breu* ~ *brew* 'brew'
	[-æəw]	[-ew]	OE *hēawan*, ME *hew(e)* 'hew'
	[-ɑw]	[-ɒw]	OE *þawian*, ME *thaw(e)* 'thaw'
	[-ɒːw]	[-ɔw] ~ [-ow]	OE *cnāwan*, ME *cnowe(n)* 'know'
	[-oːw]	[-ow]	OE *stōw*, ME *stou* 'spot'
	[-ʊw]	[-uw]	OE *fugol*, ME *foul* ~ *fowel* 'fowl'
	[-uːw]	[-uw]	OE *būgan*, ME *bouen* ~ *buwe(n)* 'bow down'

Input	OE/EME	LME	Examples
(c) V (front) + [ç]	[ɪç]	[ijç] ~ [ij]	OE *miht*, ME *might(e)* ~ *mit* 'might'
	[eːç]	[e˔jç] ~ [ɪj]	OE *nēh* > ME *neh, nei(h)* 'nigh'
	[ɛç]	[ɛjç-] ~ [ej]	OE *ehta*, ME *ehte* ~ *eihte* 'eight'

Input	OE/EME	LME	Examples
(d) V (back) + [x]	[ʊx]	[uwx] ~ [uw]	OE *druhþ*(e), ME *droute* 'drought'
	[uːx]	[uwx] ~ [uw]	OE *rūh*, ME *ruhe* ~ *rowe* 'rough'[14]
	[ɔx]	[owx] ~ [ow]	OE *sohte*, ME *sohte, soute* 'sought'[15]
	[ɔːx]	[ɔwx] ~ [ow]	OE *dāh*, ME *do(u)h* 'dough'
	[ɑh]	[ɒwx] ~ [ɒw]	ON **slahtr*, ME *slauhter* 'slaughter'

Figure 7.8 continued

Glide vocalisation is a function of syllabification. In OE [j], [ɣ] and [w] were consonantal and syllabified as onsets, possibly as ambisyllabic, but not as pure codas. Thus OE *cnāwan* 'to know' syllabified as [knɑː.wən] ~ [knɑː[w]ən], where the second syllable would be unstable; in some paradigmatic forms ending in a single deletable vowel in ME, the

[14] The short vowel in PDE *rough* has to be attributed to an early, pre-Long Vowel Shift, shortening of [uw]/[uː] to [ʊ] (see Luick 1964: §525; Dobson 1968). Other items in this subgroup are *enough, slough* 'snake skin' (early ME *slohu*/*slouh*), but *slough* '[slaʊ] 'muddy ground' (OE *sloh*), also *slew* [sluː] 'body of water', *clough* 'ravine' (OE **cloh*), both [klʌf] and [klaʊ]. In *cough* (ME *cowhen*) and *trough* (ME *trouȝ*) the back glide is unstable and the result is [ɔ].

[15] The LME [owx]~[ow] in *sought*, also *brought, bought, thought, fought, daughter* must have been lowered to [ɒw] in late ME-EModE.

syllable division changed to strengthen the [w]/[ʊ] coda position: 1st p. sg. pr. tense or imp. [knɔ(ː)w.(ə)] > [know]. The parentheses around the length diacritic and the final vowel indicate variable pronunciations: vowel length matters only if the word is pronounced as disyllabic. The original vowel length was neutralised in the process: the nuclear vowels of ME <dei> from an original short vowel + [j] and ME <grei> from a long vowel + [j], are both bimoraic. There is no indication in the metrical treatment or the later history to suggest that diphthongs originating in short vowel + glide were treated differently from those originating in long vowel + glide. Moreover, the adjacency of [j] and [w] to the original non-peripheral short vowels neutralises the height difference between the original vowels: OE *fugol* [-ʊɣ-] 'fowl', and OE *būgan* [-uːɣ-] 'bow down' merge into [-uw-] in ME.

The great diversity of inputs shown in Figure 7.8 can make one's head spin, but if we focus on the outputs in late ME, we will see immediately that the resulting diphthongs are quite straightforward. The sets in 7.8(a) and in 7.8(c) overlap, and so do the sets in 7.8(b) and 7.8(d). We can describe the general pattern as vocalisation of [j] and [w] or epenthesis in the sequence V + [ç/x], resulting in [Vj] or [Vw].

The diphthongs formed through glide vocalisation merge with the diphthongs found in borrowings from Scandinavian: [aj], [ej], [ɑw], [ou], [uw] as in ON *waive* 'turn aside', ON *hreinn* 'rein(deer)', ON *sweinn* 'swain', ON *þei-r* 'they', ON *vindauga* 'window', ON *þōh* 'though', ON **drugna*, ME *droun(en)* 'drown'.[16] The model of diphthongal nuclei in [-j] and [-w] was augmented by the presence in ME of Romance borrowings with the same diphthongs: OFr [aj] as in *grain*, *vain*, AN [ej] as in *obey*, *prey*, *(h)eir*, OFr [ɑw] as in *faut(e)* 'fault', *assaut* 'assault', *cause* 'cause', [ow] from /-l/-vocalisation (see 5.2.5), as in ME *sauder*, *sawder* < OFr *soud(i)er*, *saudier* 'soldier'; OFr *soud-*, *saud-*, *soldure* 'solder' > PDE ['sɒldə(r)] ~ ['sɑːdə(r)]; [ew] as in *beute* 'beauty', *dew*, *du* 'due'; and [iw] ~ [ju] as in *duc* 'duke', *frut* ~ *fruit* 'fruit'. All of these were absorbed in the native set of diphthongs.

In addition, two new diphthongs were added from the French: OFr [oj] and its AN counterpart [uj], as in *choys* 'choice', *destruie* ~ *destroi* 'destroy'. The practice of avoiding the letter <u> in conjunction with other vertical-stroke letters, including <i> (see 7.2), makes the difference between [oj] and [uj] hard to trace. The complexities of the dialectal and lexical distribution of the two diphthongs in ME are not relevant to their later history; they merge under [oj]. One reason why the end result was [oj] may be that [oj] was a possible native diphthong,

[16] See further Dance (2003: 126–30) for evidence of merger of the ON and ME diphthongs.

as in OE *croġen-denu*, *Croidene* (Domesday Book 1086) 'saffron-valley' (Ekwall 1960: 134). Some Dutch loanwords also had [oj]: *loytren* 'loiter', *toye* 'toy', possibly *boy*.[17] The number of items with [oj] is higher; the relative sparseness of [uj] items could also have contributed to the loss of [uj]. As noted above, the <oi> spelling for [uj] loanwords could also be a factor, especially for 'learned' words such as *foison* < AN *fuisun*. The dating of the merger is uncertain, but it must have been under way in the second half of the fourteenth century.

Ignoring the chronological depth and the diversity of sources, Figure 7.9 summarises the late ME diphthongal system and shows the incipient mergers which will be the input to the EModE changes involving diphthongal vowels.

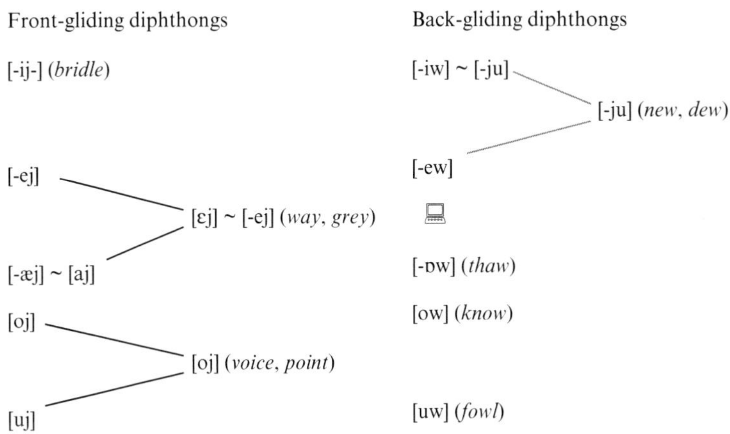

Figure 7.9 Late ME diphthongs

The long vowel changes and the substantial enrichment of the diphthongal system created a set of bimoraic nuclei quite different from the late OE system. The interaction between long vowels and diphthongs will be addressed in Chapter 8. Now we turn to changes which affect the length of vowels in ME.

7.5 Quantitative changes: why do they matter?

Any description of PDE recognises the existence of two sets of vowels: short/lax/non-peripheral and long/tense/peripheral (see 2.2.1).

[17] The etymology of *boy* remains uncertain. The two most likely sources are Anglo-Norman or Dutch (see the entry for *boy*, n. in the OED and the references there).

Although vowel duration is an unstable predictor for the taxonomy in PDE, from a historical point of view the distinction between the two sets is best expressed in terms of quantity. This section covers the major quantity shifts in Middle English and their role in shaping the pronunciation and orthography of PDE.

A literate speaker of English can easily correlate the quantitative properties of the vowel in an unfamiliar word to its spelling. The made-up words in (5) illustrate this correlation.

(5) Spelling cues for vowel length in PDE:

Spelling	**Presumed pronunciation**
<skl**i**pe/skl**y**pe>	[kl**aɪ**p] but not *[klɪp]
<spl**o**ne>	[spl**oʊ**n] but not *[splɑn]
<cl**u**nzer>	[kl**ʌ**nzər] but not *[claʊnzər]
<str**e**cked/str**e**ckt>	[str**ɛ**kt] but not *[striːkt]
<br**ou**t>	[br**aʊ**t] but not *[brʌt]
<bl**ee**m>	[bl**iː**m] but not *[blɪm]

How do we know that *clipe*, *splone*, *brout*, *bleem* have long vowels, but *clunzer* and *strecked* have short vowels? What suggests that the stressed vowels in *restilence*, *switter*, *utmer*, *hosked* would all be short, even though we have not seen those nonce-forms before? Alternatively, for *clanes*, *dyter*, *lote*, *hoiged*, we are likely to guess that the stressed vowels belong to the set of long or diphthongal vowels. This is not a silly spelling-pronunciation game: we know how to translate spellings into sounds and sounds into reasonable spellings because we make analogies to words that we already know, but that does not tell us much beyond the fact that we have learned what the most frequent patterns of English spelling are. Our goal in the next two sections will be to take that primary school-acquired knowledge one step further and explore the historical rationale behind the choices.

Let us start by rehearsing the factors involved in the enhancement or loss of vowel length. Long vowels in *unstressed* syllables are shortened and further reduced (see 3.4.3–4, 6.5.4). Recall from 2.3.3 that long or diphthongal vowels in the peak make a syllable heavy, and English aligns with the well-attested cross-linguistic preference for heavy syllables to attract stress. The co-occurrence of stress and weight goes back to OE, where stress was placed on a heavy syllable in approximately 80 per cent of the lexicon. The relation is commutable: the 'ideal' stressed syllable is heavy. We can expect therefore that short vowels in light stressed syllables (C)V- will be under some pressure to lengthen, heavy syllables of the type -(C)V(V)C would be stable and the long vowel in (C)VVCC syllables might get shortened. Syllable weight is determined both by the length of the vowel and the presence or absence of a syllable coda: codas add to the syllable weight, so that a long or diphthongal vowel plus a tautosyllabic consonant will have some extra weight that could be shed without damaging the overall distinction between light and heavy syllables. Moreover, the contribution of different types of peak vowels and coda consonants, that is, rhyme duration, to the weight of the syllable can be gradient, although the full effect of the gradience for all of the quantitative processes discussed here remains under-studied (see 9.2). 💻

Yet another important parameter is the syllabic composition of the entire word: numerous studies have confirmed the observation (Lehiste 1970) that there is a negative correlation between the number of syllables in a word and their duration: syllable durations shrink as their number increases, for example [ʌ] in *luck* is phonetically shorter in *lucky*, *luckily*. Projected onto vowel length, this means that an original long vowel can be under pressure to shorten in longer words.

A fourth factor influencing stress is the syntactic function of a word: function words such as prepositions, articles, conjunctions, pronouns and auxiliaries are weaker prosodically and of shorter duration than the major class/content words: nouns, adjectives, adverbs and verbs.

In summary: the main linguistic factors involved in the enhancement, maintenance or loss of vowel quantity in the history of English are:

- prosodic prominence
- syllable structure
- word length
- syntactic specification.

The list is not exhaustive. Stress, syllable structure and word length intersect with foot-structure. The changing membership of the short–long vowels sets in English is also influenced by vowel quality and the type of coda consonant. Lexical frequency – base alone, or base vs derivative(s) – can also play a role in quantitative changes. These numerous factors are in competition. Apart from showing how historical phonology can enlighten us about English spelling, discovering the conditions for vowel shortenings and lengthenings is an enterprise of serious theoretical consequence. The perception and recategorisation of vowel length bears on every aspect of the sound system: the featural composition of individual segments, the principles of their distribution, their interaction on higher linguistic levels and the role of vowel quantity in verse meter.

The following two sections address the vowel quantity changes responsible for the main sound-spelling correspondences in PDE.

7.5.1 Shortenings: CREEP-CREPT, MOON-MONDAY, MOUTH-PORTSMOUTH, LEEK-GARLIC

The PrG system is reconstructed as having a three-way quantitative contrast: vowels could be short, long and overlong (Ringe 2006: 214). The distribution of vowel length was unpredictable. Long or short vowels were found in both stressed and unstressed syllables. By the time of the split of North-West Germanic into its dialects, the quantity contrast for vowels became binary: short vs long/diphthongal. As discussed in 3.4.3 and 6.5.4, the reduced stress on syllables following the first root syllable in pre-OE led to recursive reduction of vowel length in that position. As a result, long vowels were no longer found in fully unstressed syllables in OE. This is the first instance of vowel shortening in the history of the language. It sets up a correlation between lack of stress and vowel shortness – the first step in a long process of vowel reduction and loss that changed the shape of the lexicon in ME (see 7.6). The elimination of long vowels from fully unstressed syllables was the initial move towards predictability of vowel length in the English lexicon.

Two vowel-shortening changes, first occurring in OE, contributed further to the transparency of vowel length: pre-consonantal shortening and shortening in some trisyllabic words. The rationale of dealing with these quantity shifts in the context of ME rather than with the OE changes in Chapter 6, is that the patterns of shortening in OE are sporadic and difficult to test. The shortening straddles Old and Middle English, and even early ME shows a great deal of variability. The results are stabilised gradually in ME and it is only in later ME that one can muster sufficient orthographic and metrical evidence to reconstruct the process as categorical.

7.5.1.1 Pre-consonantal shortening: FEED-FED, WIDE-WIDTH, SHEEP-SHEPHERD

Beginning in the seventh century, and continuing through Old and early Middle English, long vowels in stressed syllables were shortened before three or before two consonants, other than the homorganic clusters such as *-ld*, *-nd* which caused lengthening (see 6.4). The process was probably initiated in the environment of three consonants, or geminates followed by another consonant, that is, -VVCCC-, thus **brǣmblas* > *bræmblas* 'brambles', *nǣddre* > *næddre* 'adder'. A less restrictive environment for the shortening is the sequence of a long vowel followed by two consonants, not necessarily in the same syllable. In addition to syllable structure, the shortening is sensitive to word-length: the occurrence of shortening in monosyllables in OE is rare.

In OE, as in PDE, coda clusters show falling sonority (see 2.3.1). Like PDE, in the earlier stages of English the most common first consonant in coda clusters in simplex words was a sonorant or [s], and the second consonant typically a stop, naturally limiting the subset of monosyllabic lexical items eligible for shortening. Only about a dozen OE monosyllables ending in -VVCC show a short vowel in PDE and half of them end in *-st*, as in OE *blǣst* 'blast', *brēost* 'breast', *dūst* 'dust', *fȳst* 'fist', possibly PDE *mist*, *rust*. As we will see with the lengthening data in 7.5.2, the cluster [-st-] behaves inconsistently – in some words, especially those with high vowels, coda [-st] triggers shortening, as in OE *dūst* 'dust', *fȳst* 'fist', but in the overwhelming majority of monosyllabic content words in *-st* the original vowel length is preserved: *Christ*, *east*, *least*, *priest*, *ghost*, *roost*. ME borrowings from Anglo-Norman, as well as later borrowings, also preserve the original vowel length before [-st]: *beast*, *feast*, *host*, *coast*.

The two most stable and productive sub-patterns of pre-consonantal shortening emerge in two quite specific morphological sets: before the past tense dental [–d/-t] suffix (over forty verbs), and before the derivational *-th* or *-t* suffix (about twenty nouns). These two patterns are illustrated in (6) and (7).

(6) Vowel shortening in [-d/-t] preterites:

Early OE	ME	Gloss
mǣn-an [mæːnən]	menen [mɛːn(ən)]	'intend, mean'
mǣnte [mæːntə]	ment(e) [mɛnt(ə)]	'meant'
crēop-an [kreəpən]	crepen [kreːp(ən)]	'creep'
crēpte [kreːptə]	crept(e) [krɛpt(ə)]	'crept'

The pattern in (6) is robust – shortening in the set of weak verbs, such as *mǣnan* 'intend, mean', also *dǣlan* 'deal', *lǣdan* 'lead', *mētan* 'meet', *hȳdan* 'hide', is practically exceptionless, though in some verbs the long vowel is later restored by analogy with the present stem, as in PDE *heal*, *deem*, *need* < OE *hǣlan*, *dēman*, *(ge)nēodian*. By the beginning of the fourteenth century the regularity with which the dental suffix of the past tense causes shortening is shaken – along with *healed*, *deemed*, we get new weak forms without shortening, such as older *bereft* ~ *bereaved*, *cleft* ~ *cleaved*, *crept-creeped (out)*. Since only about a quarter of the OE verbs were strong, that is, forming their past tense by changing the root vowel, some strong verbs tended to develop 'weak' past tense forms, whereby the root vowel was shortened, as in OE *crēopan* in (6), for which had the strong preterite *crēap* competed with the weak form *crepte*. This is especially true of dental-final strong verb stems, where the back-to-back dentals result in geminate [-tt] or [-dd], simplified word-finally to a singleton: thus *bītan-bāt* ~ *bitte* 'bite-bit', *slīdan-slād* ~ *slidde* 'slide-slid'.

Following the principles of syllable division, the originally disyllabic forms such as OE *mǣnte*, *crēpte* (syllabified as *mǣn.te*, *crēp.te*) would have a heavy stressed syllable by virtue of the filled coda: the preferred matching of syllable weight to stress would not be damaged by shortening the vowel. In fact, the pattern in (6) shows a phonologically conditioned vowel shortening reinterpreted as a signal of a grammatical distinction: long vowel in the present, short vowel in the past tense. This creates the apparent 'irregularity' in the paradigms of *sleep-slept*, *meet-met*, *lead-led*, and so on. Pre-consonantal shortening is also the source of etymological doublets such as *screed-shed*, based on OE *scrēadian*, past tense (ME) *s(c)hredde*. The evidence that this pattern of shortening became 'morphologised' is of course strengthened by the addition of instances of originally strong verbs which developed dental preterites as alternative forms and the long vowel of the present stem was shortened, as in attested *rid*, *strid* for *rode*, *strode*.

All other pre-consonantal shortenings of surviving words occur in derived words, but not all affixes have the same effect on the stem. The addition of the suffix *-th* ~ *-t* to a VVC stem produces another systematic set of shortenings; indeed, all pre-1250 eligible forms undergo the shortening, a very different picture from that in forms derived by other affixes. The examples in (7) illustrate the effect of this type of affixation on the quantity of the input vowel.

(7) Vowel shortening in *-th* ~ *-t* derivatives:

Early OE	**ME**	**Gloss**
f**ū**l [fu:l]	foul [f**u**:l]	'foul'
*fūl + (iþ) >fȳlþ	filth [f**ɪ**lθ]	'filth'
dēop [de:p]	dep [d**e**:p]	'deep'
*dēop + þ > *dēopþ	depth(e) [dɛpθ]	'depth'

The early productivity of this shortening gives us pairs such as *dear-dearth*, *five-fifth*, *heal-health*, *steal-stealth*, *slow-sloth*, *thief-theft*, *weal-wealth* with *-th*, and *drive-drift*, *heave-heft*, *shrive-shrift*, *weave-weft* with *-t*. In this set, as in the preterite forms in (6), shortening of the vowel aligns the syllable weight of the derived forms with the majority of bimoraic monosyllabic content words. The shortened derivatives in (7) may be reinterpreted as independently stored lexical items: if we test PDE speakers on the association between *filth*, *shrift*, *sloth*, *wealth* and the base forms, only speakers with training or interest in etymology would connect them to *foul*, *shrive*, *slow*, *weal*. The suffix continued to be marginally productive in ME: only *mild-milth* (c. 1300) and the rare dialectal *side-sidth* (1855) show shortening (OED), while the majority of more recent forms preserve the long vowel: *coolth* (1547), *growth* (1557), *blowth* (1602), *gloomth* (1753), *greenth* (1753), *zeroth* (1896). Note that *-th* with ordinal numerals causes shortening in *fifth*, *tenth* but not in *ninth*, nor in any *-eenth* forms.

The results in (6) and (7) prompt the observation that shortening occurred with regularity in -VVC stems followed by a non-sonorant dental-initial suffix in Old and early ME. The addition of other derivational suffixes generally leaves the quantity of the stem intact. Except for OE *wīs* [wiːs] 'wise' – *wīsdōm*(e) [wiːsdoːm(ə)] 'wisdom', ME [wɪzdəm] – there are no other examples of shortening before *-dom*, neither before *-ful*, *-hood*, *-less*, *-ship*, *-some*, *-ster*, though many eligible derivatives are recorded in OE; words like *cheerful*, *priesthood*, *lifeless*, *township*, *loathsome* go back to the pre-Conquest records.

Compounds are another set of words where the shortening of the vowel with primary stress is attributed to the sequence -VVC followed by a consonant-initial syllable as in (8).

(8) Vowel shortening in historical compounds:

OE	ME	Gloss
gōd [goːd]	[goːd]	'good'
gōd + spel(le)	['gɔ(d)spəl]	'gospel'
OE hwīt [hwiːt]	[(h)wiːt]	'white'
hwīt + Sunnandæg	['(h)wɪtsʊndæj]	'Whitsunday'
stān [stɒːn] 'stone'	[stɔːn]	'stone'
stān [stɒːn] + ford	['stanfərd]	'Stanford'

Other pairs illustrating the same process are *bone-bonfire*, *sheep-shepherd*, *house-husband*, *shire-sheriff*, *moon-Monday*, *cheap-Chapman*, *goat-Gatwick*, *down-Dunton*, *deep-Dep(t)ford*, *foul-Fulford*. No regularity can be established in compounding in general, however: *chapman* but *footman*, *Eastman*; *shepherd* but *cowherd*, *goatherd*, *swineherd*, also *sheepskin*; *husband* but *housewife* (1225), later *hussy* (1530).

In concluding this section: the period when shortening was most active was late OE–early ME – the results are in evidence in the later twelfth-century orthographic system of the *Ormulum*. After that, identity with the base in derived forms becomes a powerful factor inhibiting, and even reversing the shortening. The clearest phonological trigger of pre-consonantal shortening is the presence of a dental obstruent in the coda.[18] In the verbal tense system, where the model of present-past stem allomorphy is already in evidence with the strong verbs, vowel shortening before the dental suffix becomes reinterpreted as (one) of the possible ways of signalling grammatical tense. This is the part of the grammar where the otherwise fossilised shortening continued as a marginally productive rule, a case similar to the plural fricative voicing (*roof-roofs ~ rooves*) discussed in 4.4. Thus from the very start, describing the shortening as occurring in extra-heavy stressed syllables, -VVCC, is insufficient to define the conditions for the loss of vowel length, nor is 'closed syllable shortening' a productive phonological rule in PDE. The probability of shortening in the historically inherited cases depends on the nature of the coda consonants, and quite possibly the interaction of all factors named in 7.5, plus the rather elusive, but potentially significant factor of density of occurrence – why [-st] clusters cause shortening in some items and not others, why *wisdom* but *leechdom*, why *meet-met* but *greet-greeted*, *feed-fed* but *need-needed*? Once again we find ourselves asking more questions than we have answers to; once again the hope is that the new electronic corpora will come to the rescue.

7.5.1.2 *Trisyllabic shortening:* HOLY-HOLIDAY, SOUTH-SOUTHERN

Trisyllabic shortening means that original long vowels were shortened in a stressed syllable followed by two unstressed ones. The process is featured most prominently in accounts of the type of paradigmatic alternations found in loanword pairs such as *divine-divinity*, *cone-conical*, *prime-primitive*, *nation-national*, *profound-profundity*. To the extent that such alternations are regular, they are commonly linked to the nature of the derivational suffix attached to the borrowed root; compare *prime-primary*, *legal-legalise*, *frequent-frequency*, *favour-favourable*, *account-accountancy*.

How the *divine-divinity* pattern of shortening the stressed vowel of the base before some suffixes came to be one of the features of PDE is a complex story, often used to illustrate and test specific theoretical paradigms. We will not rehearse the positions and the polemics regarding this aspect of the phonology of PDE; our focus is to trace the roots of this process in the earlier history of the language prior to the influx of Romance loanwords in early Modern English.

Since the classic historical quantitative study by Luick (1898), all phonological accounts of English include trisyllabic shortening as one of the major prosodic changes in English. Moreover, it is regularly

[18] Dentals are also the most frequent environment for the sporadic shortening of vowels in monosyllables, as in PDE *head*, *dead*, *death*, *foot*, *blood* (see further 8.3.1).

integrated into a macro-perspective teleological 'conspiracy' aimed at regularisation of the stressed syllable weight in English (see Lass 1992a: 70–6). The two most frequently cited examples of the change are the pairs in (9).

(9) Early instances of trisyllabic shortening

OE	**ME**	**Gloss**
h**ā**liġ [hɒːlij]	[hɔːli]	'holy'
h**ā**liġ + dæg [hɒːlijdæj]	[hɔli]	'holiday'
s**ū**þ [suːθ]	[suːθ]	'south'
s**ū**þ + erne	[sʊðərnə]	'southern'

However, a solid empirical premise for positing trisyllabic shortening as an active shortening process at any time in Old or Middle English is missing. The presumed effects of trisyllabic shortening can often be attributed to other causes, such as pre-consonantal shortening, as in *Whitsunday* in (8), *swine* - *Swinburne*, *stepfather* (OE *stēop* 'orphan'), *Tadmarton* (Oxfordshire) < OE *tād-mere-tūn* 'toad-pool farm', *Shepperton* (Middlesex) < *scēap-hierde-tūn* 'shepherd's farm'.

Since OE did not have uninflected and underived words of more than two syllables, the eligible pool of items would be very small anyway.[19] Including inflected disyllabic forms in the set of inputs, as is sometimes done, is problematic. Inflected forms of disyllabic words with a long stressed vowel, if not syncopated (*hēafod* – *hēafdu* 'head, nom. pl.') typically resist shortening: nom. pl. *sċēotunga* 'shootings', *īdelu* 'idle'. Another empirical difficulty arises from the lengthening of short vowels in disyllabic base forms: OE *æcer* 'acre', *beofor* 'beaver', *cradol* 'cradle', *hæsel* 'hazel'. The number of such items is also limited for reasons addressed in 7.5.3 below, but the meagreness of the shortening data combined with the lengthenings is sufficient to throw doubt on the assumption that trisyllabic shortening was indeed a prosodic optimisation strategy characteristic of the phonology of Old or Middle English. This is not a rejection of the more general principle (see 7.5) that word-length, or, more precisely, the way the word is 'prosodified' can interact with the weight of the stressed syllable and/or the length of the vowel in it. All that is argued here is that it is impossible to generalise the shortening to the lexicon of pre-Renaissance English: the isolated examples cited in the literature are insufficient for positing a trisyllabic shortening rule going back to Old English.

[19] The restriction applies to the native vocabulary of OE and excludes early loans such as *basilica* 'basilisk', *baptista* 'baptist', *comēta* 'comet', *cucumer* 'cucumber', *December*.

Nevertheless the pattern noted at the beginning of the section – *divine-divinity*, *cone-conical*, *humane-humanity*, *profound-profundity* – is pervasive and productive: *vine-vinegar*, *chaste-chastity*, *court-courtesy*, *compare-comparison*, *vile-vilify*, *line-linear*, *Spain-Spaniard*, *vain-vanity*, *abound-abundance*. As argued in Minkova and Stockwell (1998), the loan vocabulary where the paradigmatic alternations are exclusively located entered the language piecemeal, so that in many cases the earlier 'base' long form and the shorter derivative just kept their original vowel length. The dates of entry could be centuries apart.

(10) Date of entry and vowel length in Romance loanwords:

Long	**Short**
brief (1330)	*brevity* (1509)
cave (c. 1220)	*cavity* (?1541)
grade (c. 1400)	*gradual* (?1541)
profound (1300)	*profundity* (?1475)

Immediate source could also be a factor: Latin had vowel quantity contrasts which would have been familiar to the educated population who were the first, and also the prestigious, users of the loanwords. Pre-consonantal shortening characterises many of the Latin loans, whether they are recycled through Anglo-Norman or not, so that pairs such as *redeem-redemption*, *resume-resumptive*, *deduce-deductive*, borrowed with the allomorphy already in place, reinforce the model. Old French had no functional vowel-length distinctions after c. 1400. However, many of the items borrowed directly from French were interpreted as having a *long* stressed vowel at the right edge: *degree*, *delight*, *profound*, while inside the word the vowels were assigned to the short set: *gradual*, *delicious*, *profundity*. Ultimately, the sheer bulk of Renaissance borrowings and the concurrent adoption of stress-sensitive and vowel-shortening suffixes such as *-ity*, *-ic* bring about the establishment of allomorphy labelled trisyllabic shortening in PDE. Productive trisyllabic shortening in English is thus an early Modern English innovative pattern confined to forms derived with a subset of borrowed Romance suffixes.

Although the idea of historical continuity of trisyllabic shortening in English cannot be supported on empirical grounds, the process is an important aspect of the PDE loan phonology, whose interpretation requires reference to some universal prosodic principles. Eschewing complex theoretical notions, there is a very general linguistic principle which favours the surfacing of a short vowel in a stressed antepenultimate syllable followed by two unstressed syllables. This relates to the word-length factor listed in 7.5: long vowels are much more stable in mono- and disyllabic words than in words where two or more unstressed syllables need to be 'packed in' before the end of the word. It is also part of a complex interplay of the other quantity-regulating factors discussed before: degree of stress and syllable structure.

7.5.1.3 Vowel shortening in unstressed syllables: BUT-ABOUT, LEEK-GARLIC

Unstressed vowel reduction was already under way in Old English (see 6.5.4). Recall that 'reduction' involves both loss of distinctive height and backness specifications, and loss of length – fully reduced vowels are short/lax by definition. In OE and ME unstressed syllables are typically inflectional, or the second syllables in monomorphemic words. Lack of stress is associated also with morphological and syntactic specification: verbal and adverbial prefixes were always unstressed; the prefixes *ge-*, *be-*, *for-* were always unstressed; and prepositions, conjunctions, pronouns and auxiliaries, especially if they were monosyllabic, would also be weakly stressed. Some notable historical shortenings attributed to the weak prosodic position of the lexical item are shown in (11).

(11) Vowel shortening in weakly stressed words:

OE	**ME**	**Gloss**
ǣfre [æːvər]	[ɛvər]	'ever'
būtan [buːtən]	[bʊt(ən)]	'but'
(on)būfan [əbuːvən]	[əbʊv(ən)]	'above'
mōste [moːstə]	[mɔst(ə)] ~ [mʊst(ə)]	'may, must'
tōdæġ [toːdæj]	[tədæj]	'today'
ūs [uːs]	[ʊs/əs]	'us' 💻

The shortening is untestable for (late) OE. However, had the input long forms not been shortened in ME prior to the vowel shift, the PDE forms would be *[iːvər] for 'ever', *[əbaʊv] for 'above', *[tuːdej] for 'today' and *[aʊs] for 'us' – the way that the stressed vowel in the OE disyllabic adverb *onbūtan* [əbuːtən] 'about' developed.

Vowel shortening can also occur in the unstressed parts of compounds. There is good evidence that already in OE compounding preserved primary stress on the initial element, while the second element would have a lower degree of prominence (see 9.4.1). If the semantic link between the original components of the compound and the end product became obscured, that is, if the compound was lexicalised, original long vowels were subject to shortening. Lexicalisation accompanied by vowel reduction is particularly common in the onomastic data, but it is also found in ordinary nominal compounds. 💻

(12) Vowel shortening in historical compounds:

OE	**ME**	**Gloss**
dæġes ēage	dayesye	'day's eye, dais**y**'
scīrġerēfa	scherive	'shire reeve, sher**i**ff'
gār-lēac	garlic(e)	'spear-leek, garl**i**c'
upp-tūn	Upetone	'higher-town', Upt**o**n
grāf-hām	Grafham	'grove-home', Graffh**a**m (Sussex)
swīn-dūn	Swindone	'pig-down', Swind**o**n (Staff.)

For more on vowel reduction in unstressed syllables see 7.6. Now we turn to another set of quantitative changes in the history of English: lengthenings.

7.5.2 Lengthenings: GAME-GAMMON, GRAZE-GRASS

Throughout the history of English stressed syllables have behaved in line with the universal tendency towards co-occurrence of stress and weight. The hierarchy of weight: CV < CVC < CVV < CVVC, where CV is lightest and CVVC heaviest, is confirmed by the changes we have already examined. The lengthening of final vowels in stressed monosyllabic words in North-West Germanic, whereby the final vowels of lexical CV monosyllables became uniformly CVV: Goth. *nu*, OE *nū* 'now', Goth. *swa*, OE *swā* 'so', was covered in 3.4.4 This process is the inverse of the reduction of final vowels in unstressed syllables: having a long vowel in a *stressed* monosyllabic word increases the word's perceptual salience. The constraint on final vowels in lexical monosyllables is a feature of PDE too. It excludes stressed CV monosyllabic words: *buy* [baj], *low* [loʊ], *see* [siː], *rue* [ruː] are well-formed, but *bi* *[bɪ], *lo* *[lɔ], *se* *[sɛ], *ru* *[rʊ] are not. The prosodic constraint on the *minimal word* for content words in English is therefore defined as either (C)VC, as in *sit*, *it*, *cup*, *up*, or (C)VV, as in *sigh*, *eye*, *row*, *owe*.

The lengthening of final vowels in stressed monosyllables is the only quantitative process in the history of English which has been carried through systematically. All other processes have the effect of increasing the predictability of vowel quantity in PDE, but they apply selectively to subsets of the original long or short vowels, depending on their position in the word and their quality, more specifically on their height. We saw in 6.4 that the results of pre-cluster lengthening were constrained by both the nature of the vowel and the nature of the coda, and a word-level -VCCC- sequence blocked lengthening, thus *child* but *cildren*, *hound* but *hundred*. We now turn to another lengthening whose results are also variable depending on the type of vowel and the prosodic structure of the entire word.

7.5.2.1 ME open-syllable lengthening

The process known as open-syllable lengthening in ME is illustrated in (13).[20]

(13) Middle English open-syllable lengthening (non-high vowels)

OE	ME	Gloss
talu [tɑlə]	tal(e) [taːl(ə)]	'tale'
nosu [nɔzə]	nos(e) [nɔːz(ə)]	'nose'
medu [mɛdə]	med(e) [mɛːd(ə)]	'mead'

Here are the main descriptive facts: roughly between the end of the twelfth century and the end of the fourteenth century the stressed short mid and low vowels in open syllables were lengthened in disyllabic words when only one consonant intervened between the first and the second syllable of the word. The lengthened [ɛ] merged with [ɛː] < OE [æː] or [æə] (see 7.3.2), the lengthened [ɔ] merged with [ɔː], the reflex of OE [ɒː] in the non-Northern dialects. The lengthened [ɑ] in the Southern dialects, or OE [æ], emerged as [aː], which fills the low-vowel slot in the long-vowel set vacated by the raising of OE [ɒː] (see 7.3.2).

The lengthening was very inconsistent with high vowels, which are inherently shorter in duration. Some frequently cited examples are given in (14).

(14) Middle English open-syllable lengthening (high vowels):

OE	ME	Gloss
wicu [wɪkə]	[weːk(ə)]	'week'
yfel [ʏvəl]	[eːvɪl]	'evil'
wudu [wʊdə]	[woːd(ə)]	'wood'

High-vowel lengthening is chiefly Northern, and its results in PDE are very limited, so that we find OE *wicu* > PDE *week*, but OE *hype* > PDE *hip*, OE *dile* ~ *dili* ~ *dyle*, PDE *dill*; OE *wudu* > PDE *wood*, but OE *cuman* –> PDE *come*, OE *hulu* > PDE *hull*.

The subset in (14) is of considerable interest nevertheless, because its results show the lengthened short vowels merging *not* with the high vowels [iː] and [uː] but with the upper mid vowels [eː] and [oː]. Paired with the reverse development, the sporadic shortening of [eː] and [oː] resulting in (lower) high [ɪ] and [ʊ] (OE *wēoc(e)* > ME *week(e)* ~ *wik(e)* 'wick', OE *mōnaþ*, ME *mon(e)th(e)* 'month', OE *flōd* > ME *fludmarke* 'high-water mark' (1291), the qualitative change of the vowels in (14) is a

[20] For a complete list of OE lexical items eligible for open-syllable lengthening surviving in PDE, the results of the lengthening and an account of its causes see Minkova (1982).

strong argument in favour of positing a pan-chronic English distinction of height for the long and short vowels, supporting the reconstruction shown in Figure 6.2.

A precise dating of the lengthening is impossible to establish because of inconsistent spellings, dialectal differences, possible coarticulatory effects and lexical diffusion. It is generally accepted that the lengthening started earlier in the Northern dialects (Luick 1964: §§391–6; Jordan 1974: 47–8). Thirteenth-century poets rely predominantly on self-rhymes, but in the late thirteenth-century Northern *Cursor Mundi* we find rhymes indicating length such as *name*: *blame* (OE *nama*, OFr *blā(s)me*), *fare*: *mare* (OE *faru* 'journey, fare', OE *māra* 'more'). The southward spread of the change in the first half of the fourteenth century is not fully documented, but pairings such as *blame*: *name*, *trone*: *anon* (AN *tron(e)* 'throne', OE *on ān* 'anon'), *before*: *sore* (OE *beforan* 'before', OE *sār* 'sore') are found in *The King of Tars*. The chronological beginning and end points of the change are thus fuzzy and fall roughly between the end of the twelfth and the end of the fourteenth century, allowing for lexical idiosyncrasies.

The very name of the process, *open-syllable lengthening*, seems to define a prerequisite for its operation: in an onset-maximal syllabification one and only one consonant can intervene between the short stressed vowel and the second syllable peak: (C)V.**C**V-. In any weight hierarchy, input (C)V- syllables are at the bottom of the scale; only open syllables whose peak is filled by a syllabic sonorant (r̩, l̩, m̩, n̩) could be lighter, but in English such syllables are, and have always been, stressless. Cross-linguistically, vowels tend to be longer in open syllables than in closed syllables, everything else being equal (Maddieson 1985: 213–14). Given the universal tendency of co-occurrence of weight and stress, the vowels in the first syllables in, for example, OE *no.su* [nɔ-] 'nose', *me.du* [mɛ-] 'mead' would be likely to have longer realisations, where vowel duration goes hand-in-hand with the extra prominence required for stress. The lengthening must have started as allophonic. To illustrate: the first syllable in early ME *nose* would be [nɔzə] ~ [nɔˑzə] ~ [nɔˑz] ~ [nɔːzə] ~ [nɔːz] (where the symbol ˑ is the IPA diacritic for half-long). Indeed, there are good arguments that the short-long allophony for the low vowel [ɑ] ~ [ɑˑ] ~ [aˑ] was already in place in late West Saxon (Hogg 1996).

Important as it is, the occurrence of a short vowel in an open stressed syllable is not a sufficient condition for the operation of the lengthening. The input for the lengthening has to be an original disyllabic base. Occasionally, the disyllabic base is provided by an inflected form, as OE *stæf* (nom. sg.), *stæfe* (dat. sg.), *stafas* (nom. pl.) 'staff, letter, stave', *hwæl*

- *hwæle(s)* 'whale'. The restriction of the input to disyllables indicates that the process requires reference to a prosodic domain larger than the individual syllable – it is a foot-based phenomenon (Minkova 1982, 1985). However, the most interesting aspect of open-syllable lengthening in Middle English, which makes English different from other Germanic languages where similar processes are observed, is the strong correlation between the type of input and the survival of the lengthening. A database including all OE and ON lexical items eligible for lengthening of the mid and low vowels, ((C)VCV(C)) words, shows a striking imbalance of the results in favour of lengthened forms that also become monosyllables by word-final schwa loss. In 90.5 per cent (220 out of 243) of the OE input forms which become monosyllables due to schwa loss – the *tale, nose, mead* type – the long vowel is stabilised and survives in PDE (see 7.5.3 for the orthographic consequences of this correlation). On the other hand, only 15.2 per cent (22 out of 126) OE disyllabic forms which remain disyllabic in ME and PDE – the *acorn* (OE *æcern*), *over* (OE *ofer*) type – have lengthened forms. Put differently, 84.8 per cent of the disyllabic input forms with stable second syllables resist the lengthening.[21] This disproportionate preference for lengthening in conjunction with historical weakening and loss of the second syllable provides a strong empirical base for describing the process in compensatory terms: the chances of incrementing the stressed syllable weight are much enhanced by concomitant reduction of the weight of the second syllable.

Additional factors at play are the height of the vowel and the nature of the unstressed syllable. Lengthening of #(C)VCV# words, where the stressed vowel is low and the unstressed syllable is coda-less [-ə] – the *name, tale* type of word – occurs in 95.8 per cent of the cases, while the mid vowels show greater instability. On the other hand, 97.6 per cent of the items in which the second syllable is closed by an obstruent – the type represented by OE *ganot*, PDE *gannet*, ***haddock***, ***radish*** – retain the short vowel. Unstressed syllables with potentially variable sonorant peaks r̩ ~ ər (*acre*), l̩ ~ əl (*navel*), m̩ ~ əm (*besom*) and n̩ ~ ən (*open*) are significantly more likely to undergo lengthening: nearly one-quarter of the eligible items (39 out of 166) do in fact show lengthened forms in PDE (see Bermúdez-Otero 1998, who extends the compensatory account to these cases).

When the number of syllables in the inflectional paradigm varied: *stæf-stæfe*, and in cases of syncope which closes the initially open syllable: *hefen-hefnes* 'heaven', note the <-ea-> spelling in PDE, one can

[21] See Minkova (1982). The numbers cited here are very slightly modified in Kim (1993).

expect variable results. In most cases only one of the forms survived, though it is still easy to find PDE pairs showing the early variability of the lengthening.

(15) Variable open-syllable lengthening results in mono- and disyllables:

OE	**ME**	**Gloss**	**OE**	**ME**	**Gloss**
gamen	gam(e)	'game'	gamen	gamen	'gammon'
hræþe	rað(e)	'rathe'	hraþor	raþer(e)	'rather'
læt(e)	lat(e)	'late'	lator	later(e)	'latter'
sceadu	shad(e)	'shade'	scead(u)we	shadew(e)	'shadow'
blæc	blak	'black'	blæce	blak(e)	Blake
dæl	dal/del	'dell'	dalu (pl.)	dale	'dale'
græs	gras	'grass'	grasian	grase	'graze'
stæf	staf	'staff'	stæfe	stav(e)(s)	'stave'

The addition of consonant-initial derivational suffixes or second elements of compounds can preserve the short vowel: OE *þrote*, PDE 'thr**oa**t', but late ME *throtel* < *throt(e)* + *-le* suffix, 'thr**o**ttle' with the short/shortened vowel; OE *stelan* PDE 'st**ea**l', but ME *stel* + *-th* suffix 'st**ea**lth'; similarly OE *nosu* 'n**o**se', but *nose* + *þyrl* 'hole' > 'n**o**stril'; early ME *dal(e)* 'd**a**le', but *D**a**lwood* (East Devon); compare *St**a**ffield*, Cumberland (< *staf-* 'boundary mark') with *St**a**veley* Derbyshire (< ME *stave-ley* 'wood where staves were got') (Ekwall 1960: 435, 440). Absence of stress can also affect the lengthening; compare auxiliary *have* vs *behave*, *are* vs *care*.[22]

A considerable body of scholarship on ME open-syllable lengthening reveals further complexities. The interested reader should consult Lass (1985, 1992a); Liberman (1992b); Kim (1993); Ritt (1994); Fulk (1998); Bermúdez-Otero (1998); Lahiri and Fikkert (1999); Murray (2000); and Page (2006, 2012), who addresses all previous scholarship, treats ME open-syllable lengthening as compensatory, and proposes an account based on listener-based hypo-correction. Along with the shortenings discussed in 7.5.1.1 and 7.5.1.2, open-syllable lengthening is a central anchor for teleologically oriented accounts of the quantitative changes in the history of English, addressed in all of these studies, a fertile research area.

[22] The lengthened, also so-called 'strong' forms of the auxiliaries, are used in verse until much later. In EModE we find such rhymes as *spare* : *are* (Donne), *have* : *grave* (Herbert), *were* : *bear* (Shakespeare), examples from Barber (1997: 129), and Dryden rhymes *are* : *pair*.

7.5.3 Orthography and quantitative changes

As noted in the opening of 7.5, the quantitative changes of the *stressed* vowels (see 7.5.1, 7.5.2) have made the distribution of vowel length transparent in many environments today. With some exceptions, for example before /ʃ/, vowel quantity remains predictably contrastive in PDE only in #(C)VC#: #(C)VVC# non-function words: *bin-bean, cot-coat, mat-mate, fit-feet, fuss-fuse*, SSBE *bud-bird.* Even in this relatively limited lexical scope of unpredictable vowel quantity, the spelling of a word can be a fairly solid clue as to how a vowel should be classified.

The historical association between vowel shortness and the presence of two consonants after the vowel goes all the way to West Germanic gemination which occurred *only* after short vowels, as in OE *tellan* 'to tell', *settan* 'to set', *cynn* 'kin' (see 3.4.5). In OE (see 7.5.1), long vowels followed by geminates could be shortened: early OE *fǣtt* 'fat', ME *fat*; also the past tense forms of weak verbs with a dental geminate: *bīten-bitt(e)-bit* 'bite-bit', *mēten-mett(e)-met* 'meet-met', *slīden-slidd(e)-slid* 'slide-slid' (7.5.1.1). Pre-consonantal shortening strengthened the association between shortness of the vowel and two consonants to the right of it. Already in OE orthographic doubling of consonants appears, albeit as a 'not wholly consistent indicator of a preceding short vowel' (Hogg 1992a: §2.78, n. 1). A much more systematic recognition of the usefulness of double-consonant spellings to mark short vowels goes back to the last decades of the twelfth century, when the monk Orm became the first spelling reformer in the history of English. In his autograph versified homilies covering special calendar days, known as *The Ormulum*, he devised a system of marking a short vowel in a closed syllable by doubling the consonant after it. The first lines of Orm's *Preface* illustrate his practice:

> Þiss boc iss nemmnedd Orrmulum
> forrþi þatt Orrm itt wrohhte
> 'this book is named *Ormulum*
> because Orm created it' (*Preface*, ll.1–2)

This system is a good diagnostic of length: the double consonants in *þiss* 'this' ***nemm**.nedd* 'named', ***wrohh**.te* 'created, wrought' indicate that the preceding vowel is short; *boc* 'book' has a long vowel, and the second syllable of Orr.**mu**.lum is open, so the length of the vowel is ambiguous. Although there is no direct continuation between the Ormian system and PDE spelling, the phonological changes associated with pre-consonantal vowel shortening feed into an important orthographic convention in PDE: within the paradigm of a single word, the orthographic doubling of consonants is expected only after short vowels, as in PDE <spite-spiting> but <spit-spitting>, <coat-coating> but <cut-cutting>, <brave-braved> but <rev-revved>. In monosyllables the letters <f, l, s, z> are usually doubled after short vowels.

Orthographic geminates can also be associated with specific properties: while <c> in PDE can be both [s] and [k] (*city-college*), double-c <-cc-> never stands for [s]; it can only represent [k] (*accord, hiccup*), [ks] (*success, vaccine*), or [tʃ] in Italian loans (*capriccio, fettuccine*). Double-s, <ss>, shows restrictions on voicing: a single <s> can represent both [s] and [z]: (*mouse-rise*), while <-ss> is associated with voicelessness, a pattern mirroring the behaviour of OE fricatives (see 4.4), thus *lesser, bliss, grass.* This pattern carries over into the sound-spelling correspondences of loanwords in which [s] is palatalised to [ʃ] as in *mission, session*, making the spellings of *Aussie, scissors, dessert, hussar, Missouri, possess* – this is an exhaustive list of the items where <ss> stands for [z] – distinct oddities.

Yet another orthographic convention which mirrors phonological change is the use of the <-e> to mark vowel length, the so-called 'discontinuous' V-e (Lass 1992a: 38), a direct link between open-syllable lengthening and PDE spelling conventions. Apart from affecting vowel quantity and therefore subsequent quality through the long vowel shift (see 8.2.2), as in *game* vs *gammon*, *Blake* vs *black*, open-syllable lengthening paved the way for the 'silent *-e*' convention of English spelling. The logic of marking long vowels followed by a single consonant with a final *-e* is evident: if /-VCə/, orthographically <-VCe>, produces /-VVCØ/, the letter sequence <-VCe> can be adopted for the representation of long vowels; <-Ce> becomes a letter sequence associated both with historically lengthened vowels and *any* long vowel, of whatever origin.

A note on the chronological ordering of the <-Ce> spellings: open-syllable lengthening occurred earlier in the Northern dialects (see 7.5.2.1); not surprisingly, the special diacritical use of <-Ce> is also earlier in the North, so that the base forms of words such as OE *wīf* 'wife', OE *stān* 'stone', OE *ǣr* 'ere', OE *þǣr* 'there' start appearing with <-e> (Smith 1994: 436). The practice of adding 'inorganic' <-e>'s spread southwards in late ME, and it is part of the EModE spelling conventions. In his widely used and influential *Elementarie* (1582), the spelling reformer Mulcaster advocated the use of <-e> as a marker of length. Today<-Ce> is a fairly solid indication of length, hence the intuitions that written <sklipe/sklype>, <spone>, <dake>, <bume> correspond to [sklaip], [spoʊn], [deik], [bjuːm].[23] Combined with the

[23] One notable exception is the <-ve> sequence, which follows both long (*drive, save*)

two-vowel spellings (see 7.2), the representation of etymological long vowels in PDE is unproblematic. The qualification 'etymological' is needed to exclude cases of shortened long vowels not picked up by the spelling, as in *read*, pr. t. - *read* past t., *breath-breadth*, *mouth-Monmouth*. Conversely, the expectation for a <(C)VC(C)> sequence is that the vowel in such a word is short: *pit*, *pet*, *pat*, *pot*, *put*; this makes pronunciations of orthographic *troth*, *Job* with [oʊ] striking and unexpected. The loanword pattern of trisyllabic shortening (*divine-divinity*, *cone-conical*) is also predictive in terms of spelling: <skl**i**pical, sp**o**nity> are more likely to have short vowels. Further discrepancies are addressed in the next chapter, but barring those, the historical phonological information covered here provides *some* justification for vowel quality marking, and *good* justification for vowel quantity marking in PDE spelling.

7.6 Reduction and loss of unstressed vowels in ME

Typically, in languages distinguishing stressed and unstressed syllables, the inventory of the vowels that can appear in unstressed syllables is much smaller than that of the vowels in stressed syllables. The phonetic basis for the reduced vowel inventory in unstressed position is well studied: vowels in such positions are very short; this makes the maintenance of F1 and F2 difficult and characteristically results in the neutralisation of contrasts. In PDE the inventory of vowels occurring in stressless syllables is severely constrained: only [ə, ɪ,] come close to being contrastive in that position. All other realisations of the peaks in unstressed syllables alternate with [ə]. How far back does this situation go?

The elimination of contrast is a function of lack of stress. In early Germanic the position of the stress in the word was fixed on the first syllable of the root (see 3.4.3), but unstressed syllables could still have long or short vowels. During the next chronological stage, early OE, the vowels in unaccented syllables underwent progressive reduction accompanied by loss of vowel length distinctions. In 6.5.4 we listed the unstressed vowels found in early OE, repeated here as (16).

(16) The unstressed vowels of early OE (pre-c. 700):

Front	Example	Back	Example
/i/	*cyning* 'king'	/u/	*duru* 'door'
/æ/	*endæþ* 'ends'	/ɑ/	*nefa* 'nephew'

and short vowels (*live*, *breve*, *above*), though recently the tendency is to dispense with the <e-> after short vowels: *rev* (1851), *derv* (1948), *marv* (1964), *improv* (1979), *chav* (1998).

This inventory is subject to further reduction. Orthographic interchangeability of the unstressed vowels in late OE suggests that the spoken realisation of the unstressed vowels converged to a neutral unstressed vowel, some kind of schwa [ə]. The most common representation of the unstressed vowels was <e>, which was particularly common in the spelling of inflections. In Ælfric's *Lives of Saints* (c. 1000), for example, one finds <-e> for <-a>, <-es> for <-as>, <-en> for <-an, -on> and inverted spellings of <-a> for <-e>. Word-medially, vowel reduction is attested throughout OE in the widespread syncope and epenthesis of word-internal <-e->, especially when the etymological unstressed vowel is next to a sonorant, thus <myc(e)le> 'much', <heof(e)nes> 'of heaven', <feaxnæd(e)l> 'hairpin'. In the next two hundred years <-e> was established as the default spelling for post-tonic final vowels in monomorphemic words too: <bane> 'killer' (OE <bana>), <deme> 'judge' (OE <dema>), <nose> (OE <nosu>).

Reduction and loss of vowels in final unstressed syllables proceeded unevenly in ME. Among the system-internal factors instrumental in the rate of reduction and ultimately apocope, are the nature of the unstressed syllable: part of the stem, inflectional or derivational; the syntactic specification of the word: content or function word; the phonotactic interactions between the unstressed vowel and adjacent segments, both within the same word and across a word boundary in cases of cliticisation.

Another important aspect of the process is the strong presence of bilingual English–Old Norse speakers in the transitional period between OE and ME. Language-contact situations typically favour simplification of the morphological system: the use of two Germanic languages side by side would have created communication pressures to ignore the language-specific inflections and concentrate on the semantics of the stem. Although not actually testable, this language-contact factor must be recognised in any attempt to track the course of inflectional reduction and loss in ME.

In ME the grammatical distinctions of case, gender and in some instances number for nouns and adjectives, were no longer signalled by different inflections; homophonous, or nearly homophonous inflections were used for more than one function. Abstracting from a much more complex system, (17) illustrates the treatment of the 'ideal' Classical OE inflections, shown in their orthographic forms, by the end of ME.

(17) Homophony of OE inflections in ME:

Expected (Classical OE)	**Late ME**
<-**e**> for dat. sg. (masc., fem., neuter)	<-e>[-(ə)]
<-**a**> for gen. pl. (masc., fem., neuter)	<-e>[-(ə)]
<-**u**> for nom. acc. sg. (fem., neuter)	<-e>[-(ə)]
<-**es**> for gen. sg. (masc., neuter)	<-es>[-(ə)s]
<-**as**> for nom. acc. pl. (masc.)	<-es>[-(ə)s]
<-**an**> for weak nominal declensions	<-en>[-(ə)n]
<-**um**> for dat. pl. (all nouns)	<-en>[-(ə)n]
<-**on**> for pret. ind. pl.	<-en>[-(ə)n]
<-**aþ**> for pres. indic. imp. pl.	<-eth>[-(ə)θ]
<-**od**> for past part. (weak verb)	<-ed> [-(ə)d]

A look at the second column in (17) makes it obvious that the distinctive features of the vowels in the OE inflections have been neutralised. The set of inflections is reduced to [-(ə)], [-(ə)s], [-ən], [-(ə)θ], [-(ə)d]. Along with the loss of phonological distinctiveness, the grammatical distinctiveness of the inherited inflections was in jeopardy.

The presence or absence of a coda in the unstressed syllable is important. A bare inflectional schwa is least stable: the <-e>, <a>, <u> in the first three rows in (17) were joined by <-**e**> in the verb paradigms, marking pres. ind. sg., 1st pers., or subj. pres. sg, all persons, or subj. pret. sg, all persons, or 1st and 3rd pers. sg. pret. indic. of weak verbs, **or** 2nd pers. pret. ind. of strong verbs. The situation was unsustainable: reliance on [-ə] as a grammatical marker was no longer a viable option; phonological and morphological change reinforced each other, triggering further changes in the grammatical system: increased use of prepositions and word-order changes. In late ME, the functions of the final schwa in native lexical items were considerably reduced: if not in elision environment (see below) or in trisyllabic words, <-e> continued to be written and possibly variably realised, in the dat. sg. of nouns, the plural of adjectives and 1st pers. sg. of verbs, and as adverbial markers.[24]

An independent factor, which serves to undermine further the shaky status of final unstressed vowels, is the variable realisation of [-ə] in hiatus with another vowel (earlier) or before an initial [h-] (later): the <-e> is occasionally dropped/elided already in OE, thus <*wene ic*> 'I hope' ~ <*wen ic*>, <*sæġde ic*> 'I said' ~ *sæġd ic* (Luick 1964: §452).

[24] One regional detail concerning the orthographic representation of unstressed vowels is the use of <i> or <y> in final (closed) unstressed syllables in ME. John Barbour's *The Bruce*, a Northern poem composed in 1375 but copied later (1487 and 1489), has *hundis* 'dogs', *lordis* 'lords', *fayis* 'foes', *askyt* 'asked', *lufit* 'loved', *nakit* 'naked', *evir* 'ever', *mekill* 'much', *othir* 'other', and so on.

Elision of an unstressed vowel before another vowel in speech is a well-attested cross-linguistic phenomenon. In principle, the evidence for elision can be orthographic or based on verse. OE verse tends to be rather conservative and it is not a good testing ground for elision (see 10.2.1), but the earliest ME texts, both prose (*The Peterborough Chronicle*) and syllable-counting verse (*The Ormulum*, *The Owl and the Nightingale*), provide ample evidence for the instability of [-ə] in elision environments. In all of ME verse, elision of *-e* before another vowel or a weak [h-] is the 'rule', as the following examples show.

(18) Elision of -e before another vowel or a weak [h-] in ME verse:
Ic em nu alder þen***e*** **i**c wes, a wintre ent a lare *Poema Morale* 1
Þeȝȝ wurrdenn swiþ***e*** **o**ffdredde *Ormulum* 3343
vor riȝte niþ***e*** & for ful***e*** **o**nde *O&N* 1096
To the clep***e*** **I**, thow goddess***e*** **o**f torment *Troilus* I, 8
That Lov***e*** **h**em bryng***e*** **i**n hevene to solas *Troilus* I, 31

The syntactic specification of a word is crucially related to its prosodic prominence; function words and pronouns are weakly stressed and the instability of the final vowels in them is expected. In Chaucer <-e>'s in such words are 'silent' even before consonants:

(19) Apocope of <-e> in words of low prosodic prominence:
That by his fortune hath hir**e** faire ywonne *KT* 2659
Upon this**e** steedes, that weren grete and white *KT* 2892

The overall syllabic structure of a word is also of consequence. Final schwa loss occurs in trisyllabic words. The earliest evidence for that loss is orthographic: in the *Peterborough Chronicle* (1132–54), weak preterites occur regularly without <-e>: *macod he* 'made he', *henged up*, 'hanged/hung up', *bebyred him* 'buried them'. The metrical evidence for loss in words such as *goddess(e)*, *maner(e)*, *answer(e)*, *wepyng(e)*, *almes(se)*, *countes(se)*, *hostes(se)*, *lover(e)*, and so on is also solid.

(20) Apocope of <-e> in trisyllabic words:
To the clep***e*** **I**, thow goddess***e*** **o**f tormént *Troilus* I, 8
Lest it were wist on any maner***e*** syde *Troilus* I, 321
And of som goodly answer***e*** yow purcháce *Troilus* II, 1125
He somwhat is fro wepyng***e*** now withdrawe *Troilus* IV, 886

The loss of schwa in word-final position, both inflectional and stem-final, was more advanced in the Northern dialect areas, where by the middle of the fourteenth century its realisation would have been an archaism. In the Southern dialects the apocope must have occurred somewhat later. Chaucer, whose pronunciation as reconstructed from verse shows other conservative features, often relies on final schwa for metrical purposes. By the beginning of the fifteenth century consistent pronunciation of schwa in word-final position was becoming a marker of 'foreignness', as it is today. For a fifteenth-century speaker of English, OE loans such as *Noah*, *manna*, *Messiah*, *charta*, *podagra*, *Ursa* and later loans such as *aroma* (1220), *(Ave) Maria* (1225), *hyena* (1340), *contra* (1362), *alpha* (1382), *chimera* (1382), *cholera* (1382), *asthma* (1398), *aura* (1398), *mania* (1398), *omega* (1398), *delta* (1400), *kappa* (1400), *uvula* (1400), *santa* (1450) would have been recognisable as non-native by the presence of [-ə]. In PDE this can still be the case for rhotic speakers, for whom the unstressed syllables of *fauna* (1771), *koala* (1808), *retsina* (1920), *bazooka* (1935) carry the mark of foreignness.[25]

Final schwa loss proceeded gradually across the lexicon, occurring first in the environments shown in (18)–(20). It was probably the norm in the spoken language in all dialects by c. 1450. With the exception of [-i] in the affix <-y> (> OE *-iġ*), all uncovered vowels in final unstressed syllables in native words were dropped.

Parallel to schwa apocope in open final syllables was the reduction and eventual syncope of schwa in the inflectional suffixes: <-en, -es, -eth, -ed>. The process was blocked in stems whose final consonants would create phonotactic incompatibilities: [-s, -z, -ʃ, -ʒ, -tʃ, -dʒ] for the <-es> suffix and [t, d] for the <-ed> suffix; this gives rise to the PDE patterns *rates* vs *aces*, *faked* vs *lauded* – recall the discussion of the allomorphy of the morpheme /-d/, spelled <-ed> in 4.4.

Unlike coda-less final unstressed syllables, where *all* final vowels were subject to pre-1400 apocope, including OFr and AN words (*cause*, *cure*, *noise*, *rule*, *obey*), unstressed vowels in closed syllables were syncopated only in inflectional endings, not in syllables which are part of the stem: so *lettuce*, *foetus*, *common*, *orchid*, *mattress*, *tepid* are disyllabic. The spread of inflectional syncope is uneven across the various word classes, and a full coverage of the process in ME is still outstanding. In PDE the verb and noun inflections, if surviving, show phonotactically driven allomorphy, while superlative *-(e)st*, which used to be syncopated, is now restored to [-əst/-ɪst].

With respect to the weak verbal preterite <-ed>, there is ME verse evidence that the /-əd/ realisation is least favoured in vowel-final stems, thus *di.en* 'die', p.t. *dey.d*, *plei.en* 'play', p.t. *pley.d*. This is a predictable consequence of avoidance of hiatus – an optimal syllable will have

[25] For non-rhotic speakers final schwa is associated with the spelling <-er> (see 5.2.4), so that the author of this book has been addressed in writing by SSBE speakers as both <*Donker*> and as <*Minkover*>.

a filled onset. The next most frequent attestation of /-əd/ syncope occurs in -VR stems (*callen*, *dwellen*, *flouren*) – a -VRd coda would be well tolerated in terms of the sonority profile of the cluster since ideally sonority rises in onsets and falls in codas. Most resistant to syncope are verb stems ending in consonant clusters (*thanken*, *busken*, *trompen*) and stops (*clepen*, *knokken*). This type of loss was very gradual: syncope can be traced in Northern texts already in the thirteenth century, yet syllabic inflections in environments that would support syncope can be found until the eighteenth century.

The positioning of a lexical item within a larger prosodic domain should also be considered. In the case of final *-e*, monosyllabic adjectives preceding initially stressed nouns have been shown to hang on to the [-ə] much longer than disyllabic adjectives in the same frame, as in *a clene maydyn*, *a riche feste* vs *a wrongful thing*.[26] The preservation of the extra syllable in that frame is a matter of prosodic well-formedness: apocope would create a stress-clash, and at least for some time towards the end of ME, this was a factor maintaining the otherwise obsolete inflectional syllable. Similarly in closed unstressed syllables, there is evidence that the <-ed> of the past participle remained syllabic longer than in the preterite, most likely due to its frequent adjectival use where a syllabic suffix <-ed> acts as a prosodic buffer between an initially stressed noun and the preceding adjective. In early Modern English syllabic <-ed> was used in adjectival participles which have a non-syllabic suffix in PDE.

(21) Prosodic preservation of syllabic <-ed> in adjectival participles:[27]
With fix***ed*** Anchor in his skaly rind 206
Invests the Sea, and wish***ed*** Morn delayes 208
And leave a sing***ed*** bottom all involv'd 236
Of that inflam***ed*** Sea he stood, and call'd 300
Thus drooping, or with link***ed*** Thunderbolts 328

Indeed, the pattern persists: *aged*, *beloved*, *blessed*, *crabbed*, *crooked*, *cursed*, *learned* have different pronunciations for the preterite and the adjectival participle in PDE.

Unstressed vowels appear also in prefixes. By far the most frequent fully unstressed OE prefix was *ġe-* [jə-], used both in the verbal system and as a nominal and adjectival prefix. Its ME continuation is <i->, probably [ɪ-/ə], increasingly replaced by zero, though deliberate archaising continues in EModE, especially with Spenser: *yclad*, *ytold*, *yglanced*. OE

[26] Minkova (1991: 171–91).

[27] All examples are from Book One of Milton's *Paradise Lost*.

ġenoh > *ME inough* 'enough' is an exception to the general loss of the prefix, and so are some *a-* reflexes of OE *ġe-* in *alike*, *along*, *aware*. OE *and-/on-/a-* survives as [ə-] in *answer*, *along* < OE *and-swaru*, *and-lang*. Here belong also adjectives from prepositional *on* + a nominal base: *abed*, *afield*, *ashore*, *aglow*, *athrob*, *asleep*, *aghast*, *afloat*, *aslant*, and so on. In this connection it is interesting to observe the phenomenon of *a-prefixing* in PDE, an archaic feature surviving in East Anglia, Welsh English, South-East of England, South-West of England, Southeastern AmE, Ozark English, Appalachian English, Earlier AAVE, Newfoundland English and Cameroon English (Kortmann and Szmrecsanyi 2004: 1151–2). In those varieties there is a tendency to retain a schwa initial syllable, spelled <a->, the historically reduced reflex of the preposition *on* before *-ing* forms (*I was a-minding my business*). The occurrence of *a-* is a morphological relic, but its realisation is tightly constrained by phonological conditions: it can only be used before an initially stressed *-ing* form, making **I was a-relying on them* ungrammatical and the schwa cannot be used before a vowel-initial verb, excluding **a-opening*, **a-eating* (Wolfram 1976; Wolfram and Schilling-Estes 2006: 77, 334). This pattern provides a good parallel to the case of final *-e* preservation in specific prosodic frames in late ME discussed above (*a clene maydyn*), and to the early schwa dropping in hiatus. Many more instances of interplay between phonological reduction, rhythmic alternation and morphological form in the history of English are discussed in Schlüter (2005).

8 Vowel quality and quantity in Early Modern English and later

MOTH-MOTHER, DULL-BULL, LOST-POST, FEAR-BEAR, HERE-THERE, MOOD-STOOD-BLOOD, DEAD-BEAD

8.1 Information glut. New sources of phonological reconstruction

The closer we get to PDE, the more daunting the task of describing any aspect of the history of the language becomes. *All* of the surviving OE manuscripts have been digitised and they are accessible in searchable form from the OEC. For ME, the ratio of digitised to surviving materials is in favour of the latter, but the very extensive samples included in the MED, LAEME and LALME give us some confidence that the generalisations we come up with have some basis in the historical reality. Tracing the development of the language after the sixteenth century is both easier and more challenging in view of the exponential growth of available information. In addition to the analysis of written sources, spelling deviations and rhyming practice, the student of EModE phonology is both assisted and hampered by 'metalinguistic' evidence: numerous contemporary commentaries and manuals on spelling and pronunciation, homophone lists, puns, informal private letters, court transcripts and literary references, all of which can be both illuminating and contradictory.

The seeds of a fixed spelling system are recognisable already in late ME, and during the fifteenth century documents written in London show clear signs of orthographic regularisation. Regularisation brings about a separation of spelling and pronunciation. In the early sixteenth century the gap between the visual and the phonetic form of sounds widened. Printing made books available to a broader readership; the ensuing increase in literacy prompted the necessity of explaining the connections between letter and sound, and resulted in many attempts to describe the sounds of English in relation to spelling both for native and foreign learners. Prominent grammarians and literary figures, commonly referred to as *orthoepists* (Gk *ortho* - 'correct' + *-epi* < *epos* 'word'), strove to create a consistent spelling system. Their descriptions are a major source for the study of the sound structure of EModE. The orthoepists were aware of the disjunction between sound and spelling and they were troubled by the inconsistencies of the orthography; writers on matters of pronunciation were also strongly biased in favour of specific socially prestigious pronunciations, which they endorsed. As Richard Mulcaster writes in his famous *Elementarie* (1582):

> it is pretended, that the writing thereof [of English] is meruellous vncertain, and scant to be recouered from extreme confusion, without som change of as great extremitie. I mean therefor so to deall in it, as I maie wipe awaie that opinion of either vncertaintie for confusion, or impossibilitie for direction, that both the naturall English maie haue wherein to test, & the desirous stranger maie haue whereby to learn.
>
> ... letters can expresse *sounds* withall their ioynts & properties, no fuller then the pencill can the form & lineaments of the face, whose praise is not life but likenesse: as the letters yeld not alwaie the same, which *sound* exactlie requireth, but allwaie the nearest, wherwith *custom* is content. (Mulcaster [1582] 1925: 35, 99)

Mulcaster himself had little to say about pronunciation, but the *General Table* in his *Elementarie* lists 7,000 of the most common words in EModE and sets the stage for further attempts at codification. The information that can be extracted from contemporary observations is invaluable; it is also conflicting and controversial. None of the orthoepists had the benefit of the kind of training and knowledge that only became available after the introduction of instrumental phonetics. Many of the early commentators confused sounds with letters and were inclined to conflate pronunciation and spelling. Their philological training was in the Classics, they tended to be pedantic and conservative, and they often tried to adjust their descriptions to fit the norms of Latin pronunciation. Not surprisingly, codification of spelling and pronunciation and the next stage, prescription, take until the second half of the eighteenth century.

Another difficulty in reconstructing EModE comes from the imbalance of information on the variety of English spoken by educated upper-class Londoners and the varieties spoken in other parts of the country. It was the former that became codified and prescribed; the latter is traceable mostly in correspondence, local records, and poetry in a local dialect, though regional pronunciations can be 'borrowed' by the standard, as has happened with *uncouth*, *bury*, *break*, *great*. A comprehensive coverage of regional forms and the mechanism of dialectal transfers is beyond the scope of this book. Constructing a coherent narrative requires that much of the available material has to be kept outside the narrow focus of the emergence of a 'national' language. So, bearing in mind that an all-encompassing coverage of the available records is unrealistic within the limits of a book chapter, or even of a whole book, we will deal with the individual changes selectively, focusing on some more salient features of PDE that can be illuminated historically.[1]

8.2 Qualitative changes

The phonology of Old and Middle English provides numerous examples of the interaction between vowel quality and quantity. Open-syllable lengthening of OE [ɪ] and [ʊ] involved lowering of the vowel: OE *wicu* [wɪkə] > ME [weːk(ə)] 'week', OE *wudu* [wʊdə] > ME [woːd(ə)] 'wood'. The reverse process, shortening of [eː] and [oː] accompanied by raising to [ɪ] and [ʊ] – OE *wēoc(e)* > ME *week(e)* ~ *wik(e)* 'wick', OE *mōste* > ME *moste* ~ *muste* 'must' – also shows the possibility of simultaneous change of quantity and quality of the vowel. This is to be expected in view of the intrinsic durational difference between high and low vowels, but sometimes the variability remains allophonic, and sometimes, as in the cases cited above, the length difference triggers qualitative recategorisation. In EModE the realisation of height and backness continue to show the interaction between vowel quality and vowel quantity.

8.2.1 Short vowels: QUASH-QUACK, WASH-WAX, GOD-EGAD, PUTT-PUT

Section 7.3.1 covered the development of the OE short vowels up to, roughly, late ME. Figure 8.1 shows the necessarily idealised and homogenised five short vowels of late ME and their corresponding PDE reflexes.

Now we turn to the individual histories, starting with the front vowels. The high front non-peripheral /ɪ/ continued unchanged. It is the reflex of OE [ɪ] as in OE *fisc* 'fish'; OE [ʏ] as in OE *cyning* 'king', OE *bysiġ* 'busy'; the raising of <-e(ng)> to <-i(ng)> as in *England* (see 7.3.1). EModE [ɪ] can also be the result of ME shortening of either [iː], as in *fifteen*, *wisdom*, or of [eː], as in *sheriff*, *garlic* (see 7.5.1). Saying that the /ɪ/ 'continued unchanged' is of course a statement only about the stability of the phonemic distinctiveness of the /ɪ/-type vowel in PDE. Like every other phoneme, /ɪ/ has different allophonic realisations depending on the phonetic and prosodic environment; for example, the typical duration of the vowel of KID is twice as long as that of the vowel

[1] A survey of the sources of study in EModE is found in Nevalainen (2006: ch. 2). For the history of standardisation see Nevalainen (2006: ch. 3) and Nevalainen and Tieken-Boon van Ostade (2006).

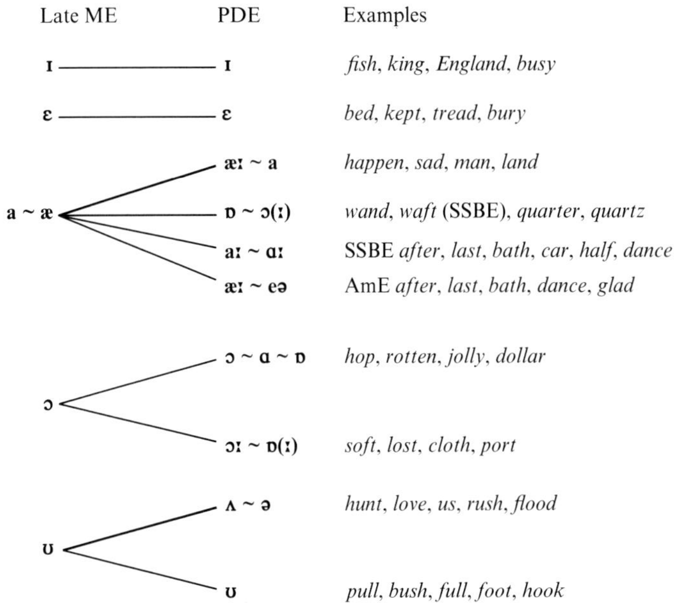

Figure 8.1 The short stressed vowels from Late Middle to Modern English

of KIT (Cruttenden 2008: 96); unstressed [ɪ] is shorter than stressed [ɪ]. Recall also the effect of the nasal coda, the PIN-PEN merger observed in AmE (see 7.3.1). Then, there are regional and social differences not linked to phonotactics. To sample just a few: in different parts of the English-speaking world today the allophonic realisations of [ɪ] can show a tendency towards centralisation and lowering. In North America (Thomas 2001: 16), a centralised [ɨ] is reported for the North and in old-fashioned Southern speech. Centralisation to [ɨ] is a twentieth-century NZE innovation which is on the increase (Trudgill et al. 1998). Lowering of [ɪ] in the direction of [ɛ] is part of the Northern Cities Shift (Labov 1994); it also occurs in California and in Canada. Scottish English also has realisations of /ɪ/ as a lower or central vowel in the direction of [ɛ̈] ~ [ʌ], with the possibility in some varieties that /ɪ/ and /ʌ/ are not distinct (Wells 1982, II: 404). Fronting to [i] and even a glide insertion [iə] is characteristic of the Southeastern states, AAVE and Caribbean English. Fronted [i] is found also in AusE and SAE. Here belongs also the phenomenon of 'HAPPY-TENSING' (Wells 1982, II: 294–319), which refers to the realisation of the second vowel of *happy* as a more peripheral vowel, a compromise between [ɪ] and [iː].

The other short vowel that has remained stable is [ɛ], the continuation of OE [ɛ]: OE *bedd* 'bed', OE *helpan* 'help'. Other sources are the shortened OE [eː] as in OE *cēpte* 'kept'; OE [eə] as in OE *stēopcild* 'stepchild'; OE [æː] as in OE *flǣsc* 'flesh'; OE [æə] as in OE *mǣnte* 'meant'. Among the survivors of the ME Southeastern regional forms of OE [ʏ] (see 7.3.1) are *bury*, *merry*, *left*. AN and OFr <e> also joins the set: *accept*, *debt*, *medal*, *tenor*, *sever*, except that when followed by a nasal, [ɛ̃] is adopted either as [ɛ], as in *defend*, *gentle*, *tense*, or as [æ], as in *example*, *pansy*; this is parallel to the historical variation of [æn] ~ [ɛn] in some very high-frequency native lexical items: *then* (OE *þanne*, *þǫnne*, *þænne*, *þenne*); *when* (OE *hwanne*, *hwǫnne*, *hwenne*, *hwœnne*); *any* (OE *æniġ*, *ęniġ*, *aniġ*, *ani*, *eniġ*); *many* (OE *mæniġ*, *moniġ*, *meniġ*). For the behaviour of [ɛ] + tautosyllabic /r/ see 7.3.1 and 8.3.2.

As with /ɪ/, the historical 'stability' of the short mid front vowel becomes suspect if one looks into the PDE realisations of /ɛ/. A backing to [ʌ] or lowering towards [a] occurs as part of the Northern Cities Shift; it is also reported for the San Francisco Bay Area and Canadian English. Younger RP speakers are also producing more open allophones of [ɛ] (Hawkins and Midgley 2005). A strong tendency for raising of [ɛ], especially in the younger generation, characterises NZE (Trudgill et al. 1998), illustrated by the confusability of, for example, *check-in-counter* ~ *chicken counter*. Raising is also common in the Southern US dialects and in north-eastern Newfoundland (Thomas 2001: 18–19). Another allophone involves the insertion of a diphthongal glide, especially in stressed monosyllables before a voiced coda, so that in popular London *bed*, *leg* can have [-eᶦ-], and in the American South it can be a fully diphthongal vowel, so that *dead* is pronounced [deʲəd] (Thomas: 2001: 18–19).

The two possible outcomes of OE short [æ] in ME were [a] or [æ] (see 7.3.1), hence the 'dual' input for the low vowel in the ME column in Figure 8.1. Recall also that orthographic <a> was subject to regional variation when followed by a nasal, resulting in ME West Midlands forms such as *mon* 'man', *onswere* 'answer'; that difference was levelled out in favour of <-an> in the fifteenth century. In EModE <a>, phonetically [a] ~ [æ], and possibly [ɑ], underwent further phonotactic changes. (1) reproduces the relevant section from Figure 8.1.

(1) Orthographic <a> and its reflexes in PDE:

a ~ æ	æ ~ a	*happen, sad, man, land*
	ɒ ~ ɔ(ː)	*wand, waft* (SSBE), *quarter, quartz*
	aː ~ ɑː	SSBE *after, last, bath, car, half, dance*
	æː ~ eə	AmE *after, last, bath, dance, glad*

The default reflex of ME [a] ~ [æ], highlighted by the heavier connector line, is a continuation of the variable ME pronunciation as in PDE *happen*, *sad*, *man*, *land*. The representation of the sound with <a> in late ME, the merger of the OE [æ] with ON and OFr [a], as well as the continuity of [a] in the modern varieties of Northern English, suggest that the input to EModE is /a/. The evidence for [a] or for a more fronted and raised allophone is mixed and the orthoepists' testimony allows conflicting interpretations. The dating of the categorical raising in the literature ranges between the fifteenth century (Kökeritz 1953; Wyld 1953) and the eighteenth century (Jespersen 1909). Lass (1999: 85–6) dates the 'stabilisation' of [æ] to about the 1650s. As argued in 7.3.1, however, the possibility of continuing allophonic [æ] in ME cannot be dismissed. Therefore, our account replaces the traditional formulation of the ME change /a/ > EModE /æ/ by ME [a] ~ [æ] > EModE [æ] ~ [a]; the assumed raising is reinterpreted as a switch of the dominant allophone from [a] to [æ], where 'dominant' is defined in terms of the size of the geographical area where a particular variant was used.[2]

The variability of /æ/ in PDE was addressed in 7.3.1. Further, a lowered allophone [a] occurs in Caribbean and Gullah; it used to be considered 'old-fashioned' in the US, but now seems to be undergoing a sudden spread in some varieties of North American English, reported for western Pennsylvanian, central Ohioan, 'young' Texan, Californian and Canadian (Thomas 2001: 20–1); the lowering is also associated with 'younger, urban, or innovative' RP speakers.

A different type of allophony, based on the phonotactic effect of the onset or the coda on the low vowel, resulted in recategorisation. The first shift, from [a] to [ɒ], as in *wand*, *quarter*, *quartz*, is attributed to the presence of a /w/-onset, which triggers backing and assimilative *rounding*.

Chaucer rhymes freely <wa->-words with other <Ca->-words: *can*: *wan*, *warm*: *harm*, so the rounding of /a/ cannot be dated before c. 1400. It probably started in the fifteenth century; some early evidence for rounding can be found in *The Cely Letters* (1472–88), where we find *w(h)as* ~ *w(h)ose* 'was', and inverse <a> spellings in *warsse* ~ *worsse* 'worse', *w(h)arke* ~ *w(h)orke* 'work'. The variable pronunciation continues through the sixteenth and seventeenth centuries. Shakespeare rhymes *ward*: *guard*, *can*: *swan*, Milton rhymes *wand*: *land*, and as late as

[2] Whether the reflex of the historical <a> is phonemicised as PDE /æ/, on the basis of number of speakers, or as /a/ as in Giegerich (1992: 72), 'for reasons of simplicity and cross-accent uniformity', is not important; in either case regional allophones will deviate from the 'basic' vowel specifications.

the first half of the nineteenth century one finds rhymes such as *wand*: *expand*: *land* and *war*: *far* (Byron 1788–1824). The spread of the rounded pronunciation was gradual, starting with prosodically weak words (*was*, *what*). Walker (1791–1826) cites variable pronunciations for *waft*, *wan*, *wasp*, *quality*, and the stressed vowel in *water* is still the vowel of MAT. The rounding is inhibited by a following velar, hence *quash* but *quack*, *wash* but *wax*, similarly *wag*, *whack*, *swagger*, *twang*, *wrangle*. When the vowel is flanked by a [w-] in the onset and a fricative in the coda, the outcome may be a long vowel in BrE as in *waft*, *quaff*, *wrath*. In those dialects of AmE that have merged the vowels of words like *cot*, *pod*, *Don*, *knotty* with the vowels of words like *caught*, *pawed*, *Dawn*, *naughty* (see below), the result in words of the *quart*, *quarter*, *quartz* type is variable. By normal historical development in the environment [Cw--rC], as in *quart*, the resulting vowel in (General) AmE would be [ɔ]. But where the merger has occurred, some further adjustment is required, and in fact the vowel of the *quart* words is closer; the word *ports* rhymes with *quartz* in such dialects.

The next two realisations of the input low vowel in (1) illustrate the difficulty of separating qualitative from quantitative processes. Here the original short open vowel was lengthened when followed by a tautosyllabic voiceless fricative: /-f/, /-θ/ or /-s/. Two factors seem to be contributing to the lengthening: longer vowel duration before fricatives as compared with stops (House 1961), and the intrinsic duration of low vowels. Both factors are relevant to the pre-fricative lengthening of the ME [ɔ] vowel, as in *soft*, *lost*, *cloth* (see (3) below). Some questions remain, of course: vowels 'gain' length before voiced codas, so we should expect *jazz*, *pizzaz* or *chav* with a long vowel, but it is not the case. Why is lengthening before [-ʃ] restricted to AmE? If [æ] and [ɔ] could be lengthened in pre-fricative contexts, why was/is [ɛ] not affected: we get AmE [deʲəd] for *dead*, [heʲəd] for *head*, but not *[beʲəst] for *best*, or *[beʲəθ] for *Beth*, or [leʲəft] *left*?

Pre-fricative lengthening of /a/ ~ /æ/ has an important distributional consequence: recall from 7.3.2 that Northern ME maintains [aː] < OE [ɒː] (OE *āc* 'oak', Scots and Northern Irish *aik*), while the Southern varieties lack a long unrounded open vowel (Figure 7.5). Today SSBE, associated southern hemisphere Englishes and AmE show some variety of a long unrounded open vowel in the range of [æː ~ aː ~ ɑː] in words which had a short [a ~ æ] in ME: *after*, *last*, *class*, *bath*.

Another environment in which a new long open vowel emerged in EModE was a rhotic in the coda, as in *car*, *bar*, *hard*; the long [ɑː] ~ [aː] is characteristic of non-rhotic varieties of BrE, as well as New England AmE, New York and some AAVE. A rounded [ɒː] is dominant in Southern r-less AmE speech, while r-ful speakers in the same areas have [-ɒɹ], so that *car* and *core* are homophones (Thomas 2001: 45–7). Pre-consonantal loss of the liquid in /-ɫC/ codas, as in *half*, *calm*, can also result in a lengthened nucleus; if the lengthening occurs early (see 5.2.5), the vowel will undergo the expected long vowel shift, as in *halfpenny* [heɪp(ə)nɪ], *Ralph* [reɪf]. The intermediate stage for the lengthening before /-lC/ involves the replacement of the dark [ɫ] by a back glide, resulting in a diphthong [-ɑʊ], later monophthongised to a long back vowel [-ɑː] or [ɔː]. Lengthening before [-ɫC] is unstable, and it is hard to draw dialect boundaries for the variants because of high sensitivity to additional phonotactic factors and lexical inconsistency; compare *half*, *calf*, *calm*, *walk*, *talk* and *salve-valve* [sɑːv]-[vælve]. Generally, the lengthened variant is not the expected realisation in North American English.

Yet another environment where we get a mixed output in PDE is the string of etymological short /a/ followed by /-NC/, especially in Romance loanwords, where the results may vary depending on the source of the borrowing. One difference is based on the rivalry between Northern OFr and AN <-aun> and Central/Parisian OFr <-an>, for example *launch* < AN *launcher* (13. . .) vs *lance* < OFr *lancier* (1330). The AN forms survive in *gaunt*, *haunt*, *laundry*, *saunter*, while *aunt*, *grant*, *slander*, *sample* go back to the <-an> input forms. The nature of the consonant following the nasal also matters: a following voiceless fricative, as in /-ns/, appears to have the strongest lengthening effect: *advance*, *chance*, *dance*, *enhance*, *lance*, *stance*, and so on, but notice *sans*, *pansy* with [-ænz]. A nasal followed by a tautosyllabic stop does not cause lengthening: *lamp*, *champ*, *blank*, *flank*, *bland*, *grand* (but *grant*, AN *graunter*, (1250), with both [ɑː] ~ [æ], also *Alexander* [-æ-] but *Saunders*). Finally, the early diphthongisation of OFr and AN /a/ + (mostly) palatal obstruents to [-ɑʊ] as in ME *daunger* 'danger', *chaunge* 'change', *raunge* 'range', also *chaumbere* 'chamber', results in late ME West Midlands and Northern [aː], which then goes through the expected long vowel shift to [eɪ]. The developments of /a/ + /NC/ are summarised in (2).

(2) Etymological /a/ + /-NC/ in the loan vocabulary:

	Source	**Output**	**Examples**
/a/ +	/-NC/ (AN <-aunC>)	[ɔː ~ ɑː]	*gaunt, haunt, laundry, saunter*
	/-NC/ (OFr <-anC>)	[ɑː ~ æ(ː)]	*aunt, grant, slander, sample, dance*
	/-NC#/	[æ(ː)]	*lamp, champ, blank, flank, bland*
	/-NC (palat. obstr.)/	[eɪ]	*danger, change, range, chamber*

It is evident that the trajectories and the results of the lengthening vary greatly. The timing of the lengthening is of interest: the lengthened vowels are kept separate from the vowels that constituted an input to the long vowel shift, so that an [aː] resulting from open-syllable lengthening, for example ME [taːl] (see 7.5.2.1), continues on the path to raising and diphthongisation, while the [æː ~ aː ~ ɑː] of, for example, *bath* remains monophthongal. The lengthening must have started in the seventeenth century and on the testimony of contemporary authorities, it was still stigmatised as 'bordering on vulgarity' in the eighteenth century.[3]

The pronunciation of the vowels in *after*, *last*, *bath*, *car*, *half*, *dance* is an important dialect criterion today. The input [a] ~ [æ] is lengthened and later backed and occurs as [ɑː] in SSBE and East Coast AmE, though that vowel is not the outcome in most of AmE. The low back vowel characterises southern hemisphere varieties. New York City, many New Englanders and Canadians have [æː] in words of the *after*, *fast* group. For further details on AmE see Thomas (2001: 21–3); Labov et al. (2006).

The development of ME [ɔ] is another instance where AmE and BrE differ; the difference is based on independent post-seventeenth-century histories of the two varieties. The split is illustrated in (3), repeating the relevant portion of Figure 8.1.

(3) EModE developments of ME [ɔ]:

Late ME	PDE	Examples
ɔ	ɔ ~ ɑ ~ ɒ	*hop, rotten, jolly, dollar*
	ɔː ~ ɒ(ː)	*soft, lost, cloth, port*

The main sources of ME [ɔ] are: OE and ON [ɔ] (OE *god* 'God', ON *rotinn* 'rotten'); OFr [ɔ] (OFr *jolif*, ME *jolie* 'jolly'); the shortening of OE [oː] (OE *gōd* + *spel(le)*, ME ['gɔ(d)spəl] 'gospel'); the shortening of early ME [ɔː] from OE [ɒː] (OE *hāliġ* + *dæg*, late ME ['hɔlidæj] 'holiday'; and the shortening of ME [ow] (ME *cowhen* 'cough') (see Figure 7.8(d)).

The PDE reflex of [ɔ] as [ɔ ~ ɒ] in *dollar*, *hop*, *rotten* may suggest an uninterrupted realisation of the vowel with a certain degree of rounding. There is good evidence that the vowel was lowered to [ɒ] and possibly unrounded to [ɑ] in the seventeenth century – it is found in

[3] See Lass (1999: 103–8) for an excellent account of the complex variability of the outcomes in EModE.

spellings such as <crass> for 'cross', <last> for 'lost', in Elizabethan rhymes and, interestingly, the inverted <o> spellings of EModE Continental loanwords: *dollar* (1553) < Dutch *daler*, *boss* (1653) < Dutch *baas* 'master'. Words borrowed from English into other languages also suggest an unrounded pronunciation: ME *box* 'punch' > Low German *baksen*, *baaksen*, German *baxen*, Danish *baxe*, Swedish *baxas* (OED), ME *frok(ke)* < French *froc*, German *Frack.*

The EModE lowering and unrounding of late ME [ɔ] can result in further fronting to [a] in forms like <Gad> 'God'; compare *egad* (< oh God), <plat> for 'plot', <Tam> for 'Tom', *drat* (< 'God rot'), the pair *strop-strap*, both from ME *stroppe.* In Scots *strap* for 'strop', *tap* for 'top', *drap* for 'drop' are the norm. The dating and the regional distribution of the [ɑ] ~ [a] forms is complex, and there was a definite sociolinguistic dimension to the choices along the [ɔ] ~ [ɒ] ~ [ɑ] ~ [a] scale. The frequent use of fronted [a] for ME [ɔ] in the seventeenth century is described as a 'mark of an affected style of speech', exemplified by the character of Lord Foppington in Vanburgh's comedy *The Relapse*, who uses <lard> for 'lord', <marning> for 'morning', <navelty> for 'novelty', <packet> for 'pocket', <rat> for 'rot' and <stap> for 'stop' (Barber 1997: 110). As late as the nineteenth century, William Barnes (1801–86), whose Dorset dialect generally has [ɒ] for the LOT vowel, allows *drop*: *clap*, *lap*, *nap*; *beyond* spelled <beyond>: *band*; *Johnny*, spelled <Jahnny>: *Fanny*; *John* also spelled <Jahn>: *stan* 'stand' (Burton 2010: 58–9).

In BrE the unrounding was reversed, possibly under the influence of spelling. The more rounded pronunciation with [ɔ] in PDE is mostly restricted to the inventory of BrE, though a great deal of variability continues to exist. The lowered [ɒ] ~ [ɑ] (but apparently not the fronted [a]) vowel was exported and maintained in Newfoundland, most likely carried by settlers from Ireland and south-western England (Thomas 2001: 25). Lexical idiosyncrasies are also common.

(4) Lexical idiosyncrasies of short vowels in the low back region:

Item	**OED**	**Dictionary.com**
LME mokk 'mock'	Brit. /mɒk/, US /mɑk/	/mɒk/
ME dogg(e) 'dog'	/dɒg/, US/dɔg/, /dɑg/	/dɔg/, /dɒg/
ME fogg(e) 'fog'	/fɒg/	/fɒg/, /fɔg/
OE malt 'malt'	Brit. /mɔːlt/, /mɒlt/, US /mɔlt/, /mɑlt/	/mɔlt/
ME salt(e) 'salt'	/sɒlt/ /-ɔː-/	/sɔlt/

The situation in AmE is complicated further by a widespread merger of [ɑ] and [ɔː], the *COT-CAUGHT* merger, which results in a partially, or fully unrounded [ɑ]. The merger occurs in large parts of North America (see Maps 1 and 2 in *Companion*, Appendix 8.3). This 'reverts' AmE to the seventeenth-century BrE realisation of the vowel.

As with ME [a], late ME [ɔ] can be lengthened in the environment of a tautosyllabic voiceless fricative: /-f/, /-θ/ or /-s/: *off*, *cloth*, *lost*, most commonly pronounced with a rounded monophthong [ɔː] ~ [ɒ(ː)].[4] Like the corresponding lengthening of /æ/ before fricatives, the process is gradual and produces variable results. Walker slams the lengthened vowel in *broth*, *froth*, *moth* as used 'frequently by inaccurate speakers, and chiefly those among the vulgar' (1791–1826: 32).

Tautosyllabic /-r/ also lengthens and lowers the preceding etymological [ɔ] as in *horse*, *port*, *lord*. Walker considers the vowel in *for*, *former* 'perfectly equivalent to the diphthong *au* [as in *taught*]; and *for* and *former* might, on account of sound only, be written *faur* and *faurmer*' (1791–1826: 33). The lowering to [ɒː] was variable in the eighteenth century: Walker cites *borne*, *corps*, *force*, *forge*, *form*, *fort*, *port*, *sport*, and so on, as having the sound of *bone*, *alone*. The length- and height-neutralisation of mid and low back vowels + /r/ is an ongoing process, so that in some BrE varieties and in some earlier AmE we find the merger of the NORTH and START vowels.[5] A Northern English merger ('broadest Geordie') of the NORTH-NURSE vowels (Wells 1982, II), earlier involving lowering and centralisation, is currently modified to a front rounded [ø] 'amongst young women in particular', as reported in Wales (2006: 173–4). For AmE the merger of the HORSE and HOARSE vowels is the norm for most speakers.

The etymological cluster <-ng>, PDE [ŋ], can also result in allophonic lengthening of [ɔ], merging the vowels of *lost* and *long*. For the influence of coda /-l/ see 5.2.5; the loss of /l/ and the attendant vowel lengthening can be lexically specific, for example ME *folk*, *golfe*, *bolt* > PDE [foʊk], [gɒlf] ~ [gɒf], [boʊlt].

The last short vowel in Figure 8.1 is the late ME high back rounded [ʊ]. PDE reflexes are shown again in (5).

[4] NYC older-generation and working-class speakers, also New Jersey and Philadelphia, have raising and ingliding diphthongisation of [ɔː] to (often stigmatised) [oʊə ~ ʊə] in, for example, *off*, *bought*; compare also the NY and Mid Atlantic states diphthongisation of [æː] in, for example, *fast* to [fɪəst] through these steps: [æː] > [æə] > [eə] > [ɪə]. For more details on the diphthongisation of [æː] see Thomas (2001: 21–3).

[5] William Barnes (nineteenth-century Dorset) rhymes *storm* : *harm*, *corn* : *barn*, *short* : *heart* (Burton 2010: 266). In AmE homophony of LORD-LARD is reported for the lower Mississippi valley, the area from St. Louis to Evansville, Indiana, Texas, Newfoundland and Utah (Thomas 2001: 47–8).

(5) EModE developments of late ME [ʊ]:

Late ME	PDE	Examples
ʊ	ʌ ~ ə	*hunt, love, us, much, rush, flood*
	ʊ	*pull, bush, full, foot, hook*

There are multiple sources of the short close non-peripheral [ʊ]. It is the direct continuation of OE [ʊ], as in ME *hunt(en)* 'hunt', *luve* ~ *love* 'love' (see 7.2.1); it can be the result of shortening of [uː], as in *dove*, n., *husband, us, but* (see 7.5.1.1, 7.5.1.3). As noted in 7.3.1, late ME [ʊ] is also one of the common developments of OE [ʏ], as in *clutch, much*, or OFr and AN <u(i)>, as in *punish(en)* 'punish', *ruser, ruiser* 'rush'. AN and OFr close [o] is adopted in English as [ʊ], thus *colour, covet, glutton, stomach, subtle, supper*; unstable vowel length is suggested by the spelling *country, cousin* (but *coz*), *trouble, double, couple.*

The fifteenth-century input [ʊ] was unrounded, lowered and centralised, starting probably around the beginning of the seventeenth century. The resulting vowel is a lower-mid back unrounded [ʌ]. The process must have been still ongoing in the first half of the seventeenth century; the first solid contemporary evidence is from the 1640s (Lass 1999: 89). The association between the letter <u> and a short non-high unrounded vowel is shown by the different accommodation of Indian loanwords spelled with <a> in English and other European languages: *curry* (1598) < Tamil *kari*, Portuguese *caril*, French *cari*; *pundit* (1661) < Sanskrit *paṇḍita*, French and Italian *pandit*; *bungalow* (1676) < Hindustani *banglā*; *Punjab* (1833) < Urdu *Panjāb.*

The lowering and unrounding is considered the 'default' development, indicated by the heavier line in (5). The realisation varies in the different PDE standards between [ʌ] (Southern BrE, SSE, Irish English) and a somewhat higher and more central [ə] ~ [ɜ] (AmE). Indeed, an exact characterisation of the phonetic properties of the reflexes of [ʊ] is impossible; the use of [ʌ] ~ [ə] ~ [ɜ] here covers what Lass calls 'a rather vague range of opener centralised-to-central vowel qualities' (1999: 90).

Lowering and centralisation to [ʌ] is not the only reflex of ME [ʊ]. As shown in (5), the ME quality of the vowel can be maintained, as in *pull, bush, full, foot, hook.* The PDE vowel in *pull*, also *pulley, Pulman, put, push*; *bush, bullion, bullet, bulletin, bushel, butcher*; *full*, also *Fulham*; *wolf, wood* is attributed to the influence of the labial onsets [p-], [b-], [f-], [w-], which could inhibit the unrounding. The phonetic rationale is clearly the maintenance of the labiality feature in the transition from the onset to the nucleus. If the pattern was clean-cut, it might suggest an allophonic distribution: [-ʌ] after all other onsets and [-ʊ] after labials, but an elementary 'minimal-pair' test shows immediately that the seventeenth-century shift of [ʊ] to [ʌ] introduced a new contrastive unit in the system. That /ʌ/ is an independent phoneme is evident from the fact that the presence of a labial has been ignored in numerous lexical items: *pulse*, *pulp*, *punish*, *pulmonary*, *but*, *butter*, *buttock*, *bulb*, *bulge*, *bulk*, *fumble*, *fudge*, and so on. Some items show [ʊ] in other environments: *cushion*, *sugar*, *should*, *would*, *gooseberry*, and some words show variability: AmE *pulpit* [ˈpəlpət] ~ [ˈpʊlpət], *mush* [məʃ] ~ [mʊʃ]. Then, there are the minimal pairs such as *PUT-PUTT*, *PUSS-PUS*, whose number is increased by the items whose ME [oː] was raised and shortened to [ʊ], as in *TOOK-TUCK*, *LOOK-LUCK*, *ROOM-RUM*, *BOOK-BUCK*, *COULD-CUD*. Some of these shortened forms undergo further unrounding to [ʌ] in spite of the labial onset as in *FLOOD*, *BLOOD* (see 8.3.1).

The seventeenth-century split of the input vowel [ʊ] was characteristic of the Southern and South-Western dialects of English. It occurred also in Scottish and Irish English. In a large dialect area south of the Scottish Borders and north of an isogloss running from the Wash to the Welsh border (*The Wash-Severn line on FOOT-STRUT*, Wells 1982, II), the vowel has preserved its closeness to [ʊ], providing a salient dialect criterion for separating Northern from Southern English. The importance of this dialect marker was recognised early. Kirkby (1746) comments on the vowel of *skull*, *gun*, *supper* thus: 'This Sound is scarce known to the Inhabitants of the North, who always use the short Sound of the eighth Vowel [the vowel of *too*, *woo*, *food*, DM] instead of it' (Kirkby [1746] 1971: 7). Commenting on the preservation of [ʊ] in some words, Walker calls it a:

> whimsical deviation . . . sufficient to puzzle Englishmen who reside at any distance from the capital, and to make the inhabitants of Scotland and Ireland (who, it is highly probable, received a much more regular pronunciation from our ancestors) not infrequently the jest of fools. (Walker 1791–1826: 34)

He reports that 'some speakers have attempted to give *bulk* and *punish* this obtuse sound [ʊ, DM], but luckily have not been followed' and opines that 'we cannot be too careful to check the growth of so unmeaning an irregularity'. Variability and cross-dialectal borrowing continued in the in the nineteenth century, when comparisons with the vowels of other languages are very common in the description of this new phoneme in English for which there was no corresponding letter. It is likely that the lowering and opening of the vowel was very widespread

Figure 8.2 The [ʌ]-[ʊ] isogloss in England, Map 11 'But' in Trudgill (1999a), *The Dialects of England*, Wiley-Blackwell

in the nineteenth century, affecting items which were later reverted to [ʊ] in the south. Cockney is one variety where the increasingly lower realisation of the CUT vowel results in (IPA [ɐ]).[6]

Figure 8.2 shows a map of the *but* vowel in England at the end of the twentieth century.

[6] Unexpected [ʌ] in nineteenth-century Dorset and southern Somerset is attested by rhymes such as ***put***: *nut, shut, pudding*: ***blood*** *in*, ***roof***: *buff, stuff, enough* (see Burton 2010: 60).

For PDE, the [ʌ]-[ʊ] divide remains an important regional identifier, though, as can be expected, there is ample evidence of continuing variability: in the twentieth century, the RP variant of the CUT vowel has been moving forward towards [a] (MacMahon 1998: 410–11, 456–7). Wales (2006: 172–3) reports that Northern English speakers participating in 'the growth of suburbanization' and born since 1938, have pronunciations 'which are neither RP phonemically or traditionally local: so for Hull speech as well as Merseyside and Newcastle, a schwa-vowel in *mud*, . . .that is neither /u/ *nor* /ʌ/'.[7] While unrounding may affect the upwardly mobile speakers of Northern English, the opposite, a tendency for [ʊ] in the vowel of *cut*, is reported in AmE for Detroit; backing and rounding is also part of the Northern Cities Shift in AmE (Thomas 2001: 27–8).

8.2.2 The Great/Long/English Vowel Shift

La, a note to follow sol . . .
LA, The City of Angels

This section turns to the most emblematic of all phonological changes in the history of English: the set of long-vowel changes that started in late ME and led to the renaming of the vowel letters <a, e, i, o> from labels identified with the Latin values to their current names [eɪ, iː, aɪ, oʊ]. English is the only European language using the Roman alphabet in which the reference to the vowel letters in FACE, FLEECE, PRICE, GOAT differs significantly from the value assigned to them in Latin, or German, Spanish, Hungarian, for example. This English-specific naming started out as reflecting the pronunciation of the letters representing historically long vowels /aː/, /eː/, /iː/, /oː/. Their realisation was in the process of changing in late ME, though the dominance of Latin in the elementary language-education curriculum and in the universities delayed the recognition and acceptance of the innovations. The very popular didactic verse treatise *The Prick of Conscience* (Northern, probably mid fourteenth century), in a section heavily interspersed with Latin lines and even couplets, plays on the association between <a> - /aː/, and <e> - /e/ː.

(6) Rhyming <a>: <swa> and <be>: <e> (Northern):

And by þat cry men may knaw þan
Whether it be man or weman,

[7] See also Lass (1987: 250): 'Northerners who "standardize" without going all the way to adopting RP or a general SBE [SSBE in this book] profile will normally "correct" the *foot*/*but* identity (sometimes with a "compromise" [ə] in *but*) . . .'

For when it es born it cryes **swa**;
If it be man, it says **'a, a,'**
Þat þe first letter es of þe nam
Of our forme-fader **A**dam.
And if þe child a woman **be**,
When it es born, it says **'e, e.'**
E es þe first letter and þe hede
Of þe name of **E**ue þat bygan our dede.
(Morris 1863: 14)

Similarly, it is commonly held that the realisation of the long vowels in Chaucer was close enough to their Latin pronunciation. The evidence cited for that is that he could rhyme the name of the letter *A* with *omnia.*

(7) Rhyming <a>: <Lat. *omnia*> (Southern, Chaucer):

On which was first i-write a crowned A,
And after, *Amor vincit omnia.* CT *Prologue* 161

Rhymes can be a good source of evidence for phonological change, yet when a rhyme clearly echoes a Latin sound or word, its reliability can be questioned. In both instances the interpretation of strictly low monophthongal [aː] is not the only option: the rhyme <a>: <swa> in (6) could have been on [æː] or even [ɛː] in the North,[8] and A: *omnia* in (7) could be a spelling-based stretch and the final vowel in *omnia* could also be [æː] under secondary stress. As for <be>: <e> in (6), it is hard to tell how raised the [eː] of *be* was; the rhyme does not preclude a diphthongal [ej], as is suggested already in OE, where the names of the consonant letters of the alphabet are recorded as both *be* or *bei* for <b>, *ce* or *cei* for <c>, *de* or *dei* for <d> and *ge* or *gei* for <g> (DOE).

Before we look further into chronological details, it will help to take a long-term view and clarify the scope of the events and the labels they have been given. The change of the OE long vowels to their current pronunciations affects *all* vowels in the system reconstructed for ME in Figure 7.5, used as the ME base in Figure 8.3.

The vowel correspondences between late ME and PDE, which nineteenth-century philologists reconstructed and described, are listed in Figure 8.4.

The arrows in Figure 8.4 are a crude approximation of the reconstructed input–output correspondences. Some version of this set of

[8] On early raising of /aː/ in the North see Smith (1996: 99–100); Stenbrenden (2010: 80–1, 532).

Middle English		Examples	
iː	**uː**	[m**iː**s] 'mice'	[m**uː**s] 'mouse'
eː	**oː**	[s**eː**] 'see'	[f**oː**l] 'fool'
ɛː	**ɔː**	[s**ɛː**] 'sea'	[**ɔː**k] 'oak'
aː		(N, Sc.) [**aː**k]'aik/oak', [b**aː**k(ə)] 'bake'	

Figure 8.3 Long-vowel inheritance in Middle English

Middle English		PDE[9]	Examples
iː	------------▶	**aɪ**	*price, mice, bind, wife, sign*
eː	------------▶	**iː**	*fleece, see, tree, be, fiend*
ɛː	------------▶	**iː/e**	*sea, meal, break*
aː	------------▶	**eɪ**	*face, bake, strange, save*
ɔː	------------▶	**oʊ**	*goat, oak, boat, nose, stone*
oː	------------▶	**uː**	*goose, fool, do, moon, scoop*
uː	------------▶	**aʊ**	*mouth, mouse, how, cow*

Figure 8.4 Long-vowel changes from ME to PDE

changes, known collectively as the *Great Vowel Shift* (GVS), a moniker first found in Jespersen (1909: 231), appears in all histories of the English language and all descriptions of Chaucerian English.

The term 'shift' with reference to these changes is used in a highly specific meaning: except for the *SEE-SEA* homophony in most varieties of PDE, the phonemic contrasts between the original entities have been preserved, in spite of the change in their phonetic realisations. This kind of input–output maintenance of contrast is typical of

[9] Transcription practices for the diphthongs resulting from the shift can vary, especially for the vowels of *FACE* and *GOAT*. Some the common alternatives are:
[**eɪ**]: [eː] ~ [e] ~ [ej] ~ [ey]
[**oʊ**]: [oː] ~ [o] ~ [ow] ~ [əʊ] (BrE)

'**chain** shifts'; the label implies a lock-step development of a whole set of related sounds. The structural appeal of all seven long vowels behaving in a very similar fashion, within the same time frame, with comparable results, is undoubtedly strong and the last century has generated a huge amount of scholarship on the construct of *the* 'Great' vowel shift.[10] Starting with Karl Luick (1898) and Otto Jespersen (1909), the changes in Figure 8.4 have been treated as a unified set of phonological events, where each new value is supposed to be the result and the trigger of a chain-like reaction affecting all ME long vowels. The position is well represented by Jespersen's summary statement:

> The great vowel-shift consists in a general raising of all long vowels with the exception of the two high vowels /iˑ/ and /uˑ/,[11] which could not be raised further without becoming consonants and which were diphthongized into . . . [ai, au]. (Jespersen 1909: 231)

The structural connectedness among the changes is represented in the often-cited chart in Figure 8.5 from Jespersen (1909: 232), where <ˑ> marks vowel length:

All ME long vowels: the ones that were long in OE, the ones that acquired length through homorganic cluster lengthening (see 6.4) or open-syllable lengthening (see 7.5.2.1), participate in the raising and diphthongisation shown in Figure 8.5. This all-encompassing, chain-shift view of the GVS dominated the scholarship throughout the early parts of the twentieth century. Hypotheses addressing the initiation, causation

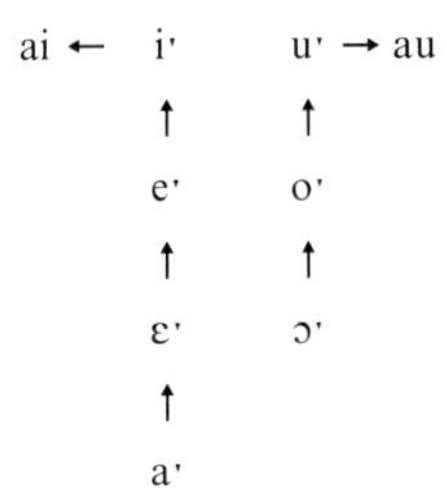

Figure 8.5 Directionality of the *Great Vowel Shift* according to Jespersen (1909: 232)

[10] Placing 'Great' in scare quotes is now common in the literature. For the myth of 'greatness' and the history of its debunking see Watts (2003, 2011). Stenbrenden (2010) avoids 'Great' in the title of her extensive research project on the shift, and keeps references to the 'Great' vowel shift in scare quotes – a practice adopted here.

[11] Jespersen uses the pre-IPA symbol [ˑ] (= IPA [ː]) for length.

and propagation of the putative massive chain shift have been proposed in terms of numerous phonological theories, including structuralism, generative phonology, lexical phonology, dependency phonology, particle phonology, lexical diffusion and optimality theory. With rare exceptions, a representation of the changes from Middle to Modern English, with each long vowel linked to an arrow pointing upwards or outwards, it is still repeated in textbook accounts of the history of English phonology.

The twentieth century also saw the 'deconstruction' of the events associated with the shift. One shortcoming of the early discussions of the shift as a unified chain, with the front and the back vowels advancing in harmony, is that the scrutiny of the end results was confined to SSBE. Another difficulty with the construct in Figure 8.5 is that that it presupposes a beginning and an end to long vowel shifting, although, as we will see below, the written records of the various innovations are a challenge to the traditionally assumed time span of 1400–1750. Yet another serious source of discomfort is the treatment of the processes affecting the long vowels in isolation, without reference to the coexisting diphthongal nuclei.

The problem of regional variants and local sub-shifts is acknowledged in all or most accounts of the 'Great' vowel shift; analysts are aware that neither the ME input vowels nor the output vowels are uniform across the varieties of English. It is still the case, nevertheless, that the PDE values shown in Figure 8.4 and 8.5 represent roughly the pronunciation of the long vowels in current 'General' AmE and SSBE, and this is also the pronunciation recognised and used in 'global English'. It is therefore possible to confine the account to these varieties and set aside the dialect differences. In the next sections the focus will be on the chronology, the mechanism and the motivation of the changes that produced the supra-regional long-vowel system of PDE.

8.2.2.1 Chronology and dating

The term 'chronology' can be used both in reference to the arrangement of 'events in the order of time' and to the 'assignation of events to their correct dates' (OED). The two temporal dimensions are interrelated; the ordering of the changes with respect to each other cannot be divorced from the dating of those changes, but for the sake of clearer exposition we will consider them separately.

Chronological ordering is essential in determining system-internal causal relationships. Establishing the chronology of phonological change is directly linked to the adaptation of loanwords in the language. Loanword phonology is a useful test for the existence of a particular vowel realisation at the time of borrowing. One can be fairly sure that the words *price*, AN *price*, *priese* (c. 1225) and *sign* (?c. 1225), AN *seigne*, *sein(e)* had vowels that were identified with the native vowels of *mice*, *bind*, *wife* (see Figure 8.4) – all of them having been shifted. Similarly, borrowings from French with etymological [eː] such as *friar* (c. 1290), OFr *frere*; *require* (1312), AN *requere*, *requerer*; *die*, n. pl. *dice* (c. 1330), OFr *dé*, pl. *dés*, must have had a vowel identical or very similar to the *MICE* vowel in order to get through the shift. On the other hand, *police* (1450), *machine* (1545), *tambourine* (1579), *magazine* (1583), *caprice* (1673), *critique*, v. (1751), all with etymological stressed [iː], are either too late or too rare, or both, to join the general diphthongisation of [iː].

For the shift in Figure 8.5, locating the initial impetus is central to the overall account of the events. If the impulse for the diphthongisation of the high vowels /iː/ and /uː/ came from the raising of the high-mid vowels /eː/ and /oː/, the closeness of the raised allophones to the historical /iː/ and /uː/ could be a trigger of diphthongisation of the high vowels. This is the '*push-chain*' theory which originates with Luick. If the high vowels /iː/, /uː/ started to diphthongise first, one can imagine that the resulting vacant vowel areas would enable the raising of /eː/ and /oː/; this is the '*drag-chain*' theory which originates with Jespersen. Further, if we look at the low vowels, the fronting and raising of OE [ɒː] to [aː] in the North, as in 'aik/oak', could have been the initiation of a more general push-chain front-vowel shift in the northern dialects, unrelated to the changes in the South (Smith 1996: 99–101). Yet another chronological option is to consider the raising of OE [æː] to [ɛː] in early ME (see 7.3.2, Figure 7.5) as a precursor of the whole push-chain process of the long vowel shifting in ME and EModE.

The metaphors of 'pushing' – avoidance of merger, or 'pulling' – avoidance of large gaps in the phonological space, dominated the discourse on the shift in the last century, but their usefulness is limited: the new data on the *dating* of the high and upper-mid vowel changes examined in Stenbrenden (2010) show that the raising of [eː] and [oː] *and* the diphthongisation of [iː] and [uː] started simultaneously in parts of the East Midlands and the West Midlands in the course of the thirteenth century.[12] This leaves us with a chronology of the changes in Figure 8.5 which bundles together the high and the upper-mid long vowels /iː/, /uː/, /eː/ and /oː/ as the 'leaders' of the shift. Further identification of lexical frequency and phonetic and sociolinguistic factors may lead to new insights on the chronological ordering, but the available evidence makes both the 'push' and the 'drag' shift scenario suspect.

[12] Earliness of the shift is argued for in Stockwell and Minkova (1988, 1997a); Minkova and Stockwell (1997a: 33–5, 2003a *passim*); Johnston (1992).

Dating the events is a separate matter; it is of practical consequence for editing, teaching and reading Middle English texts. While pegging a date onto a particular sound change will always be open to dispute, especially the initial stages, the availability of LAEME and LALME allow the type of close scrutiny of the written records that was unavailable to earlier scholarship. Extensive studies of these records by Stenbrenden, culminating with Stenbrenden (2010), show that a hypothesis of a thirteenth-century incipience and fourteenth-century vigorous spread of the new values of the historical long monophthongs is robustly supported by irregular spellings.

As noted in 8.2.2, the assumption in most sources is that the beginning of the shift should be dated to the *late* fourteenth century, hence the common reconstruction of Chaucerian pronunciation with fully unshifted /iː/, /uː/, /eː/ and /oː/. Dissenting opinions expressed early come from Wyld (1953) and Kökeritz (1961), who famously described the reconstruction of fully unshifted long vowels for Chaucer as 'a pronunciation [which] would probably sound old-fashioned to Chaucer, could he hear it, perhaps reminding him of the speech of his grandparents' (Kökeritz 1961: 9). Wyld proposed a bold early dating: ME [eː] was [iː] before the end of the fourteenth century, ME [oː] approximated [uː] in the early fourteenth century in the East, whence it spread to London. Stenbrenden, who refers to Wyld's hypothesis with approval (2010: 542), has now presented persuasive arguments and testable orthographic data which are the most thorough substantiation of the earliness of the change. These conclusions should find their way into the manuals on Chaucer's language.[13]

It is clear that the initial stages of the restructuring of the long-vowel system can be detected much earlier than the traditional 'Early Modern' dating in the literature. Another question regarding chronological boundaries is, when does the shift end? As noted in 8.2.2, the date of entry of a word in the language may correlate with the non-operation of the change; recall *caprice* (1673), *critique*, v. (1751). The shifting of a vowel interacts also with the quantitative changes covered in 7.5: if the vowel was long in OE, but remains unshifted, it must have been shortened prior to the shift; *meant*, *stealth*, *wisdom* had long vowels in OE, but they have not gone through the process of shifting (see 8.3.1). On the other hand, the original short vowels in OE *child*, *hound* and ME *tale*,

[13] The evidence for the early stages of the shift is primarily from orthography. Rhyme evidence for early fifteenth-century diphthongisation of the high vowels is adduced in Jordan (1974: 239–40); for the upper-mid back vowel we find OE *dōm*, ME *dome* 'doom': *meum* Lat. pronoun stressed as meúm (*Everyman*).

nose were lengthened; these 'new' long vowels were subject to shifting. Vowels which were lengthened in early Modern English: *dance*, *bath*, *lost*, *half* (see 8.2.1) generally do not undergo the shift, except for isolated cases such as *halfpenny* [heɪp(ə)nɪ], *Ralph* [reɪf].[14] Thus in one sense, the vowel changes discussed here do fit within a chronological frame, albeit a rather flexible one. This is especially true of the native lexicon, the definition of which must also be flexible in order to include early loanwords.

As regards the local manifestations of the long-vowel changes in the modern dialects, and the behaviour of *post-ME borrowings*, the long vowel shifting is very much part of the phonology of PDE. An important aspect of the historical shifting is that it created a pattern of allomorphic alternations which can be applied to borrowed words. Thus the native vowel-patterning in *heal-health*, *knee-knelt*, *wide-width*, *five-fifth*, *bone-bonfire* (see 7.5.1) is replicated in such pairs of loanwords as *serene-serenity*, *please-pleasure*, *deprive-deprivation*, *resign-resignation*, *phone-symphonic*, and so on. The second words in these pairs are suffixed formations coming directly from Latin and French. The pairing here is between the preservation of length in the borrowed stressed vowel, as in *serene*, *please*, *deprive*, *resign*, *phone*, in which case the long vowel shifts like any long vowel in the native vocabulary, and the lax vowel in derived forms, either inherited as lax or laxed after borrowing. Shifted and unshifted (and further reduced) vowels in the loan vocabulary frequently alternate depending on stress. If the borrowed long vowel preserves stress, it is shifted, but if the stress falls away from the vowel in a form derived with a stress-shifting suffix, the vowel is not only shortened, but further reduced to [ə]: *a**b**le-a**b**ility*, *m**a**son-M**a**sonic*, *le**g**al-le**g**ality*, *ar**o**ma-ar**o**matic*, *hori**z**on-hori**z**ontal*. These synchronic allomorphic patterns present many challenges and are much discussed in the literature.[15]

Like every other phonological change, long vowel shifts stretch over a considerable period of time, affecting different items at a different rate. Useful lexical diffusion information for some long vowels in native words is presented in Ogura (1987), but many unknowns remain. To frame the problem: a loanword such as *police* (1450) keeps [iː] unchanged, while *profile*, n. (1638) is 'anglicised'. Walker (1791–1826: 26) cites Pope rhyming *besieg'd*: *oblig'd* on [iː], where the vowel of *besiege*

[14] There is variability in the adaptation of OFr/AN low back vowels before nasals, where AN had the diphthong [au] and OFr [a], both merging in possibly nasalised [ɑ̃ː]. The latter tends to diphthongise to [eɪ], especially before palato-alveolars, as in *angel*, *change*, *ancient*, *danger*, *strange*. The results may vary; compare *ancient-pansy*, and before labials *chamber-lamp*.

[15] See Minkova and Stockwell (1998) and references there.

(1297) is from OFr [eː], and the vowel of *oblige* (c. 1325) is from AN [iː] and should have been diphthongised. Some of Walker's 'unshifted' words with borrowed [iː] coincide with the PDE forms: *antique*, *caprice*, *critique*, *quarantine*, *magazine*, and so on but not *vertigo* (1528).[16] What is the rationale behind the shifting, or lack thereof, in the combining forms *macro-* (1821) (unshifted) vs *micro-* (1849) (shifted), while *macron* (1851) allows both [æ] and [eɪ]? The word *route* (1225) can be both [uː] and [aʊ].[17] The name *Levi* may be unshifted, but both vowels shift in *Levis* (1926). Using examples with just the low vowel, doublet forms exist for *pater* (1400), *mater* (1425), *data* (1646), *gala* (1625), *qua* (1647), but not for *aleph* (1300), the note *la* (1325), *lama* (1654), *façade* (1656), *lager* (1855). These examples show both the persistence and the apparent haphazardness of the application of the shift to new vocabulary.

8.2.2.2 Mechanism and causation

The developments bundled together under the general umbrella of the long vowel shift are not as unilinear or straightforward as Figure 8.5 may suggest. The shift is a subset of a complex series of long nuclei changes and mergers which do not occur at the same time, in the same regions or for the same reasons. The great diversity of intermediary steps and outcomes cannot be dealt with in every detail here; moreover, many changes indicating continuity of the shift are still under way (see 8.4).

Limiting the focus on changes extracted as the 'Great' vowel shift, the consensus is that the high and the upper-mid long vowels /iː/, /uː/, /eː/ and /oː/ were the 'leaders' of the shift, with the high vowels becoming diphthongal and the high-mid vowels reaching their PDE height by c. 1550 in the variety of Southern English that was recognised as 'standard' after the seventeenth century. There is also consensus that there was as much as a whole century between these earlier changes and the rest of the long-monophthong changes: the 'peak' period for the shifting of the low-mid [ɛː], [ɔː] and the low [aː] was around the middle of the seventeenth century. This chronological gap prompts accounts which 'set these later developments aside, and restrict the term "GVS" to the original high/higher-mid chain shift of the 15th–16th centuries' (Lass 1992a: 153).

[16] The fashionable pronunciation well into the nineteenth century was [və'tiːgəʊ] (OED). For *profile* Walker allows both [iː] and [aɪ]. PDE *cation* (1834) is now ['kætaɪən], most likely on the analogy of *ion*, but the earlier pronunciation was ['kætɪən] (OED).

[17] 'The pronunciation with a diphthong is recorded from the second half of the 18th c. and preferred by some, but not all commentators . . .; it disappears from standard British English in the course of the 19th cent., but is still widespread in North America' (OED).

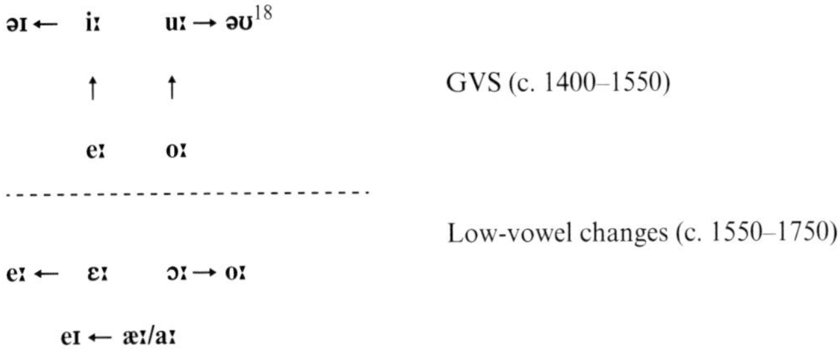

Figure 8.6 Phases of the long vowel shift in Southern Standard English

The point of Figure 8.6 is that the historical details do not justify the reconstruction of a step-by-step, cause-and-effect unified 'Great' event. Since initiation of the shift of the high and upper-mid vowels cannot be separated chronologically (see 8.2.2.1), assumptions that high-vowel diphthongisation 'causes' mid-vowel raising, or that mid-vowel raising 'causes' high-vowel diphthongisation are unwarranted: both processes 'appear to have started in parts of the E Midlands and W Midlands in the course of the thirteenth century' (Stenbrenden 2010: 542). Nevertheless, it is an incontrovertible fact that the letters <i>, <e>, <a>, <o>, <u> represented different long nuclei in the early thirteenth century and today, and like all other changes surveyed here, this one invites inquiry into the reasons for the selection, maintenance and codification of the variants that emerged and spread in later English.

Starting with the early ME high vowels /iː/ and /uː/, the generalisation is that they were diphthongised. Focusing first on /iː/, recall from 7.4 that already in OE the palatal glide [-j] formed a diphthong with a preceding front-vowel nucleus when it was in the same syllable or the same stem. Examples with a high front vowel include early OE **briġdel* > late OE *brīdel* 'bridle', *drȳġness* ~ *drīġness* > late OE *drīness(e)* 'dryness', *flȳġan* ~ *flȳan*, p.t. *flīġde* '(cause to) fly', all with [-ij]. The perceptual distance between the [ij] of, for example, *brīdel* 'bridle' and the [iː] of, for example, *wīf* 'wife' would be minimal; it is therefore quite logical to treat [ij] and [iː] as allophones already in late OE. Support for this allophony is found in variable spellings of historical [-ij] forms as in *drȳġness* ~ *drīġness*, *flȳġan* ~ *flȳan*, and in 'reverse' spellings where both <i> and <ig> stand for etymological [iː] in final position: <bi ~ big ~

[18] The diphthongal realisations [əɪ] and [əʊ] represent intermediate pronunciations of /iː/ and /uː/ – they are the closest to what philologists think of as the 'authentic' Elizabethan/Shakespearean pronunciation of these vowels.

bii> 'by, prep.', <hwy ~ hwig> 'why', <sie ~ sy ~ sig> 'be, pres. subj.' (see 7.4). This minimally diphthongal [ij] can be posited as the primary allophone of the long high front vowel in early ME, that is, as the input to the later change of OE /iː/.

The situation with the high back vowel was parallel: if an OE back vowel was followed by the OE voiced velar fricative [ɣ] (see 4.2.1), the result was a diphthongal nucleus with a second element [-w]: OE *būgan*, ME *bouen* ~ *buwe(n)* [buw-(ən)] 'bow down'; OE *(for)suwod* ~ *(for)sugod* [suw-(ə)d] 'silenced'; OE *sugu*, ME *suw(e)* 'sow, female swine', where [uw] would be an allophone of [uː] in, for example, *mūs* [muːs] 'mouse'. The number of lexical items with [uw] was increased in ME through the loss of the voiceless glottal fricative /h/, as in OE *druhþ(e)* > ME *druȝt* ~ *droute* [drʊxt] ~ [druwt] 'drought' (see 5.1.4). This allophonic [uw] serves as the proto-diphthongal realisation of the original long /uː/. In the case of the high vowels, then, diphthongal and monophthongal variants merged toward a more perceptually salient diphthongal realisation. These initial diphthongs were further optimised by differentiation of their end points, reaching the values [əɪ] > [aɪ] for *mice*, *bind*, *bridle*, *dry*, *wife*, *sign*, and [əʊ] > [aʊ] for *mouse*, *bow*, *cow*, *crown*, *sow*, *fowl*.

The increase of the distance between the elements of the nucleus proceeds gradually, and each stage is attested historically. Schematically, this part of the long vowel shift can be represented as in (8).[19]

(8) The mechanism of high-vowel shifting in ME:

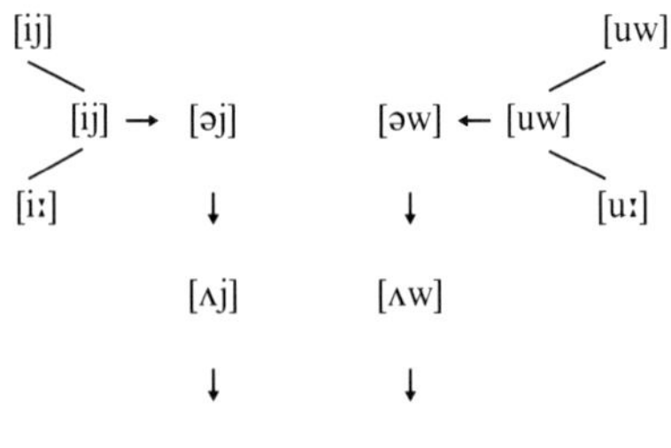

This sequence of events, labelled the 'Center Drift' (Stockwell 2002b: 267), is not the only possible way of reconstructing the intermediate historical phonetic values of the diphthongs.[20] In all accounts, however,

[19] It is assumed that diphthongal transcriptions using the IPA high front glide [-j] and the high back rounded glide [-w] are functionally equivalent to transcriptions using [-ɪ] and [-ʊ] (see Cruttenden 2008: 94; also 2.2.2, n. 9).

[20] A very good survey of the positions is offered in Wełna (1978: 184–7); Lass (1999: 80–1). The strikingly diverse dialectal detail on the realisations of OE [iː] (17 vari-

a monophthongal input becomes a diphthongal entity with the original short trajectory within the nucleus getting extended. In the inputs [ij] and [uw] the glides are at the same general height. The subsequent lowering of the first element produces a 'better' diphthong in terms of perceptual distinctiveness by height-dissimilation: the first element is lowered and centralised while the end point remains at the same height.

For reasons which are still being studied, different varieties of English today show 'arrested' development in maintaining the incremental dissimilation of the diphthongs: for example, [əɪ] for PRICE and [əʊ] for MOUTH occur in Welsh, Irish and Dorset; [ʌɪ] for historical [ij] before voiceless codas is found in Scots (also [ɑ˙e]) and famously in Canadian English (see 8.4.1). In popular London the PRICE vowel nucleus is retracted to [ɑɪ], and rounded to [ɒɪ] in Cockney.

The opposite tendency is towards assimilation of the end points of the diphthong, in which case the underlying phonetic impetus is minimisation of effort, as in 'extreme' Cockney [ɑ̟ə ~ ɑ̟ː] (Wells 1982, II: 306–10), NZE [ɑe] (Bauer 1994a: 389), Northern US [æɪ ~ ɜɪ]), or Southern US [ae ~ aː], where the result is ultimately a monophthong (Thomas 2001: 34–8; see also Thomas 2001: 39–43 for the 'bewildering array' of /aʊ/ realisations in AmE). These attestations of historically intermediate stages and the ongoing reversals of diphthong optimisation make it very clear that the assumption of an overarching directionality of the long-vowel changes in the second millennium in English is problematic: the stressed long vowels of English, as in other Germanic languages, become diphthongal, and diphthongs become monophthongised, justifying the metaphoric description of their state as 'diachronic *perpetuum mobile*' (Minkova and Stockwell 2003a: 174).

At the same time as the high-vowel incipient diphthongs were becoming less monophthongal and more perceptually salient, the upper-mid long vowels [eː] and [oː] were raised, becoming more similar to [iː] and [uː]. Two considerations should be included in the account of the raising. First, the vowels which we reconstruct as [eː] and [oː], following a long philological tradition, may have been allophonically higher than the spellings with <e> and <o> suggest.[21] Occasional spellings

ants) and [uː] (45 variants) in Ogura (1987: 30–109) leaves no room for doubt that the realisations posited in (8) are realistic.

[21] Paradigmatic alternations of [eː] ~ [ɪ] and [oː] ~ [ʊ] also provide the speaker/learner with a pattern of alternations that support the assumption of 'raised' upper-mid vowels, as in *Grimstead* (Wiltshire, 1242) < OE *grēn* 'green' + *-styde* '-stead', *Brumstead* (Norfork, 1165) < OE *brōm* 'broom' + stede 'place'. The shortening of ME [eː] as [ɪ] (see 7.5.2.1) is attested in such Chaucerian rhymes as *fil* (pret.sg.) < OE *fēoll*: *wil, n.* (*KT* 1103).

such as OE <fyt>/<fiet> for <fēt> 'feet' and early ME spellings such as <shipe> for <shēp> 'sheep' (*Cursor Mundi*), <sliep> for <slep> 'sleep' (*Vices and Virtues*) point in that direction.

Another consideration comes from the structure of the phonological system. In principle, overlapping realisations of adjacent phonemes are not surprising; the denser the overlap, the higher the probability of merger. However, once the allophonic cloud of original [iː] and [uː] had started shifting away, the allophonic realisations of raised [eː˔] ~ [eɪ] and [oː˔] ~ [oʊ] would not impinge on the distinctiveness of the original entities. The boundaries of the clusters of allophonic realisations remain crisp and the identification of raised [eː˔] and [oː˔] with original /iː/ and /uː/ does not result in merger, as is indeed the case with the vowels of MICE-FEET, MOUSE-MOON. Metaphorically speaking, the diphthongisation of the earlier [iː] ~ [əj] and [uː] ~ [əw] 'vacates' the high-front and high-back slots in the vowel system and allows raising of the upper-mid vowels. The logic of this correlation makes the upper part of the changes in Figure 8.6 the only part of the GVS that can legitimately be claimed to be a *chain shift*, a lock-step change of contrastive units which preserve the original contrast but change their properties. This is shown in (9), which combines the centre drift of the high vowels with the raising of the mid vowels.

(9) The mechanism of high- and mid-vowel shifting in ME (non-Northern):

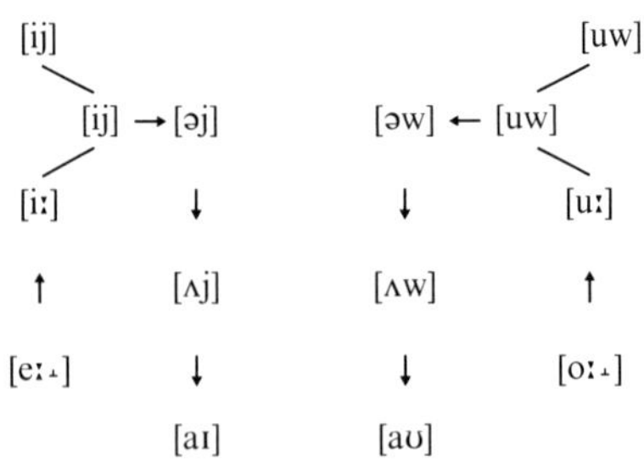

The hypothesis about the correlation of the events in (9) is supported by an interesting regional development in ME. During the thirteenth century in the North the upper-mid [oː] was fronted and raised in the direction of [yː], rhyming with OFr [yː], so we get *rude* < AN *rud(e)*: *gud(e)* < OE *gōd* 'good' (Jordan 1974: 86). It is also a fact that in the same areas where [oː] was fronted, the [uː] remained unchanged, which results in the Northern realisation of [uː] for the MOUSE vowel and [ɪə] ~ [ɪʊ] for the MOON vowel. This simplified description is instructive in terms of the mechanism and structural relatedness of the changes in the mid- and high-vowel part of the system.

The mid- and high-vowel changes in (9) were pretty much complete by the end of the sixteenth century. The other long-vowel changes in Figure 8.6 involve early ME [ɛː], [æː], [aː] and [ɔː]. As noted in 8.2.2.1, the emergence in early ME of [ɛː] and [ɔː] from raising of [æː] or [ɒː] (see 7.3.2), or from open-syllable lengthening of [ɛ] and [ɔː] (see 7.5.2.1), is also part of the larger picture of events. Acknowledging that, here we focus on the subsequent history of [ɛː], [aː] ~ [æː] and [ɔː] – the changes that result in their PDE values also have their roots in ME, but appear to have taken longer to spread and become incorporated into the incipient standard.

The first thing to note here is that unlike the high vowels [iː] and [uː] in (9), the lower-mid front [ɛː] (OE *slǣp*, ME [slɛːp] 'sleep', OE *medu*, ME [mɛːd(ə)] 'mead') and the lower-mid back [ɔː] (OE *nosu*, ME [nɔːz(ə)] 'nose') do not behave in a parallel fashion. In the front series [ɛː], in the variety later codified as the Southern Standard, was raised further to [eː] and merged with the historical [eː], so that it is only the not fully reliable PDE spelling that signals that the vowels of *sea* and *see*, *meat* and *meet*, *heal* and *heel* were originally distinct (see 7.3.2). The dating of this merger is difficult to test because it is dialect- and item-specific. There is rhyme evidence for it in the fourteenth century, though the merger was still not completed before the end of the seventeenth century. The earliest examples of the merger are in word-final position as in *se(e)* 'sea' (OE *sǣ*): *me* 'me' (OE *mē*), but there are also rhymes involving [ɛː] in closed syllables, as in *del* 'deal' (OE *dǣl*): *stel* 'steel' (OE Angl. *stēl*), *grete* 'great' (OE *grēat*): *fet* 'feet' (OE *fēt*).

The historical merger of the front mid vowels [ɛː] and [eː] can be seen as functionally undesirable; the justification for it is often sought in the avoidance of 'crowding' in the vowel space: a four-vowel height system could be less stable than a three-vowel height system, which minimises the allophonic overlap between adjacent phonemes and guarantees greater perceptual salience.

The merging proceeded gradually; the range of allophones for the front lower-mid vowel was apparently quite broad. The picture is extremely complex and involves cross-dialectal and cross-social class and register variation. The 'middle' position of early ME [ɛː] allows reconstructed realisations ranging from [æː] ~ [ɛː] ~ [eː] ~ [eː˔] ~ [eɪ], and indeed there is evidence well into the eighteenth century that all these variants were available from the fifteenth and sixteenth century; the final stage of codification had not been reached for Dryden and even

Pope.[22] Potential confusion between historically distinct vowels exists in words containing early ME [eː], [ɛː] and [aː], further complicated by the possibility of mergers with the diphthongal [-æj] ~ [ɛj] ~ [ej] (see below). A sociolinguistic interpretation of the changes and distribution of these vowels c. 1600 presents the pattern in (10) for OE *mētan* 'to meet' with OE [eː], OE *mete* 'meat' with [ɛː], and ME *mate* 'defeat' (AN *mater*) with [æː].

(10) Social dimensions of the long vowel shift c. 1600:[23]

Aristocracy	**Bourgeoisie**	**Lower class**
meet [iː]	meet [iː]	meet [iː]
meat [ɛː] ~ [eː]	meat [eː]	meat [iː]
mate [æː] ~ [ɛː]	mate [eː]	mate [eː]

Even the most conservative pronunciation in the first column allows homophony of *meat* and *mate*; that homophony is well attested in the middle column. The dominant pattern is a two-way, rather than the input three-way distinction, that is, the vowel space has been optimised. Given the pre-existing diphthongs [ɛj] ~ [ej], which merge with [ɛː], the realisation of the *MEAT* vowel c. 1600 would still quite commonly be [eː] ~ [ej]. In most cases the raising continues on to [iː], as in the third column in (10), leaving only a handful of words in the Southern standard preserving the earlier diphthongal realisation: *great*, *break*, *yea*.[24] Again, this is only the outcome in the Southern standard, distilled from a variety of competing realisations. The merger of the long mid vowels did not occur in the North Midlands, where OE [æː], as in OE *lǣst* 'least', and the lengthened OE [ɛ], as in OE *etan* 'to eat', did not merge, so that *LEAST* is [lɪəst] but *EAT* is [ej], neither of them joining ME [eː] in the raising to [iː].[25]

The mechanism of the change of the long low [aː] ~ [æː] and the lower-mid [ɔː] also involves raising and merger with highly similar diphthongs, both old and new, discussed in 7.4 (see also Figures 7.7, 7.8).

[22] Dryden (1631–1700) rhymes *make: speak*, *great: seat*, and Pope (1688–1744) rhymes *shade: mead* (cited in Barber 1976: 293).

[23] The schema was proposed by Leith (1983: 148–9). This allows Shakespeare the flexibility of rhyming *meat: mate* either as [ɛː] or as [eː], with lower-class characters more likely to rhyme *meat: meet*. On the long front-vowel overlaps in early ModE see also Barber (1976: 292–3/1997: 114–15).

[24] The word *steak* is commonly included in this set, but it could be a continuation of the ON form *steik* 'steak'. Walker (1791–1826: §240) identifies the vowel of *steak*, *break*, *great* with the vowel of *bear*, *pear*, *swear*.

[25] The history and scholarship on the North Midlands shift is discussed in Stockwell and Minkova (1999: 90–8) and Minkova and Stockwell (2003a: 171).

As a reminder, selecting only the relevant units, late ME had a set of diphthongs that come from the sources presented in (11).

(11) Sources of ME diphthongs relevant to the history of the low long vowels:

(a) Vocalisation or epenthesis in the OE sequence V + /-j, -w, -h/:
[-ej] (OE Angl.) *grēġ*, ME *grei* 'grey')
[ɛjç-] ~ [ej] (OE *ehta*, ME *ehte* ~ *eihte* 'eight')
[-æj] ~ [ɛj] ~ [ej] (OE *dæġ*, ME *dai* 'day')
[ow] (OE *stōw*, ME *stou* 'spot, -stow')
[ɔw] ~ [ow] (OE *cnāwan*, ME *cnowe(n)* 'know')
[ɔwx] ~ [ɔw] ~ [ow] (OE *dāh*, ME *do(u)h* 'dough')

(b) Scandinavian loans:
[ej] (ON *megen* 'main, strength', ON *þeir* 'their')
[ow] (ON **þōh* 'though')

(c) French loans:
[ej] (OFr *deis* 'dais' (a. 1259), OFr *delei* 'delay' (1275)

The presence of these diphthongal allophones in the system is important since it destabilises the perceptual difference between the presumably monophthongal [æː] and [ɔː] and the clearly diphthongal nuclei [-æj] ~ [ɛj] ~ [ej] and [ɔw] ~ [ow]. English stressed long vowels become diphthongal readily, and the availability of falling diphthongs with peaks identical to the monophthongs makes the task of discrimination between overlapping realisations harder. In this scenario the diphthongal vowels provide the basis of the mergers in (12).[26]

(12) Low and lower-mid vowel mergers with pre-existing diphthongs in late ME:

[26] This part of the 'traditional' 'Great' vowel shift account is based on Stockwell and Minkova (1988), Stockwell (2002b), and Minkova and Stockwell (2003).

[27] The source of the low-front [æː] is open-syllable lengthening of OE and OFr [a] as in OE *tale*, ME [taːl(ə)] ~ [tæːl(ə)] 'tale', OFr *age, blame, grace, place, scale* (see 7.5.2.1).

[28] The sources of [ɔː] are the raising of OE [ɒː] as in OE *āc*, ME southern [ɔːk] 'oak' (see 7.3.2) and open-syllable lengthening of OE [ɔ] and OFr [o] as in OE *nosu*, ME [nɔːz(ə)] 'nose', OFr *cloke* 'cloak' (see 7.5.2.1).

Along with the possible merger of [ɛː] with [ɛj] ~ [ej] (as in *break*, *yea*, *great*), the continuum of lower-mid long front vowels allows the same diphthongs to be identified with [æː]. The raising and possible diphthongisation of [æː] is attested only sporadically in ME. Occasional early rhymes such as *seyde: made* (*Guy of Warwick*); *hayte* 'hate': *fayt* 'dissemble' < OE *feġan: waite* < AN *waitier* might be imperfect rhymes or, alternatively, they are early indications of imperfect discrimination of the vocalic entities in that corner of the vowel space.

The appearance of the raised vowel in the north before 1500 is found first before the anterior coronal /-s/, as in Scottish rhymes of *place*, *grace*, *case* and others in *-ness*, *-less* (Jordan 1974: 238), which is what one would expect: there is a well-established bidirectional interaction between anterior coronals and vowel frontness.[29] Ignoring possible early indications and dialect differences, the raising of long [aː] to [æː] is a reliably attested feature of *late* ME. The identification of historical [aː] with a mid vowel in the fifteenth century is common: the mid-fifteenth century *Paston Letters* (Norfolk) show spellings such as <hest> 'haste' and <mek> 'make'. The diphthongal allophone is recoverable from the spelling of OFr *male* 'mail', appearing as <mayl/mail> in late ME, rhyming with *taylle* 'tail', OE *tæġl*, *tæġel* (*Townley Plays*, Lincoln (?) a. 1500 (a. 1460)).

The history of late ME [ɔː] is comparable. Here too the first inklings of the raising are found in rhymes involving historical [oː] and [ɔː]: *so* 'so', OE *swā*: *to* 'to', OE *tō*; *wo* 'woe', OE *wā*: *do* 'do', OE *dōn*. The raising of [ɔː] seems to be more advanced in word-final position, though it is not clear why this particular environment should be conducive to height neutralisation. The merger of the raised [oː] with the diphthongs shown in (12) is recognised in the first half of the seventeenth century, though earlier phonotactically conditioned diphthongisation of [ɔː] to [ɔw] ~ [ow] before tautosyllabic dark [ɫ] is indicated by MED spellings such as <owld> 'old' (c. 1376, a. 1400), <could> 'cold, n.' (1440).

One can thus say that both the upper and the lower half of the traditional 'Great' vowel shift underwent not just raising or independent diphthongisation, but a series of mergers with the pre-existing diphthongs (shaded in 13), ultimately favouring diphthongal realisations as the primary allophones which define the rising standard and the shape of the PDE vowel system. Merging (9) and (12), (13) summarises the main events discussed in this section.

[29] The phonetic and phonological basis and the typology of the interaction between coronals and vowel frontness is discussed in Flemming (2003).

(13) A summary of the major long-vowel changes in ME and EModE:[30]

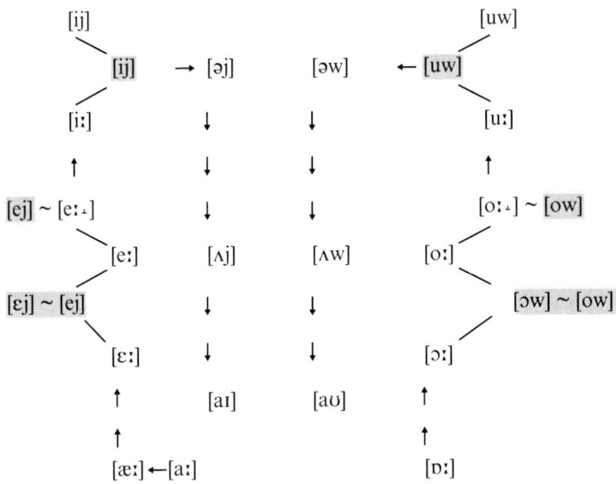

In some ways the schema in (13) supports the traditional assumption that the mechanism of the shift involves raising and diphthongisation of the long vowels: but it crucially refers also to the ambient phonological system: 'pure' long vowels and diphthongal long vowels coexist and alternate historically. In the mid-vowel area a set of two or three or more contrastive entities within a relatively restricted vowel space merge to a single unit. This is in fact the opposite of a chain shift: there is no displacement of contrasts. This means that the fundamental condition for a chain, namely the no-merger condition, can only be supported for the high vowels.

In conclusion: it is true that all long vowels underwent some kind of change in ME and EModE. Nevertheless, any representation of the mechanism of the changes ignoring the coexisting long vocalic nuclei in ME is too restrictive. The shaded diphthongal variants of the long vowels in (13) existed in OE or arose in ME from coarticulatory changes and from borrowing. The diphthongal and the monophthongal variants of neighbouring allomorphic clouds merged towards either a diphthongal or a monophthongal realisation. Some diphthongs were optimised by differentiation of their end points: [aɪ] for *bind*, *design*, *wife*, *sty*, and [aʊ] for *cow*, *crown*, *how*, *fowl*. Thus [aɪ] and [aʊ] are the attested SSBE results of the gradual change of both pure long vowels and minimal diphthongs of high vowel followed by a homorganic glide; it was the diphthongal realisations that were formative in terms

[30] This is an elaboration of the schema proposed in Stockwell (2002a: 267).

of the later history of these vocalic units. Similarly, the history of the ME mid long vowels [ɛː] as in OE *brecan*, ME [brɛːk(ə)] 'break'; /aː/ as in OE *bacan*, ME [baːk(ə) ~ bæːk(ə)] 'bake'; and /ɔː/ as in OE *āc*, ME Southern [ɔːk] 'oak' cannot be separated from the history of pre-existing diphthongs as in *day, play, weigh, blow, stow, dough.* Any description of the reorganisation of the vowel system of ME should take into consideration both the history of the long vowels proper and the diphthongal entities with which the long vowels merged in the course of the long vowel shift.

In this 'deconstructive' approach to the mechanism of 'Great' vowel shift, the changes were early, often simultaneous, and fully integrated within the vocalic system. Lexical diffusion is a main, and not yet fully understood component of the process: some environments are more conducive to change, and there is ample evidence that the frequency of a lexical item is of consequence.

Addressing the causation of the changes is more challenging. Some possible linguistic cause-and-effect factors in the initiation and diffusion of individual changes have already been identified. There is no single motivation that applies to all changes, but one can summarise the processes in (13) with reference to the interplay of four factors that jointly define the output. These four factors are:

1. Diphthong optimisation in perceptual terms.
2. Diphthong optimisation in articulatory terms.
3. Optimal spacing of adjacent entities – merger avoidance.
4. Optimal spacing of adjacent entities – merger.

The perceptual optimisation of diphthongs is illustrated by the progressively longer diphthong-internal trajectory as in [ij] > [aɪ] and [uw] > [aʊ]. Diphthong optimisation in articulatory terms is the minimisation of effort in terms of number of gestures, the necessity to coordinate the gestures, economy of time and muscle energy, that is, the realisation of diphthongs with shorter trajectories. An example of the minimisation of effort is the assimilation of the end points of the diphthong in the PRICE vowel; as noted above, it appears as [ɑ̟ə ~ ɑ̟ː] in 'extreme' Cockney, as [ɑe] in NZE and [ae ~ aː] in Southern AmE. Merger avoidance is the principle that maintains the contrast between historically contrastive entities: OE *hȳdan* 'to hide' and OE *hēdan* 'to heed' were not homophones, neither are their PDE reflexes. Changes resulting in merger are also attributable to optimal spacing of the vowel entities: phonemic distinctions based on small acoustic and articulatory differences are hard to maintain – in the account presented here this was the case with the overcrowded mid-vowel space in (13).

In addition to these linguistic structural forces at work, motivation for the selection of a particular variant pronunciation can be sought in the historical sociolinguistic setting of the process. From the start, all scholarship on the 'Great' vowel shift emphasises that the system described in, for example, Figure 8.4 can be applied only to a variety of English that was spoken in the southern part of the country that eventually became codified as the standard variety. The regional dialects of England and Scotland underwent their own long vowel shifts, some of them very different from the 'Great' vowel shift. Moreover, many current developments of the long vowels in American, British and Australian English are also 'shifts' – we will return to some specifically North American changes at the end of this chapter. The sociolinguistic aspects of the long vowel shifting are outside the scope of this book, but it must be acknowledged that the interaction among the regional varieties in essentially 'oral', pre-literate and pre-standard times is an important component of the historical record. The introduction of the printing press, the rise in literacy and the involvement of the orthoepists in the standardisation of written English is another key step towards the selection and diffusion of particular pronunciations in London and in the areas around London in the sixteenth and seventeenth centuries. It was the establishment of a written standard that provided the background for the codifying and prescriptive work of such writers as Thomas Sheridan and John Walker that culminated in 'Southern Standard British English'.

8.2.2.3 Further instability and enrichment: BREW-NEW, DO-DUE, AUNT-HAUNT

The picture of the long vowel nuclei in EModE in (13) is incomplete: it focuses on monophthongal vowels becoming diphthongal. The absorption of long vowels by pre-existing diphthongs suggests the potential for the opposite process, historical diphthongs becoming monophthongs, and it is indeed a type of change encountered in the monophthongisation of OE diphthongs in ME (see 7.4, Figure 7.6). Monophthongisation is also attested during the early and late Modern English periods. In addition, the English long vowel system was enriched with two diphthongs from French, /oi/ and /ui/. Figure 8.7 outlines the main diphthongal changes from late ME to PDE.

Figure 8.7 conceals some of the complexity of the processes involved in view of the multiple sources of the merging diphthongs: Middle English, Old Norse, Anglo-Norman and (Old) French. Some the details

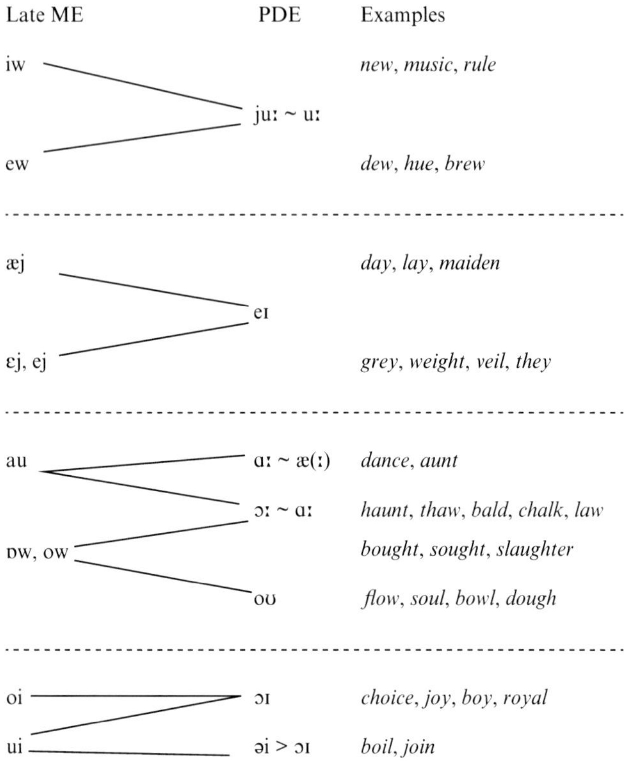

Figure 8.7 Diphthongal changes from Middle to Modern English

on <auNC> were touched upon in 8.2.1 and (11) lists the main sources of the ME diphthongs, but some clarification is still in order.

In the case of the [iw] and [ew] merger at the top of Figure 8.7, the native sources were joined by a large set of French words with a high front rounded vowel close to [y], which was probably reanalysed and adopted as [iu]: *due*, *duke*, *sugar*, *sure*. A very similar diphthong was already in existence in ME both as a continuation of [i] + [w] (as in *Tuesday* < OE *Tiwesday*) and from a raised ME [ew] as in *brew*.

The change from a rising diphthong to a monophthong – [iu] > [juː] > [uː] – has been ongoing since c. 1600. It is most advanced in words in which the vowel is preceded by the sonorants [r-] and [Cl-] and the affricates [tʃ-], [dʒ-]: *rude*, *clue*, *chew*, *June*. In some other coronal environments – [s-], [z-], [θ-]: *suit*, *assume*, *resume*, *enthuse*; after single onset [l-]: *lute*, *absolute*; and after [t-], [d-] and [n-] there continues to exist widespread variation across regional accents, registers and individual lexical items.

The merger of [æj], [ɛj], [ej], if they were ever really kept apart (see 7.4), occurred probably already in Southern ME, though the orthographic record is, as usual, more conservative and, indeed, quite inconsistent. The raised realisations [ɛj] and [ej] for <ai>, though not acknowledged until the middle of the sixteenth century, must have been common in the fourteenth century. Chaucer's rhyming practice suggests that for his variety of English the two diphthongs were already merged, allowing flexibility in the choice of rhymes.[31]

For the ME diphthong [au] the two outcomes are [ɑː] ~ [æ(ː)] as in *dance, aunt,* or [ɔː] ~ [ɑː] as in *haunt, thaw, bald, law, straw, sauce, laundry.* The split is often along etymological lines: Old French vs Anglo-Norman (see 8.2.1). In the sixteenth century <a> + [-m, -n], as in *dance, lamp, angel, flame, danger,* was pronounced as [ɑː] (vulgar or dialectal) or [aʊ] (elegant). As in the case with the [ɛː] and [eː] mergers in the course of the long vowel shift, it appears that the originally less prestigious, provincial pronunciation became codified; the variant with [eɪ] (*angel, strange, danger*) was a shifted version of [ɑː] after the seventeenth century.

The [ɔː] ~ [ɑː] set is joined by words with the ME diphthong [ɒw], [ow] before historical [-h], as in *bought, sought, slaughter.* Here belong also some late ME forms with [ɑw] from <a> + <l>, where the diphthong is due to the development of a back glide before the liquid, as in *all, hall, call, false, salt,* and so on (see 5.2.5). Before velars the /-l/ is dropped, for example *chalk, stalk, talk.* These forms were identical with the forms containing /l/ + labial (*calf, calm, half*) until the seventeenth century. The pronunciation with [æː] in *calf* and *half* is recorded from the early eighteenth century in British English; it is also the standard American pronunciation.

The last pair of diphthongs in Figure 8.9 represent the only vocalic nuclei in the late ME sound system that have no native pedigree. The large majority of <oi> and <ui> words in PDE come from French (*choice, employ, loin, moist, turmoil, soil, join, poison*) and Dutch (*buoy, foist, loiter*), and occasionally from other languages: Greek *hoi polloi,* Algonquian *Illinois,* Bengali *poisha,* Chinese *hoisin,* Dinka *toich,* imitative *ahoy, boink, oink.* The original [ui] has an unusual history in that, like the more recent history of /h-/ (see 5.3.1), it is one of the rare well-documented instances of a sound change in progress inhibited and partially reversed by the

[31] In the *Canterbury Tales* we find rhymes *they* [ej]: *awey* 'away' (ParT 541–2, The Hengwrt ms), *away: day* ([ɛi] (?)) (MT 3553–4, The Cambridge ms).

influence of spelling. Many of the words with PDE <oi> – *loin, boil, coy, oil, join, point, choice, poison* – had variant pronunciations with [oi] and [ui], the latter commonly from Anglo-Norman. The 'normal' development of [ui], involving lowering and centralisation of the first element of the diphthong (see 8.2.1), was towards [əi], which in the seventeenth and into the eighteenth century was also a possible realisation of historical [iː]. That the two etymologically distinct entities were treated as identical is shown by rhymes like *loin: line, boil: bile, point: pint* as late as the second half of the eighteenth century. In spelling the [ui] > [əi] words alternated between <ui> and <oi>. Eventually the centralised pronunciation [əi] for historical [ui] was abandoned in favour of [ɔi], no doubt supported by the spelling and pronunciation of the majority of the loanwords in that group.

The incorporation of the new diphthong in *boy, joy, coin* into the English phonological system is commonly described as incomplete. Vachek (1976: 162–7, 265–8) argued that lack of parallelism with the other diphthongs ([eɪ-oʊ], [aɪ-aʊ], but not *[ɛɪ-ɔɪ]) and lack of morphophonemic alternations involving [ɔɪ] in the PDE system, makes [ɔɪ] a 'peripheral' phoneme in SSBE. He hypothesised that the survival of [ɔɪ] is associated with its pragmatic function of differentiating synchronically foreign words from native words, especially polysyllabic words. Lass (1992a: 53) also emphasises the 'foreignness' of [ɔɪ] and its structural isolation, and concludes that it [ɔɪ] 'has just sat there for its whole history as a kind of non-integrated "excrescence" on the English vowel system'. While there are certainly asymmetries and restrictions on the distribution of [ɔɪ], in PDE the diphthong is as variable as other diphthongs, possibly in response to the ambient system. In AmE (as in London and Cockney English, where [aɪ] is [ɑɪ]) there is widespread raising of [ɔɪ] to [oi] and occasionally [ui] in the younger generation of speakers. In the American South the diphthong can be realised as triphthongal [ɔoi] ~ [ɑoɨ]. African American speakers show lowering of the second element to [oɛ] ~ [oæ] or [oɤ] ~ [ɔʌ]; merger of [oi] and [ai] is also recorded in Jamaican, Caribbean and Newfoundland English (Thomas 2001: 38–9). The continuity of the foreign status of [ɔɪ] is doubtful also in view of the fact that many of the original loanwords were monosyllabic and thus fit the prosodic pattern of the native vocabulary. The high productivity of the suffix *-oid* in the last two centuries would be another argument against the special nature of the diphthong. To what extent newly created items such as *oik* (1917), onomatopoeic *oink* (1935), *boing* (1952), *boink* (1963), as well as catchy clippings such as *droid* (1952), *roid* (1978), earmark [ɔɪ] as exotic is an issue that will profit from psycholinguistic testing.

8.3 The effect of phonotactics on long vowel shifting

One of the most reliable signals of historical vowel length in English orthography is the representation of a vowel with two vowel letters or digraphs; the use of these in *boat*, *read*, *keep*, *loud*, *moon*, *fear*, and so on is an indication that the vowel was long prior to the vowel shift (see 7.5.3). Yet matching English spelling to pronunciation may appear erratic; compare *booth-book*, *bear-fear*, *mood-stood-blood*, *dead-bead*. In all these sets of words the input is a historically long vowel, but the outcome is different.

Pre-vowel shift lengthenings are usually marked by a digraph or by the sequence <-VCe>: OE *medu* 'm**ea**d, OE *talu* 't**a**l**e**'. In contrast, shortenings, especially in derived words, may not be orthographically marked: *south-southern*, *clean-cleanse*; being short prior to the shift, the vowels in *southern*, *cleanse* are exempt from it. In addition to such shortenings (see 7.5.1), the nuclei of monosyllabic words tend to shorten before specific codas. In these cases too, the orthography remains unchanged, but the outcome is a short vowel, as in *book*, *stood*, *dead*. Tautosyllabic /r/ is also a special factor, responsible for, for example, *bear* vs *fear*. The next two sections address these special cases.

8.3.1 *Shortening in monosyllabic words:* LEAD *(Pb)-*LEAD, *V.,* DEAF*-*LEAF*,* MOOD*-*STOOD*-*BLOOD

The most noticeable environment for shortening in monosyllabic items is before dentals, as found in, for example, PDE *bread*, *dead*, *deaf*, *death*, *head*, *lead* (Pb), *shred*, *thread*, *sweat*, *threat*.[32] As the <-ea-> spellings suggest, the vowels in these monosyllables go back to ME [ɛː]; the shortening must have occurred prior to the shift to [iː] in the varieties that were later accepted as 'standard'. In ME the shortened variants were in rivalry with the historical long variants; long variants of *head*, *bread*, *dead* are attested into the seventeenth century, and they are amply attested in the regional varieties of English today. For the front mid vowels, statistics show that the shortening was most advanced before [-d], spreading to [-t], [-θ] in the seventeenth century, while *deaf* continued to have a long vowel until the late eighteenth century. Within a given set, the vowel of the most frequent word changed first, thus

[32] Other monosyllables with long front vowel nucleus that went through pre-shift shortening are *red* < OE *rēad*, *wet* < OE *wǣt*, *ten* < OE Angl. ***tēn****(e)*, compare *fifteen* with the original long vowel shifted; *hot* < OE ***hāt*** 'hot', compare *hǣtan* 'to heat'. Note that *hot*, *red*, *wet*, *ten* would tend to be prosodically weaker in a noun phrase where the noun is also monosyllabic.

dead, *head* were shortened earlier than *spread*, *stead* (Ogura 1987: 148–9, 185–90, 196–9). Many questions remain: the pairs *death-lead*, v. inf., *sweat-treat*, v., *deaf-leaf* have approximately the same frequency, so while frequency is a factor within the group of items that did change, a full account of the shortening is still needed.

Vowel shortening in monosyllables occurs sporadically also in words with late ME–early ModE [uː], the raised reflex of ME [oː]. Thus in the sixteenth and seventeenth centuries *book*, *cook*, *look*, *took*, *nook*, *rook*, *forsook*, *crook* are all recorded with [uː], and so are *good*, *stood*, *food*, *foot* (Dobson 1968: §§35–9). The centralised/laxed and shortened variants with [ʊ] gradually gained ground in the seventeenth century. For some items the change occurred early enough for them to participate in the further qualitative change of [ʊ] to [ʌ ~ ə], as in *flood*, *blood*, *glove* (see 8.2.1). Within the set of shortened items, a coda [-d] seemed to induce the shortening first, followed by [-v], followed by [-t, -θ, -k]. Within those subsets, lexical frequency and the presence of an initial cluster also favoured the change (Ogura 1987: 145).

The shortening before dentals, both before the high back vowel and the mid-front vowel, has been a puzzle for a long time, prompting explanations based on syntactic context, syllable well-formedness, analogy, semiotics and coarticulation (see Ritt 1997; Phillips 2002; Ritt 2007). The probabilistic basis of all these hypotheses is still debated; the leading trigger of the shortening, coda /-d/, should not be conducive to shortening in view of the general tendency of the preservation of phonetic duration before voiced obstruents.

Shortening also occurs before the voiceless velar coda [-k], as in *book*, *cook*, *look*, *took*, *nook*, *rook*, *forsook*, *crook*. The phonetic mechanism of this seventeenth-century shortening can be related to the inherent likelihood of a shorter vowel before a voiceless stop, but the consistency with which this particular shortening occurred before the voiceless velar in English is surprising. Note that monosyllabic words in PDE which ended in [-uːk] in the seventeenth and eighteenth centuries and which maintained the original length of the vowel are practically non-existent. It is possible that once the shortening occurred on a single word, the fashion for [-ʊk] in the eligible monosyllables spread and affected all such words. How and whether this development relates to the complete absence of [-uːg] or [-ʊg] codas in stressed monosyllables is difficult to determine; the gap in the phonotactic system may be completely accidental.

The chronological sequence of shortening [uː] > [ʊ] presented here is not the only logical possibility. In the items undergoing shortening of the high back vowel, [uː] is the raised reflex of ME [oː], as in OE *bōc* 'book', OE *gōd* 'good', OE *fōd* 'food', OE *glōf* 'glove'. Recall, however, that if lengthened, OE [ʊ] > [oː], as in OE *duru* > ME *dōr(e)* 'door' (see 6.5.1), and that shortened of [oː] could result in ME [ʊ], as in *moon* (OE *mōna*) - *Monday* (OE *mōnandæġ*) (see 6.5.1); similarly, the stressed [oː] in OE *mōnað* 'month', *mōðor* 'mother' show EModE shortened [ʊ], later non-Northern [ʌ].[33] These examples suggest the analytical possibility of OE [oː] being directly shortened to its height-partner [ʊ].

Figures 8.8 and 8.9 show how the items with shortened vowels discussed in this section compare with items resisting the shortening.

	OE *dēaf* 'deaf'	OE *lēaf* 'leaf'
Input	[æː], [æə]	[æː], [æə]
Shortening	[ɛ]	---
Vowel shift	---	[iː]
PDE	[dɛf]	[liːf]

Figure 8.8 The DEAF-LEAF contrast in PDE

	OE *mōd* 'mood'	OE *stōd* 'stood'	OE *blōd* 'blood'
Input	[oː]	[oː]	[oː]
Vowel shift	[-uːd]	[-uːd]	[-uːd]
Shortening	---	[-ʊd]	[-ʊd]
[ʊ] > [ʌ ~ ə][34]	---	---	[-ʌd]

Figure 8.9 The MOOD-STOOD-BLOOD contrast in PDE

The values of the vowels in the three items in Figure 8.9, *mood-stood-blood*, were in place by the eighteenth century, but for some items the variability continues to this day: *hoof, roof, root, soot* can be either [uː] or [ʊ], *groom* and *broom* are also variable, but not *gloom*; *soon* and *spoon* are variable, but not *moon* and *noon*; *hoop* and *whoops* vary, but not *stoop*. These rather disparate data do not point to a particular pattern – a full

[33] The pair *moth-mother* is sometimes cited as an example of erratic English spelling. *Moth* is from OE *moððe* > PDE [mɒθ], [mɔθ], [mɑθ] (see 8.2.1). *Mother* belongs to the set of common words such as *other, brother*, also *smo(r)ther*, for which Jespersen (1909: 332) attributes the shortening to the cluster /-ðr-/ in inflected forms.

[34] The lowering is dated after the first half of the seventeenth century (see 8.2.1).

set of regional variables may reveal the reasons behind the selection of a particular realisation. Why monosyllabic shortening targets ME [ɛː] and (late) ME [uː] < [oː] words but other long vowels are unaffected, is yet another unanswered question.

8.3.2 *Vowels in relation to /r/:* PERSON-PARSON, TEAR, *v.* - TEAR, *n.*, FLOOR-POOR

Figure 8.10 *I Lost My Khakis* (from <http://weknowmemes.com>

There are no sections on 'Vowels in relation to [-p]' or 'Vowels in relation to [-z]', so the heading of this section must be justified. Our starting point is the properties of /r/ discussed in 5.2.1. In PDE the consonant in question is a member of the class of rhotics, a complex class of sounds collectively represented as /r/, a continuant with variable realisations of which the alveolar approximant [ɹ] is most common. Additionally we find the alveolar coronal trill [r] in some accents of Scots, alveolar tap [ɾ] intervocalically in 'Refined RP', also the most common rhotic in

Scots, the retroflex [ɻ] (South-West BrE, North American, similar to [ɹ]), the uvular continuant [ʀ], or the uvular fricative [ʁ] (North-East England, Lowland Scots), and a labiodental continuant [ʋ] or [ɰ], the velar approximant similar to an unrounded [w] in London/Estuary English.

The most likely allophones of /r/ for late OE are the central approximant [ɹ] or the coronal trill [r] in the syllable coda (see 5.2.2). The early changes involving short vowels plus coda /r/: Breaking, metathesis, epenthesis and the very early ME pre-consonantal loss point to the significant coarticulatory effect of /-r/ codas, but they did not trigger a restructuring of the vowel system (see 6.5.3). The possible effect on long vowels can be illustrated as in (14), acknowledging that some of the scribal variants are rare, or specific to a particular set of texts.

(14) Scribal variants for OE long vowel + /-r/ coda:
OE *dēor* 'deer': <deor ~ dior ~ dyor ~ dear ~ dær>
OE *fȳr* 'fire': <fyr(r) ~ fyer ~ fir ~ fur ~ fer ~ feer ~ fier ~ fares ~ fære>

The early pre-consonantal loss of /-r/ (see 5.2.3) can be seen as the beginning of a process stretching over more than six centuries and affecting different dialects and different lexical items unevenly. The nature of the rhotic, the most sonorous of the consonants, contributes to its weakening in coda position, leading to its confusability with schwa and eventual reanalysis to schwa, or loss in the non-rhotic varieties of English. As this section shows, loss of coda /-r/ emerges as one of the most important triggers of phonotactically conditioned vowel lengthening and diphthongisation in EModE, changing the composition of the vocalic system.

Before discussing lengthening and new types of diphthongs in relation to /-r/, we turn to a process covered briefly in 7.3.1 in the context of late ME short vowel changes. In the course of the fourteenth century, the sequence <-er-> [-ɛr-] became <-ar-> [-ar-], as shown in (15).

(15) Late Middle English [-ɛr] > [-ar]:

OE	EME	LME	PDE
herġan [hɛrjən]	[hɛrj(ən])]	[hari]	'harry'
steorra [stɛrrə]	[stɛr(rə)]	[star]	'star'
	[fɛrm] < Fr. *ferme*	[farm]	'farm'

EME	LME	PDE
[(h)ɛrb] < AN *(h)erb-*	[arbər]	'arbor' (1300)
	[(h)ɛrbəl]	'herbal' (1516)
[pɛrsən] < OFr *persone*	[parsən]	'parson'
	[pɛrsən]	'person'

The innovative forms were first observed in the North:

> *ĕ* before *r* began to change to *ă* in the early fourteenth century in the North, and by the end of the century the new sound had begun to appear in the South. . . . The lowering was probably in the first instance to [æ], and subsequently to [a]. (Dobson 1968: §64, n.2; §§67–69 and notes)

The change occurs later than pre-consonantal shortening: OE *dēor* 'dear' > *darling*, OE *fēorþing* > *farthing*, OE *stēor* 'steer' + *bord* > *starboard*.

In some of the French loanwords the spelling with <e> continued to be used after the fifteenth century, as in *sergeant* (c. 1200, OFr *sergent*). Under the influence of spelling, [-ɛr] (subsequently [-ər] ~ [-ɜː] ~ [ɚ][35]) was reinstated in many words, quite likely with reinforcement from Latin, as in *perfect*, *serve*, with late ME variants *parfit*, *sarve*. The existence of competing pronunciations in EModE accounts for Shakespearean rhymes such as *starve*: *deserve*, *desert*: *part*. This incomplete change created interesting pairs such as *university-varsity*, ***Berkeley*** [-ɚ] - ***Berkshire*** [ar-], ***clerk*** [-ɚ] (AmE) - ***clerk*** [-ar] (BrE). Interestingly, *err*, v. (1303, OFr *errer*), recorded as <arr(en)> in the fifteenth century, shows two spelling pronunciations, the earlier [ɜː] and both [ɚ] and [ɛr] in AmE, the latter possibly supported by more frequent *error* (1300 < OFr *error*).

(16) Orthography and the variable results of fourteenth-century [ɛr] > [ar]:

Source	**Expected [-ar]**	**Unchanged/restored [ɛr]/[ɜː] ~ [ɚ]**
OE *beorc* 'birch'	Barkham (Berkshire)	Berkeley (CA)[36]
OE *dēorby* 'deer-by'	Derbyshire[37]	derby (AmE)

[35] The rhotacisation right-hook on schwa is very similar to the IPA right-hook reversed epsilon [ɝ]. We use only the former for the NURSE vowel in PDE AmE.

[36] Compare *Berkley* (Somerset), UK.

[37] Compare *Darby* Lodge (Lincolnshire), UK; *Darby*, MT, *Darby* PA in the US.

OE *heort* 'hart'	Hertford (Herts)	Hertford (NC)
Gmc **sker-*	shard	sherd
OE *clerec* ~ *clerc*	clerk (BrE)	clerk (AmE)
OFr *errant*	arrant	errant
OFr *mercant*	Marchand	merchant
OFr *sergent*	sergeant	
	varmint	vermin

The lowering and centralisation of retained, reinstated or newly borrowed [-ɛr] > [-ər]/[ɚ] was under way during the seventeenth century. It seems to have been preceded by a parallel change of the high vowels, a merger of [-ɪr] and [-ʊr] into [-ər] in progress already in the sixteenth century. In (Southern) EModE words such as *fir* < OE **fyre* 'fir', *circle* OE < Lat. *circul* 'astronomical circle', *further* < OE *furðra*, ME *cursor* 'runner' had the same stressed vowel. The three-way merger of historical <-*ir*, -*er*, -*ur*> is attested in Shakespeare's rhymes of the type *birds: herds*, *curse: first.* The merger is illustrated in (17).[38]

(17) <-ir, -er, -ur> merger in EModE:

Source	**ME**	**EModE**
OE *gyrdel* 'girdle'	*gir(r)del*	
AN *surgien* 'surgeon'	*surge(y)n*	[-ə(r)-]
OFr *certain* 'certain'	*certe(i)n*	

(*gir(r)del*, *surge(y)n*, *certe(i)n* → [-ə(r)-])

A coda /-r/ is a neutralising environment. For the short vowels neutralisation of [ɪ], [ʊ], [ɛ] results in merger into the featurally neutral schwa outcome. The phonetic rationale behind this is the coarticulation of the short vowel + /-r/ which affects both segments: it lowers and centralises the vowel, while the adjacent sonorant coda becomes more schwa-like; its further weakening can eliminate the consonantal cues, leading to complete loss of the consonantal properties of /r/. The difficulty of perceiving the distinctive features of pre-/r/ vowels is attributed to the acoustic similarity of the first two formants of [ɹ], [ɹ̩], and [ə ~ ɨ] (see 5.4.2). The next step, associated with the vocalisation of /-r/ in the

[38] The difference between the original short vowels is preserved in Scots, where [-r] has not had the same neutralising effect. This follows from the fact that Scots post-vocalic [-r] is a tongue-tip trill, which is incompatible with simple retroflex coloration of the preceding vowel. Irish English merges [-ɪr] and [-ʊr], but keeps [-ɛr] distinct (Lass 1987: 259, 264).

Southern varieties, is compensatory lengthening to [ɜː] in SSBE, and merger with the possibly unshifted [ɛː] in, for example, *earl* (OE *eorl*), *earth* (OE *eorðe*) (see below).

Note that unlike the [-ɛr] > [-ar] change, where /-r-/ has the same effect whether it is tautosyllabic (*farm, darling*) or ambisyllabic (*barry, arrant*), the mergers of the short vowels before /-r/ in (17) occur *only* if the consonant is fully tautosyllabic. Thus words like *terror* (1375), *terrace* (1575), *serif* (1830), *mirror* (1300), *squirrel* (1366), *pyramid* (1398), *syrup* (1398), *lyric* (1581) preserve the quality of their original stressed short vowels.

Turning to the influence of /r/ on the preceding long vowel, recall from 6.4 that some ME spellings indicate sporadic lengthening before /-rC/ clusters, treated in the literature as part of the lengthening before homorganic clusters: *board* (OE *bord*), *hoard* (OE *hord*), *earl* (OE *eorl*), *earth* (OE *eorðe*), *hearken* (OE *he(o)rcnian*), *heart* (OE *he(o)rte*), *mourn* (OE *murnen*). The extent of the lengthening is unclear; as long as /r/ was realised with some friction, the tendency towards lengthening would be counteracted by the tendency for long vowels to shorten when followed by /-CC/ (see 7.5.1.1). The [-ɛr] > [-ar] change discussed above can be a diagnostic of length: *hearken, heart* must have had the short [ɛ] for it to be lowered to [a], while in *earl, earth* the input to EModE [-ə(r)-], PDE [ɜː] ~ [ɚ] could have been either [ɛ] or [ɛː].

It was noted in 8.2.1 that loss of /r/ was one of the sources for the introduction of 'new' vowels, [ɑː] and [ɒː] ~ [ɔː], in PDE. In the long-vowel subsystem the most interesting effect of a following /-r/ is the rise of a new set of diphthongs in conjunction with the loss of /-r/ in the non-rhotic varieties. The dating of /r/-loss (see 5.2.3) varies depending on the social background of the data source. Dobson (1968: §332) found that 'only sources which reflect vulgar pronunciation give evidence of the change before 1700, and even they give little'. The switch from 'vulgar' to accepted in 'good' speech took at least a century. In stressed syllables 'the change could not have occurred in good speech before c. 1800' (Dobson 1968: §427).

The loss of /-r/ after long vowels follows upon two analytically separable processes, schwa-insertion (breaking) and pre-schwa-laxing (Wells 1982, I: 214–16), though the exact timeline is hard to ascertain. Bearing in mind that the chronology and the exact phonetic nature of these transitional stages are hard to reconstruct, we can offer a schema of the effect of coda /-r/ on the long vowels in EModE as in (18).[39]

[39] See Lass (1999: 108–12) for a more detailed account of the dating of the transitional stages with reference to the orthoepistic testimony.

(18) The effect of /-r/ loss on long vowels in non-rhotic Englishes:[40]

Late ME to EModE	Schwa-insertion	Length adjustment	/-r/ -loss	Examples
-əir ~ -ʌir	-aiər	-aɪər	-aɪə	*fire* (OE *fȳr*)
-eː˔r ~ -iːr	-iːər	-ɪər	-ɪə	*deer* (OE *dēor*)
-ɛːr ~ -e˔ːr ~ -iːr	-iːər	-ɪər	-ɪə	*ear* (OE *ēare*)
-ɛːr ~ -eːr	-eːər	-ɛər	-ɛə	*pear* (OE *pere*)
-æːr ~ - ɛːr	-ɛːər	-ɛər	-ɛə	*hare* (OE *hara*)
-ɔːr	-ɔː(ə)r	-ɔ(ː)(ə)r	-ɔ(ː)(ə)	*oar* (OE *ār*)
-oːr	-ɔː(ə)r	-ɔ(ː)(ə)r	-ɔ(ː)(ə)	*floor* (OE *flōr*)
-oː˔r ~ -uːr	-uːər	-ʊər	-ʊə	*poor* (AN *pover, pour*)
-əur ~ -ʌur	-auər	-aʊər	-aʊə	*bower* (OE *būr*)

Schwa-insertion occurs also in the inherited diphthongs, for example OE *fæġer* 'fair, adj.', OE *leġer* 'lair', where the palatal glide was lowered before /-r/, resulting in merger with the new centring diphthongs from etymological [-ɛːr] as in *pear, hare.* As noted above, an important consequence of the processes in (18) is the introduction of the new diphthongs [ɪə], [ɛə], [ɔə], [ʊə] in the non-rhotic varieties of English.

Another observation about the data in (18) is that as with the short vowels in (17), the presence of /-r/ in the coda can have a strong neutralising effect, evidenced by the merger in the etymologically distinct pairs *deer-ear, pear-hare, oar-floor* (and currently *poor, pore* in some varieties). The mergers affect mostly the long mid vowels and they are not carried through with consistency. While historical long [eː] as in *deer* (OE *dēor*) generally participates in the raising of [eː] to [eː˔] ~ [iː] (see 8.2.2), <ea> spellings as in *hear* (OE Angl. *hēran*), *dear* (OE *dēore*) suggest that the vowel was identified with historically lower-mid front [ɛː] as in *ear* (OE *ēare*). However, ME [-ɛːr] can either emerge as the raised [eː˔r] ~ [iːr] as in *ear*, or the /r/ acts as a deterrent to raising, so that the outcome is [-ɛə], which merges with the reflex of ME [-æːr] ~ [-ɛːr] as in *hare* (OE *hara*). Merger occurs with the mid back vowels too, producing homophones from historical [-ɔːr] as in *oar* (OE *ār*) and [-oːr] as in *floor* (OE *flōr*). Once again, the /-r/ may or may not inhibit the raising of the high mid back vowel, so that an input [-oːr] can emerge as either

[40] The glides [j] and [w] used for the second part of the reflexes of historical [iː] and [uː] are replaced by [i] and [u] on the assumption of some positional lengthening before /r/. The exact history of [j]-[ɪ]-[i] and [w]-[ʊ]-[u] in this context needs further clarification.

[ɔːə] as in *floor* or as [ʊə] as in *poor.* Going back to the key pairs in the heading of this section, we can describe, if not explain, the difference between *tear,* v. - *tear,* n. and *floor-poor.* in *tear,* v. (OE *teren*) and *floor* ME [-ɛːr] and ME [-oːr] remained at their original height, while in *tear,* n. (OE *tēar*) and *poor* the same vowels participated in the long vowel shift. These pre-schwa-insertion patterns are shown in (19).

(19) *TEAR*, v. - *TEAR*, n. and *FLOOR-POOR*:

	***tear*, v.**	***tear*, n.**	***floor***	***poor***
ME	[-ɛː-]	ME [-ɛː-]	ME [oː]	ME [oː]
Effect of [-r]	[-ɛ-]	---	[oː]	---
Long vowel shift	---	[-iː-]	---	[-uː-]

The possible articulatory basis of /-r/ vocalisation (see 5.2.4) is a separation of the gestural components of constricted /r/. Phonetically, the change from a rhotic to a non-rhotic state is from a bi-gestural [ɹ], to bi-gestural [əɹ], to uni-gestural [ə]. An important contributing factor is also the perceptual similarity between the sonorant /r/ to schwa. In the non-rhotic varieties of English, the transition from [-əɹ] to [-ə] is carried through, while rhotic varieties preserve bi-gestural [-əɹ], usually rendered as [ɚ]. It should also be added that the effect of /r/ is not the same in all rhotic varieties. In SSE a coda /-r/ does not involve schwa-insertion, thus *bee* and *beer* both have [iː], similarly *hay* and *hair* both have [eː] (McMahon 2000: 232).

While loss of /r/ may be described as 'natural' in a phonetic sense, it is still unclear why some communities of speakers preserved it when others did not. One reason why the change may have taken off in the first place, not usually considered in the textbook accounts, is loan phonology. In Later Old French (eleventh to fourteenth century) and Middle French (fourteenth to sixteenth century), pre-consonantal [r] was assimilated to the following consonant and thereby lost in the spoken language (it is retained in spelling to this day), producing rhymes such as *sage* : *large, fors* : *clos, ferme* : *meesme.* Thus English orthography was at odds with the functional factor of ease of articulation and with the possibly prestigious pronunciation of recent loanwords in which pre-consonantal [-r] had been lost. This may account for the considerable lag time for the diffusion and codification of [r]-loss in early Modern English. Rhotic and non-rhotic pronunciations must have coexisted for over three centuries, even in the same dialects. As noted above, conservatism based on spelling maintained rhoticity in the Southern standard until just after the first quarter of the nineteenth century.

A historical note on the spread of rhoticity: the main rhotic varieties are spoken in Scotland, Ireland, South-West England, extreme West

Lancashire, most of the USA and Canada (see 5.2.4). The development of North American rhotic accents is to a considerable extent a function of settlement patterns in colonial times. Though the original settlers on the East Coast were mostly from the south and east of England, which are now non-rhotic, they arrived in the Colonies long before 'dropping the -r' had become fashionable and codified there. The problem is not explaining where American rhoticity came from, – it came from Southern and East Midland England originally, and later waves of settlers from Scotland and Ireland vigorously reinforced it – but rather why non-rhoticity shows up anywhere in America. Since it only shows up in centres of education along the East Coast, not including Philadelphia, which has always been, and continues to be, rhotic, it may be that in the major political and trading centres, namely Boston, New York, Norfolk, Savannah, Alexandria and Charleston, the newly fashionable British r-less accent took root and was reinforced by regular travel to Britain. The Civil War is a watershed in the perception of rhoticity as prestigious: prior to it r-lessness was associated with the Bostonian and Virginian elite, but after 1870 New York was increasingly rhotic, the British model was much less important and rhoticity gained prestige.

8.4 Continuity or reinvention

The survey of the segmental histories of consonants and vowels in earlier English revealed many parallels with ongoing changes in the varieties of English spoken today. There is nothing surprising about history repeating itself – language change is inherent in language use, and language users are guided by the same principles of speech production and perception. Before we move on to the description of stress placement in the history of English, we go briefly over a topic which illustrates the way in which one phonological pattern can straddle historical and ongoing phonological change.

8.4.1 Canadian or long-vowel 'Raising': ICE *[ʌɪs] -* EYES *[aɪz] ~ [aɛz] ~ [aᵊ] ~ [aː]*[41]

In Canadian English (CE) the PRICE vowel has two realisations depending on the voicing of the coda consonant: [ʌɪ] before voiceless codas, as in *price*, *right* (referred to as 'Canadian Raising'), and [aɪ] before

[41] This section will focus only on the [ʌɪ]-[aɪ] alteration, though the pattern is observed also with [ʌʊ]-[aʊ]. For details on the research history, the geographical range and updates on the various findings see Chambers (2006).

voiced codas, as in *prize, ride.* As the reconstruction of the long-vowel changes in (13) shows, [ʌɪ] was an intermediate value in the history of inherited [iː]. The logical question, then, is whether CE is conservative or innovative. Moreton and Thomas (2007) argue that the existing alternations associated with the so-called Canadian Raising 'have been independently re-innovated and show a systematic typology: The voiceless environment selects the higher allophone.' They focus on the asymmetry between the first element and the offglide in response to voicing: diphthongs assimilate to the first element before voiced codas, hence [aɪz] ~ [aɛz] ~ [aᵊ] ~ [aː], and to their offglides before voiceless ones, hence [ʌɪs]. They find a modern parallel of the effect of the coda consonant in CE on this vowel and the ongoing /ai/-alternation in the Cleveland area in Ohio.[42] This leads them to dismiss the hypothesis that the alternations are a 'more likely retentions of earlier values, related to similar qualities in Scots and Hiberno English' (Lass 1987: 285); recall that the BITE vowel in southern Hiberno English is [ʌɪ], in Standard Scottish English [ʌi][43] and in Mid Ulster English [əi]. Lass further points out that [ə-] and [ʌ-] as first elements of the diphthong based on ME [iː] were 'normal' in SSBE in the seventeenth and eighteenth centuries (see 8.2.2.2), and the fully open [a-] was a later innovation. In that scenario, the alternation is inherited and should be labelled a non-lowering 'archaism' rather than 'raising'.

Moreton and Thomas's point that the innovations observed in PDE that appear to replicate the 'Canadian Raising' and the phenomenon in CE must be related by common phonetic motivation is beyond dispute. In their account, that motivation is the tendency of diphthongs to be dominated by the offglide before voiceless codas, and by the first element of the diphthongs elsewhere. No matter what the motivation, however, we have to assume that the same linguistic factors can be at work at different times and places, and therefore dismissing the possibility that the [ʌɪ]-[aɪ] alternation in CE is ancestral is not a logical

[42] Further 'Canadian Raising' features are found in Rochester, New York, with extrapolations to the Great Lakes basin on the American side, Ann Arbor, Michigan, Detroit, Newcastle-on-Tyne and in the Fens of eastern England (see Chambers 2006 for full references).

[43] The literature on the issue of [ʌi] vs [a·e], which is a sub-part of a more general 'Scottish Vowel Length Rule', or 'Aitken's Law' is very rich, starting famously with Aitken (1962). It refers to the process whereby in Scots before /r/, voiced fricatives and before major boundaries there is also lengthening and lowering:

[ʌi]: *tight, fine, time, Fife, mice, tide*

[a·e]: *tie, fire, five, rise, tied*

Note the exclusion of voiced stops from the lengthening environment.

necessity. Parallel, and innovative, developments in US English are phonetically based, and so can be the 'innovative' lowering of the [ʌɪ] > [aɪ] before voiced codas in CE. It is important to recognise that 'both /au/- and /ai/-raising were well established in Ontario among people born as early as 1860' (Chambers 2006: 111). Surveys of the settlement history of Canada (Finegan 2006: 414) identify the Irish and the Scots as the largest immigrant groups in Canada in the 1830s and 1840s, peaking in 1851–61. Another wave of Scottish immigration occurred between 1901 and 1911. Evaluating the contribution of these demographic factors to the formation of the CE vowel system against the likelihood of independent innovation is far from straightforward. It certainly allows for a reversal of the direction of change – from raised realisations in all environments to lowered realisations before voiced codas. The source, or more likely sources, of 'Canadian Raising' cannot therefore be considered fully determined.

This brief excursion into the roots of a well-known regional characteristic concludes the survey of the segmental histories of English sounds. The next two chapters will address patterns of stress and the early history of English versification in relation to phonological history.

See further reading and appendices on *Companion* website.

9 The evolution of the English stress system[1]

ALWAYS-CAUSEWAYS, PRÉSENT, N. - PRESÉNT, V. HARÁSS ~ HÁRASS

This chapter shifts the focus from segmental histories to the history of word- and phrasal stress in English. We first define some terms used in the description of the prosodic patterns of speech and revisit (see 2.3) the ways in which syllable structure and syllable weight interact and influence the assignment of stress. A brief sketch of the patterns of stress assignment in PDE is followed by notes on the methodology of prosodic reconstruction. Sections 9.4–9.6 turn to the description of Old and Middle English word- and phrasal stress. The last two sections discuss the effect of lexical borrowing from French and Latin on the prosody of English and some interesting prosodic changes in post-Renaissance English.

9.1 Preliminaries: definition of some terms

It is customary in linguistics to approach phonological issues from two angles: the study of individual segments, or **segmental** phonology, or the study of **prosodic** structures. The term 'prosody', as used here, refers to the 'suprasegmental' domain of linguistic description and analysis, attending to the properties of individual segments only if relevant to the structure and function of higher-level units, such as syllables. Very importantly, syllables are the carriers of 'stress', the contrastive intensity that marks some syllables as more or less prominent. The term 'accent' can also be used with reference to syllable prominence, so an 'unaccented syllable' and an 'unstressed syllable' can be synonymous.

The goal of prosodic description is to identify the properties and the organisation of syllables into words, phrases and utterances in speech. This area of inquiry is also referred to as 'metrical phonology'. In order to avoid confusion between the 'metrical' properties of speech and the properties of poetic meter, we will use 'prosody' for the structures in

[1] Parts of this chapter are based on Minkova (2012) and Minkova (2013).

'ordinary' spoken language. For the structures found in verse, we will use 'poetic meter', or simply 'meter'. Both prosody and meter refer to **rhythm**, the regularity of recurrence of stresses, which can interact with the prosodic realisation of words and phrases. To illustrate: in PDE rhythmic well-formedness accounts for the lack of word-internal three unstressed syllables in a row, known as the 'lapse' constraint. Rhythm is involved in stress-clash avoidance, as in 'The Arab Rule' (Ross 1972), whereby a secondary stress in PDE is demoted after a light, main-stressed syllable – the case of the alternation in *Arab*: ['eɪˌɹæb] vs ['æɹəb], or in the lack of secondary stress in [-rɪz-] in *charismatic*, though the syllable is heavy and the input *charisma* is stressed on the penultimate syllable. Rhythm is also instrumental in versification, where the distance between prominent metrical positions tends to be tightly regulated.

Prosody is also the linguistic bridge between phonology and morphology – linguistic units such as words and phrases have prosodic structure which interacts with the unit's morphosyntactic status. To illustrate: *présent*, n. - *presént*, v., *sóft pòrn*, compound - *sòft táp*, phrase. Stress is one of the main cues for speech segmentation into individual words: a speaker of English will associate stress with the left edge of a word, hence the familiar joke *Be alert – your country needs lerts*. The interaction between rhythmic constraints and the word-delimiting function of stress in English is seen in the absence of words that have more than a single fully unstressed syllable word-initially: *saguáro* [sə'gwɑroʊ] is fine, but *saguarésque* *[səgwə'rɛsk] must have secondary stress on the initial syllable, *Japan* [dʒə'pæn] is fine, but *Japanése* has to have initial secondary stress: [ˌdʒæpə'niːz]; *Magéllan* [mə'dʒɛlən], but *Magellánic* [ˌmædʒə'lænɪk].

Outside of linguistics, the term 'prosody' can also be used with reference to the study of verse and its properties; again, for the conventionalised rhythmic structures of verse we reserve the term 'meter', the topic of Chapter 10.

Individual speech sounds are the building blocks of prosodic units that are independently pronounceable, namely syllables.[2] One important property of syllables is that they have *prosodic weight*. The contribution of an individual sound to the prosodic weight of a syllable can be measured in terms of *moras*: recall from 2.3.3 that all short vowels in English are associated with a single mora, all long vowels and

[2] The unity and independence of the syllable in speech has been recognised for a very long time. Ælfric's pedagogically oriented *Grammar* (995) offers a definition which can still be used today: '*SYLLABA* is stæfgefēg on anre orðunge geendod' [A syllable is a stave/letter-conjunction completed in one breath].

diphthongs are bimoraic, and consonants are moraic or non-moraic depending on their position in the syllable. The ability to divide an utterance into syllables, and, for English, the ability to perceive syllable weight, is part of the intuitive knowledge that speakers have of their language.

In addition to being the smallest independently pronounceable units of speech, English syllables are the domains of stress-placement. Phonetically, stress is associated with the use of increased respiratory energy, increased tension of the vocal folds and loudness. Though stress is technically not a phonological feature, it can be described as binary in the sense that syllables are either [+ stress] or [- stress]. However, within the domain of an English word there may be more than one syllable designated as [+ stress], and if so, those syllables will have different levels of stress. The most prominent syllable in a word carries *primary* or *main* stress, marked either with a *superior vertical stroke* [ˈ] before the stressed syllable (IPA), or, informally in orthographic forms, with an acute accent, ˊ over the vowel, so [ˈlætɪn] is the transcription of *Látin.* Secondary and tertiary stresses, most common in our loan vocabulary, here bundled together here as *non-primary* stress, are marked either with the IPA *inferior vertical stroke* [ˌ], or with a grave accent, ˋ, in orthographic forms, so [ˌtɛrəˈdæktəl] is the transcription of *ptèrodáctyl.* Although informally we speak of 'stressed' and 'unstressed' vowels, and place the acute and grave diacritics over the vowel-letters for typographic convenience, it is important to bear in mind that stress is a property of the entire syllable.[3]

The relationship between vowel reduction and stress was discussed in 2.3.3 and 7.6; in PDE lack of stress can be recognised by the presence of unstressable peaks: [ə, n̩, m̩]; some degree of stress is always associated with [eɪ, ɛ, æ, ɑ, ɔ, ʊ, uː, ʌ] peaks, and the remaining peaks can appear in both stressed and unstressed syllables.[4]

9.2 Syllable structure and syllable weight

Recall from 2.3.2 and 2.3.3 that the syllable is a structurally complex unit in that it is further decomposable. At the core of the syllable is its

[3] Dictionaries vary in stress notation; stress diacritics can be placed before or after the stressed syllable, thus for *poster* one finds OED: [ˈpoʊstər] (IPA), *The American Heritage Dictionary.* [pōˊstər], similarly *Chambers 21st Century Dictionary.* Alternative ways of orthographic indication of stress are using bold (*Dictionary.com.* [**poh**-ster]), capitalising a particular syllable or word (*POster, Was it THIS level we parked on?*) or italicising.

[4] This taxonomy follows Hayes (1995: 15). The OED transcription system allows many of the 'stressed only' peaks to appear in unstressed syllables.

'nucleus' or 'peak', the segment of highest sonority in the string. The nucleus is the only obligatory component of the syllable – it is usually filled by a vowel or a diphthong, but sometimes also by a syllabic sonorant /r̩, l̩, m̩, n̩/. Consonants or consonant clusters to the left of the nucleus constitute the syllable onset, and the consonants following the nucleus make up the coda. The onset and the coda can be empty (indefinite article *a*), filled by a single consonant (***be***, ***it***, ***bit***) or filled by a consonant cluster (***stay***, ***east***, ***crest***). Together, the peak and coda, if there is one, constitute the syllable rhyme. Universally, there is an asymmetry between the onset and the coda: a filled onset is preferred to a filled coda. The preference is known as *Onset Maximalism*, or the *Maximal Onset Principle.*

Syllables vary in weight depending on the segment in the peak and the composition of the syllable. Syllables with rhymes consisting only of a short vowel V are light. All other syllables are heavy, but not equally so: the higher the weight of the syllable, the more likely it is that it will attract stress. Historically, syllables that carry stress are likely to become heavy (see 7.5).

The usual binary division into light (V) and heavy syllables is useful, but it is also insufficiently predictive. It has always been recognised that heavy syllables attract stress; some studies of English have also recognised -VVCC(C) syllables as superheavy (Lass 1992a, 1994). Current studies show additional significant contrasts among the subtypes of heavy syllables. As established by Ryan (2011a), the probability of a syllable being stressed in English increases from a light syllable V (lowest probability) to VC to VV to VVC (highest probability). Moreover, the different weights are not distributed evenly on the continuum: the VC to VV contrast is over twice as great in magnitude as the VV to VVC contrast. Independently, the effect of coda size also increases from a single consonant C to CC to CCC, where every contrast is statistically significant.

English onsets have traditionally been considered weight-neutral. While this has been the position in the handbooks, recent research reveals some fine-grained distinctions between syllabic onsets and stress. Kelly (2004), reports on tests both on existing lexicon and on nonce/wug words which show a strong correlation between onset complexity and stress attraction in English. His results are corroborated in Ryan (2011a: 172–90).

In addition to syllable structure, the morphological structure of a word can determine stress placement. Root stress is commonly preserved after the addition of affixes: *bóther-bóthersome*, *unbóthered*; *válue-váluate*, *inváluable*. Some borrowed affixes have special properties, however: they can be always unstressed, always stressed or they can attract stress on a particular syllable of the word. The effect of affixes on stress may also be unstable, depending on conflicting factors, for example *-ic* will normally attract stress to the immediately preceding syllable, as in *patriótic*, *symbólic*, *galáctic*, but not in *cátholic*, *lúnatic*, *rhétoric*. The morphosyntactic nature of a word – nominal vs verbal – can also be involved in determining the stress placement, as in pairs of the type *áddict-addíct*, *présent-presént*.

The description of the PDE prosodic system requires reference to all of these factors, and even then there are numerous exceptions. Accounting for English stress is a challenging undertaking, beyond the remit of this volume. The goal here is to present the facts, to the extent that they are recoverable, of the evolution of the prosodic system. The description will be limited to word- and phrasal stress – the only domains for which there is testable historical evidence.

9.3 Historical sources of information for prosodic reconstruction

Without the help of speech-recording and -analysing technology, without contemporary commentary, and without the visual props of italics, bold or capitalisation in the older texts, any prosodic information extracted from the surviving manuscripts and early printed materials is by definition secondary. Among the important sources that can lead to prosodic inferences are: typological comparisons, scribal evidence for stress-sensitive segmental change, verse evidence and, after the sixteenth century, contemporary descriptions.

English is a member of the Germanic language group. In all early dialects of Germanic stress became fixed on the first syllable of the root (see 3.4.3). The function of stress as a word-boundary signal continues to be an important prosodic characteristic of all Germanic languages today; it is therefore safe to start with the assumption that OE underived words shared that pattern. Words inherited from OE – *áfter*, *hállow*, *blóssom*, *abróad*, *becóme* – follow the *Germanic Stress Rule* (GSR). With respect to OE, the validity of the GSR is uncontroversial, and if the vocabulary consisted solely of underived words of Germanic descent, the typological evidence would have been all that one needed to reconstruct OE word-stress. This is obviously not the case – the OE derivational morphology is very rich and we have to account for the stress of derived items, compounds and the higher-level prosodic contours of phrases. Moreover, non-Germanic lexical items are well attested already in OE, and for them typological comparisons are impossible or unreliable.

9.3.1 Orthographic evidence for word-stress

For morphologically complex and borrowed words additional information from spelling can help in the recovery of prosodic patterns in the earlier stages of English. For the Germanic vocabulary, vowel reduction and loss are expected in unstressed syllables. The spelling evidence for that is ample in post-tonic syllables (see 6.5.4); similarly, the reduction and loss of the prefix *ge-*: OE *geriden* > ME *iriden* > 'ridden'. Alternative spellings for the preposition *for* in OE are <*for, far, fur, fær, fer, fr, f*>. Such spellings support the assumption that *ge-* and *for* were unstressed in OE.

The situation with non-Germanic words is more complex. The proportion of loans in OE was low compared with PDE, yet the records show close to a thousand borrowings from Latin, or Greek through Latin, in Old English, about 3 per cent of the surviving vocabulary. In the disyllabic and many of the trisyllabic loanwords the original stress was serendipitously the same as the stress assigned by the GSR: *cánker, cránic* 'chronicle', *círcle, fénix, Jácob, Lúcifer, mártyr, órgan.* With some trisyllabic words spelling is a window into their adaptation to the native pattern: the variable spelling of the second and third syllable of, for example, Lat. *cucúlla* 'cowl' in OE: <cug**ele**, cu**ele**, cu**le**, cuh**le**>, suggests that the original penultimate stress was ignored in OE. The evidence is not ample, but orthographic forms attesting lack of stress on originally stressed syllables do exist, as in (1).

(1) Scribal evidence for early stress-shifting in Old English loanwords:

Latin	**OE**	**Gloss**
abb**ā́**dem	<ab**u**d ~ ab**o**d ~ ab**e**d>	'abbot'
alt**ā́**re	<alt**e**r ~ altr**e**>	'altar'
ac**ḗ**tum	<ec**e**d ~ ec**i**d>	'vinegar'
coqu**ī́**na	<cyc**ene**>	'kitchen'
mort**ā́**rium	<mort**e**re>	'mortar'
sext**ā́**rius	<sest**e**r ~ seoxt**e**r>	'a measure'

Such spellings can be compared with the more stable spelling of proper names such as *Abraham, Augustus, Babylon, Philippus, Saturnus,* whose lower frequency would be a factor in the slower rate of assimilation to the native stress pattern.

Scribal evidence for stress-placement in ME loans is of the same type: variable spellings or spellings with <e> of original long vowels in the penultimate syllables, as well as loss of unstressed syllables. One can infer that the word *corúne* 'crown' (OFr *corone, corune,* Lat. *corōna*) maintained stress on the penultimate syllable, as in Latin, because already

Orm (c. 1200) wrote <**cr**uness> 'crowns'; the initial syllable could be syncopated only if it was unstressed.[5]

(2) Scribal evidence for stress-shifting in Middle English loanwords:

Loanword	ME	Gloss
AN caboge	*<cabache ~ caboch ~ cabish ~ cabech ~ cabush>*	'cabbage'
Lat. form**ā**lis	*<formal(l) ~ formel>*	'formal'
Lat. ol**ī**va	*<oleu(e) ~ olefe>*	'olive'
Lat. pict**ū**ra	*<picter ~ pictor ~ pictar ~ pictre>*	'picture'

The closer we get to PDE, the less likely it is that a new loanword will be subject to orthographic and/or phonological adaptation: *kar**a**kul* (1853), *bacc**a**ra(t)* (1866), *autog**o**ny* (1870), *taig**a*** (1888) preserve the original vowel letters in unstressed syllables in English.

The types of segmental changes in stressed and unstressed syllables are very different. Shifting the focus from unstressed to stressed syllables, the orthographic records of processes such as vowel lengthening, vowel shifting and consonant gemination are also useful, albeit self-evident. The shifted vowels in PDE in *silence* (1225, < OFr *silence*, Lat. *silentium*), *l**i**bel* (1297, < OFr *libelle* (fem.), Lat. *libellus*), *m**ou**ntain* (1275, < AN *mountaine ~ muntaine*, Lat. *montāna*) suggest that the initial stress in these words was in place prior to the long vowel shift (see 8.2.2.1), unlike loans such as *mach**i**ne* (1545), *tambour**i**ne* (1579), *t**ou**can* (1568), *b**ou**levard* (1769).

Stress patterns above the domain of the simplex word can also be inferred from synchronic scribal variation, as with the shift from *phrase > compound > obscure compound > simplex word* (see 9.5).

9.3.2 Verse evidence for stress

The deployment of words and phrases in verse is an important source of information regarding the history of stress, yet verse texts are also notoriously controversial as an evidential basis for phonological reconstruction. The greatest challenge for the researcher is circularity: there are no contemporaneous records of 'rules' governing early versification, so we have to rely on templates extrapolated from the surviving poetic corpus. The range of allowable templatic variation is founded on statistical probabilities, which lead to inferences about the interplay between language and meter with no possibility of speaker verification. The way to avoid explaining the unknown by means of the more unknown

[5] LAEME records only thirteen tokens of <cor-, cur-> against 109 tokens of <cr-> for both the verb and the noun.

is by applying rigorous quantitative tests including comparisons with non-verse material.

Parametrical verse features, such as rhyme and alliteration, are also central, but must be used with caution. The data on OE alliteration, for example, are strikingly consistent: in 26,088 verses of OE poetry, only thirty-six, or 0.001 per cent, lack alliteration (Hutcheson 1995: 169). The onsets of testably unstressed syllables, such as inflectional syllables, never alliterate; therefore, we can use alliteration as a reliable indicator of stress. No matter what theory of OE meter one adopts, there can be no doubt that *gefrǽtwade*, *fóldan*, *grímma*, *Gréndel*, *gerúmlicor* and *rǽste* in (3) have the main stress on the first root syllable (alliterating onsets are in bold).

(3) Alliteration and main stress in OE verse:

ond gef**r**ǽtwade / **f**óldan sceatas	*Beowulf* 96
'and adorned / earth's regions'	
Wæs se **g**rímma gæst / **G**réndel haten	*Beowulf* 102
'was the grim ghost / Grendel called'	
ge**r**úmlicor / **r**ǽste sohte	*Beowulf* 139
'in roomier space / rest sought'	

On the other hand, the very fact that alliteration as a metrical device that keeps the two halves of the line together was so prominent in the Germanic tradition suggests the possibility that composers and copiers of verse could occasionally resort to alliteration on syllables that would normally have lower prominence than the neighbouring syllables, as in (4).

(4) Alliteration on non-primary stress in OE:

on **þ**ǣm dæge / **þ**ysses līfes	*Beowulf* 197[6]
'on that day / of this life'	
Ðȳs dōgor **þ**ū / ge**þ**yld hafa	*Beowulf* 1395
'On this day you / patience have'	

Elsewhere in the OE verse corpus determiners do not alliterate, so we can assume that, as in PDE, the need for special emphasis in speech and in verse can override other factors such as normal right-prominence in the determiner-noun phrases 'this day', 'this life'.

Violations in matching main stress to alliteration in the classical

[6] Compare the treatment of the demonstrative in line 197 with the *Beowulf* line 1216:

> **B**ruc ðisses **b**eages, / **B**ēowulf lēofa
> 'Enjoy this ring, / dear Beowulf'

OE poetic corpus are infrequent. The situation changed in ME: the composers of alliterative verse became more liberal with the use of visual alliteration, both because of the gradual shift from oral to written composition and because of the greater density of non-initially stressed words. The extent to which ME alliterative verse can be trusted with respect to stress on prefixed native and borrowed words is controversial: initial alliteration on native words as in ***behold*** or ***forsake*** is as suspicious as initial alliteration on ***enthrone***, ***rejoice***, ***remove***. While the most common interpretation of such instances is that they are based on orthography rather than on stress, there are arguments in the literature that with some prefixes the alliterative practice reflects acceptable ME pronunciations.

In ME the use of end-rhyme became the dominant mode of keeping verse lines together. Here again the requirement of prosodic identity can be useful for the recovery of the stress-pattern. As shown in (5), Chaucer's rhyme practice indicates that the loanword *philosóphre* 'philosopher' (c. 1330) had penultimate stress, which is confirmed by the use of the same word line-medially, as in (6).

(5) Rhyme evidence for stress in ME end-rhymed verse:[7]
But al be that he was a philo**sóphre**,
Yet hadde he but litel gold in **cófre**; *GP* 279–98:
In name of crist, to wexe a philo**sóphre**.
Ther been ful fewe to whiche I wolde **prófre** *CYT* 1122–3

(6) Metrical evidence for stress supporting rhyme evidence in ME:
Was thér no phílo**sóphr**e in ál thy tóun? *MLT* 310
This wíse phílo**sóphre**, thús seyde hée. *PardT* 620

A cautionary note is needed in this case too: because end-rhyme in this tradition marks the line end, and because it keeps larger structures such as couplets and stanzas together, 'liberties' can be taken with the actual prosodic contour of a word: verse-specific promotions of unstressed syllables occur commonly in ME even for native items whose stress in the contemporary spoken language cannot be assumed to have been anything but root-initial. Compare the contrasting prominence contours in *sweryng* 'swearing' in lines 635 and 638 with line 643 in Chaucer's *Pardoner's Tale*.

(7) End-rhyme as non-evidence for ME stress:
Of swéryng séith the hóoly jéremýe, 635

[7] All Chaucerian citations and abbreviations are from *The Riverside Chaucer* (Benson 1987).

Thou shalt swere sooth thyne othes, and nat lye,
And swere in doom, and eek in rightwisnesse;
But ýdel swéryng ís a cursednesse.
. . .
Lo, rather be forbedeth swich swe**ryng**
Than homycide or many a cursed **thyng**; *PardT* 635–44

Similarly, the rhymes *felawe: ydrawe* (*GP* 395–6); *biddyng: thing* (*CYT* 1144) are not good evidence that *fellow* or *bidding* had final stress in speech. Compare the use of the same items in (8), where they are clearly initially stressed.

(8) Mid-line metrical evidence for stress in ME verse:
Lat évery **fé**lawe télle his tále abóute *KnT* 890
His **fé**lawe wénte and sóughte hym dóun in hélle *KnT* 1200
Ay **bí**ddynge ín hire órisóns ful fáste *SNT* 140

The literature on stress reconstruction in English often uses the evidence of ME rhymes as a categorical indicator of the contemporary realisation of stress in the spoken language. However, rhyme evidence has to be evaluated carefully and compared with the evidence of the placement of such words in line-medial position, where the matching of prosodic to metrical prominences is much more reliable. The metrical constraints on early English verse are covered in greater detail in Chapter 10; here one should note that the unreliability of end-rhyme as a source of stress reconstruction is paralleled by the positioning of words at the left edge of the line, where prominence inversions (placing, for example, *réady, únder, máketh* in the first iambic foot (W S) can be a deliberate stratagem to avoid the monotony of repeated identical structures – it is not prima facie evidence of final stress in these native words). On the other hand, if confirmed by mid-line behaviour, items such as *citées, justicé, poynáunt* at the left edge of the early pentameter line are good evidence for retention of the final stress. Decisions on the prosodic history of loanwords have to be based on fine-grained and comprehensive coverage of all data – another area in the history of the language that remains underexplored.

This brief discussion of the methodology of stress reconstruction focused on Old and Middle English sources. The task of tracing stress patterns in early Modern English is facilitated by the appearance of contemporary lists of rhymes. The first more systematic such record is Peter Levins's *Manipulus Vocabulorum: A Rhyming Dictionary of the English Language* (1570). 💻 Later attempts culminated in the descriptions of the patterns found in Walker's monumental dictionary (1791–1826), including the first extensive comments on secondary stress (ibid.: 73–4). There is much more to be discovered about the situation after the eighteenth century: stress alternations have continued to occur and variability of stress is part of the complexity of the PDE prosodic system, but at least for the last two centuries there are reliable first-hand records in pronouncing dictionaries and, in the twenty-first century, practically unlimited web-based opportunities for research on current prosodic patterns.

9.4 OE stress placement

The typology of stress-assignment recognises languages that have *free* or *fixed* word-stress. Further, stress can be determined by the morphological or by the phonological properties of the host syllable. Stress can also be regulated by the proximity to a boundary or to another stress (Hayes 1995: 31–2). Recall from 3.4.3 that Germanic stress became fixed on the first syllable of the root; OE therefore is characterised as a language with a word-bounded, morphologically assigned fixed stress, though as will be seen below, the blurry distinction between prefix and root could obscures the predictability and the 'fixed' nature of the stress. In other systems, most relevantly Latin, it is syllable weight in relation to the word-edge that governs stress-distribution. The types of stress assignment are rarely found in 'pure' form. It is quite common for morphological and prosodic factors to interact, and indeed English has never belonged exclusively to one type. The rest of this chapter will survey the interaction of the principles of stress placement in earlier English.

9.4.1 OE word-stress

In OE the *Germanic Stress Rule* (GSR) (see 3.4.3) results in native words having main stress on the first syllable of the root, leaving grammatical affixes completely unstressed, and derivational affixes either unstressed or weakly stressed. The stability of the primary stress on the first root syllable was maintained in the entire derivational set, unlike PDE where suffix-induced stress-shifts can leave root-initial syllables completely stressless: *ídiot-idiótic*, *Málta-Maltése*, *sólid-solídity*. (9) illustrates the fixedness of main stress on OE root-initial syllables.

(9) The maintenance of OE root-initial primary stress in derivatives:

Base	**Derivatives**
béalu 'bale, evil'	*béalufull* 'baleful', *béaluleas* 'innocent'

dḗma 'judge' — *dḗmend* 'God', *dḗmere* 'judge', *dḗmedlic* 'subject to judgement'
dḗofol 'devil' — *dḗofolscipe* 'devil-ship', *dḗofollic* 'devilish'
eald 'old' — *éaldan* 'to age', *éaldordom* 'power, authority'
fǣ́der 'father' — *ġefǣ́dere* 'godmother', *fǣ́derlice* 'fatherly'

The weight of the root-initial syllable is irrelevant for the placement of the main stress. Both heavy and light syllables attract stress root-initially: in *dēma* [deː.mə], *dēofol* [deə.v(ə)l], *ealdan* ['æl.dən] in (9) stress is on a heavy syllable, and in *bealu* ['bæ.lə], *fæder* ['fæ.dəɹ] stress is on a light syllable. This justifies a characterisation of OE stress-placement as *morphologically* governed; however, syllable weight in OE is not completely irrelevant.

The addition of *suffixes* in Old English never affects the primary prominence. Inflectional suffixes throughout the history of English have always been unstressed. Some derivational suffixes, on the other hand, can be assigned non-primary stress and appear in strong metrical positions (ictus) in verse, though such weakly stressed syllables never carry the alliteration. It is likely that the prosodic prominence of derivational suffixes in speech was gradient, ranging from secondary stress to complete lack of stress, depending on phonological factors: syllable weight, distance from the right edge of the word and distance from the main stress. The examples in (10) illustrate the variability of stress on suffixes depending on phonological factors.

(10) Variability of secondary stress on derivational suffixes in OE:
(a) wís***dòme*** héold 'with wisdom ruled' — *Beowulf* 1959b
(b) wórd ond wís***dom*** 'word and wisdom' — *Andreas* 569a

(a) *of cíld**hàde*** 'from childhood' — *Elene* 914a
(b) mǽgð***had*** se mícla 'maidhood great' — *Christ A, B, C* 86a in

In the (a) examples *-dōm-* '-dom' and *-hād-* '-hood' are word-internal and have to be matched to strong verse positions, otherwise the verses will have only three metrical positions – adjacent unstressed syllables in OE verse fill a single weak metrical position (see 10.2.1). In the (b) examples matching the same suffixes to weak positions results in scansions aligning the verses with frequent types in the corpus: the pattern S w S w of *wórd ond wís**dom*** (*Andreas* 569a) is attested very robustly, 16 per cent of the entire corpus, while a potential S w S s (*wórd ond wísdòm*) is much rarer.[8] When followed by an inflectional syllable, *-lēas-* '-less', *-dōm-* '-dom', *-fæst-* '-fast', *-hād-* '-hood' are regularly placed in strong positions, but if

[8] Hutcheson (1995: 175).

uninflected, they can be in weak positions. All of these suffixes are heavy syllables, an additional factor facilitating stressability.

Any full prosodic history of native suffixes has to take into account rhythmic factors and frequency as well. The two equally productive OE suffixes *-hād* and *-dōm* would be expected to emerge either both with a full vowel or both with a reduced vowel in EModE. However, in ME close to 70 per cent of the *-dom* derivatives followed a monosyllabic root (*earldom*, *freedom*, *kingdom*, *wisdom*), where stress-clash avoidance resulted in de-stressing of the suffix to [-dəm/-dm̩], while during the same period 73 per cent of *-hood* derivatives had a disyllabic stem (*bishophood*, *maidenhood*, *womanhood*), allowing the preservation of secondary stress on the suffix and raising of the vowel to [uː] prior to seventeenth-century shortening to [-ʊ].[9]

The morphological status of the suffix is also of consequence. Quite often in OE it is hard to assign suffixal status to morphological units which are also attested as independent words: *dōm*, *fæst*, *full*, *hād*, *lēas* are separate lexical entries and their autonomy elsewhere in the vocabulary could factor in the preservation of stress; compare the divided spelling of *childhood* in *Elene* 336a, 775b *in cíldes hàd* with *Elene* 914a: *of cíldhàde*. Thus an array of factors: syllable weight, rhythmic preferences and morphosemantic independence must be considered in the account of OE suffixal stress.

Like derivational suffixes, prefixes can originate from independent words. Within the larger family of affixes, suffixes are cross-linguistically more likely to lose their independent word status than prefixes, and therefore one would expect more root-like behaviour from prefixes. Identifying the exact range of prefixes in OE is problematic, because outside of the clearly prefixal bound forms – *æf-*, *and-*, *be-*, *ed-*, *fær-*, *for-*, *ge-*, *mis-* – it is hard to determine whether forms such as *ofer* 'over', *on* 'on', *wiþ* 'against', *ymb* 'about' are prefixes or roots. The prosodic treatment of these forms in OE shows further complexity: in nouns and adjectives most of the heavy prefixes exhibit root-like prosody, while light prefixes (*ge-*, *be-*) remain unstressed. For verbs and adverbs prefixation does not affect the main stress, so that we get minimal pairs as in (11).

(11) OE prefixal stress on nominal vs verbal derivatives:
 (a) ðæt ðu **ó**ndsware / mid **ófer**hỳgdum — *Andreas* 319
 'That thou an answer / with arrogance'
 (b) Ofer**h**ógode ða / **h**ringa fengel — *Beowulf* 2345
 'Scorned then / the rings' ruler'

[9] Based on Minkova and Stockwell (2005).

(a) Sumes ýmbhògan, / **ú**ngemet gemen. *MB* 7.28
'Of some consideration / excessive'
(b) **S**ylf in þam **s**olere / ond ymbséteð utan *Phx* 204
'self in that solarium / and surrounded from outside'

(a) swylce óncỳþðe / **é**alle gebette, *Beowulf* 830
'also distress / all allayed'
(b) **f**eond mid **f**olme; / he on**f**éng hraþe *Beowulf* 748
'fiend with open palm / he took hold of quickly'

In the (a)-type examples in (11) the nouns ***óferhỳgd-um*** 'arrogance' '***ýmbhòga-n*** 'consideration', ***óncỳþð-e*** 'distress' have the stress contour of compounds: leftmost primary stress and secondary stress on the first syllable of the second element. Attached to verbs, the same prefixal elements in the examples in (b) – *oferhógode* 'scorned', *ymbséteð* 'surrounded', *onféng* 'took hold of' – are non-alliterating; primary stress and alliteration is on the first root syllable. Thus both syllable weight and the grammatical nature of the base are active in determining the stressability of OE prefixes.

In compounds the stress on the first element is primary, marking off the left boundary of the entire word, while the stress on the second root is non-primary. In the verse, the obligatory alliteration is consistently placed on the first stressed syllable onset.

(12) Compound stress and alliteration in OE:
(a) **w**uldres **w**ealdend, / **w**óroldàre forgeaf *Beowulf* 17
'of the glory ruler / worldly honour gave'
ac he **s**ígewæ̀pnum / for**s**woren hæfde *Beowulf* 804
'but he victory-weapons / forsworn had'

(b) geond **w**íd**w**ègas / **w**undor sceawian *Beowulf* 840
'beyond wide-ways / wonder to examine'
æfter **d**éað**d**æ̀ge / **d**om unlytel, *Beowulf* 885
'after death-day / fame un-little'
héard**h**ìcgende / **h**ider wilcuman. *Beowulf* 394a
'hard-minded / hither welcome.'

In the verse the second stressed syllable in a compound may alliterate *only* if its onset is identical with the onset of the first syllable of the first root, as in the (b) examples in (12). In the (a) examples the onsets of *ār* 'honour' in *wóroldàr-e*, and *wæpn-um* 'weapon' in *sígewæ̀pn-um* do not alliterate. This implies that compounds with identical root-initial onsets like *wídwèg-as*, *déaðdæ̀g-e* will not appear in the second half-line in OE verse (see 10.2.1).[10]

[10] This restriction does not extend to suffixal elements; for example, *láðlìce* 'hatefully' is

Doubly alliterating compounds in OE verse present an interesting dilemma for stress reconstruction: when positioned in the on-verse they do not constitute evidence for left-edge prominence within the word. Their behaviour is compatible with the reconstruction of equal levels of stress on both elements. Compounding was a favourite stylistic choice for the OE scops and it is not too far-fetched to assume that the 'secondary' stresses in these and possibly other compounds were on the level of primary stresses, especially in recitation and especially for the compounds in which the first part was disyllabic. In novel compounds both roots could retain their semantic independence and strong prosodic prominence, blurring the line between compounds and syntactic phrases. Creativity and language play lies behind the fact that many of the self-alliterating compounds in the OE corpus are *hapax legomena*, single-instance forms.

(13) Self-alliterating *hapax legomena* in *Beowulf*:

béarn-gebỳrdo 'child-bearing'	*héoro-hòcyhte* 'savagely hooked'
éall-ìren 'all of iron'	*hílde-hlæ̀mm* 'battle crash'
fén-frèoðo 'marsh refuge'	*sǽsìð* 'sea voyage'
grýre-gèatwe 'terrifying armour'	*swát-swàðu* 'bloody track'
grýre-gìest 'terrible visitor'	*sýn-snæ̀d* 'huge cut'
héardhìcgend 'hard-minded'	*þéodþrèa* 'people-calamity'

The status of these constructions is an area deserving further inquiry. Were the various names for the Danes in *Beowulf* – *East(-)Dena*, *West(-)Dena*, *Beorht(-)Dena* and (uniquely) *Healf(-)Dena* – compounds or freely formed phrases? As argued below, the alliterative tests in this case are unhelpful, and there is indeterminacy between left-prominence, right-prominence and equal prominence.[11]

9.4.2 OE stress above the word level

The prosodic properties of units above the word level in a dead language are even more challenging to reconstruct than word-stress. Morphosyntactic structures larger than the word form their own hierarchy of prosodic domains: word, clitic group, phonological phrase, intonational phrase and utterance (Hayes 1989). Attempting to recover intonational phrase and utterance prosody for OE would be purely

found at the right edge of the off-verse, a further confirmation of the importance of morphological status in stress assignment.

[11] See further Giegerich (2009), who shows that end-stress on noun-noun compounds in PDE of the type *steel bridge*, *apple pie*, *Madison Avenue* may reflect the syntactic provenance of incompletely lexicalised forms and that nominals of the form attribute-head can be both lexical and syntactic.

speculative, but some evidence for the historical treatment of clitic groups and phonological phrases is available.

A clitic group is a combination of a stressed major-class headword and one or more unstressed function words such as articles, prepositions, conjunctions and pronouns – *the bóok, at a schóol, lóved it*, and so on – are clitic groups. The adjunction of clitics to a host word, known as cliticisation, is not obligatory in English; it depends on the syllabic structure of the function word, and on the strength of the syntactic boundaries in the sequence. Cliticisation does not occur if there is special discourse emphasis on a normally unstressed function word. Articles are the most common types of clitics in English, but even they can be promoted from clitics to fully stressed items, for example 'You mean *a* [eɪ] gas station or *the* [ðiː] gas station on Highway 5?' Cliticisation implies the presence of a single strong stress in the clitic group.

Although prominence relations in clitic groups are typically not reflected in our word-based orthographic system, we are familiar with spellings such as *fill'er* for *fill her*, *the flight's* for *the flight is*, *a-milking*, *a-leaping* for historical *on milking*, *on leaping*. A good example of an original clitic group where the clitic has lost its independent status is the PDE form *gonna* (1913), for *going to*, also earlier Scottish *ganna*, *gaunna* (1806, OED).[12] Scribal evidence for clitic group formation is scanty in Old and Middle English, quite possibly because of the learned nature of the texts that we have to draw on. One place where clitics and hosts merge is in the formation of lexicalised adverbs from prepositional phrases: *on* + *weġ* 'way' > *onwéġ* 'away'; *tō* + *gædre*, adv. > *togǽdre* 'together', where the final stress is testable in the verse and persists to this day.

Another place where cliticisation appears with regularity in OE is in negative contraction when the host word is vowel-initial, or [w-] initial, as in (14a). In (14b) continuous spelling also indicates that there is no internal boundary between the clitics and the hosts.

(14) Scribal evidence for OE and ME clitic group formation:

(a) OE			(b) ME		
ne + *ealles*	→	*nealles* 'not at all'	*þe* + *oþre*	→	*þoþre* 'the other'
ne + *wāt*	→	*nāt* 'not know'	*to* + *eke(n)*	→	*teken* 'in addition'
ne + *ǣnig*	→	*nǣnig* 'none'	*the* + *array*	→	*tharray* 'the array'

Cliticisation in OE is testable in the verse. Clitics, even when they are orthographically merged with the host, do not affect the alliteration patterns.

[12] The OED describes *gonna* not just as 'colloquial (esp. U.S.)', but also as 'vulgar pronunciation of *going to*'.

(15) OE clitic groups and alliteration:
nealles **sw**æslice / **s**ið alyfed *Beowulf* 3089
'not at all in a friendly way / a passage allowed'
in **C**aines **c**ynne – / þone **c**wealm gewræc *Beowulf* 107
'in Cain's kin – / the killing avenged'

The next level in the prosodic hierarchy is the phonological phrase (P-Phrase). In PDE P-Phrases have final prominence, which is 'a common but not invariant pattern across languages' (Hayes 1995: 368). The most easily testable type of P-Phrase historically is a syntactic noun phrase, where the material to the left is adjoined to the head noun: *a fine teacher*, *on the village green*, *former student*. Other common phrases incorporating material to the left are adjective phrases: *strongly supportive*, *overly cautious*; adverb phrases: *very energetically*, *admirably well*; and verb phrases where subjects are adjoined to the left: *Mary smiles*, *the ship sailed*, and complements are adjoined to the right: *stop the presses*, *speak slowly*. The final prominence in PDE phrasal units is known as the *Nuclear Stress Rule*, or the *End Rule*. The End Rule applies only to unmarked, not contrastive or specially focused phrases. The prominence assigned by the End Rule adds to the prominence of the stressed syllable of the rightmost word: in *fórmer stúdent* the first syllable of *stúdent* is prosodically stronger than the first syllable of *fórmer*.

Reconstructing the assignment of phrasal stress in OE is challenging and many issues relating to phrasal prosody are under-researched and controversial. Spelling is uninformative, and there are no early grammarians commenting on phrasal prosodic contours. The choice and distribution of alliterating words in the verse remains the only testable base of hypotheses about the prominence relations on the P-Phrase level. However, the arrangement of alliterating elements across the OE alliterative line is not necessarily 'natural', in the sense that the conventions of verse composition and recitation may override and thus obscure the prosodic patterns of speech.

One area of uncertainty is the prosodic behaviour of the inflected verb within a verb phrase in OE. It is easy to ascertain statistically that the OE scops treated finite verbs differently from nouns. In a verse where the strong positions are filled by a noun and a verb, the noun will consistently carry the alliteration.

(16) Finite verb alliteration in OE verse:

(a) Him ða **Sc**yld gewat / to ge**sc**æphwile *Beowulf* 26
'then Scyld departed / at the destined time'
Gebad **w**intra **w**orn, / ær he on **w**eg hwurfe *Beowulf* 264
'lived to see of winters many / before he away turned'

(b) þenden **w**ordum **w**eold / **w**ine Scyldinga *Beowulf* 30
'when with words ruled / friend of Scyldings'
ne ge**f**eah he þære **f**æhðe, / ac he hine **f**eor forwræc *Beowulf* 109
'not enjoyed he of that hostility / but he him far banished'

(c) Hi hyne þa æt**b**æron / to **b**rimes faroðe *Beowulf* 28
'they him then carried / to briny sea's current'

The alliterative patterns in (16) show that in both NP-VP strings as in *Beowulf* 26a, 264b and VP-NP strings as in *Beowulf* 264a, the highest *metrical* prominence is on the noun, not on the verb, even if it is phrase-final as in *Beowulf* 26a, 264b. This alliterative regularity in (16a) is known as Sievers' *Rule of Precedence*: it states that 'if an inflected verb precedes a noun, it does not have to alliterate, that it must not alliterate if the noun does not alliterate too, and that a non-alliterating noun can never be followed by an alliterating finite verb' (Sievers 1893: §§22–9). The rule does not exclude double alliteration as in *Beowulf* 30a, 109a (16b). The only circumstance in which the finite verb carries the structural alliteration (16c) is when all other words in the verse are prosodically weaker, as in *Beowulf* 28a: *Hi hyne þa ætbæron* 'they him then carried'.

The extent to which the linear conventions of alliteration with respect to the verb match the prosody of speech is thus hard to determine, but the fact that clause-initial finite verbs are regularly skipped in alliteration, while this does not happen to clause-initial nouns, suggests that verbs were indeed less prominent than nouns. Throughout the modern Continental West Germanic languages and therefore presumably in PrG, complements are stronger than their verbs, irrespective of the linear order. This typological comparison and the consistency with which complement-verb prosodic relations are respected in the verse – the complement always alliterates – is a good argument for projecting the complement-strong prosodic contour to OE. By itself, however, the argument from verse – lack of alliteration on phrase-final finite verbs if there are other major-class words in the same verse – remains uninformative. OE verse-ends and phrase-ends typically coincide, and the last stress in the a-verse does not have to alliterate and may not alliterate in the b-verse, irrespective of the morphosyntactic category of the item filling that position.

Prominence in noun and adjective phrases and coordinate phrases is not directly recoverable from the verse. In this area the linear rules of alliteration may be more of a handicap than actual help: alliteration on the first adjective or noun in an OE verse line is obligatory. However, identifying a metrical convention that privileges linear order of alliterative signals for the purpose of keeping the line together, with the prosodic realisation of the same sequences in speech is unjustified. First, in noun and coordinate phrases, the normative syntactic order overlaps with the linear alliteration on the first stressed word in the phrase. This takes instances such as *lange hwile* 'a long while' (*Beowulf* 16a), *hond ond rond* 'hand and shield' (*Beowulf* 656a) out of the evidential basis for prosodic reconstruction. Second, projecting the metrical convention onto the prosody is made suspect by the freedom with which the poet switches components to fit the scheme in the line.

(17) NP modifier-head positioning in OE verse:

Head-final	**Non-head-final**
Geata dryhten (*Beowulf* 2561b) 'lord of the Geats'	*dryhten Geata* (*Beowulf* 2901a)
Leofa Biowulf (*Beowulf* 2663a) 'Dear Beowulf'	*Wiglaf leofa* (*Beowulf* 2745a) 'Wiglaf dear'

The unstable internal order of such syntactically equivalent phrases suggests very strongly that the principle of selection is based not on prosodic prominence, but on the alliterative needs in the rest of the line. The absence of double alliteration in the b-verse is clearly metrically determined because all types of words can be positioned there.[13] Some other facts also prompt scepticism about the link between alliteration and linguistic prominence: as noted above, phrasal right-prominence is typologically very common. Moreover, the default contour for noun phrases and coordinate phrases in the modern Germanic languages is right-prominent.[14] Right-hand prominence is attested also in copulative combinations of the type *Anglo-Sáxon*, *Native Canádian*; they also typically align with syntactically coordinated phrases. The density of double alliteration in on-verses coextensive with noun + prepositional phrase (*bat under beorge* 'boat under cliff', *Beowulf* 211a) and in conjoined phrases (*word ond wísdom* 'word and wisdom', *Andreas* 569a) exceeds by far the overall 47 per cent ratio of double alliteration in the on-verse, as reported in Hutcheson (1995: 112). This asymmetrical distribution precludes a linguistic bias towards left-prominence in such phrases, but does not rule out equal or right-hand prominence. The most economical account that does not require a historical shift, therefore, is that the right-prominent prosodic contour of phrasal stress has been in the language since Old English times.

[13] See Russom (1987: 114); Hutcheson (1995: 271).

[14] For German see Selkirk (1984: 225–30).

9.5 ME stress placement: the native component

The prosodic system of Middle English continues to show stability of the GSR, aligning primary stress with the left edge of all words and with the left edge of the root for prefixed verbs and adverbs. This is easily demonstrated in verse: the first syllables of all disyllabic words in Chaucer's *Wife of Bath's Tale* (*WBT*) 278–9 are in strong metrical positions. Confirmation comes also from the alliteration of disyllables, as in *Sir Gawain and the Green Knight* (*SGGK*) 49–50.

(18) Continuity of the GSR in Middle English:
Thow seyst that *dróppyng hóuses*, and eek smoke,
And *chídyng wýves máken* men to flee *WBT* 278–9
With *lórdez* and *ládies*, as *léuest* him þoȝt.
With all þe *wéle* of þe *wórlde* þay *wóned* þer sámen *SGGK* 49–50

Words derived by native suffixation also show the expected main stress on the leftmost root syllable, as in *kíngship*, *wísdom*, *wítness*, *hóly*, *blíssful*. In words in which the derivational suffix follows a disyllabic stem the suffix may preserve a rhythmically induced degree of stress. This non-primary suffixal stress can be used in verse with the suffix in a strong metrical position, most often in rhyme, for example *présse*: *wantow**nésse*** (*GP* 263–4), *sóbre**lý***: *cóurtepý* (*GP* 289–90), but also in other positions, as in: *And spécial**lý** from évery shíres énde* (*GP* 15).

The prosodic contour of compounds in ME can be inferred from synchronic scribal variation and from the deployment of compounds in the verse line. ME variant spellings for <cuppe bord> (1375), <copard> (1400), <copberd> (1450), <coberd> (1474) 'cupboard' indicate a window of only a century between the first attestation of the word and its reanalysis as a simplex initially stressed word. Similarly, *necklace*, first attested in 1577, appears as <neklas>, <necles> in the seventeenth century (OED), indicating rapid loss of stress on the second element of the compound. The pair *ALWAYS-CAUSEWAYS* illustrates well two options: loss of secondary stress and reinterpretation of the compound as a monomorphemic word, as in *always* ending in either (formal) [-weɪz] or (casual) [-wɪz], and preservation of the secondary stress as in *causeway* (1440) ending in [-weɪ]. Initial stress is stable in the well-known instances of compound obscuration as in (19).

(19) Compound stress and obscure compounds:

Source	**ME/EModE**
OE dǽʒes ḕaʒe 'day's eye'	ME <daysy> (1440) 'daisy'
OE *hū́swī̀f* 'housewife'	EModE <hussy> (1647) 'hussy'
ON *víndàuga* 'wind-eye'	ME <wind**o**(u)(e), wind**ew**(e)> 'window'

The salience of the secondary stress is an important factor in the preservation of the orthographic transparency of the etymology in compounds such as *breakfast*, *Christmas*, *gunwale* [-nəl], *island*, *brimstone* [-stən]. Of interest is also the fact that items such as *whetstone*, *starboard*, *waistcoat* used to have reduced vowels in the second element, but since their spelling highlights the morphological structure of the compound, the secondary stress in them is restored. A good example of spelling-induced reinstatement of secondary stress comes from the realisation of *-day* in the weekdays. Early reduced forms are well attested; compare fourteenth-century spellings <Sonde>, <Sonede> for *Sunday*, fifteenth- and sixteenth-century spellings <Mundy>, <Mondy> for *Monday*, <Tysdy> for *Tuesday*. Walker (1791–1826: §223) endorses '*Sunday*, *Monday*, &c. as if written *Sundy*, *Mundy* &c.' Secondary stress on *-dày* [-deɪ] is still in competition with the reduced form [-di] in AE, where [-deɪ] is definitely the preferred realisation in slow, careful speech.

In the verse, predictably, the first root syllable of compounds is usually aligned with a strong metrical position. The dominant pattern of placement of compounds in alliterative verse also supports initial main stress.

(20) Compound stress in ME verse:
Ful thr**é**dbare was his overeste courtepy; *GP* 290
A sh**í**pman was ther, wonynge fer by weste *GP* 388
And þe **g**réhòundez so **g**rete, þat **g**eten hem bylyue *SGGK* 1171
And **m**ore he is þen any **m**on vpon **m**ýddelèrde, *SGGK* 2100

In contrast to OE, in the ME alliterative corpus secondary stresses in compounds are occasionally allowed to carry the alliteration, with the first element of the compound completely out of the alliterative schema.

(21) Salience of secondary stress in ME alliterative verse:
And hit **l**yfte vp þe ỳȝe-**l**ýddez and **l**oked ful brode, *SGGK* 446
Dòuble-**f**élde, as hit **f**allez, and **f**ele kyn **f**ischez *SGGK* 890

In the iambic compositions in ME the testability of secondary stress is dependent on the syllabic structure of the components.

(22) Compound stress in ME iambic verse:[15]
(a) If éven-sòng and mórwe-sòng accorde *GP* 830
His hérte-blòod hath bathed al his heer *KnT* 2006

[15] The hyphenation in the cited forms is editorial.

(b) And póudre-màrchant tart and galyngale *GP* 381
But by hir cóte-armùres[16] and by hir gere *KnT* 1016

Compounds in which an unstressed syllable separates the two roots normally start in even (strong) positions in the iambic verse line, both in native (22a) and in non-native forms (22b). In these examples the relative prominence of the two parts of the compound is not testable; both stresses are aligned with strong metrical positions. If a buffer unstressed syllable separating the left edges of the roots is not available, the compound can be left-aligned either with a strong or with a weak metrical position, as in (23).

(23) Compounds with monosyllabic first part in ME iambic verse:
(a) A lóve-knòtte in the gretter ende ther was *GP* 197
That hadde a fýr-rèed cherubynnes face *GP* 624

(b) Grèhóundes he hadde as swift as fowel in flight *GP* 190
He was shòrt-shóldred, brood, a thikke knarre *GP* 549

In (23a) the compounds are left-aligned with even/strong positions, mirroring the compound stress in speech. In (23b), however, the first stress is subordinated and appears in an odd/weak metrical position, while the second root is in a strong position. Such 'inversions' are found most commonly in the first foot, as in *GP* 190, but not exclusively. Further study of the distribution of compounds with a monosyllabic first element in both types of ME verse has the potential of revealing the strength of the 'compound stress' principle in earlier English.

The testability of phrasal stress in ME verse is limited. In an iambic line, if there is a buffer weak syllable between the stressed syllables, and if the left edge of the phrase aligns with a strong metrical position, as in (of) *sóndry fólk* . . . (*GP* 25), (and) *máde fórward* . . . (*GP* 33), . . . *týme and spáce* (*GP* 35), the relative prominence of the two stresses cannot be ascertained. Monosyllabic adjectives in noun phrases do provide some corroboration for continuing right-prominent phrasal stress – *ne pólax, né short knýf* . . . (*KnT* 2544), *Gret swéryng is* . . . (*PardT* 631) – but the stress-alternating nature of the verse, the availability of optional *-e* and metrical slot-fillers, as well as the flexibility of monosyllabic items in metrical matching obscure the picture. As argued in Minkova and Stockwell (1997a), there are no good arguments in favour of positing dramatic changes in the prosody of phrasal stress from Old English to Present-Day English. Even if we assume a more level phrasal stress in

[16] 'A garment embroidered or painted with heraldic arms', OFr *cōte*, n. and *armūre* (MED). The first root is monosyllabic: <-e> in *cōte* is elided before <a->.

Old English than in Present-Day English, the right-hand prominence of Old French and Anglo-Norman would have contributed to the present contour.

9.6 ME prosodic innovations

The non-native component in the OE vocabulary was never higher than about 3 per cent (see 9.3.1). The population was relatively homogeneous, with OE the dominant language, even if we assume marginal Old English–Insular Latin bilingualism for a portion of the educated population. The prosody of Old English remained firmly Germanic.[17]

The situation changed gradually after 1066 (see 1.3). The control of the administrative, economic and sociocultural resources was transferred to speakers whose primary language was not English. A considerable non-native component was introduced into the vocabulary of Middle English. Within three hundred years after the Conquest the portion of the non-Germanic, primarily Romance vocabulary had grown to about 25 per cent. Many of the new words, especially the earliest borrowings, were 'core' vocabulary: *beauty*, *colour*, *danger*, *diet*, *jealous*, *journey*, *liquor*, *mountain*, *river*, *season*, *story*, *tender*. OE words associated with government and military power were either duplicated or replaced by Romance borrowings: *army*, *council*, *empire*, *mayor*, *navy*, *parliament*, *record*, *soldier*, *statute*. Words from the spheres of literature, art, science and medicine came into the language in large numbers, including the words *sphere*, *literature*, *art*, *science*, *medicine*, *language*, *large*, *number*; also *figure*, *grammar*, *image*, *logic*, *music*, *poet*, *remedy*, *romance*, *study*, *surgeon*, *tragedy*. Many of these items did not have initial stress in the source language and their entry into English raises the question of their rate of adaptation to the native Germanic stress-pattern and their potential effect on the system of stress-placement in ME.

One type of evidence for initial stress in loanwords was noted in 9.3: participation of the stressed vowel in the long vowel shift, thus ***cou**ncil*, n. (1125), ***mou**ntain* (1275), ***si**lence* (1225), ***li**bel* (1297), ***sea**son* (1300), ***la**bour* (1300), ***sci**ence* (1340), ***na**vy* (1375). Another important source of information is the placement of the new items in verse. Looking again at Chaucer's practice, we can illustrate the methodology of reconstruction with the word *season*.

[17] In neighbouring or substratum Celtic, too, primary word-stress was fixed on initial syllables excluding proclitics (Bennett 1970: 465).

(24) Testing word-stress in Chaucer's verse:

Bifil that in that **séson** on a day	*GP* 19
After the sondry **sésons** of the yeer	*GP* 347
And eek the lusty **séson** of that May	*KnT* 2484

The word *season* appears fifteen times in Chaucer's verse. In all but one of the attestations the first syllable matches an even/strong metrical position, as in (24). The single exception where the second syllable is matched to a strong position is ... *thy déclináción: his tyme and his sesón* (*FrT* 1033–4). The end-stressed *sesón* in rhyme position allows two interpretations. One is that the Anglicised 'normal' pronunciation *séson* was artificially changed to fit the prominence required by the rhyme position, as in native *swerýng: thyng* in (7); such stress-shifts were a common verse convention and they tell us nothing about the actual word prosody (see 9.3.2). Another interpretation is that an 'unshifted' pronunciation *sesón* could still be heard in the last decade of the fourteenth century, so that Chaucer had two alternate realisations to choose from. The likelihood of these hypotheses has to be tested on a word-by-word basis, on the assumption that prosodic accommodation of loanwords is lexically diffuse. Thus *country* (1275) is used forty-five times in Chaucer's pentameter verse, twenty-one of which are in rhyme position and are realised as end-stressed. Of the twenty-four line-internal attestations, however, there is not a single example of end-stress on the word; they are all of the type illustrated by *SumT* 1710: *A mérsshy* ***cóntree*** *cálled hóldernésse.* The absence of finally stressed variants in mid-line position is a strong indication that the initial stress was 'normal' in the language of London speakers at the end of ME. A comprehensive and statistically testable database of the stress-patterns of ME borrowings is still missing, but as argued in Minkova (2000, 2006a), the methodology of data-gathering from rhymed verse has to be revised to control for the convention of matching a prosodically weak syllable to a metrically strong rhyme position in the final foot of the verse line.

When rhyme position is kept out of the picture, the rate of assimilation of the early ME loanwords to the native stem-initial prominence is remarkably steady. This is partly due to a serendipitous overlap between the *Germanic Stress Rule* and the *Latin Stress Rule*, according to which stress falls on the penultimate syllable if it is heavy, otherwise, on the antepenultimate syllable. The final syllable is invisible to the stress rule and CV syllables are light, while all other syllables are heavy. (25) shows how this works for disyllabic and trisyllabic words.

(25) The Latin Stress Rule:

Heavy penult	Disyllabic	*fā́.ma* 'fame', *ér.gō* 'ergo, therefore'
	Trisyllabic	*co.mḗ.ta* 'comet', *co.lū́m.na* 'column'
Light penult	Disyllabic	*cró.cus*, *ó.nyx*
	Trisyllabic	*á.ba.cus*, *Lú.ci.fer*

In words of more than three syllables the stress fell on the penult or the antepenult depending on the penult's weight: *co.ri.án.der*, *ba.sí.li.ca*. Disyllabic words get initial stress by default: *fama*, *ergo*, *crocus*, *hérpes*, *mórtar*, *onyx*, *sphére*, *stúpor*, etc. would require no accommodation. The same is true of trisyllabic words with a light penult, the type exemplified by *abacus*, *Lucifer*. It was only the subset of trisyllabic words with a heavy penult like *cometa*, *columna*, *cucumber*, and words of more than three syllables like *coriander*, *mediator*, *memorandum*, *paralysis*, that did not fit the Germanic pattern. For that portion of the lexicon the position of the stress was determined by syllable weight. The adoption of such words provides the foundation for phonologically assigned primary stress as a new prosodic model in PDE.

Words borrowed in ME after the Conquest could be direct transfers from the Classical languages, or they could be entering English via Anglo-Norman or Old French. Many early Latin borrowings lost their inflectional markers (*-a*, *-(t)is*, *-us*, *–um*, and so on), so the source of the loan was often obscured. AN and OFr words were stressed depending on the weight of the final syllable, or the *ultima*.

(26) Stress in Old French and Anglo-Norman loans:

Heavy ultima	Final stress in disyllables: *pité*, *barón*, *reál*, *merchánt*
	Alternating stress in polysyllables: *dàngerús*, *comàndemént*
Light ultima	Initial stress in disyllables: *frére*, *dánce*, *róuge*, *ríme*
	Penultimate stress in trisyllables: *madáme*, *servíse*, *piéce*
	Alternating stress in polysyllables: *crèatúre*, *pìlgrimáge*

The most notable prosodic outliers in the loan vocabulary coming from OFr and AN would have been disyllables with a heavy final syllable, like *pité*, *barón*, *reál*, *merchánt*, and the trisyllabic words with penultimate stress, like *madáme, servíse, piéce, folýe, mirácle, viságe.* Since final syllables ending in schwa are unstressable, in originally polysyllabic words with a heavy penultimate syllable like *bataille* the stress was on the penultimate, as in Latin. Additionally, the loss of the final schwa in OFr and AN, well under way in the thirteenth century (Short 2007), results in more finally stressed disyllabic items. Throughout ME, however, these disyllabic borrowings show a strong tendency towards leftward stress-shifting, in conformity with the GSR, as in *pity, baron, battle, merchant, madam, service, piece, visage, juncture, human, chaplain, novice.* The leftward stress-shift disregards syllable weight; indeed in many cases the stress shifts leftwards from a heavy to a light syllable, as in *chaplain* (Lat. *cappellān-us*, OFr *chapelain*), also *battle, folly, miracle, novice.*

Polysyllabic words with a heavy final syllable, like *dàngerús, ìnnocént, comàndemént, cònsecratión, justìficatión,* or words of more than three syllables ending in schwa, like *crèatúre, pìlgrimáge, vìlanýe,* have their right edge stressed depending on the weight of the ultima. The distribution of the prominences to the left of that first window appears to follow the principle of rhythmic alternation. This is very similar to the preservation of prominence on derivational affixes in the native vocabulary, where the rhythmically induced prominence of native suffixes is utilised in verse: the suffixes in *sóbrelỳ, nórissỳng drónkenèsse, dóutelèes, mártyrdòm* are aligned with strong metrical positions (see 9.5). The combination of dominant word-initial stress and the rhythmic preference for stress alternation in borrowed words produces a comparable effect in the new loan vocabulary. The difference between native *sóbrelỳ, nórissỳng* and borrowed *dàngerús, ìnnocént,* or between *drónkenèsse* and *pìlgrimáge* is in the relative strength of the stresses: in the native words the stress on the affix is subordinate, while the rightmost stress in the loanwords is primary, and additional stresses to the left are less prominent, at least initially.

Once again, verse provides the basis for testing and confirmation. In iambic verse, polysyllabic loanwords are hard to fit to a metrical frame of alternating prominences. Ignoring morphological structure for the moment, one can observe that the linguistic sequence /w w s/ in the source language is realised in ME as /s w s/: *àrgumént, chàritée, làxatíf, gènerál, òpposít, òrisóun, plèntevóus, règióun.* As noted above, it is possible that in such cases, at least for words of lower frequency, it was the leftmost syllable of the word that carried the secondary stress at first, judging from the strong preference for placement of such words in rhyme position.

(27) Romance polysyllables in rhyme position in Chaucer:

aváunt: rèpentáunt	*GP* 227–8	*hóus: plèntevóus*	*GP* 343–4

dìgestíble: Bíble	*GP* 437–8	*whít: òpposít*	*KnT* 1893–4
wróoth was shé: chàritée	*GP* 451–2	*adóun: règióun*	*KnT* 2081–2
comàndemént: ysént	*KnT* 2869–70	*màriáge: ìn myn áge*	*WBT* 23–4
of blóod roiál: in gènerál	*Tr* III: 1800–2	*dýe: of bìgamýe*	*WBT* 85–6

On the other hand, the initial syllables of many trisyllabic loans with original rightmost prominence can alliterate: ***áudience***, ***bénefys***, ***béneson***, ***élementz***, ***équite***, ***órisouns*** are attested in Langland's *Piers the Plowman* (Tamson 1898: 72–3). It is probable, therefore, that the switch from word-initial secondary to primary stress in such trisyllabic words started in Middle English. A more precise dating is not recoverable from iambic verse, where both primary and secondary stresses may fill strong positions. Since ME alliterative verse was no longer orally composed and transmitted, scribes could have used eye-alliteration, so the evidence from alliterative verse is suggestive but not compelling.

The preservation of some degree of stress on the final syllable in polysyllabic Romance loans beyond Middle English is documented in Dobson (1968: §§265–92). The pattern of alternating stress as in *grácìous*, *submíssìon*, *rèsolútìon*, *éxcellènce* is found in the poetry throughout the seventeenth century.

Danielsson (1948: 26–9, 39–54) attributes the eventual demotion of the original primary rightmost stress in loanwords of more than three syllables to the school pronunciation of Latin in Middle English and Early Modern English. He uses the term 'countertonic accentuation' to describe the shift of, for example, Gk *melancholía* > Lat., AN *melancolie* (1375) to *mélanchòly*, similar to the native model of *máidenhòod*, *drúnkennèss*. The picture is complicated by the fact that along with borrowing entire words, English 'nativised' some Latin and French derivational affixes. Such affixes can attach to native roots without affecting the stress placement, thus AN *-able*, ME *singable* (1340), *believable* (1382); OFr *-ard*, ME *wizard* (1440) < *wise*, adj. + *-ard*; AN, OFr diminutive *-erel*, ME *pykerell* (1290) < *pike* + *-erel*; OFr *-age*, ME *bondage* (1330) < OE *bonda* + *age*, also *brewage* (1542), *leafage* (1599). Other affixes can be attached only or mainly to borrowed bases: *-acy*, *-ate*, *-ee*, *-erie*, *-ment*, *-ous*, *-ic(al)*. We return to the innovative stress-patterns related to non-native suffixation in 9.8.

9.6.1 Grammar, meaning and stress-shifting: PERFÉCT-PÉRFECT, CANÁL-CHÁNNEL

The examples of the variable treatment of main stress in prefixed nouns and prefixed verbs in OE (see 9.4.1) seem to be identical to PDE *upload*, v. [ˌʌp'loʊd] (1870) vs *upload*, n. ['ʌpˌləʊd] (1979); *overhang*, v. [ˌoʊvər'hæŋ] (OE) vs *overhang*, n. ['oʊvərˌ(h)æŋ] (1853). The process is known as *functional stress-shifting*. For the native vocabulary, the prosodic marking of morphosyntactic category requires the presence of a recognisable prefix. Although many details remain unexplored, it seems safe to assume that borrowed words in ME could also fit the pattern of prosodic differentiation of the morphosyntactic nature of the stems. Verbs in which the prefixation is transparent behave like the native prefixed verbs, that is, main stress on the first syllable of the root: ***Perfóurme** it out* . . . (*Tr* III 417), *ye nát* ***discóvere*** *me* (*MerT* 1942). Prefixed nouns and adjectives vary. Chaucer uses both initial and final stress on *proverb*, a word first recorded in his works (OED): *Wel may that be a* ***próverbe*** . . .(*WBT* 284), *And therfore this* ***provérbe*** *is* . . . (*RvT* 4319). Etymologically non-transparent prefixed nouns and adjectives tend to follow the native rule: *Ben humble* ***súbgit*** . . . (*Tr* II. 828), . . . *in joye and* ***pérfit*** *heele* (*KnT* 1271). Of greater interest are, however, the loanwords which are synchronically monomorphemic, which nevertheless are also subject to functional stress-shifting, as in the examples in (28), with first-recorded dates from the OED.

(28) Functional stress shifts in synchronically monomorphemic ME loans:

	Verb	**Noun/Adjective**
ally	1297	1380
augment	1400	1430
ferment	1398	1420
frequent	1477	1531
rebel	1340	1297
record	1225	1300
torment	1290	1290

Notice that the dates for the verb tend to be earlier than for the corresponding noun or adjective. The direction of the shift in the loans is almost always from end-stress for verbs to initial stress for nouns and adjectives, confirming the observations on the strength of the GSR in ME (see 9.6). The full history of stress-shifting in ME is an area which has not been fully researched yet; it is an inquiry that promises to throw light on the continuity and/or reintroduction of a prosodic pattern in English which has been has been growing steadily since the second half of the sixteenth century, as in *ábstract-abstráct*, *récord-recórd*, *rébel-rebél*, *pólice-políce*.

In addition to differentiating word-class, stress-shifting can involve semantic differentiation, with or without word-class change. There is nothing surprising about variant pronunciations of polysemous words resulting in the split of the original base into two separate lexical entries. A famous case in point is the semantic bifurcation in the pair: *palace-palate* < Lat. *palātum* 'roof of the mouth, one of the seven hills of Rome, the house of Augustus situated there, any roof-like form', where the [-s] form is from AN and OFr; similarly the history of *person-parson*, *arrant-errant* (see 8.3.2). Variable prosodic forms can also result in a lexical split. One of the earliest examples of transfer of meaning, accompanied by a stress-shift for one of the meanings is the pair *Áugust* (OE) - *augúst* (1664). (29) shows more instances of historical stress variability producing semantically independent lexical entries, either because of repeated borrowing or because of synchronic variability in ME.

(29) Stress-shifts related to meaning-shifts:

drágon, n. (c. 1220) < OFr *dragon*, Lat. *dracōn*	*dragóon* (1622)
crític, adj. (1543); †*crític* 'criticism' (1656)	*critíque* (1719)
chánnel (1300) < OFr *chanel*	*canál* (1449) < Lat. *canāl-em*
húman (1450) < AN *humane* (fem.)	*humáne* (1500) < Lat. *hūmānus*
úrban (1634) < Lat. *urbānus*	*urbáne* (1533)[18]
trável, v. (1270) < OFr *travaillier*	*traváil* (1250)
pétty (1372) ~ *pétit* (1390) < AN *petit*, masc.)	*petíte* (1766) < *petite*, fem.
ínvalid, n. (1642)[19] < Lat. *invalid-us*	*inválid* (1635)
tóilet (1540) < Fr. *toilette*	*toilétte*, post-16th c. var. of *toilet*

9.7 ME compound and phrasal stress

Section 9.4.2 touched on the problem of proving or disproving the hypothesis of different prosodic contours for compounds and phrases in OE: while left-edge prominence in compounds is solidly supported by the evidence, right-hand prominence, or the End Rule, for phrases, cannot be tested reliably in the verse. The alliterative compositions in ME are somewhat more informative, primarily because of the

[18] *Urbáne* was originally a variant of *úrban*; the meaning differentiation (*urbane* 'refined') is first recorded in the seventeenth century. The same variation occurred with *travel* and *travail*.

[19] Originally, it was a special sense of the adj. *invalíd*. The switch to initial stress occurred in the nineteenth century in AmE; Webster (1828) has *ínvalid*, a 'pronunciation ... commonly heard in England also' (OED).

relaxation of the classical OE matrix of obligatory alliteration on the linearly first member of a noun phrase, whether it is the head or the modifier. Already in the thirteenth century, the alliterating portions of some lyrics show right-hand prominence, thus *helle* ***stenches***, *lustes* ***stench***, *godes word*, *godis wille*, all alliterating on the head noun.[20] The phrasal End Rule is supported also by the frequency of right-hand alliterative prominence in fourteenth-century verse. Some examples from *Sir Gawain and the Green Knight* are shown in (30).

(30) The End Rule in fourteenth-century alliterative verse (*SGGK*):
So **b**isied him *his ȝonge blod* and his **b**rayn wylde 89
Talkkande bifore *þe hyȝe table* of **t**rifles ful hende 108
Þen *þe first cors* come with **c**rakkyng of trumpes 116
To *þe grene chapel* þou **ch**ose, I **ch**arge þe, to fotte 451

Alliteration on the head noun in noun phrases (NPs) is regular with semantically weak modifiers – *good*, *great*, *many*, *such*, *other* – but it can go both ways with more distinct adjectives. This suggests that while phrasal stress is subject to the overall preference for right-hand prominence, it is also susceptible to other factors such as semantic load and lexicalisation.

Testing compound and phrasal stress in ME syllable-counting verse is complicated by the optional phrase-internal unstressed syllables. Looking at the NPs in the opening of Chaucer's *General Prologue*, we find: . . .with his *sweete breeth*, . . . in *every holt*, The *tendre croppes*, . . .the *yonge sonne*, . . .his *halve cours*, And *smale foweles* (*GP* 5–9), where all of the italicised phrases are aligned with S W S metrical positions. This is uninformative because both compounds and phrases fit the same metrical frame. The sequence S W S can be satisfied in several ways: the modifier is disyllabic, for example in *every holt*; the modifier is monosyllabic and follows a determiner (weak declension), so there is an extra buffer syllable before the noun, for example his *sweete breeth*; the noun is not initially stressed, for example . . . *an hard requeste* (Tr III, 148); or the monosyllabic modifier is plural, preserving the inflectional *-e*, for example *smale foweles*. The relative strength of the two prominences is indeterminate.

EModE shows a somewhat clearer distributional evidence for compound and phrasal stress. The matching of these units to metrical positions in Elizabethan iambic pentameter tends to mirror the linguistic difference between the two types of structures. Compounds with a monosyllabic first element (*long-lived*, *first-born*, *tongue-tied*) and

[20] Examples from Brown (1932/1962: 4, 15, 27, 46).

NP phrases of comparable syllabic composition (*sweet brood*, *old Time*, *tall building*) are distributed predictably in verse: the former type are aligned overwhelmingly with S W / even positions, while the phrases appear mostly in W S W positions. Compare the examples in (31) from Shakespeare's sonnets.

(31) Compound vs phrasal placement in Shakespeare's *Sonnets*:

(a) Compounds in S(trong)-Weak metrical position:

And burn the long-lived phoenix in her blood	*Sonnet 19*
With April's first-born flowers, and all things rare	*Sonnet 21*
To make me tongue-tied speaking of your fame	*Sonnet 80*

(b) Phrases in W(eak)-(S(trong) metrical position:

And make the earth devour her own sweet brood;	*Sonnet 19*
Yet, do thy worst, old Time: despite thy wrong,	*Sonnet 19*
He of tall building, and of goodly pride	*Sonnet 80*

In summary, ME compound and phrasal stress cannot be shown to be 'innovative'. There is no reason reject the assumption that both the left-prominent compound stress contour and the right-prominent phrasal stress contour posited for Old English remained stable in ME. By the end of ME, phrasal stress would have been reinforced by exposure to French prosodic patterns, with dominant right-headedness on the phrasal level. Although the claim is only weakly supported in the verse material, not fully recoverable from the meter of the earlier periods, it would appear that the most reasonable position is that 'Alfredian, Ricardian, Elizabethan, Jacobean, and even Clintonian English obey and have always obeyed the same rules of phrase internal prominence assignment' (Minkova and Stockwell 1997b: 320).

9.8 Post-ME prosodic innovations

EModE is a period characterised by higher literacy rates, a sharp rise in book production and a parallel rapid expansion of the lexicon. Over 20,000 classical loanwords first recorded between 1500 and 1700 survive to this day. This exceeds by far the rate of borrowing in Middle English. Two thirds of the new forms in EModE were based on already recorded roots and affixes and about one third were straight borrowings. Latin and French continued to be the main donors of new words. Of note is also that while late ME loans from French outnumbered those from Latin, the proportion of loans from Latin increased steadily and peaked between 1575 and 1675. Parallel to the entry of 'whole' lexemes, there is also a striking increase of the relative frequency of Latinate affixes in the overall number of new affixed forms from 20 per cent in the fifteenth century to 70 per cent in the third half of the eighteenth century.

The large majority of the new items were scientific and technical terms adopted or coined by English speakers who were proficient in Latin. Such speakers would tend to preserve the *Latin Stress Rule* (25) as in *ablátion*, *compéndium*, *máximum*, *meánder*, *términus*. The density of these forms and the shared literate understanding of their prosody gave rise to a new, parallel model of stress in English, which is weight sensitive, and which can apply productively to new words such as *Óregon* (1765, possibly Connecticut pidgin Algonquian, OED), *kaínga* 'village' (Maori, 1820), *carráncha* 'carrion-hawk' (South American Indian language, 1839), *Anímikie* 'thunderer' (1873, Ojibwa), *mazúrka* (Polish, 1818), *palachínka* 'pancake' (Serbian, 1884). The process of integrating a right-to-left weight-sensitive stress placement stretches over the whole EModE period, but it was not until the mid-eighteenth century that the new model was fully recognised. Lass (1999: 130) dates 'the shift in grammarians' typological intuitions' between the 1740s and the 1780s. From then on, 'English begins to feel more like a language with a Latinate accentual system than one with a Germanic type' (ibid.). The statement is justified by the limited share of native items in the lexicon of an adult English speaker, approximately 25–30 per cent (Minkova and Stockwell 2006: 466–7).

The recognition of a new model of stress-placement for polysyllables never completely obscured the tenacity of the GSR. As is common in any body of loanwords, the EModE borrowed lexicon was composed primarily of nouns and adjectives. The relative share of nouns in the new lexicon of EModE was consistently above 50 per cent and reached 70 per cent in 1760–4. The proportion of adjectives is also significant, ranging from 20 per cent to 28 per cent in 1660–74. Verbs, on the other hand, are borrowed at a lower rate, rarely up to 20 per cent and down to 8 per cent at the end of the period.[21]

Since the GSR applied without exception to native nouns and adjectives throughout the earlier history of English, even in prefixed forms (see 9.4.1), it is not surprising that left-edge prominence continued to be a salient and active principle in the adaptation of borrowed nouns and adjectives. Consolidation of the primary stress on the initial syllable of the stem went beyond the disyllabic shifts recorded in 9.6, as in *hérpes*, *mórtar*, *sphére*, *stúpor*, and affected trisyllabic nouns and adjectives. Words such as *ámorous*, *cálendar*, *chárity*, *génial*, *ínfantry*, *láxative*, *mércury*, *ópposite*, *órient*, *órison*, *pléenteous*, *région* changed their Chaucerian 'double-stressed'

[21] Statistics from Nevalainen (1999: 353).

realisation in favour of a GSR-type stress. Stress-shift to the initial syllable often proceeded in spite of the etymological heaviness of the penultimate syllable, as in the ME loans *ámorous*, *fórtunate*, *ínfantry*, *ínterval*, *órient* and many post-ME forms such as *órchestra* (1596), *vértebra* (1615), *bálcony* (1618), *tálisman* (1638), *cóquetry* (1656), *sýnergy* (1660), *mónocle* (1772), *Cávendish* (1839), *bádminton* (1845), *állergy* (1911).

The emerging picture is complexly layered: the prosody of native unprefixed words follows the OE left-alignment of the word or stem with the main stress. The non-native vocabulary displays hybrid patterns, and no single model covers all realisations without multiple exceptions, so that only strong tendencies can be defined. New words can fall in with the native left-strong Germanic model, or they can follow a weight-sensitive model whereby stress in non-derived words is assigned by syllable weight. The weight of the penultimate syllable is responsible for *agénda*, *Torónto*, while *cánopy*, *ínfidel* fit both models. Although the considerable overlap between the patterns noted in 9.6 for disyllabic nouns and adjectives continues, end-stressed nouns like *abýss*, *baróque*, *cabál*, *canál*, *duréss*, *elíte*, *maláise*, *ravíne* do occur. Verbs with heavy final syllables are generally end-stressed, for example *paráde*, *dený*, *maintáin*, *oblíge*, *protéct*, but the realisations of the verbal affix *-ate* may vary: *cóncentrate*, *dévastate*, *éxcavate*, but *demonstrate*, *elongate*, *contemplate* allow penultimate stress.

Variable stress in borrowed words is very much a feature of the prosody of English in the last couple of centuries. MacMahon (1998: 493–517) presents detailed chronological tables of words susceptible to stress-shifts since the end of the eighteenth century. He uses twenty-four pronouncing dictionaries: from Johnston (1764) and Sheridan (1781) to the 1990 *Longman Pronouncing Dictionary* and the 1992 OED2. He establishes six patterns of main stress variation, set out in (32).

(32) Post-eighteenth-century patterns of variation and change:[22]

Description	**Examples**
Type 1: Zero or limited variability	*énterprise*, *predícament*
	súbstantive ~ *substántive* (BrE)
Type 2: Competing forms (A ~ B)	*décorous* ~ *decórous*
	cóntroversy ~ *contróversy*
Type 3: Shorter-term changes (A > B > A)	*shérbet*, *sherbét*, *shérbet*

[22] From MacMahon (1998: 493); the examples are from his tables 5.1–5.6. The tabulation records only primary stresses; other levels of stress are conflated with absence of stress.

	splenétic, splénetic, splenétic
Type 4: Clear change, no reversal (A > B)	*accéss*, n. > *áccess*, n. *balcóny* > *bálcony*
Type 5: Multi-stage change (A > B > C . . .)	*cómplaisance, complaisánce, compláisance*
Type 6: Variation and reversal (A > B ~ A > A)	*panthéon, pántheon*

Focusing only on the twentieth century, Bauer (1994b: 96–103) records items which have undergone a recent shift to penultimate stress, for example *ábdomen, ácumen, ánchovy, étiquette, molýbdenum, précedence, quándary, sécretive, sónorous, vágary.* 💻 The continuing variability of main-stress placement and the concomitant degree of vowel reduction for some items is well illustrated by the OED pronunciation entry for *quadruple*, n., adj., adv.: Brit. /ˈkwɒdrʊpl/, /kwɒˈdruːpl/, /kwəˈdruːpl/, US /kwɑˈdrup(ə)l/, /kwəˈdrup(ə)l/, /kwɑˈdrəp(ə)l/, /kwəˈdrəp(ə)l/. As is clear from this and many other entries, the extent to which individual loanwords favour morphological vs syllable weight-based stress can differ in British and American English. Some well-known examples with first attestation dates from the OED are shown in (33); some of these are simply 'majority' pronunciations in variation with the alternative pronunciation.

(33) Stress differences between American and British English:

(a) GSR in AmE:

American English	**Date**	**British English**
ínquiry	(1440)	*inquíry*
pólice (also *polı́ce*)	(1450)	*polı́ce*
frústrate	(1447)	*frustráte*
móustache	(1585)	*moustáche*

(b) GSR in BrE:

American English	**Date**	**British English**
premı́er	(1500)	*prémier*
debrı́s	(1708)	*débris*
café	(1802)	*cáfe*
miráge	(1812)	*mı́rage*
garáge	(1902)	*gárage*

The examples in (32) and (33) leave no doubt as to the hybridity of the PDE prosodic system. As is the case for ME too, however, the prosodic behaviour of new words in EModE and PDE has not been fully documented and analysed. What is still needed is a full-scale statistical overview of the patterns of adaptation, controlled for factors such as word-class, number of syllables, the place of the item in a derivational set and frequency of the morphemes in non-monomorphemic items, though Berg's (1999) comparison between stress in British and American English offers both valuable data and some interesting conclusions.

Before we conclude the survey of the prosodic adaptation of loanwords in English, we must note a further complicating factor: the role of suffixes in stress placement. As noted in section 9.4.1, OE suffixation was never associated with main-stress reduction; the highest level of prominence in a suffixed word was always inherited from the stem: *bérend* 'bearer, pregnant' - *bérendnes* 'fecundity', *fǽder* 'father' - *fǽderlic* 'fatherly'. Through ME, and into PDE, the suffixes listed in (34) never carry the primary stress in a derivative.

(34) Stress-neutral native derivational suffixes:
-dom: as in *mártyr - mártyrdom*
-en: as in *forgíve - forgíven*
-er: as in *intérpret - intérpreter*
-ful: as in *regrét - regrétful*
-hood: as in *néighbour- néighbourhood*
-ish: as in *yéllow - yéllowish*
-less: as in *compássion - compássionless*
-ly: as in *mátron - mátronly*
-ness: as in *invíncible - invíncibleness*
-some: as in *advénture - advénturesome*
-ward(s): as in *héaven - héavenward(s)*
-wise: as in *óther - ótherwise*

Persistence of primary stress in words derived with native suffixes continued in ME. At the same time, the adoption of a large number of foreign suffixed words triggered the introduction of suffix-specific main-stress placement at the right edge of the word.

The behaviour of the Latinate suffixes in PDE has been the subject of intense linguistic scrutiny, yet none of the analyses can be considered conclusive.[23] Some of the more general patterns exemplified in (35)–(38) include suffixes which behave like the native suffixes, that is, they are stress-neutral; suffixes that always attract stress; and suffixes that push the stress onto a particular syllable to their left. We will ignore secondary stress, noting that some suffixes, for example *-ise*, *-oid*, are stress-neutral with respect to the stem but they attract secondary stress.

[23] A good descriptive coverage is found in Fudge (1984); the analytical problems are addressed in Giegerich (1999).

Also, the process of derivation with suffixes that are not stress-neutral may involve preservation of the stress of the original base, so the initial primary stress on *móuntain*, *pícture*, *vélvet* is inherited as secondary stress in the derivatives *mòuntainéer*, *pìcturésque*, *vèlvetéen.*

(35) Stress-neutral borrowed suffixes:
-ist: *(e)vangelist* (1175), *exorcist* (1382), *dogmatist* (1541)
-ty: *specialty* (1330), *mayoralty* (1387–8), *admiralty* (1419)
-ise: *authorise* (1383), *crystallise* (1600), *generalise* (1425)

(36) Stress-attracting borrowed suffixes:
-ade: *grenáde*, *lemonáde*
-air: *debonáir*, *corsáir*
-ane: *arcáne*, *mundáne*, *germáne*, *urbáne*
-ee: *payée*, *devotée*
-een: *velvetéen*, *cantéen*
-eer, -ier: *mountainéer*, *brigadíer*
-elle: *bagatélle*, *villanelle*
-esce: *effervésce*, *acquiésce*
-esque: *statuésque*, *grotésque*, *picturésque*
-ese: *journalése*, *viennése*
-ette: *majorétte*, *serviétte*
-oon: *tycóon*, *ballóon*, *dragóon*, *picaróon*

(37) Penultimate stress with borrowed suffixes:
-ic: *numéric*, *idiótic*, *históric*, *económic*
-id: *carótid*, *myópsid*
-ion: *rebéllion*, *compánion*

(38) Antepenultimate stress with borrowed suffixes:
-(cra)cy: *demócracy*, *aristócracy*
-ast: *icónoclast*, *enthúsiast*
-ity/-ety: *tranquílity*, *humílity*
-ose: *cómatose*, *béllicose*
-tude: *similitude*, *áttitude*

The antepenultimate is stressed also in combining forms such as *-ólogy*, *-ósophy*, *-ógraphy*, *-ólatry*, *-ócracy*, and so on. These new patterns of stress-assignment extend to native roots under foreign suffixation as in *Icelándic* (1674), *weatherólogy* (1823), *speedómeter* (1904), *Chàplinésque* (1921). Then there are patterns that are not based on an actual affix, for example *-eau*, which tends to be stress-attracting, but the final stress may be shifted in *chateau*, *tableau*, *plateau*, *trousseau*, *bureau*, especially in British English. Similarly, *-oo* attracts stress: *bambóo*, *shampóo*, *tabóo*, although the etymology of the <-oo> words is quite disparate, so the fixing of the stress on the final syllable is within English, where [uː] is always a stressed vowel.

The examples in (35)–(38) are selected to illustrate some general patterns, but they are far from exhaustive. They are indeed only slightly better than a bewildering laundry list, and there are exceptions galore in each group: in (35) we list *-ise* as stress-neutral, but *chastíse* (1325) has alternated with initially stressed *chástise* from the beginning.[24] In (36) with *-ade*, we find *grenáde*, *lemonáde*, but AmE also *lémonàde*, and both BrE and AmE allow initial main stress in *prómenàde*; with *-air* we find *debonáir*, *corsáir*, but AmE also *córsair*; with *-ee* we find *payée*, *devotée*, but both *employée and emplóyee*, and both *refugée* and *réfugee* in AmE. Some highly productive suffixes, for example *-able*, are hard to fit in the taxonomy because they produce variable results: *-able* can be stress-neutral: *colléctable*, *excúsable*, *récognisable*, *réplicable*; it can go against the stress of the base: *irréparable*, *cómparable*, *préferable*, *ádmirable*, *demónstrable*; and the stress varies in *applicable*, *despicable*, *hospitable*, *(in)explicable*. The productive suffix *-age* has two forms: unstressed [-ədʒ/-ɪdʒ] in *pilgrimage*, *steerage*, *orphanage*, [-eɪdʒ] in verbs: *engage*, *rampage*, *presage*; and stressed [ɑ(ː)ʒ] as in still unassimilated *barrage* (1859).

The difficulty of describing stress in derived words in PDE is exacerbated by the tendency for the prosody of the base to be inherited in the derivative. Stress placement in derived words can ignore the nature of the suffix and preserve the prosody of a pre-existing and frequently used base, thus *cápital*, *prefér* are the bases which trigger the change of old *capítalist* to current *cápitalist*, and of old *préferable* to AmE *preférable*.

In summary, stress-placement in PDE is a mixture of prosodic patterns, some inherited from Old English, some introduced in Early Modern English. With Old English we share left-edge prominence in disyllabic noun and adjective bases, left-edge marking of compounds, lack of stress on function words, head-prominence in clitic groups and, most probably, right-hand phrasal prominence. The loan vocabulary of Middle and Modern English complicates the picture by introducing weight-sensitive stress assignment, suffix-driven stress assignment, tolerance for final stress in nouns, and specific rhythmic constraints for the avoidance of stress-clashes and strings of unstressed syllables. Many relevant details in the prosodic history of English remain under-

[24] 'The stress was originally always on the first syllable: ˈ*chastise*, is generally so with Shakespeare (7 times against 2), and also in later poets, as still in ˈ*chastisement*; but already in Chaucer sometimes, and Gower often, on the second, as now' (OED). The etymology of the word is unclear – it may have final stress on the analogy of *comprise*, *demise*, *despise*, *devise*.

researched: the prosodic behaviour of borrowings in Middle English needs fuller documentation, and the relevance of competing factors such as phonological composition, frequency, morphological marking and transparency, social prestige and spelling have to be evaluated. The relationship between innovations in verse form and prosodic innovations is also of considerable linguistic and cultural interest. Other areas that invite further inquiry are the prosodic patterns in the regional and ethnic varieties of English, and the contact-induced changes in English spoken as a second language.

The historical diversity of the stress-patterns in English is related directly to the rise of new word-formation models. The loss of post-tonic syllables goes back to OE; it is unremarkable in a language with stress on the first root syllable. Though the loss normally affects inflectional syllables (see 7.6), a process of 'back-clipping' in English is attested early and its productivity grew in EModE.

(39) Back-clipping of initially stressed words:

trent < *tréntal* (1389)	*ult* < *últimum* (1750)
chat < *chátter*, v. (1440)	*vis* < *vísit*, v. (1754)
coz < *cóusin*, n. (1559)	*bod* < *bódy* (1788)
mob < *mobile* (1688)	*lunch* < *lúncheon*, n. (1829)
hack < *háckney*, v. (1721)	*beaut* < *béauty* (1866)

In (39) the clippings preserve the stressed syllable of the input, and the output words can be both nouns and verbs. A somewhat different model of back-clipping is illustrated in (40), where the main stress is ignored.

(40) Back-clipping of non-initially stressed words:

Oxon < *Oxónian*, n., adj. (1439)	*extra* < *extraórdinary* (1776)
sol < *solútion*, n. (1588)	*prof* < *proféssor*, n. (1800)
phyz < *physiógnomy*, n. (1687)	*advert* < *advertisement* (1814)
gin < *Genéva*, n. (1714)	*math* < *mathemátics* (1847)
ally < *alabáster*, n. (1720)	*perk* < *perquísite*, n. (1869)

In the set in (40) it is the left edge of the word that is preserved, in spite of the lack of primary stress, or *any* stress on the remaining portion. If the remaining portion is disyllabic, it has initial stress. The process appears to be almost categorically restricted to nouns and adjectives. Thus, along with the introduction of new vocabulary, we can discern a tendency for adapting the polysyllabic words to the mono- and disyllabic initially stressed mould of the native word-stock. Shortened forms, for example *rep(utation)* (1677), *rep(ublic)* (1701), *mob(ile)* (1688), *penult(imate)* (1490), were the target of complaints by some eighteenth-century language commentators, yet such forms have continued to enter the language and the model is very much in vogue in PDE. *Bio*, *econ*, *lit*, *math*, *psych* are in the vocabulary of any college student, the *telly* has *ads* and *sitcoms*, we use our *cells* to download *apps*. There are clearly two distinct factors at work: stress-preservation, as in *zine* (1965), and left-edge alignment/first-syllable anchoring, as in *app* (1985). Their interaction is an important component of the prosodic morphology of English (see further Lappe 2007).

The loss of pre-tonic syllables is known as **aphesis**.[25] Pre-tonic loss of unstressed stem vowels (*gýpsy* < ***E****gyptian*, n. (1514), *Mér(ri) kin*, n. < *American* (1872), *lectric* < *electric* (1955)), is an innovation which can be associated with the adoption of the weight-based model of stress-placement and conformity to the preferred word-length in English. Deletion of initial unstressed prefixes did occur in OE, especially with the prefix *ge-*, thus *fere* < *gefere* 'companion' (975), *mung* < *gemong* 'mixture', n. and adj. (1175), but the frequency of attested forms increased significantly from early ME on. Not surprisingly, in view of the native model of unstressable verbal prefixes (***be****spéak*, ***for****gét*, ***with****stánd*) and the variable use of the *a-* prefix (*down* ~ *adown*, *mid* ~ *amid*, *mend* ~ *amend*, *rise* ~ *arise*), the most frequent new aphetic forms are Latinate prefixed verbs (*spute* < *dispute*, v. (1225), *dite* < *endite*, v. (1300), *stall* < ***in****stall*, v. (1300)). There are, however, some instances of aphesis in nouns – *merlin* < *esmerilun* (1382), †*colet* (1382) < *acolyte*, *larum* (1533) < *alarum*, *cello* (1848) < *violoncello*, *zine* (1965) < *magazine* – where the deletable part is not prefixal. Here belong also the truncated forms of some names such as *Bert*, *Ria*, *Gene*. The early history of these forms is not yet fully documented and analysed, but there is some evidence that the process peaked between 1300 and 1500 and has been gradually getting more marginal.

The recessiveness of pre-tonic syllable loss in English has not been discussed in the literature. Possible directions of inquiry are (a) the uneven historical rate of unstressed syllable loss at the right or the left edge of the word as a diagnostic of the dominant prosodic model, and (b) the sociolinguistic implications of the chronological fluctuation in the productivity of aphesis in English. A full exploration of the data promises to be quite revealing about the interplay between weight-based stress and left-edge prominence, a rivalry which has been characteristic of English prosody for many centuries.

Suggested further reading on *Companion* website.

[25] The usual definition of 'aphesis' refers to the pre-tonic loss of a vowel (see 2.5), but here the term is used more broadly to cover the loss of any pre-tonic syllabic material.

10 Early English verse forms: from Cædmon to Chaucer

This chapter offers an overview of the main verse forms in the early history of English. After defining some terms specific to the study of poetic meter, it addresses the evolution of alliterative verse: its structure in Old English, the continuity of alliterative versification in early Middle English and the reinvention of alliterative verse in the fourteenth century. Section 3 turns to the introduction of rhyme and syllable-counting. Section 4 focuses specifically on Chaucer's contribution: the iambic pentameter. The principles of matching stress to meter outlined in the chapter are applicable to post-Chaucerian verse forms as found in the works of Skelton, Lydgate, Wyatt, Shakespeare, Milton, Wordsworth, Byron, Shelley and Keats, to name only some of the great poets of the previous millennium.

10.1 Preliminaries: speech prosody vs poetic meter, stress vs ictus

The term **prosody**, as used here is restricted to stress phenomena in the spoken language, so 'prosody' is short for 'speech prosody' (see 9.1). **Meter** describes the modes of versification, where linguistic material is arranged in specific recursive frames; as used here, 'meter' is short for 'verse or poetic meter'. Meter always draws on the prosodic structures available in the language. The two systems rely on the same fundamental distinctive categories and relations, though meter obeys verse-specific conventions such as repetition, alliteration and end-rhyme, and not all prosodic features have to be harnessed into a specific verse form. Nevertheless, there are important correspondences between the structure of verse and the structure of the ambient language. This makes meter a valuable source of information about language. The linguistic competence of the poet provides the raw material for verse; the way in which that material is manipulated to fit the metrical constraints of a particular tradition reveals the poet's, or the copyist's intuitions about prosody. 💻

The study of poetic meter relies on characteristics defined on the basis of linguistic primes: segments, syllables, words, stress, weight, rhythmic preferences and hierarchical relations. For English the syllable, the carrier of linguistic stress, is the main constituent that forms the basis for the historical study of prosody and meter. As shown in 9.1 and 9.3, word-stress can be seen as a gradient property, with absence of stress at one end of the continuum and primary stress at the other end. The prominence of an individual syllable is also a function of the position of the word in a larger domain: the first syllable of *léather* ['lɛðə(ɹ)] in the phrase *leather handbag* is less prominent than the first syllable in *handbag*, but in the compound *leather-coated* ['lɛ-] is more prominent than [koʊ-] in *coated*. Prosodic prominence relations are most stable at the level of the word; in a word like *leather* the first syllable has to be stronger than the second. Commonly the same prominence relationship persists irrespective of the embedding of the stem in a derivative, for example *leatherette* [ˌlɛðə'rɛt].

The syllable is also the basic building block of the verse units in the various English metrical forms. In verse, syllables fill *metrical positions*; metrical positions are the prime constituents of verse. The metrical positions in the line differ in their prominence. A prominent, or strong metrical position is called an **ictus**, here marked with S(trong); ictic positions are usually, but not always, filled by stressed syllables, while **non-ictic** W(eak) positions attract unstressed syllables. S and W metrical positions are further organised into higher-level constituents known as metrical **feet**. All metrical feet contain an ictus. Within the foot, the strong position must be either initial as in S W or **trochee**, S W W or **dactyl**, or final as in W S or **iamb**, W W S or **anapaest**. The number of weak positions in a foot varies in the different metrical forms. The weak/non-ictic position in a metrical foot can be left unfilled; this is the case in the so-called 'headless' lines (see 10.4).

Above the level of the foot the unit that includes one or more feet is usually known as a **colon** (pl. **cola**), or a **hemistich**, though for OE the accepted term for a hemistich is **verse** (see 10.2). Hemistichs are usually separated by a **caesura**, a metrical pause commonly coterminous with a syntactic boundary. The structure uniting the cola is the **metrical line**: the lines in the verse-types we will be looking at are made up of two colas. In English alliterative compositions, the two verses make up the **alliterative long line**.

The overall number of syllables per line can be the same for each line, as is the case in Chaucer's or Shakespeare's verse: such verse is known as **isosyllabic**. The number of feet per line in isosyllabic verse determines whether a line is a **monometer** (one), **dimeter** (two), **trimeter** (three), **tetrameter** (four), **pentameter** (five), **hexameter** (six) or **heptameter** (seven). Alternatively, the number of syllables per line can be flexible – this is true of English alliterative verse and of **free verse**, both of which are **non-isosyllabic**. Our discussion of the early forms of English verse will stop at the level of the line, though clearly lines can build larger verse units such as couplets, triplets, quatrains, stanzas and cantos.

In 'ideal' syllable-counting verse, single metrical positions are filled by single syllables, S-positions align with stressed syllables and W-positions align with unstressed syllables. This important constraint on matching prominences in speech and verse is a valuable historical diagnostic for stress. Further alignments of linguistic units to metrical constituents are optional. This includes word boundaries coinciding with metrical foot boundaries, phrase boundaries coinciding with hemistichs, and clause boundaries matching line-ends. A simple alignment between meter and prosody is shown in Figure 10.1; prosodically stressed syllables are marked *s*, unstressed syllables are *w*.

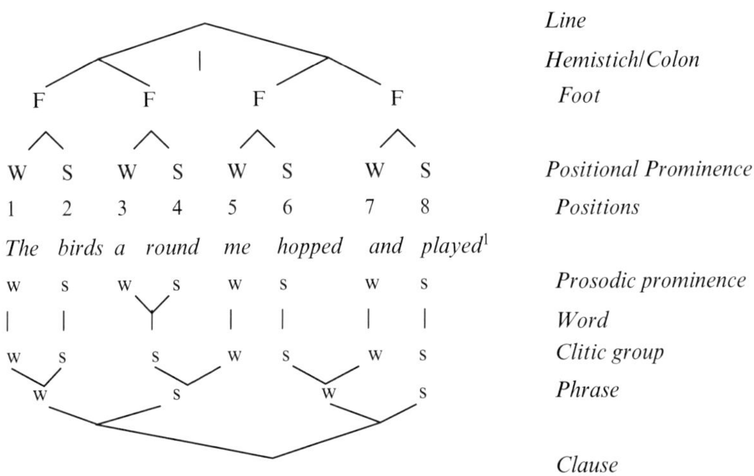

Figure 10.1 Matching meter to prosody

[1] Wordsworth, *Lines Written in Early Spring* (1798).

In this example, the alignment on the syllabic level – syllabic prominence to prosodic prominence – is perfect: all metrical S's are filled by stressed syllables (*birds*, *-round*, *hopped*, *played*) flanked by weakly stressed syllables within a word (a-) or a clitic group (*the*, *me*, *and*). All word boundaries coincide with the metrical foot boundaries in positions 2, 4, 6 and 8. The clause boundary appears at the end of the line. The only mismatch is between phrase and colon: *the birds around me* straddles the hemistich, so that the caesura is heard *after* the fifth, and not after the fourth position. This type of mismatch is common and benign; the verse is well-formed and the mismatch avoids monotony. On the other hand, the iambic tetrameter line in Figure 10.1 would be metrically much less acceptable if it started with **Around me the birds*. . . because *the* would be in the S position in the second foot. Moreover, if there were no mismatches, as in the construct *The birds around, they hopped and played*, where phrase and hemistich boundaries align, the line would be rhythmically less interesting. Thus the mismatch in the actual line is not just metrically tolerated, it contributes to the aesthetic value of the line by introducing a small irregularity. The example also illustrates an important analytical principle: metrical well-formedness is a gradient property of all types of verse.

The simplicity of the correspondences in Figure 10.1 is deceptive; the forms of English verse covered in the following sections are much more complex, but the principles remain the same. The metricality of a verse piece is evaluated on the basis of matches and mismatches between the abstract metrical template and the properties of the linguistic material used in the verse.

10.2 Alliterative verse

As is evident from the name of this type of versification, **alliterative verse** relies on **alliteration**, defined for the purpose of Germanic and OE meter as identity of the onsets of stressed syllables. More specifically, the recurrent alliterating linguistic units are equivalent along three parameters: phonetic properties, onset position in the syllable and placement in a prosodically prominent syllable.

The etymological relation between Lat. *littera* 'letter' and *alliteration* can be taken too literally; the reference to identity of initial *letters* was pervasive in the early definitions of the term. The orthographic aspect of alliteration should be kept out of the linguistic analysis: <f> in *folc* 'folk' and <ph> in ***Pharaon*** 'pharaoh' alliterate in OE, and PDE *city slicker* is an alliterating phrase, while *giant gorilla* is not. Although the dictionary definitions today emphasise the phonological rather than the visual identity in alliteration, the restriction to stressed syllables is often ignored, so that strings such as *you **b**etter **b**elieve it*, ***b**elow the **b**elt*, are considered 'alliterating' in the broader sense of the term, satisfying two out of the three parameters listed above: phonetic identity and onset position. 💻

As will become clear in this section, the interpretation of what constitutes identity in alliterative verse is not static. The requirements can be more or less restrictive; the practice of the poets may shift depending on the modes of composition and consumption: primarily oral, as in Germanic and OE, or mixed oral and written, as in ME.

Proto-Germanic and all of the older Germanic languages were characterised by the placement of primary stress on the first root syllable (see 3.4.3). Against this prosodic foundation the choice of left-edge identity as a unifying feature of the verse line appears to be a natural artistic extension of the left-prominent prosodic patterns of Germanic. Put differently, in a language with initial word-stress, the development of a verse form organised around alliteration corresponds to one of the most basic principles of the interface between language and meter, the 'fit' between stress and ictus. Our starting point, then, is the assumption that the prosodic structure of the Germanic languages, placing highest prominence on the initial syllable of the root, is ideally suited for alliteration. 💻

10.2.1 Classical OE alliterative verse

The OE alliterative tradition is part of the indigenous Germanic verse tradition. Attempts to look for the origin of OE alliteration outside Germanic are unconvincing; 'cultural' borrowing of the model is ruled out by the alliterative inscriptions from Anglian territory before AD 400.[2] Alliteration flourished in Germanic both for the mnemonic and aesthetic reasons that generate it in the poetic models of other languages, and for internal linguistic reasons.

The composition of alliterative verse in Anglo-Saxon times stretches over the entire OE period. The datable chronological end points of the surviving material range from 737, the Northumbrian 'Moore' manuscript of *Cædmon's Hymn*, the verse account of the miraculous invention of alliterative meter by an illiterate cowherd, to the 1065 poem *The Death of Edward*, the last OE composition which can be described reasonably as belonging to the classical metrical tradition of Anglo-Saxon

[2] See Lapidge (1979: 219–20) for a summary of the arguments and a vigorous defence of the indigenous nature of OE versification.

versification. The entire OE poetic heritage was meticulously edited and annotated in the monumental six-volume collective edition of *The Anglo-Saxon Poetic Records* (Krapp and Dobbie 1931–53).[3]

Germanic and OE versification is notoriously difficult to model. Although new theories of OE meter continue to appear, no new approach rivals the descriptive adequacy and broad scholarly acceptance of the observations and patterns in Sievers (1893). Although there are no agreed principles of interpretation of all the relevant parameters determining the metrical structures of OE alliterative verse, the obligatory presence of alliteration as a structural binding factor and as a central linguistic means of creating an artistic effect is (almost) universally recognised. As noted in 9.3.2, the vanishingly rare occurrence of verse lines lacking alliteration, amounting to as little as 0.001 per cent in the poetic corpus, allows us to rely on alliteration as a basic correlate of stress. Other regularities in the metrical structure of OE verse are listed in (1).

(1) Some basic descriptive features of OE alliterative verse:

- A (long) line consists of two verses the 'on-verse' ('a-verse') and the 'off-verse' ('b-verse').
- Each verse/half-line has two feet and *at least four* positions.[4]
- Each foot must contain an ictus (S), also known as a 'lift', and at least one non-ictic position (W), also known as a 'dip'.
- The first foot is stronger than the second.
- The verses are linked by alliteration. The on-verse may have two alliterating strong positions. In the off-verse, only the ictic syllable of the first foot participates in the structural alliteration.

This allows us to represent the structure of the line as in Figure 10.2, where F stands for FOOT and the numbers at the bottom stand for POSITIONS.

The binary representation in Figure 10.2 is an abstract template based on the minimal line structure in terms of syllable count. Verses shorter than four syllables are defective. Four-syllable verses like *ne leof ne lað* 'not friend nor enemy' are not the most common type; not exceeding 25 per cent in the corpus.[5] The foot-internal prominence relations have to be left unspecified; S's (lifts) and W's (dips) can appear in either order, allowing a mid-verse stress-clash, where positions 2 and 3 are filled by stressed syllables, as in *beléan míhte* 'dissuade could'.

[3] Accessible as public domain at <http://www.sacred-texts.com/neu/ascp/> (last accessed 30 May 2013).

[4] Verses of more than four positions are considered 'hypermetric'.

[5] The estimate is based on the statistics in Hutcheson (1995: 175–269).

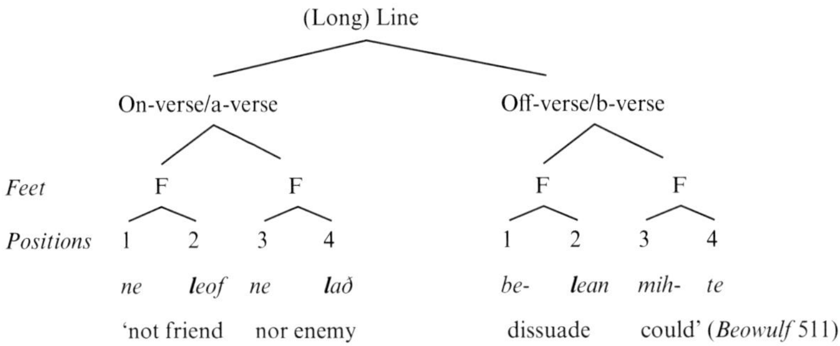

Figure 10.2 The structure of the Old English verse line

One of the most striking features of OE meter, making it speech-like, is that the length of the long line is variable and can contain from eight to as many as fifteen syllables. This is related to the uneven size of the lifts – one or two syllables, and especially the dips – zero to three, four, very occasionally even more syllables.

As stated in the third bullet in (1), each foot must contain an ictus (S). A monosyllabic foot, where the W position is empty (optionally analysed as filled by a zero syllable), is allowed only if the adjacent foot is minimally trisyllabic; otherwise a foot must have at least one syllable filling a non-ictic position W.

The size of W positions varies. If a W position is filled by more than one syllable, it is known as an 'expanded' dip, that is, W = [ww], [www], and so on. Verse-final weak positions cannot be expanded: $W \neq [ww]_{verse}$. Expanded W positions are preferred in the first foot of a verse: [wws], [wwws], or [sww], [swww] are very common in the first foot of the verse. Expanded dips appear in the second feet of verses only in 2–3 per cent of the verses. Note that foot-boundaries never separate a string of weak syllables – adjacent w's are always subsumed under a single non-ictic position. This is a metrical convention: for the purpose of meter, in, for example, *ǣnne ofer ȳðe* 'alone over waves' (*Beowulf* 46a), scanned as [swww / sw], the syllables . . . *ne o.fer* are not distinguished in metrical strength, though in speech the first syllable of *ófer* would be realised as more prominent than the adjacent syllables to the left and the right.

A strong position S is typically filled by a single syllable, and it must be filled by at least one syllable. The one-to-one correspondence between a syllable and a position may be disregarded for S-positions under a special metrical convention known as 'resolution'. Resolution is a metrical equivalence: one and only one stressed *heavy* syllable (H) can fill a lift, but a *light* stressed syllable (L) and any other unstressed syllable (X) may jointly fill a lift to avoid an unacceptable metrical violation, such as two unstressed syllables/an expanded dip at the right edge of the verse. This metrical equivalence, under which, for example, the words *cyning* 'king' and *ēa* 'river' are 'the same', requires onset-maximal syllabification, that is, intervocalic singleton consonants are syllabified as onsets of the vowel to the right (see 2.3.2). The convention is verse-specific and suggests that the recitation style observes onset-maximality, which may not have been true in casual speech. Thus in the verse ***réceda under róderum*** 'of halls under heavens' (*Beowulf* 310a), the syllables *ró.de-* are metrically subsumed under the S position to avoid the unacceptable verse-final [ww] in-*de.rum.* One notation for resolution is the insertion of a hyphen between the light stressed syllable and the following syllable, so *ró.de* is [s-ww].

Verse-internal resolution is illustrated in (2) where slashes separate feet, lower-case s's and w's match syllables, and upper case S's and W's represent positions in the abstract metrical template.

(2) Verse-internal resolution in OE verse:

ond ***féo rum gú me*** *na* → [w s-w / s-w w] = W S / S W
L H L L
'and lives of men' *Beowulf* 73b

hǽ leð *under* ***héo fe*** *num* → [s-w w w / s-w w] = S W / S W
L H L L
'heroes under heaven' *Beowulf* 52a

The norm of four positions in the verses in (2), marked with the capitalised equivalent scansions (W S / S W for *Beowulf* 73b and S W / S W for *Beowulf* 52a), is achieved only if the light stressed syllables in these verses fill an ictic position together with the following syllable. When this adjustment is made verse-initially or after an unstressed syllable, the resolvable syllable may be heavy, as in *féorum* 'lives' and *hǽleð* 'heroes'. Indeed, the examples in (2) can be taken as illustrating another specificity of OE verse: in some frameworks resolution is considered obligatory if the first ictic position in the verse is aligned with a light syllable and if the word is *not* a finite verb – we will return to the special status of inflected verbs below. On the other hand, subsuming a heavy syllable under a resolved ictus is generally prohibited verse-finally: an unstressed heavy syllable blocks resolution with a preceding light stressed syllable, as shown in (3).

(3) Verse-final suspension of resolution:

*gúð rìnc mó. **nig*** → [s s / s w] = S W / S W, not *[s s / s-w] or *S W / S

L H

'battle-man many' *Beowulf* 838b

*wið wrāð wé. **rod*** → [w s / s w] = W S / S W, not *[w s / s-w]

L H

'against hostile troops' *Beowulf* 319a

The restriction illustrated in (3) is known as *Kaluza's Law*. Structurally ***féorum*** 'lives' and ***hǽleð*** 'heroes' in (2) and ***mónig*** 'many', ***wérod*** 'troops' in (3) are identical, yet the heavy second syllable in these items counts as filling an independent weak position only at the verse-end. This is not to say that resolution is precluded from occurring at verse-ends; compare with *Beowulf* 478a: *on Gréndles grýre* 'in Grendel's terror', where *grýre* 'terror' has two light syllables and the verse scans [w s / w s-w] = W S / W S. It is hard to see how such complex metrical conventions reflect linguistic realities. It is more likely that the general principle of closure in metrical composition – flexibility at the left edge, and tighter constraints at the right edge of the verse or the line – is at play in this case.[6]

Creative compounding was a defining stylistic feature of OE versification. In compounds the primary stress is on the first root syllable with secondary stress on the first syllable of the second root, thus *báncòfa* 'bone-chamber', *méodosètla* 'mead-benches, *lándfrùma* 'land-ruler (see 9.4.1). In the meter the secondary stress is preserved and a polysyllabic compound can occasionally fill a whole verse.

(4) Compounds as whole verses in OE:

wílġesī̀þas	'willing companions'	(*Beowulf* 23a)	[s w / s w] = S W / S W
híldewæ̀pnum	'with battle-weapons'	(*Beowulf* 39a)	
lándgemỳrcu	'shore-boundaries'	(*Beowulf* 209b)	

In (4) the second elements *-sī̀þas* 'companions' and *-wæ̀pnum* 'with weapons' function as prosodically independent entities, and it is only on the verse level that the prosodic strength relations are reflected – the first foot is stronger than the second. When embedded within a longer

[6] See Hayes (1983: 373) for the principle of closure in other verse traditions.

verse, the second elements of compounds can be within the same foot as the first element. In such cases – for example *médoærn micel* 'mead-room big' (*Beowulf* 68a), *wiġes wéorðmỳnd* 'battle's honour' (*Beowulf* 65a) – the second elements *-ærn* 'room', *-mỳnd* '-mind' are metrically subordinated on the foot level, leading to a somewhat different foot-internal prosodic contour *in performance.* With this in mind, and allowing for the syllabic expansions within the metrical foot, we can posit three types of foot cadences, shown in (5), where parentheses indicate the optional recurrence of unstressed syllables within a single metrical W.

(5) Types of foot cadences in OE verse:

Falling	[s w (w)] = S W	***monegum** (mǣgþum)* 'from many tribes'
Rising:	[w (w) s] = W S	*on **bearm** (scipes)* 'in the ship's bosom'
Cascading:	[s-w s w(w)] = S W	***méodosètla** (oftēah)* 'meat-benches seized'

As already noted, the arrangement of the feet in a verse is only minimally linearly regulated in the sense that a syllabically short foot is balanced by a longer foot; there are never two feet within a verse both missing a filled weak position. Since the W position in the first foot is most commonly the one that hosts multiple unstressed syllables, the first foot tends to be longer, containing more syllables. In terms of metrical prominence, the first foot in a verse is considered stronger, because normally its ictus carries the structural alliteration – this is recorded in the fourth bullet in (1) above. The left-hand prominence can be taken one level further: the selection of alliterating ictic positions across the long line suggests that the a-verse is metrically stronger than the b-verse, because only the former allows both ictic positions to be filled by alliterating syllables. The second ictus in the b-verse, or the fourth ictus in the long line, does not contribute to the structural alliteration – alliteration is systematically avoided in that position, the fifth bullet in (1).

Trivial as it may sound, this statement needs further elaboration. Identity of the onsets of the syllables in ictic position in at least the first foot of each verse is a requirement for the line to be metrical. Double alliteration is allowed only in the a-verse; the occurrence of double alliteration can be quite high, ranging up to 69 per cent of the a-verses in some poems, 49 per cent in *Beowulf* and a mean of 46 per cent across the corpus.[7] In some verse-types, notably some A-, D- and all E-type verses (see (9) below), double alliteration is the norm.

Further alliteration conventions which refer to segmental identity in the stressed-syllable onsets are shown in (6).

[7] The statistics are from Hutcheson (1995: 271).

(6) Alliteration conventions for OE meter:

(a) Singleton onset consonants in ictic positions must be identical:

bēaga **b**ryttan, / on **b**earm scipes
mǣrne be **m**æste. / Þǣr wæs **m**ādma fela *Beowulf* 35–6
'the bestower of rings / in the bosom of the ship,
mighty by mast / there were treasures many'

(b) Vowels alliterate with each other:

īsig ond **ū**tfūs, / **æ**þelinges fær *Beowulf* 33
'icy and out-keen, / hero's vessel'
Þā þæt **O**ffan mǣg / **ǣ**rest onfunde
þæt se **eo**rl nolde / **y**rhðo geþolian *Maldon* 5–6
'when Offa's kinsman / first understood
that the earl would not / slackness endure'

(c) *sp-*, *st-*, *sc-* alliterate as groups:

<sp>: <sp>:
ond on **sp**ēd wrecan / **sp**el gerāde *Beowulf* 873
'and on success create / a skilful tale'

<st>: <st>:
Þā **st**od on **st**æðe, **st**īðlīce clypode *Maldon* 25
'stood then on the place / sternly called'

<sc>: <sc>:
Oft **Sc**yld Scēfing / **sc**ēaþena ðrēatum *Beowulf* 4
'oft Scyld Scefing / from bands of enemies'

The identity of the onsets in (6a) is straightforward. The only complication arises with the velar and palatal <g>'s, which alliterate freely with each other only in the early verse, for example *Beowulf.*

(7) Alliteration on voiced velars in early OE verse:
Swā sceal **ġ**eong **g**uma / **g**ōde ġewyrcean *Beowulf* 20
'So shall young man / good deeds work'

In Beowulf 20 *ġeong* 'young' has the allophone [j] from PrG /ɣ/, while *guma* 'man' and *gode* 'good deeds' have the [ɣ] allophone, which became a separate phoneme /g/ in the tenth century (see 4.2.1, 5.1.2). Syllables beginning with the consonant spelled <c>, occasionally <k>, alliterate freely throughout the corpus, irrespective of the later history of the consonant, so we get *ćȳneriċe* 'kingdom' matching *ċild* 'child' (*The Death of Edgar* 975). Initial <h->, either alone or in clusters, alliterates with itself.

Vowel alliteration is based not on the quality of the vowel peak in the stressed syllable, but on the insertion, especially in slow declamatory performance, of a glottal stop [ʔ-] in the onset. Indeed, calling the examples in (6b) 'vowel' alliteration is a misnomer – the identity is based on a consonant characterised by the laryngeal feature of constricted glottis.

Cluster alliteration, as in (6c), points to the strong cohesiveness of the [s-]-initial clusters when the second consonant in the cluster is a voiceless stop. There are no cases of splitting these clusters in the OE poetic corpus: alliteration of <sp-> with <sm->, or <st->, or just <s-> does not occur. The cohesiveness of [sp-, st-, sk-] in English is a salient phonological property: these are the only clusters that tolerate a third consonant in the onset: *spl-*, *str-*, *skw-* are well-formed onsets in English, but there no other CCC- onset clusters. The tradition of treating [sp-, st-, sk-] the same way as singletons in alliteration continued in ME (see 10.2.2), although it was not as rigorously observed as in OE.

There are also conditions on alliteration which have to do with the relative prominence of syntactic constituents. As discussed in 9.4.2, Sievers' Rule of Precedence stipulates that 'if an inflected verb precedes a noun, it does not have to alliterate, that it must not alliterate if the noun does not alliterate too, and that a non-alliterating noun can never be followed by an alliterating finite verb' (1893: §§22–9). (8) illustrates some of the options; the alliteration is marked in bold.

(8) Alliteration involving finite verbs in in OE verse:

(a)	hē þæs 'he of the	**fr**ōfre relief	gebād experienced'	*Beowulf* 7b
(b)	þenden 'when	**w**ordum with words	**w**ēold wielded'	*Beowulf* 30a
(c)	in 'in the	**w**orold world	**w**ōcun were born'	*Beowulf* 60a
(d)	ne hyrde 'heard not	ic I	**c**ymlicor comelier'	*Beowulf* 38a
(e)	**w**ēox 'grew	under under	**w**olcnum the skies'	*Beowulf* 8a
(f)	Hī hyne 'They him	þā then	æt**b**ǣron carried'	*Beowulf* 28a

The higher strength of complements in relation to their verbs is a shared and persistent feature of Germanic prosody. The alliterative behaviour of the verb in OE verse reflects this situation. When the verb is in clause-final position, its complement carries the alliteration as in (8a), *Beowulf* 7b; in this case the linear Rule of Precedence and the prosodic relations of complement-verb overlap, and the verb alliterates *only if* the complement does too, as in (8b), *Beowulf* 30a. Intransitive verbs are no exception to the reluctance of predicates to be stressed over arguments, as in (8c), *Beowulf* 60a. When the verb is in clause-initial position, the alliteration can skip it, as in (8d), *Beowulf* 38a; or the verb can co-alliterate as in (8e), *Beowulf* 8a. If the finite verb is the most prominent word in the string, and there are no nouns, adjectives or heavy adverbs in the same verse, the verb carries the alliteration, as in (8f), *Beowulf* 28a.

The type represented in (8f) is known as Type A3; the most remarkable aspect of this type is that if one posits an ictus earlier in the verse, it would be a non-alliterating ictus. The single alliterating ictus in such verses does not have to be a finite verb. Since the alliterating ictic syllable is always preceded by at least two monosyllables, the question of whether one of them carries higher stress is open; what unifies the pattern is the unambiguous alliteration on the first syllable of the last word in the a-verse. Predictably, verses with single alliteration on the last ictic position in the verse are almost entirely restricted to the a-verse. Such verses can either be classified as a separate type or they can be subsumed under type A; we will follow Hutcheson (1995: 198–203) in bundling those together with the common Type A.

Although the principles of scansion are still debatable, and the typology of verses based on Sievers' original classification has been critiqued and modified numerous times, the classical division into alphabetically named types continues to dominate the discourse on OE meter. The Sieversian taxonomy is shown in (9), with one addition, the three-stress type.

(9) Sievers' Five Types (expanded):

	Scansion	**Mnemonic**	**Examples**	
Type A:	[s w (w) / s w]	*Arnie's* ***army***	Adam ærest	*Glc* 826a
Type B:	[(w) w s / (w) w s]	*in* ***briny baths***	þurh þæs beornes breost	*Andreas* 1279a
Type C:	[(w) w s / s w]	*by* ***cost-cutting***	ofer cald cleofu	*Andreas* 310
Type D_1:	[s (w) / s s w]	***dumb dogcatchers***	deorc dēaþscua	*Beowulf* 160a
Type E:	[s s w / s (Ø)]	***egg-laying*** *hen*	eallisig tungl	*MB* 24.23
Type 3:	[s / s w / s]	***fierce fighting*** *tribe*	holm heolfre weoll	*Beowulf* 2138a

Again, parenthesised w's indicate the possibility of expansion of the dip. The phrases in the middle column are PDE constructs intended to imitate the cadences of the verses and possibly help with the type identification.

The variety of verse-types may seem bewilderingly rich, and indeed it is, but it has to be acknowledged that statistically Type A verses are by far the best represented type, amounting to 47 per cent of the a-verses and 39 per cent of the b-verses in the corpus.[8] A second observation about the density of types is that the first three types, A, B and C together comprise 76 per cent of the a-verses and 82 per cent of the b-verses. Types D and E always involve compounds: in Type D the compound is to the right, and in type E the compound is initial in the foot. In spite of their relative rarity overall, these two types represent a major characteristic property of OE meter. Their abandonment is an important diagnostic of 'the end' of the Classical OE meter.[9] Type 3 ['three'], introduced by Hutcheson (1995), is distinguished from all other types in that it has three independent lexical stresses, and the items bearing the stresses are not identifiable as compounds. The overall number of such verses is not high: 2.7 per cent in the a-verse and 2.6 per cent in the b-verse.

Nearly all verses are complete syntactic units. The smallest morpho-syntactic units that occupy a verse are compounds, as shown in (4). Most often, however, a verse is coextensive with a phrase or a clause: *Hī hyne þā ætbǣron* / *tō* ***brimes*** *faroðe* 'they him then carried / to the sea's current' (*Beowulf* 28).

Classifying a particular verse according to the typology shown in (9) is not always straightforward, and the descriptive details are complex. In order to fit the linguistic material under the idealised four positions in Figure 10.2, one needs to accommodate the uneven matching of syllables to metrical positions. One such accommodation is resolution. Another one is the expandability of the non-final weak position in the verse. Additionally, there is a consensus in the OE metrical scholarship that certain unstressed syllables are 'invisible' to the meter; they are *extra-metrical.* Extrametricality is commonly associated with the prefixes *ġe-*, *be-* and the negative proclitic *ne.* Occasionally the same proclitics have to be counted to get the obligatory fourth position, for example *Fyrst forð g̱e̱wat* 'time forth passed' (*Beowulf* 210a), where *ġe-* has to fill a weak metrical position. The placing of extrametrical syllables, not just clitics but any unstressed syllables, *before* the first foot of the verse is known as *anacrusis.* An initial S W foot in an a-verse may be preceded by at most two extrametrical weak syllables. Anacrusis is rarer in the b-verse and there can be at most one unstressed syllable in anacrusis there.

[8] Percentages from Hutcheson (1995: 297), calculated from a database of 13,044 long lines, representing approximately 40 per cent of the extant OE poetic texts.

[9] For statistics and discussion of the loss of these types in early ME see Cable (1991: 52–65).

Assigning syllabic structure and prosodic values to OE verse, like scanning *any* verse extant only in written form, involves judgements based on the reader's understanding of the template, the independently reconstructed phonology, and the reader's interpretation of what needs to be foregrounded in the line – aesthetic and semantic preferences that can be intentionally emphasised in performance. The latter aspect of verse lies outside the narrower limits of the linguistic correspondences of prosodic to metrical units, as idealised in Figure 10.1. The matching of the template to the phonology is less problematic when the phonology is categorical about a certain property, as are the stress contours of the words in the examples in (10).

(10) Unambiguous stress-to-ictus and syllable-to-position correspondences:

strēamas wundon 'streams wound' [s w / s w] = S W / S W *Beowulf* 212b

cealde strēamas 'cold streams' [s w / s w] = S W / S W *Beowulf* 1261a

In such verses a word like OE ***strēamas*** 'streams' will always have its initial syllable more prominent than the second syllable containing the plural inflection. The syllable *-mas* in this word *must* be placed in a metrically weak position, it cannot be ignored in scansion, it cannot be resolved because the preceding syllable is heavy: the word is unambiguously disyllabic and its syllables must be placed in metrically distinct positions.

In many instances, however, the phonological underpinning may be ambiguous; compare the PDE options of *hárass-haráss*, or the variable syllable-count in *botany*, *natural*, *Indian* – three or two syllables depending on the rate and style of speech. The competition of variables is always present in language and it is an important part of the process of language change. There can be no doubt that poets are aware of the options in the ambient language and can take advantage of them in order to conform more closely to the chosen metrical template. The 'metrically relevant range of phonological representations' of the forms used in verse is known as **paraphonology** (Kiparsky 1977: 190). The paraphonology refers to non-categorical properties used selectively in the verse. It is the 'phonology of opportunity', drawing on the variability of spoken forms, available to poets at all times.

Reference to optional features is essential to the reconstruction of both the metrical forms and the linguistic forms in ME verse (see 10.2.2, 10.4), where the statistical preponderance of unambiguous matches gives us a basis for formulating hypotheses about segmental and prosodic change. For the OE corpus, we can mention two paraphonological properties that are of interest: the varying syllabicity of post-obstruent coda sonorants, because it is valuable in reconstructing the date of composition of a poetic piece; and elision of final <-e>, because it plays a central role in the later verse forms.

In OE, original monosyllables with codas in obstruent + sonorant could be treated either as monosyllabic or as disyllabic, where the second syllable peak was either the sonorant, which became syllabic, or a schwa, followed by the sonorant; the development of a second syllable is labelled **parasiting**. The 'parasitic' schwas can be reflected in the orthography, for example <*wǣpn* ~ *wǣpen*> 'weapon' < Goth. **wēpn*, ON *vapn*, Modern Icelandic *vopn*. As shown convincingly by Fulk (1992, 2007), the monosyllabic forms are most common in poems that 'have traditionally been regarded as likeliest to be relatively early compositions' (Fulk 2007: 306). Other items that can have monosyllabic realisations in verse are *bēcn* 'monument', *hleahtor* 'laughter', *winter* 'winter', *wundor* 'wonder'. The 'parasitic' schwas in such words survive to this day, and they alternate with syllabic sonorants in fast speech.

Elision involves the deletion of an unstressed final [-ə] before another vowel to the right; the avoidance of two unstressed vowels in hiatus is common cross-linguistically; PDE disallows word-internal adjacency of two vowels, of which the first one is schwa or *any* short vowel.[10] As noted in 7.6, the orthographic evidence for unstressed vowel elision goes back to OE; for example, the 'correct', expected forms of the verbs in <*wene ic*> 'I hope', <*sæġde ic*> 'I said' appear as <*wen ic*, <*sæġd ic*>. In the verse final [-ə] elision appears to have been optional.

(11) OE elision optional; ambiguous scansions:

ǣnn*e* *o*fer ȳðe [s w w **w** / s w] or [s w w / s w] = S W / S W
Beowulf 46a
'alone over waves'

wanod*e* *o*nd wyrde [s-w w **w** / s w] or [s-w w /s w] = S W /S W
Beowulf 1337a
'lessened and destroyed'

rǣsd*e* *o*n ðone rōfan [s w w w **w** / s w] or [s w w w / s w] = S W /S W
Beowulf 2690a
'rushed at the renowned'

[10] Allerton (2000) discusses the current tendency to avoid such sequences in morphologically complex words and across word boundaries in BrE.

The examples in (11) illustrate that in most cases where elision can be posited, the verse will be well-formed with or without the extra weak syllable, so the performance/realisation of the verse is open-ended. The choice can be based on the relative frequency of either option, so that for *Beowulf* 2690a the second option, with a shorter dip in the first foot ([s w w / s w]), would be statistically better attested. Alternatively, one can argue that elision would be avoided in the formal declamatory style of oral poetry, giving preference to the first, more extended-dip scansions in (11).

A more detailed account of OE verse was given here partly because of the general unfamiliarity of the topic, and partly because OE verse provides a basis for comparison with later forms of versification, the topic of our next section.

10.2.2 Continuity and reinvention of alliterative versification in ME[11]

The 1065 poem *The Death of Edward* is the last composition that can be described reasonably as belonging to the Classical metrical tradition of Anglo-Saxon versification. Very revealing in this respect are the statistics and the comments presented in Cable (1991: 54–5). He notes one single metrically dubious verse (*soþfæste sawle* 'soothfast soul' (28a)) in the sixty-eight verses of *The Death of Edward*, while on the other side of the 1066 chronological divide the next extant poem with prominent alliteration, *Durham*, composed c. 1100, shows a very high level of unmetricality. In *Durham* 38.1 per cent of the forty-two verses fail to conform to the classical rules. Thus, while the cataclysmic effect of the Norman Conquest with respect to changes affecting phonology and morphosyntax can be questioned, the demarcation line in terms of versification modes is clearer, at least within the inevitable limitations imposed by the surviving texts.

The absence of records showing that alliterative verse continued to be composed after the Conquest leaves us in the dark as to the familiarity and popularity of this kind of versification in the next two centuries. Some superficial formal similarities, such as the use of alliteration and free distribution of unstressed syllables, have been seen as a link between some late tenth-century Ælfrician prose texts and early ME verse compositions such as *The Proverbs of Alfred*, *The Worcester Fragments of the Soul's Address to the Body*, *The Bestiary* and Lagamon's *Brut*. However, the link is tenuous, and positing continuity of an oral poetic form on the basis of vague analogy to literary prose is unjustified, as Fulk (2004) has

[11] This section uses material and arguments from Minkova (2009a, 2009b).

argued persuasively. It is much more probable, though not testable because of the nature of oral traditions, that a body of alliterative verse compositions did exist in the twelfth and thirteenth centuries. The early ME compositions mentioned above are 'hybrids' both in structure and genealogy: they mix rhyme, alliteration and syllable-counting in often erratic patterns, and they combine features of the traditional oral alliterative versification with the more literary features of rhyme and syllable-counting which were gaining prestige in the Anglo-Norman cultural setting.

In the fourteenth century a significant portion of the literary activity in many northern, western and south-western areas was channelled into the composition of alliterative verse, culminating in masterpieces like *Winner and Waster* (*W&W*), *Sir Gawain and the Green Knight* (*SGGK*), *The Wars of Alexander* (*WA*), *Piers Plowman* (*PP*) and *The Alliterative Morte Arthure* (*MA*). These works are associated with a literary period in English known as the *Alliterative Revival.* The Revival flourished for about a century, starting around the 1330s and dying out in Scotland in the fifteenth century.

If we accept the logical premise that a body of oral alliterative verse must have existed in post-Conquest England continuously until the fourteenth century, our description of the meter of the Revival metrical forms can start with a comparison of the features of OE verse with the features of ME alliterative verse. Before proceeding with the structural similarities and differences, we will survey the ways in which the technique of the ME versifiers matched or differed from the technique of the Old English scops. The patterns of onset identity observed in OE, shown in (6a–c), were still present in ME: singleton onsets have to be identical, different vowels may alliterate with each other, and [sp-, st-, sk-] alliterate cohesively. However, all three patterns are subject to further qualifications in ME which reflect new phonological variables in the language. Singleton onsets have to alliterate in ME verse, but some poets or copyists resort to dialectal borrowing in alliteration, so we find /f-/ : /v-/, where /v-/ is the south and south-west Midlands pronunciation of /f-/, and /w-/ : /v-/, also dialectal variants of the fricative in initial position in the south (see 4.4). Another innovation is the occasional matching of <h->-initial words with vowel-initial words, indicating the instability of onset /h-/ (see 5.1.3).

One of the most interesting aspects of the choice of alliterating words in ME verse is the systematic avoidance of vowel alliteration. In OE the rate of vowel alliteration is within the expected range: 15.5 per cent of the lines in *Beowulf* have vowel alliteration. The ME corpus shows a dramatic drop in vowel alliteration, ranging from 1.1 per cent to at most 5 per cent of the lines, which is significantly below the expected random distribution of alliteration on consonants vs alliteration on vowels.[12] Moreover, even in the rare cases of vowel alliteration, the poets strongly prefer identical vowels, as illustrated in (12).

(12) ME alliteration on identical vowels:

And his **a**rsounz al **a**fter / and his **a**þel skyrtes,	*SGGK* 171
There **a**lienes, in **a**bsence / of **a**ll men of armes	*MA* 273
Offirs all his **o**ld gods / his **ho**nour þam thankis	*WA* 3658
Of **A**ppils & **a**lmands / & **a**ll manere of frutis	*WA* 4718

The rationale for these choices is best explained with reference to the obligatory nature of stressed-syllable onsets in OE (see the discussion of (6b) in 10.2.1). In OE the glottal stop provided the basis of onset identity in orthographically vowel-initial stressed syllables. In ME the realisation of a glottal stop in the same position became optional. Anglo-Norman does not mandate a filled onset and it is likely that this could influence the realisation of vowel-initial stressed native words too, especially for non-monolingual speakers. Although some residual mixing of vowels across the line survives, loanword phonology would be an incentive for the selection of identical vowels.

Another aspect of ME alliteration that goes hand in hand with the change in the onset-constraint on stressed syllables is the so-called *Liaison Alliteration* or *Stab der Liaison*, illustrated in (13).

(13) Liaison Alliteration (*Stab der Liaison*):

'Þat schal I **t**elle þe **t**rwly,' quoþ þa**t o**þer þenne	*SGGK* 2444
Takis þam with him to his **t**ent & þam a**t e**se makis	*WA* 1955
Vmquile he **n**oys as a **n**owte, as a **n**ox quen he lawes	*WA* 4871

In these examples the poet relies on resyllabification within the clitic phrase: the clitic coda becomes an onset to the stressed vowel-initial heads in the groups *that other*, *at ease*, *an ox*. That onset is then the one that carries the alliteration, as in ***tell***, ***truly***: *(tha)****tother***, ***take***, ***tent***: *(a)****tease***, ***noys*** 'annoys', ***nowte*** 'bull': *(a)****nox***. The reality of this reassignment in speech can be confirmed independently; for example, the phrase '*at an oven*' is attested in the surnames *Roger atte* **N***ovene of Walyngford* (1323), *Rico ate* **N***ouene* (1327) (MED entry under 'oven'). No such examples are found in OE verse, which suggests that the resyllabification in ME is enabled by an ongoing change in the realisation stressed vowel-initial words.

[12] See the discussion in Minkova (2003: 239–40 and *passim*).

The speech-based innovative alliterative techniques discussed here point to the survival of a strong oral component in ME alliterative verse. This is not to say that the visual image of a letter can be excluded completely from the alliterative techniques, especially as 'orality' may be more a matter of delivery than of composition. In other words, one should ask the sceptical question, how much of alliteration was 'literal', also ME 'letterall' (1450)? By definition, all of the alliterative material we have inherited has survived by virtue of being written down or copied, mostly anonymously. The only reliably identifiable 'author' of OE poems was Cynewulf (post-Beowulf, pre-Alfredian, late eighth century, Mercian), who left his signature in the poems. Other attributions (Cædmon/Bede, Wulfstan, Aldhelm) are questionable. All of the major Anglo-Saxon poems are anonymous, and so are the ME alliterative poems. Authorial anonymity is not synonymous with oral composition, however, and the possibility of influence of the written shape of words on the selection of matching onsets cannot be fully excluded.

Already in OE, the difference between a letter and the sound it represents would have been familiar to any well-educated cleric. Two aspects of the ME alliterative technique suggest that the identity of letter-shape should also be considered in evaluating the poets' craft. The first one is the apparent stress-promotion of prefixes as in *rewarde*: ***R**ome*; *persayfede*: ***P**eter*, where the allure of letter-sameness seems a better explanation of the matching than positing initial stress on **pérceived* or **réward*. The second point, admittedly negative, is the absence of 'erroneous' alliteration of consonants that are phonetically very close. If, as noted above, cross-dialectal /f-/ : /v-/ and /w-/ : /v-/ could be matched in alliteration, we would expect highly confusable spirants in the same dialect, such as /f/ and /θ/ to be paired in alliteration, albeit rarely.[13] That such alliterations are not found in ME suggests that the poets or copyists tolerated letter over sound identity and cross-dialectal forms, but they did not deviate from the sound-identity norm if the letters were not identical.

A comparison of the OE and the ME alliterative long line reveals both similarities and differences. The basic descriptive features of the Classical OE compositions, listed in (1), are all identifiable in ME too: a line consists of a-verses and b-verses, each verse has a minimum of two feet and four positions, each foot contains an ictic (S) and a non-ictic (W) position, the first foot is stronger than the second and the verses are

[13] On the confusability of /f/ -/θ/ and <th->-fronting see Wells (1982, II: 329); Tabain (1998).

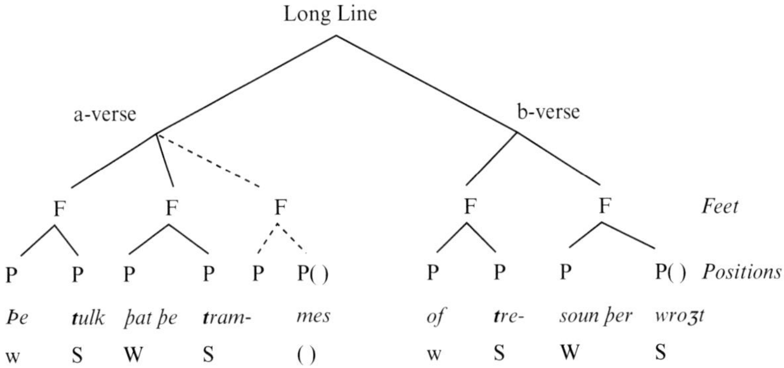

Figure 10.3 Structure of the Middle English alliterative long line in fourteenth-century verse:
S = a strong position, W = a weak position filled by two or three syllables, w = a weak position filled by a single syllable, ( ) = an optional verse-final w(eak) position

linked by alliteration. Within these general properties, however, there are important aspects in which the two traditions differ.[14] Using the same primes as Figure 10.2, Figure 10.3 shows the structure of the ME alliterative long line.

In addition to the familiar line-constituents – a-verse, b-verse, feet and positions – the ME material justifies separate treatment of weak metrical positions filled by a single syllable, which we can mark as [w], and a 'strong' dip, corresponding to the 'expanded' weak position of OE, marked [W]. The parentheses at the end of the verse indicate that a single unstressed syllable at the end of the verse is not part of the template – it is 'extrametrical'.

Now we turn to the metrical frames in ME, bearing in mind that each generalisation covers only statistically dominant attestations. The first, and probably most conspicuous metrical difference between Old and ME, recognised by several generations of metrists, is that within the ME alliterative long line the a-verse and the b-verse are rhythmically different. The concrete manifestations of the rhythmic difference are shown in (14) and (15).

[14] Imprecise as it is to refer to the entirety of the OE poetic records as fitting a single monolithic metrical template, it is even more of an idealisation to subsume all ME alliterative compositions under a single template. Some differences are ignored here in favour of presenting a more general schema applicable to the majority of the texts and the lines.

(14) Three alliterating S-positions in the a-verse in ME:

And **m**eled þus **m**uch with his **m**uthe / as ȝe **m**ay now here *SGGK* 447

A lowde **l**aȝtir he **l**oȝe / and to þe **l**ede said *WA* 96

To **l**aite þaire **l**ord at was **l**ost / with **l**atis vnblythe *WA* 152

First, the a-verse is heavier than the b-verse because it allows up to three strong metrical positions, and all three may, but do not have to alliterate. Verses with three ictic positions are known as 'extended'. The dashed line for the rightmost branch in the a-verse in Figure 10.3 marks the optionality of the third foot. Extended verses are avoided in the second half-line.

Second, the a-verse and the b-verse differ in the distribution of W's, weak positions filled by two or more unstressed syllables: two W's are common in the a-verse, while the percentage of b-verses with two heavy dips is very low.

(15) Avoidance of two strong dips in the b-verse:

And bot the **l**engthe of a **l**aunde / thies **l**ordes bytwene *W&W* 54

Quen he was **s**emely vp **s**et / with **s**eptour in hand *WA* 198

With alle þe **m**ete and þe **m**irþe / þat **m**en couþe avyse *SGGK* 45

The b-verse is more tightly constrained. It requires two lifts. As in OE, the first of these lifts carries the obligatory alliteration, but unlike the OE schema, alliteration on the second ictus is not unusual.

(16) Second ictus alliterating in the b-verse:

In a **s**omer **s**eson, / whan **s**ofte was the **s**onne *PP* P.1

Gawayn **g**ly3t on þe **g**ome / þat **g**odly hym **g**ret *SGGK* 842

Double-**f**elde, as hit **f**allez, / and **f**ele kyn **f**ischez *SGGK* 890

The stricter limits on the arrangement of syllables in the b-verse warrants a summary statement on the types that can be labelled 'metrical'. The optional verse-final weak syllables are excluded.

(17) Metrical patterns in the b-verse in decreasing frequency:

w S W S:	of trésoun þer wroȝt	*SGGK* 3b
S W S:	flákerande with wýnges	*W&W* 92b
W S w S:	vndyr the **h**éuene rýche	*MA* 108b
W S S:	that one the **b**ent houes	*W&W* 105b

The rare types are listed in (18), again in decreasing frequency. Only the types attested above 1 per cent are illustrated.

(18) Rare or unmetrical b-verse types:

W S W S:	when the **p**úrpos was takyn	*MA* 415b
w S w S:	with **g**éntill knyghtes	*MA* 372b

S w S
w S S
w S w S w S
S w S w

Clearly, the composition of alliterative verse in England in the fourteenth century is based on a system that imitates closely, but does not replicate the design of OE verse. There are new techniques of alliteration, new constraints on the length of the verses and the distribution of syllables in the dips. In addition to the overall rhythmic asymmetry of the a- and b-verses, the preferred verse-internal cadences are different. One of the most striking discontinuities is the rarity in ME of four-syllable verses, which, though not *the* most frequent type in OE, still make up about one-quarter of the verse data in OE (see 10.2.1). Another remarkable difference is that the pattern **S w S w** is unmetrical in Middle English, while this is a common (sub-)A-Type in OE.[15] The common OE (sub-)B-Type **w S w S** is at most marginally metrical in ME. Note that in both of these types the intervals between single strong and weak syllables are identical; these are types where the foot structure can be labelled purely trochaic or purely iambic. This throws into relief the *avoidance* of simple stress-alternating rhythm: the presence of a 'strong' dip is practically obligatory, making this a salient characteristic of this tradition of versification, both in comparison with OE, and in comparison with the contemporary iambic meters.

10.3 Introduction of rhyme, syllable-counting and binary foot structure

Grounded in the prosodic pattern of stress on the first root syllable, alliteration as a cohesive device survived in Middle English, but at the same time new modes of versification based on rhyme and syllable counting were gaining popularity. Early instances of occasional ornamental rhyming can be found in the OE alliterative corpus.

(19) Rhyme as ornamentation in OE alliterative verse:
fylle ge<u>fǣgon</u>; / **f**ægere ge<u>þǣgon</u> *Beowulf* 1014
'rejoiced in the feast / partook of it with relish'
Byrhtnoð maþe<u>lode</u> / **b**ord hafe<u>node</u> *Maldon* 42
'Byrhnoth spoke / raised his shield'

[15] The S w S w subtype in OE amounts to 16 per cent of the data in Hutcheson (1995: 175).

Such lines are rare and it is clear that rhyming, exact and inexact, including assonance, was not an obligatory cohesive device. One famous exception is the so-called *Rhyming Poem*, which combines alliteration and rhyme, sometimes in consecutive lines, in what has often been described as a tour de force of metrical technique.

(20) Combining alliteration and rhyme in OE (*The Rhyming Poem*):
Scrifen **scr**ād glād / þurh ge**sc**ād in brād;
wæs on **l**agustrēame lād, / þær me **l**eoþu ne biglād
Hæfde ic **h**ēanne hād, / ne was mē in **h**ealle gād 13–15
'The appointed ship glided through the distance into the broad sea;
there was a path upon the ocean stream, where I was not without guidance.
I had high rank; I lacked nothing in the hall'

Scealcas wǣron scearpe, / **sc**yl wæs hearpe,
hlūde hlynede, / **hl**eoþor dynede 27–8
'The servants were active, / the harp was resonant,
loudly rang; / sound pealed'

Swā nū **w**orld wendeþ, / **w**yrde sendeþ 59
'thus now the world goes, fate brings'

The West European tradition of rhyming is associated with Church Latin, starting with some rather crude correspondences in the second century AD. McKie describes three stages in the acceptance and spread of rhyme in England:

> Initially, rhyme was imported from Church Latin by Anglo-Saxon versifiers steeped in the culture of the Church. . . . Yet such use was occasional, and in no sense prosodic. In the second stage, under the pressure of linguistic changes brought about by the Conquest, narrative verse in rhymed couplets emerged. . . . In the final stage . . . the simplicity of couplet-rhyme was overtaken by the more highly prized complexity of stanzaic rhyme-patterning. (McKie 1997: 829)

The Latin 'rhythmi', variously impure, are an important source for the adoption of rhyme in Old English. The memory-aiding nature of rhyming also contributes to the process. A good example of how the Latin practice of rhyming was taken over by the Anglo-Saxon clerics is the translation of a Latin proverb.

(21) Rhyming in Latin-English translation:
Ardor frigesscit, nitor squalescit, amor abolescit, lux obtenebrescit.

Hat ācolað, / hwit āsolað,
leof ālaðaþ, / leoht āðystrað
'Heat cools / white(ness) tarnishes
Love becomes hateful, / light darkens'

By the eleventh century end-rhyme had become an essential feature of Medieval Latin verse. That feature is never absent from Old French verse. English versifiers, who were probably also good Latinists, could not escape the influence of rhyme – they made increasing use of rhyme for both aesthetic and mnemonic purposes. A possibly humorous entry in *The Anglo-Saxon Chronicle* for 1076 tells us: *he [Raulf] þa lædde þæt wif to Norðwic, þær wæs þæt brȳdealo, þæt wæs manegra manna bealo* ('He led the wife to Norwich, there was that bridal that was the destruction of many men'). The early rhymes were commonly *feminine rhymes*: a stressed syllable followed by an unstressed syllable, and often involved inflectional and derivational suffixes, as in the examples in (21). In the twelfth century the practice of rhyming was firmly established in England, its popularity enhanced by the troubadour poets patronised by Henry II and Eleanor of Aquitaine (McKie 1997: 828). In bi- and trilingual England the versifiers sometimes mixed languages in choosing the rhyming words: '*in tabulis / la vile de Paris / so wel me is*'.[16] As the use of rhyme spread, the matching was perfected, and the identity of endings became a way of keeping verse lines together, giving rise to the *couplet*.

(22) The short rhymed couplet in early ME:
Ure feder þet in heouene is,
þet is al soð ful iwis,
weo moten to þes wordes iseon
þet to liue and to saule gode beon *Paternoster* (12th c.)[17]

By the beginning of the thirteenth century the rhyming couplet had become a form completely native to English versifiers, producing vernacular masterpieces such as the anonymous *Owl and the Nightingale*. At the same time, techniques combining alliteration and rhyme are used well into the thirteenth century, as in the lines in (23) from *The Proverbs of Alfred*.[18]

16 The macaronic example is from the love poem '*Dum ludis floribus*', cited in McKie (1997: 821). Further mixed rhyming AN-English (*et leal* 'and faithful': *it fele* 'feel it', *sovent* 'often': *ysend*), or English-Latin (*Kyng of Blys*: *virginis* 'by the Virgin'), and a discussion of code-switching in medieval English poetry is found in Schendl (2001).

17 *Old English Homilies*, First Series (Early English Text Society OS 29), p. 55.

18 Another text which famously bridges the techniques of alliteration and rhyme is

(23) Mixing alliteration and rhyme in ME:
þe **l**ond to **l**eden / mid **l**aueliche dedin 74–5
þat þe **ch**ireche habbe gryþ. And þe **ch**eorl beo in fryþ 87–8

Histories of English versification frequently emphasise 'the pressure of linguistic changes brought about by the Conquest' (McKie 1997: 829) as the impetus behind the second stage in the evolution of rhyming. Optimally, there is a 'fit' between metrical form(s) selected by an individual artist or a group of people and the language (see 10.2). However, there is nothing 'suboptimal' in OE in terms of availability of rhyming words, the ease of counting syllables or placing beats at regular intervals. Therefore the repeated references to 'language change' are too general; not every type of linguistic change can be associated with the adoption of rhyme in English.

The relationship between the loss of inflections in ME and the acceptance of rhyme is dubious; numerous verse traditions, including the oldest known tradition of rhyming in Chinese, dating back to the fifth century BC (McKie 1997), employ rhyme. The gradual perfection of the rhyming patterns in Latin in the first millennium proceeded without the crutches of newly developed analyticity, and rhyming characterises the verse tradition in a strongly synthetic language like Russian. The very existence of occasional rhymes, including some monosyllabic or *masculine* rhymes in OE, makes the dependence of rhyming on loss of inflections a difficult hypothesis to defend. The borrowing of Romance vocabulary is a different matter; the presence in the language of adjectives and nouns with final stress and the fact that many polysyllabic loanwords had alternating stress might indeed have facilitated rhyming by increasing the pool of available items, but it should not be considered the determining factor. Twelfth- and thirteenth-century rhyming compositions, for example *Poema Morale*, *Havelok the Dane*, *The Owl and the Nightingale*, use vocabulary that is almost exclusively Germanic. The primary reason why rhyme became the verse-line marker of choice in ME was the cultural model of Latin and Anglo-Norman.

Another important innovation in ME versification was the introduction of syllable-counting, also an imported metrical feature. Verses of equal numbers of syllables, 'isosyllabic' verses, are found in OE poetry, but their recurrence was not structurally regulated; a verse could have from a minimum of four to fourteen syllables (see 10.2.1). The first notable compositions based on the iteration of isosyllabic lines in ME

Lawman's *Brut*, where one finds 'pure' alliterative lines, 'pure' rhyming couplets and hybrid lines such as: *he is **k**ing & heo is quene; of þine **k**ume nis na wene* (14,046).

are the mid-twelfth-century *Poema Morale*, which does what it says – gives moral advice in 270–400 lines, depending on the manuscript – and the autograph 19,000-line long poem *The Ormulum* (late twelfth century). The pieces are monotonously regular, with fifteen syllables in each long line, divided by a caesura after the eighth syllable. The form is known as *septenary* or *septenarius*, a popular form in classical Latin versification, illustrated with the first lines of these poems in (24).

(24) The septenary in early Middle English:

Ic em nu alder þene ic wes,	a wintre ent a lare	*Poema Morale* 1
'I am now older than I was	in years and in knowledge'	
Þiss boc iss nemmnedd Orrmulum	forrþi þatt Orrm itt wrohhte	*Preface* 1
'this book is named Ormulum	because Orm wrote it'	

These compositions were the work of highly trained monastics who must have had exposure to the Latin form, which the monk Orm, for one, applied with considerable care and precision. The septenary line can also be analysed as a sequence of four and three iambic feet or eight plus seven syllables, with a special constraint at the right edge of the long line: the fourteenth syllable is always heavy and it is invariably followed by a weak syllable which belongs to the same word.[19] The vocabulary of both texts is almost exclusively Germanic.

Another schema based on the iteration of isosyllabic lines is the octosyllabic line, practised with various precision from the end of the twelfth century onwards. The earliest extended poem of lasting literary value which is in octosyllabic rhymed couplets is *The Owl and the Nightingale*, whose composition is dated early rather than late in the period 1189–1216 (Stanley 1972: 19). The opening lines of the poem are given in (25).

(25) *The Owl and the Nightingale*, lines 1–6:
ICH was in one sum*ere* dale,
In one suþe diȝ*ele* hale,
Iherd*e* ich holde grete tale
an Hul*e* and one niȝtingale.
Þat plait was stif & starc & strong,

[19] The rightmost edges of any type of verse are known to be especially rigid metrically (see note 6). In *The Ormulum* the letter of the fifteenth-syllable vowel is always <-e(-)>, most likely a kind of schwa. The metrical significance of this fact is discussed in Minkova (1996: 102–4).

sum wile soft*e* & lud among;
(Stanley 1972: 49)

In addition to the prevocalic elision of <-e>, as in *iherde ich* 'heard I' (3), *hule and* 'owl and' (4), and so on, the octosyllabic frame suggests the possibility of word-internal weak-vowel syncope, as in *sumere* 'summer' (1), though both in this case and in the case of diȝ*ele* 'hidden' either elision or syncope will get to the right number of syllables.

Exact syllable-counting cannot be claimed for all of the verse written outside the ME 'Alliterative Revival' tradition. Even the highly skilled early poets, and the author of *The Owl and the Nightingale* was certainly one of them, allow syllabic ambiguity and occasional clear violations of the syllabic count. But the target of isosyllabicity is undeniable: even a conservative approach to the flexibility of the final unstressed vowel in early ME shows that the syllabic regularity in this text reaches 70 per cent. A less restrictive approach to the paraphonology of the unstressed vowels will undoubtedly indicate even higher regularity. The issue of counting syllables will be revisited after a discussion of a related feature of ME syllable-counting poetry, namely the organisation of syllables into metrical feet.

The distribution and the syllabic content of weak and strong positions in OE verse was flexible, and it is only after disassociating the numerical correspondence of syllable(s) from metrical positions that we can get to the abstraction of W S and S W metrical sequences, as in (5) above. Verses exhibiting one-to-one correspondence of syllable to position did exist in OE, but they were not the statistical norm. The adoption of isosyllabic versification in ME is linked to the rise of a new structural component of verse: the binary foot. Using the terminology of classical Greek and Latin versification, we will refer to the unit of a S(trong)/ictic + W(eak)/non-ictic position as a *trochee* (S W), and to the unit of a weak + strong position as an *iamb* (W S).[20] The two metrical feet have ready counterparts in the prosody of speech: unprefixed disyllabic words (*silver*, *scatter*, *holy*, *seldom*) and monosyllables followed by clitics (*heard it*, *milk and*, *found them*) are trochaic, prefixed verbs, adverbs, and groups with monosyllabic clitics (*beseech*, *outdid*, *about*, *the king*) are iambic. In OE verse the occurrence of the left-strong type (S W) was more frequent than the (W S) type.

[20] Originally, the terms are applied to quantitative meter, where S stands for 'long' and W for 'short' syllables. Tri-positional feet: S W W (dactyl) and W W S (anapest), will not be discussed here, because regular dactylic and anapestic versification in English is outside the scope of this chapter.

In Middle English isosyllabic verse the iamb became the dominant metrical foot, making it the cadence of choice for English poetry for the entire second millennium. The regular alternation of weak and strong prominences, each one associated with a single syllable, is characteristic even of the earliest post-Conquest syllable-counting compositions such as *The Ormulum* and *The Owl and the Nightingale.*

(26) Iambic footing in early ME verse:

W	S /	W	S /	W	S /	W	S /
An	*énn-*	*gell*	*comm*	*off*	*béoff-*	*ness*	*ærd;*
'An	angel		came	from	heaven's		region

W	S /	W	S /	W	S /	(W)
inn	*á-*	*ness*	*wé-*	*ress*	*hé-*	*we*
in	one		man's		likeness'	*Ormulum* 3336–7

The lines in (26) illustrate the default matching of syllables to positions: strong (S), or even, positions are filled by stressed syllables: *énngell* 'angel', *béoffness* 'heaven's', *áness* '(of) one', *wéress* 'man's', *héwe* 'likeness' are aligned with S W positions. Lexical monosyllables – *comm* 'came', *ærd* 'region' – also occupy S positions. The unstressed syllables of disyllabic lexical words and function words – *an, off, inn* – are placed in weak (W) or odd-numbered positions. Some derivational morphemes such as *-dom, -ing, -like, -ness* can be treated as second elements of compounds and like them, they can fill a strong metrical position; compare (27a) and (27b), where the former illustrates the S-matching of *-dom.*

(27) Derivational suffixes in strong metrical position in early ME iambic verse:

And ec forr þatt he wollde swa

(a)	W	S	W	S	W	S
	Þurrh	*hiss*	*þeww-*	***dom***	*ut*	*lesen*
	'through	his	thraldom		release'	

(b)	W	S	W	S	W	S	W	S	
	Off	*def-*	*less*	*þeww-*	*dom*	*al*	*le*	*þa*	
	'from	devil's		thraldom		all		then'	*Ormulum* 3618–20

As in OE (see 10.2.1, (4)), compounds such as *twifald* 'twofold', *mannkinn* 'mankind', *summwhatt* 'somewhat' allow the placement of either the first or the second element in a strong metrical position; compare Orm's *All mánnkinn forr to lokenn* (3283) with *Off all mannkínn onn eorþe* (3273).

An important principle of matching speech prosody to meter relevant to the establishment of a binary foot structure in English verse is that the matching of monosyllabic lexical items to metrical positions is flexible. Monosyllables in isolation do not really have 'stress'; their prominence is determined in relation to adjacent syllables. In the early isosyllabic verse placing a prosodically weak monosyllable in S is not a violation of the metrical template, as in lines 3409 and 3411 of *The Ormulum* in (28), where ***and*** in line 3409 and ***þurrh*** in line 3411 fill strong positions.

(28) Unstressed monosyllables in strong positions in *The Ormulum*:

& tokenn innwarrdlike godd;

W	S	W	S	W	S	(W)
To	*lo*	*fenn*	***&***	*to*	*þann*	*kenn*
'To	praise		and	to	thank'	

All þatt teȝȝ haffdenn herrd off himm;

W	S	W	S	W	S	
&	*se*	*ȝhenn*	***þurrh***	*his*	*are*	
'and	seen		through	his	grace'	3408–11

The observation that monosyllables are flexible in syllable-counting binary-footed meters has been around for a long time. George Gascoine (1575: 469) noted that 'woordes of one syllable will more easily fall to be shorte or long as occasion requireth, or wilbe adapted to become circumflexe or of an indifferent sound'.[21] The free correspondence between monosyllabic words and metrical positions in the pentameter was formalised as the *Monosyllabic Rule* in generative metrics. The rule permits the scansion of lines such as in (29) as fully metrical, though the italicised words correspond to odd-numbered positions in the metrical template (see 10.5).

(29) The Monosyllabic Rule in syllable-counting verse (Chaucer):
Ne no *man* shal unto his felawe ryde
But o *cours* with a sharpe ygrounde spere *KnT* 2548–9
I wole han twelf *pens*, though that she be wood *FrT* 1576

[21] From 'Certayne Notes of Instruction' (Gascoine 1575: 465–73).

The fashion for iambic versification in ME was another cultural import from the Continent, but, as noted above, it could not have been adopted with such ease if the prosodic conditions had not been favourable. Again, the correlation between the prosodic shape of the majority of the vocabulary items and the choice of verse form was recognised early. Gascoine's advice to prospective versifiers is:

> I thinke it not amisse to forewarne you that you thrust as few wordes of many sillables into your verse as may be: and hereunto I might alledge many reasons: first the most auncient English wordes are of one sillable, so that the more monasyllables that you use, the truer Englishman you shall seeme, and the lesse you shall smell of the Inkehorne. (Gascoine 1575: 468)

The gradual loss of final <-e> and vowel syncope in inflectional endings made the native vocabulary predominantly monosyllabic, allowing flexibility in the prosody-to-meter matching. Increased use of prepositions compensating for inflectional loss created new W S clitic groups: *at níght, to rést, with chéer.* Prefixed verbs and adverbs supplied another set of natural iambic structures: *befóre, forgíve, perfórm, asléep.* Phrasal stress continued to be right-strong; phrases made up of stressed monosyllables easily match an iambic foot: *five bóoks, tall mén, full glád, God knóws.* The poets also draw from an inventory of handy 'fillers', semantically dispensable monosyllabic words, for example *and, now, for, full, some*; past tense *did* marking; and the grammatically redundant 'pleonastic' *this, that.* Thus, although individual underived disyllabic words (*summer, weapon, silver*) had root-initial stress, in connected speech metrical W S cadences were frequent and easy to construct; this permits an effortless 'fit' between language and the iambic meter.[22]

The gradual adoption of isosyllabic versification in early ME proceeds against the background of unstable realisation of unstressed vowels. Some accommodations, such as pre-vocalic elision of <e->, are commonly recognised in the scholarship on the history of English metrical forms (see (25) above, 7.6). Some further paraphonological options whose application affects the syllabic count in a verse line are illustrated with Chaucerian examples in (30)–(35) below.

An extension of the pre-vocalic loss of final <-e> in disyllables is the

[22] The lasting appeal of the iambic form is recognised by the earliest English prosodists. Gascoine (1575: 466) writes: 'note you that commonly now a dayes in english rimes (for I dare not cal them English verses) we use none other order but a foote of two sillables, wherof the first is depressed or made short, & the second is elevate or made long: and that sound or scanning continueth throughout the verse'.

loss of final <-e> in monosyllabic clitics followed by a vowel-initial word. This can be termed **apocope** within the domain of the clitic group. After apocope, resyllabification places the consonant of the clitic in the onset of the following syllable. Apocope is more likely when the lexical head starts with an unstressed syllable as in (30a).

(30) Apocope within clitic groups:
(a) *Th*estaat, *th*array, the nombre, and eek the cause *GP* 716
*T*espien where he myghte wedded be *MerT* 1257
(b) In th*e e*nde of which an ounce, and namoore *CYT* 1266
And to th*e y*mage of Juppiter hem sente *SNT* 364

Apocope is a remedy against a string of unstressed syllables and against onsetless syllables; it is confirmed by spellings such as <*thestaat*>, <*thespien*> for 'the estaat', 'to espien' in the Chaucerian manuscripts, as well as by the poet's metrical practice even when the scribes preserved <-e>, as in *the ende* (*CYT* 1266) and *the ymage* (*SNT* 364) in (30b).

Another phonological option is **synizesis**, the fusion of two syllables into one, when an unstressed [ɪ, ʊ] is followed by an unstressed vowel.

(31) Synizesis ([ɪ, ʊ] + [ə]):
Nowher so bis*y a* man as he ther nas
And yet he semed bis*ie*r than he was *GP* 321–2
This Pardoner hadde heer as yel*ow a*s wex *GP* 675

Loss of word-internal schwa occurs when [-ə-] is adjacent to the sonorants [r, l, m, n], as in PDE *mystery*, *summoner*, *asterisk*, *lingering*. Syncope can occur within a word or it can be triggered by a following vowel-initial or weak /h/-initial unstressed word.

(32) Contraction/syncope ([ə] + [r, l, m, n]):
And everemoore he hadde a sov(*e*)*r*eyn prys *GP* 67
By wat(*e*)r *he* sente hem hoom to every lond *GP* 400
Which cause is of my deth for sor(*o*)we and thought *Tr* I 579

Like apocope and synizesis, word-internal syncope avoids the placement of two syllables in a single metrical position.

Decisions on syllabicity in (31)–(32) rest primarily on the segmental environment of the unstressed vowel. Other paraphonological adaptations can be triggered by the inherent low prosodic prominence of a word, or by the position of schwa in the word, without reference to what the adjacent vowels or consonants are. Predictably, lack of stress on function words, pronouns and auxiliaries will increase the probability of dropping -*e*.

(33) Loss of <-e> in words of low prosodic prominence:
That down were̱ sent in scornynge of nature *Tr* I 105
As don thise̱ foles that hire̱ sorwes eche *Tr* I 705

In speech, long strings of unstressed syllables are rhythmically undesirable; instability of final *-e* in potentially trisyllabic words with initial stress is therefore expected, see 7.6 (20).

(34) Final schwa loss in trisyllabic words:
Lest it were wist on any máner*e* syde *Tr* I 321
And of som goodly ánswer*e* yow purchace *Tr* II 1125
He somwhat is fro wépyng*e* now withdrawe *Tr* IV 886

Within the native vocabulary trisyllabic words are either compounds, or they are inflected forms of originally disyllabic roots. Therefore, the processes of pre-vocalic elision and trisyllabic loss may affect final vowels in which the unstressed vowel is an inflection.

(35) Inflectional loss of schwa:
With buttok*es* brode, and brestes rounde and hye *RT* 3975
For I lou*ed* ek, though ich vnworthi were *Tr* IV 329

ME isosyllabic verse was composed and copied at a time when the syllabicity of the inflections *-ed*, *-es*, *-eth* still depended on the prosodic and segmental context. Inflectional syncope is more likely in a disyllabic stem, in elision environments, and depends also on the nature of the stem-final consonant: liquids leading nasals, followed by fricatives and stops.[23]

Clearly, statistics on the strictness of syllable-counting will differ depending on the way the optional syllables are treated. The uncertainties are both linguistic and textual. Linguistically, a decision on what counts as a syllable hangs on the application or non-application of paraphonological options. The presumed dialect and chronology of the poem and the modes of its transmission are also barriers to ironclad conclusions: what we have in the extant texts are often copies of poems, not authorial compositions. Random survival of variant texts, possibly influenced by intermediate oral transmission from memory, is another obstacle. With all of these caveats in mind, it is still reasonable to describe the development of new metrical modes in ME as resting on

[23] These results for the weak preterits are reported in Minkova (2009c: 325–31). For earlier verse attestations of syncope in *-es* see Fitzgerald (2008) and Putter (2005: 292, esp. fn. 22). The evidence from syllable-counting verse is supported by scribal evidence for inflectional syncope (see LALME vol. III, questionnaire items 56, 59, 60 and vol. IV: 108–14).

three important innovations: the extended use of rhyme as a cohesive structural device, the adoption of syllable-counting and the increasingly sophisticated use of binary metric feet. Skipping over some hard questions about violations of isosyllabicity, correspondence violations, especially the difference between singly filled weak positions and doubly filled weak positions, we will move to the last section of our survey: Chaucer's metrical art.

10.4 Chaucer and the invention of the iambic pentameter

The poetic work of Geoffrey Chaucer (?1342–1400) is universally recognised as the highest achievement of Middle English isosyllabic versification. In the *Introduction to The Man of Law's Tale* the author draws attention to his own success as a storyteller and famously comments on his metrical skills:

> . . . but nathelees certeyn
> I kan right now no thrifty tale seyn
> That Chaucer, thogh he kan but lewedly
> On metres and on rymyng craftily,
> Hath seyd hem in swich Englissh as he kan
> Of olde tyme, as knoweth many a man. *MLI* 45–50

The obligatory modesty convention forces Chaucer to play down his verse-craft, which in his words *he kan but lewedly*, 'he knows only poorly'. His protestations notwithstanding, his superior command of meter and rhyme, as well as his pioneering approach to the Continental model, have made him one of the major innovators in the history of English verse.

In some of his early work Chaucer was using a familiar verse form. He must have been acquainted with the octosyllabic line both from native and from Latin, Anglo-Norman and French versification. Trochaic or iambic tetrameter meter is widespread across the world's verse traditions. Its binarity on both the foot level and the colon level (Figure 10.1) makes it easily accessible and replicable – it is the preferred model for nursery rhymes, and it can be described as the 'unmarked' mode of footed syllable-counting meter. It is also the type of meter that can easily lapse into monotony. Fragments of Chaucer's early translation of the Romaunt of the Rose, his poem *The Book of the Duchess*, dating from 1368–9, as well as *The House of Fame*, completed 1378–80(?), are in iambic tetrameter. Chaucer approached the inherited template with originality. His lines are generally metrically smooth, the syllable count is more consistent than the earlier octosyllabic verse, allowing for occasional *headless line* (empty W position in the first foot) and a feminine rhyme, which adds an extrametrical ninth syllable at the right edge of the line. While in the previous English tetrameter compositions line-ends coincided with a major syntactic break, Chaucer diversified the rhythm by introducing a large number of run-on lines, or lines with **enjambment**, in which single syntactic units straddle two lines. In the following examples this is the case with *ne may slepe* (*BD* 22–3), *cam to do*, *take good herte* (*HF* 602–5).

(36) Enjambment in Chaucer's octosyllabic verse:
And I *ne may*, ne nyght ne morwe,
Slepe; and thus melancolye — *BD* 22–3

And whider thou shalt, and why I *cam*
To do thys, so that thou *take*
Good herte, and not for fere quake — *HF* 602–5

After Chaucer turned to the pentameter as his meter of choice, which he used in *Troilus and Criseyde* (1381–6) and *The Canterbury Tales* (1387–1400), he must have regarded the tetrameter as an inferior metrical scheme. Echoes of the tetrameter are heard in *The Tale of Sir Thopas*, a parody inserted in the *Canterbury Tales*, described by Chaucer himself as being in 'a rym I lerned longe agoon' (Pro *Thop* 709). The Host's rude interruption of the tale, dismissing it as 'rym doggerel' (*Thop* 925) and 'drasty ryming' (*Thop* 930), and his disparaging 'Thou dost noght elles but despendest tyme' (*Thop* 931), suggest that like his fictional mirror-image of a rhymester, the mature Chaucer considered the previously popular form a good target of ridicule.

There is no known body of iambic pentameter verse in English prior to Chaucer. *Troilus and Criseyde* is the first long, self-contained, finished major work in the iambic pentameter in the English language. The individual components of the iambic pentameter were not original with Chaucer: as discussed in 10.3, iambic verse had been composed in English since the end of the twelfth century, but the earlier iambic feet were used in either eight- or fourteen-syllable lines. Decasyllabic lines were known in France, Portugal and Spain, and were a popular form in fourteenth-century Italian verse, though the rhythmic contour of the Continental models was not strictly iambic. Chaucer's metrical innovation, then, consisted in combining the iambic rhythm of the English tradition with the decasyllabic line borrowed from the Continent. Chaucer himself identifies Dante as his metrical source in *The Wife of Bath's Tale*.

(37) Chaucer's familiarity with decasyllabic verse:
Wel kan the wise poete of florence,
That highte Dant, speken in this sentence.
Lo, in swich maner rym is Dantes tale . . . *WBT* 1125–7

The two main features that define the template of Chaucer's pentameter verse line are a fixed number of syllables per line and iambic feet. Ideally, each foot includes a weak syllable followed by a strong syllable. The line is often split in two parts by a **caesura**. The caesura occurs commonly after the second foot, but also (with diminishing frequency) after the third foot, the fourth and the first foot, and, occasionally, even within the third and the fourth foot. As in every other type of verse, internal line-breaks tend to coincide with syntactic breaks, but the correspondence is not obligatory.

Some of the nuances of scansion can be helpful to the reader of Chaucer's poetry. Looking at the syllabic count first, the model iambic pentameter line has ten syllables, each one of which corresponds to a single metrical position. Weak (W) and strong (S) positions alternate in strict succession. There may be an optional eleventh syllable, which is not part of the template; as in other verse-forms an unstressed syllable after the last ictus can be extrametrical; the isosyllabicity of the line is not affected by its presence or absence. The canonical iambic pentameter matching is illustrated in (38).

(38) Canonical iambic pentameter in Chaucer:

∧		∧		∧		∧		∧			Foot
W	S	W	S	W	S	W	S	W	S		Position
1	2	3	4	5	6	7	8	9	10	(11)	Syllabic count
In	*al*	*this*	*world*	*ne*	*was*	*ther*	*noon*	*hym*	*lik*		*GP* 412
I	*hold~~e~~*	*hym*	*rich~~e~~*	*al*	*hadd~~e~~*	*he*	*nat*	*a*	*sher*	*(te)*	*WBT* 1,192

The treatment of unstressed syllables follows the patterns discussed in 10.3 (30)–(35): loss of <-e> before vowels and weak <h->, synizesis and all the various contractions should be taken into consideration when scanning the line; the crossed <e->'s in *holde*, *riche*, *hadde* in *WBT* 1192 have to be elided. The basic syllabic count is not affected by extrametricality at the right edge, as the boxed eleventh syllable <-te> in *WBT* 1192, where the extra syllable is the second syllable of a feminine rhyme.

Headlessness occurs at the left edge of the line when the initial foot is missing its weak syllable. Again, this variation of the schema is shared with other types of iambic verse, resulting in seven syllables for the tetrameter line, or nine syllables for the pentameter. Headless lines must start with a stressed syllable.

(39) Headless iambic pentameter lines in Chaucer:

	^		^		^		^		^	Foot
W	S	W	S	W	S	W	S	W	S	Position
1	2	3	4	5	6	7	8	9	10	Syllabic count
Ø	*Swere*	*and*	*ly*	*en,*	*as*	*a*	*wom*	*man*	*kan*	*WBP* 228
Ø	*Wom*	*men*	*may*	*go*	*sauf*	*ly*	*up*	*and*	*doun*[24]	*WBT* 878

If a line is headless, it can never have more than ten syllables, and if a tenth syllable is present, it is extrametrical. Extrametricality and headlessness can be combined in a ten-syllable line, as in (40).

(40) Combining headlessness and extrametricality in a ten-syllable line:

	^		^		^		^		^		Foot
W	S	W	S	W	S	W	S	W	S		Position
1	2	3	4	5	6	7	8	9	10	11	Syllabic count
Ø	*'Glad*	*ly',*	*quod*	*she,*	*'sith*	*it*	*may*	*yow*	*li*	*(ke)'...*	*WBP* 188

The appearance of ten syllables in such cases is deceptive: only nine of the basic metrical positions are filled, and the lines are headless; any other scansion would result in unnatural stressing within the line, for example *gladlý*, and a strange placement of an unstressed *-e* in the strong tenth position.[25] Besides, the previous line of the couplet is: *And teche us yonge men of your praktíke*, so that **liké* would destroy the rhyme. From this follows an observation which should guide the reader in scansion: whether the leftmost position is filled or empty, the tenth position must always be matched to a stressed syllable – we return to this constraint on stress alternation in the iambic pentameter below.

Over 98 per cent of the lines in Chaucer's pentameter verse conform to the decasyllabic norm if the scansion incorporates the adjustments

[24] This is the syllabic structure of the line both in Hg and El – the two best manuscripts. Some editions have *now* inserted after *go*, a questionable emendation.

[25] The fact that the line can be scanned as fully trochaic is irrelevant; as noted above, what matters is that it is embedded in iambic metrical context.

to the syllable count described in (30)–(35) and (39)–(40). Bad lines do occur, but those are genuinely rare and attributing them to the poet or to one of his later scribes remains speculative, especially if comparing manuscripts is uninformative.

Besides isosyllabicity, the iambic template presupposes regular stress alternation: odd positions filled by unstressed syllables, and even positions by stressed syllables. With respect to this parameter too, there is variation in the realisation of the basic schema. Any deviation from the schema is a mismatch; the mismatches between stress and metrical position are known as **labelling mismatches** (Kiparsky 1977), or simply **stress mismatches**.

Stress mismatches are not of the same severity, nor are they equally tolerated across the verse line. Word-stress mismatch, for example placing *summer* in metrical W S or placing *behold* in S W metrical sequence, is more disruptive than placing *find it* in W S or *his belt* in S W, which is more disruptive than placing *brimstone* in W S, and so on. A hierarchy of stress mismatches is proposed in (49), but first we survey the distribution of mostly word-stress mismatches across Chaucer's pentameter line.

The most common type of stress mismatch, which breaks the monotony and produces a more interesting prosodic contour is the reversal of the strength relations in the first foot, known as **iambic reversal** or **trochaic substitution**. This means that an unambiguously stressed syllable is placed at the left edge of the line, followed by two unstressed syllables, resulting in what is known as a rhythmic **triple**.

(41) Trochaic substitution at the left edge of the iambic line:

^		^		^		^		^		Foot
W	**S**	W	S	W	S	W	S	W	S	Position
Un-	*der*	*his*	*belt*	*he*	*bar*	*ful*	*thrif-*	*ti-*	*ly*	*GP* 105
S	**W**	W	S	W	S	W	S	W	S	Stress

Unless one posits a completely artificial delivery: **undér his belt* . . ., the inversion in the first foot creates a triple. Trochaic substitution in the first foot must be considered a valid prosodic option even in the case of French loanwords.

(42) Trochaic substitution involving French loanwords:
(a) *Jústice* he was ful often in assise *GP* 314
Compare:
(b) Now was ther thanne a *jústice* in that toun *PhysT* 121

The type of trochaic substitution shown in (41) and (42a) is most common in the first foot; it is associated with metrical and syntactic boundaries. Post-pausal mismatches are characteristic of all types of isosyllabic meter. Predictably, the next highest incidence of trochaic substitution is in the third and the fourth foot, which corresponds to the frequent division of the Chaucerian pentameter line in colas of 2 + 3 or 3 + 2 feet.[26] Pre-pausal feet, either the last foot of the line or line-internally the last foot of the first colon, are locations where the prosodic and the metrical prominences are much more strictly matched. In Chaucer's iambic pentameter the second foot undergoes substitution rarely, in under 2 per cent of the lines (Youmans and Li 2002: 157), and when the second foot is matched to a trochaic word, it usually follows another trochee or two monosyllables.

(43) Second-foot trochaic substitution in the iambic line:
Of his *óffryng* and eek of his substaunce. *GP* 489
Whan myn *hóusbonde* is fro the world ygon *WBP* 47
Under that *cólour* hadde I many a myrthe *WBP* 405

Third- and fourth-foot substitutions are in the range of 3.6–3.7 per cent (Youmans and Li 2002: 157). As the examples in (44) show, the substitutions occur after syntactic breaks.

(44) Third- and fourth-foot trochaic substitutions:
If that I speke *áfter* my fantasye *WBP* 190
What nedeth yow, *Thómas*, to maken stryf? *SumT* 2000
The smylere with the knyf *únder* the cloke *KnT* 1999
I governed hem so wel, *áfter* my lawe *WBP* 219

Occasionally, there will be more than one reversed foot in a decasyllabic headless line, creating a strikingly different prosodic cadence in an otherwise fully iambic metrical context.

(45) Multiple substitutions in the iambic line:
Bácyns, *lávours*, er that men hem bye,
Spóones and *stóoles*, and al swich housbondrye *WBP* 287–8

Bléssinge hálles, *chámbres*, *kíchenes*, *bóures*
Cítees, *búrghes*, *cástels*, *hýe tóures* . . . *WBT* 869–70

The fifth foot disallows substitution; in practice it can accommodate only iambic sequences. In that position compounds must shift the main

[26] About half of Chaucer's pentameter lines show a syntactic break after the second foot. Statistical details and comments on the uneven distribution of inversions across the line are found in Tarlinskaja (1976: 279–80), Youmans and Li (2002: 156–8).

stress from the first to the second element, and derivational suffixes are metrically promoted.

(46) Strictness of the fifth foot in the iambic pentameter:
Right so a wyf destroyeth hire *housbónde* *WBP* 377
And al was fals, but that I took *witnésse* *WBP* 382

The strong position in the rightmost foot of the line, where the rhyme is located, is metrically demanding in that it enforces prominence on the syllable filling that position. This is a verse convention, possibly observed in performance, but its implications for reconstructing speech prosody are limited. In ME rhyming practice, suffixes are allowed to fill the rhyme position: ... *sette at réste: the worthiéste* (*Tr* II 761), *and make a thyng: ... at his writýng* (*GP* 325–6), *drónkenèsse: witnèsse* (*WBT* 381–2). The metrical strictness of the last strong position is such that it can even invert the prosodic contour of a native word by suppressing its primary stress – ... *upon a mére: ... and a millére* (*GP* 541–2), *answèrde: hérde* (*CIT* 21–2) – although this is rare in Chaucer. The convention is linguistically constrained only to the extent that inflectional syllables are not allowed to fill the last strong position in the line.

The uneven distribution of trochaic inversions and the very strong tendency for the alignment of syntactic breaks with even metrical positions, especially after the second foot, supports the claim that the pentameter line invented by Chaucer is not just a sequence of W's and S's. The prototype iambic pentameter structure is hierarchical: different feet have different strength indices for the strong positions. 💻

(47) The prototypical iambic pentameter line:
[W 2S] [W 3S] // [W 2S] / [W 2S] [W 5S]

The description of Chaucer's pentameter, or any type of non-free verse, raises the question of the difference between meter and performance. The template of Chaucer's iambic pentameter, as presented here, requires that at least four weak and exactly five strong metrical positions in the line must be filled. If weak positions are filled by unstressed syllables, and strong positions by stressed syllables, the fit between prosody and meter is perfect. However, in PDE, as well as in earlier English, weak and strong syllables do not alternate at absolutely regular intervals: strings of unstressed syllables, as well as stress-clashes between two or more stressed syllables occur commonly in speech. This inevitable discrepancy between the rhythm of speech and the abstract metrical schema is sometimes taken as an argument against the metrical regularity of Chaucer's iambic pentameter. One of the much-debated issues in Chaucerian metrical studies is whether Chaucer's ten-syllable line can legitimately be described as a five-stress line. It is indeed the case that Chaucer's narrative verse naturally reflects the imperfect stress alternation found in the spoken language, so that the number of full stresses in a line realised in recitation can be four or even three.

(48) Discrepancy between prosodic peaks and metrical S's in Chaucer:
For **of** góod náme and wís*dom and ma*nére — *TC* 1.880
Póynaunt and shárp, and ré*dy* ***al*** *his* géere — *GP* 352
Thanne ***wolde*** *he* spéke and críe *as* ***he*** *were* wóod — *GP* 636

It is laughable to advocate reading these lines as mechanically mirroring the meter, for example 'For **ó**f good náme and wísdom ***ánd*** manére', matching pedantically the surface string of syllables to the metrical W's and S's. This does not mean that the lines in (48) are not perfect instantiations of the iambic pentameter. In verse performance, as in speech in general, the underlying categories and their surface realisation can differ within some well-defined limits. In this case, the limits are set by the syllabic composition of the words and by their grammatical function. As pointed out in 10.3, monosyllabic words can occupy both strong and weak positions, though in practice nouns, verbs and adjectives gravitate towards the strong positions, while function words are placed in the weak positions. Strings of unstressed monosyllables, also known as lapses – *<u>But</u> <u>as</u> <u>a</u> [child of twelf month oold, or lesse]* (*PrT* 484); *[I wole han twelf pens,] though <u>that</u> <u>she</u> <u>be</u> wood* (*FrT* 1576) – are freely accommodated by the meter; such strings do not constitute evidence against the abstract stress-alternating schema used by Chaucer. The same logic of performative freedom applies to adjacent full lexical monosyllables, which some metrists interpret as 'spondaic' stress-clashes, as in [*But as a child of*] *<u>twelf</u> <u>month</u> oold, [or lesse]* (*PP* 484), [*I wole han*] *<u>twelf pens,</u> [though that she be wood]* (*FrT* 1576). In this case too, the schema is observed, whether the prominence of one of the items is adjusted up or down or not in performance.

Mismatches of prosodic prominence to metrical positions are differently evaluated not just by where they occur in the line, but also in terms of the domain of the violation, where a mismatch on the word-level is most noticeably disruptive. A possible hierarchy of the severity of matching violations is shown in (49), where matching the syllable prominence of underived words to the corresponding metrical positions is most strictly enforced, and the matching for phrasal stress is most easily ignored.

(49) Gradient violability of stress-to-ictus matching:
Underived words (*father*, *lyved*, *speken*, *muchel*, *under*)
↓
Clitic groups (*a lord*, *the best*, *in swich*)
↓
Derived words (*ending*, *childhood*)
↓
Compounds (*brimstone*, *offspring*, *col-blak*)
↓
Phrases (*old men*, *brend gold*, *white thing*)

The hierarchy is tentative and it includes only disyllabic sequences. It correlates with the morphological and semantic independence of the syllables in the string. The categories are rather crude. Unstressed syllables belonging to the stem will be least likely to fill a strong position; this type of mismatch triggers trochaic substitution. Noun and verb inflections are similarly resistant to metrical promotion, but the comparative *-est* and the gerundial *-yng* are occasionally found in the tenth position, for example *almageste*: *hyeste* (*WBP* 325–6); *thyng*: *grucchyng* (*WBP* 405–6). The placement of French derivational suffixes in rhyme position (*-able*, *-aunce*, *-ioun*, *-ie*, and so on) is much more frequent than the use of native suffixes in rhyme. There are subtler differences in the behaviour of different clitics, and of different derivational affixes. Determiner clitics (*a*, *the*) are very rarely placed in S metrical position. Prepositions and pronouns, as well as auxiliaries (*be*, *have*, *wol*) and conjunctions (*and*, *or*) are more flexible. Not least, the line separating derived items from compounds and compounds from phrases is often blurry. Nevertheless, the hierarchy provides a basis for testing the Chaucerian verse corpus, a task which has not been undertaken yet.

In the idealised schema in Figure 10.1 the edges of most prosodic domains are aligned with the edges of the metrical divisions: clause boundaries match line boundaries, and word boundaries and clitic group boundaries match foot boundaries. Deviations from these 'ideal' alignments are known as *bracketing mismatches*. Bracketing mismatches avoid the monotony of the line: the more bracketing mismatches there are, the more metrically interesting a line is. As in the case of stress mismatches, mismatches of prosodic and metrical domain boundaries are of different severity. Typically, bracketing mismatches are hierarchised in the order given in (50).

(50) Hierarchy of bracketing mismatches:
(a) Clause boundary – line-end
That they were maked for <u>purgacioun</u>

Of uryne . . . *WBP* 120–1

↓

(b) Phrase boundary – colon

But, lord crist! whan that it remembreth me *WBP* 469

↓

(c) Clitic group and word boundary – foot

A bettre envyned man was nowher noon *GP* 342

The rarest of the bracketing mismatches in Chaucer's pentameter involves enjambment, as in (50a). Non-observance of the alignment at the right edge of the line makes for a looser verse-form and bridges the gap between verse and prose. In (50b) the syntactic breaks after the first and the third positions are quite unusual – as noted above, Chaucer's pentameter cola-breaks occur most commonly after the fourth position, or after the fifth and the sixth position. In (50c) the second foot starts inside the second word with elision of *-e* on <bettre>: [-tren-], the third foot straddles <. . . -ned man> and the fourth foot ends inside <nowher>. All three examples, in fact, show word-to-foot misalignment, yet all three examples are within the range of metrically well-formed lines. Bracketing mismatches are more common in Chaucer's narrative verse than in his lyric verse.

The cumulative effect of both stress-to-ictus matching and the matching of prosodic to metrical units in the earlier syllable-counting verse has not been explored for Chaucer or Gower. Sophisticated mathematical modelling of constraints, their interrelation and predictability, as proposed by Hayes et al. (2012) for Shakespeare and Milton, has yet to be attempted on pre-Elizabethan verse. What is evident from the survey in this chapter, however, is that isosyllabic verse and iambic footing have been an option in the language since before the end of the twelfth century. Even the modern reader of poetry is aware of the continuity of this tradition:

> . . . the iamb has been the predominant foot in metrical English poetry for upwards of seven centuries and will remain so for the forehearable future. The oft-anthologized pieces in *The Classic Hundred: All-Time Favorite Poems* show a good deal of metrical and stanzaic variety, but in ninety-nine of the poems the fundamental rhythm is iambic, with the remaining lone exception a poem in free verse. (Harmon 1997: 15)

The principles of metrical template construction for isosyllabic verse have been the same from Orm to this day, and the variability in line length, stress matching and domain alignment that characterises individual poets and compositions can all be addressed in terms of the parameters discussed here. And before we take leave of this all too hasty survey, we should reiterate the advantages of familiarity with the structure of early verse for the historical phonologist. Alliterative verse is an essential source for formulating and testing hypotheses about segmental inventories, their categorisation and their phonological function. All measured verse is a primary testing ground for prosodic reconstruction: theories of early English syllable structure, word- and compound stress, and phrasal prominence are strengthened or invalidated by parallel, yet independently learned and replicated metrical systems.

Bibliography

Ahn, Sang-Cheol (2003), 'Towards an optimal account of diachronic chain shifts: part I (Grimm's law)', in J. Spenader, A. Eriksson and Östen Dahl (eds), *Variation within Optimality Theory*. Proceedings of the Stockholm Workshop on 'Variation within Optimality Theory', April 2003, at Stockholm University, Sweden, Stockholm: Stockholm University, 7–16.

Aitken, A. J. (1962), 'Vowel length in modern Scots', unpublished mimeograph, Edinburgh: Department of English Language, University of Edinburgh.

Albright, Adam (2009), 'Feature-based generalisation as a source of gradient acceptability', *Phonology* 26, 9–41.

Alexander, James D. (1985), 'R-methathesis in English: a diachronic account', *Journal of English Linguistics* 18.1, 33–40.

Algeo, John (ed.) (2001), *The Atlas of North American English*, Cambridge: Cambridge University Press.

Allerton, D. J. (2000), 'Articulatory inertia vs "Systemzwang": changes in liaison phenomena in recent British English', *English Studies* 81:6, 574–81.

Anderson, John (2001), 'A major restructuring in the English consonant system: the de-linearization of [h] and the de-consonantization of [w] and [j]', *English Language and Linguistics* 5:2, 199–212.

Anderson, John and D. Britton (1997), 'Double trouble: geminate versus simplex graphs in the *Ormulum*', in Jacek Fisiak (ed.), *Studies in Middle English Linguistics*, Trends in Linguistics. Studies and Monographs 103, Berlin: Mouton de Gruyter, 23–58.

Aroui, Jean-Louis and Andy Arleo (eds) (2009), *Towards a Typology of Poetic Forms*, Language Faculty and Beyond, 2, Amsterdam: Benjamins.

Barber, Charles (1976), *Early Modern English*, London: André Deutsch.

Barber, Charles (1997), *Early Modern English*, Edinburgh: Edinburgh University Press.

Bauer, Laurie (1992), 'The Second Great Vowel Shift revisited', *English World-Wide* 13, 253–68.

Bauer, Laurie (1994a), 'English in New Zealand', in Robert Burchfield (ed.), *The Cambridge History of the English Language, Vol. V: English in Britain and Overseas, Origins and Development*, Cambridge: Cambridge University Press, 382–428.

Bauer, Laurie (1994b), *Watching English Change*, London: Longman.

Bauer, Laurie (2002), *An Introduction to International Varieties of English*, Edinburgh: Edinburgh University Press.

Becker, Michael, Andrew Nevins and Jonathan Levine (2012), 'Asymmetries in generalizing alternations to and from initial syllables', *Language* 88:2, 231–60.

Beddor, Patrice Speeter, Rena Arens Krakow and Louis M. Goldstein (1986), 'Perceptual constraints and phonological change: a study of nasal vowel height', *Phonology Yearbook* 3, 197–217.

Bell, Alan, Jason M. Brenier, Michelle Gregory, Cynthia Girand and Dan Jurafsky (2009), 'Predictability effects on durations of content and function words in conversational English', *Journal of Memory and Language* 60, 92–111.

Bennett, William H. (1970), 'The stress patterns of Gothic', *PMLA* 85:3, 463–72.

Benson, Larry D. (ed.) (1987), *The Riverside Chaucer*, 3rd edn, Boston: Houghton Mifflin.

Berg, Thomas (1999), 'Stress variation in British and American English', *World Englishes* 18:2, 123–43.

Bermúdez-Otero, Ricardo (1998), 'Prosodic optimization: the Middle English length adjustment', *English Language and Linguistics* 2:2, 169–97.

Bermúdez-Otero, Ricardo (2005), Review of *Alliteration and Sound Change in Early English* by Donka Minkova, *Diachronica* 22, 438–45.

Bermúdez-Otero, Ricardo (2006), 'Phonological change in Optimality Theory', in Keith Brown (ed.), *Encyclopedia of Language and Linguistics*, vol. 9, 2nd edn, Oxford: Elsevier, 497–505.

Bermúdez-Otero, Ricardo (2007), 'Diachronic phonology', in Paul de Lacy (ed.), *The Cambridge Handbook of Phonology*, Cambridge: Cambridge University Press, 497–517.

Bermúdez-Otero, Ricardo and Richard Hogg (2003), 'The actuation problem: phonologization, rule inversion and rule loss', in Holt (ed.) (2003), 91–119.

Bermúdez-Otero, Ricardo and April McMahon (2006), 'English phonology and morphology', in Bas Aarts and April McMahon (eds), *The Handbook of English Linguistics*, Oxford: Blackwell, 382–410.

Bermúdez-Otero, Ricardo and Graeme Trousdale (2012), 'Cycles continua: on unidirectionality and gradualness in language change', in Terttu Nevalainen and Elizabeth Closs Traugott (eds), *The Oxford Handbook of the History of English*, Oxford: Oxford University Press, 691–720.

Berndt, Rolf (1965), 'The linguistic situation in England from the Norman Conquest to the Loss of Normandy (1066–1204)', *Philologica Pragensia* 8, 145–63.

Berndt, Rolf (1972), 'The period of the final decline of French in medieval England (fourteenth and early fifteenth centuries)', *Zeitschrift fur Anglistik und Amerikanistik* 20, 341–69.

Berndt, Rolf (1992), 'The history of the English language and social history: French vs. English', in Wilhelm G. Busse (ed.), *Anglistentag 1991*, Düsseldorf: Proceedings, Tübingen: Niemeyer, 276–92.

Bibire, Paul (2001), 'North Sea language contacts in the early Middle Ages:

English and Norse', in Thomas Liszka and Lorna E. M. Walker (eds), *The North Sea World in the Middle Ages*, Dublin: Four Courts Press, 88–108.

Bigham, Douglas Stephen (2008), *Dialect Contact and Accommodation among Emerging Adults in a University Setting*, PhD thesis, The University of Texas at Austin.

Blevins, Juliette and Andrew Garrett (1998), 'The origins of consonant-vowel metathesis', *Language* 74:3, 508–56.

Boersma, Paul (1998), *Functional Phonology*, The Hague: Netherlands Graduate School of Linguistics (LOT).

Bondar, Vladimir A. (2006), 'On hit-it variation in Old English', paper delivered at the *Central European Student Conference in Linguistics* (CESCL), Budapest, May–June 2006.

Bosworth, Joseph and T. Northcote Toller (1898, 1921), *An Anglo-Saxon Dictionary* (1898) and *Supplement* (1921), <http://www.bosworthtoller.com> (last accessed 3 June 2013).

Bradley, Travis G. (2007), 'Morphological derived-environment effects in gestural coordination: a case study of Norwegian clusters', *Lingua* 117:6, 950–85.

Branchaw, Sherrylyn (2010), *Survival of the Strongest: Strong Verbs in the History of English*, PhD thesis, University of California, Los Angeles.

Bredehoft, Thomas (2005), *Early English Metre*, Toronto Old English Series, Toronto, Buffalo and London: University of Toronto Press.

Brinton, Laurel and Margery Fee (2001), 'Canadian English', in John Algeo (ed.), *The Cambridge History of the English Language, Vol. VI: English in North America*, Cambridge: Cambridge University Press, 422–40.

Britton, Derek (2007a), 'The dialectal origins of the language of Henry Machyn', in Christopher M. Cain and Geoffrey Russom (eds), *Studies in the History of the English Language III. Managing Chaos: Strategies for Identifying Change in English*, Berlin: Mouton de Gruyter, 251–67.

Britton, Derek (2007b), 'A history of hyper-rhoticity in English', *English Language and Linguistics* 11:3, 525–36.

Browman, Catherine P. and Louis Goldstein (1990), 'Gestural specification using dynamically-defined articulatory structures', *Journal of Phonetics* 18, 299–320.

Brown, Carleton (ed.), [1932] (1962), *English Lyrics of the XIIIth Century*, Oxford: Clarendon Press.

Brunner, Karl (1963), *An Outline of Middle English Grammar*, trans. Grahame Johnston, Cambridge, MA: Harvard University Press.

Burling, Robbins (1966), 'The metrics of children's verse: a cross-linguistic study', *American Anthropologist* 68, 1418–41.

Burton, T. L. (2010), *William Barnes's Dialect Poems: A Pronunciation Guide*, Adelaide: Chaucer Studio Press.

Bybee, Joan L. (2007), *Frequency of Use and the Organization of Language*, Oxford: Oxford University Press.

Bybee, Joan and Dan I. Slobin (1982), 'Rules and schemas in the development and use of the English past tense', *Language* 58, 265–89.

Cable, Thomas (1991), *The English Alliterative Tradition*, Philadelphia: University of Pennsylvania Press.

Cable, Thomas (2009), 'Foreign influence, native continuation, and metrical typology in alliterative lyrics', in Jefferson and Putter (eds) (2009), 219–34.

Campbell, Alistair (1959), *Old English Grammar*, Oxford: Clarendon Press.

Carter, Paul and John Local (2007), 'F2 variation in Newcastle and Leeds English liquid systems', *Journal of the International Phonetic Association* 37:2, 173–82.

Cercignani, Fausto (1981), *Shakespeare's Works and Elizabethan Pronunciation*, Oxford: Clarendon Press.

Chambers, J. K. (2006), 'Canadian Raising retrospect and prospect', *The Canadian Journal of Linguistics* 51:2/3, 105–18.

Ching, Marvin, K. L. (1996), 'GreaZy/GreaSy and other /Z/-/S/ choices in Southern pronunciation', *Journal of English Linguistics* 24, 295–307.

Chomsky, Noam and Morris Halle (1968), *The Sound Pattern of English*, New York: Harper and Row.

Clark, Cecily (1992) 'Onomastics', in Norman Blake (ed.), *The Cambridge History of the English Language, Vol. II: 1066–1476*, 542–606.

Clarke, Sandra (2006), '*Nooz* or nyooz?: The complex construction of Canadian identity', *Canadian Journal of Linguistics* 51:2/3, 225–46.

Cohn, Abigail (1993), 'Nasalization in English: phonology or phonetics', *Phonology* 10:1, 43–81.

Cohn, Abigail (2003), 'Phonological structure and phonetic duration: the role of the mora', *Working Papers of the Cornell Phonetics Laboratory*, vol. 15, 69–100.

Collie, Sarah (2007), *English Stress Preservation and Stratal Optimality Theory*, PhD dissertation, University of Edinburgh.

Collie, Sarah (2008), 'English stress preservation: the case for "fake cyclicity"', *English Language and Linguistics* 12:3, 505–32.

Colman, Fran (1983), 'Old English /ɑ/ ≠ /æ/ or /ɑ/ ~ /æ/?', *Folia Linguistica Historica* 4:2, 265–85.

Colman, Fran (ed.) (1992), *Evidence for Old English: Material and Theoretical Bases for Reconstruction*, Edinburgh: John Donald.

Côté, Marie-Hélène (2004), 'Syntagmatic distinctness in consonant deletion', *Phonology* 21, 1–41.

Crisma, Paola (2009) 'Word-initial *h*- in Middle and Early Modern English', in Minkova (ed.) (2009), 130–68.

Crosswhite, Katherine (2004), 'Vowel reduction', in Hayes et al. (eds) (2004), 191–231.

Cruttenden, Alan (2008), *Gimson's Pronunciation of English*, 7th edn, London: Hodder Education.

Crystal, David (2006), 'English worldwide', in Hogg and Denison (eds) (2006), 420–40.

Crystal, David (2008), *'Think on my Words': Exploring Shakespeare's Language*, Cambridge, Cambridge University Press.

Culpeper, Jonathan and Phoebe Clapham (1996), 'The borrowing of Classical and Romance words into English: a study based on the electronic *Oxford English Dictionary*', *International Journal of Corpus Linguistics* 1:2, 199–218.

Curzan, Anne and Kim Emmons (eds) (2004), *Unfolding Conversations: Studies in the History of the English Language II*, Berlin: Mouton de Gruyter.

Cutler, Anne and Sally Butterfield (1992), 'Rhythmic cues to speech segmentation: evidence from juncture misperception', *Journal of Memory and Language* 31, 218–36.

Dance, Richard (2003), *Words Derived from Old Norse in Early Middle English: Studies in the Vocabulary of the South-West Midland Texts*, Medieval and Renaissance Texts and Studies, vol. 246, Tempe, AZ: Arizona Center for Medieval and Renaissance Studies.

Danchev, Andrei [1975] (1976), *On the Phonemic and Phonetic Values of the Short* ea *and* eo *Diagraphs in Old English*. Annuaire de l'Université de Sofia. Faculté des Lettres. Langues et littératures romanes et germaniques. Vol. LXX, Sofia: Naouka I Izkoustvo, 1, 37–88.

Danielsson, B. (1948), *Studies on the Accentuation of Polysyllabic Latin, Greek, and Romance Loan-Words in English with Special Reference to those Ending in -able, ate, -ator, -ible, -ic, -ical, and -ize*, Stockholm: Almqvist and Wiksell.

Daunt, Marjorie (1939), 'Old English sound changes reconsidered in relation to scribal tradition and practice', *Transactions of the Philological Society* 38, 108–37.

Davenport, Mike and S. J. Hannahs (2010), *Introducing Phonetics and Phonology*, 3rd edn, London: Hodder Education.

Delattre, Pierre and Donald C. Freeman (1968), 'A dialect study of American r's by x-ray motion picture', *Linguistics* 44, 29–68.

Denton, Jeannette Marshall (1999), *North and West Germanic Consonant Gemination: A Philological and Phonetic Reanalysis*, PhD thesis, University of Chicago.

Denton, Jeannette Marshall (2003), 'Reconstructing the articulation of Early Germanic *r', *Diachronica* 20:1, 11–43.

Diamond, Jared and Peter Bellwood (2003), 'Farmers and their languages: the first expansions', *Science* 300:5,619, 597–603.

Dobson, Eric John (1957), *English Pronunciation 1500–1700*, vol. 1, Oxford: Clarendon Press.

Dobson, Eric John [1957] (1968), *English Pronunciation 1500–1700*, vol. 2, 2nd edn, Oxford: Clarendon Press.

DOE, *Dictionary of Old English: A to G*, online, ed. Antonette diPaolo Healey, Toronto: Dictionary of Old English Project, University of Toronto, <http://www.doe.utoronto.ca/pages/pub/fasc-a-g-web.html> (last updated 22 July 2011, last accessed 3 June 2013).

Dresher, B. Elan [1978] (1985), *Old English and the Theory of Phonology*, PhD dissertation, University of Massachusetts, Amherst. 1985 reprint, New York: Garland.

Dresher, B. Elan (2009), *The Contrastive Hierarchy in Phonology*, Cambridge: Cambridge University Press.

Dresher, B. Elan and Nila Friedberg (eds) (2002), *Formal Approaches to Poetry: Recent Developments in Metrics*, Berlin: Mouton de Gruyter.

Duffell, Martin (2008a), *A New History of English Metre*, Legenda, Studies in Linguistics 5, London: Modern Humanities Research Association and Maney Publishing.

Duffell Martin J. (2008b), 'Some observations on English binary metres', *Language and Literature* 17, 5–20.

Duggan, Hoyt N. (2001), 'Some aspects of a-verse rhythms in Middle English alliterative poetry', in Robert F. Yeager and Charlotte Morse (eds), *Speaking Images: Essays in Honor of V. A. Kolve*, Ashville, NC: Pegasus Press, 479–503.

Eckert, Penny (n.d.), 'Vowel shifts in Northern California and the Detroit suburbs', <http://www.stanford.edu/~eckert/vowels.html> (last accessed 3 June 2013).

Eddington, David and Michael Taylor (2009), '*T*-glottalization in American English', *American Speech* 84:3, 298–315.

Eddington, David and Caitlin Channer (2010), 'American English has goʔ a loʔ of glottal stops: social diffusion and linguistic motivation', *American Speech* 85:3, 338–52.

Ekwall, Eilert (1960), *The Concise Oxford Dictionary of Place-names*, 4th edn, Oxford: Clarendon Press.

Ellis, Lucy and William J. Hardcastle (2002), 'Categorical and gradient properties of assimilation in alveolar to velar sequences: evidence from EPG and EMA data', *Journal of Phonetics* 30:3, 373–96.

Erickson, Blaine (2002), 'On the development of English *r*', in Minkova and Stockwell (eds) (2002), 183–207.

Evans, Arthur Benoni (1881), *Leicester Words, Phrases, and Proverbs*. Edited with Additions and an Introduction, by Sebastian Evans. London: Published for the English Dialect Society by Truebner and Co., 57 and 59, Ludgate Hill.

Fabb, Nigel (2010), 'Is literary language a development of ordinary language?', *Lingua* 120:5, 1,219–32.

Fabricius, Anne (2002), 'Weak vowels in modern RP: an acoustic study of happY-tensing and KIT/schwa shift', *Language Variation and Change* 14, 211–37.

Ferragne, Emmanuel and François Pellegrino (2010), 'Formant frequencies of vowels in 13 accents of the British Isles', *Journal of the International Phonetic Association* 40:1, 1–34.

Fikkert, Paula (2007), 'Acquiring phonology', in P. de Lacy (ed.), *Handbook of Phonological Theory*, Cambridge, MA: Cambridge University Press, 537–54.

Filppula, Markku, Juhani Klemola and Heli Paulasto (2008), *English and Celtic in Contact*, New York and Abingdon: Routledge.

Filppula, Markku, Juhani Klemola and Heli Pitkänen (eds) (2002), *The Celtic Roots of English*. Studies in Language, vol. 37, Joensuu: Faculty of Humanities, University of Joensuu.

Finegan, Edward (2006), 'English in North America', in Hogg and Denison (eds) (2006), 384–420.

Finkenstaedt, T., E. Leisi and D. Wolff (eds) (1970), *A Chronological English Dictionary*, Heidelberg: Carl Winter Universitätsverlag.

Fischer, David Hackett (1989), *Albion's Seed: Four British Folkways in America*, Oxford: Oxford University Press.

Fisher, John Hurt (2001), 'British and American, continuity and divergence', in John Algeo (ed.), *The Cambridge History of the English Language, Vol. VI: English in North America*, Cambridge: Cambridge University Press, 59–85.

Fisiak, Jacek (1968), *A Short Grammar of Middle English*, Warsaw: Państwowe Wydawnictwo Naukowe.

Fitzgerald, Christina (2008), '"Ubbe dubbede him to knith": the scansion of *Havelok* and ME *-es*, *-ed*, and *-ede*', in Susan Fitzmaurice and Donka Minkova (eds), *Studies in the History of the English Language IV: Empirical and Analytical Advances in the Study of English Language Change*, Berlin: Mouton de Gruyter, 187–205.

Flasdieck, Hermann F. (1958), 'Die Entstehung des engl. Phonems [ʃ], zugleich ein Beitrag zur Geschichte der Quantität', *Anglia* 76, 339–410.

Flemming, Edward (1995), *Auditory Representations in Phonology*, PhD dissertation, University of California, Los Angeles.

Flemming, Edward (2003), 'The relationship between coronal place and vowel backness', *Phonology* 20, 335–373.

Flemming, Edward (2004), 'Contrast and perceptual distinctiveness', in Hayes et al. (eds) (2004), 232–77.

Flemming, Edward (2009), 'The phonetic weakness of schwa vowels', in Minkova (ed.) (2009), 78–99.

Flemming, Edward and S. Johnson (2007), 'Rosa's roses: reduced vowels in American English', *Journal of the International Phonetic Association* 37, 83–96.

Fridland, V. (2000), 'The Southern Shift in Memphis, Tennessee', *Language Variation and Change* 11, 267–85.

Fromkin, Victoria (ed.) et al. (2000), *Linguistics: An Introduction to Linguistic Theory*, Oxford: Blackwell.

Fudge, Eric, (1984), *English Word-Stress*, London: George Allen and Unwin.

Fulk, Robert D. (1992), *A History of Old English Meter*, Philadelphia: University of Pennsylvania Press.

Fulk, Robert D. (1997), 'Ambisyllabicity in Old English: a contrary view', in Irmengard Rauch and Gerald F. Carr (eds), *Insights in Germanic Linguistics II: Classic and Contemporary*, Trends in Linguistics. Studies and Monographs 94, Berlin: Mouton de Gruyter, 29–45.

Fulk, Robert D. (1998), 'The role of syllable structure in Old English quantitative sound changes', *NOWELE: North-Western European Language Evolution* 33, 3–35.

Fulk, Robert D. (1999), 'Evaluating the evidence for lengthening before homorganic consonant clusters in the *Ormulum*', in G. F. Carr and W. Harbert (eds), *Interdigitations: Essays for Irmengard Rauch*, New York: P. Lang, 201–9.

Fulk, Robert D. (2002), 'Early Middle English evidence for Old English metrics: resolution in *Poema morale*', *Journal of Germanic Linguistics* 14, 331–55.

Fulk, Robert D. (2004), 'Old English poetry and the alliterative revival: on Geoffrey Russom's "The evolution of Middle English alliterative meter"', in Curzan and Emmons (eds) (2004), 305–12.

Fulk, Robert D. (2007), 'Old English meter and oral tradition: three issues bearing on poetic chronology', *The Journal of English and Germanic Philology* 106:3, 304–24.

Fulk, Robert D. (2012), *An Introduction to Middle English: Grammar: Texts*, Peterborough, ON: Broadview Press.

Garrett, Andrew and Juliette Blevins (2009), 'Analogical morphophonology', in Kristin Hanson and Sharon Inkelas (eds), *The Nature of the Word: Essays in Honor of Paul Kiparsky*, Cambridge, MA: MIT Press, 527–45.

Gascoine, George (1575), *The Posies*, Printed at London for Richard Smith, and are to be solde at the Northweast doore of Paules Church. (Edited by John W. Cunliffe, MA, DLit (London) Professor of English in the University of Wisconsin, USA. Cambridge: at the University Press 1907).

Geist, Robert J. (1948), 'Notes on "The King of Tars"', *The Journal of English and Germanic Philology* 47:2, 173–8.

Getty, Michael (2002), *The Metre of* Beowulf, Berlin: Mouton de Gruyter.

Gick, Bryan (1999), 'A gesture-based account of intrusive consonants in English', *Phonology* 16:1, 29–54.

Gick, Bryan (2002), 'The American intrusive L', *American Speech* 77, 167–83.

Giegerich, Heinz (1992), *English Phonology: An Introduction*, Cambridge: Cambridge University Press.

Giegerich, Heinz (1997), 'The phonology of /ɔ:/ and /ɑ:/ in RP English: Henry Sweet and after', *English Language and Linguistics* 1:1, 25–79.

Giegerich, Heinz (1999), *Lexical Strata in English: Morphological Causes, Phonological Effects*, Cambridge: Cambridge University Press.

Giegerich Heinz J. (2009), 'Compounding and lexicalism', in Rochelle Lieber and Pavol Štekauer (eds), *Handbook of Compounding*, Oxford: Oxford University Press, 178–200.

Gimson, A. C. (1970), *An Introduction to the Pronunciation of English*, 2nd edn, London: Edward Arnold.

Gnanadesikan, Amalia E. (2009), *The Writing Revolution: Cuneiform to the Internet*, Chichester: Wiley-Blackwell.

Goldsmith, John (1995), 'Phonological theory', in J. Goldsmith (ed.), *The Handbook of Phonological Theory*, Oxford: Blackwell, 1–23.

Gordon, Matthew J. (2001a), 'Small-town values and big-city vowels: a study of the Northern cities shift in Michigan', *Publications of the American Dialect Society* (PADS) 84, Durham, NC: Duke University Press.

Gordon, Matthew J. (2001b), 'Investigating chain shifts and mergers', in J. K. Chambers, P. Trudgill and N. Schilling-Estes (eds), *The Handbook of Language Variation and Change*, Malden, MA: Blackwell, 244–66.

Gordon, Matthew Kelly (2004), 'Syllable weight', in Hayes et al. (eds) (2004), 277–312.

Gordon, Matthew Kelly (2006), *Syllable Weight: Phonetics, Phonology, Typology*, New York: Routledge.

Grant, Colin (2011), An Acoustic Analysis of Anglian Smoothing (MA thesis, Indiana University).

Greenberg, Joseph (1978), *Universals of Human Language, Vol. II Phonology*, Stanford: Stanford University Press.

Greenfield, Stanley and Daniel Calder (1986), *A New Critical History of Old English Literature. With a Survey of the Anglo-Latin Background by Michael Lapidge*, New York and London: New York University Press.

Gussmann, Edmund (2002), *Phonology: Analysis and Theory*, Cambridge: Cambridge University Press.

Hall, Nancy (2006), 'Cross-linguistic patterns of vowel intrusion', *Phonology* 23, 387–429.

Hall, Tracy A. and Silke Hamann (2010), 'On the cross-linguistic avoidance of rhotic plus high front vocoid sequences', *Lingua* 120, 1,821–44.

Halmari, Helena (2011), 'Alliteration in inaugural addresses: from George Washington to Barack Obama', in Roper (ed.) (2011), 45–61.

Hamann, Silke (2005), 'The diachronic emergence of retroflex segments in three languages', *Tijdschrift voor linguistiek te Utrecht* 15, 29–48.

Hammond, Michael (1997), 'Vowel quantity and syllabification in English', *Language* 73:1, 1–17.

Hammond, Michael (1999), *The Phonology of English: A Prosodic Optimality-Theoretic Approach*, Oxford: Oxford University Press.

Hanham, Alison (ed.) (1975), *The Cely Letters 1472–1488*, EETS 273, London: Oxford University Press.

Hanson, Kristin and Paul Kiparsky (1996), 'A parametric theory of poetic meter', *Language* 72:2, 287–336.

Harmon, William (1997), 'English versification: fifteen hundred years of continuity and change', *Studies in Philology* 94:1, 1–37.

Harrington, Jonathan, Felicity Cox and Zoe Evans (1997), 'An acoustic phonetic study of broad, general, and cultivated Australian English vowels', *Australian Journal of Linguistics* 17:2, 155–84.

Haugen, Einar (1938), 'Notes on "voiced t" in American English', *Dialect Notes* 6:16–17, 627–34.

Hawkins, Sarah and Jonathan Midgley (2005), 'Formant frequencies of RP monophthongs in four age groups of speakers', *Journal of the International Phonetic Association* 35:2, 183–99.

Hay, Jennifer and Andrea Sudbury (2005), 'How rhoticity became /r/-sandhi', *Language* 81:4, 799–824.

Hayes, Bruce (1983), 'A grid-based theory of English meter', *Linguistic Inquiry* 14, 357–93.

Hayes, Bruce (1988), 'Metrics and phonological theory', in Frederick Newmeyer (ed.), *Linguistics: The Cambridge Survey*, Cambridge: Cambridge University Press, 220–49.

Hayes, Bruce (1989), 'The prosodic hierarchy in meter', in Paul Kiparsky and Gilbert Youmans (eds), *Phonetics and Phonology, Vol. 1: Rhythm and Meter*, San Diego: Academic Press, 201–60.

Hayes, Bruce (1995), *Metrical Stress Theory: Principles and Case Studies*, Chicago: University of Chicago Press.

Hayes, Bruce (2009a) 'Syllabification in English', <http://linguistics.ucla.edu/people/hayes/251English/Readings/HayesAmbisyllabicity.pdf> (last accessed 3 June 2013).

Hayes, Bruce (2009b) *Introductory Phonology*, Oxford and Malden, MA: Wiley-Blackwell.

Hayes, Bruce and Donca Steriade (2004), 'Introduction: the phonetic bases of phonological markedness', in Hayes et al. (eds) (2004), 1–34.

Hayes, Bruce, Robert Kirchner and Donca Steriade (eds) (2004), *Phonetically Based Phonology*, Cambridge: Cambridge University Press.

Hayes, Bruce, Colin Wilson and Anne Shisko (2012), 'Maxent grammars for the metrics of Shakespeare and Milton', *Language* 88:4, 691–731.

Hebda, Anna (2002), 'Open syllable lengthening before /t/ and /k/ in the language of *Cursor Mundi* – the evidence from rhyme vowels', *Studia Anglica Posnaniensia* 38, 229–37.

Heselwood, Barry (2009), 'R vocalization, linking R and intrusive R: accounting for final schwa in RP English', *Transactions of the Philological Society* 107:1, 66–97.

Hickey, Raymond (1986), 'Possible phonological parallels between Irish and Irish English', *English World-Wide* 7, 1–21.

Hickey, Raymond (1998), 'The *Dublin Vowel Shift* and the historical perspective', in Jacek Fisiak and Marcin Krygier (eds), *Advances in English Historical Linguistics 1996*, Trends in Linguistics. Studies and Monographs 112, Berlin: Mouton de Gruyter, 79–106.

Hill, Archibald A. (1940), 'Early loss of [r] before dentals', *PMLA* 55:2, 308–59.

Hogg, Richard M. (1992a), *A Grammar of Old English, Vol. I: Phonology*, Oxford and Cambridge, MA: Blackwell.

Hogg, Richard (1992b), 'Phonology and morphology', in Hogg (1992a), 67–168.

Hogg, Richard (1996), 'Old English open-syllable lengthening', *Transactions of the Philological Society* 94:1, 57–72.

Hogg, Richard (2000), 'On the (non-)existence of High Vowel Deletion', in Aditi Lahiri (ed.), *Analogy, Levelling, Markedness*, Berlin: Mouton de Gruyter, 353–77.

Hogg, Richard (2002), *An Introduction to Old English*, Edinburgh: Edinburgh University Press.

Hogg, Richard (2006a), 'English in Britain', in Hogg and Denison (eds) (2006), 352–84.

Hogg, Richard (2006b), 'Old English dialectology', in Kemenade and Los (eds) (2006), 395–416.

Hogg, Richard M. (gen. ed.) (1992–c. 2001), *The Cambridge History of the English Language in 6 volumes*, Cambridge: Cambridge University Press.

Hogg, Richard and David Denison (eds) (2006), *A History of the English Language*, Cambridge: Cambridge University Press.

Hogg, Richard and Robert D. Fulk (2010), *A Grammar of Old English, Volume II: Morphology*, Chichester: Wiley-Blackwell.

Holt, D. Eric (ed.) (2003), *Optimality Theory and Language Change*, Studies in Natural Language and Linguistic Theory 56, Dordrecht: Kluwer.

Honeybone, Patrick (2005), 'Diachronic evidence in segmental phonology: the case of obstruent laryngeal specifications', in M. van Oostendorp and J. van de Weijer (eds), *The Internal Organization of Phonological Segments*, Berlin: Mouton de Gruyter, 317–53.

Honeybone, Patrick and Joseph Salmons (eds) (2014), *The Oxford Handbook of Historical Phonology*, Oxford: Oxford University Press.

Hoover, David (1985), *A New Theory of Old English Meter*, New York: Peter Lang.

Horn, Wilhelm and Martin Lehnert (1954), *Laut und Leben. Englische Lautgeschichte der neueren Zeit (1400–1950)*, 2 vols, Berlin: Deutscher Verlag der Wissenschaften.

Horobin, Simon and Jeremy Smith (2002), *An Introduction to Middle English*, Edinburgh: Edinburgh University Press.

House, Arthur S. (1961), 'On vowel duration in English', *The Journal of the Acoustical Society of America* 33:9, 1,174–8.

Howell, Robert B. (1987), 'Tracing the origin of uvular R in the Germanic languages', *Folia Linguistica Historica* 7:2, 317–49.

Howell, Robert B. (1991), *Old English Breaking and its Germanic Analogues*, Tübingen: Max Niemeyer.

Howell, Robert and Katerina Somers Wicka (2007), 'A phonetic account of Anglian Smoothing', *Folia Linguistica Historica* 28:1, 187–214.

Hughes, Geoffrey (2000), *A History of English Words*, Oxford: Blackwell.

Hume, Elizabeth and K. Johnson (eds) (2001), *The Role of Speech Perception in Phonology*, New York: Academic Press.

Hutcheson, Bellenden Rand (1995), *Old English Poetic Metre*, Cambridge: D. S. Brewer.

Hyman, Larry (2002), 'Is there a right-to-left bias in vowel harmony?', paper presented at the 9th International Phonology Meeting, Vienna, 1 November 2002, <http://www.linguistics.berkeley.edu/~hyman/Hyman_Vienna_VH_paper_forma.pdf> (last accessed 3 June 2013).

Ikegami, Masa T. (1984), *Rhyme and Pronunciation: Some Studies of English Rhymes from* King Alisaunder *to Skelton*, Tokyo: Hogaku-Kenkyu-Kai.

'Indo-European languages' (2009), in *Encyclopædia Britannica Online*, <http://search.eb.com/eb/article-74551> (last accessed 5 July 2009).

Ingham, Richard (2012), 'The decline of bilingual competence in French in medieval England: evidence from the PROME database', in Nils Langer, Steffan Davies and Wim Vandenbussche (eds), *Language and History, Linguistics and Historiography: Interdisciplinary Approaches*, Studies in Historical Linguistics 9, Frankfurt am Main: Peter Lang, 271–92.

IPA Handbook (1999), *Handbook of the International Phonetic Association: A Guide to the Use of the International Phonetic Alphabet*, Cambridge: Cambridge University Press.

Ito, Junko and Armin Mester (2001), 'Structure preservation and stratal opacity in German', in L. Lombardi (ed.), *Segmental Phonology in Optimality Theory*, Cambridge: Cambridge University Press, 261–95.

Iverson, Gregory K. and J. C. Salmons (1995), 'Aspiration and laryngeal representation in Germanic', *Phonology* 12, 369–96.

Iverson, Gregory K. and J. C. Salmons (2005), 'Filling the gap. English tense vowel plus final /š/', *Journal of English Linguistics* 33:3, 1–15.

Iverson Gregory K. and Sang-Cheol Ahn (2007), 'English voicing in dimensional theory', *Language Sciences* 29, 247–69.

Jefferson, Judith and Ad Putter (eds) (2009), *Approaches to the Metres of Alliterative Verse*, Leeds Texts and Monographs New Series 17, Leeds: University of Leeds.

Jespersen, Otto (1909), *A Modern English Grammar on Historical Principles. Part I, Sounds and Spellings*, Heidelberg: Carl Winter's Universitätsbuchhandlung.

Johnson, Wyn and David Britain (2007), 'L-vocalisation as a natural phenomenon: explorations in sociophonology', *Language Sciences* 29, 294–315.

Johnston, Paul A., Jr. (1992), 'English vowel shifting: one great vowel shift or two small vowel shifts?', *Diachronica* 9:2, 189–226.

Jones, Charles (1989), *A History of English Phonology*, London: Longman.

Jones, Daniel (1924), *An English Pronouncing Dictionary (showing the pronunciation of over 50,000 words in international phonetic transcription)*, New York: E. P. Dutton.

Jordan, Richard (1974), *A Handbook of Middle English Grammar: Phonology*, trans. and rev. by Eugene Joseph Crook, Janua Linguarum Series Practica 218, The Hague: Mouton.

Kastovsky, Dieter (1992), 'Semantics and vocabulary', in Hogg (1992a), 290–408.

Kastovsky, Dieter (ed.) (1994), *Studies in Early Modern English*, Berlin: Mouton de Gruyter.

Kaun, Abigail (1995), *The Typology of Rounding Harmony: An Optimality-Theoretic Approach*, PhD thesis, University of California, Los Angeles.

Kawahara, Shigeto (2007), 'Sonorancy and geminacy', in *University of Massachusetts Occasional Papers in Linguistics 32: Papers in Optimality III*, Amherst: Book Surge Publishing, 145–86.

Keenan, Edward (2002), 'Explaining the creating of reflexive pronouns in English', in Minkova and Stockwell (eds) (2002), 325–55.

Kelly, Michael (2004), 'Word onset patterns and lexical stress in English', *Journal of Memory and Language* 50, 231–44.

Kemenade, Ans van and Bettelou Los (eds) (2006), *The Handbook of the History of English*, Oxford: Blackwell.

Kenyon, John S. and Thomas A. Knott (1949), *Pronouncing Dictionary of American English*, <http://www.archive.org/details/pronouncingdicti00unse> (last accessed 3 June 2013).

Keyser, S. J. and W. O'Neil (1985), *Rule Generalization and Opacity in Language Change*, Dordrecht: Foris.

Kim, Myungsook (1993), 'On lengthening in the open syllables of Middle English', *Lingua* 91, 261–77.

King, Anne (1992), 'You say [æjðər] and I say [æjhwæðər]? Interpreting Old English written data', in Colman (ed.) (1992), 20–43.

Kiparsky, Paul (1973), 'The role of linguistics in a theory of poetry', *Daedalus*

102, 231–45. [Reprinted in Donald C. Freeman (ed.) (1981), *Essays in Modern Stylistics*, London: Methuen, 9–23].

Kiparsky, Paul (1977), 'The rhythmic structure of English verse', *Linguistic Inquiry* 8, 189–247.

Kiparsky, Paul and W. O'Neil (1976), 'The phonology of Old English inflexions', *Linguistic Inquiry* 7, 527–57.

Kirchner, Robert (2004), 'Consonant lenition', in Hayes et al. (eds) (2004), 313–46.

Kirkby, John [1746] (1971), *A New English Grammar, or Guide to the English Tongue, with Notes . . .*, facsimile reprint, Menston: Sclar Press.

Kirwin, William J. (2001), 'Newfoundland English', in John Algeo (ed.), *The Cambridge History of the English Language, Vol. VI: English in North America*, Cambridge: Cambridge University Press, 441–55.

Kitson, Peter (1997), 'When did Middle English begin? Later than you think!', in Jacek Fisiak (ed.), *Studies in Middle English Linguistics*, Trends in Linguistics. Studies and Monographs 103, Berlin: Mouton de Gruyter, 221–71.

Knappe, Gabrielle (1997), '*Though* it is *tough*: on regional differences in the development and substitution of the Middle English voiceless velar fricative [x] in syllable coda position', in Heinrich Ramisch and Kenneth Wynne (eds), *Language in Time and Space: Studies in Honour of Wolfgang Viereck on the Occasion of his 60th Birthday*, Zeitschrift für Dialektologie und Linguistik, Beihefte, Heft 97, Stuttgart: Franz Steiner, 139–63.

Kökeritz, Helge (1953), *Shakespeare's Pronunciation*, New Haven, CT: Yale University Press.

Kökeritz, Helge (1959), 'English *i* for Old French *ü*', in J. Vendryes (eds), *Mélanges de linguistique et de philologie, Fernand Mossé in memoriam*, Paris: Didier, 218–25.

Kökeritz, Helge (1961), *A Guide to Chaucer's Pronunciation*, New York: Holt, Rinehart and Winston.

Kortmann, Bernd and Benedikt Szmrecsanyi (2004), 'Global synopsis: morphological and syntactic variation in English', in Bernd Kortmann and Edgar Schneider (eds), *A Handbook of Varieties of English*, Berlin: Mouton de Gruyter, 1,142–202.

Krapp, George Philip and Elliot van Kirk Dobbie (1931–53), *The Anglo-Saxon Poetic Records*, 6 vols, New York: Columbia University Press.

Kreidler, Charles (2004), *The Pronunciation of English: A Coursebook*, Oxford and Malden, MA: Blackwell Publishing.

Krygier, Marcin (1996), 'Plural markers of the Old English nouns of relationship in the two manuscripts of Laȝamon's *Brut*', in Jacek Fisiak (ed.), *Middle English Miscellany: From Vocabulary to Linguistic Variation*, Poznań: Motivex, 47–69.

Kuryłowicz, Jerzy (1970), *Die sprachlichen Grundlagen der altgermanischen Metrik*, Innsbruck: Institut für vergleichende Sprachwissenschaft der Universität Innsbruck.

Labov, William (1991), 'The three dialects of English', in P. Eckert (ed.), *New Ways of Analyzing Sound Change*, New York: Academic Press, 1–44.

Labov, William (1994), *Principles of Linguistic Change. Vol. I, Internal Factors*, Oxford: Blackwell.

Labov, William (2008), 'Triggering events', in Susan Fitzmaurice and Donka Minkova (eds), *Studies in the History of the English Language IV: Empirical and Analytical Advances in the Study of English Language Change*, Berlin: Mouton de Gruyter, 11–54.

Labov, William, Paul Cohen, Clarence Robins and John Lewis (1968), *A Study of the Nonstandard English of Black and Puerto Rican Speakers in New York City*, Cooperative Research Report no. 3288, Washington DC: United States Office of Education.

Labov, William, M. Yaeger and R. Steiner (1972), *A Quantitative Study of Sound Change in Progress*, Philadelphia: US Regional Survey.

Labov, William, Sharon Ash and Charles Boberg (2006), *The Atlas of North American English* (ANAE), Berlin: Mouton de Gruyter.

Ladefoged, Peter (1982), *A Course in Phonetics*, 2nd edn, New York: Harcourt Brace Jovanovich.

Ladefoged, Peter (2005), *Vowels and Consonants*, Oxford: Blackwell Publishing.

Ladefoged, Peter and Ian Maddieson (1996), *The Sounds of the World's Languages*, Oxford and Malden, MA: Wiley-Blackwell.

LAEME, *A Linguistic Atlas of Early Middle English, 1150–1325*. Compiled by Margaret Laing. [http://www.lel.ed.ac.uk/ihd/laeme1/laeme1.html] (Edinburgh: © 2008– The University of Edinburgh).

Lahiri, Aditi and Paula Fikkert (1999), 'Trisyllabic shortening in English: past and present', *English Language and Linguistics* 3:2, 229–67.

Laing, Margaret (1999), 'Confusion *wrs* confounded: litteral substitution sets in early Middle English writing systems', *Neuphilologische Mitteilungen* 100, 251–70.

Laing, Margaret (2009), 'Orthographic indications of weakness in early Middle English', in Minkova (ed.) (2009), 237–316.

Laing, Margaret and Roger Lass (2003), 'Tales of the 1001 nists: the phonological implications of litteral substitution sets in some thirteenth-century South-West Midland texts', *English Language and Linguistics* 7:2, 257–78.

Laing, Margaret and Roger Lass (2006), 'Early Middle English dialectology: problems and prospects', in Kemenade and Los (eds) (2006), 417–51.

Laing, Margaret and Roger Lass (2009), 'Shape-shifting, sound-change and the genesis of prodigal writing systems', *English Language and Linguistics* 13:1, 1–31.

LALME, *A Linguistic Atlas of Late Middle English* (1986), ed. Angus McIntosh, Michael L. Samuels and Michael Benskin, with the assistance of Margaret Laing and Keith Williamson, Aberdeen: Aberdeen University Press.

Lamb, Sydney and E. Douglas Mitchell (eds) (1991), *Sprung from Some Common Source: Investigations into the Prehistory of Ancient Languages*, Stanford: Stanford University Press.

Lapidge, Michael (1979), 'Aldhelm's Latin poetry and Old English verse', *Comparative Literature* 31, 209–31.

Lapidge, Michael (1986), 'The Anglo-Latin background', in Greenfield and Calder (1986), 5–37.

Lappe, Sabine (2007), *English Prosodic Morphology*, Dordrecht: Springer.

Lass, Roger (1976), *English Phonology and Phonological Theory*, Cambridge: Cambridge University Press.

Lass, Roger (1980), *On Explaining Language Change*, Cambridge: Cambridge University Press.

Lass, Roger (1985), 'Minkova *noch einmal*. MEOSL and the resolved foot', *Folia Linguistica Historica* 6, 245–66.

Lass, Roger (1987), *The Shape of English: Structure and History*, London: J. M. Dent and Sons.

Lass, Roger (1992a), 'Phonology and morphology', in Norman Blake (ed.), *The Cambridge History of the English Language, Vol. II: 1066–1476*, 23–155.

Lass, Roger (1992b), 'Front rounded vowels in Old English', in Colman (ed.) (1992), 88–116.

Lass, Roger (1992c), 'What, if anything, was the Great Vowel Shift?, in Matti Rissanen, Ossi Ihalainen, Terttu Nevalainen and Irma Taavitsainen (eds), *History of Englishes: New Methods and Interpretations in Historical Linguistics*, Berlin: Mouton de Gruyter, 144–55.

Lass, Roger (1994), *Old English: A Historical Linguistic Companion*, Cambridge: Cambridge University Press.

Lass, Roger (1999), 'Phonology and morphology', in Roger Lass (ed.), *The Cambridge History of the English Language, Vol. III: 1476–1776*, Cambridge: Cambridge University Press, 56–186.

Lass, Roger (2000), 'Language periodization and the concept "middle"', in Irma Taavitsainen, Terttu Nevalainen, Päivi Pahta and Matti Rissanen (eds), *Placing Middle English in Context*, Berlin and New York: Mouton de Gruyter, 7–42.

Lass, Roger (2009), 'On schwa: synchronic prelude and historical fugue', in Minkova (ed.) (2009), 47–77.

Lass, Roger (2014), 'Interpreting alphabetic orthographies: early Middle English spelling', in Patrick Honeybone and Joseph Salmons (eds), *The Oxford Handbook of Historical Phonology*, Oxford: Oxford University Press.

Lass, Roger (ed.) (1969), *Approaches to English Historical Linguistics*, New York: Holt, Rinehart and Winston.

Lass, Roger and John Anderson (1975), *Old English Phonology*, Cambridge: Cambridge University Press.

Lass, Roger and Susan Wright (1985), 'The South African chain shift', in Roger Eaton, Olga Fischer, Willem Koopman and Frederike van der Leek (eds), *Papers from the 4th International Conference on English Historical Linguistics*, Amsterdam: John Benjamins, 137–62.

Lass, Roger and Margaret Laing (2005), 'Are front rounded vowels retained in West Midlands Middle English?', in Nikolaus Ritt and Herbert Schendl (eds), *Rethinking Middle English: Linguistic and Literary Approaches*, Frankfurt am Main: Peter Lang, 280–90.

Lauttamus, Timo (1981), 'A note on the development of Old English [x] to Middle English [f]', *Neuphilologische Mitteilungen* 82, 1–5.

Lavoie, Lisa (2009), 'Testing consonant weakness phonetically', in Minkova (ed.) (2009), 29–46.

Lawson, Eleanor, Jane Stuart-Smith and James Scobbie (2008), 'Articulatory insights into language variation and change: preliminary findings from an ultrasound study of derhoticization in Scottish English', in K. Gorman (ed.), *University of Pennsylvania Working Papers in Linguistics* 14:2: *Selected Papers from NWAV 36*, 102–10.

Leach, Alfred (1880), *The Letter H Past, Present, and Future*, London: Griffith and Farran.

Lehiste, Ilse (1970), *Suprasegmentals*, Cambridge, MA: MIT Press.

Lehmann, Winfred P. [1956] (1971), *The Development of Germanic Verse Form*, New York: Gordian Press.

Leith, Dick (1983), *A Social History of English*, London: Routledge and Kegan Paul.

Lewis, M. Paul, Gary F. Simons and Charles D. Fennig (eds) (2013) *Ethnologue: Languages of the World*, 17th edn, Dallas: SIL International. Online version available at <http://www.ethnologue.com> (last accessed 16 May 2013).

Liberman, Anatoly (1965a), 'K istorii dolgoty v sredneangliiskom' [On the history of length in Middle English], *Filologicheskie nauki* 1, 125–35.

Liberman, Anatoly (1965b), 'K voprosu o sredneangliiskom udlinenii v otkrytom sloge' [On the question of Middle English lengthening in open syllable], *Vestnik Leningradskogo Universiteta* 8, 129–37.

Liberman, Anatoly (1992a), 'Vowel lengthening before resonant + another consonant and svarabhakti in Germanic', in Irmengard Rauch, Gerald F. Carr and Robert L. Kyes (eds), *On Germanic Linguistics: Issues and Methods*, Berlin: Mouton de Gruyter, 163–217.

Liberman, Anatoly (1992b), 'A bird's-eye view of open syllable lengthening in English and in other Germanic languages', *NOWELE: North-Western European Language Evolution* 20, 67–87.

Liberman, Anatoly (1995), 'The beginning and end of the (great) vowel shifts in Late Germanic', in Irmengard Rauch and Gerald F. Carr (eds), *Insights in Germanic Linguistics: Methodology in Transition*, Trends in Linguistics. Studies and Monographs 83, Berlin: Mouton de Gruyter, 203–31.

Liebl, Christian (2006), 'The A and O of a medieval English sound change: prolegomena to a study of the origins and early geographical diffusion of /ɑː/ > /oː/', in Nikolaus Ritt, Herbert Schendl, Christiane Dalton-Puffer and Dieter Kastovsky (eds), *Medieval English and its Heritage: Structure, Meaning and Mechanisms of Change*, Studies in Medieval Language and Literature 16, Frankfurt am Main: Peter Lang, 19–35.

Luick, Karl (1898), 'Beiträge zur englischen Grammatik III. Die Quantitätsveränderungen im Laufe der englischen Sprachentwicklung', *Anglia* 20, 335–62.

Luick, Karl [1914, 1921–40] (1964), *Historische Grammatik der englischen Sprache*, 2 vols, Leipzig: Tauchnitz.

Lutz, Angelika (1991), *Phonotaktisch gesteuerte Konsonantenveränderungen in der Geschichte des Englischen*, Tübingen: Niemeyer.

Lutz, Angelika (1994), 'Vocalization of "post-vocalic *r*" – an Early Modern English sound change?', in Kastovsky (ed.) (1994), 167–85.

Lutz, Angelika (2002), 'When did English begin?', in Teresa Fanego, Belén Méndez-Naya and Elena Seoane (eds), *Sounds, Words, Texts and Change: Selected Papers from 11 ICEHL, Santiago de Compostela, 7–11 September 2000*, Amsterdam: John Benjamins, 145–71.

Lutz, Angelika (2004), 'The first push: a prelude to the Great Vowel Shift', *Anglia* 122:2, 209–24.

Maclagan, Margaret and Jennifer Hay (2007), 'Getting *fed* up with our *feet*: contrast maintenance and the New Zealand English "short" front vowel shift', *Language Variation and Change* 19, 1–25.

MacMahon, Michael K. C. (1998), 'Phonology', in Suzanne Romaine (ed.), *The Cambridge History of the English Language, Vol. IV: 1776–1997*, Cambridge: Cambridge University Press, 373–535.

Maddieson, Ian (1984), *Patterns of Sound*, Cambridge: Cambridge University Press.

Maddieson, Ian (1985), 'Phonetic cues to syllabification', in Victoria Fromkin (ed.), *Phonetic Linguistics. Essays in Honor of Peter Ladefoged*, Orlando: Academic Press, 203–21.

Maddieson, Ian (1993), 'Splitting the mora', *UCLA Working Papers in Phonetics* 83, 9–19.

Magnuson, Thomas J. (2007), 'The story of /r/ in two vocal tracts', *Proceedings of the 16th International Congress of the Phonetic Sciences*, 6–10 August 2007, Saarbrucken, Germany, 1,193–6.

Malone, Kemp (1930), 'When did Middle English begin?', in James T. Hatfield, Werner Leopold and A. J. Friedrich Zieglschmid (eds), *Curme Volume of Linguistic Studies*, Language Monograph No. 7, Philadelphia: Linguistic Society of America, 110–17.

Marchand, Hans (1969), *The Categories and Types of Present-Day English Word-Formation: A Synchronic-Diachronic Approach*, Munich: Beck.

Mayr, Robert (2010), 'What exactly is a front rounded vowel? An acoustic and articulatory investigation of the NURSE vowel in South Wales English', *Journal of the International Phonetic Association* 40:1, 93–112.

McCully, Christopher B. (1997), 'Stress, survival and change: Old to Middle English', in Jacek Fisiak (ed.), *Studies in Middle English Linguistics*, Trends in Linguistics. Studies and Monographs 103, Berlin: Mouton de Gruyter, 301–35.

McDavid, Raven I., Jr. (1952), 'Some social differences in pronunciation', *Language Learning* 4:3–4, 102–16.

McKie, Michael (1997), 'The origins and early development of rhyme in English verse', *The Modern Language Review* 92:4, 817–31.

McMahon, April (1994), *Understanding Language Change*, Cambridge: Cambridge University Press.

McMahon, April M. S. (2000), *Lexical Phonology and the History of English*, Cambridge: Cambridge University Press.

McMahon, April (2002), *An Introduction to English Phonology*, Oxford: Oxford University Press.

McMahon, April (2006), 'Restructuring Renaissance English', in Linda Mugglestone (ed.), *The Oxford History of English*, Oxford: Oxford University Press, 147–77.

McMahon, April (2009), 'Perspectives on weakness from English /r/', in Minkova (ed.) (2009), 99–115.

Menken, H. L. (1910), 'The two Englishes', *Baltimore Evening Sun*, 15 September.

Milroy, James (1983), 'On the sociolinguistic history of /h/-dropping in English', in Michael Davenport and Erik Hansen (eds), *Current Topics in English Historical Linguistics*, Odense: Odense University Press, 37–54.

Minkoff, Marco [1967] (1972), *English Historical Grammar*, 3rd edn, Sofia: Naouka I Izkoustvo.

Minkova, Donka (1982), 'The environment for open-syllable lengthening in Middle English', *Folia Linguistica Historica* 3, 29–58.

Minkova, Donka (1985), 'Of rhyme and reason: some foot-governed quantity changes in English', in Roger Eaton, Olga Fischer, Willem Koopman and Frederike van der Leek (eds), *Papers from the 4th International Conference on English Historical Linguistics*, Amsterdam: John Benjamins, 163–78.

Minkova, Donka (1991), *The History of Final Vowels in English*, Berlin and New York: Mouton de Gruyter.

Minkova, Donka (1992), 'Verse structure in the Middle English "Genesis and Exodus"', *Journal of English and Germanic Philology* 91:2, 157–78.

Minkova, Donka (1993), 'On leap-frogging in historical phonology', in *Papers from the Tenth International Conference on Historical Linguistics Amsterdam*, ed. Jaap van Marle, Amsterdam Studies in the Theory and History of Linguistic Science, Series IV, Current Issues in Linguistic Theory, vol. 107, Amsterdam: John Benjamins, 211–29.

Minkova, Donka (1996), 'Non-primary stress in early Middle English accentual-syllabic verse', in Chris McCully and J. J. Anderson (eds), *English Historical Metrics*, Cambridge: Cambridge University Press, 95–120.

Minkova, Donka (1997), 'The credibility of Pseudo-Alfred: prosodic insights in post-Conquest mongrel meter', *Modern Philology* 94:4, 427–54.

Minkova, Donka (2000), 'Middle English prosodic innovations and their test-ability in verse', in Irma Taavitsainen, Terttu Nevalainen, Päivi Pahta and Matti Rissanen (eds), *Placing Middle English in Context*, Berlin and New York: Mouton de Gruyter, 431–461.

Minkova, Donka (2003), *Alliteration and Sound Change in Early English*, Cambridge Studies in Linguistics 101, Cambridge: Cambridge University Press.

Minkova, Donka (2004), 'Philology, linguistics, and the history of [hw] ~[w]', in Curzan and Emmons (eds) (2004), 6–46.

Minkova, Donka (2006a) 'Old and Middle English prosody', in Kemenade and Los (eds) (2006), 95–125.

Minkova, Donka (2006b), 'Phonetic naturalness vs. orthography in the formation of a standardized consonantal inventory of English', in Ursula Schäfer (ed.), *The Beginnings of Standardization. Language and Culture in Fourteenth Century England*, Frankfurt am Main and New York: Peter Lang, 147–75.

Minkova, Donka (2007), 'The forms of verse', in Peter Brown (ed.), *A Companion to Medieval English Literature and Culture c. 1350–1500*, Oxford: Blackwell Publishing, 176–96.

Minkova, Donka (2008a), 'Prefixation and stress in Old English', *Word Structure* 1:1, 21–52.

Minkova, D. (2008b), Review of *Early English Metre* by Thomas Bredehoft, Toronto, Buffalo, London: University of Toronto Press, *Speculum* 83, 673–5. Full text at <http://www.english.ucla.edu/faculty/minkova/BredehoftSpeculumlong.pdf> (last accessed 3 June 2013).

Minkova, Donka (2009a) 'Diagnostics of metricality in Middle English alliterative verse', in Jefferson and Putter (eds) (2009), 77–115.

Minkova, Donka (2009b), 'On the meter of Middle English alliterative verse', in Aroui and Arleo (eds) (2009), 207–25.

Minkova, Donka (2009c) 'Inflectional syncope vs. epanthesis. Notes on the history of weak preterites in English', in Minkova (ed.) (2009), 316–46.

Minkova, Donka (2011a), 'Syllable weight and the weak-verb paradigms in Old English', in David Denison, Ricardo Bermúdez-Otero, Chris McCully and Emma Moore (eds), *Analysing Older English*, Cambridge: Cambridge University Press, 194–213.

Minkova, Donka (2011b) 'Phonemically contrastive fricatives in Old English?', *English Language and Linguistics* 15:1, 31–60.

Minkova, Donka (2012a), 'Prosody', in Alexander Bergs and Laurel Brinton (eds), *Historical Linguistics of English*, Handbücher zur Sprach- und Kommunikationswissenschaft, Berlin: Mouton de Gruyter, 113–29.

Minkova, Donka (2012b), 'Functional stress-shifting in Old English', handout from ICEHL 17, Zürich, August 2012, <https://www.researchgate.net/profile/Donka_Minkova/publications/> (last accessed 18 June 2013).

Minkova, Donka (2013), 'Reconstructing stress in Old and Middle English', in Manfred Krug and Julia Schlüter (eds), *Research Methods in Language Variation and Change*, Cambridge: Cambridge University Press, 260–78.

Minkova, Donka (2014), 'Establishing phonemic contrast in written sources (with reference to Old English)', in Patrick Honeybone and Joseph Salmons (eds), *The Oxford Handbook of Historical Phonology*, Oxford: Oxford University Press.

Minkova, Donka (ed.) (2009), *Phonological Weakness in English: From Old to Present-Day English*, Basingstoke: Palgrave Macmillan.

Minkova, Donka and Robert Stockwell (1992), 'Homorganic clusters as moric busters in the history of English: the case of *-ld, -nd, -mb*', in Matti Rissanen, Ossi Ihalainen, Terttu Nevalainen and Irma Taavitsainen (eds), *History of Englishes: New Methods and Interpretations in Historical Linguistics*, Berlin: Mouton de Gruyter, 191–206.

Minkova, Donka and Robert Stockwell (1994), Review of Norman Blake (ed.), *The Cambridge History of the English Language, Vol. II: 1066–1476*, *Journal of Linguistics* 30:2, 528–66.

Minkova, Donka and Robert Stockwell (1997a), 'Chaucerian phonemics: evidence and interpretation', in Raymond Hickey and Stanisław Puppel (eds), *Language History and Linguistic Modelling*, Trends in Linguistics. Studies and Monographs 101, Berlin: Mouton de Gruyter, 29–58.

Minkova, Donka and Robert Stockwell (1997b), 'Against the *emergence* of the nuclear stress rule in Middle English', in Jacek Fisiak (ed.), *Studies in Middle English Linguistics*, Trends in Linguistics. Studies and Monographs 103, Berlin: Mouton de Gruyter, 301–35.

Minkova, Donka and Robert Stockwell (1998), 'The origins of long-short allomorphy in English', in Jacek Fisiak and Marcin Krygier (eds), *Advances in English Historical Linguistics*, Berlin: Mouton de Gruyter, 211–40.

Minkova, Donka and Robert Stockwell (eds) (2002), *Studies in the History of the English Language: A Millennial Perspective*, Berlin: Mouton de Gruyter.

Minkova, Donka and Robert Stockwell (2003a), 'English vowel shifts and "optimal" diphthongs: is there a logical link?', in Holt (ed.) (2003), 169–90.

Minkova, Donka and Robert Stockwell (2003b), 'Emendation and the Chaucerian metrical template', in Donka Minkova and Theresa Tinkle (eds), *Chaucer and the Challenges of Medievalism*, Frankfurt am Main: Peter Lang, 129–40.

Minkova, Donka and Robert Stockwell (2005), 'Clash avoidance in morphologically derived words in Middle English. (Why [-hʊd] but [-dəm])?', in Nikolaus Ritt and Herbert Schendl (eds), *Rethinking Middle English: Linguistic and Literary Approaches*, Frankfurt am Main: Peter Lang, 263–80.

Minkova, Donka and Robert Stockwell (2006), 'English words', in Bas Aarts and April McMahon (eds), *The Handbook of English Linguistics*, Oxford: Blackwell, 461–83.

Minkova, Donka and Robert Stockwell (2009), *English Words: History and Structure*, 2nd edn, Cambridge: Cambridge University Press.

Minkova, Donka and Kie Ross Zuraw (forthcoming), 'Testing ambisyllabicity in early English', in Merja Kytö and Päivi Pahta (eds), *The Cambridge Handbook of English Historical Linguistics*, Cambridge: Cambridge University Press.

Moen, Per (1979), 'The laxing of the high-back vowel: historical development and recent trends in Minnesota speech', *American Studies in Scandinavia* 11, 67–79.

Montgomery, Michael (2001), 'British and Irish antecedents', in John Algeo (ed.), *The Cambridge History of the English Language, Vol. VI: English in North America*, Cambridge: Cambridge University Press, 86–153.

Montgomery, Michael and Connie Eble (2004), 'Historical perspectives on the *pen/pin* merger in Southern American English', in Curzan and Emmons (eds) (2004), 415–34.

Moore, Samuel and Albert H. Marckwardt (1951), *Historical Outlines of English Sounds and Inflections*, Ann Arbor, MI: George Wahr.

Morén, Bruce (2003), 'Weight typology: an Optimality Theoretic approach', *The Linguistic Review* 20, 281–304.

Moreton, Elliott and Erik Thomas (2007), 'Origins of Canadian Raising in voiceless-coda effects: a case study in phonologization', *Papers in Laboratory*

Phonology 9, ed. Jennifer Cole and José Ignacio Hualde, Berlin: Mouton de Gruyter, 36–74.

Morris, Richard (ed.) (1863), *The Pricke of Conscience (Stimulus Conscientiae), A Northumbrian Poem by Richard Rolle de Hampole*, Berlin: A. Asher.

Mossé, Fernand and James Walker (trans.) [1952] (1968), *Handbook of Middle English*, Baltimore: Johns Hopkins University Press.

Mugglestone, Lynda (2003), *Talking Proper: The Rise and Fall of the English Accent as a Social Symbol*, New York: Oxford University Press.

Mulcaster, Richard [1582] (1925), *THE FIRST PART OF THE ELEMENTARIE WHICH ENTREATETH CHEFELIE OF THE right writing of our English tung, set furth by RICHARD MULCASTER*. Imprinted at London by Thomas Vautroullier dwelling in the blak-friers by Lud-gate. 1925 reprint, Oxford: Clarendon Press.

Murray, Robert W. (2000), 'Syllable cut prosody in early Middle English', *Language* 76, 617–54.

Muthmann, Gustav (1999), *Reverse English Dictionary Based on Phonological and Morphological Principles*, Berlin: Mouton de Gruyter.

Nagy, Naomi and Patricia Irwin (2010), 'Boston (r): Neighbo(r)s nea(r) and fa(r)', *Language Variation and Change* 22, 241–78.

NED, *New English Dictionary on Historical Principles* (1884–1928), Oxford: Clarendon Press.

Nevalainen, Terttu (1999), 'Lexis and semantics', in Roger Lass (ed.), *The Cambridge History of the English Language, Vol. III: 1476–1776*, Cambridge: Cambridge University Press, 332–458.

Nevalainen, Terttu (2006), *An Introduction to Early Modern English*, Edinburgh: Edinburgh University Press.

Nevalainen, Terttu and Ingrid Tieken-Boon van Ostade (2006), 'Standardisation', in Hogg and Denison (eds) (2006), 271–311.

Nevanlinna, Saara (2007), 'The loss of final plosive consonant in Late Middle English rhyme words', in Hans Sauer and Renate Bauer (eds), *Beowulf and Beyond*, Frankfurt am Main: Peter Lang, 271–92.

Oakden, J. P. [1930, 1935] (1968) *Alliterative Poetry in Middle English*, Hamden, CT: Archon Books.

Ogden, Richard (2009), *Introduction to English Phonetics*, Edinburgh: Edinburgh University Press.

Ogura, Mieko (1987), *Historical English Phonology: A Lexical Perspective*, Tokyo: Kenkyusha.

Oppenheimer, Stephen (2006), *The Origins of the British: A Genetic Detective Story*, London: Constable and Robinson.

Ostler, Nicholas (2005), *Empires of the Word: A Language History of the World*, New York: HarperCollins.

Page, B. Richard (2006), 'The diachrony and synchrony of vowel quantity in English and Dutch', *Diachronica* 23:1, 61–104.

Page, Richard (2012) 'Regular vowel lengthening versus sporadic vowel lengthening in Middle English', paper presented at GLAC 18, Bloomington, IN, April 2012.

Pająk, Bożena (2009), 'Contextual constraints on geminates: the case of Polish', *Proceedings of BLS 35*, Berkeley: University of California.

Palsgrave, John (1530), *Lesclarcissement de la langue francoyse*, London: J. Haukyns.

Parkes, M. B. (1983), 'On the presumed date and possible origin of the manuscript of the *Orrmulum*', in E. G. Stanley and D. Gray (eds), *Five Hundred Years of Words and Sounds: A Festschrift for Eric Dobson*, Cambridge: Cambridge University Press, 15–27.

Petrova, Olga (2000), 'Grimm's Law in Optimality Theory', in Karlene Jones-Bley, Martin E. Huld and Angela Della Volpe (eds), *Proceedings of the Eleventh Annual UCLA Indo-European Conference*, Los Angeles, 4–5 June 1999, Washington DC: Institute for the Study of Man, 45–67.

Petrova, Olga (2004), 'Perceptual contrast in Verner's Law', in Curzan and Emmons (eds) (2004), 371–411.

Phillips, Betty (1981a) 'The phonetic basis of a Late Old English sound change', in *Phonologica 1980*, ed. W. U. Dressler, Oskar Pfeiffer and John Rennison, Innsbruck: Institut für Sprachwissenschaft, 337–41.

Phillips, Betty (1981b), 'Lexical diffusion and Southern *tune, duke, news*', *American Speech* 56:1, 72–8.

Phillips, Betty (1983), 'Constraints on syllables and quantitative changes in early English', *Linguistics* 21, 879–95.

Phillips, Betty (2002), 'Lexical diffusion and competing analyses of sound change', in Minkova and Stockwell (eds) (2002), 231–43.

Phillips, Betty (2006), *Word Frequency and Lexical Diffusion*, Basingstoke: Palgrave Macmillan.

Polka, Linda and Megha Sundara (2012), 'Word segmentation in monolingual infants acquiring Canadian English and Canadian French: native language, cross-dialect, and cross-language comparisons', *Infancy* 17:2, 198–232.

Pope, Mildred [1934] (1961), *From Latin to Modern French with Especial Consideration of Anglo-Norman*, Manchester: Manchester University Press.

Proctor, Michael (2010), *Gestural Characterization of a Phonological Class: The Liquids*, PhD thesis, Yale University.

Pullum, Geoffrey and William Ladusaw (1986), *Phonetic Symbol Guide*, Chicago: University of Chicago Press.

Purnell, Thomas C. and Malcah Yaeger-Dror (2010), *Accommodation to the Locally Dominant Norm*, special issue of *American Speech* 85:2.

Putter, Ad (2005), 'Weak *E* and the metre of Richard Spalding's *Alliterative Katherine Hymn*', *Notes and Queries* 52, 288–92.

Putter, Ad, Judith Jefferson and Donka Minkova (2014), 'Dialect, rhyme, and emendation in *Sir Tristrem*', *Journal of English and Germanic Philology* 113:1.

Pyles, Thomas (1943), 'The pronunciation of Latin learned loan words and foreign words in Old English', *PMLA* 58:4, 891–910.

Quirk, Randolph and C. L. Wrenn (1957), *An Old English Grammar*, 2nd edn, New York: Holt, Rinehart and Winston.

Restle, David and Dietmar Zaefferer (eds) (2002), *Sounds and Systems: Studies in*

Structure and Change: A Festschrift for Theo Vennemann, Trends in Linguistics. Studies and Monographs 141, Berlin: Mouton de Gruyter.

Reszkiewicz, Alfred (1973), *A Diachronic Grammar of Old English*, Warsaw: Państwowe Wydawnictwo Naukowe.

Riera, María, Joaquín Romero and Ben Parrell (2009), 'Schwa in American English V+/r/ sequences', in Vigário et al. (eds) (2009), 15–35.

Ringe, Don (2006), *A Linguistic History of English. Volume I: From Proto-Indo-European to Proto-Germanic*, Oxford: Oxford University Press.

Ritt, Nikolaus (1994), *Quantity Adjustment: Vowel Lengthening and Shortening in Early Middle English*, Cambridge: Cambridge University Press.

Ritt, Nikolaus (1997), Early Modern English vowel shortenings in monosyllables before dentals: a morphologically conditioned sound change?', in Raymond Hickey and Stanislav Puppel (eds), *Language History and Linguistic Modelling*, Berlin and New York: Mouton de Gruyter, 65–72.

Ritt, Nikolaus (2007), 'It seemed like a good idea at the time: why there may not have been any early Modern English shortening before dentals after all', in Ute Smit, Stefan Dollinger, Julia Huettner, Gunther Kaltenboeck and Ursula Lutzky (eds), *Tracing English through Time: Explorations in Language Variation: In Honour of Herbert Schendl on the Occasion of his 65th Birthday*, Vienna: Braumüller, 315–31.

Roberts, Jane (2006), *A Guide to Scripts Used in English Writings up to 1500*, London and Boston Spa: British Library Publishing.

Robinson, Orrin W. (1992), *Old English and its Closest Relatives: A Survey of the Earliest Germanic Languages*, Stanford: Stanford University Press.

Roper, Jonathan (ed.) (2011), *Alliteration in Culture*, Houndmills: Palgrave Macmillan.

Ross, John Robert (1972), 'A reanalysis of English word stress', in M. Brame (ed.), *Contributions to Generative Phonology*, Austin: University of Texas Press, 229–323.

Rothwell, W. (2001), 'English and French in England after 1362', *English Studies* 82:6, 539–59.

Rusch, Willard (1994), 'When rhymes go bad: recontextualizing Chaucer's rhymes with the mid front long vowels', *American Journal of Germanic Linguistics and Literatures* 6:1, 1–50.

Russom, Geoffrey (1987), *Old English Meter and Linguistic Theory*, Cambridge: Cambridge University Press.

Russom, Geoffrey (1998), Beowulf *and Old Germanic Metre*, Cambridge Studies in Anglo-Saxon England 23, Cambridge: Cambridge University Press.

Russom, Geoffrey (2004), 'The evolution of Middle English alliterative meter', in Curzan and Emmons (eds) (2004), 279–304.

Ryan, Kevin (2011a), *Gradient Weight in Phonology*, PhD thesis, University of California, Los Angeles.

Ryan, Kevin M. (2011b), 'Gradient syllable weight and weight universals in quantitative metrics', *Phonology* 28:3, 413–54.

Saintsbury, George [1906] (1923), *A History of English Prosody from the Twelfth Century to the Present Day*, vol. I, 2nd edn, New York: Macmillan.

Salmons, Joseph (1992), *Accentual Change and Language Contact: A Comparative Survey and a Case Study of Northern Europe*, Oxford and New York: Routledge.

Samuels, Michael (1963), 'Some applications of Middle English dialectology', *English Studies* 44, 81–94.

Sandved, Arthur O. (1985), *Introduction to Chaucerian English*, Cambridge: D. S. Brewer.

Schaefer, Ursula (ed.) (2006), *The Beginnings of Standardization: Language and Culture in Fourteenth-century England*, Bern: Peter Lang.

Schendl, Herbert (2001), 'Code-switching in medieval English poetry', in Dieter Kastovsky and Arthur Mettinger (eds), *Language Contact in the History of English*, Frankfurt am Main: Peter Lang, 305–37.

Schendl, Herbert (2002), 'Mixed language texts as data and evidence in English historical linguistics', in Minkova and Stockwell (eds) (2002), 51–79.

Schlüter, Julia (2005), *Rhythmic Grammar: The Influence of Rhythm on Grammatical Variation and Change in English*, Topics in English Linguistics 46, Berlin and New York: Mouton de Gruyter.

Schlüter, Julia (2009), 'Consonant or "vowel"? A diachronic study of initial <h> from early Middle English to nineteenth-century English', in Minkova (ed.) (2009), 168–99.

Schreier, Daniel (2005), *Consonant Change in English Worldwide: Synchrony Meets Diachrony*, New York: Palgrave Macmillan.

Schrijver, Peter (2009), 'Celtic influence on Old English: phonological and phonetic evidence', *English Language and Linguistics* 13:2, 193–211.

Schrijver, Peter (2011), 'From Proto-Celtic to Old Irish: relative chronology', handout for University of California, Los Angeles (UCLA) mini-course, 11–15 April 2011.

Scobbie, James and Alan Wrench (2003), 'An articulatory investigation of word final /l/ and /l/-sandhi in three dialects of English', in *Proceedings of the XVth International Conference of Phonetic Sciences*, 1871–4.

Scragg, Donald (1970), 'Initial *H* in Old English', *Anglia* 88, 165–96.

Scragg, Donald G. (1974), *A History of English Spelling*, Manchester: Manchester University Press.

Selkirk, Elisabeth O. (1984), *Phonology and Syntax: The Relation between Sound and Structure*, Cambridge, MA: MIT Press.

Sharf, Donald J. (1962), 'Duration of post-stress intervocalic stops and preceding vowels', *Language and Speech* 5:1, 26–30.

Short, Ian (2007), *Manual of Anglo-Norman*, Occasional Publications Series no. 7, London: Anglo-Norman Text Society.

Sievers, Eduard (1893), *Altgermanische Metrik*, Halle: Niemeyer.

Simon, Ellen (2008), 'Phonological transfer of voicing and devoicing rules: evidence from L1 Dutch and L2 English conversational speech', *Language Sciences* 32:2,010, 63–86.

Smith, Jeremy (1994), 'The Great Vowel Shift in the North of England, and some forms in Chaucer's *Reeve's Tale*', *Neuphilologische Mitteilungen: Bulletin of the Modern Language Society*, 95:433–7.

Smith, Jeremy (1996), *An Historical Study of English: Function, Form and Change*, London: Routledge.

Smith, Jeremy J. (2007), *Sound Change and the History of English*, Oxford: Oxford University Press.

Smith, Jeremy J. (2009), *Old English: A Linguistic Introduction*, Cambridge: Cambridge University Press.

Sóskuthy, Márton (2010), Analogy in the emergence of intrusive-*r* in English. Richard M. Hogg Prize winning essay, <http://www.isle-linguistics.org/prize/> (last accessed 3 June 2013).

Stanley, Eric (ed.) (1972), *The Owl and the Nightingale*, Manchester: Manchester University Press.

Stanley, Eric G. (1988), 'Rhymes in English Medieval verse: from Old English to Middle English', in *Medieval English Studies Presented to George Kane*, ed. Edward Donald Kennedy, Ronald Waldron and Joseph S. Wittig, Cambridge: Brewer, 115–38.

Stenbrenden, Gjertrud (2003), 'On the interpretation of early evidence for ME vowel-change', in Barry Blake, Kate Burridge and Jo Taylor (eds), *Historical Linguistics 2001: Selected Papers from the 15th ICHL, Melbourne, 13–16 August 2001*, Amsterdam and Philadelphia: Benjamins, 403–16.

Stenbrenden, G. F. (2010), *The Chronology and Regional Spread of Long-Vowel Changes in English, c. 1150–1500*, PhD dissertation, University of Oslo.

Stenroos, Merja (2005), 'Spelling conventions and rounded front vowels in the poems of William Herebert', in Nikolaus Ritt and Herbert Schendl (eds), *Rethinking Middle English: Linguistic and Literary Approaches*, Frankfurt am Main: Peter Lang, 291–309.

Steriade, Donca (1991), 'Moras and other slots', *Proceedings of the Formal Linguistics Society of the Midamerica* 1, 254–80.

Steriade, Donca (2001), 'Directional asymmetries in place assimilation: a perceptual account', in E. Hume and K. Johnson (eds), *The Role of Speech Perception in Phonology*, New York: Academic Press, 219–50.

Stockwell, Robert (1961), 'The Middle English "long close" and "long open" mid vowels', *Texas Studies in Literature and Language* 2, 259–68. [Reprinted in Lass (ed.) (1969), 154–63].

Stockwell, Robert (1985), 'Assessment of alternative explanations of the Middle English phenomenon of high vowel lowering when lengthened in the open syllable', in Roger Eaton, Olga Fischer, Willem Koopman and Frederike van der Leek (eds), *Papers from the 4th International Conference on English Historical Linguistics*, Amsterdam: John Benjamins, 303–18.

Stockwell, Robert (2002a), 'Retraction and rounding in Old English Breaking', in Restle and Zaefferer (eds) (2002), 121–37.

Stockwell, Robert (2002b), 'How much shifting actually occurred in the historical English vowel shift?', in Minkova and Stockwell (eds) (2002), 267–81.

Stockwell, Robert (2006), 'The status of Late Middle English <*ei*> spellings as early evidence of the English Vowel Shift', in Schaefer (ed.) (2006), 175–80.

Stockwell, Robert P. and C. Westbrook Barritt (1955), 'The Old English short di-graphs: some considerations', *Language* 31:3, 372–89.

Stockwell, Robert P. and C. Westbrook Barritt (1961), 'Scribal practice: some assumptions', *Language* 37:1, 75–82. [Reprinted in Lass (ed.) (1969), 133–42].

Stockwell, Robert and Donka Minkova (1988), 'The English Vowel Shift: problems of coherence and explanation', in Dieter Kastovsky and Gero Bauer (eds), *Luick Revisited*, Tübingen: Günter Narr, 355–94.

Stockwell, Robert and Donka Minkova (1997a), 'On drifts and shifts', *Studia Anglica Posnaniensia* 31, 283–305.

Stockwell, Robert and Donka Minkova (1997b) 'Prosody', in Robert Bjork and John Niles (eds), *A* Beowulf *Handbook*, Lincoln, NE: University of Nebraska Press, 55–85.

Stockwell, Robert and Donka Minkova (1997c), 'Old English Metrics and the phonology of resolution', *Germanic Studies in Honor of Anatoly Liberman, NOWELE: North-Western European Language Evolution* 31/32, 389–406.

Stockwell, Robert and Donka Minkova (1999), 'Explanations of sound change: contradictions between dialect data and theories of chain shifting', *Leeds Studies in English* 30, 83–103.

Stockwell, Robert and Donka Minkova (2001), 'The partial-contact origins of English pentameter verse: the Anglicization of an Italian model', in Dieter Kastovsky and Arthur Mettinger (eds), *Language Contact in the History of English*, Frankfurt am Main: Peter Lang, 337–62.

Stockwell, Robert and Donka Minkova (2002), 'Interpreting the Old and Middle English close vowels', *Language Sciences* 24:3–4, 447–58.

Strandberg, Otto (1919), *The Rime-Vowels of Cursor Mundi: A Phonological and Etymological Investigation*, Uppsala: Almqvist and Wiskells.

Sweet, Henry (1877) *Handbook of Phonetics*, vol. 2, Oxford: Clarendon Press.

Sweet, Henry (1888), *History of English Sounds, Transactions of the Philological Society for 1873–4*, Oxford: Clarendon Press.

Sweet, Henry (1890), *A Primer of Spoken English*, Oxford: Clarendon Press.

Sweet, Henry (1922), *An Anglo-Saxon Reader in Verse and Prose*, 9th edn, Oxford: Clarendon Press.

Szemerényi, Oswald J. L. [1970] (1999), *Introduction to Indo-European Linguistics*, Oxford: Oxford University Press.

Taavitsainen, Irma (2000), 'Scientific language and spelling standardisation 1375–1550', in Laura Wright (ed.), *The Development of Standard English 1300–1800*, Cambridge: Cambridge University Press, 131–54.

Tabain, M. (1998), 'Non-sibilant fricatives in English: spectral information above 10 kHz', *Phonetica* 55, 107–30.

Tagliamonte, Sali and Rosalind Temple (2005), 'New perspectives on an ol' variable: (t, d) in British English', *Language Variation and Change* 17:3, 281–302.

Tamson, George J. (1898), *Word-Stress in English. A Short Treatise on the Accentuation of Words in Middle English as Compared with the Stress in Old and Modern English, Studien zur englischen Philologie III*, Halle an der Saale: Dr Martin Sändig.

Tarlinskaja, Marina (1976), *English Verse: Theory and History*, The Hague: Mouton.

Tarlinskaja, Marina (1987), *Shakespeare's Verse: Iambic Pentameter and the Poet's Idiosyncrasies*, New York: Peter Lang.

Tarlinskaja, Marina (forthcoming), *Shakespeare among Others: English Drama 1541–1642.*

Terajima, Michiko (1985), *The Trajectory Constraint and 'Irregular' Rhymes in Middle English*, Tokyo: Shinozaki Shorin.

Thomas, Eric (2001), *An Acoustic Analysis of Vowel Variation in New World English*, Publication of the American Dialect Society no. 85, Durham, NC: Duke University Press.

Throop, Priscilla (2008), *Ælfric's Grammar and Glossary: The Complete English Translation*, Medieval MS Box 363: Charlotte, VT.

Tieken-Boon van Ostade, I. (2009), *An Introduction to Late Modern English*, Edinburgh: Edinburgh University Press.

Tottie, Gunnel (2002), *An Introduction to American English*, Oxford: Blackwell.

Tristram, Hildegard (2002), 'Attrition of inflections in English and Welsh', in Markku Filppula, Juhani Klemola and Heli Pitkänen (eds), *The Celtic Roots of English*, Joensuu: University of Joensuu, Faculty of Humanities, 111–49.

Trudgill, Peter (1983), *On Dialect: Social and Geographical Perspectives*, Oxford: Blackwell.

Trudgill, Peter (1986), *Dialects in Contact*, Oxford: Blackwell.

Trudgill, Peter (1999a), *The Dialects of England*, 2nd edn, Oxford and Malden, MA: Wiley-Blackwell.

Trudgill, Peter (1999b), 'A window on the past: "colonial lag" and New Zealand evidence for the phonology of nineteenth-century English', *American Speech* 74:3, 227–39.

Trudgill, Peter (ed.) (1984), *Language in the British Isles*, Cambridge: Cambridge University Press.

Trudgill, Peter, Elizabeth Gordon and Gillian Lewis (1998), 'New-dialect formation and Southern Hemisphere English: the New Zealand short front vowels', *Journal of Sociolinguistics* 2:1, 35–51.

Trudgill, Peter and Elizabeth Gordon (2006), 'Predicting the past. Dialect archaeology and Australian English rhoticity', *English World-Wide* 27:3, 235–46.

Uffmann, Christian (2007), 'Intrusive [r] and optimal epenthetic consonants', *Language Sciences* 29:2–3, 334–59.

Vachek, Joseph (1976), *Selected Writings in English and General Linguistics*, Prague: Academia and The Hague: Mouton.

Vennemann, Theo (1988), *Preference Laws for Syllable Structure and the Explanation of Sound Change*, Berlin: Mouton de Gruyter.

Vennemann, Theo (2010), 'The source of the *Ing* rune and of the futhark', *Sprachwissenschaft* 35, 1–14.

Vigário, Marina Cláudia, Sónia Frota and Maria João Freitas (eds) (2009), *Phonetics and Phonology: Interactions and Interrelations*, Current Issues in Linguistic Theory 306, Amsterdam: John Benjamins.

Wakelin, Martyn (1972), *English Dialects: An Introduction*, London: Athlone Press.

Wakelin, Martyn (1988), *The Archaeology of English*, London: B. T. Batsford.

Wales, Katie (2006), *Northern English: A Social and Cultural History*, Cambridge: Cambridge University Press.

Walker, John (1791–1826), *Critical Pronouncing Dictionary. A critical pronouncing dictionary and expositor of the English language ≈: to which are prefixed, principles of English pronunciation≈with observations etymological, critical, and grammatical≈with directions to foreigners, for acquiring a knowledge of the use of this dictionary*, London and Leipzig: Ernest Fleischer.

Watkins, Calvert (1985), *The American Heritage Dictionary of Indo-European Roots*, Boston: Houghton Mifflin.

Watkins, Calvert (1992), 'Indo-European and the Indo-Europeans', in *The American Heritage Dictionary of the English Language*, 3rd edn, Boston: Houghton Mifflin, 2,081–9.

Watts, Richard J. (2003), 'Was the Great Vowel Shift really "great"? A reappraisal of research work on an elusive linguistic phenomenon', in Cornelia Tschichoid (ed.), *English Core Linguistics, Essays in Honour of D. J. Allerton*, Bern: Peter Lang, 13–30.

Watts, Richard J. (2011), *Language Myths and the History of English*, Oxford: Oxford University Press.

Wells, John (1982), *Accents of English*, vols 1–3, Cambridge: Cambridge University Press.

Wells, John (1984), 'English accents in England', in Trudgill (ed.) (1984), 55–69.

Wełna, Jerzy (1978), *A Diachronic Grammar of English. Part One: Phonology*, Warsaw: Państwowe Wydawnictwo Naukowe.

Wełna, Jerzy (1987), *A Critical Survey of a Historical Phonology of English Vowels* (with special reference to Karl Luick's 'Historische Grammatik der englischen Sprache'), Warsaw: Wydawnictwa Uniwersytetu Warszawskiego.

Wełna, Jerzy (2004), 'Middle English ē-raising: a prelude to the Great Vowel Shift', *Studia Anglica Posnaniensia* 40, 75–83.

Wełna, Jerzy (2007), 'The loss of [ei]: [ai] opposition in Middle English', *Studia Anglica Posnaniensia* 43, 3–16.

Wetzel, Claus-Dieter (1981), *Die Worttrennung am Zeilenende in altenglischen Handschriften*, Frankfurt am Main: Peter Lang.

Wheatley, Henry B. (ed.) (1867), *Manipulus Vocabulorum: A Rhyming Dictionary of the English Language by Peter Levins* (1570). Edited, with an alphabetical index by Henry B. Wheatley, London: Published for the Early English Text Society by Trübner and Co., 60, Paternoster Row.

White, David (2004), 'Why we should not believe in short diphthongs', in Curzan and Emmons (eds) (2004), 57–84.

Wiggins, Alison (2003), '*Guy of Warwick* in Warwick?: Reconsidering the dialect evidence', *English Studies* 84:3, 219–30.

Williams, Fionnuala Carson (2011), 'Alliteration in English-Language versions of current widespread European idioms and proverbs', in Roper (ed.) (2011), 24–44.

Windross, Michael (1994), 'Loss of post-vocalic *r*: were the orthoepists really tone-deaf?', in Kastovsky (ed.) (1994), 429–48.

Wogan-Browne, Jocelyn (ed.), with Carolyn Collette, Maryanne Kowaleski, Linne Mooney, Ad Putter and David Trotter (2009), *Language and Culture in Medieval Britain: The French of England, c. 1100–c. 1500*, Woodbridge and Rochester, NY: York Medieval Press.

Wolfram, Walt (1976), 'Toward a description of a-prefixing in Appalachian English', *American Speech* 51:1/2, 45–56.

Wolfram, Walt and Natalie Schilling-Estes [1998] (2006), *American English: Dialects and Variation*, 2nd edn, Cambridge and Oxford: Basil Blackwell.

Wright, Joseph and Elizabeth M. Wright (1928), *An Elementary Middle English Grammar*, 2nd edn, London: Oxford University Press.

Wyld, Henry Cecil [1927] (1949), *A Short History of English*, London: John Murray.

Wyld, Henry Cecil (1953), *A History of Modern Colloquial English*, Oxford: Basil Blackwell.

Youmans, Gilbert (1989), 'Milton's meter', in Paul Kiparsky and Gilbert Youmans (eds), *Phonetics and Phonology, Vol. 1: Rhythm and Meter*, San Diego: Academic Press, 341–79.

Youmans, Gilbert (1996), 'Reconsidering Chaucer's prosody', in C. B. McCully and J. J. Anderson (eds), *English Historical Metrics*, Cambridge: Cambridge University Press, 185–210.

Youmans, Gilbert and Xingzhong Li (2002), 'Chaucer: folk poet or littérateur?', in Minkova and Stockwell (eds) (2002), Berlin: Mouton de Gruyter, 153–75.

Zec, Draga (1995), 'Sonority constraints on syllable structure', *Phonology* 12:1, 85–129.

Zuraw, Kie (2009), 'Treatments of weakness in phonological theory', in Minkova (ed.) (2009), 9–29.

Word Index

The word index includes items whose pronunciation is discussed in the hard copy portion of the book. It does not include words discussed in the Online Companion. It excludes high frequency words which occur in the main text: function words, pronouns, core vocabulary items. Colons in the entries indicate a rhyming pair, other pairs are linked with – or ~. Accents are preserved only when relevant to the context.

a-, 182
ábacus, 308
abbot, 78, 289
abide, 203
ability-habilitation, 107
-able, 310, 320
able-ability, 255
able-habilitate, 105
abnormality, 147
abound-abundance, 218
about, 191
above, 219
abridge, 141
abróad, 288
absolute, 268
ábstract-abstráct, 311
abysm, 58
account-accountancy, 216
acorn, 223
acre, 217, 223
-acy, 310
adder, 79, 125, 212
áddict-addíct, 288
-ade, 319–20
adze, 135
afford, 125
again, 8
against, 49, 150
-age, 310, 320
age, 263
aged, 232
aggravate, 32
agnostic, 67
ahoy, 269
aik/oak, 201, 250
Aike-Oake 200, 203, 240
-air, 319–20
-al, 47
alderman, 125
aleph, 256
Alexander, 66
Alexander-Saunders, 241
all, 129
állergy-allérgic, 13
allow, 32
ally, 311
almesse, 140
alóha, 101, 115
alone, 32
altar, 289
alum, 136
alumnus, 15, 136
always-causeways, 284, 303
ambi-, 187
amidst, 49, 150
amnesia, 142
among(st), 49, 150, 192
ámorous, 315–16
-an, 49
ancient, 140, 150, 255
ancient-pansy, 255
-ancy, 15
and- (OE), 233
-ane, 319
angel, 182, 255, 269
animal, 12–13
ante-, 15
antenna, 15
antique, 256
ape, 73, 78
aplomb, 135
apple, 72–3, 78, 104, 120, 179, 199–200, 298
appreciate, 144
April, 160
apse, 134
-ar, 47
Arab, 108, 160, 285
arbour, 200
arbour-herbage, 107
-ard, 310
are : pair, 224
area-aerial, 129
ark, 183
arm, 117, 124, 178
aroma-aromatic, 255
arrant, 277–8
arrant-errant, 312
arrow, 126
arse, 122
art, 169
ash, 44, 154
ask~ax, 48
assault, 208
assembly, 12–13
assume, 268
-ast, 319
asterisk, 354
asthma, 57, 231
at ease, 25, 147, 341
ataxy, 187
-ate, 310, 316
attain, 27
attribute, 32
augment, 311

Áugust-augúst, 312
aunt, 169, 241, 268–9
aunt-haunt, 267
Aussie, 226
autogony, 290
autumn(al), 136, 140
await : white, 110
awe, 83
axe, 134

baccara(t), 290
Bach, 100
back, 198–200
bad, 180
bairn, 68, 117
bake, 250, 266
balanced, 34
bald, 268–9
bale-baleful, 294
ban, 155
ban-bang, 138
band, 169
Bangor, 138
bank, 7
banner, 32
baptist, 217
bar, 240
barber, 200
bark, 200
barn, 121
barrier-reef, 32
barrow, 84
base, 191
basilisk, 217
bass-bass, 20
bath, 28, 81, 179, 188, 198–9, 238, 242, 255
bath-bathe-baths, 74, 89, 90
bathe, 28, 81, 93, 97
battle, 309
be, 191
be-, 182, 219, 296, 336
beam me, 32
bear, 63, 68
bear-fear, 271
beast, 213
beat-beet, 190
beauty, 38, 208, 306
beaver, 120, 217
bed, 80, 237, 238
bedchamber, 13
beef, 97
beer, 206
beership, 182
beet, 190
beetle, 195
beetle-bitter, 78
behave, 29, 102
behest, 150
behind, 166, 168
beige, 50, 142
being, 191
belief-beliefs-believe, 74, 89, 96, 156, 159
beloved, 232
bench, 85
bench-bank, 86
bend, 169
bereft~bereaved, 213
Berkeley-Berkshire-Berkley, 276
berry, 179
besiege, 255
besom, 223
best, 149
bestial, 144
Beth, 240
bethink, 91
betide, 203
betoken-behave, 27
betwixt, 49
beyond, 28
bid, 72–3
bidder, 147
bidding, 293
bin, 155
bin-bean, 225
bind, 166, 250, 253, 258, 265
bingo, 138
birch, 120
birch-birk, 86
bird, 35
bishop, 182
bit, 78
bite, 45, 78
bite-bit, 214, 225
bitter, 24, 72
black, 172
black-Blake, 224, 226
bladder, 125
blame, 263
bland, 241
blank, 241
blast, 213
blend, 169
bless, 93
blessed, 232
blind, 165, 168
bliss, 226
blitz, 134
blood, 160, 190, 246, 272
blood-bleed, 162
blossom, 49, 288
blow, 175, 266
blowth, 215
blue, 191
blush, 194, 197
board, 124, 165, 278
boat, 155, 188, 190, 202, 250, 271
boil, 191, 268, 270
boil : bile, 270
boing, 270
boink, 269–70
bold, 167
bolt, 169, 244
bomb, 135
bomb-bombable, 135
bone, 26, 45, 244, 331
bone-bonfire, 215, 255
book, 81, 190, 225, 271, 272, 273
book-buck, 246
booth-book, 271
born, 155
borne, 244
borough, 48
borrow, 12, 67, 87, 126, 160
boss, 243
botany, 337
both, 190
both~baith, 203
bóther-bóthersome, 287
bottom, 31, 34, 40, 69, 192
bough, 48, 113, 114, 140
bought, 206, 207, 268, 269
boulder, 169
boulevard, 290
bound for, 168
bow, 205, 207
bow down, 205, 258
bower, 279
bowl, 268
boy, 98, 190, 191, 209, 268, 270
brambles, 48, 120, 129, 212
brass-brazen, 97
brave-braved, 226
bread, 41, 45, 271
break, 250, 262, 264, 266
breakfast, 304
breast, 213
breastplate, 13
breath-breadth, 227
breathe, 93, 97

breeches~burches, 119
brethren, 161
brew, 205, 207, 268
brew-new, 267
bridge, 77, 81, 86, 129, 141, 194, 197
Bridgestowe-Bristol, 128
bridle, 205–6, 209, 257–8
brief, 92, 97, 202
brief-brevity, 218
bright, 113, 206
brimstone, 304
bring-brought, 163
brisk-brusque, 194
broad-braid, 203
broom, 273
broth, 244
brother, 66, 69, 91, 120, 161
brought, 207
bud-bird, 225
buf(f)et, 194
bugle, 193
build, 167
bulb, 246
bulge, 246
bulk, 246
bull, 7
bullet, 245
bulletin, 245
bullion, 245
bungalow, 245
buoy, 269
burden, 125, 137, 145
-burgh, 84, 103, 113
burn, 119
-bury, 196
bury, 195–6, 235, 237–8
bush, 50, 194, 237, 245
bushel, 245
busy, 196, 236
but, 219, 246
but-about, 219
butcher, 245
butter, 246
buttock, 246
buy, 72, 220
buy-bought, 163
by, prep, 205

cabbage, 290
cage, 141
Cajun, 30
Calder-called her, 104
cálendar, 315
calf, 241, 269
call, 7, 68, 269
calm, 241, 269
cambric, 167
Cambridge, 167
camouflage, 142
camp, 198
canál-chánnel, 310
candēla, 5
candle, 58
cánker, 289
capitalise, 25, 147
caprice, 253–4, 256
car, 240, 242
carafe, 97
car-core, 241
cardiac, 63
care, 82, 85, 88
cast, 7
-caster vs -chester, 86
castle, 49
cat, 24, 172
catch-chase, 86
cattle, 12
cattle-chattel, 86
caught, 33, 50
cause, 208
cave-cavity, 218
ceiling, 34
celestial, 144
cell, 82
cerebellum, 15
certain, 277
chair, 28
chalice, 159
chalk, 268, 269
chamber-lamp, 255
champ, 241
chance, 169
change, 241
channel canál, 312
chaplain, 309
charisma-charismatic, 285
chárity, 315
Charles, 12
chary, 85, 86, 88
chaste-chastity, 218
chattel, 12
chav, 227, 240
cheap-Chapman, 215
check-in-chicken, 238
cheese, 81
chef, 98
cherub, 34
chess, 29, 49
chest-kist, 86
chew, 197, 268
chief, 92
child, 41, 81, 85, 166–7, 172, 179, 220, 254, 333
child-children, 151, 165
childhood, 296
children, 125, 166
chimney, 30
chin, 85
choice, 38, 50, 58, 151, 208, 268, 269, 270
choose, 82, 201, 204
chorus, 57, 63
Christ, 213
Christmas, 304
chthonic, 57
church, 8, 85, 194, 196
church-kirk, 88
churn, 194
chutzpah, 100
cigar, 30
Cindi~Cindy, 187
circle, 277
círcle, 289
Citi, 187
city, 82
clatter, 68
claw, 191
clean, 202
clean-cleanse, 271
cleave-cleft, 96
cleft~cleaved, 213
clergy, 124
clerk, 82, 277
clerk-clerk, 276
climb, 43, 135, 166–7
climber, 135
climbing, 135
cloak, 263
close-close, 88
cloth, 35, 237, 240, 242
cloth-clothe, 89
cloth-clothes-cloths, 96
clothe, 94
clough, 207
clue, 268
clutch, 194, 245
coal, 202
coast, 213
coat-coating, 226
coffin, 92
coffin-coven, 50
cognition, 63
coif, 97
coin, 270

cold, 167, 264
cold-chill, 86
colour, 245
colourless, 13
colours, 124
column, 136, 308
comb, 135, 167
combi, 187
come, 69, 82, 189, 221
comet, 5, 58, 217, 308
comma, 34, 151
commute, 32
compare-comparison, 218
complain, 190
compound, 140
con, 67
condemn, 136
cone-conical, 216, 218, 227
connateness, 32
cook, 272
cool, 129
coolth, 215
coomb, 167
cord, 169
cordial, 63
cordial-hearty, 74
corps, 244
cortège, 142
cot, 33, 50
cot-caught, 240, 243
cot-coat, 225
cough, 105, 112, 114, 207, 242
could-cud, 246
council, 306
country, 307
couple, 245
courage, 141
court-courtesy, 218
cousin, 45, 245
cove, 92
cover, 189
covet, 245
cow, 250, 258, 265
cowl, 289
coy, 270
crabbed, 232
(cra)cy, 319
cradle, 217
craft, 81
cramp, 102
creature, 144
creature~critter, 144
creep(s)-crept, 39–40, 43, 212–13
cress, 119
Cristal, 187
critic-critíque, 312
critique, 253–4, 256
crook, 272
crooked, 232
cross, 243
cross~corse, 119-20
crown, 49, 258, 265, 289
crutch, 194
cucumber, 217, 308
cuddle, 27
cudgel, 194, 197
cul(minate)-hill, 62
culver, 92
cumin, 137
cunning, 67
cupboard, 303
curd, 35
cure, 37, 206
curriculum, 15
curry, 245
curse, 124, 169
cursed, 232
cursor, 277
cushion, 246
cut, 65, 189
cut-cute, 190
cut-cutting, 226
cute, 38

dais, 263
daisy, 220, 303
dale, 224
Dalwood, 224
Dalziel, 83
damn, 136
damn-damnation, 134, 136
dance, 22, 237–8, 241–2, 255, 268–9
danger, 241, 255, 269
darling, 276, 278
Darlington, 122
daughter, 57, 113–14, 161, 207
dawn, 84
-day, 304
day, 177–8, 81, 190–1, 205–6, 263, 266, 268
day-dawn, 74
dead, 238, 240, 271
dead-bead, 234, 271
deaf, 271, 273
dead-leaf, 271–3
deal, 213
steel, 261
dealer, 155
dear, 206
dear-dearth, 214
dear-darling, 276, 278
death, 271
debt, 238
December, 167, 217
decision, 82
deduce-deductive, 218
deed, 174
deem, 12, 201, 213
deep, 214
deep-Dep(t)ford, 215
deer, 12, 275, 279
degree, 58, 218
delay, 263
delight-delicious, 218
dell-dale, 224
deprive-deprivation, 255
depth, 214
derision, 143
derv, 227
desert : part, 276
design, 265
despair, 65
dessert, 66, 93, 226
destroy, 208
devil-devilish, 295
dew, 191, 205, 209, 268
diagnosis, 67
dice, 253
digestif, 97, 98
digestive, 97
dill, 221
din, 173
dinghy, 139
dinner-time, 13
diphthongal, 138
disciple, 87
discipline, 87
discus, 88
dish-disk-discus, 74, 88
dissatisfied, 32, 77
disservice, 32
dissolve, 66, 93
ditch, 82, 85
dive, 194
divine-divinity, 216, 218, 227
division, 141
dizzy, 173, 182
dizzy-busy, 184, 192, 195
-dj, 144
do, 155

do~dae, 203
do-due, 267
dog, 243
doldrum(s), 167
dollar, 237, 242–3
-dom, 138, 215, 295–6, 318, 351
Don-Dawn, 240
doohickey, 101, 115
doom, 157, 254
doom-deem, 162
door, 63, 172, 181, 227
double, 245
doug, 207
dough, 81, 103, 114, 263, 266, 268
dough-duff, 114
dove, 189, 245
down, 30
down-Dunton, 215
drag, 84
drágon-dragóon, 312
drat, 243
drau, 191
draught, 113
draw, 83
draw-drag, 88
dray, 84
dream, 202
dreich, 100
dress, 34, 151
drink, 183
drink-drench, 86
drive, 92
drive-drift, 214
droid, 270
drop, 243
drought, 47, 206, 207, 258
drown, 208
drunk, 155
dry, 144, 258
dryad, 63
dryness, 205, 257
due, 38, 143, 268
duke, 144, 193, 197, 208, 268
dull-bull, 234
dumb, 135, 140, 167
dune, 143
dung, 194
dust, 213
duty, 38
Dvořák, 66
dwarf, 96, 114–15
dwarfs/dwarves, 96
dwell, 163
each, 86, 130
ear, 183, 279
ear (of corn), 146
earl, 124, 165, 278
earth, 165, 278
east, 170, 213
eat, 191, 262
-eau, 319
edge, 86, 101, 141
-ee, 310, 319–20
-een, 319
-eenth, 215
-eer, -ier, 319
effect-feckless, 149
Egypt, 149
eight, 206–7, 263
elbow, 49
elder, 125, 163, 167
eldest, 163
electrizity for electricity, 94
Elene, 105
eleven, 49, 129
elf-elfs-elven, 74, 96
-elle, 319
ellipse, 134
Elysian, 142
ember, 167
Emma, 128, 132
-en, 49, 318
-ence, -ency, 15
end, 169
ends, 227
endure, 63, 195
eng, agma, angma, 136
-e(ng), 192, 236
English~Inglis(s), 192
enough, 48, 113, 114, 207, 233
enthuse, 268
entire, 58
-er, 138, 163, 318
-er/-re, 18
ere, 226
-erel, 310
-erie, 310
errant, 277
error, 276
-es, 49
escalade~scale, 48
-esce, 319
-ese, 319
especial~special, 48
espionage, 142
espouse~spouse, 48
-esque, 319
-est, 49, 138, 163
estate~state, 48
-ette, 319
euphoria, 63, 68
even(ing)-eve, 49
ever, 120, 219
every, 49
evil, 157, 221
example, 66
exclusive vs excluzive, 94
excusable, 12
excuse, 12
exemplar, 12
exemplary, 12
expound, 140
eye, 220

fa, 127
fa[r], 127
façade, 256
face, 34, 38, 94, 151, 248, 250
fáham, 101, 115
fair, 279
fajita, 59, 115
fall, 95, 131
false, 169, 269
family, 49
fan, 30, 92, 156
fang-fan, 75
fangless, 138
fan-van, 24
far, 118
fared, 189
farm, 140, 278
farthing, 276
farthingale, 137
-fast, 295
fast, 198
fast, 91
fasten, 49, 91
fast-vast, 91
fat, 225
father, 66, 69, 124, 145, 198
father-fatherly, 295, 318
faucet, 129
fault, 131, 208
favour-favourable, 216
fear, 271
fear-bear, 234
feast, 213
feather, 7
feature, 144
feck, 149
feed-fed, 212, 216
feel, 129

feet, 191, 260
fell, 166, 168
fellow, 126, 293
ferment, 311
ferry-very, 91
ferther, 140
fertile, 68, 224
fetter, 147
fiddle, 92, 125
field, 166–8, 172
fiend, 161, 191, 202, 250
fiend-fiends, 159
fierce, 122
fifteen, 236
fifth, 215
fight, 41, 49
fill, 155
filth, 170, 214
fine-vine, 89
fir, 277
fire, 155, 188, 191, 275, 279, 282
first, 120, 169, 193
fish, 86–8, 95, 139, 236–7
fishes, 86
fish-piscatorial, 87
fist, 213
fit-feet, 225
five, 169
five-fifth, 96, 214, 255
flame, 269
flank, 241
flea, 188
flee, 188
fleece, 34, 37–8, 151, 248, 250
flesh, 75
fling, 192
flood, 237, 245–6, 272
floor, 279
floor-poor, 274, 280
flow, 268
flow, 65
flung, 45
fly, 205, 257
fodder, 125
fog, 243
foison, 209
foist, 269
-fold, 91
fold, 167
folk, 22, 131, 189, 244
folly, 309
food, 246, 273
food-feed, 162
fool, 250
foot, 34, 45, 54, 63, 68, 151, 173, 197–8, 216, 237, 245, 248, 272
foot-feet, 151, 157, 161
foot-podium, 54, 67
foot-strut, 246
for-, 219, 296
force, 244
foretaste, 13
forge, 244
formal, 290
forsook, 272
fort, 244
fortune, 144
forum, 63, 68
fought, 207
foul, 214
foul-filth, 163
foul-Fulford, 215
foul-defile, 162
foundry, 167
four, 177
fowl, 190, 207–8, 258, 265
fox, 95, 163
fox-vixen, 163–4
fray, 49
Frederick, 119
freemason, 13
frequent, 311
frequent-frequency, 216
friar, 253
Friedman, 119
Friedrich, 119
friend, 22, 161
frog, 79
frontier, 144
froth, 244
fruit, 208
fudge, 246
-ful, 91, 215, 318
Fulham, 245
full, 129, 192, 237, 245
full-fill, 151, 157, 161
full-length, 32
full-to fill, 162
fumble, 246
fume, 45, 195
fungation, 138
fur, 151
furry, 32
fury, 32, 38
fury-bury, 184, 192, 195
furze, 194
fuss-fuse, 225
gae-go, 200
gaffe, 98
gala, 256
game-gammon, 184, 220, 224, 226
gammon-game, 49
gannet, 223
gape, 7
garage, 141
garlic, 220, 236
gather, 83, 124
gaunt, 241
ge- (OE), 182, 219, 232, 289
gendarme, 142
ġenoh (OE), 232
genre, 142
georgette, 142
get, 8
get úp, 147
ghost, 213
ghost, 81
gigolo, 142
gigue, 142
gild, 167
giraffes~gira[v]es, 98
gird, 63
girdle, 119, 120, 277
girl, 124
give, 8, 83, 156
give-gift, 96
glad, 180, 199, 237
glasnost, 68
glass-glaze, 89, 97
glazing, 91
gloom, 273
gloomth, 215
gloss, 160
glove, 189, 272, 273
glowing, 28
glutton, 245
gnat, 81
gnaw, 49, 205
God, 22, 154, 183
gnawing, 140
go, 156
go~gae, 203
goat, 34, 37–8, 83, 102, 151, 162, 248, 250
goat-Gatwick, 215
God, 22, 44, 65, 155, 172, 242–3, 295
God-egad, 236
goddess, 164
golden, 80
gold-gild, 162

golf, 97
golfe, 244
gonna-going to, 299
good, 83, 154, 190–1, 215
goose, 34, 37–8, 97, 151, 161, 169, 173, 198, 250
goose-gosling, 97
gooseberry, 246
gorse, 119, 120, 121, 124
gosling, 94
gospel, 154, 215, 242
gotcha, 143
Goth, 83
grace, 263
grade-gradual, 218
gradual, 218
Graffham, 220
graft, 93, 150
grand-grant, 241
grass, 226
grass~garston, 119
grass-graze, 89, 90, 96–7, 184, 220, 224
grasshopper, 79
grave, 93
gravel-stone, 13
grease, n. (c. 1340 < OFr graisse)-(variable) grease, 97
greasy, 94
great, 264
green, 41
greenth, 215
greet-greeted, 216
grey, 177–8, 205–6, 209, 263, 268
grief, 36
grief-grieve, 89, 96
grieve, 36
grin~girn, 119
grind, 168
groom, 273
gross, 94
ground, 103, 168, 172
ground, 81
grove, 83
grow, 83
growth, 215
guarantee, 12
guarantee-guardian, 86
guardian, 12
guess, 7
guest, 65, 68
guild, 167
gun, 246
gunwale, 304
gymnasium, 142
gypsy, 49

habítual, 102
hallúcinate, 102
Havána, 102
haddock, 223
hag(g), 84
hagio-, 107
hair, 153
(h)aitches, 99
half, 129, 140, 179, 238
halfpenny, 131, 241, 255
hall, 156, 198, 269
hállow, 288
halo, 107
hand, 169, 198
handiwork, 104
hangar, 139
hap, 7
happen, 237, 238–9
happy, 91, 102, 237
hárass-haráss, 284, 337
harbinger, 137
hard, 103
hardy, 106
hare, 279
harmony, 107
harrow, 84
harry, 84, 200, 278
haste, 106, 264
hat, 30, 199
hate, 199
haunt, 241, 268, 269
have-behave, 224
have : grave, 224
haven, 7
haw, 84
hay, 84, 178
hazel, 199, 217
hellénic, 102
helló, 102
head, 45, 190, 217, 271
heal, 213
heal-health, 214, 255
heal-heel, 261
hear, 153
hearken, 124, 278
heart, 63, 117, 278
heathen, 137
heather, 102
heave-heft, 96, 214
heaven, 7, 106, 182, 223
heavens, 181
hecatomb, 135
heed, 266
heel, 202
height, 47
heir, 99, 108, 208
helix, 107
help, 140
hemato-, 107
hemi-, 107
hence, 95
hept(a)-, 107
herald, 106
herb, 99, 108
Hercules, 105
here-there, 234
heritage, 99, 108
hermit, 106
heron, 106
hetero-, 107
hew, 207
hex(a)-, 107
hiccup, 226
hide, 193–4, 213, 266
high, 104, 106, 113, 163
hill, 29, 54, 68, 71, 73, 84, 103, 113–14, 196
hill-culminate, 54, 67
hip, 221
historic, 99
hither, 125
hoard, 124, 165, 278
hog, 79
hoi polloi, 269
hoist, 150
hold, 106, 167
hole, 105
holiday, 242
holiday, 83
holy-holiday, 216
home, 175
home~hame, 203
honest, 108
honey, 99, 189
honorarium, 108
honour, 99
flour, 22
hónour-honourée, 13
-hood, 115, 138, 215, 295–6, 318
hood, 102
hoof, 273
hoof-hoofs/hooves, 96
hook, 237, 245

hoop, 273
hop, 237, 242
hope, v. 165
hope-hop, 78
horæ, 108
horary, 108
horitculture, 63
horizon-horizontal, 255
horology, 108
horrible, 106
horse, 48, 244
horse-hoarse, 244
hospital, 99
hospitality, 68
host, 68, 99, 213
hostler, 99
hot, 102, 271
hot-heat, 162
hound, 48, 166, 168, 254
hound-hundred, 151
hour, 108, 140
house, 47, 114, 121, 155, 179, 188, 190–1
householder, 7
house-house, 89
house-husband, 215
hous-ing, 91
hover, 189
how, 104
hue, 268
huge, 28, 197
hull, 221
humane-humanity, 218
human-humáne, 312
humble, 99, 106, 141
humorous, 99
humour, 99, 106, 140
hundred, 166
hung, 30
Hungárian, 102
Hungary, 138
hunger, 21, 104
hungry, 138
hunt, 237, 245
hurdle, 194
husband(ry), 7, 13, 47, 215, 245
hussar, 226
hussy, 303
hydrangea, 34
hydro-, 107
hymnal, 136
hyper-, 107
hypo-, 107
hysto-, 107

iamb, 135
iamb-iambic, 99, 132, 134, 136
-ian, 84
-ic, 218, 288, 319
-ic(al), 310
ice cream, 149
ice-eyes, 281
ichthi(o), 57
-id, 319
idea, 58, 128
idea-ideal, 129
idiom, 58
idiot~eejit, 144
ídiot-idiótic, 294
idle, 217
if, 83
-ig, 88, 164
ignore, 67
-il, 160, 164
ilk, 129
improv, 227
-in, 160
-incel, 164
inch, 160
(in)dent-tooth, 55
Indian, 337
Indian~Injun, 144
Infiniti, 187
-ing, 136, 138, 164, 233, 351
inherit, 108
inhibit, 102
injun, 143
ink, 192
invalid-inválid, 312
-ion, 319
ion-cation, 256
-ir, 160, 163
Irene, 108
-isc, 164
-ise, 318–19, 320
-ish, 138, 318
island, 304
-ist, 319
isthmus, 57
-ity, 218
-ity/-ety, 319

Jácob, 289
jam, 30
-jan, 72
Japan-Japanése, 285
jargon, 141
jazz, 28, 240
jealousy, 141
Jew, 197
jewel, 197
jig-juice-jest, 142
Job, 227
join, 268, 270
jojoba, 59, 115
joke, 29
jolly, 237, 242
Joni~Jony, 187
joy, 268, 270
joyful, 13
judge, 12, 13, 194
Judi~Judy, 187
juice, 141
June, 268
just, 194

karakul, 290
Karl, 12
Karl-Charles, 86
keep, 190
Kelli~Kelly, 187
ken, 67
kenning, 67
kerchiefs~kerchieves, 96
kettle, 34, 40, 69
kettle-chettel, 86
key, 183
kibbutz, 134
kid, 37, 236
kind, 193
kindred, 168
king, 15–16, 75, 85, 160, 181, 227, 236–7, 330, 348
kingdom, 138, 333
kingling, 138
kin-king, 138
kirk, 8, 85
kirk-church, 74
kiss, 78
kissed, 193
kit, 34, 37, 151, 237, 372
kitchen, 289
kitten, 31
kitty-kiddy, 147
knave, 133, 199
knealt, 129
knee, 82, 204
knee-knelt, 255
kneeled, 132
knew, 133
Knievel, 133
knife, 7, 132
knight, 49, 132
kiss, 22

knobs, 133
knotty-naughty, 240
know, 63, 108, 175, 207, 209
know-ignorant, 67
know-no, 20

la, 256
labour, 306
lacuna, 15
ladder, 25, 41, 125, 147, 202
lager, 256
lair, 279
lama, 256
lamb, 135, 156, 167, 198
lamb's wool, 135
lambskin, 135
lamp, 241, 269
lance, 241
land, 169, 237, 239
language, 34
larst for last, 124
larynx, 135
late-latter, 224
laugh, 72, 80, 105, 112–14, 178
laughter, 113, 338
launch-lance, 241
laundry, 167, 241, 269
law, 103, 205, 269
law, 81, 83
lay, 268
lead, v. 36, 78, 201, 213
lead(Pb)-lead, v. 271
lead-led, 78, 214
leaf, 273
leaf-leave, 50
leafy-Levy, 24
learn, 117
learned, 232
lease [-z]-lease [s], 94
least, 213, 262
leave-left, 96
lectern, 124
ledge, 30
leechdom, 216
leek-garlic, 212, 219
left, 238
leg, 7, 238
legal-legalise, 216
legal-legality, 255
leisure, 10, 50
lemon, 32
-less, 138, 215, 264, 295, 318
lesser, 226
-let, 138
letter, 24
letters, 124
Levi, 256
libel, 290, 306
lid, 36
life, 189
life-live, 91
-like, 351
limb, 135
lineage, 12
lineation, 12
line-linear, 218
-ling, 138
linger, 192
lingering, 354
lip, 128
lisp, 133
listless, 162
literature, 144
lithe, 94
live, 79
loaf-loaves, 74, 89
loan, 7
loath, 190
loathe, 94
loch, 29, 100
loin, 269–70
loiter, 209, 269
long-length, 163
look, 165
look-luck, 246
lord, 243, 244
lord-lard, 244
lore, 66
lost, 240, 242
lost-post, 234
lot, 33–5, 44, 105, 108, 115, 132, 151, 243
loud, 271
louse, 161
love, 165, 172, 182, 237, 245
loveable, 13
low, 30, 220
lubricate, 38
Lúcifer, 289
luck, 189
luck-lucky-luckily, 211
lung, 192
lush, 45, 50
lust-list(less), 162
lute, 268
-ly, 49, 139, 318
lyric, 278
lyric – lyre, 190
machine, 253, 290
macro-, 256
macron, 256
mad, 180
mæcca, 77
magazine, 253, 256
Magéllan-Magéllanic, 285
magnesium, 142
maharaja, 99, 101–2
maiden, 81, 83, 268
maiden-maid, 49
mail, 264
main, 263
mája, 115
malt, 243
Málta-Maltése, 294
man, 30, 155, 198
mane-man, 78
mango-mangle, 129
man-men, 151, 157, 161
mannerly, 13
many, 83
Marchand, 277
margin~margent, 48
mark, 179
marrow, 103
marrow, 81
mártyr, 289
marv, 227
mash potato, 149
mason-Masonic, 255
mat, 240
match, 28
mater, 256
mat-mate, 225
matter-madder, 147
mature, 143, 144
maxi, 187
may, must, 219
mead, 221–2, 261, 271
meal, 155, 175, 202, 204, 250
mean, 202
mean-meant, 213
meant, 254
measure, 28, 142, 143
meat, 36, 190, 202
medal, 238
meed, 121
meet, 47, 78, 154, 162, 190, 202, 213
meet-meat-mate, 262
meet-met, 78, 214, 216, 225
melange, 141
ménage, 142

menage-manage, 142
-ment, 310
Menzies, 83
merchant, 277
merchant-marchand, 200
merry, 196, 238
merry-mirth, 192, 195
mesh, 45
mesh-mask, 87
messenger, 137
mice, 82, 161, 174, 201, 250, 253, 258, 282
micro-, 256
midday, 71
midden, 137
middle, 71
might, 206, 207
mighty, 105
mild, 166, 168
mild-milth, 215
milk, 82
milk-milch, 86
mill, 196
mine, 201
miracle, 12, 13, 309
mirror, 125, 278
mirth, 196
mis-, 183, 296
mission, 143
missive, 71
Missouri, 226
misspell, 71
mist, 213
mnemonic, 58, 347
mock, 243
moist, 269
mojo, 115
mold, 167
monk, 4, 164, 189, 225
monk-minchen, 164
month, 189, 221, 273
mood, 273
mood-stood-blood, 234, 271, 273
moon, 175, 188, 250, 260, 271, 273
moon-Monday, 184, 212, 215, 273
moor, 206
moot, 12, 162
more~mair, 203
morning, 243
mornings, 122
mortar, 289
mórtar, 315
moth, 244
mother, 124, 125, 161, 273
moth-mother, 234, 273
motive, 92
mountain, 290, 306
mourn, 124, 278
mouse, 161, 250, 258, 260
mouth, 38, 94, 151, 162, 169, 191, 250, 259
mouth-Monmouth, 227
mouth-mouth, 89, 97
mouth-Portsmouth, 212
Mrs, 94
much, 130, 194
muckle-much, 86
mud, 248
murder, 69, 125
muscle, 31
mush, 246
music, 268
must, 236
mutter, 34, 39, 69
mutual, 143
mystery, 354
myth, 98

nah, 44
naif~naïve 97
namby-pamby, 187
name, 182, 223
nap, 105, 108
narrow, 126
nation-national, 216
natural, 337
nature, 144
nausea, 142
navel, 223
navy, 306
necklace, 303
need, 213
needle, 125
need-needed, 216
negotiate, 144
nephew 181, 227
nerd, 25
-ness, 138, 264, 318, 351
new, 191, 205, 207, 209, 268
news, 38
newt, 146
nigh, 206, 207
night, 103, 206
nightingale, 103, 137
ninth, 215
nook, 272
noon, 273
North-nurse, 244
nose, 91, 94, 182, 202, 221–2, 224, 228, 250, 255, 261, 263
nose-nostril, 44
nostalgia, 34
nostril, 224
nothingism, 138
nought, 44
novelty, 243
novice, 309
now, 191, 201
numb, 30
nuncle, 146
nurse, 34–5, 198, 276, 383

oaf, 97
oak, 170, 189, 202, 250, 263, 266
Oake-Aike, 200, 203, 240
oar, 279
oaths, 91
obey, 208
occasion, 143
-oid, 270, 318
oik, 270
oil, 270
oink, 269, 270
old, 163, 167
olive, 290
-on, 49
-ong, 192
only, 139
-oon, 319
ooze, 109
open, 223
opera, 66
opus, 66
-or/-our, 18
ordure, 144
órgan, 289
órison, 315
-ose, 319
ostler-hostel, 107
-ous, 310
out, 39, 189
over, 91–2
overhang-overhang, 311
overture, 144
owe, 220
own, 175

pa, 44
pace, 32
pace-setter, 77

pageant, 150
pahit, 102
pal-pale, 190
palace-palate, 312
palm, 34–5, 151
palmer, 131
pandit, 245
pang, 45
pansy, 241
Parisian, 144
park, 148
parsley, 200
pass, 32
passenger, 137
passim-pass him, 104
passion, 143
pat-hat, 27
pater, 256
paw, 44, 129, 132
peace n. (1160)-appease, 97
peace-appease, 89
pear, 279
peasant, 140, 150
pedal, 63
pence, 95
pennant, 150
Pennines, 71
people, 129
perfect, 276
perfect-parfait, 200
perféct-pérfect, 310
person-parson, 274, 312
pet-Pete, 190
petty-petíte, 312
pharaoh, 22, 111, 326
phase, 94
pheasant, 150
philharmónic, 107
Phillipp, 111
phone-symphonic, 255
photographs~photogra[v]es, 98
phthisic, 58
phthisis, 57, 134
physics, 57
picture, 290
piece, 202
pig, 79
pill, 128
pillows, 126
pin, 27
pin–pine, 190
pin-pen, 192, 237
pin-ping-pink, 138
pitcher, 30
piteous, 144
pizzaz, 240
place, 263
plaid, 45
plaintiff, 98
plank, 138
play, 266
please-pleasure, 255
plenary-full, 74
plenteous, 144
plough, 84
plunge, 141
ply, 49
pneo-, 58
pneu-, 134
pneumonia, 57
pocket, 243
pod(ium)-foot, 62
podiatry, 63
pod-pawed, 240
point, 191, 209, 270
point : pint, 270
poison, 191, 269, 270
police, 253, 255
pólice-políce, 311
pontiff, 98
poor, 190, 279
poor, pore, 279
porridge, 147
port, 237, 242, 244
posh, 45
possess, 66, 93, 226
post-, 15
pouff, 98
pound, 48, 140, 168
preposition with, 94
présent-presént, 284–5
prestige, 141
presume, 38
pretty, 121
pretty~purty, 48, 119
prey, 208
price, 38, 151, 248, 253, 259, 266, 281
priest, 170, 190, 213
prime-primary, 216
prime-primitive, 216
prize, 282
procedure, 143
profile, 255, 256
profound-profundity, 216, 218
prognosis, 63, 67
prohibition, 99
prolong, 139
prolongate, 139
prolongation, 139
prolonging, 139
proof-prove, 89, 96
prosper, 65
psychology, 58
psychopaths, 98
pterodactyl, 58
pull, 131, 237, 245
pulmonary, 246
pulp, 246
pulpit, 246
pulse, 246
punish, 194, 246
punish(en), 245
Punjab, 245
pure, 38
pursue, 143
puss-pus, 246
put-putt, 246
putt-put, 50, 236
pyramid, 278

qua, 256
quack, 240
quaff, 240
quarantine, 256
quart, 240
quarter, 237, 239–40
quartz, 237, 239–40
quash-quack, 236
queen, 202
question, 47

race, 82
race-raise, 91
radish, 223
radius, 15
rag, 30
rage, 141
rain, 81
Ralph, 241, 255
rang-ran, 136
rapture, 143
rather, 81
rathe-rather, 224
ray, 30
realm, 191
rear, 66
rébel-rebél, 311
récord-recórd, 311
red, 271
redeem-redemption, 218
reduce, 144
reel-real, 20

refer, 63
reif-reave, 96
rein(deer), 208
relief-relieve, 96
rend, 169
rescind, 87
resign-resignation, 255
resign, 66
resume-resumptive, 218
resume, 268
rev-revved, 226
rev, 227
rhomb, 135, 136
rib, 30
rice, 78
rick-rich, 86
ridden, 289
ride, 155, 282
ridge, 26, 28, 141, 147, 196, 198
righteous, 144
ring, 45, 69, 105, 108, 128, 132, 231, 291
ringette, 138
ringlet, 138
rioha, 115
rioja, 59
rise, 66
rivalless, 32, 77
river, 6, 306, 330
riverside, 13
road-rood, 190
rob–robe, 190
Robin~Robyn, 187
rode, 214
roid, 270
roof, 273
roof-roofs-rooves, 96, 216
rook, 272
room-rum, 246
roost, 213
root, 273
Rosa's, 34
roses, 34
rot, 243
rotten, 237, 242
rough, 113, 115, 207
rough-though, 20
route, 256
row, 220
royal, 268
rude, 268
rue, 197, 220
rule, 268
run-rung, 138
rush, 194, 237, 245
rust, 213

sack, 24
sacrifice, 92
sad, 199, 237, 238, 239
safe, 131
safe-keeping, 13
safe-save, 24
saga, 84
saguáro-saguarésque, 285
said, 45
salad, 34
sale-sell, 157, 162
salt, 243, 269
salve-valve, 241
same, 45
sand, 169
sandwich, 34
saner, 32
sans, 241
sap, 24, 78
Saturday, 49
sauce, 269
Saul : saw, 129
saunter, 241
save, 250
saw, 44, 84
say-saw-saga, 74
scab, 65, 87
scabrous, 65
scale, 87, 263
scan, 140
scarves/scarfs, 96
scene-seen, 20
sceptic, skeptic, 87
sceptre, 87
schism, 87
schizo-, 87
schmeer, 148
science, 306
scissors, 124, 226
score, 7
scot, 87
screed-shed, 214
sċrift, 87
script, 87
scripture, 87
scrod, 87
scrub, 87
scuffle, 87
sculpture, 143
sea, 188–9, 191, 250
seal, 78, 129, 178
seal-zeal, 91
sea-see, 261
season, 306
seat, 130, 188
sedge, 81
see, v. 188, 190, 220
see, v. 104, 156
seed, 174
seek, 202
seek-beseech, 86
seek-sought, 163
seen, 202
see-saw, 129
see-sea, 250
seethe, 66, 93, 97
ségment-segmentátion, 13
seldom, 167
sell, 72–3
sell-sold, 163
send, 169
serene-serenity, 255
Sereniti, 187
serf, 92
serf-serfs, 74
serf-serve, 96
sergeant, 276–7
serif, 97, 278
serve, 276
set, 155, 172
setting, 147
sever, 238
sewer, 143
shade, 75
shade-shadow, 44, 224
shard, 277
sharp, 75
shave, 87
she wolf, 129
shear, 154
shed, 87
sheep, 204, 260
sheep-shepherd, 212, 215
shelf-shelves, 89
shell, 87
shelving, 91
Shepperton, 217
sherd, 277
sheriff, 220, 236
shield, 167
ship, 28, 76, 81, 87, 132, 215
shire, 87
shire-sheriff, 215
shirt, 8, 87
shirt-skirt, 74, 88
shlep, 148
shlock, 148

shoot, 177
shootings, 217
short, 41
shot, 87
shoulder, 168
shove, 87
shred, 87, 271
shrift, 214
shrift-script, 74, 88
shrive-shrift, 96, 214
shrub, 87
shtetl, 148
shtick, 148
shuffle, 87
shut, 194
shuttle, 194
sib(b), 80
side-sidth, 215
sieve-sift, 96
sift, 172
sigh, 220
sight, 114
sign, 253, 258
silence, 290, 306
silly, 91
silvery, 49
sin, 77, 138, 188, 192, 195, 197
sing, 39, 49–50, 136
singer-linger, 134
single, 138
sink, 138
sink-zinc, 91
sin-sing-sink, 138
sip, 30
sir, 35
sister, 7
sit, 72
sit-zit, 89
skewer, 38
skill, 7
skim, 194
skin, 7
skipper, 87
Skirlaugh, 87
skirt, 8, 87
skirt-shirt, 74, 88
skulk, 131
skull, 246
sky, 7
slander, 241
slangy, 138
slaughter, 207, 268–9
sleep, 41, 174, 175, 260–1
sleep-slept, 214
sleight, 47
slew, 207
slide-slid, 214, 225
slough, 207
slow-sloth, 214
smo(r)ther, 273
smooth, 93
smurf, 98
sock, 30
sodden, 66
soft, 237, 240, 242
Soho, 115
soil, 269
sold, 167
solder, 208
soldier, 131, 143, 208
solemnity, 136
sole-soul, 22
sólid-solídify, 13
sólid-solídity, 294
-some, 215, 318
some, 91, 189
son, 188–9
song, 140
soon, 175, 197, 273
soot, 273
soothe, 94
sought, 49, 103, 113, 206, 207, 268, 269
soul, 268
sound, 48, 140, 166
south-southern, 216, 271
sow, 258
Spain-Spaniard, 218
spare : are, 224
speak(s), 85, 121
speech, 85, 121
speed, 65
spend, 169
sphére, 315
spider, 125
spindle, 48
spinach, 34
spit-spitting, 226
spittle, 130
spoof, 98
spoon, 273
sport, 244
square, 37
squirrel, 278
staff, 222
staff-stave, 224
stag, 83
stain-glass, 149
stalk, 269
stance, 65, 241
stand, 65
Stanford, 215
star, 71, 200
starboard, 276, 304
stark, 200
start, 244
starve : deserve, 276
static, 65
statistics, 65
status, 65
stave, 222
stave-staff, 44
stead, 11, 65, 259, 272
steal, 202, 224
steal-stealth, 184, 214
stealth, 254
steer>starboard, 276
stelan, 224
stepchild, 238
stepfather, 217
-ster, 215
sthenic, 57, 134
stink-stench, 86
stomach, 245
stone(s), 175, 181, 189, 190–1, 215, 226, 250
stone-stane, 203
stood, 45, 271, 273
stool, 65
stoop, 273
stop, 243
stow, 191, 205, 263, 266
strange, 250, 255
straw, 269
stream, 156, 159, 176, 201, 204, 337
street-Stratford, 173, 174
stretch, 72, 82, 163
Stretham, 174
strode, 214
strong, 192
strongish, 138
strong-strength, 163
strop-strap, 243
strut, 33–44, 151
stúpor, 308, 315
sty, 265
sub-, 15
subbie, 32
subbrachial, 32
succumb, 135
such, 30, 194
sucker, 30
sue, 38, 197

suffer, 32
sugar, 143, 268
suit, 38, 143, 268
sulphur, 92
summon, 32
summoner, 354
sunder, 166
sundry, 194
sung-sun, 136
super-, 15
supper, 245, 246
sure, 30, 143, 268
surf, 97
surgeon, 277
sw-, 139
swagger, 240
swain, 208
swathe, 93
sway, 28
sweat, 271
sweat-treat, 272
sweet, 155, 188
Swindon, 220
swine, 95
swine-Swinburne, 217
sword, 139
symposium, 142
syrup, 278

Tadmarton, 217
taiga, 290
tail, 264
tale, 157, 221, 223, 254, 263, 271
tale-tell, 162
talk, 49, 241, 269
talkative, 13
tambourine, 253, 290
tango, 138
tango-tangle, 129
tar, 200
tarpaulin, 137
taught, 206
taxi, 187
teach-taught, 163
teethe, 94
teething, 91
tell, 157
tell-told, 163
ten, 271
tend, 49
tender, 169
tenor, 238
tenth, 215
terrace, 278
terror, 278
-th, 213
that, 199
thaw, 65, 207, 209, 268, 269
theatre, 58
theft, 163, 170
there, 206
thick, 28
thief, 163, 191, 201–2
thief-theft, 47, 214
thigh, 114
thimble, 130
thin, 30
thine, 81
thing, 49, 50
thinghood, 138
thing-thin, 75, 136
think, 189
think-thought, 163
third, 79, 119
thirst, 119, 120
this, 28, 30
thistle, 49
thistle-this, 91
thither, 125
though, 105, 113, 115, 208
thought, 33–5, 75, 136, 151, 207
though-tough, 99, 112–13
thread, 271
threat, 271
three, 54, 63, 68, 81, 94, 139
three-triple, 54, 67
threshed, 119
thrice, 95
thrive-thrift, 96
throat, 224
throttle, 224
through, 105, 113, 115
thrush, 194
thud, 194
thunder, 48, 168
thyroid, 26, 63, 68, 94
tide, 189
tilde, 34
timber, 167
time, 189
tmesis, 134
toad, 202
today, 219
toe, 191
toes~taes, 203
together, 125
toilet-toilétte, 312
tomb, 135
tombic, 136
tongue, 136, 189
took-tuck, 246
tooth, 54, 68, 161
toothache, 91
tooth-dental, 54, 67
torment, 311
tother, 146
toucan, 290
tough, 114
town, 30, 160, 191
town-clerk, 13
township, 160
toy, 50, 209
transact, 66
transcend, 32
trap, 34, 151
travel-traváil, 312
tread, 237
treasure, 141
tree, 63, 176, 191, 250
tri(ple)-three, 62
triad, 63
triple, 63
triplex, 68
troth, 177, 227
trouble, 245
trough, 207
truce, 95
trust, 194
truth, 12
try, 144
tsar, 148
-tude, 144, 319
Tuesday, 38, 143, 268, 304
tuft, 150
tug, 112
tumble, 167
tumour, 144
tumult, 144
tune, 38, 143
Tunesia, 144
turf, 124
turfs/turves, 96
turmoil, 269
turve, 96
tutor, 144
twang, 240
twice, 95
twine, 121
two, 139
-ty, 319
tyrant, 140, 150
tyre~tire, 187

un-, 183
uncouth, 235
(un)couth-kithe, 162
under, 69, 188, 189
unison, 94
university-varsity, 276
unnamed, 32
unneeded, 77
upload-upload, 311
upon, 30
Upton, 220
urban-urbáne, 312
us, 219
usage, 94
use, 195, 197
usual, 141

vaccine, 226
vagrant, 98
vahana, 98
vain-fain, 92
vain-vanity, 218
valet, 98
válue-váluate, 287
van, 30
vane, 95, 182
varmint, 277
vase, 98
vast-fast, 50
vat, 95
vault, 131
veal, 92
vehement, 99
vehicle, 99
veil, 268
verdure, 143
verity, 12, 13
vermin, 277
vermin~varmint, 48
vermouth, 98
verse, 58
vertigo, 256
victor, 85
vile-file, 92
vile-vilify, 218
village, 141
vinegar, 289
vine-vinegar, 218
violence, 12
violent, 12
Virgil, 22
Virgilius, 58
virgin, 124
visage, 12
visceral, 87
vision, 12
vixen, 95
vodka, 98
voice, 209

wa-, 239
wāfer, 92
waft, 237, 240
wag, 240
waistcoat, 304
waiter, 41, 147
wake, 72, 77
wake-watch, 86
walk, 49, 241
wan, 240
wand, 237, 239
-ward(s), 318
warden, 12
-wards, 124
warm-to warm, 159
warn, 200
warranty, 12
warranty-warden, 86
warsh for wash, 124
wash-wax, 236
wasp, 240
watch, 72, 82
water, 120, 147, 199, 240
wavering, 92
way, 178, 206, 209
weal-wealth, 214
weapon, 34, 40, 69, 182, 297, 338, 353
weather, 124
weave-weft, 96, 214
wed-red, 134
week, 172, 221, 236
weigh, 266
weight, 268
welcome, 34
well, 190
wench, 130
wend, 169
were : bear, 224
west, 28
wet, 271
whack, 240
whale, 28, 64, 76, 102, 109, 223
whale-wail, 76, 109
wharf, 30, 50, 109
wheat, 109, 140
whereon, 110
whether, 81
whetstone, 304
whet-wet, 76
which, 130
which-witch, 99, 105, 109, 111
whiff, 109
while, 140
whilst, 49, 150
whine, 22, 28, 50, 102
whine-wine, 105, 109
whip, 109
whisk, 109
whistle, 28, 102
white, 21, 64, 76, 105, 108–9, 115, 215, 230, 347
white-wit, 21
whither, 125
Whitsunday, 215
whole, 189
whole~hail, 203
whole-heal, 162
whoop~hoop, 109
whoops, 273
why, 205
wick, 221, 236
-wick vs. -wich, 86
wide-width, 212, 255
wife, 96–7, 189, 226, 250, 253, 257–8, 265
wife-wives, 89
win, 30
wince, 192
window(s), 126, 208, 303
wind-wind, 169
wine-whine, 22
wing, 7, 192
winter, 338
wisdom, 215, 236, 254
-wise, 318
wise, 93, 215
wizard, 13
wiþ-, 183
woe, 191, 264
wolf, 69, 245
wolf-wolves, 90
woman, 47
woman-women, 161
womb, 135, 167
wonder, 12, 189, 338
woo, 246
wood, 221, 236, 245
wool, 71
work-wrought, 163
worse, 189

wrangle, 240
wrath, 134, 240
wreak-wretch, 86
wreathe, 94
wreck-reck, 134
wrenches, 134
wretch, 133
wrinkle, 134
writ : wonder, 22
write-right, 99, 132
wrong, 7, 49
wrought, 105, 119–20, 133, 140, 163, 225

Xavier, 139
X-ray, 139

-y, 15
yard, 8
yarn, 83
yawn, 83
yea, 83, 262, 264
year, 103, 175
yearn, 83, 165
yeast, 83
yeehaw, 101, 115
yell, 103
yellow, 28, 145, 156, 178–9
yes, 8, 30, 83
yet, 81
yield, 154
yogurt, 124
yoke, 83
yon, 83
yonge, 140
you two, 83
young, 83, 103
youngness, 138

zeal, 93
zephyr, 93, 98
zeroth, 215
zeugma, 93, 143
Zeus, 143
Zhivago, 30
zip, 30
zloty, 98
zombie, 98
zone, 93, 98

Names Index

Page numbers in the Names index refer to the main hardcopy volume. Entries in bold refer to the sections in the Online Companion where the sources are cited or discussed. The Companion is available at: www.euppublishing.com/page/ETOTELAdvanced/Minkova

Ahn, Sang-Cheol, **3.4.1**
Albright, Adam, **5.6**
Alexander, James D., **5.2.2**
Algeo, John, **1.6 (Further Reading)**
Allerton, D. J., 338
Anderson, John, **5.6 (Further Reading)**
Anderson, John and D. Britton, 167
Aroui, Jean-Louis and Andy Arleo, **10.1**, **10.4**

Barber, Charles, 15, 224, 243, 262, **1.6 (Further Reading)**
Bauer, Laurie, 111, 259, 317, **1.6 (Further Reading)**
Becker, Michael, Andrew Nevins and Jonathan Levine, 98, **4.4**
Beddor, Patrice Speeter, Rena Arens Krakow and Louis M. Goldstein, 175, **7.3.1**
Bell, Alan, Jason M. Brenier, Michelle Gregory, Cynthia Girand and Dan Jurafsky, **7.5.1.3**
Bennett, William H., 306
Benson, Larry D., 292, **10.4**
Berg, Thomas, 318, **9.8**
Bermúdez-Otero, Ricardo, 223–4, **2.5 (Further Reading)**, **4.1.1**, **5.3.2**, **7.5.1.2**, **7.5.2.1**
Bermúdez-Otero, Ricardo and April McMahon, **7.5.1.1**
Bermúdez-Otero, Ricardo and Richard Hogg, 121
Bermúdez-Otero, Ricardo and Graeme Trousdale, **5.3.2**
Berndt, Rolf, **1.6 (Further Reading)**
Bibire, Paul, 6, **6.2**, **7.3.1**
Bigham, Douglas Stephen, **Appendix 8.3**
Blevins, Juliette and Andrew Garrett, 120
Boersma, Paul, **3.4.1**
Bondar, Vladimir A., **5.1.3**
Bosworth, Joseph and T. Northcote Toller, **5.2.2**
Bradley, Travis G., **5.2.3**
Branchaw, Sherrylyn, **7.5.1.1**
Bredehoft, Thomas, **10.2.1**
Brinton, Laurel and Margery Fee, 111
Britton, Derek, 125–6, **5.2.3**
Browman, Catherine P. and Louis Goldstein, **5.2.2**
Brown, Carleton, 313
Brunner, Karl, **7.3.1**
Burling, Robbins, **10.4**
Burton, T. L., 243–4, 247, **5.3.2**, **Chapter 8 (Further Reading)**
Bybee, Joan and Dan I. Slobin, **6.3**
Bybee, Joan L., **6.3**

Cable, Thomas, 336, 339, **10.2.2**, **10.3**
Campbell, Alistair, 58, 157, 181, **1.6 (Further Reading)**, **3.4.5**, **4.1.2**, **5.2.2**, **6.2**, **6.5.3**, **7.5.1.1**, **9.3.1**
Carter, Paul and John Local, **2.3.1**
Chambers, J. K., 281–3
Ching, Marvin K. L., 94
Chomsky, Noam and Morris Halle, 196
Clark, Cecily, **7.5.1.3**
Clarke, Sandra, **8.2.2.3**
Cohn, Abigail, 169, **6.4.1**
Collie, Sarah, **9.8**
Colman, Fran, 155, **6.2**
Côté, Marie-Hélène, 150
Crisma, Paola, **5.6 (Further Reading)**
Crosswhite, Katherine, 181
Cruttenden, Alan, 34, 36, 77, 116, 134, 141, 146–7, 199, 237, 258, **2.2.1**, **2.5**

(**Further Reading**), **4.1.2**, **5.1.1**, **5.1.3**, **5.6** (**Assignments**), **6.4**, **6.5.4**, **7.5**
Crystal, David, **8.2.2**, **Appendix 8.1**
Culpeper, Jonathan and Phoebe Clapham, **9.8**
Cutler, Anne and Sally Butterfield, **9.1**

Dance, Richard, 6, 173, 177, 208, **7.6**
Danchev, Andrei, **6.5.3**
Danielsson, B., 310
Daunt, Marjorie, **5.2.2**, **6.5.3**
Davenport, Mike and S.J. Hannahs, 116
Delattre, Pierre and Donald C. Freeman, 117
Denton, Jeanette Marshall, 118, 120, **3.4.5**, **3.4.5** (**Further Reading**), **5.2.2**, **5.6** (**Further Reading**)
Diamond, Jared and Peter Bellwood, **3.4.5** (**Further Reading**)
Dobson, Eric John, 114, 123, 126, 130–1, 137, 200, 207, 272, 276, 278, 310, **2.5**, **5.2.4**, **5.4**, **7.3.1**, **7.5.2.1**, **8.1**, **8.2.2.2**, **Appendix 8.1**, **Chapter 8** (**Further Reading**)
Dresher, B. Elan, **3.4.5** (**Further Reading**), **7.3.1**
Dresher, B. Elan and Nila Friedberg, **10.1**
Duffell, Martin, **10.3**, **10.4**
Duggan, Hoyt N., **10.2.2**

Eckert, Penny, **Appendix 8.3**
Eddington, David and Caitlin Channer, 147
Eddington, David and Michael Taylor, 147
Ekwall, Eilert, 195, 209, 224, **7.3.1**
Ellis, Lucy and William J. Hardcastle, **5.3.2**
Erickson, Blaine, **5.2.2**

Fabb, Nigel, **10.2**
Fabricius, Anne, **8.2.1**
Ferragne, Emmanuel and François Pellegrino, **7.6**, **8.2.1**
Fikkert, Paula, **5.3.2**
Filppula, Markku, Juhani Klemola and Heli Paulasto, **1.2**
Finegan, Edward, 283, **1.6** (**Further Reading**)
Finkenstaedt, T. E. Leisi and D. Wolff, 12
Fischer, David Hackett, **1.4**
Fisher, John Hurt, **8.3.2**
Fisiak, Jacek, **7.2.1**, **7.6**, **Chapter 8** (**Further Reading**)
Fitzgerald, Christina, 355
Fitzmaurice, Susan and Donka Minkova, **Appendix 8.3**
Flasdieck, Hermann F., **4.3**
Flemming, Edward, 90, 197, 264, **2.2**, **7.6**, **8.2.2.2**
Flemming, Edward and S. Johnson, **2.2**
Fridland, V., **Appendix 8.3**
Fromkin, Victoria, **4.4**
Fudge, Eric, 318
Fulk, Robert D., 42, 167, 224, 338–9, **1.6** (**Further Reading**), **5.2.2**, **6.4**, **7.5.1.1**, **7.5.1.2**, **9.4.1**

Garrett, Andrew and Juliette Blevins, **5.3.2**
Gascoine, George, 352–3, **10.2.1**, **10.3**
Getty, Michael, 170, **10.2.1**
Gick, Bryan, 129, **5.2.5**
Giegerich, Heinz, 28, 31, 43, 239, 298, 318, **2.1**, **2.2.1**, **2.5** (**Further Reading**), **5.1.1**, **5.2.4**, **5.3.2**, **5.6** (**Further Reading**), **7.5.1**, **9.8** (**Further Reading**)
Gimson, A. C., 199, **7.5.1**
Gnanadesikan, Amalia E., 154
Goldsmith, John, 179–80
Gordon, Matthew J., **Appendix 8.3**
Gordon, Matthew Kelly, 171, **4.1.2**, **7.5**, **7.5.2**
Grant, Colin, **5.1.2**
Greenberg, Joseph, **5.1.2**
Greenfield, Stanley and Daniel Calder, **10.3**
Gussmann, Edmund, **5.3.2**

Hall, Nancy, **5.2.2**
Hall, Tracy and Silke Hamann, 128
Halmari, Helena, **10.2**
Hamann, Silke, 123, **5.2.3**
Hammond, Michael, **2.2.2**, **4.1.2**, **6.4.1**, **6.4.1**, **7.5**
Hanham, Alison, **5.2.4**
Hanson, Kristin and Paul Kiparsky, **10.2**
Harmon, William, 365, **10.3**
Harrington, Jonathan, Felicity Cox and Zoe Evans, **7.6**
Haugen, Einar, 148, **5.5.2**
Hawkins, Sarah and Jonathan Midgley, 238, **8.2.1**
Hay, Jennifer and Andrea Sudbury, 126, **5.2.3**, **5.6** (**Further Reading**)
Hayes, Bruce, 42, 97, 286, 294, 298, 300, 331, **2.5** (**Further Reading**), **5.1.1**, **5.2.5**, **7.5.1**, **8.2.1**, **9.8** (**Further Reading**), **10.1**, **10.3**, **10.4**
Hayes, Bruce and Donca Steriade, 79, **2.5**
Hayes, Bruce, Colin Wilson and Anne Shisko, 365
Hebda, Anna, **7.5.2.1**
Heselwood, Barry, 118, 127, **5.2.2**, **5.2.4**
Hickey, Raymond, **1.2**, **Appendix 8.3**
Hill, Archibald A., 121–4, **5.2.3**, **5.6** (**Further Reading**)

Hogg, Richard, 8, 19, 79, 119, 121, 130, 154–7, 159, 173, 176, 181, 184, 198, 222, 225, **1.6** (**Further Reading**), **1.6** (**Further Reading**), **3.4.5**, **4.2.1**, **5.1.2**, **5.2.2**, **5.2.2**, **5.2.5**, **6.2**, **6.3**, **6.5.1**, **6.5.3**, **6.5.4**, **7.3.1**, **7.5.2.1**
Hogg, Richard and Robert D. Fulk, **1.6** (**Further Reading**)
Honeybone, Patrick, **2.1.1** (**Further Reading**)
Hoover, David, **9.4.1**
Horn, Wilhelm and Martin Lehnert, **5.2.4**
Horobin, Simon and Jeremy Smith, **1.6** (**Further Reading**), **7.2**, **7.4**
House, Arthur S., 240
Howell, Robert B., 117, 120, **5.1.2**, **5.2.2**, **5.2.5**
Howell, Robert and Katerina Somers Wicka, **5.1.2**, **5.2.2**, **5.2.2**
Hughes, Geoffrey, **1.6** (**Further Reading**)
Hutcheson, Bellenden Rand, 291, 295, 302, 328, 332, 335–6, 345, **6.5.4**, **10.2.1**
Hyman, Larry, 164

Ikegami, Masa T., 122, 192, **7.4**, **7.5.2**, **7.5.2.1**
Ingham, Richard, 11
Ito, Junko and Armin Mester, **5.1.2**
Iverson, Gregory K. and J. C. Salmons, **3.4.1**, **4.3**
Iverson Gregory K. and Sang-Cheol Ahn, **2.1.1**

Jefferson, Judith and Ad Putter, **10.2.2**
Jespersen, Otto, 125, 131, 134–5, 147, 239, 250–1, 253, 273, **8.1**, **8.2.1**, **Chapter 8** (**Further Reading**)
Johnson, Wyn and David Britain, **5.2.5**
Johnston, Paul A., Jr., 253, 316
Jones, Charles, 169
Jones, Daniel, 23, **2.1.2**, **9.8**
Jordan, Richard, 122, 133, 136, 194, 197–8, 200, 222, 254, 260, 264, **1.6** (**Further Reading**), **7.3.1**, **7.4**

Kastovsky, Dieter, **6.3**, **Chapter 8** (**Further Reading**)
Kawahara,Shigeto, **4.1.2**
Kaun, Abigail, 197, **7.3.1**
Keenan, Edward, **7.5.1.3**
Kelly, Michael, 287
Kenyon, John S. and Thomas A. Knott, 23, **8.2.1**
Keyser, S. J. and W. O'Neil, **3.4.5** (**Further Reading**)
Kim, Myungsook, 223–4
King, Anne, **6.2**
Kiparsky, Paul, **10.1**, **10.3**
Kiparsky, Paul and W. O'Neil, **3.4.5** (**Further Reading**)
Kirchner, Robert, 79
Kirkby, John, 246
Kirwin, William J., 95
Kitson, Peter, 9
Knappe, Gabrielle, **5.1.4**
Kökeritz, Helge, 239, 254, **8.2.2.2**, **Appendix 8.1**, **Chapter 8** (**Further Reading**)
Kortmann, Bernd and Benedikt Szmrecsanyi, 233
Krapp, George Philip and Elliot van Kirk Dobbie, 328
Kreidler, Charles, 28, **2.1**, **2.5** (**Further Reading**), **5.1.1**, **8.2.1**
Krygier, Marcin, 161
Kury˜lowicz, Jerzy, **9.4.1**

Labov, William, 35, 237, **Appendix 8.3**
Labov, William, Paul Cohen, Clarence Robins and John Lewis, 150
Labov, William, Sharon Ash and Charles Boberg, 242, **1.6** (**Further Reading**), **2.2.1**, **2.5** (**Further Reading**)
Labov, William, M. Yaeger and R. Steiner, **Appendix 8.3**
Ladefoged, Peter, 37, 101, 141, **2.1.1**, **2.1.2**, **2.2.1**, **5.1.4**
Ladefoged, Peter and Ian Maddieson, 25, 77, 79, 101, 116, 118, **7.3.1**
Lahiri, Aditi and Paula Fikkert, 224, **7.5.1.1**, **7.5.1.2**
Laing, Margaret, **7.2**
Laing, Margaret and Roger Lass, 184, **5.1.4**, **6.4.1**, **7.2**, **7.2.1**, **7.2.2**
Lamb, Sydney and E. Douglas Mitchell, **3.4.5** (**Further Reading**)
Lapidge, Michael, 327, **10.2.1**
Lappe, Sabine, 322, **9.8**
Lass, Roger, 11, 123, 126, 131, 133, 137–8, 144, 157, 170–1, 173, 176–7, 179, 185, 217, 224, 226, 239, 242, 245, 248, 256, 258, 270, 277–8, 282, 287, 315, **1.3**, **1.6** (**Further Reading**), **2.2**, **2.3.1**, **3.4.5**, **3.4.5** (**Further Reading**), **5.2.2**, **6.2**, **6.3**, **6.4**, **6.4.1**, **6.5.4**, **7.2.1**, , **7.3.1**, **7.5.2.1**, **8.1**, **8.2.2**, **8.2.2.2**, **8.2.2.3**, **Appendix 8.3**, **Chapter 8** (**Further Reading**), **9.3.2**
Lass, Roger and John Anderson, 117, **5.2.2**, **7.4**
Lass, Roger and Margaret Laing, 194, **7.2.2**
Lauttamus, Timo, **5.6** (**Further Reading**)
Lavoie, Lisa, 169

Lawson, Eleanor, Jane Stuart-Smith and James Scobbie, 126, **5.2.3**
Leach, Alfred, 108, 111
Lehiste, Ilse, 211
Lehmann, Winfred P., **10.2**, **10.2.2**
Leith, Dick, 262
Lewis, M. Paul, Gary F. Simons and Charles D. Fennig, 56
Liberman, Anatoly, 165, 224, **6.4**, **6.5.3**, **7.5.2.1**
Liebl, Christian, 202
Luick, Karl, 138, 165, 170–1, 207, 216, 222, 229, 251, 253, **5.4**, **6.4**, **6.4.1**, **8.1**, **Chapter 8** (**Further Reading**)
Lutz, Angelika, 120, 131, **1.3**, **5.2.4**, **5.6** (**Further Reading**), **8.2.2.1**

Maclagan, Margaret and Jennifer Hay, **Appendix 8.3**
MacMahon, Michael K. C., 248, 316
Maddieson, Ian, 118, 222, **3.4.1**, **6.4.1**
Magnuson, Thomas J., 116
Malone, Kemp, 9, 182–3
Marchand, Hans, **9.8**
Mayr, Robert, 198, **7.3.1**
McCully, Christopher B., **9.4.2**
McDavid, Raven I., Jr., **8.3.1**
McKie, Michael, 346–8, **10.3**
McMahon, April, 28, 31, 36, 37, 116, 280, **2.1**, **2.2.1**, **2.5** (**Further Reading**), **5.6** (**Further Reading**), **Chapter 8** (**Further Reading**)
Menken, H. L., 2
Milroy, James, **5.6** (**Further Reading**)
Minkoff, Marco, 130, 167, **5.6**, **6.5.3**, **8.2.2**
Minkova, Donka, 85, 105, 109, 111, 1323, 178, 183, 221, 223, 232, 284, 307, 339, 341, 349, 355, **1.6** (**Further Reading**), **4.1.1**, **4.4**, **5.1.2**, **5.1.4**, **5.1.4**, **5.3.2**, **5.5.1**, **5.6** (**Further Reading**), **6.5.4**, **7.5.2.1**, **7.6**, **9.3.2**, **9.4.1**, **9.4.2**, **9.6.1**, **9.8**, **10.2**, **10.2.1**, **10.2.2**, **10.3**
Minkova, Donka and Kie Ross Zuraw, 42, **4.2.1**, **5.5.2**, **6.4**
Minkova, Donka and Robert Stockwell, 61, 167, 218, 253, 255, 259, 262–3, 296, 305, 314–15, 378, 390, **1.6** (**Further Reading**), **5.3.2**, **6.4.1**, **7.5.1.1**, **8.2.2**, **Appendix 8.3**, **9.4.2**, **10.4**
Moen, Per, **8.3.1**
Montgomery, Michael, 111, 148
Montgomery, Michael and Connie Eble, **7.3.1**
Morén, Bruce, **6.4.1**
Moreton, Elliot and Erik Thomas, 282
Morris, Richard, 249
Mossé, Fernand and James Walker, **1.6** (**Further Reading**), **7.3.1**
Mugglestone, Lynda, 107–8, 111, 126, **5.1.3**, **5.6** (**Further Reading**)
Mulcaster, Richard, 226, 235
Murray, Robert W., 224
Muthmann, Gustav, **5.1.4**, **5.2.3**

Nagy, Naomi and PatriciaIrwin, 126, **5.2.3**, **5.2.4**
Nevalainen, Terttu, 15, 236, 315, **1.4**, **1.6** (**Further Reading**), **9.8**
Nevalainen, Terttu andIngridTieken-BoonvanOstade, 19, 236
Nevanlinna, Saara, **5.6**

Oakden, J. P., **10.2.2**
Ogden, Richard, 26
Ogura, Mieko, 255, 259, 272, **7.3.2**, **8.2.2**, **8.2.2.2**, **8.3.1**, **Chapter 8** (**Further Reading**)
Oppenheimer, Stephen, 3, **3.4.5** (**Further Reading**)
Ostler, Nicholas, 11

Page, Richard, 224
Pająk, Bożena, **4.1.2**
Parkes, M. B., **7.2.1**
Passy, Paul, **2.1.2**
Petrova, Olga, **3.4.1**, **15**
Phillips, Betty, 51, 169, 171, 272, **5.4.1**, 7.3.1, **8.2.2.3**, **8.3.1**, **9.8**
Polka, Linda and Megha Sundara, **9.1**
Pope, Mildred, 106, 122, 131, 141, **4.1.2**, **5.2.5**, **8.2.1**
Proctor, Michael, 117, **5.2.5**
Purnell, Thomas C. and Malcah Yaeger-Dror, **1.2**
Putter, Ad, 355
Putter, Ad, Judith Jefferson and Donka Minkova, **7.4**, **8.2.2.2**
Pyles, Thomas, 105

Quirk, Randolph and C. L. Wrenn, **5.2.2**

Reszkiewicz, Alfred, 157, 181, **5.2.2**
Riera, María, Joaquín Romero and Ben Parrell, **5.2.2**
Ringe, Don, 180, 212, **3.4.1**, **3.4.5** (**Further Reading**)
Ritt, Nikolaus, 224, 272, **6.4**, **7.5.1.1**, **7.5.2.1**, **8.3.1**
Roberts, Jane, **7.2**
Robinson, Orrin W., **3.4.5** (**Further Reading**), **8.2.2.2**

Rusch, Willard, **7.3.2**
Ross, John, 285
Rothwell, W., 11
Russom, Geoffrey, 302, **6.5.4**, **9.4.1**, **10.2.1**, **10.2.2**
Ryan, Kevin, 171, 287, **6.4.1**, **7.5**, **7.5.2**

Saintsbury, George, **10.2**
Salmons, Joseph, 70, **2.5** (**Further Reading**) **3.4.3**
Samuels, Michael, 184, **7.2**
Sandved, Arthur O., **7.3.2**
Schaefer, Ursula, **1.6** (**Further Reading**)
Schendl, Herbert, 185, 347
Schlüter, Julia, 233, **5.1.1**, **5.1.3**, **5.6** (**Further Reading**)
Schrijver, Peter, 150, **4.1.2**, **6.5.3**
Scobbie, James and Alan Wrench, **5.2.5**
Scragg, Donald G., 82, 111, 202, **5.1.2**, **7.3.2**
Selkirk, Elisabeth O., 302
Sharf, Donald J., **7.5**
Short, Ian, 309
Sievers, Eduard, 301, 328
Simon, Ellen, 90
Smith, Jeremy, 19, 179, 186, 203, 226, 249, 253, **5.2.2**, **6.5.3**, **7.2**, **8.2.2.1**, **8.2.2.2**
Sóskuthy, Márton, 128–9, 131
Stanley, Eric, 349, 350, **10.3**
Stenbrenden, Gjertrud, 202, 249, 251, 253–4, 257, **7.3.2**, **8.2.2.2**, **8.3.1**, **Chapter 8** (**Further Reading**)
Stenroos, Merja, **7.3.1**
Steriade, Donca, 123, **4.1.2**
Stockwell, Robert, 118, 180, 258, 263, 265, **5.2.2**, **7.3.2**, **7.5.2.1**, **Appendix 8.3**, **Chapter 8** (**Further Reading**)
Stockwell, Robert and Donka Minkova, 253, 262–3, **6.5.1**, **8.2.2**, **Chapter 8** (**Further Reading**), **10.2.1**, **10.4**
Stockwell, Robert P. and C. Westbrook Barritt, **6.5.3**
Strandberg, Otto, **7.5.2.1**
Stuart-Smith, Jane, **5.6** (**Assignments**)
Sweet, Henry, 9, 108, **5.1.3**, **10.2.1**
Szemerényi, Oswald J. L., **3.4.5** (**Further Reading**)

Taavitsainen, Irma, **7.2**, **111**
Tabain, M., 101, 342, **3.4.1**
Tagliamonte, Sali and Rosalind Temple, 149–50
Tamson, George J., 310, **9.5**
Tarlinskaja, Marina, 361, **5.4.1**, **9.6**, **10.3**, **10.4**
Terajima, Michiko, **8.2.2.2**
Thomas, Eric, 35, 180, 199, 237–9, 241–4, 248, 259, 270, **2.5** (**Further Reading**), **7.3.1**, **8.2.1**
Throop, Priscilla, 154, **10.2.2**
Tieken-Boon van Ostade, I., **1.6** (**Further Reading**)
Tottie, Gunnel, **7.5.1.1**
Tristram, Hildegard, 3
Trudgill, Peter, 19, 95, 126, 138, 147, 247, **5.2.4**
Trudgill, Peter, Elizabeth Gordon and Gillian Lewis, 237–8

Uffmann, Christian, **5.2.4**, **5.2.5**

Vachek, Joseph, 270, **5.3.2**
Vennemann, Theo, 123, **1.6**, **2.5** (**Further Reading**)

Wakelin, Martyn, 3, 63, 96, 116, **8.2.2.2**
Wales, Katie, 147, 244, 248, **1.4**, **8.2.2.2**, **Appendix 8.2**
Walker, John, 23, 99, 107–8, 135, 143–4, 240, 244, 246, 255–6, 262, 267, 304, **5.4.1**, **8.2.1**, **8.2.2.1**, **8.3.2**
Watkins, Calvert, 56, 69, **3.4.5** (**Further Reading**), **3.4.5** (**Assignments**)
Watts, Richard J., 251,
Wells, John, 63, 127, 129, 137, 198, 237, 244, 246, 259, 278, 342, **5.2.3**, **8.2.2.2**, **8.2.2.3**
Wełna, Jerzy, 176, 258, **7.4**, **7.5.1.1**, **8.2.2.1**, **8.2.2.2**
Wetzel, Claus-Dieter, **7.4**
Wheatley, Henry B., **6.4**
White, David, 176
Williams, Fionnuala Carson, **10.2**
Windross, Michael, 120, 126, **5.2.3**, **8.3.2**
Wogan-Browne, Jocelyn (ed.) et al., **1.6** (**Further Reading**)
Wolfram , Walt and Natalie Schilling-Estes, 35, 138, 233
Wolfram, Walt, 233
Wolfram, Walt and Natalie Schilling-Estes, 150, **8.2.1**
Wright, Joseph and Elizabeth M. Wright, **7.5.2.1**
Wyld, Henry Cecil, 95–6, 122–3, 130, 239, 254, **5.5.2**, **8.2.2.2**

Youmans, Gilbert, **9.7**, **10.1**, **10.2.1**
Youmans, Gilbert and Xingzhong Li, 36, **10.4**

Zec, Draga, **6.4.1**
Zuraw, Kie, **2.5**

Subject Index

Ælfric, 19, 67, 86, 154, 179, 184, 187, 228, 285, 339
  Lives of Saints, 228

AAVE, 17, 150, 233, 237, 240
accidental gap, 79
affix,inflectional, 91
affix <-y>, 231
affricates, 29–30, 74–5, 77, 90, 142, 144, 197, 268
affrication, 74, 84–6, 88, 99, 144–5
  dating, 85
Afrikaans, 59–60, 100, 118
Aidan, Bishop, 4
Akzentumsprung, 177
Aldhelm, 342
Alfred, King of Wessex, 6, 10
alignment, 326
alliteration, 13, 22, 76, 94, 291–2, 295, 297, 299, 300–4, 310, 313, 323, 326–8, 332–5, 339–48
  and stress, 291
  liaison alliteration, 341
  OE <hw>, 76
alliterative long line, 324, 342–3
Alliterative Revival, 340, 350
allograph, 21, 90
allomorph(s), 52, 88
allophone, 21, 25, 29, 50, 66, 83, 85, 102–3, 116, 118, 135–6, 138, 141, 166, 173, 177, 180, 199, 205, 238–9, 258, 264, 282, 333
alveolar, 28
ambisyllabicity, 41
American English
  colonial, 17
Americanism, 17
anacrusis, 336
analogy, 49
anapaest, 324
anaptyxis, 48, 120–1, 129, 132–3
Andreas, 76, 87, 295–6, 302, 335
Anglo-Saxon Chronicle, 5
Anglo-Norman, 10–12, 53, 58, 82, 86, 107, 131, 178, 185, 190–1, 200, 213, 218, 267, 270, 306, 308, 340–1, 348, 356
Anglo-Saxon, 2, 5, 8–10, 20, 67, 76, 82, 86, 106, 327, 328, 339, 342, 346–7
aphe(re)sis, 49, 322
apocope, 49, 228, 230–2, 354
a-prefixing, 233
articulation, 27
assimilation, 15, 47, 71, 75, 78, 85, 122–4, 128, 135, 137, 143–5, 157, 198, 259, 266, 289
Atlas of North American English (ANAE), 35
athematic noun, 161
Augustine, 4
AusE, 17, 129, 147, 237
<-aun>, 241, 268
Australia, 17, 127, 149

back-clipping, 321
Barnes, William, 243–4
Battle of Maldon, 76, 86, 333, 345
Bede, 2–4, 342
Beowulf, 76, 94, 145, 183, 291, 295, 297–8, 300–2, 329–40, 342, 345
bilabial, 28, 62
bilingualism, 4, 11, 17, 58, 115, 306
binary foot, 345, 350, 352
borrowed, 7, 13, 15, 20, 22, 41, 53–4, 58, 63, 65, 67, 86–8, 92, 94, 106–7, 135, 141, 178, 191, 216, 218, 235, 243, 255–6, 287, 289, 292, 308–16, 319, 357
borrowings, 8, 12, 15, 50, 105, 148, 200, 241, 246, 252, 255, 265, 284, 310, 312, 314, 327, 348
Breaking, 117–19, 129, 275
Britain, Roman, 3–4
Bullokar, William, 123
Byron, Lord, 137, 240, 323

Cædmon, 323, 342
  Caedmon's Hymn, 24, 327
caesura, 324, 326, 349, 358
Canada, 17, 127, 149, 237, 281, 283
Canadian English, 17, 111, 238, 259, 281–3
Canadian Raising, 281–3
Caribbean English, 18, 237, 239, 270
Caxton, William, 14–15, 82
<-cc>, 226
Celtic, 1, 3, 4, 8, 53, 57–8, 80, 306
Cely Letters, 125, 143, 239
chain shift, 35, 64–5, 203, 251–2, 256, 260, 265
Chancery Standard, 187
Chaucer, Geoffrey, 14–15, 95, 144, 168, 200, 202, 204, 230, 239, 249, 250, 254, 259, 292, 303, 306–7, 309, 311, 313, 315, 320, 323–4, 352–4, 356–65
  Canterbury Tales, 269, 292–3, 303–5, 307, 309–11, 313, 352, 354, 357–8, 360–3, 365
  Troilus and Criseyde, 230, 357
Chaucerian English, 204, 250
Chaucerian rhyme, 259, 269, 292
Christ A, B, C, 295
Christianity, 4, 20, 58
clippings, 187, 270, 321
clitic (group), 51, 139, 145–6, 298–300, 320, 325–6, 353–543, 364
cliticisation, 299
cluster, 28, 32, 40, 42–3, 48–50, 57, 76, 86–7, 102, 109–10, 112, 119–21, 123–4, 131–6, 139, 149, 165–72, 213, 220, 232, 244, 251, 272–3, 287, 334
  coda clusters, 213
  bi-segmental, 108
  medial cluster, 42
  non-native, 57
  simplification, 49
Cockney, 17, 63, 95, 247, 259, 266, 270
codification, 14, 19, 21, 48–9, 107, 126, 148, 179, 184, 235, 257, 261, 267, 269, 280–1
cognate, 54–5, 69, 87–8, 101, 163
colon. See hemistich
Colonial English, 16
combining form, 57–8, 319, 149
complementary distribution, 90–1, 93, 97, 155
compound, 91, 140, 160, 161, 164, 166, 174, 183, 215, 219–20, 290, 297–8, 303–5, 313, 324, 331, 336, 366
compound stress, 297, 312, 314
consonant
  approximant, 27, 29–31, 37, 77, 79, 105
  coronal, 29, 38, 85, 116–18, 122–3, 134, 142, 165, 169, 264, 268, 274–5
  dorsal, 29, 85, 117, 131
  fortis, 27
  geminate, 31–2, 71, 73, 77–9, 80, 83, 93, 112, 118, 132, 214, 225
  glottal, 27
  heterorganic, 122
  lenis, 27
  nasal, 27, 29, 30–1, 48, 136, 152, 169, 192, 255, 355
  oral, 29
  singleton, 31, 41, 49, 72–3, 75, 77, 80, 87, 334
  voiced, 21–2, 25–8, 31, 36, 44, 48, 50, 52, 62–7, 74–5, 79, 81–4, 89–95, 97–8, 101–5, 112–13, 124, 134–8, 141–2, 165, 169, 177, 205, 238, 240, 258, 272, 282–3, 333
  voiceless, 21–2, 27–9, 31, 36, 40, 49, 50, 52, 62–5, 72, 74, 76, 80, 82–3, 85, 89–90, 92–3, 95, 101–3, 105, 112, 114, 138, 142, 146, 148, 177, 205–6, 241, 244, 258–9, 272, 281–2, 334
consonants of OE, 71, 74, 76
continuant, 30, 116–17, 140, 274–5
Cornwall, 3, 95
coronal stop deletion, 149
countertonic accentuation, 310
creolised vernacular
creolised, 7
Cursor Mundi, 222, 260
Cynewulf, 342

/d/, 28–9, 40–1, 47–8, 52, 54, 66, 89, 102, 125, 142, 145, 147, 163, 168, 180, 231, 272
dactyl, 324, 350
Danelaw, 6
Danish, 5, 7, 21, 59–61, 243
Death of Edgar, 333
Death of Edward, 327, 339
degemination, 80–1, 93
dental, 28, 54, 67
dental-final verbs, 78
[-d(ə).r], 124
derivational affix, 84
[dʒ], 74, 77, 79, 81, 84, 86, 122, 141
diacritic, 152, 154, 179, 189–90, 202, 208, 222, 226, 286
digraph, 22, 43, 45, 82, 86, 88, 111, 124, 156, 159, 176, 178–80, 187, 190–1, 202, 271
  digraph controversy, 179
  spelling, 117
dip, 328–30, 335, 339, 343–5
  expanded dip, 329

diphthong, 35, 37–8, 45, 47, 50, 58, 83, 103, 159, 170, 175–8, 201, 204–5, 208, 241, 244, 255–7, 259, 266, 268–70, 282, 287
  centring, 206, 279
  falling, 177, 263
  rising, 177
dissimilation, 47–8
  height dissimilation, 259
Domesday Book, 122, 209
Donne, John, 1, 224
doublets, 83, 87, 96, 104, 214
drag-chain theory, 253
Dryden, John, 224, 261–2
Durham, 8, 85, 111, 339
Dutch, 59–60
  Pennsylvania Dutch, 59–60

-ed, 89, 229, 231–2
edh, 20, 82, 90, 94
Elene, 105, 295–6
elision, 229–30, 338–9, 350, 353, 355, 365
Elizabeth, 137
End Rule *see* Nuclear Stress Rule
end-stressed nouns, 316
enjambment, 357, 365
epenthesis, 48, 119–20, 130, 137, 206, 208, 228, 263, 275
[ɛr] > [ar], 275–6
-(e)st, 231
eth, 20, 229, 231, 355
etymology, 12, 23, 45–6, 69, 75, 83, 86–7, 103, 106–7, 109–10, 116, 124, 128, 149, 152, 154, 156, 167, 175, 178, 188–9, 194–5, 214, 227, 241, 244, 253, 257, 269, 279, 316, 326
  etymological spelling, 45, 153
  unetymological, 49
extrametrical, 336, 357

-ə, 34, 69, 80, 93–4, 126, 206, 223, 229, 230–2, 277–8, 280, 338, 354
əm-, 139

[f], 241
Faroese, 60
final <-e>, 189, 338, 353–4
flap, 147
Flemish, 59, 60
'focused' variety, 179, 184
foreignness, 142–3, 231, 270
fortition, 50, 75, 103
French, 7, 10–13, 15, 17, 23, 48, 53, 55, 57–8, 86–8, 92, 95, 97, 99, 106–7, 131, 136, 141–3, 146, 148, 152, 158, 185–7, 193–5, 197, 200, 202–3, 208, 218, 243, 245, 253, 255, 263, 267–9, 276, 280, 284, 306, 308, 310, 314, 347, 356, 360, 364
  Old French, 22
frequency, 51
fricative, 30, 75, 102; *see also* spirant
tautosyllabic voiceless fricative, 240
fricative voicing, 66, 74, 83, 88, 91, 95–6, 216
Frisian, 21, 59–60, 73, 118
function word, 71, 83, 94, 211, 225, 230, 299, 320, 351, 354, 363
functional stress-shifting, 311

/ɣ/, 75, 77, 79, 81, 83–4, 86, 102–3, 105
gap, 79, 253, 272
gemination, 93
  new in OE, 78
  West Germanic Consonant Gemination, 71–3, 76–9
German
  High, 21, 60–1, 73
  Old High, 61
Germanic, 1–5, 7, 10, 12–13, 17, 47, 54–5, 57–63, 65–73, 75, 79, 82, 84–7, 103, 106, 113, 116, 118–19, 129–30, 139, 145–6, 153–5, 159, 162–5, 174–6, 178, 180–1, 212, 220, 223, 225, 227–8, 259, 288–9, 291, 294, 301–2, 306, 308, 315–16, 326–8, 334, 348–9
  diaspora, 3
  East Germanic, 59
  Germanic invasion, 3
  North Germanic, 59–60
  Old Germanic, 66
  Proto-Germanic, 8, 36, 57, 59–62, 65–6, 68–73, 77–8, 82–7, 104, 112, 121, 129, 156–9, 161–3, 169, 173, 177, 199, 212, 301, 327, 333
  West Germanic, 60–1, 63, 72, 78, 84, 175–6
Germanic Stress Rule (GSR), 70, 288–9, 294, 303, 307, 309, 311, 315–16
  in AmE and BrE, 317
-gg-, 72, 79
Gil, Alexander, 16
glide vocalisation, 207–8
glides, 25, 30–1, 37, 113, 119, 168, 177, 190, 259, 279
global English, 252
globalisation, 142
glottal, see stop, glottal
glottalisation, 146–7
grapheme, 21
Greek, 15, 54–8, 60, 62–3, 65, 67, 87, 93, 100, 107, 111, 115, 134, 148, 154, 269, 289, 350

Grimm's Law, 61–2, 66–8; *see also* First Germanic Consonant Shift
Guy of Warwick, 264

hapax legomena, 298
Havelok the Dane, 149, 348
h-dropping, 100–1, 107–8, 111
  orthographic, 104
headless line, 324, 357–8, 361
hemistich, 324–5
heptarchy, 5
hiatus, 93, 146, 229, 233, 338
avoidance of, 231
High Vowel Deletion (HVD), 73
Holofernes, 131
homophone, 22, 104, 129, 134, 167, 179, 241, 279
homophony, 64, 111, 149, 169, 244, 250, 262
homorganic cluster lengthening, 124, 135, 157, 165–6, 168–9, 171
<hw> - [ʍ], 21–2, 28, 50, 64, 74, 76, 102, 109–12
hybrid
  prosodic patterns 316–17
  verse 340, 348
  word-formation, 13
hypermetric, 328

iamb, 324, 350
iambic pentameter, 14, 313, 323, 356–9, 361–3
iambic reversal *see* trochaic substitution
-lC-loss, 130
ictic, 324, 328, 330, 332–3, 335, 342, 344, 350
ictus (ictic), 295, 323–4, 327–30, 332, 335, 337, 344, 358, 364–5
I-Mutation/I-Umlaut, 73, 85, 153, 156–64, 172–3, 176, 193
Indian English, 18
Indo-European, 2, 54–9, 61–2, 67–9, 74, 79, 180
inflectional suffixes, 182, 295
International Phonetic Alphabet (IPA), 25, 28, 30, 33–6, 38, 41, 46, 69, 82, 103, 152, 154, 158, 222, 247, 251, 258, 276, 286
  vowel chart, 33
  vowel symbols, 36
interrogative, 109
intrusive r, 127
inverse spelling, 135, 167
-ir, -er, -ur, 277
Ireland, 4–5, 16, 127, 243, 246, 280–1
Irish, 4, 16, 20, 111, 125, 131, 147, 240, 245–6, 259, 277, 283
Irish English, 4
irregularity, 246
isosyllabic, 324, 348–53, 355–6, 361, 365
Italian, 23, 55, 154, 245, 357
Italian loans, 226
Italic, 57–8, 63

Jamestown Colony, 16

Kaluza's Law, 331
Keats, John, 137, 323
Kent, 2, 4–5, 95, 203
Knight's Tale, 230

<l-> insertion, 130
labelling mismatches *see* stress mismatches
labiodental, 28
labiovelar, 28
LAEME, 15, 92, 108–9, 132, 135, 179, 185, 189, 192, 234–4, 290
LALME, 15, 122, 185, 234, 254, 355
language contact, 8, 47, 80, 106
laryngeal *see* glottal
Latin, 1–2, 4–5, 7–8, 10–12, 15–16, 20, 22–3, 35, 48, 53–5, 57–8, 60, 62–3, 65–7, 80, 86–7, 92–3, 104–5, 107, 111, 131, 139–41, 146, 148, 153, 160, 167, 185–7, 200, 218, 235, 248–9, 255, 276, 284, 289, 294, 306, 308–10, 314–15, 346–50, 356
Latin borrowing
  Latin *see* loanwords
Latin Stress Rule, 307–8, 315
Latino/Chicano English, 17
lengthening before /-lC/, 241
lenition, 50, 83, 103–4, 106, 113–14, 149, 205
Levins, Peter, 293
lexical frequency, 124, 136, 253, 272
lexicon, 44, 61, 71, 79, 89, 133, 157, 182, 210, 212, 217, 231, 255, 287, 308, 314–15
lift, 328–30, 344
'linking' /r/, 127
liquid, 30
loans, 7, 12, 48, 58, 65, 84, 87, 92, 96–7, 107, 139, 141, 193, 194–5, 218, 231, 263, 289–90, 308, 310–11, 314, 316
  early loans, 217
loanword adaptation, 13
loanwords, 4–5, 12–13, 15, 32, 66, 70, 92–3, 98, 100, 107, 111, 135, 137, 141, 148, 159, 195, 197, 200, 202, 209, 216, 218, 226, 241, 243, 245, 252, 255, 270, 276, 280, 289–90, 293, 306–7, 309–11, 314–15, 317, 348, 360
  Classical, 15
  Greek, 57
  Romance *see* Romance vocabulary

London, 9, 16, 19, 63, 116, 122, 134, 146, 198, 202, 234, 238, 254, 259, 267, 270, 275, 307
loss of [-n], 146
Lothian, 3
Love's Labour's Lost, 131
Lowland Scots, 116–17, 185, 190, 275

Machyn, 125
macron, 33, 45, 155, 156, 174, 180, 256
major-class words, 94
markedness, 64, 197, 198
Maximal Onset Principle, 41, 287
MB, 297, 335
merger, which-witch, 111
metathesis, 48, 86, 119–20, 130, 275
metrical feet, 324, 350
metrical positions, 285, 295, 305, 309, 313, 324–5, 336, 343–4, 350, 352, 359, 362–3
metricality, 326
Milton, 232, 323, 365
Milton, John, 239
minimal pairs, 77–8, 80, 89, 92–3, 136, 179, 246, 296
mismatches, 326
  bracketing, 364–5
Mondegreen, 145
monophthong, 37–8, 157–8, 201, 254, 263, 267
monophthongisation, 153, 176, 241, 259
Monosyllabic Rule, 352
mora, 43–4, 170–1, 180, 285
moraic
  bi, 43, 45, 168, 170–1, 177, 208–9, 214, 286
  mono, 43, 45
morphemes, 49, 51–2, 83, 89, 318
morphophonemic, 52, 89, 160, 163
Mulcaster, 226, 235

nativisation, 13, 92, 142
New Zealand, 17, 100–11, 127, 148, 198
New Zealand English, 17
-ŋg, 41, 49–50, 75, 136–9, 165, 192
[ŋ], 29, 41, 50, 74–5, 99, 136, 138–9
non-ictic, 324, 328–9, 342
non-isosyllabic, 325
Norman
  Conquest, 9–10, 12–14, 82, 106, 121, 130, 182, 184, 185, 190, 215, 306, 308, 339, 340, 346, 348, 351
  Norman French *see* Anglo-Norman
Northumbria, 4–5
-ns, 241
Nuclear Stress Rule *see* End Rule
NZE, 126, 129, 147, 237–8, 259, 266

obstruent, 30–1, 61, 64, 67, 90, 101–2, 135, 142–3, 145, 169, 241, 272
octosyllabic, 349–50, 356–7
OE Breaking, 116–18, 129
OFr <-an>, 241
[oi], 191, 209, 269–70
Old Norse, 5–8, 10, 21, 53, 60, 65, 72, 83–7, 103, 109, 122, 167–8, 172, 177–8, 192, 203, 207–8, 223, 228, 239, 242, 262–3, 267, 303, 338
onomastic data, 219
onset
  Onset Maximalism *see* Maximal Onset Principle
onset-maximal syllabification, 330
open-syllable lengthening, 199, 221–4, 226, 242, 251, 261, 263
Orm, 80, 154, 167, 189, 225, 290, 349, 352, 365
Ormulum, 215, 225, 230, 349, 351–2
orthoepist, 23, 126, 146, 234–5, 239, 267
orthographic evidence for word-stress, 289
orthographic geminates, 226
orthographic standard, 18
Owl and the Nightingale, 230, 347–51

ɔi, 35, 38, 45, 50, 58, 151, 268, 270

pagan, 4–5
palatal assimilation, 142
palatalisation, 74, 81, 83–8, 99, 141–5
  eModE, 143
palato-alveolar, 28
Paradise Lost, 232
paraphonology, 337, 350, 353–5
Paston Letters, 143, 264
Pearl, 95
pentameter, 293, 307, 325, 352, 357–62, 365
periodisation, 9
peripherality, 36, 151
Persian, 55
Peterborough Chronicle, 185, 230
phonaesthemes, 149
phoneme, 21, 24–5, 28, 31, 40, 45, 50, 83, 104, 138, 149, 180, 199, 200, 236, 246, 270, 333
phonemic merger, 50–1
phonemic split, 50, 91
phonological phrase, 298, 300
phonotactics, 99, 134, 140, 237, 271
phrasal stress, 312, 314
Phoenix, 297
Piers Plowman, 132, 134, 340, 344
plosive. See stop
Poema Morale, 130, 230, 348–9

poetic meter, 284–5, 323–4
post-ME borrowings, 255
pre-consonantal shortening, 168, 212–15, 217, 225, 276
pre-fricative lengthening, 240
prestige, 235, 269; *see also* stigmatisation
Prick of Conscience, 248
pro(s)thesis, 48
pronominal word, 94
pronunciation norm, 153
prosody, 4, 12, 14–15, 18, 39, 44, 51–3, 55, 58, 61, 66, 69–70, 106, 112, 130, 145, 152, 160, 164, 170–1, 181, 211, 216–20, 223, 230, 232–3, 236, 270, 284–5, 288–9, 292–6, 298, 300–3, 306–8, 311–12, 314, 317–18, 320–4, 326–7, 331–2, 337–8, 345–6, 353–5, 360–6
  weight, 285
Proto-Indo-European (PIE), 56, 61–5, 67–9, 129
  accent, 65
Proverbs of Alfred, 339, 347
push-chain theory, 253

Received Pronunciation (RP), 18–19, 36, 116, 118, 129, 134, 146, 153, 198–9, 206, 238–9, 248, 274
reduplication, 149
Renaissance, 144, 217–18, 284
  Greek, 141
  Latin, 107
resolution, 77, 329
resources, 8, 14, 45, 306
  for the study of Middle English, 14
r-ful. See *rhoticity*
rhotacism, 66, 121
rhotic
  non-rhotic. *See* r-less
rhoticity, 99, 115–17, 121, 125, 128, 274
  hyper-rhoticity, 124, 126
rhyme, 22, 95, 249
  feminine rhyme, 357
Rhyming Poem, 346
rhythm, 285
r-less *see* non-rhotic
Roman, 3–4, 20–1, 36, 106, 115, 146, 153, 248
Romance vocabulary, 12, 84, 97, 106–7, 141, 148, 208, 216, 218, 241, 306, 309–10, 348
Romans, 1, 3, 55
rounding, 239
/-rðər, -rð.r/ > /rd.r/, 125
rune, 20, 59, 76, 116, 154

SAE, 40, 237
St Augustine, 106
sandhi, 126, 128, 132
Sanskrit, 55–6, 245
Scandinavia, 5, 10, 59
Scandinavian, 5–8, 10, 60, 67, 87, 208, 263
schwa, 34–5, 37, 50, 69, 93, 120, 124, 127–9, 132, 139, 176, 180, 182–3, 223, 228–31, 233, 248, 275–8, 280, 309, 338, 349, 354–5; *see also -ə*
  in word-final position, 230–1
  loss in trisyllabic words, 355
Scotland, 5, 16, 83, 100, 110–11, 127, 149, 246, 267, 280–1, 340
Scots, 16, 86, 116, 131, 147, 194, 203, 240, 243, 259, 274–5, 277, 282–3
semivowel *see* glide
septenary, 349
Shakespeare, William, 22, 50, 161, 224, 239, 262, 277, 314, 320, 323–4, 365
Sheridan, Thomas, 144, 267, 316
shibboleth, 100, 108
Shift
  First Germanic Consonant Shift, 61–6; *see also* Grimm's Law
  Great Vowel Shift, 201, 248, 250–1, 256–7, 260
  Long Vowel Shift, 38, 124, 175, 203, 207, 226, 241–2, 252–3, 255–6, 257–8, 262, 266–7, 269, 271, 280, 290, 306
  Northern Cities, 35, 203, 237–8, 248
Sievers' Five Types, 334–5
  Type A3, 335
Sievers' *Rule of Precedence*, 301; *see also* 335
  Type A3, 334
silent *-e*, 226
silent words, 230
similarity
  avoidance, 136
simplification, 40, 49, 80, 99, 109, 122–4, 132–6, 139, 141, 148–9, 167, 173, 197
singleton, 40, 42, 75, 77, 80, 93, 104, 118, 143, 170, 214, 330, 340
Singletons, 74, 78
Sir Gawain and the Green Knight, 143, 303–4, 313, 340–1, 344
Sir William Jones, 55
[sk], 86–7
slashed o, 158
sociolinguistic, 47, 52, 111–12, 253, 262, 267, 322
sonority, 31, 39, 40, 50, 95, 106, 119, 121, 123, 128, 131, 133–5, 169, 181, 232, 287
  falling, 40, 135, 213
  rising, 40

sonorant, 30–1, 34, 48, 50, 69, 75, 83–4, 91, 101, 103, 113, 121, 129, 132, 169, 268, 338, 354
sonority scale, 31
South Africa, 18, 60, 100, 127
Spanish, 17–18, 55, 58, 115, 248
Spenser, Edmund, 232
spirants *see* fricative
spoken standard, 18
spread glottis, 31, 112
-ss, 226
SSBE, 16–18, 20, 28, 34–7, 40, 44, 106, 126, 128, 137, 139, 146, 151–2, 173, 184, 225, 231, 237–8, 240, 242, 248, 252, 265, 270, 278, 282
SSE, 38, 100, 129, 173, 245, 280
Standard English, 18–19, 174, 184, 257
standard written, 14
standardisation, 52, 107, 140, 195, 236, 267
stigmatisation, 242, 244
stigmatised, 106–8, 114, 131, 146
stop, 30; *see also* plosive
aspirated, 27, 40, 62–4, 67
glottal, 24–5, 27, 29, 62, 74, 76, 99, 102–5, 112, 145–6, 205–6, 258, 334, 341
palatal, 28
unreleased, 149
velar, 28
stress, 1, 13, 15, 22, 34, 39–40, 42, 44, 49, 51, 58, 65–6, 69–70, 91, 93, 95, 107, 115, 142, 145, 170, 180–1, 183, 210–12, 214–15, 218–19, 220, 222, 224, 227, 232, 249, 255, 281, 283–7, 288–313, 315–25, 327–8, 331, 335, 337, 345, 348, 352–5, 359–60, 362–6
Germanic, 5
non-primary, 286, 295
root-initial, 58, 353
secondary and tertiary, 286
stress mismatches, 360
stress-attracting suffixes, 319
stress-neutral suffixes, 318–19
stress-shift, 294, 307, 316
suprasegmental, 284
sw-, 139
syllabic sonorant, 39, 222, 287
syllable, 39
closed, 44
coda, 39–44, 70, 84–5, 92, 112–13, 117–18, 120–1, 123–8, 130–1, 134–40, 146, 149, 165–7, 170, 176, 178, 192, 198, 205–6, 208, 211, 213–14, 216, 220, 223, 229, 231–2, 237–40, 244, 272, 275, 277–82, 287, 338, 341
definition, 39
length, 44
loss of coda, 275
nucleus, 39
onset, 32, 38–42, 48, 72–3, 76, 85, 91, 101–2, 104–6, 108–9, 112–13, 115, 118, 120–1, 124–6, 128, 133–6, 139, 143, 145–6, 148–9, 165, 222, 231, 239–40, 246, 268, 287, 297, 326–7, 330, 333–4, 340–1, 354
open, 44
peak, 37–9, 43, 113, 135, 222, 338
rhyme, 39
stressed, 34, 40, 44–5, 71, 85, 102, 126, 138, 145–6, 152, 165, 170, 210, 212, 216, 220, 227, 278, 289, 295, 305, 324–8, 330, 341, 351, 360, 362
structure, 39, 286
superheavy, 170, 287
vowel-initial, 29, 146
weight, 43–4, 210
syllable structure, 1, 39, 41, 43, 120, 123, 211–12, 219, 284, 287, 366
syllable(s)
unstressed, 9, 34, 45, 66, 70–1, 85, 93, 102, 106, 115, 121, 124–5, 136–7, 143, 181–3, 210, 212, 218–20, 227–9, 231–2, 285–6, 289–91, 295, 313, 320, 324–5, 330, 332, 336, 339, 344, 351, 354–5, 358, 360, 362
syncope, 49, 80, 182, 223, 228, 231–2, 350, 353–5
synizesis, 354, 358

ʃ, 28, 75, 132, 142–3, 225
ʃ-ʒ contrast, 142
ʃl-, 53, 149
ʃm-, 53, 149
ʃm- ʃl- ʃt-, 60, 148

tap, 25, 99, 145, 147–8
Tautosyllabic /-r/, 244
tautosyllabicity, 75, 118, 166, 169, 177, 200, 211, 238, 241, 244, 264, 278
Tennyson, Alfred Lord, 137
tetrameter, 325–6, 356–7, 359
The Alliterative Morte Arthure, 340, 341
The Pickwick Papers, 96
The Sowdone of Babylon, 137–8
The Wars of Alexander, 340–1, 344
thorn, 20, 82, 90
[tj] ~ [tʃ], 144
Tolkien, J.R.R., 96
Townley Plays, 264
trisyllabic shortening, 216–18, 227
trisyllabic words, 212, 229–30, 289, 307–8, 310, 355

trochaic substitution, 360–1, 364
trochee, 324, 350, 361
tʃ, 74, 77, 81–2, 85–6, 88, 122, 144, 226
spelling, 86
ts-, 42, 53, 148–9
Tudor, 15
typology, 44, 47, 196, 264, 282, 294, 336

[-uɣ-], 208
[ui], 187, 190–1, 193, 195, 269–70
Unstressed syllables, 9, 34, 41, 45, 48, 66, 70–1, 80, etc.; *see also* syllable(s), unstressed
Unstressed vowels, 49, 51, 180, 232; *see also* schwa, vowel reduction

Vanburgh, 243
variable stress, 316
-ve, 226
vernacular, 10–12, 14, 185, 187
vernaculars, 55
Vernay Letters, 126
Verner's Law, 66, 70, 116
  in English, 66
verse, 22
  Old English, 5, 41, 73, 77, 86, 105, 109, 230, 291, 295, 297–8, 300–2, 328, 330, 332–4, 337, 339–41, 345, 350
versification, 13–14, 22, 283, 285, 290, 323, 326–8, 339–40, 345, 348–50, 353, 356
Vices and Virtues, 260
vocal tract, 25–7, 29–32, 50, 101, 105, 116
vocalisation, 73, 114, 126–7, 131, 165, 177–8, 205–6, 208, 277, 280
voicing, 26, 47, 91, 147
vowel
  backness, 32, 36
  checked, 44
  free, 44
  height, 32, 34, 36
  lax, 35–6, 44, 70, 151, 171, 209, 219, 255, 272
  length, 35, 212
  neutralisation, 9
  quality, 32
  reduction, 9, 165, 180–2, 212, 219–20, 228, 286, 289, 317
  round, 33
  tense, 35–6, 38, 151, 166, 179, 209, 378
  unround, 33
vowel alliteration, 334
vowel harmony, 157
Vowel shortening in unstressed syllables, 219
vulgar, 108, 114, 126, 242, 244, 269, 278, 299

w-, 109, 111–12, 115, 134, 140, 240, 245, 299
Wales, 3, 16, 147, 198, 244, 248
Walker, John, 23, 99, 107–8, 135, 143–4, 240, 244, 246, 255–6, 262, 267, 293, 304
Webster, Noah, 17
Welsh, 4, 16, 58, 111, 233, 246, 259
Welsh English, 4
West Germanic (Consonant) Gemination, 71–3, 76–9
Whitby, Synod of, 4
Winchester, 8, 179, 184
Winner and Waster, 340, 344
word-minimality, 71
Wordsworth, William, 137, 323, 325
written standard, 14, 18–19, 185, 187, 267
wug test, 97
Wulfila, 60
Wulfstan, 19, 342
Wycliffite texts, 187
wynn, 20, 76, 190

y, 37–8, 152, 154–5, 173, 187, 193–8, 236, 238, 245, 268
Yiddish, 59–60, 148–9
yod-dropping, 197
yogh, 82

[z] ~ [ʒ], 142
/ʒ/, 28, 41, 50, 53, 99, 141–3